Cornell Woolrich
from Pulp Noir to Film Noir

ALSO BY THOMAS C. RENZI

*Jules Verne on Film:
A Filmography of the Cinematic Adaptations
of His Works, 1902 through 1997*
(McFarland, 1998; paperback 2004)

Cornell Woolrich from Pulp Noir to Film Noir

Thomas C. Renzi

McFarland & Company, Inc., Publishers
Jefferson, North Carolina, and London

LIBRARY OF CONGRESS CATALOGUING-IN-PUBLICATION DATA

Renzi, Thomas C., 1948–
    Cornell Woolrich : from pulp noir to film noir / Thomas C. Renzi.
    p.   cm.
    Includes bibliographical references and index.

    ISBN 0-7864-2351-X (softcover : 50# alkaline paper)

    1. Woolrich, Cornell, 1903–1968 — Criticism and interpretation   2. Woolrich, Cornell, 1903–1968 — Film and video adaptations.   3. Noir fiction, American — History and criticism.   4. Film noir — History and criticism. I. Title.

PS351.O455Z85   2006
813'.52 — dc22   2005031453

British Library cataloguing data are available

©2006 Thomas C. Renzi. All rights reserved

No part of this book may be reproduced or transmitted in any form or by any means, electronic or mechanical, including photocopying or recording, or by any information storage and retrieval system, without permission in writing from the publisher.

On the cover: Susan Hayward and Paul Lukas in *Deadline at Dawn*, RKO 1945 (National Screen Service Corp., courtesy William Thailing)

Manufactured in the United States of America

McFarland & Company, Inc., Publishers
  Box 611, Jefferson, North Carolina 28640
    www.mcfarlandpub.com

For my family, relatives, and friends
who have kept me from being
totally engulfed by my *noir* fantasies

Acknowledgments

To identify the specific moment that inspired a piece of writing would normally be difficult: the genesis of the creative process can depend on any infinite number of sources. For me, however, I know exactly when I decided to write this book — when my brother-in-law suggested that I should. Right here, I'd like to express my gratitude formally to Roger Pijacki for playing the muse and prompting me with that subtle challenge. Thanks, Rog.

I also made a couple of long-distance friends who were very kind and helpful to me along the way. I exchanged emails with Francis M. Nevins, Jr., author of the only comprehensive biography on Cornell Woolrich. His book was a rich source of information, both about Woolrich and about the films adapted from his works.

Mr. Nevins put me in touch with another avid Woolrich connoisseur and scholar, William Thailing, who became a good friend as a result of our mutual admiration for the author's extraordinary fictions. Mr. Thailing most generously shared with me several of the more difficult-to-find films adapted from Woolrich's writings, *Convicted*, *Fall Guy*, *The Guilty*, and *The Boy Cried Murder*. In addition, as owner of an extensive collection of photographs from these films, he provided many of them in this book. Sadly, Mr. Thailing passed away at the end of 2003, but I'd like to believe that he is in a fine and well-lighted place where he can appreciate his contribution to this study and still read the Woolrich stories for which he had such an ardent passion.

Lastly and of greatest significance, I'd like to thank the two people most dear to me. My wife Deborah showered me with generous amounts of tolerance, not only by showing patience with the time I needed to work on this project but also by humoring me for my occasional homilies on an author who was about as crucial to her life as Brussels sprouts. I also must thank my son Matthew who, at eighteen years old, keeps me vitalized with his spirit, his sense of humor, and his strength of character.

Table of Contents

Acknowledgments — vi
Preface — 1
Introduction — 3

"The Corpse Next Door" (January 23, 1937) — 25
   Union City (1979) — 27
"Face Work" (October 1937) — 31
   Convicted (1938) — 34
"I'm Dangerous Tonight" (November 1937) — 39
   I'm Dangerous Tonight (1990) — 42
"I Wouldn't Be in Your Shoes" (March 12, 1938) — 47
   I Wouldn't Be in Your Shoes (1948) — 51
"All at Once, No Alice" (March 20, 1940) — 57
   The Return of the Whistler (1948) — 60
"C-Jag" (October 1940) — 67
   Fall Guy (1947) — 71
The Bride Wore Black (1940) — 78
   The Bride Wore Black (1967) — 84
"He Looked Like Murder" (February 8, 1941) — 93
   The Guilty (1947) — 97
"Nightmare" (March 1941) — 107
   Fear in the Night (1947) — 114
   Nightmare (1956) — 122
The Black Curtain (1941) — 130
   Street of Chance (1942) — 134

"Rear Window" (February 1942) — 143
   Rear Window (1954) — 150
   Rear Window (Television, 1998) — 170

Black Alibi (1942) — 175
   The Leopard Man (1943) — 179

"Dormant Account" (May 1942) — 190
   The Mark of the Whistler (1944) — 196

Phantom Lady (1942) — 200
   Phantom Lady (1944) — 205

The Black Angel (1943) — 213
   Black Angel (1946) — 219

Deadline at Dawn (1944) — 230
   Deadline at Dawn (1946) — 234

The Black Path of Fear (1944) — 242
   The Chase (1946) — 249

Night Has a Thousand Eyes (1945) — 261
   Night Has a Thousand Eyes (1948) — 266

Waltz into Darkness (1947) — 276
   Mississippi Mermaid (1969) — 285
   Original Sin (2001) — 295

"The Boy Cried Murder" (March 1947) — 303
   The Window (1949) — 307
   The Boy Cried Murder (1966) — 318
   Cloak & Dagger (1984) — 322

I Married a Dead Man (1948) — 324
   No Man of Her Own (1950) — 328
   J'ai épousé une ombre (1982) — 337
   Mrs. Winterbourne (1996) — 340
   She's No Angel (Television, 2003) — 343

"For the Rest of Her Life" (May 1968) — 345
   Martha (German television, 1973) — 349

Bibliography — 355
Index — 359

Preface

Cornell who? This question — very possibly the same question you are asking yourself right now — is the one I asked when I first ran across this author's name. The question kindled my curiosity, which in turn fired my eagerness to explore the man further. The result is this book, *Cornell Woolrich from Pulp Noir to Film Noir*. The birth of this project depended on the intersection of three diverse and incongruent elements: Alfred Hitchcock, *film noir*, and an off-hand remark by my brother-in-law.

A colleague once asked me one of those classic philosophical questions: If you were told that all films must be destroyed and you were allowed to save only one, which would it be? *The Birth of a Nation? The General? King Kong? Citizen Kane? Singin' in the Rain? Shane? The Searchers? The 7th Voyage of Sinbad?* These titles are among the two or three dozen I include on my top-ten favorites list, so truthfully, I couldn't make a clear choice. However, if I were pressed — *really* forced into such an unlikely situation — I can admit a slight bias that enables me to answer that hypothetical question. One particular film has mesmerized me from the first time I saw it and, over time, has held an even greater fascination for me the more I study it: *Rear Window*. Oddly, I had already viewed it many times before I finally noticed that the story was credited to some obscure author, one Cornell Woolrich. I had never heard of him, but I made a mental note of the name. Then, in a coincidence very much like a fateful accident in one of Woolrich's stories, I was loitering in a bookstore when I came across *The Cornell Woolrich Omnibus*. Compelled to see how his "Rear Window" compared with Hitchcock's masterpiece, I scooped up the copy and, after reading that one short story, became addicted to the author's Svengali-like ability to draw his reader into his fiction. He had a keen sense of irony and a creative knack for unraveling bizarre plots in a captivating style. In this one collection, however, I reached a dead end because nearly all of his work, I subsequently learned, was out of print.

I might have put it to rest there and then, but I told my brother-in-law how I "discovered" Cornell Woolrich whose nifty little story Hitchcock had expanded into an astounding film. Roger Pijacki said very casually, more in jest than in seriousness, "Sounds like an idea for your next book." His statement took root and grew, not quickly but methodically, into the work you have before you.

As for motivation to complete this project, the essential thing was my learning that Cornell Woolrich, among the pulp fiction writers of the 1930s and 1940s, was the one whose works were adapted most often to *film noir*. Now, *noir* has always intrigued me, even when I was a youngster going to Sunday matinees. I was too young at the time to appreciate or understand these films totally, but even so, my memories still resonate with the deep impact they made on me, films like *The Window* and *Vertigo*. (Shamefacedly, I will share one example of my naiveté related to my initial viewing of *The Harder They Fall* when I was seven or eight. Boxer Toro Moreno was knocked down in the ring, and as he crawled agonizingly across the canvas, something dropped out of his mouth. I thought he had bitten off his tongue! That image haunted me until I saw the film years later and realized that that something wasn't his tongue after all but his mouth guard. This was lucky for him because he still had some speaking lines later on.)

The present book, then, is as much a study of Cornell Woolrich as it is a study of *film noir* and of one man's literature that impacted the style and themes of this emerging 1940s film genre. Structurally, the book is organized in sections according to the chronological publication dates of Woolrich's written works (short stories and novels). A discussion of each Woolrich story is followed by separate discussions of the film or films adapted from that source. Twenty-two primary works serve as source material for thirty films. In the process, the discussions take into consideration many Woolrich novels and short stories, broadening our overview of the man and his artistry. At the same time, the book includes a look at numerous *films noirs*, even if not directly adapted from Woolrich, to show how far-reaching were his tonal nuances and plot ideas in affecting that remarkable film style and genre.

At the beginning of each discussion of the 22 works is a brief synopsis of that novel's or short story's publication history. Preceding the examination of each of the 30 films is a detailed list of the film credits, including the main cast, with each actor's name and the character he/she plays, and the production crew, noting the director, producer, screenwriter, editor, and so on. All in all, *Cornell Woolrich from Pulp Noir to Film Noir* accomplishes two primary objectives: it offers a comprehensive study of one of the leading pulp writers responsible for the *noir* phenomenon; and it singles out and examines many of the thematic elements and stylistic techniques that have contributed to defining *film noir*.

Introduction

Once in the vanguard of mystery-suspense pulp fiction, Cornell Woolrich today has faded from must-read classics lists, yet retains notoriety as a cult icon among the more ardent aficionados. Film critics praise him for the vital role he played in laying the literary foundation for *film noir* and frequently mention him in the company of Chandler, Hammett, and Cain. However, they much too often skim over the extent of his contributions. Not that theirs is a sin of omission. Woolrich's life lurks furtively in the same opaque shadows as his characters. He led a relatively quiet, unassuming, uneventful existence that did not draw much attention to itself. Yet commentators generally agree they cannot overlook him entirely, and so, sensing the dint of his influence on *noir* yet suffering from a dearth of knowledge about his background, they generously place him a notch above footnote status.

There are, however, some studies that offer more than a cursory acknowledgement of the man who helped define the style and content of pulp *noir* and *film noir*. Foster Hirsch, for instance, in *The Dark Side of the Screen: Film Noir*, devotes several pages to Woolrich's prominence as a literary source for *films noirs*. Andrew Dickos, author of *Street with No Name*, offers a concise and informative overview of Woolrich and his contribution to the *noir* genre. Occasional articles, such as those by Tom Flinn (1972) or Barry N. Malzberg and Donald A. Yates (1998), and the substantial forewords to Woolrich's books by the likes of Harlan Ellison and Francis M. Nevins, Jr., provide insightful perspectives. The most significant seminal sources on the man are two book-length works, Nevins's comprehensive and meticulously researched biography, *Cornell Woolrich: First You Dream, Then You Die* (with an invaluable "checklist" of Woolrich's published works compiled by Nevins, Harold Knott, and William Thailing) and Woolrich's own pseudo-autobiography *Blues of a Lifetime* (with incisive introduction and end notes by editor Mark T. Bassett). Still, no matter how much one reads about him, one inevitably confronts the translucent façade Woolrich wore like a mask to protect his private self. His reclusive life, for all its apparent simplicity, raises many unanswerable questions.

Whatever documented facts we have about the author hardly do more than plot out a crude timeline of his life. He was born Cornell George Hopley-Woolrich in New York City, December 4, 1903. (The moniker is of family origin, a conglomerate of names from his maternal grandfather, Jewish immigrant Gyorgi Tarler; from his mother's brother, George Cornell Tarler; and from his father.) His father, Genaro Hopley-Woolrich, a tepid Roman Catholic, may have been either a metallurgist or a civil engineer. (The uncertainty about his occupation is consistent with the other indefinite details of Woolrich's life.) In contrast, his mother, Claire Attalie Tarler, hailed from an affluent Jewish family. When the boy was three, the father's work took them down to Mexico. Whether from the strain of relocating, or from Claire's discomfort away from her family and her familiar life style, or from irreconcilable personal differences, the marriage fizzled. Claire returned to New York to live with her parents while Cornell remained in Mexico with his father, who agreed to send the boy to her when he reached adolescence.

Blues of a Lifetime offers some brief and cryptic allusions to that period in Woolrich's history. Unlike a conventional chronological biography, the book is a collection of five vignettes, each centered on a different climactic moment in his life. Incoherent and incomplete as a biographical whole, *Blues* fittingly complements Woolrich's inventive and experimental approach to story structure and narrative style, transforming his "real" life into a biofictional account: the first-person narrator says many things that are specious as fact, but make for darn good entertainment.

In the first vignette, "Remington Portable NC69411," Woolrich pays tribute to the first typewriter he fingered as a young, fledgling writer. During the telling, he makes a couple of digressions to his childhood spent in Mexico. When he was eight years old, for instance, he and his displaced family were visited by his maternal grandfather who took him to see *Madama Butterfly* for the first time. *Madama Butterfly* becomes an allusive device in several of Woolrich's future works; more than that, the pathos of the opera, heartfelt loss coupled with stinging irony, becomes a tonal quality he infuses into many of his stories.

A second digression takes Woolrich from his homage to his typewriter to a reflection on the antipodal relationship between a brief period in his young adult life and an incident in Mexico where, when he was 11, he witnessed an exceptionally violent thunderstorm:

> This credo of escape from responsibility, of fun and of the unserious, was in the atmosphere, the climate of the times [i.e., the 1920s, notoriously labeled the Jazz Age, when Woolrich was in his early twenties]....
> ... It became locked into my heart.... It was the perfect counterpoint to the sense of personal, private doom that had been in me..., ever since one night when I was 11 and ... [I] looked up at the low-hanging stars of the Valley of Anahuac, and knew I would certainly die finally, or something worse. I had that trapped feeling, like some sort of a poor insect that you've put inside a downturned glass, and it tries to climb up the sides, and it can't, and it can't, and it can't [15–16].

In this passage, the author eloquently expresses a childhood fear marked by intense anxiety and desperation, but one has to wonder whether Woolrich the Adult is rendering truthfully the paralyzing paranoia of Woolrich the Boy or is describing a morbid philosophy honed over years of disheartening disappointments and frustrations. To recall and relate the event at all suggests it must have deeply affected him, and even if it does not coincide accurately with his youthful impression, it certainly reflects the *noir* sensibility of the mature author.

In this same excerpt, Woolrich credits the Jazz Age as a primary influence on his development as a person — and thus as a writer. For one thing this is the productive period of the exemplary Francis Scott Fitzgerald, the man who most epitomized the Jazz Age in his work and his life, and the man whom Woolrich, the young emerging writer, tried most to emulate. Understandably, this decade is also nostalgic for Woolrich: not only does he get his first book published during this time (*Cover Charge*, 1926), but he also sees his second book *Children of the Ritz* (1927) made into a movie (produced by First National in 1929, directed by John Francis Dillon). Fitzgerald's thumbprint is visible on these and the subsequent realistic novels that Woolrich writes in trying to negotiate the waters of mainstream literature: *Times Square*, 1929; *A Young Man's Heart*, 1930; *The Time of Her Life*, 1931; and *Manhattan Love Song*, 1932 (this last made into a Monogram film in 1934).

When Woolrich says that the twenties served to counter his feelings of some ineffable doom, he acknowledges that era as a time when he felt more carefree, optimistic, hopeful, and contented than at any before or since. Ironically, the Jazz Age, sandwiched between the two international cataclysms of World War I and the Great Depression, spawned its own strain of social upheaval: people became more hedonistic, less morally restrained. Living in this materialistic society, balanced precariously on the knife-edge of experiential freedom, one finds the world exciting and invigorating, even if morally corrupting.

Woolrich further confesses that this lifestyle, although but a momentary ray of sunshine in his otherwise gloomy life, imbedded itself permanently in his psyche. Yet what he actually did during those years to make himself a part of the times is not detailed. His publications and film adaptations prove the period productive for him, financially and creatively, but what was his personal life like?

Through several reflections in *Blues of a Lifetime*, Woolrich enlightens us — although to what extent we can believe these accounts is another matter. In "Remington Portable NC69411," he confesses that his love for writing — and for his typewriter — surpasses anything he felt for a woman, and he declares, with rather stoic indifference, that he had only three romantic affairs in his life, each "a kick in the jaw":

> The first time, it was just puppy love, but it ended disastrously for at least one of us, through no fault of mine. The second time, somebody else married her.... The

third time, I married her, and it was only after it happened that I realized I wished it hadn't [4].

Because much of Woolrich's autobiographical commentary exhibits the writer's prerogative to interweave fiction with fact, this revelation of a pathetically barren love life must, from one perspective, be viewed with amused wariness. He may, in truth, have had only these three passing infatuations, but we have to wonder it he actually had more — or less. He equivocates when he says that three failed affairs led him to lose his "incentive." Most of us experience far more rejections than that and never stop trying. He seems to be rationalizing his failures to justify his decision to remain isolated, alone, supposedly celibate. But we know his dark secret. Revelations from other evidence (and verified by Bassett and Nevins) tell us that Woolrich was homosexual, which seems to validate his reticence for getting involved with a girl, obviously shunning romantic entanglements with women because he preferred the company of men.

On the other hand, if we can assume as true that Woolrich experienced only these three poignant affairs, we can also try to speculate about them. The "puppy love" fiasco, for example, would seem to refer to his romantic encounter described in "The Poor Girl," the second story of *Blues of a Lifetime*, where he tells how he met Vera (short for Veronica) Gaffney. Although his "puppy love" label connotes youthful naiveté and innocence, he candidly describes his feeble attempt one night to seduce her. The attempt in itself suggests that his perception of romance has evolved beyond the "puppy" stage. Vera casually deflects his overture with philosophical words about reputation, mutual respect, and meaningful relationships. (Vera is a name that, perhaps for this delicate reason, Woolrich assigns to more than a few female characters in his stories.)

The episode is supposed to show Woolrich as an ordinary young man with normal libidinous cravings, yet it raises questions about the truth of his supposedly uncensored confession. Chronologically, the Vera Gaffney story, although following "Remington Portable," should have come first: Woolrich's relationship with Vera must have occurred sometime during 1922 and 1923, when the 18 year old turned 19; the events of "Remington" happened a little later, between spring and fall of 1925 (Bassett in *Blues* 31, 144.6n, 145.15n). Arguable as Woolrich's reason may be for reversing this sequence, it raises a curiously significant contradiction. In the first story, Woolrich explains how his good friend Ken, like a well-meaning older brother, arranged his initiation into the world of sex. Woolrich says he gained his knowledge of women in the "scriptural sense" through a rite of passage resembling that of "primitive tribes where ... the striplings had to face up to certain tests and ordeals before they were allowed to claim full manhood" (*Blues* 17). Woolrich's deft skill with word play should not go unnoticed — the pun on "stripling" with its implied sexual relevance, and the ironic contrast between biblical euphemism and primitive ritual.

In the second story, his presumptuous attempt to seduce Vera indicates that he has already had sexual experience, that he has already known a woman in the "scriptural sense." It is hardly likely, although admittedly not impossible, that this reputedly shy, young milquetoast should go out with a young girl and, on their first date, make blatant sexual advances toward her. Either he is fantasizing about his male prowess or he is describing the aggressive behavior of a man with more sexual experience and more definite sexual expectations. Whichever category he falls into, his calling his relationship with Vera "puppy love" subtly distorts reality, manipulates and compromises truth in the service of his writer's craft. That is, these confessions about his sexual awakening may be fundamentally true, but in their details, they hint at something more fictitious and less innocent.

There is also the matter of that first sexual encounter. By equating lovemaking with an "ordeal," he blunts what should have been an ecstatic initiation into sexual awareness and twists it into a trial to be endured:

> I have a recollection of a completely blacked out living room.... And ... a record that never stopped playing...: "I'm Just Wild About Harry."
> ... I never again could hear that piece without remembering that pitch-black room, though everything else is gone now, the girls' names, their very faces, and even Ken himself [*Blues* 17–18].

His tone is remote, even aloof, and given that the "first time" for most people, for better or worse, cannot help but stand out as a momentous occasion, it is queer how he stumbles through vague, shadowy recollections of an experience that should have been more vivid in his memory (How can he *not* remember the girl's name?). Like a magician, he creates the illusion of presenting personal events in sufficient detail. But when we look closer, we see that this defining moment has been narrated in such general and apathetic terms that we have to question whether he has told us anything at all — or at least whether he's told us anything explicit. Implicitly, the omission of precise details tells us more about him than about the event itself. Instead of the indelible imprint on memory that this climactic experience has for most of us, Woolrich remembers chiefly the darkness and the music. If true, the literal blackness covering his illicit deed symbolizes the shroud of oblivion that prevents him from recalling or relating certain specifics, probably because he doesn't want to. His may not have been the rapturous euphoria a sexual encounter was rumored to elicit. His cynical comments on heterosexual sex make more apparent the reality of his hidden homosexuality. His forgetting the girl's name but remembering the song title, "I'm Just Wild About Harry," incidentally suggests which gender he favors for sexual liaisons.

Woolrich's second love affair remains his secret. There is no evidence to identify his lover or the circumstances of their relationship. Even so, what could have been a simple throwaway comment becomes cryptically captivating because he implies that, looked at in retrospect, she might have been the love of his life. Whether she exists in fact or fancy, as a real figure or an idealistic fable, is anybody's guess.

It is Woolrich's third affair, however, which is the most telling, especially in respect to his sexual orientation. Information is more reliable and impressive than that about the other two because it comes from an objective source, Nevins's biographical opus on the author. Before elaborating on the marriage debacle, Nevins outlines the whirlwind career of J. Stuart Blackton, the filmmaking pioneer, whose Vitagraph Company at the turn of the century rivaled Edison in output, influence, and profits. Woolrich met and married one of Blackton's two daughters, Violet Virginia (nicknamed Gloria, and at times, for some unexplained reason, called Bill). Nevins theorizes that Woolrich met Gloria sometime in 1930 after he had come to Hollywood to observe the film adaptation of his first novel *Children of the Ritz* (Nevins 71–72). Considering that Woolrich attended theaters regularly, that he was strongly influenced throughout his life by the movies, and that his early novel was adapted to film, it seems fitting that he should have married into a family associated with the film industry.

However, like the outcome in many of his stories, this event was to produce ironic consequences radically different from any conventional scenario. According to Nevins, the marriage on December 6, 1930, two days after Woolrich's 27th birthday, was never consummated. Woolrich turned out to be a back-street homosexual. Not until after he left her did his abandoned new bride discover the truth. From a personal diary he had left behind, its pages rambling with sordid accounts, and from a suitcase spilling out its evidence, she learned to her horror that, on occasion, he would dress in a sailor suit and comb the derelict dives and dens of the seedy waterfront for the kind of entertainment he could never find at home. The marriage was annulled and Woolrich exorcised the trauma of this experience by taking a two-year hiatus to Europe with his mother Claire, where he completed his sixth novel, *Manhattan Love Song*, his last in the Fitzgerald vein. Nevins makes the case that this realistic novel already bears a strong foreshadowing of the *noir* style and plot devices Woolrich will infuse into his future work as a pulp fiction writer (88–100).

Woolrich and Claire return to New York in 1932 or 1933. In "Even God Felt the Depression," the third vignette in *Blues of a Lifetime*, he tells how he tries to maintain his independence, living alone in a hotel room and struggling to support himself four years after The Crash. At this time, his cash flow has dwindled to a trickle and he gamely resists his mother's enticing offers of money that could insulate him from financial insecurity. When he learns that she has paid his hotel bill without his knowing, he expresses his resentment with a passing show of proud indignation. At bottom, he seems to cling to his self-sufficiency more on the basis of social propriety than on his need to adhere to some great self-defining principle. We know that ultimately he cannot persist in this separation. His personality is too inextricably bound with hers.

In 1933, he moves with his mother into a hotel, the Hotel Marseilles at Broadway and 103rd, where they live together until her death in 1957. For insights into that relationship, the fifth story of *Blues*, "President Eisenhower's Speech," tells of Woolrich's attempt to protect his mother from needless distress during a minor fire in their hotel. Bassett notes that there is no record of a fire at the Marseilles anytime during 1957, when this story supposedly takes place (148.3n). Once again, Woolrich appears to be cloaking his biography in plausible fiction. The story moves forward with the rapidity of a glacier floe. In one respect, it exhibits the machinations of a fiction writer: a cast of characters represents the different strata of society, all remarkably living side-by-each in this one hotel. In another respect, it is tediously trite, but it happens to expose some of the sensitive nerve endings that have kept mother and son emotionally dependent, one on the other, and complicates our speculations on his motives for living with her. He may have depended on her money or needed reassurance from her physical presence. Or he may have been responding to a lifetime of conditioning that trained him to do her bidding. This notion was inferred by a college classmate, the writer Jacques Barzun, who had the impression that, during their college years, Claire dominated her son (Nevins 19). A fellow pulp writer, reminiscing about his brushes with Woolrich, tells how, one night, he and Steve Fisher called him at home to join them for a drink at a local bar: "His mother answered the phone and gave us holy hell — and refused to put him on the phone" (Gruber 101). Then again, Woolrich may have felt obligated to take care of her out of genuine love or some ineffable feeling of allegiance or responsibility. Friend Barry N. Malzberg writes in a eulogistic essay what Woolrich told him about his decision to stay with her:

> I tried to move out. In 1942 I lived alone in a hotel room for three weeks and then one night she called me and said, "I can't live without you, I must live with you, I need you," and I put down the phone and I packed and I went back to that place and for the rest of her life I never spent a night away from her, not one. I know what they thought of me, what they said about me but I just didn't care. I don't regret it and I'll never regret it as long as I live [164].

There is a discrepancy in the date given here. According to *Blues*, Woolrich's flight to independence occurred in 1933 — unless in 1942 he made a second attempt for a few weeks and couldn't sustain it. Whichever the circumstances, this latter remark makes it sound as if his was a deliberate decision. But who can tell if it is a sign of devotion, obsession, love, subservience, guilt, or something else? Becoming his mother's lifelong companion may be no more than an excuse for clinging to her consolatory apron strings or a means for eradicating his own tormenting loneliness or a justification for his anti-social behavior. The complexities of their relationship defy summation and closure.

It is during those cloistered years in that hotel room that he redefines himself as an author and gains the fame which had eluded him earlier. In 1934, he begins to write a certain species of story for the pulp magazines, short tales of mystery and suspense, often exercises in the preposterous, the grotesque, and the exotic, meant to shock and horrify the reader. The genre has an emancipating effect on him: crossing into this realm of the bizarre and the perverted, he is able to fashion a style that suits him better because of his inclination toward the dark, gruesome, cynical side of life.

"Walls That Hear You" (1934), "Preview of Death" (1934), "The Body Upstairs" (1935), "Kiss of the Cobra" (1935), and "Dark Melody of Madness" (1935) are among these early stories. Their plots include complex murder methods, severed limbs, gory deaths, erotic rituals, and repulsive characters. Meanwhile, in churning out these fantastic story lines, Woolrich begins to develop a style that epitomizes the *noir* world in mood and tone, a surreal, nightmarish world in which his characters are manipulated like inconsequential game tokens. Thematically, too, he proposes the notion of a coldly indifferent and unfathomable power — fate or providence, coincidence or chance — that controls human lives. Although some of his characters aspire to virtuousness, many others are wicked, vile, self-serving creatures inhabiting the dismal crannies of foul urban environs. Woolrich keeps evoking the ambience of Gothic horror stories by descending again and again into the same squalid settings: seedy dance halls, remote dwellings, derelict hotels, and dark, deserted streets and alleyways — the underworld of modern civilization, the *noir* labyrinth.

So after eight years of writing realistic literature, Woolrich doused his dream of joining the ranks of mainstream fiction writers and turned instead to writing for pulp magazines. The specific reason for this divergence is not very clear, since he had already achieved some success as a serious novelist. Six published novels and two adapted films suggest that he was well entrenched in his career path. Not so. He seemed to feel the need for a change; he was a committed writer, and so he carried on in that same profession, just in a different genre.

When he first became interested in writing as a young college student at Columbia, motivated by accolades from his creative writing teacher Harrison R. Steeves, he may have harbored an inflated opinion of himself. His skills with a diverse vocabulary and descriptive detail lifted him above the rank and file of other student writers. Then, when he first published, he surely must have had visions of nudging his way up into the rarefied company of Fitzgerald and Hemingway. But somewhere, somehow, something changed all that.

In "Remington Portable NC69411," Woolrich speaks of his fascination with writing as if some creative demon or badgering muse had taken possession of him and could only be exorcised through the act of writing itself:

> The stream of words was like an electric arc leaping across the intervening space from pole to opposite pole, from me to paper, later on from me to machine.... and it wouldn't let go....
> I couldn't tell what it was.... Some kind of energy ... [9].

This passage resonates with the ardent, all-consuming enthusiasm a writer feels for his craft. Woolrich so effusively expresses the driving force behind the artist, the need to fulfill some ineffable creative urge within. Yet his excitement over the act of writing is tempered only a few pages later by his blaming drink for keeping him from becoming what he could have been:

> ... I was already beginning to drink sporadically [in the 1920s].... trying to cover up *from* something, or cover *up* something, or both.
> It is a wrong thing ... to pervert yourself like this.... You destroy the you that was meant to be, that was placed there to be, that would ... and should have been....
> I would have been a great writer ... a great and good man. I would have left a name.... And ... I would have led a happy life [15].

Woolrich juxtaposes writing and morality, as if they were implicitly connected, and he condemns liquor for undermining them both: it prevented him from achieving literary success and it diluted his spiritual integrity. Literally, alcohol had a detrimental effect on his creative faculties. (Whether his self-assessment, that he could have been "a great writer," is false humility or an accurate evaluation is open to debate.) But in a figurative sense, alcohol also serves as a scapegoat for guilt over his submission to worldly temptations too strong to resist and too corrosive to leave him unscarred.

It is difficult not to see alcohol as a metaphor for his homosexuality. He calls drinking a perversion, which was the general (and probably his own) perception of homosexuality at that time. (Consider how *films noirs*, from *The Maltese Falcon* to the present, frequently portray homosexual characters as symbols of social and moral corruption and human perversity.) He may be making a subliminal admission of his homosexuality, holding up liquor as a straw man for his sexual deviance. He may also be denouncing liquor for some literal connection to his homosexuality, as if it contributed in some way to his transformation from a heterosexual male to a homosexual "pervert." Was he under the influence of alcohol when he had his first homosexual experience? Did he need to couple his drinking binges with his homosexual encounters? His pathetic self-recriminations suggest that he is confessing to more than just a weakness for whiskey.

The above passage from "Remington" contains other shadowy implications roiling in Woolrich's mind. Alcohol could be a symbol for money. Woolrich often complained that whatever he received for his writing or sold to film companies was never enough (a complaint which might have been justified). High literature did not pave a direct path to financial rewards, and so he might have turned to the pulps, hoping they would be more lucrative. Thus, he "perverted" or "prostituted" his talent by forsaking art for something less noble and fine (money and pulp fiction).

Even if he didn't write for the pulps purely for money, it must have been bitterly frustrating to let go of his grandiose dream, finally admitting that he was not as gifted a writer as he had originally thought. Turning to the pulps after a semi-successful run at authorial fame suggests this. It was easier to blame alcohol for his failure to scale the lofty literary peaks than to admit that his talent could not make the higher grade, not that writing on a lower plane should have been considered all bad. In his shift from realistic novels to sensationalized fiction, he could appeal to a different, wider audience.

He was very conscious of why an idealistic, ambitious artist might have to temper his dream and amend his content, style, and expectations. Consider what one character says in his last book, *Into the Night*. (This unfinished work was completed by Lawrence Block and published posthumously). Giving professional advice to her songwriting protégée Madeline, Adelaide Nelson explains why talent and desire must coexist in an artist:

> Anything that gets in your blood that way, it's hard to find a way to say no to it. If you're lucky, the desire and the talent come in the same package. But some unlucky people get the one without the other. Of course, if you get the talent and not the desire, it's not necessarily the worst thing in the world [because it's easier to quit at any time].
> ... When it's the other way around, you got a lifetime of disappointment. Well, what the hell — that's what you get when you've got the drive *and* the talent, too, because this is a business where even the winners lose most of the time. But at least there are a few victories along the way, something to keep your hopes up."

One does not have to plunge too deeply into this passage to recognize it as a self-reflective comment on Woolrich's own situation. For one thing, Adelaide's words most likely express Woolrich's opinion — a plausible inference simply because every artist, at one time or another, considers these same things about talent, desire, and opportunity. The question is not really whether the character is speaking for Woolrich (although she certainly does), or whether Woolrich had the persistence to succeed (although he certainly did). The question is whether that persistence complemented a genuine talent or compensated for naive mediocrity. Woolrich must have concluded that he fit in the second category, for he chose to stop writing for mainstream fiction in favor of the pulps.

If Woolrich considered the fact that, despite his determination, he did not have the talent, he might have seen his persistence not as an indefatigable effort to succeed but a prolonged struggle toward failure. Failure in an occupation that consumed him for the past 40 years would have been difficult to accept. And so the subtitle of Nevins's book, "First You Dream, Then You Die," one of Woolrich's working titles never linked to a story, can fittingly be applied to his life, the dream perpetually deferred until time — and life — ran out.

Woolrich deserted his dream of literary fame and made the tactical but humbling decision to write for the lowly pulps. These publications may have offended the dignity of the literati, but they enjoyed significant notoriety within their own sphere of influence. In the 1930s, besides the esteemed *Black Mask*, founded in 1920 as a Mencken-Nathan collaboration (Dickos 98), leading magazines such as *Detective Story, Argosy, Detective Fiction Weekly,* and *Dime*

Detective provided markets for Woolrich's new output of morbid and macabre suspense stories. Even if cynicism and pessimism sprang from his having to give up his original expectations, he learned quickly that, although he was a crude acolyte among the Hemingways and Fitzgeralds, he became a high priest among pulp writers. "I wasn't that good, you know," he tells a friend near the end of his life. "What I was was a guy who could write a little, publishing in magazines surrounded by people who couldn't write at all. So I looked pretty good. But I never thought I was that good at all. All that I thought was that I tried" (Malzberg 165).

What some people may take as false modesty is actually a fair assessment of himself. Critics (myself included) will often point out, with self-conscious ambivalence, Woolrich's works show him to be a highly gifted wordsmith, a capable mood-spinner and storyteller, but not an exceptional writer destined to compose great literature: "...although Woolrich had a genius for inventing extraordinary situations (Raymond Chandler called him 'the best idea man'), he wrote in a bloated purple prose that thuds like overemphatic movie music..." (O'Brien 91). Actually, Woolrich does not drift so much into the florid style of "purple prose" as he does the bathos of maudlin melodrama. But whether called "purple prose" or an exaggerated emotional pitch, his densely packed descriptions associated with despair, darkness, and death are what most effectively engage us. Chandler is exactly right: as an "idea man," Woolrich creates the most spellbinding of premises. Consider: an innocent man is found guilty of murder because the only woman who can corroborate his testimony has disappeared, and his Girl Friday has to play "beat-the-clock" to save him; a man, confined to his bedroom, whiles away the time by spying on his neighbors and, on circumstantial evidence, comes to believe that one of them has murdered his wife; a young boy witnesses a murder, and the only ones who believe his story are the murderers trying to kill him. The list goes on. Woolrich may have resented the lowly status of his new creations, but writing for the pulps gave him an outlet for expressing his perversions more freely. Many of his core story ideas deal with surrealistic nightmares of a febrile but intelligent mind, hence Nevins's equating him with Poe. These two key components, idea and style, fused together in a blend of psychotic frenzy, neurotic fear, and debilitating cynicism, produce the perverted, paranoid world that is not only his but ours, for we at times must identify disconcertingly with it.

Although he gave up his original ambitions for a more modest career among the pulps, he could not abandon the writer's life, which consumed him intensely. Toward the end of his life, he tells Malzberg, in a strange non sequitur, his feelings about writing: "It isn't dying I'm afraid of...; I know what it is to die, I've died already. It is the endless obliteration, the knowledge that there will never be anything else. That's what I can't stand, to try so hard and to end in nothing. You know what I mean, don't you? ... I really loved to write" (163). Writing seems somehow linked to salvation, to an immortality that defies dying and "endless obliteration." Yet he expresses a fear whether writing is enough. Maybe it comes to nothing; that is, maybe his writing isn't good enough, that it will "end in nothing."

Late in 1967, Woolrich failed to treat a foot infection, which became gangrenous. In January of the following year, he faced amputation of his leg above the knee. Later that year, on September 19, he suffered a stroke and collapsed in his hotel room. After a week in a coma, he died on September 25, 1968. When his body was laid out for one night, on September 27, five people attended, an irony Woolrich might have appreciated because he could now identify with the most famous character created by his mentor, F.S. Fitzgerald: Jay Gatsby was an outsider whose funeral was attended by a mere three people. A further irony is that a foot ailment had launched his career, and a foot ailment contributed to his demise.

From Woolrich's perspective, perhaps his life did "end in nothing." But not from ours. The undiluted despair and nihilism in the six books of his Black series, the amusing originality of such works as *Phantom Lady* and *I Married a Dead Man*, and the mesmerizing inventiveness of his numerous short stories are much more than the "nothing" he loved to wallow in. Whether a well-conceived story or the weakest of his potboilers, all of his writings are sources of entertainment, interesting studies of human nature, and inspirations for introspection.

Few people would deny that, when it comes to suspense writers, Cornell Woolrich ranks among the most proficient. He has a knack for incorporating his own paranoia, neuroses, and psychoses into his stories, amplifying them to excessive proportions. "Nightmare" and "He Looked Like Murder," for instance, flirt with homosexual implications; *Night Has a Thousand Eyes* and *Into the Night* touch on that ultimate taboo, incest, one suggesting it, the other overtly admitting it; "Rear Window" and "The Boy Cried Murder" include acts of voyeurism; "For the Rest of Her Life" flaunts the viciousness of sadism. Woolrich exposes these secret perversions of private lives, regardless of whether they are festering in the decrepit corners of a skid row slum (the indigent alcoholic Marty Blair in *The Black Angel*) or metastasizing behind the luxurious façades of the very rich (plantation owner Louis Durand in *Waltz into Darkness*). For sheer inventiveness of plot, his stories are the nonpareil. His central ideas, his basic premises, can be so ingeniously original: their unique "what-if" speculations grab our curiosity, snag our imagination (What if a man cannot tell whether the murder he committed in a dream is a murder he committed in reality? What if a man suddenly wakes from an amnesiac state and, unable to remember what he did during those lost years, realizes he may have killed someone? What if a woman survives a train wreck and is mistaken for the wife of a man who died in the accident?). Originality is one of his most outstanding virtues. Raymond Chandler acknowledged this attribute in his contemporary, calling him "one of the oldest hands there are at the pulp detective business. He is known in the trade as an idea writer...." He qualified his compliment, adding that Woolrich is "not much of a character man. I think his stuff is very readable, but leaves no warmth behind it" (Hiney and MacShane 33).

In addition to not being "much of a character man," Woolrich is also inconsistent in regard to the construction and cohesiveness of his stories. His plots are, in fact, something of an artistic paradox because the brilliance of his originality is too often compromised by his incomprehensible lapses in logic. In the actual telling, Woolrich is willing to distort all logic in character and action if it allows him to accommodate a sequence of actions or enables him to cram his ending into some hastily devised resolution. At times it is obvious that, after a captivating premise has set events into motion, he is not sure how to end the story, and so he hastily finagles situations, motives, and options that enable him to tie up all the unraveled plot threads.

For this reason, a Woolrich narrative sometimes requires more imaginative latitude than the normal suspension of disbelief. To enjoy such stories as *The Black Angel* and *Deadline at Dawn*, we must ignore implausible circumstances, outrageous coincidences, or unlikely character psychology. Of course, such failings, though prevalent, are not always present, and many of Woolrich's stories are completely satisfying in logic and common sense. That said, we don't read Woolrich strictly for his storyline anyway. More important is what his stories have to offer in stylistics, tonalities, and tensions, the same elements for which Chandler praised Hammett in *The Simple Art of Murder*. These are the essentials that reflect Woolrich's strengths and merit our loyalty as his readers.

Besides succumbing now and again to faulty logic, Woolrich occasionally counters his creativity with a personal approach to plot inspiration: he recycles his own stories. For whatever reason—fending off writer's block, maintaining momentum in his literary output (for financial or artistic purposes), exploiting a successful formula, or something else—Woolrich has the blatant audacity to steal from himself. Anyone who has consumed a fair quantity of Woolrich can't help but notice how, from time to time, one story is a regurgitated version of an earlier story or the amalgam of several previous stories. For instance, the female avenging angel in *The Bride Wore Black* is reincarnated as a young man in *Rendezvous in Black*. *Phantom Lady* evolved into novel form after first appearing as the short story "Those Who Kill" (1939) and then undergoing expansion into a six-part serial, "Phantom Alibi" (1942). Meanwhile, *The Black Angel* is derivative of several stories, including *Phantom Lady*, "Murder in Wax" (1935), and "Face Work" (1937). "They Call Me Patrice" (1946) provides the germinal idea for the lengthier *I Married a Dead Man* (1948). "Momentum," "From Dusk to Dawn," and "Marihuana" follow an identical trajectory: an innocent, law-abiding man makes one fatal error in judgment and is drawn headlong into committing a series of criminal acts.

Although this kind of plot inbreeding sometimes produces a near clone of a previous model, what Woolrich manages to achieve is a number of variations on a theme. That is, he takes his original central idea and modifies it in one or more ways, perhaps treating similar circumstances from an alternate point of view (seeking proof of innocence in *Phantom Lady* and *The Black Curtain*); or having similar events lead to a different outcome (suspecting someone of murder in "Rear Window" and "He Looked Like Murder"); or tweaking some similar plot device (the nature of the protagonist's blackout experience in "Morning After Murder," *The Black Curtain*, "Nightmare", "Marihuana", and "C-Jag"); or developing his story around closely related situations (*The Bride Wore Black* and *Rendezvous in Black*); and so on. This practice is not unique to Woolrich; many artists devote a lifetime to telling their single theme in a variety of ways. It is just that it appears more noticeable with Woolrich because his stories are generally plot-driven and he is not so tactful about disguising a previous story line. Even so, the results are not without their reward and this repetitiveness is not enough to discourage us from reading him. Those of us who are true fans keep seeking out his work, regardless of the redundancies, looking for it wherever we can find it, like thirsty wayfarers in a desert, unable to get enough of what we need. What keeps us so interested is that style of his, that ingenious flair for creating tense, overwrought situations that propel us forward in the narrative. We want as much of it as we can get, and we don't care if it means treading a bit of ground we've trod before.

One format of novel writing that becomes for Woolrich an oft-used convention is the episodic structure. Although from time to time he employs the standard linear narrative with satisfactory success (*Waltz into Darkness*, *I Married a Dead Man*, *The Black Path of Fear*), he frequently turns to the episodic form as if he feels more comfortable with it. Woolrich is like Poe in his flirtations with the bizarre, the horrific, and the macabre, but he also imitates him as an accomplished and prolific short story writer who may have preferred to string together a sequence of short episodes than have to sustain a long single narrative line (as Poe did in *The Narrative of Arthur Gordon Pym*, his sole work of novel length). After using the episodic structure in his first suspense novel *The Bride Wore Black*, he returns to it again in subsequent novels such as *The Black Angel*, *Deadline at Dawn*, and *Rendezvous in Black*.

A plot device that recurs in many Woolrich works and affects their structure is the quest formula. In these stories, one person nobly sets out to prove another's innocence or sometimes literally to redeem another's life. Generally, he has the male needing the help of the female, rather than vice versa. If a piece of writing can be analyzed as the dreamwork or wish-fulfillment of an author, we may see this as an indication of Woolrich's belief that the male depends more heavily on the female for salvation than does the female on the male. Taken further, we may even surmise that this is a reflection of his psychological dependency on his mother. In "Face Work," one of his early attempts at this type of story, a woman sets out to prove the innocence of her brother, who has been convicted of murder and sentenced to death. The pattern sets a precedent for many of Woolrich's later stories, among them *Phantom Lady*, *The Black Angel*, and *Deadline at Dawn*. *The Black Curtain* and *Nightmare* are types that also fit this category but with the ironic twist that the redeemer and the accused are one and the same person: a conscience-stricken man is on a mission to discover his own innocence or guilt. Other stories related to this quest formula include "All at Once, No Alice" and "You'll Never See Me Again," where a wife's baffling disappearance catapults the husband into a desperate search for her.

One variation on this quest story or redeemer motif deals with the bond between a brother and sister. Besides "Face Work," stories such as "Somebody on the Phone," "Bluebeard's Seventh Wife," and "One and a Half Murders" make use of this familial relationship. "Nightmare" improvises on it further: the accused's sister is married to a detective who vicariously steps in for the sister and helps his brother-in-law discover his role in an unsolved murder.

Stories involving the sister-brother relationship reach their ironic and catastrophic culmination in *Into the Night*. Formerly, the sibling relationship was built on trust, love, and loyalty. In this last of his novels, Woolrich aims for an alternate outcome where one party violates those shared values. Unfortunately, Woolrich did not finish this book, so we cannot know his intended outcome. The hopeful "happy" ending concocted by Lawrence Block totally ignores Woolrich's obvious clues that are steering the characters toward self-annihilation. Instead, the novel flounders feebly by trying to salvage redemption out of previous immoral acts of deceit, degradation, violation, and perversion.

Another personal convention Woolrich repeatedly pulls out of his writer's grab bag is the "Trivial Clue Device." At some point in a story, a protagonist, trying to solve a mystery, has nothing to go on. Suddenly, he or she discovers the slightest of clues (a matchbook cover, a slip of paper in shoe). This minor evidence becomes the inspiration for an elaborate train of logic (often specious and arguable, although Woolrich presents it as ironclad and indisputable) and sets the protagonist on the trail of a definite suspect. *Deadline at Dawn* and *Black Angel* contain many of these moments. As remarkably engrossing as "Rear Window" is, it also is filled with a plethora of ambiguous clues, particularly the vague intimations in Thorwald's mundane gestures, which the voyeuristic Jeff somehow interprets correctly to validate his suspicions about his neighbor's crime.

Finally, something must be said about Woolrich's style. While a Woolrich plot, more often than not, contains specious, unconvincing elements such as outlandish coincidences and improbable character behavior, his style, so often intriguing through language and phrasing, can enthrall us and buoy us to the end of the story. At times his writing can be quite poetic, clever, and inventive: "The death of a man is a sad enough thing to watch, but he goes by himself, taking nothing else with him. The death of a house is a sadder thing by far to watch. For so much more goes with it" (*Waltz into Darkness*, Chapter

30). Then occasionally it may collapse into amateurish awkwardness. For instance, in *The Black Angel*: "I flung out my hand quickly, struck out the red ember that had been held in it against something" (106). Here, the odd sequence of words is merely confusing, not ear- or eye-catching. The "red ember" is, of course, a synecdoche for the cigarette in Alberta's hand, but the passive voice ("that had been held") and the delayed "against something," which refers to what was done with it, create a clumsy, disjointed sequence. If Woolrich is doing this deliberately to show his creative expressiveness with sentence construction, we might appreciate the effort, but we have to wince at the result.

There are times when Woolrich stretches his poetical attempts beyond their proper bounds. Again in *The Black Angel*: "What sounded like an enamel panful of loosely rolling instruments was shifted sleazily aside to make room" (120). Is it possible that a metallic sound can give the impression of moving "sleazily"? Even though the word is meant to reflect the psychological state of the protagonist, it feels inappropriate. This is one example of Woolrich's reputation for straining his stylistics with odd and often obtrusive sounding adverbs. Consider also several examples from *The Black Curtain*: "lonelily," "troubledly," "blurredly," "sepulchrally," and (my personal favorite) "amputatedly." Although they affect the flow of the sentence (many of them are not easily pronounced aloud), he may be using them to try to establish a personal voice. One cannot defend these attempts for any artistic value, but one surely must admire Woolrich's courage in deploying them.

In his best stories, Woolrich offers some insights about human nature that, accurate or not, serve two main purposes. First, they give the plot momentum, no matter how fantastic these same comments appear if applied to reality. The narrator's logic addresses the goings-on from several angles, offers alternatives, finally settles on the one that explains the particular circumstances and gives the story its outcome. We accept these remarks as *plausible*, even if we know that in actuality they may not be possible. Thus, Jeff reaches his conclusion, that Thorwald committed murder, from an accretion of mundane evidence that no real person would have put together in that way. Yet his inferences follow such a detailed and deliberate train of logic that readers are willing to accept them on the chance that the voyeur may be right.

A second thing resulting from Woolrich's analysis of human nature is an automatic by-product of the first: it immerses readers in the story. His logic has a personal appeal that hits readers on the intimate, visceral level. Sometimes we marvel at Woolrich's attempt to explain a small gesture in terms of deeper motivations (e.g., in "Rear Window," Jeff infers that the way Thorwald wipes his forehead must be a sign of guilt, when instead it may simply be a sign of physical exertion). Even if these comments fall into the trap of an arguable either-or fallacy, they still make us wonder about some alternative we may never have thought of at all. More importantly, though, what appear to be trivial comments on minute habits and mundane ways of thinking turn out to be incisive observations about human nature. We often find ourselves identifying with many of these "trite" insights and we begin to consider how much of what Woolrich says actually applies to us.

In their excellent compilation *Film Noir: An Encyclopedic Reference to the American Style*, Silver and Ward offer an exhausting coverage of their subject, from their own perspective on this species of film, to an extraordinary collection of analyses of individual films (contributed by 18 reviewers), to a wealth of essential information on *noir's* critical history, filmmaking personnel, and related issues. They discuss the difficulty in trying to categorize noir, "whether it is called a series, style, genre, movement, cycle, or all of the above" (398), and propose their own "definition of film noir used in this work, treating it as a cycle which combines aspects of both movement (style) and genre (content)" (372).

What makes *film noir* such a slippery beast is its chimerical qualities: it is made up of all these features, so that, while it may be a series or a style or a genre, it may also be a series and a style and a genre. A critic trying to define *film noir* must feel like Jason confronting the multi-headed hydra: just when he or she has lopped off the extraneous possibilities, counter-arguments sprout anew. It would probably be easier to translate *In Search of Lost Time* into hieroglyphics.

Defining *film noir* as a "cycle" (or "series," as noted by the French cinéastes, particularly Borde and Chaumeton) works well enough when applied to those appropriate crime films bracketed between 1941 and 1958, the "classic period." In post-war Europe, French film critics noticed how a number of films recently imported from the United States mirrored the themes and content of American crime literature that had been translated into French under the heading *Serie Noire* (Silver and Ward 1). Since the likes of Chandler, Hammett, McCoy, and Cain had authored most of these works, it was obvious that contributors to the pulps, noted for their detective and crime fiction, were influencing filmmakers in some definite ways.

If the term "cycle" or "series" presupposes some common denominator linking these films, and if, as is apparent, crime alone is *not* enough to connect them, we should be able to identify a number of shared characteristics. Once we start to enumerate these shared characteristics, we begin to move toward the area of genre. True, a cycle or series is defined by a period, and it just so happens that *film noir* reflects the intersection of several socio-economic and socio-political traumas of the time (emergence from the Great Depression, entrance into World War II, post-war upheaval of social norms, Cold War tensions, threat of a nuclear holocaust). If we confine our discussion of *film noir* to the classic period, the films, with some few discrepancies, become fairly easy to contain. What complicate the discussion are the post-*noirs* and neo-*noirs* that exist outside that period. These later *noirs* copy the content and style of classic *noirs*, and because duplication of certain features and conventions is what enables one to define a genre, *film noir* suddenly edges into genre territory.

The argument that *film noir* is a style or movement also has validity. The direct relationship of *film noir* to German Expressionism, itself a movement from an earlier era, has been thoroughly documented: "Thematically, the conflict between the 'interior' world of the individual and the 'exterior' world that repels him is one of the links between Germany of the Twenties and America of the Forties" (Lloyd 142). American directors, particularly Orson Welles (with guidance from cinematographers Gregg Toland and Stanley Cortez), became proponents of the style with its dynamic lighting techniques and extensive range of camera angles and movements, but the more penetrating influence came from the Germans and Europeans, who, fleeing the horrors overrunning their homelands, emigrated to America and found a refuge where they could continue their filmmaking traditions. To call *film noir* a style, however, may be too narrow a designation if we consider that, in German Expressionism, style is not an end in itself but a means of enhancing mood, tone, and ambience while communicating content. In *noir*, too, style plays an identical role, and rather than the be-all and end-all of a film, it serves as one of many conventions contributing to the whole, another element helping to denote a "type" of film.

In defining *film noir*, Foster Hirsch uses the words "style," "genre," and "cycle" interchangeably as if they are synonyms (21). Maybe when applied to this polymorphic body of films, they are. Hirsch, however, organizes each of his chapters according to individual components peculiar to *noir*, and it is clear that, fundamentally, he considers *film noir* a genre.

While *film noir* possesses overlapping qualities that classify it as a cycle, series, style, movement, and genre all at once, treating it as a genre is the most efficient way of exploring Woolrich's contributions to its development. *Cornell Woolrich from Pulp Noir to Film Noir* looks closely at the works of the writer whose lurid tales served as the grist for many *film noir* mills of the classic era and afterward. Consequently, this book becomes at once a study of the author and an analysis of the films adapted from his writings or dependent on his themes, plot devices, and story lines.

When Nino Frank uses the term "film noir" for the first time in 1946, he applies it specifically to the American "crime film." He then goes on to say that perhaps a better term for these films would be "criminal psychology" because "the essential question is no longer 'who-done-it?' but how does this protagonist act?" (in *Film Noir Reader 2* 15, 16). Although Frank is correct in saying that the character study makes a *film noir* so much more interesting than a simple mystery, he does not distill from his generalization the precise dynamic at the core of nearly every *noir* character's dilemma, namely guilt.

As examined in *Cornell Woolrich from Pulp Noir to Film Noir*, almost every story from "The Corpse Next Door" to *I Married a Dead Man* shows that Woolrich's paranoid, troubled, wicked, or depraved characters are more complex mainly because their psychological makeup is complicated by a prickling conscience that compels them to question their options. Sensitivity to guilt — an awareness of conscience and of moral choices, the existential factor — gives *noir* characters fuller dimensions than the criminals of the 1930s mystery or gangster films and creates complexities in their motives and their relationships with society. As one of the literary influences on *film noir*, Woolrich is not alone here, but he figures most prominently. His many forays into the world of guilt, exploring its causes and effects, are a primary contribution to *film noir*, which also makes guilt an important influence on character motivation.

The treatment of guilt in a classic mystery is different from the way guilt is played out in a Woolrich story and, consequently, in *film noir*. Most mysteries, of course, rely on crime as a main ingredient in their plot; however, the element of guilt accompanies the crime, not because the criminal feels guilty for his actions but because he is blamed for the wrongdoing. Guilt in this respect is an external label outside the psychological framework of the character. The character does not necessarily feel or show any remorse, any compunction for his behavior or way of thinking. Not so with Woolrich. Guilt is essential in affecting characters' reasoning and behavior: if they commit a crime, they feel ambivalent toward the deed ("The Corpse Next Door," "Dormant Account"); and if they are innocent of the crime, they are connected to it in some way that inspires guilt, which becomes an integral part of the story (*Black Curtain, Deadline at Dawn*). Guilt must be confronted; it demands consideration and resolution. Confronting it may lead to absolution and redemption ("Nightmare"), or in the bleaker of Woolrich's stories, it may lead to punishment or death (not always deserved, such as in "The Night Reveals").

Consider the role of guilt in *film noir*, say in two examples such as *Sorry, Wrong Number* and *Night and the City*. In both films, a man has big personal plans to succeed, but feels suppressed. At a critical moment, while making a decision to further himself, he violates the ethics and morals he knows he should be obeying. Henry Stevenson plots to kill his wife. Harry Fabian cheats his acquaintances and steals money from his girlfriend. Both wage an internal battle with themselves, conscious of their wrongdoing, but they are driven by some greater need, in this case their excessive pride and pretensions that short-circuit their scruples.

Woolrich often endows his characters with two other traits common in *noir*, extreme, obsessive behavior and feelings of alienation. Whether it is the perpetual liar in "The Boy Cried Murder" or the voyeur in "Rear Window," characters frequently find themselves driven by some overwhelming psychological need, some horrific emotional fear, or some frightening physical threat, which can either be the cause or the effect of their isolation from society. In film, alienation and obsession become two of the most prominent traits defining *noir* characterization, appearing repeatedly in the protagonist (Silver and Ward 3–5). In *Night and the City*, for instance, Harry Fabian, at the

Night and the City — Harry Fabian (Richard Widmark, right), an ambitious scam artist, belongs in Woolrich's rogues gallery with its array of ill-fated scalawags and doomed confidence men (20th Century–Fox).

beginning and end of the film, is running from some indefinite pursuer who wants to do him harm. His obsession with achieving success distorts his judgment and leads to his alienation from the few friends who might have saved him.

Ambiguity and irony are key ingredients in Woolrich's stories, affecting both plot and character. Alberta's quandary after winning her husband's freedom in *The Black Angel* and Julie Killeen's odd predicament after successfully avenging her husband's death in *The Bride Wore Black* are moral dilemmas for the audience as well as the characters. Woolrich's stories often end without closure, a feature carried over to *film noir* and meant to convey to the audience the same feelings of apprehension and disorientation felt by the characters (Borde and Chaumeton). Also contributing to this ambiguity and disorientation is the flashback, which disjoints time and space within the narrative. For Woolrich, the flashback is akin to the waking nightmare, the kind of oneirism that permeates much of *film noir*. For example, in *The Black Path of Fear*, the protagonist reveals his past in a flashback, but his reliability as a narrator is suspect and his story is nothing less than a bad dream; these doubts are translated in the film adaptation, *The Chase*, as ambiguity between dream and reality.

Besides the existential protagonist, the *femme fatale* makes a prevalent appearance in the *noir* narrative, both in literature and movies. Woolrich uses many variations that become prototypes for *film noir*. In *Waltz into Darkness* appears the treacherous Spider Woman who plots the male's demise. Contrasting her is the "innocent" *femme noire* who means well, but unintentionally causes the male's downfall, such as the heroine of *The Black Angel*, the ironic title suggesting her unfortunate role. In *The Bride Wore Black*, the *femme noire* assumes her role willfully, destroying men deliberately for what she believes is a legitimate reason, while in *I Married a Dead Man*, fate maneuvers her into that role where she inadvertently destroys two dissimilar men, one her evil tormentor, the other her beloved. In these stories and in the films adapted from them, the women, divergent in their motives, have an ambiguous effect on the outcomes.

Finally, the mysterious, ambiguous, indiscriminate force that shifts characters to and fro in Woolrich's stories becomes the same one that guides and manipulates characters in *film noir*. The name usually given to this force is Fate, and it manifests itself in two different ways. In one respect, Fate can indicate predetermination: no matter what a person does, he or she cannot escape a prescribed outcome. In another respect, Fate is a capricious power that manipulates people arbitrarily, as if for its own amusement. Relying on coincidence to indicate the role Fate plays in the lives of his characters, Woolrich works with both notions, displaying Fate's hard-line inevitability in stories like *Fright* and "Too Nice a Day to Die," and its fickle and haphazard qualities in stories like "Dormant Account," *The Bride Wore Black*, and *Rendezvous in Black*.

Film noir, no less than Woolrich, depends on coincidence to suggest Fate's same two possibilities. *Out of the Past*, for instance, implies predetermination by showing how a man's sordid past contains the seeds of his doom. A hostile figure from the man's former life accidentally finds him and pulls him back into that existence he hoped to forget. *Sunset Boulevard* exemplifies Fate's randomness when a blown tire forces a down-and-out screenwriter to pull into the driveway of the *femme fatale* who will from then on rule his actions. Either way, free will becomes suspect as *noir* characters cannot help but succumb to the dictates of their destiny.

Woolrich's *pulp noir* contains all the ingredients that are directly translated to cinema's *film noir*: characters alienated from society, driven by obsessive desires, and beleaguered by guilt; *femmes noires* who tempt, seduce, and destroy their victims and usually themselves; plots teeming with ambiguity and irony; and an indifferent Fate manipulating lives with little or no consideration of justice. These elements and more indicate why Woolrich is a major inspiration in defining that most ambiguous—and therefore most fascinating—of film categories.

"The Corpse Next Door"

Short story first published in *Detective Fiction Weekly*, January 23, 1937; reprinted in *Nightwebs* (Harper & Row, 1971).

Francis M. Nevins, Jr., accurately likens "The Corpse Next Door" to Poe's "The Tell-Tale Heart." In both, a murderer's guilt gradually infects his imagination until he suffers an intense psychological crisis that climaxes with his exposing his crime. Considering that many of Poe's stories delve into the psyche of characters tormented by guilt and remorse, we can see that Woolrich, deliberately or not, has distinct ties to his predecessor's style and themes.

This particular treatment of guilt dovetails with Woolrich's many other variations on the guilt complex. "The Corpse Next Door" considers the morbid consequences when an impressionable conscience is plagued by guilt, and unhealthy, obsessive remorse poisons the mind and drives the perpetrator mad.

Ed Harlan is a volatile man with a hair-trigger temper. Knowing this, his wife does not tell him that the milk delivered to their door has been stolen for the fifth time in two weeks. While trying secretly to open a can of evaporated milk, she drops it and he infers the bad news, that they have no fresh milk. He sets a trap by tying a fishing line from the milk bottle to his finger. In the night, a tug on the line wakes him and he rushes out to catch the thief, an anonymous vagrant. But he cannot contain his anger. He beats the man and knocks his head against the floor. Harlan, his fury abated, disgruntledly tells the prostrate man to take the milk and leave, but then Harlan notices a thin trickle of blood seeping from the man's ears. He realizes he has killed him.

Guilt and fear compel him to cover up his crime. He sees the door ajar in a nearby apartment and assumes that the man must have come from there. He hides the body in the Murphy bed that retracts into the wall. After that, guilt prevents him from settling back into his normal routine, and in growing increments, his conscience begins to needle him more and more. Mundane comments by neighbors arouse his anxiety that they know something of his crime; he is leery that his most trivial gestures, such as a glance toward the door of the apartment where the corpse is hidden, may give him away.

When one day his wife complains of a repugnant smell in their apartment, he believes he knows the source and he fears discovery. Two newlyweds soon rent the apartment and he becomes desperate. He hears the groom complaining that he can't open the door to lower the bed. Feigning neighborliness, Harlan loans him a hammer and watches as the groom unjams the door and pulls down the bed. After he does so, Harlan, behind him, swings the hammer down on his head, killing him.

The police arrive. Harlan explains that he killed the groom to keep him from finding the body on the bed — but surprisingly, the Murphy bed is empty of its grisly contents. All the mysteries are quickly cleared up. The pungent smell came not from a dead body but from cabbage cooked in the apartment below. The milk thief Harlan had supposedly killed was a down-and-out friend of the building superintendent, who had let him sleep in the vacant apartment. The man had recuperated from Harlan's blows and managed to extricate himself from the bed and flee the building. Harlan, in his fear, commits a real murder that up to now had existed only in his imagination.

Although we don't know enough of Harlan's background to understand the root causes of his behavior, we understand his dilemma. Guilt can be an all-consuming obsession that affects the ability to think clearly and act rationally. As in Harlan's case, guilt can make a person interpret others' words and behavior as if they had some preternatural knowledge of what the person did. Motives become subject to suspicion and self-control grows precariously unbalanced.

This would seem natural in a sensitive soul, yet Woolrich does not construct his character on that obvious cliché. Instead, he adds a contradictory twist to his personality: "Harlan had a vicious temper." The implication is that guilt can take possession of anyone, hardened as well as not. Excessive guilt can reduce anyone to an abject, irrational fool.

A very human touch Woolrich gives his protagonist occurs when Harlan first beats the thief, then growls at him, "Take the lousy milk.... Only next time ask for it first!" After his rage is satisfied by his violent explosion, he is capable of showing compassion (albeit with reluctance). This is a very real reaction in people with violent tempers; they cannot control their fury, but once expended, it is replaced by guilt which prompts remorse. They will do almost anything to make amends, as with Harlan, who ironically offers his victim the milk that was the reason for the altercation in the first place.

Besides its distinct parallels with Poe's story, "The Corpse Next Door" has another not-so-obvious connection. Woolrich is familiar with Maupassant, as evidenced by his epigraphs in *The Bride Wore Black*, and his reliance on irony as a technique in ending most of his stories may also be a direct borrowing from the French short story master who is famous for this device. Consequently, Woolrich's story seems comparable to Maupassant's "The Coward" in which psychological stress compels an individual to do the very thing he's most afraid of. A man, challenged to a duel, frets so much about his fear of death that he ends up committing suicide. In "The Corpse Next Door," Harlan's fear of being discovered compels him to commit a second murder which ironically *uncovers* his initial crime, a crime that was not committed in the first place.

For Woolrich, such an ironic twist is not exclusive to this story. He also uses it in "The Night Reveals" and *The Bride Wore Black*, where the illusion of a crime compels a character to avenge it, only to find false satisfaction for his or her efforts.

"The Corpse Next Door" contains some links to other Woolrich works. In "You'll Never See Me Again," another "Ed"—Ed Bliss—clings to the needless pride that initiates a series of events leading to near-fatal consequences. After he has an argument with Smiles, his wife, she walks out on him, threatening him with the words of the title. When she disappears, his conscience feels the pain of remorse and he blames himself for her possible death.

In another connection, "The Corpse Next Door" is the inversion of "Rear Window." The latter is told from the viewpoint of a voyeur who is suspicious of his neighbor's actions; he watches diligently, trying to determine if the neighbor has murdered his wife and, if so, what he has done with her body. In "Corpse," the story is told from the viewpoint of the "murderer," who lives in fear that his neighbors may suspect his crime and discover where he has hidden his victim.

Of all the stories in which Woolrich deals with a character haunted by guilt for some misdeed, his novel *Fright* (1950, under the pseudonym George Hopley) comes very close in spirit and construct to "The Corpse Next Door." Ambitious Prescott Marshall, after an indiscreet lapse into a drunken revel, is blackmailed by the young woman with whom he had a one-night affair. Afraid that a scandal could jeopardize his opportunity to marry the socialite who may help his career, he goes into a blind rage and unconsciously strangles the blackmailer to death. Like Harlan, even after he has killed his adversary, he talks to her, throws money at her, and tells her to get out. In both cases, murder was committed inadvertently while emotions overrode rationality and the will.

Marshall follows Harlan's lead and hides the body in a closet. Physically, the corpse vanishes from view, but mentally, it is ever before the mind's eye. Conscience cannot dismiss it, so guilt taints the psyche, and during the subsequent series of events, Marshall begins to interpret innocent, meaningless occurrences as threats and plots against him. Guilt as a curse on the wrongdoer is a frequent motif in *film noir*. The individual struggles to flee physically, and may even succeed on that level, but he or she can never find total freedom because conscience metes out its own inescapable sentence.

Film: Union City

1980, Columbia Pictures, in association with Kinesis Ltd. and Monty Montgomery; released through Cantina Blues Films, Inc. *D:* Mark Reichert. *P:* Graham Belin. *Cin:*

Edward Lachman. *Sc:* Mark Reichert. *Supervising Ed:* Eric Albertson. *Mus:* Chris Stein. *Art Dir:* George Stavrinos.

Cast: Deborah Harry (Lillian), Dennis Lipscomb (Harlan), Irina Maleeva (Contessa Kafka), Everett McGill (Larry Longacre), Terina Lewis (Secretary), Sam McMurray (Vagrant), Tony Azito (Alphonse Florescu), Pat Benetar (Jeanette Florescu), Terry Walsh (Paperboy), Charles Rydell (Cab driver), Cynthia Crisp (Wanda), Taylor Mead (Walter), Sally MacLeod (Woman in bar), Paul Andor (Ludendorff), Arthur McFarland (Mr. Lewis), C.C.H. Pounder (Mrs. Lewis). 87 min.

In adapting "Rear Window" to film, Hitchcock and John Michael Hayes augment Woolrich's plot with a larger number of pithily drawn characters who are interconnected with one another. In effect, the film uses the short story as a germinal idea to turn "Rear Window" into something greater than itself. Reichert, in similar fashion, populates his film with more characters and interrelationships than we find in Woolrich's "The Corpse Next Door." Besides the main character, Harlan, there is his romance-starved wife, the building superintendent who seduces her into an affair, a quirky female neighbor, and Harlan's dutiful secretary.

Union City is not a bad film. (On this point, I differ with Nevins, who appraises the movie with nearly every negative adjective at his disposal). It contains little originality, yet displays a few striking cinematic images. It is an extremely close adaptation of Woolrich's story, adhering to his theme and offering a very similar message without going far beyond that. By remaining true to Woolrich's format, it also remains fairly true to Woolrich's *noir* vision and could be considered a neo-*noir*.

The plot is essentially the same. Harlan (Dennis Lipscomb), a middle-class, working stiff with a nasty temper, cannot tolerate having someone pilfer his milk delivery. While he is enrapt in his trite job and obsessed with catching the thief, his wife Lillian (Deborah Harry) is nurturing an affair with the building superintendent (Everett McGill). Harlan sets a trap, catches the thief in the act, and beats him, accidentally killing him. Frantic, he drags the body into a vacant apartment and stows it behind the stored Murphy bed. But fear of discovery weighs on him and his nerves grow frayed. When a newly married couple (Tony Azito and Pat Benetar) moves into the apartment, he anticipates their finding the body. Enthralled by the imminent revelation, he cannot help himself and actually becomes complicit in bringing to light the evidence of his crime. He lends the husband Alphonse a hammer to loosen the jammed door of the closet that houses the bed. Alphonse lowers the bed halfway. Without revealing the contents, he gasps at something he sees on the bed. Harlan backs toward an open window. While Alphonse gapes at the unrevealed sight, we hear Harlan (unseen outside the frame) make some garbled noises and the hammer's thud as it hits the floor. When Alphonse lowers the bed completely, we see that the sheets are stained with blood — but there is no body. He turns around and Harlan is gone. He has jumped out the window, killing himself on the pavement below. On the street, a circle of people gathers around the body, attracting the attention of another figure, the vagrant whom Harlan had beaten. His head bandaged, he is still alive and he walks over to join the group of onlookers.

One of Nevins's complaints about the film adaptation is that it changes the story's setting from the Depression era to the post–World War II period (An opening title places events in March 1953.). Situated in the Depression, the vagrant's theft of a bottle of milk appears somehow justified, so that Harlan's crime symbolizes a lack of compassion and tolerance of the Haves for the Have-nots. I am not so sure that this alteration is any kind of shortcoming in the film. The post-war period was an uncertain time for displaced, disoriented veterans, as reflected in many post-war *noir* films (which Reichert obviously tries to emulate). Some (such as the cabby) found a place in society and others (like the vagrant) did not. The film's fleeting contrast, without subsequent supportive situations, only vaguely sets up an opposition between Fate and Self-determination, but the point is that the vagrant is jobless and starving and Harlan's reaction is pitiless, selfish, and excessive. In effect, the implication for the short story and film is the same: one segment of society with a superior self-righteous attitude looks condescendingly down on another less fortunate segment.

The biggest advantage of the short story over the film is the one that literature generally has over filmed adaptations: the protagonist's viewpoint is more vividly and precisely realized in the written work. Thus, in Woolrich's story, the implications of Harlan's crime are richer, more extensive, and better developed. The film tends to limit Harlan's mental erosion to fear of discovery; the short story raises the stakes by suggesting a strong connection between Harlan's fear of discovery and his guilt over his senseless explosion.

Lipscomb's Harlan is well played as a high-strung, self-centered twerp. His insensitivity to his wife's needs is already driving her away from him even before he commits his crime. She has to satisfy her romantic fantasies in magazines and romance novels. She has also been flirting with their superintendent Larry Longacre, but not until Harlan becomes totally self-absorbed in his plight to keep the body hidden does she consummate her affair with Larry. (Deborah Harry, lead singer of Blondie, adequately personifies the disaffected "everyday housewife," the cliché lackluster female role of the fifties.)

The central symbol of Reichert's film is the milk which stands for male virility and potency. Symbolically, the theft of the milk is the theft of Harlan's virility, which accounts for his extreme outrage over the petty theft and his hysteric obsession with catching the culprit. Once he has committed his crime, however, milk becomes repulsive to him, just as he finds his wife repulsive: he calls her a whore and no longer finds the urge to make love to her. Instead, it is Larry who offers to put cream in Lillian's cup of coffee—and she accepts.

This symbolism is successful as far as it goes. The only problem is its limitations and its obviousness. The film *Rear Window* again becomes a useful comparison because one of the central issues is Jeff's impotency as signified by a number of related images and symbols (broken leg, food, long camera lens). In Hitchcock's creative hands, that motif is exploited in a variety of ways to enrich the protagonist's character and stir in the audience a deeper empathy with him. In Reichert's hands, it has a static quality and seems more a playful conceit of the director than a meaningful, well-integrated symbol in the story. That may even have been Reichert's starting place in making the film: he saw the potential of the milk symbol and built his story around it. Although mildly entertaining, the film ends up as a linear narrative without layers of meaning which could have been attained with more interconnected symbols. Lachman's photography and Stavrinos's art direction are the strongest contributions to the film, establishing the mood and visual impressions of the trite, mundane, humdrum world that Harlan lives in.

Union City is dependent on Hitchcock for other reasons besides its technical approach. After Harlan kills the vagrant, he tries to cover up his crime by hiding the body, washing the floor of blood, and disposing of his stained clothes. The detail in this effort, a visual sequence without words or music, comes directly from *Psycho* when Norman Bates cleans the bathroom after his gruesome murder.

Guilt's influence on perception, as indicated by Harlan's precipitous descent into paranoia and his fear that people already know of his shameful offense, can be found in numerous *films noirs*. A vivid example occurs in *Where Danger Lives* (John Farrow, 1950). Two fugitive lovers (Robert Mitchum and Faith Domergue) try to escape to Mexico by airplane after the man has an altercation with the woman's husband (Claude Rains) and thinks he has killed him. They see two policemen standing at the ticket counter and assume they are after them. Instead, the two officers were loitering innocently at that spot. Changing their plans, they try to escape by car, but run into a roadblock they think is set up for them. They veer off track, unaware that it is simply a routine inspection by the Department of Agriculture. Guilt alters the ability to interpret events objectively and accurately and usually leads to self-destructive complications.

The themes of social apathy and isolation (Harlan does not know his neighbors' names, much less associate with them) are reminiscent of a number of films from the fifties that preached against public indifference toward crime and social ills. One is *Captive City*, a *film noir* in which a newspaper editor (John Forsythe) gets little help in trying to expose the source of corruption in his quiet small town. A controversial film is the *noir*-laden science fiction thriller *Invasion of the Body Snatchers*. A man (Kevin McCarthy) leads a small group against an alien attempt to take over human minds and erase all signs of ambition and individuality. And there is the classic western *High Noon* (also with *noir* influences) in which the retiring sheriff (Gary Cooper), true to his sense of duty, protects his town from outlaws even though he cannot find anyone to help him. When Reichert sets his film in 1953, it appears to be with a deliberate allusion to these movies and the *noir* themes of this particular era.

"Face Work"

Short story, debuted in *Black Mask*, October 1937. Reprinted as "Angel Face" in *Ellery Queen's Mystery Magazine*, Dec. 1946; in *Ellery Queen's Anthology*, 1968; in *Crime on Her Mind*, ed. Michael B. Slung, 1975; and in *The Great American Detective*, eds. William Kitteredge and Steven M. Krauzer, 1978. Renamed "One Night in New York" as an entry in the short story collection *Six Nights of Mystery* under the pseudonym William Irish (Popular Library pbk #258, 1950).

For its diverse and dynamic contribution to plot and theme, one of the most potent conventions in *film noir* is the *femme fatale*. *Noir* did not invent her; she was throwing her destructive weight around in literature long before the French christened American crime dramas the "black films." Although no more than a pawn of Fate, Iocaste contributed to her son's tragic downfall in Sophocles' *Oedipus Rex*. Taking a more aggressive role was Lady Macbeth — conniving, ambitious, ruthless, self-serving, mad: no female character could serve as a better prototype for the likes of Phyllis Dietrichson (*Double Indemnity*) and Elsa Bannister (*The Lady from Shanghai*). Shakespeare, as if to outdo himself for personifying evil so well in *Macbeth*, upped the ante in *King Lear* and dallied with not one but two *femmes fatales*, the wicked, conspiratorial siblings Regan and Goneril, who brought devastation on their father, their country, and themselves (Cordelia, it could be argued, also contributed to the tragedy as an inadvertent *femme fatale*.). Dickens gave us Estella, Lady Havisham's protégée in *Great Expectations*, schooled by the old dame in how to retain an icy hubris while turning men's hearts to ash. And in creating Hedda Gabler and Nora Helmer, Ibsen displayed how women, insidiously or naively, wield an ineffable power over men. In pre-*noir* films, too, this kind of woman was already displaying prominent traits as vamp and spoiler. Screen icon Greta Garbo portrayed a sultry, finagling, unfaithful temptress in *Flesh and the Devil* (1927). Gangster Tony Camonte's sister, Cesca, unintentionally inspired his darker sexual instincts that contributed eventually to his downfall (*Scarface*, 1932). The *femme fatale*, then, is not a product of *film noir* but a prevalent and long-standing literary convention that happened to find a comfortable home here.

The pulp *noir* "Face Work" is a precursor to *film noir* because it contains several elements that will later help define that kind of film, chief among them the *femme fatale*. Jerry Wheeler, 27, has been dancing in nightclubs to support herself and her brother ever since she was 16. Now, when she learns that Chick is ready to desert kindly Mary Allen and run off with a gold-digging floozy, her motherly (or is it her amorous?) instincts are aroused and she becomes aggressively protective. She visits Ruby Rose Reading, but can't convince her or Chick to sever the relationship. Later that night, Ruby is found dead and police arrest Chick as the prime suspect. At the trial, the testimonies from Ruby's maid Mandy Leroy and the doorman Charlie Baker seal Chick's conviction. Jerry faints and Detective Nick Burns, who had arrested Chick, comes to her aid and takes her home. The lawyer's fees force Jerry to move to a cheaper apartment, a seedy dive she has rented under her old stage name, Honey Sebastian. Nick volunteers to help her find evidence that can reopen the trial and exonerate Chick. He calls her Angel Face, a term of endearment that indicates his romantic attraction to her.

When Mandy Leroy dies in a hit-and-run accident and Charlie Baker suddenly returns to England, supposedly to claim an inheritance, Jerry loses her two leads. She feels someone is manipulating events, but unable to identify this phantom, she admits to Nick, "There's a gap there I can't jump across to the other side." However, this gap is suddenly bridged when she attends the auction liquidating Ruby's possessions. She becomes suspicious of a man who takes an unusual interest in Ruby's jewelry case, and after a flurry of exchanges, Jerry outbids him at thirty dollars. Inside the box she discovers a secret compartment containing a letter written by notorious gangster Milton Militis in which he threatens Ruby for cheating on him. Showing the letter to Nick, Jerry reminds him that Ruby had a scar on her hip from Militis's branding her there, a sadistic rite of ownership he was famous for. She gives Nick the letters and tells him to make Photostats.

To wangle her way closer to Militis, Jerry auditions at one of his nightclubs, Hell's Bells. On the strength of her facial looks alone, she gets the job and sparks Militis's lascivious interest. She stalls him for several weeks, but with time running out for Chick, she takes desperate action and sends Militis a bogus telegram to lure him out of town. Alone in his apartment, she looks for concrete evidence to convict him. Militis returns too soon and, seeing her there, believes she has finally consented to be his girl. But Rocco, one of his henchmen, recognizes her from the auction. He steals the photo Jerry had placed in a frame for Militis and shows it to the telegraph operator who recognizes her as the one who sent the phony telegram.

Rocco exposes Jerry's identity to Militis. Nick calls on the phone at just that moment and Militis traces the call to the police station. They lug Jerry downstairs, past the sleeping doorman and out to their car to take her to Militis' house on Long Island. Jerry thinks to herself, "Maybe it's better this way ... than growing into an old lady and no one looks at your face anymore." She powders her nose one last time and throws away her compact.

At his house, Militis performs his branding ritual on Jerry. He brags aloud about killing her the same way he killed Ruby. Suddenly, Nick bursts through the door with an army of police. He shoots Militis, who, Jerry says, "went down at my feet like he wanted to apologize for what he'd done to me, but ... he didn't get up anymore." Meanwhile, "Rocco and the other guy went down into hamburger under a battery of heavy fists." Jerry recognizes the sleeping doorman from Hell's Bells, who was actually an undercover cop Nick had stationed there to protect her. The police had trailed Militis to his Long Island home and raided it in time to hear his confession. Nick says that with this information and the brand on Jerry's hip in the same place as it was on Ruby Rose, they can prove Chick's innocence.

For a short story, "Face Work" employs the *femme fatale* in a number of intricately developed ways. First, Ruby Rose makes an obvious Spider Woman trying to initiate Chick into the degenerate underworld that Jerry has all these years been trying to shield him from. Militis's branding ritual is a symbol of the sadistic depravity that goes on in that sleazy substratum and Chick's arrest shows how vulnerable the innocent are in an unjust jungle.

More complex is Jerry Wheeler as a *femme fatale*. One of Woolrich's sister-brother stories, "Face Work" depicts her in ambiguous terms as both a concerned, responsible mother figure and an incestuous lover. More than that, their names suggest a gender reversal, the masculine "Jerry" assuming the dominant role over her brother whose name is the unflattering slang expression for a young woman. She has an androgynous role, reinforced further by her former stage name, Honey Sebastian, a female-male amalgam. Jerry's female side is exhibited in her romantic relationships with Nick and Militis, simultaneous affairs that reveal the paradox in her character: she functions comfortably on both sides of the law. By the story's end, one man has died because of her duplicity and she gives the other no definite indication of where their relationship will go.

The branding is a sadistic act, literally an example of a degenerate's extreme perverted behavior with misogynistic undertones not very subtly implied. The mutilation leaves a stigma, a physical wound for betraying Militis and a symbol of the emotional scars left after undergoing her ordeal.

Both the original title "Face Work" and its revamped title "Angel Face" work well enough, readily calling attention to facial beauty as a central symbol in the story. The significance of facial beauty is its mystical, seductive power that enables the woman to dominate the man. This is what attracts Nick, and this is what allows her to get her job at Hell's Bells and win Militis's confidence. Facial beauty also relates to vanity, as suggested in the scene when Jerry, aware that the gangster intends to kill her, still takes time to primp herself in her compact mirror — and then throws it away. She welcomes death because "maybe it's better this way ... than growing into an old lady and no one looks at your face anymore." Death seems a more welcome alternative than aging and losing one's good looks.

The brief allusion to police brutality at the end of the story is a plot element Woolrich resorts to occasionally. He suggests that injustice exists on both sides of the law, that even the protectors of the law yield to brutal, illegal methods when it suits their purpose or satisfies some base sadistic yen.

Another plot device common in Woolrich stories is the clue that comes out of nowhere. When the two trial witnesses are lost to Jerry, she reaches a dead end, a "gap," in her investigation, which offers no alternative avenue to pursue. But Coincidence smiles on her, calling her attention to the auction of Ruby's effects, which leads her directly to Militis and the solution of the murder. Out of this comes another Woolrich convention: an external force is controlling and manipulating events to prevent the protagonist from succeeding in his or her quest. This device will emerge more prominently in *Phantom Lady*.

"Face Work" is a strong entry in the Woolrich canon. At the same time, it is one of those stories recycled from previous material ("Murder in Wax," which appeared two years before in *Dime Detective*), and serves as source material for later stories (especially for his stellar 1943 novel *Black Angel*).

Film: Convicted

1938, Columbia. *D:* Leon Barsha. *P:* Kenneth J. Bishop. *Cin:* George Meehan. *Ed:* William Austin. *Sc:* Edgar Edwards. *Mus:* Morris Stoloff.

Cast: Charles Quigley (Detective Burns), Rita Hayworth (Jerry Wheeler), Doreen MacGregor (Mary Allen), Bill Irving (Detective Cobble-Puss Coley), George McKay (Detective Kane), Edgar Edwards (Chick Wheeler), Noel Cusack (Agnes Leroy), Phyllis Clare (Ruby Rose), Eddie Laughton (Berger), Marc Lawrence (Milton Militis), Bob Rideout (Rocco), Michael Heppell (Pal), Grant MacDonald (Frankie), Donald Douglas (District Attorney), uncredited actor (Charlie Baker), Percy Kilbride (Maintenance man, uncredited). 54 min.

Convicted is the first film adapted from a Cornell Woolrich suspense story—but it is not the author's first film adaptation. Two of his mainstream novels had already been turned into films: *Children of the Ritz* (1927) was adapted for the silent screen in 1929 and directed by John Francis Dillon for First National; *Manhattan Love Song* (1932) was directed by Leonard Fields for Monogram in 1934. There is a nettling question as to whether Woolrich had earlier ties to the silent film industry as a title writer. The name "William Irish," the pseudonym he will begin using with the publication of *Phantom Lady* (1942), appears in the credits of several silent films. Although some researchers attribute this writing credit to him, it is unsubstantiated whether Woolrich and this earlier Irish are one and the same or whether Woolrich had anything at all to do with the film industry, other than contributing his source material.

Leon Barsha has more credits as a producer than a director, his most sustained success coming from his collaborations with actor William "Wild Bill"

Elliot who starred in a series of B-westerns in the 1940s and '50s. (As a boy going to Saturday and Sunday matinees, I thoroughly enjoyed these films. I don't know if it was the aura attached to the name "Wild Bill" or my love of westerns at that early age or the actor himself, whose stoic character exuded a quiet charisma.) At Columbia studios, Barsha was never attached to any A-project, and *Convicted*, despite the presence of Rita Hayworth, was no exception. Although the actress will eventually emerge as one of the most vibrant, sexiest products off Hollywood's image-crafting assembly line, she has to wait for a more captivating vehicle to achieve this. Not until her thirty-second picture, *Blood and Sand* (1941), does she earn that kind of notoriety. So by the time she makes her two most important *films noirs*, *Gilda* (1946) and *The Lady from Shanghai* (1948), she is already a sex symbol and box-office drawing card.

Contemporary critics were less than kind to the debut of Barsha's film. *Boxoffice* magazine claimed that the only saving grace of the film was "the beauty of Rita Hayworth" (in Ringgold, *The Films of Rita Hayworth* 93). And prominent critic Bosley Crowther of *The New York Times* lambasted it with disdainful sarcasm. Of epic stature it is not, but the movie is a competently made programmer, adequately entertaining and satisfying.

Convicted is not a full-fledged *film noir*. Although very close thematically and structurally to Woolrich's "Face Work," making similar use of the *femmes fatales* and the guilt-plagued heroine (guilt for her past and fear of failing to save her brother) and pulling us into the corrupt society of snide gangsters and loose women, the film lacks the stylistic elements necessary to evoke the appropriate *noir* atmosphere. Instead of using the camera dynamically with some off-kilter or extreme angles for expressionistic effect, the director takes all camera shots, but one, at eye level. That single exception suggests one *film noir* technique: an extreme low-angle shot shows Jerry Wheeler (Rita Hayworth) springing from her chair when she realizes Militis (Marc Lawrence) has discovered her duplicity, thereby visually reinforcing her agitation and anxiousness and lending urgency to the moment. But this is not enough to place the film squarely among the blue-blood *noirs* and the lack of dramatic camera angles for varied effects may be one reason the critics disliked the film. Although most components, such as the acting and the story continuity, work fine, and although Barsha uses a gamut of camera shots (shot reverse-shot, medium and long shots, etc.) and movements (pans and tracking shots), the shooting technique is generally very flat, monotonous, and uninspired. Even silent films had developed a much greater visual vocabulary. The Thin Man and Charlie Chan mystery series have more in common with *noir* than what Barsha offers here.

At the same time, most scenes, even if occurring at night, are uniformly lit, shot with high-key lighting and without deep shadows. However, there are two scenes that harbinger the lighting effects associated with *noir*. During the courtroom scene, faint shadows of venetian blinds appear on the wall above the witnesses while they give their testimony. And in the scene where Mary

Allen (Doreen MacGregor) visits Chick (Edgar Edwards) in his jail cell, vertical shadows of the jail bars line the left wall while the moving shadow of a guard plays along the rear wall. The shadows deployed in these instances portend an identical effect that such shadows will have in true *films noirs*, a claustrophobic sensation of a dark, menacing world closing in on and imprisoning the characters. Again, not enough to raise this programmer to *film noir* status, but enough to show that some thoughtfulness went into making the film and that it contains a few devices associated with the *noir* techniques to come.

Substantially, *Convicted* retains much of "Face Work," particularly the arc of the plot, the characters, and the hard-edged slang, this last being one of the most salient and attractive features of Woolrich's story. The differences in Edwards's screenplay contribute in some ways to elaborating on the subtle nuances implied by Woolrich. For instance, Mary Allen is given a larger role, shown sharing an apartment with Jerry and visiting Chick in his cell, which develops her character more fully as the slighted but unwavering girlfriend. Her sporadic appearances keep reminding us of the innocent side of life that counters the contemptible wickedness of the foul and fetid underworld.

By contrast, Jerry Wheeler, although the protagonist, is associated with that latter repugnant life style. When she takes the stand at Chick's trial, the district attorney (Donald Douglas) "tortures" her with questions about her past: "You were willing to lie, cheat, and starve to support him ever since you were sixteen." Even Chick is conscious of her sacrifices; he tries to silence the D.A.'s badgering by jumping up and confessing to the murder. Jerry cries out, "He's only trying to spare me the humiliation of —." Here, the scene ends abruptly and the exact nature and details of her indiscretions are left to our imagination. Depending on the limits of our creative vision, we may believe that she has spent years performing her solo rumba in various nightclubs; or considering darker possibilities, we may infer that her dancing at the Ankle Inn represents her climb from a series of dissolute dives where she had to perform dances of a more exotic nature (In "Face Work," she says explicitly that she "spent most of my girlhood in a tinseled G-string."); and if we give in to more depraved notions, we may even read the protective outbursts from the brother and sister as implications of an incestuous relationship (also implied in Woolrich). This prudent sidestepping of the details of Jerry's desperate debauchery must have been done to appease the censorship code. Her promiscuous background had to be glossed over so that she appeared an all–American girl — after all, when she and Detective Burns (Charles Quigley) engage in a romantic clinch at the finale, we want to believe she is still pure enough to find true love with a deserving man.

Thematically, the film has many parallels with Woolrich's story, probably because it follows the original so closely. However, there are a few differences, too, and these alter some of the meanings in the film. As in the short story, the power of the female visage is at the heart of the film: Jerry uses her facial beauty to influence Burns, get a job at the Scat Club, and worm her way into

Militis's life, much the same as Woolrich's heroine does. Mirrors abound in the film, a substitute for the brief moment Woolrich's character spends with the compact case. Jerry appears in front of her dressing room mirrors several times, and when she falsely confesses to the crime to save Chick, Detective Coley (Bill Irving) sarcastically declares, "She must've used mirrors." Vanity is again the implication, but with the difference that, in the film, the mirrors seem more functional than symbolic. Jerry seems less self-conscious—if only a little less—of the power of her good looks.

In Woolrich's story, Militis's branding his women is a cruel, sadistic act exemplifying the misogyny that often festers below the surface in *noir*. In the film, Edwards tactfully replaces this atrocity with a less threatening diamond bracelet. While the sadism is lost, the implication of male dominance is not. The bracelet symbolizes material temptation and bondage: the "shackle," first worn by Ruby, is handed down to Jerry, Ruby's heir apparent. The framed photograph, like the bracelet, also suggests ownership for Militis: he possesses the photo as long as he possesses the girl. After he discards Ruby along with her photo, he encourages Jerry to put her picture in it. When Jerry does so (under the pretense of capitulation), she symbolically becomes his possession and nearly suffers Ruby's fate.

The doubling between Jerry Wheeler and Ruby Rose is evident in both the short story and film. The rivalry for Chick at the beginning immediately links them. Afterwards, Jerry becomes a substitute for Ruby, becoming Militis's "possession," being branded by him (or given the bracelet Ruby once wore), and being murdered (or nearly murdered) in the same way. Barsha's film reinforces this with several additional parallels: Wheeler and Ruby are both "professional" dancers; Wheeler lives at the Mont*rose* Apartment Hotel; and when Wheeler visits Ruby to plead for Chick, she mentions that they've "both been around." The doubled women contrast with Mary Allen who represents a third party interested in Chick, the girl who is truly good for him, who can help him adhere to the values forfeited by Jerry and Ruby.

Coincidence is an important element for Woolrich and for *noir* in general. *Convicted* uses it to the extent that it appears in Woolrich's story, but does not exploit it enough to make us feel the effect of that inscrutable power controlling human destiny. One instance is Chick's being in the wrong place at the wrong time: he is with Ruby's body at the precise moment the maid (Noel Cusack) comes home, giving the impression that he just killed her. Coincidence also has a role in the auction sequence, which deviates somewhat from the original scene in Woolrich's story. Instead of Jerry's winning the jewelry box for thirty dollars, she and Rocco (Bob Rideout) run up the bid until Rocco reaches one hundred fifty dollars. This is Jerry's limit, but Mary adds a dollar, and Jerry bids one hundred fifty-one dollars. Rocco backs down, not knowing he only had to make one more bid to win the item. Significantly, the moment contains some suspense and the element of ironic coincidence plays a small part.

Considering how difficult it is to get a print of *Convicted* and how infrequently it is shown on television, it is fair to assume that this film will not enter the video or DVD market anytime soon. However, the film deserves attention as an asterisk in film history. It is a stepping stone in the career of Rita Hayworth; it foreshadows some of the *noir* conventions to come; and it is based on a story by the suspense writer whose literary works served as source material for more *films noirs* than those of any of his contemporaries.

"I'm Dangerous Tonight"

Short story, first published in *All-American Fiction*, November 1937. Reprinted in two short story collections, *The Fantastic Stories of Cornell Woolrich*, 1981, and *Vampire's Honeymoon*, 1985.

With "I'm Dangerous Tonight," Woolrich makes one of his early forays into the world of the macabre. Having abandoned his dream of succeeding as a writer of mainstream literary fiction, he groped to find a new niche, testing the uncertain potentials of the perverse and the bizarre. Some of these initial excursions, such as "Dark Melody of Madness" (1935), were innovative and fascinating; others, such as "Kiss of the Cobra" (1935), used sensationalism with the finesse of a rockslide. In "I'm Dangerous Tonight," he melds together two plot devices he had found useful for his initial experiments, gangsterism and the supernatural. Over time, as Woolrich developed his expertise in writing popular pulp, he expanded his arsenal of conventions and basic premises, but he never abandoned his inclination to resurrect motifs, scenes, and scenarios he had used in previous stories. (Even "I'm Dangerous Tonight" already contains a scene he will mimic in *The Bride Wore Black*. The moment where Mrs. Travis lures her husband to his death by making him reach too far over the ship's railing to retrieve her scarf foreshadows Julie's modus operandi for pushing Bliss off the high-rise balcony.)

Although the unmistakable merits of the Woolrich style are apparent, "I'm Dangerous Tonight" suffers the slings and arrows of outrageous logic. The story grinds forward, straining the bounds of credibility with an incoherence that is rampant and relentless. The forced, contrived quality of the storytelling makes Woolrich's venture into this new, popular genre seem a desperate attempt to find the fame and fortune that eluded him in his previous efforts at realistic fiction.

The story begins in Paris, France, at the "blue hour," when paranormal occurrences are rife. The devil himself appears to the famous French dress designer Madame Maldonado (translated with facile irony as "evil gift" or "evil giver") and offers her his cloak as material for a dress that will suborn women to serve his wicked whims. Maldonado senses the malevolence of the cloak, yet the very next day, she has her seamstresses complete her design, which bears the label "I'm Dangerous Tonight." While the seamstresses work, their model Mimi Brissard fluctuates between homicidal urges and calm normalcy as she alternately dons the dress, then removes it for alterations. That night, after the dress is completed, she wears it for her rendezvous with her drug-dealing boyfriend Belden. The night watchman catches her stealing it and she stabs him to death with a pair of shears.

American F.B.I. agent Frank Fisher is in France, obsessed with catching and extraditing Belden for killing his brother Jimmy Fisher, also an agent. Mimi knows about him, but once in the charmed dress, she develops a sudden sadistic desire to betray her lover so he will suffer the agony of facing the electric chair. She collaborates with Fisher. After her mission is accomplished, however, and she takes off her dress, she realizes what she has done. While Fisher leads the handcuffed Belden from her apartment, she leaps from her window to her death in the street below.

Unexplained is how Maldonado manages to retrieve the dress, but she does. She sells it to an American tourist, Sarah Travis. In her stateroom aboard the ship returning home, the normally shy and retiring middle-aged housewife dons the newly acquired dress. (She puts it on for the first time. Wouldn't a woman want to try on a unique designer dress *before* purchasing it?) Immediately, she begins to formulate an evil plot to kill her husband so she can benefit from his life insurance policy. She knows that the criminal Belden is aboard ship, and to carry out her plan, she enlists his help. (Mrs. Travis's need to free Belden and include him in her plot is absurd, but Woolrich tries to justify it. She wants Belden to impersonate her husband when they dock, so she can pretend he arrived safely in America. The rationale is baffling. She could have murdered Hiram without Belden's help and claimed the life insurance money without their landing in America.) Belden just "happens" to have a packet of sleeping powder hidden in his shoe. He gives it to Sarah and she administers it to Fisher. She steals his keys and sets Belden free. Then, she coaxes her husband to the railing of the ship, saying she needs him to retrieve her scarf, which has slipped from her hands and got tangled off the side. While he reaches for it, she makes him lose his balance and fall to his death. Then she helps Belden trap Fisher. Belden shoots Fisher and leaves him for dead. When Sarah removes her dress, she suddenly realizes all the mischief she has caused and the flood of guilt is too much for her conscience and mental equilibrium. She goes insane. With the ship close to shore, Belden leaps into the water and escapes.

Fisher recovers in a hospital. Because he bungled his arrest, his superior expels him from the force. Depressed, he takes to drink. At a bar, he has a fight with the beefy bartender, but singer Joan Blaine intervenes and saves him from a bad beating. He takes a hotel room next to hers. Joan looks for work and gets hired at the Chanticleer Club. Fisher, meanwhile, makes contact with a drug dealer who he hopes will lead him to Belden. Coincidentally, the contact steers him to the Chanticleer Club. At the club on the night Joan starts work, she dons a dress her agent had purchased from an estate sale, the red and black Maldonado design. When Fisher comes to the club, she betrays him, as Mimi betrayed Belden, and enables the owner Graham and his thugs to capture him.

Fisher is taken to the beach where Graham meets a boat coming in for a drug drop. Belden is among the crew. Aboard ship, Fisher throws an oil lamp at Belden and sets him afire. Belden leaps into the water. Fisher dives after him, wrestles with him, and breaks his neck. Joan by this time has taken off the dress and, realizing her mistake, called the F.B.I., who arrive in time to save Fisher from Graham. Fisher's superior tells him that the bureau is pleased with the results and he can have his old job back.

The plot of "I'm Dangerous Tonight" has so many weak links that, if it were a chain, it couldn't support air. The evil urges that overtake the women while they wear the dress are inconsistent. If the women focused exclusively on hurting the one they loved, the supernatural dementia might have seemed plausible. However, sometimes their evil obsession moves them to hurt others (Mimi kills the security man), and sometimes it doesn't (Sarah frees Belden to get his help). Also the dress will at times, by its very presence, infect people with general discontent, and at other times, it does nothing. In other words, there are no "rules" governing the dress's supposed powers. These would have to be established so as to give the story an internal relative logic and make events and character reactions more consistent.

One thing that might have helped the story would have been to give the dress an aura of mystery. That Woolrich makes the devil the obvious origin of the dress material isn't necessarily a failing. However, since ambiguity generally enriches a story, Woolrich could have omitted defining the exact nature or source of the dress and suggested it was bewitched by some unnamed power, so that any woman who wore it felt voluptuous and alluring and had to surrender to her baser, destructive instincts.

"I'm Dangerous Tonight" belongs with those Woolrich stories that exploit the goings-on among underworld figures—*C-Jag*, "Johnny on the Spot," "An Apple a Day," "The Fountain Pen," "The Number's Up," "Face Work," and the mobster segments in *Hotel Room* and *The Black Angel*, to name a few. Woolrich peoples this venal environ with stereotyped characters who have the personality and depth of a cotton ball. Although the incidents that that draw us into this unholy world may be initially intriguing, once we become acclimated, events and actions often seem contrived, phony, and wooden.

Despite its flaws, "I'm Dangerous Tonight" exemplifies an approach Woolrich applies to much of his writing, be it his best or shoddiest work. At the outset is an engaging basic premise that acts as the catalyst for the events that follow. Whether those events can sustain a logical, credible progression is another matter—a matter, which, odd as it seems, Woolrich does not give high priority. Instead, he is more concerned with the allegorical implications of his creation, a strategy that arguably may counteract the faulty logic of the narrative.

Looking at this allegorical aspect, we may realize that, although it can sometimes tax the suspension of disbelief too heavily and too often, in "I'm Dangerous Tonight" it has some merit. Of prime significance is that the devil proposes to enslave women, not men, in his service. Each woman who wears the dress cannot help but become a *femme fatale*, a Black Widow, a destroyer of men. In the three main instances here, the women profess an exceptional love or attachment to a man, yet are driven to betray or kill him for vaguely sadistic, selfish reasons. (Mimi and Sarah show exceptional dedication to their roles, giving the devil a bonus by attacking incidental males, the night watchman and agent Fisher.) The cloak, direct from Satan's shoulders, is symbolic. It represents some facet of the female's psyche that forces her, in spite of herself and her good intentions, to surrender to some inexplicable, primal urge to hurt the male. As a religious allusion, this offers a misogynistic perspective on the Eden story: like Eve, all women deliberately or inadvertently become an agent of the devil, put on this earth solely for the purpose of destroying the male. Among *noir* themes, a more compelling one would be difficult to find.

Film: I'm Dangerous Tonight

1990, TV. MCA-Universal Home Video/MTE, Inc./BBK Productions, Inc. *D:* Tobe Hooper. *P:* Bruce Lansbury, Philip John Taylor. *Ex P*: Boris Malden. *Co-Ex P:* Michael Weisbarth. *Cin:* Levie Isaacks. *Sc:* Bruce Lansbury, Philip John Taylor. *Ed:* Carl Kress. *Mus:* Nicholas Pike. *Set Des:* Leonard A. Mazzola. *F/X:* Special Effects Unlimited, Inc., coordinated by Joseph Mercurio, with Vincent Montefusco, Tom Ficke, Charles Dellardinelli.

Cast: Mädchen Amick (Amy O'Neal), Corey Parker (Eddie), Daisy Hall (Gloria), R. Lee Ermey (Capt. Aikman), Natalie Schafer (Grandmother), Jason Brooks (Mason), William Berger (Dr. Jonas Wilson), Mary Frann (Martha), Dee Wallace Stone (Wanda Thatcher), Anthony Perkins (Prof. Gordon Buchanan), Lew Horn (Coroner), Stuart Fratkin (Victor), Dan Leegant (Frank), Jack McGee (Landlord), Edward Trotta (Joey), David Carlile (Matt), Felicia Lansbury (Librarian), Henry C. Brown (Anchorman), Ellen Gerstein (Server), Ivan Gueron ("Romeo"), Juan García (Enriqué), Frank Dielsi (City Worker), Richard Penn (Paramedic), Xavier Barquet (Punk #1), Matthew Walker (Punk #2), Robert H. Harvey (Janitor), Bill Madden ("Tybalt"). 92 min.

Anthony Perkins made sixty-plus films between 1953 and his untimely death in 1992. Never a top box-office draw, he was nonetheless a truly versatile actor, playing a range of roles as diverse as callow Sheriff Ben Owens in the western *The Tin Star* (1957) and girl-shy Cornelius Hackl in *The Matchmaker* (1958). However, for him, Hitchcock's *Psycho* became both his Mt. Sinai and his Golgotha. He attained a pinnacle, and gained a degree of immortality, for his role as Norman Bates, but in the post–*Psycho* stage of his career, despite continuous work and diverse roles, he was regarded mostly for his

I'm Dangerous Tonight— Meek Amy O'Neal (Mädchen Amick) is transformed into a seductive vamp when she dons the red dress that exudes supernatural powers (USA Network).

characterizations as a paranoid, perverted, imbalanced deviate. He has a glorified bit part in *I'm Dangerous Tonight*, where, despite the trappings of a college professor, he does not stray far from his Norman Bates persona.

Tobe Hooper created some underground tremors with the cult classic *The Texas Chainsaw Massacre* (1974) and gained mainstream notoriety by directing the more popularly received *Poltergeist* (1982) for producer Steven Spielberg. "Shock value" is one of his directorial trademarks, a reliance on repulsive images to disturb his viewers viscerally and sensorially. On the basis of this work ethic, Hooper is the ideal choice to direct the film adaptation of *I'm Dangerous Tonight*.

I'm Dangerous Tonight is a throwback to the teen horror flicks of the fifties, classics like *I Was a Teenage Werewolf* (1957) and *The Blob* (1958), but with less sensitivity for teen concerns and crises. It belongs among the new wave of adolescent thrillers, a natural offshoot of the Nightmare on Elm Street and Tales from the Crypt series (both with entries directed by Hooper). Oddly, despite its stock characters and situations, the story starts out as mildly engrossing, thanks particularly to the fresh innocence of female protagonist Mädchen Amick. However, about halfway through the film, the entrance of obnoxious police captain Aikman (R. Lee Ermey) seems to mark the exact moment when the story collapses into a sequence of dull clichés: conventional horror situations are strung together like sausages and scare tactics are totally predictable. Quickly, audience empathy disintegrates.

The devil's cloak in Woolrich's story becomes, in Hooper's film, a red cloak worn by Aztec priests during their rites of human sacrifice. Jonas Wilson (William Berger), a professor at Tiverton College, extracts the cloak from a secret compartment inside an Aztec altar. He puts it on and (surprise) goes berserk, axing a museum guard and his own wife and then killing himself. Days later at school, Eddie (Corey Parker) convinces Amy (Amick) to be a gopher for his drama class. Looking for props, she purchases a trunk at the Wilson estate sale and discovers the cloak inside. At rehearsal, Eddie tries on the cloak and is transformed from a mild-mannered, fun-loving guy into a mephistophelean meanie, threatening to use his stage sword to skewer the eye of one of his co-actors. Amy realizes that the cloak is charmed. She takes it home, and demonstrates some remarkable sewing skills by transforming two square yards of cloth into a fetching Bill Blass original.

On the night she is supposed to be home watching grandma (Natalie Schafer), she instead wiggles into her slinky Victoria's Secret attire and heads for the college dance. She seduces her cousin's boyfriend and winds up with him in his truck. Once stripped of her dress, however, she regains her moral inhibitions, grabs her paraphernalia, and slips away from the grasp of the frustrated Romeo. She returns home where grandma, like most elderly mutes, is blessed with a sixth sense and divines the malevolence inherent in the red dress. She tries to take it away from Amy. When she pulls away, her wheelchair crashes through the banister and she dies in a heap at the bottom of the stairs.

Amy hides the dress in her closet, but her cousin Gloria (Daisy Hall) finds it and wears it to her boyfriend's house. After a sexually satisfying romp in bed, Mason (Jason Brooks) announces that he will be trying out for a professional football team, which puts a virtual end to their relationship. Angry and vengeful, Gloria attacks him in the shower, strangles him, and castrates him with a razorblade. Next she goes after Amy and Eddie, using Mason's pick-up truck to try to push their car off the road. Instead, she crashes and dies in the ensuing fire.

The dress, impervious to fire, now finds itself on the sultry body of the police clerk who had catalogued it as evidence. Wanda (Dee Wallace Stone) slits one man's throat before Amy is able to locate her to try to retrieve the dress. Amy fails, but Wanda finds out where she lives and attacks her at home. On the same stairs that claimed grandma, Wanda takes a bad fall, but the dress infuses her body with a supernatural energy that makes her nearly invulnerable. Luckily, Eddie happens along in time to save Amy, but his motives become lewdly selfish ones: he puts the dress on Amy while she is unconscious, hoping they can make love while she wears it. Amy miraculously fights off the spell of the dress and is able to divert Eddie's libidinous intentions into positive moral support. She feeds the dress through the wood chipper and buries the tattered scraps with Wanda's coffin. The final scene shows Wilson's colleague, Professor Gordon Buchanan (Anthony Perkins), digging up the red shreds, hoping to restore them to whole cloth and use the garment for his own diabolical purposes, whatever they may be. (Perhaps it will make an attractive cloth for covering an end table at the Bates Motel).

Deviating from the demonic connection of Woolrich's dress, Hooper links Amy's dress to religious ritual, to human sacrifice, which explains why the wearer's weapon of choice is a knife or ax. In Woolrich's scenario, despite some narrative contradictions, the fashionable female always leans toward murder. Hooper's film introduces the twist that the wearer's reaction is relative to his or her elemental nature. The garment is a conduit for releasing repressed desires, so that a person with hidden evil ambitions (Wilson, Gloria, Wanda) will suddenly explode with murderous and perverted acts, whereas a person who is basically good (Amy, Eddie) will be less drastically affected, succumbing to less destructive desires, such as lust or vanity.

Further, in Woolrich's story, the woman who wears the dress suffers extreme guilt in the aftermath of her unconscionable crime. Suicide and insanity are the only way two of the tainted women can achieve expiation for betraying their love. In Hooper's film, the women (and Eddie) suffer no such duress. After wearing it once, they want to wear it again. The enchanted garment holds a fascination for anyone who touches it, creates an obsession especially because of its appeal to the violent sadism and libidinous passions pent up within the individual. Somehow (against the logic of the story), Amy manages to defy the dress's power even while she is wearing it. She convinces Eddie to help her resist its potent urges (quite a novelty, two teenagers relying on reason to harness their hormones).

The Cinderella motif may be a bit overdone here, but it works for the story. Amy is an orphan living with her aunt and cousin. She is the do-gooder stepdaughter completely suppressed by her dominating stepmother and vain stepsister, both of who get their comeuppance. She even goes to a ball where, instead of losing a glass slipper, she is ready to lose her virginity. Her goodness overrides the power of the dress in the end and enables her to win fair prince.

Hooper's film also differs from Woolrich's story in structure. As a narrative, Hooper's film follows a conventional chronological pattern: the story begins at the so-called beginning and proceeds along a single thread to its conclusion; a main character interacts with other characters until the end, when the outcome produces some telltale change in that character. Amy is the main character. She interacts with other characters and undergoes an experience that inspires her to discover self-confidence and self-esteem at the end.

Unlike Hooper's film, Woolrich's version belongs to a specific type of story in which a certain object or locale acts as a connective for a series of episodes and a parade of diverse characters. In "I'm Dangerous Tonight," for instance, although Fisher may be considered the main character, he is actually a peripheral character in the first two episodes and does not emerge as a true central character until the last segment. Before that, his presence seems preposterously coincidental. In the film, the dress has a similar function, passing from one woman to another, but Amy remains always at the center of story, while the lives of the other wearers are treated merely as tangential. Woolrich uses this same approach in a number of stories, such as "An Apple-a-Day" and "The Fountain Pen," in which the titled objects pass from one person to another, giving us glimpses into the lives of the objects' current owners. *Hotel Room* is a "novel" told as a sequence of separate episodes (actually short stories) whose only unifying link is the one hotel room that intersects the lives of a series of transient occupants. There are numerous film counterparts to this type of story, not necessarily *noirs*: *Tales of Manhattan* (1942), *The Yellow Rolls Royce* (1965), and *Twenty Bucks* (1993).

Neither Woolrich's original story nor Hooper's film adaptation fits into the *noir* genre. Both are more appropriate for the horror category, although the *femme fatale* characters and the presence of a supernatural power (a substitute for fate) that manipulates behavior give them a tenuous link to *noir* motifs.

"I Wouldn't Be in Your Shoes"

Short story under the pseudonym William Irish, first appearing in *Detective Fiction Weekly*, March 12, 1938; reprinted in the short story collection, *I Wouldn't Be in Your Shoes*, Lippincott, 1943, and Hutchinson, 1946; first paperback edition, Armed Services pbk #1173, 1945. U.S. contents: "I Wouldn't Be in Your Shoes," "Last Night" (revised treatment of "The Red Tide"), "Three O'Clock," "Nightmare," and "Papa Benjamin" (original title "Dark Melody of Madness"). Subsequent paperback editions usually contain abridged contents from original hardcover edition: *I Wouldn't Be in Your Shoes*, Mercury pbk #82, 1944, contains "I Wouldn't Be in Your Shoes" and "Last Night"; *Nightmare*, Readers Choice Library pbk #12, 1950, contains "Nightmare," "Three O'Clock," and "I Wouldn't Be in Your Shoes."

In this short story, Woolrich integrates plot devices and motifs that become staples in many of his other writings: the Wrong Man theme, the race against time, the last-minute rescue, the sympathetic detective, outlandish coincidences that signify the arbitrariness of Fate, ambiguous situations, complex interrelationships of guilt, innocence, and justice, and the ironic outcome. Typical for a Woolrich story, "I Wouldn't Be in Your Shoes" begins with a mundane situation that evolves into a surreal nightmare for the beleaguered characters. The plot zigzags through several winding turns that keep it from settling into a simple linear tale. Tom Quinn and his wife Ann are besieged every night by a band of stray cats howling beneath their bedroom window. Quinn reacts by angrily flinging one shoe, then the other, at the noisy intruders. The shoes are expensive orthopedic ones, his wife reminds him, and he trudges downstairs to retrieve them. When he can't find them, he concludes that they must have gone through some neighbor's open window. The next day, after work, he learns from his wife that the shoes were returned by an unidentified samaritan. He is just glad he does not have to hear any more rebukes from her.

Meanwhile, the police have discovered the dead body of a local miser, Wontner, who was killed in his run-down shack, supposedly in a robbery attempt. There were rumors that he had hoarded a great deal of money. One clear footprint enables the police to trace the shoes to Quinn, whom they follow for a time to learn his routine. Coincidentally, Quinn comes home one night with a wallet containing over two thousand dollars that he found on the subway steps. Ann has misgivings, but Quinn persuades her that they should keep it. They go on a shopping spree and their sudden extravagance confirms his guilt. The police arrest Quinn, who is convicted of murder and sentenced to death.

Bob White, a conscientious detective, believes Quinn guilty, until he returns to Wontner's shack one night to investigate its decimation by tramps using the planks for firewood. Weakened by the scavenging, the floor beams give way and White plummets into the rat-infested cellar. He throws tin cans at the rats, then notices they are filled with money, obviously Wontner's hidden hoard. The fact that this money was not taken leads him to believe that Quinn must be innocent; otherwise, he would have taken the whole cache, not just two thousand dollars.

White's superior is not convinced, so White pursues his theory on his own. He visits Quinn's wife, who, after lengthy interrogation, finally remembers the shoe-throwing incident. Considering the trajectory of the tossed shoes, White locates an apartment where there once lived a fellow, Kosloff, who came into money and left abruptly for Pittsfield, Massachusetts. White accosts him there. Kosloff explains that he left because his mother was ill, and that he really did not have money but only made it appear so because he wanted her to think he was doing well. White reminds him that the money he got after his mother's death was only five hundred dollars, but again Kosloff explains that his mother distrusted banks and kept the bulk of her money in a wall safe. Although Kosloff pleads with him, saying that he is going to be married and this scandal will ruin his life, White takes him back to the city where witnesses verify his knowledge of Wontner's wealth. Kosloff is arrested and Quinn set free.

Quinn returns to Ann who tells him she is leaving. Testimony at the trial was so convincing that it filled her with doubts. She tells Quinn she had watched from the window as he searched the ground for his shoes. He said he lit matches to see, but she never saw a flame from any match. She deduces that the shoe-throwing incident may have been his ruse to get out of the house and steal money from the nearby miser. If he lied about the matches—and he admits he did—he may have lied about the murder. Just after she walks out the door, Quinn hears the caterwauling of the stray felines begin again.

Outrageous coincidences pile up ad infinitum. Of all his shoes, Quinn throws his expensive orthopedic ones at the wailing cats. If he isn't the murderer, then the potential murderer either happens to be passing by at the *exact* moment he tosses the shoes or else lives in one of the adjacent apartments where the shoes come flying *deus ex machina* style through his open window. Further, Quinn discovers a wallet containing *exactly* the same kind of old oversized bills that Wontner stockpiled. When White returns to Wontner's house, he *coincidentally* discovers the cache that was somehow overlooked earlier by police. The second suspect, Kosloff, like Quinn, comes into an unexpected windfall at just this time. The death of his mother, his leaving town, the weak, unsubstantiated explanation of where he got most of his money all intersect at the right time to make him appear as guilty as Quinn. One may argue that "I Wouldn't Be" exaggerates coincidence to the point that it undermines any realism the story contains—but then Woolrich does not always try to depict realism. At times, he is more like an allegorical writer, or an impressionistic painter, conveying ideas through a facsimile of reality—like Tennessee Williams's Tom Wingfield, he presents truth through the pleasing medium of illusion. In this instance, his multiple coincidences stress the fact that our lives are not totally under our control, that there are forces at work that interfere with our best laid plans, maneuvering us and producing consequences that are sometimes beneficial, more often disastrous. As the narrator says, "Tom Quinn loaded the dice in his favor, but it's the gods who do the casting." We see just how mischievous and capricious these "gods" can be.

Woolrich's excessive use of coincidence appears a flagrant flaw until we justify it as a purposeful motif. At times we can't; at others we can. For instance, the many coincidences in "I'm Dangerous Tonight" add up to nothing more than gross manipulation by an author trying to foist a story on us. In "I Wouldn't Be in Your Shoes," on the other hand, although they appear no less rampant, the coincidences function more substantively, contributing to irony and theme.

Another of Woolrich's plot devices that hang precariously balanced between trite contrivance and significant purpose is a character's inability to perceive the obvious. The reader understands the situation before the character does, even though the situation should be clear enough to the character as well; all he or she has to do is remember a detail, interpret a telltale sign, or choose the obvious alternative. Instead, the character behaves naïvely, obliviously, inciting in the reader this urge to enter the story, grab the character by the collar, and tell him or her what to think or do. Interestingly, this strategy resembles Hitchcock's method for creating suspense. Clarifying why he prefers suspense over surprise, the director explains to Truffaut the importance of dramatic irony, of keeping the characters unaware of dire circumstances that have the potential to cause a tragic outcome yet alerting the audience to these same circumstances as early as possible: an apparently mundane situation "becomes fascinating because the public is participating in the scene. The audience is longing to warn the characters on the screen.... The conclusion is that whenever possible the public must be informed" (Truffaut 73). Suspense is created from the anticipation of harm and the uncertainty of whether it will be prevented.

In "I Wouldn't Be," the fact that Quinn and his wife both forget the shoe-throwing incident seems unlikely, maybe even absurd, considering how crucial the footprint is to his conviction. Suspense is created in our anticipation of the moment when they *will* remember and save themselves. And it does come, but with surprising results. Although the revelation saves Quinn, the whole ordeal has shattered Ann's faith. Quinn is absolved of murder, but loses his wife. This device is used repeatedly by Woolrich, one of his primary methods for tugging at every potential plot thread and drawing out suspense. Consider how treachery is telegraphed in "Mind over Murder," *I Married a Dead Man*, and *Waltz into Darkness*. The reader reads on, anxious to see when the character will finally realize what should have been apparent all along. Sometimes the character realizes it in time, sometimes too late, sometimes not at all.

The character's inability to recognize the obvious, as contrary as it is to narrative logic, is a feature prevalent in *noir*. A sense of right and wrong should enable a man to know better. Past experience should help a woman to make the right choice. Yet people delude themselves and fall into traps regularly because they have wisdom least when they need it most. *Out of the Past, Where Danger Lives, Possessed, The File on Thelma Jordan, Pitfall, Double Indemnity*— these are a few examples of *noirs* where the dark side suddenly engulfs a character who fails to heed the warning signs that could have prevented a world of grief and regret.

"I Wouldn't Be in Your Shoes" fits in the same category as "Silhouette," "Rear Window," and "He Looked Like Murder." Appearances, although convincing, are not enough to determine guilt or innocence. Even perceptions based on strong visual proofs may be subject to error. The police follow Quinn to *watch* for changes in his life style or any *exhibition* of suspicious behavior. The doubts that drive Ann from her husband are based on her *observations* the night of the shoe-throwing: she *watched* from the window and did not *see* him light any matches as he said he did. But this should not be enough to condemn a man. Told from the viewpoint of the objective omniscient narrator, the story makes it clear that Quinn lied for an innocent reason: he only wanted to keep her from nagging him. Getting inside his thoughts, we also know that he did not know anything about who returned the shoes.

However, Woolrich constructs his story insidiously. The shoes act like a Hitchcockian maguffin, an incidental device important to plot and motivation but secondary to other thematic considerations. Nevins is correct in saying that both men, Kosloff and Quinn, are just as potentially guilty, as they are innocent, of the crime. Quinn could have used the shoes as an excuse to get out of the house to kill the miser, then made up the tale about finding the wallet later. Although his lie about the matches and his ignorance about who returned the shoes are legitimate, he still may have murdered Wontner. Similarly, Kosloff's explanation is just as logical and just as flimsy.

Because both Quinn and Kosloff may be guilty or innocent, they share a kinship with Lars Thorwald ("Rear Window") and Dixon ("He Looked Like Murder") who also tease our perception of their guilt or innocence. The latter two stories depend for their suspense on our seeing events through the eyes of a narrator-protagonist who cannot determine whether the person he is investigating did or did not commit murder. "I Wouldn't Be in Your Shoes" inverts this dilemma, makes us feel that Quinn is innocent and that the real culprit used his shoes. Then the story plays the trick of reversing this implication at the end and making us realize that Quinn, if not Kosloff, may have been guilty after all.

Assigning guilt or innocence to a person for his actions becomes almost arbitrary. Unable to fathom fully what goes on inside a person's mind, we cannot appreciate the precise motives behind that person's actions, and based on ocular evidence alone, we cannot comprehend all the circumstances surrounding the actions we observe. In "I Wouldn't Be in Your Shoes," Woolrich continues to explore guilt, innocence, and justice, and as he so often does, places it in the context of the *noir* universe, where, to Fate, such designations do not make any difference. Guilty or innocent, Quinn loses Ann, and guilty or innocent, Kosloff's life is ruined. Both men cannot be guilty — but both men's lives are destroyed.

Film: I Wouldn't Be in Your Shoes

1948, Monogram. *D:* William Nigh. *P:* Walter M. Mirisch. *Cin:* Mack Stengler. *Sc:* Steve Fisher. *Ed:* Roy Livingston, Otho Lovering (supervisor). *Mus:* Edward J. Kay. *Art Dir:* David Milton. *Set Dec:* Raymond Boltz, Jr.

Cast: Don Castle (Tom Quinn), Elyse Knox (Ann Quinn), Regis Toomey (Det. Clinton Judd), Charles D. Brown (Inspector Stevens), Rory Mallinson (First detective), Bill Kennedy (Second detective), Steve Darrell (District Attorney), Robert Lowell (John L. Kosloff), Esther Michelson (Mrs. Finkelstein), Ray Dolciame (Shoeshine boy), William Ruhl (Police Lieutenant), John Sheehan (Judge), John H. Elliott (Lawyer), Dorothy Vaughan (Mrs. Alvin), Herman Cantor (Jury Foreman), Hugh Charles (Counterman), Laura Treadwell (Mrs. Stevens), Joe Bernard (Janitor), Tito Vuolo (Grocer), Jimmy Aubrey (Tramp), John Shay (Salesman), Donald Kerr (Vaudevillian), Stanley Blystone (McGee), Matty Fain (Prisoner), John Doucette (Prisoner), Dan White (Prisoner), Bill Walker (Prisoner), Ray Teal (Guard), Paul Bryar (Guard), Walden Boyle (Priest), Wally Walker (Clerk), Eddie Parker (Policeman). 70 min.

Note: I sought this film through a variety of markets and in a variety of formats over a four-year period and was unable to locate it. Some prints may exist somewhere, but they obviously are not readily available. Woolrich enthusiast William Thailing had access to the Dialogue Sheets and was kind enough to lend them to me. Of course, the expressionistic chiaroscuro settings, an important ingredient of noir, *cannot be inferred from this limited document. However, with the dialogue, one can construct a good idea of the story line, making it possible to comment on the characters and themes and find some comparisons with Woolrich's original story.*

I Wouldn't Be in Your Shoes was one of William Nigh's two final films made in 1948, and although he cannot boast a single landmark film to his credit, he was an extremely steady and prolific director, churning out an amazing 115 films during a career that lasted 35 years. Born in 1881 as Emil Kreuske, he joined the fledgling film industry during the silent era, dividing his talents as writer, actor, and director. His first directorial opportunity came in 1914 (*Salomy Jane*), and afterwards, he contributed frequently to the mystery genre, among them entries in the Mr. Wong series of the 1930s, starring Lugosi and

Karloff. During the forties, he was a reliable workhorse in B-film productions, which made him well prepared for the *Shoes* assignment. He died in 1955.

Scenarist Steve Fisher, a contemporary writer and intimate friend of Cornell Woolrich, knows his fellow author's work. His personal twists to the original story manage to complement the general tenor of Woolrich's writing.

Tom Quinn (Don Castle) is on death row, hoping an 11th-hour reprieve from the governor will halt his imminent execution. Inmates coax him to tell his story. Instead of responding, he turns away and thinks about what led to his predicament, narrating his recollections in a voiceover. (The film's opening *in media res* is a structural deviation from Woolrich's story which starts at the beginning and moves forward chronologically. Fisher's flashback is a convention often used in forties' *noirs*— see *Criss Cross* and *Double Indemnity*, for instance — to show how past events led up to the present circumstances.) Tom and his wife Ann (Elyse Knox) are a struggling dance team. He is unemployed; she scrapes together some income by teaching ballroom dancing. When she comes home late from work one night, she explains that she was just taking advantage of an attentive customer whom she has dubbed "Santa Claus" because he usually gives her a sizable tip.

Once in bed, Tom complains of the noisy cats outside and he throws both of his tap shoes at them through the open window. Ann reminds him how expensive the shoes are. He goes to retrieve them, but can't locate them. The next morning, they reappear mysteriously outside their door. Tom and Ann assume that some neighbor must have known whom they belonged to.

Meanwhile, that same night, a murder has occurred in the neighborhood, the brutal slaying of Old Man Wontner, a notorious miser. The police arrive, and their ace investigator Clinton Judd (Regis Toomey) discovers a complete footprint, which, because of the uniqueness of the tap cleat, leads them to suspect the Quinns. Coincidentally, Tom finds a wallet filled with the old oversized bills that were discontinued at the turn of the century, the same vintage bills stolen from Old Man Wontner. When Tom and Ann start to spend their newly acquired funds, they are arrested. Ann is released, but Tom is tried, convicted, and sentenced to death.

Judd visits Ann, who instantly recognizes him as "Santa Claus," her generous dancing pupil. He confesses his intimate feelings for her and she agrees to marry him if he can scavenge some evidence to save Tom. Judd makes what appears to be a genuine effort. He discovers that a young man, John Kosloff (Robert Lowell), formerly a tenant in an apartment near the Quinns, had come into some money and left town abruptly. Judd follows him to Pittsfield, Massachusetts, and brings him back to New York. However, police inspector Stevens (Charles D. Brown) verifies that Kosloff, on the day of the murder, was in the hospital recovering from an appendectomy. Stevens releases him.

Tom's flashback ends and the story resumes in the present. With no suspects left, his doom seems inevitable.

Judd visits Ann and takes her to a romantic bungalow he had prepared

I Wouldn't Be in Your Shoes— Detective Clinton Judd (Regis Toomey) directs the guilty evidence towards the man he wants to frame, so he can go after the man's wife, the object of his warped obsession (Monogram, courtesy William Thailing).

for them. He admits that he had followed her regularly and knows all about her, including her favorite colors and perfume. Ann suddenly accuses him of framing Tom for the murder he himself had committed. She suspected him after he had accidentally tipped her with one of the unusual oversized bills. Inspector Stevens, hidden until now, overhears Judd's admission of guilt. (The convenient self-incrimination may have been inspired by the conclusion of "Face Work.") Stevens steps forward and promptly arrests him. Then he tells another detective to alert the governor who is standing by on an open line. Ann asks, "Will Tom be...?" but the story ends before she receives an answer.

Fisher's plot clearly resonates with Woolrich's tonalities; substantially, however, it is a different story. The ambiguity of guilt at the end of Woolrich's version is replaced with the ambiguity of Tom's execution, the uncertainty of whether the call to the governor will come in time. Fisher's ending suits the *noir* exigencies, the innocent man a victim of circumstance or fate. Even if he is spared the execution, he has suffered a belittling, unjust ordeal. There is closure, however, in that the mystery has been solved. Woolrich's ending, on the other hand, is more complex and thought provoking. The unsettling questions about guilt and innocence, who deserves punishment and who deserves

I Wouldn't Be in Your Shoes— Ann Quinn (Elyse Knox) holds on to her husband Tom (Don Castle) while the law personified by dectectives Stevens (Charles D. Brown) and Judd (Toomey), points the finger of guilt at an innocent man (Monogram, courtesy William Thailing).

exoneration, are impossible to answer and linger long after the story is finished. Woolrich's Tom Quinn is similar to Joe Keller in Arthur Miller's *All My Sons*: he is acquitted in the eyes of the law but not in the eyes of his neighbors. Guilt is a scarlet letter that, once affixed, is extremely difficult to remove.

Produced by Monogram, *I Wouldn't Be in Your Shoes* has some coincidental parallels with the company's production of the previous year, *Fall Guy*, adapted from Woolrich's *C-Jag*. Both films transform Woolrich's stories of desperation into romantic triangles: a conniving fraud frames an innocent man for murder so he can eliminate his rival for the attention of the girl they both love. This revision does not hurt the entertainment value of the films, but for *Shoes* at least, it simplifies the thematic complexities which, in Woolrich, are considerably richer.

As an original device, the film's Santa Claus motif works adequately. Santa Claus is the perennial gift-giver, a fantasy figure who gives without expecting anything in return. In the world of humankind, where, with few notable exceptions, such selfless philanthropy is myth, he cannot exist. Given this nickname, Judd appears a noble Samaritan, tipping Ann munificently and then making an overt attempt to help her by bringing the "real" criminal to justice. However, he already knows that Kosloff has been questioned and released. His effort is pure show, a pretense of heroism meant only to convince Ann that he has her welfare in mind. Thus, Judd is an ironic Santa Claus, a phony who gives the illusion that he is helping her when in fact he does what he does only to satisfy himself. Charles Foster Kane (Orson Welles in *Citizen Kane*) condemns the supposedly self-sacrificing side of love when he raises his glass and bitterly announces to his friend (Joseph Cotten), "A toast, Jedediah, to love on my terms. Those are the only terms anybody ever knows. His own." It is a cynical imprimatur on the self-serving motives of people who claim they are in love, a personal proclamation that, sadly, has a tinge of universal truth to it.

In 1941, Steve Fisher's *I Wake Up Screaming* was a cutting-edge entry for the classic *film noir* period. Written specifically for film and later revised for publication in novel form, *I Wake* is a precursor to Fisher's adaptation of *I Wouldn't Be in Your Shoes* in that both mysteries link a furtive lover with the murder. Police detective Ed Cornell (Laird Cregar) does not commit the murder, but he is secretly in love with the victim, Vicky Lynn (Carole Landis). He is so envious of her connection with publicity agent Frankie Christopher (matinee idol Victor Mature) that he vindictively seeks Christopher's conviction even though he knows another man did the killing. The corrupt cop manipulates opinion and outcome from his position of authority, just as in *Shoes*, where Judd, the murderous cop, also has the power to manipulate evidence and get people to believe what he wants them to believe.

As a sidelight, Fisher, in creating "Ed Cornell," appears to be paying homage to his pal Woolrich, a probability noted by Nevins in his biography on Woolrich. The novel's description of the police detective is too uncannily close to Woolrich's features to be coincidental:

> He was about 30. He had red hair and thin white skin and red eyebrows and blue eyes. He looked sick. He looked like a corpse. His clothes didn't fit him. He wore a derby.... He was a misfit.... He was frail, gray-faced and bitter. He was possessed with a macabre humor. His voice was nasal. He might have had T.B. He looked like he couldn't stand up in a wind. He was thin and his face was gaunt. He kept lighting cigarettes... [Fisher 35].

Perhaps not a flattering description, but the comparison fits. The judgmental term "misfit" certainly describes his odd, reclusive life style, and the "macabre sense of humor" is evident in many of his works, such as "Mind over Murder" or "Graves for the Living."

Both Ed Cornell and Clinton Judd deny their guilt because they believe they possess a noble motive, love. They are typical of the *noir* character who falls into the fateful vise of destruction as a victim of his own unhealthy flirtation with one or more of four primary obsessions: love, money, power, and revenge. The two cops are ill-starred lovers, pitiful romantics smitten by an Aphrodite beyond their reach. They use their legal power with the illusion that they can control the situation, overcome their limitations, and achieve success. Fate, however, will not be denied. The corrupt world they have fabricated needs only time before it implodes on them, destroying both them and their elusive dream.

"All at Once, No Alice"

Short story in *Argosy*, March 2, 1940. Reprinted as by William Irish in the short story collection *Eyes That Watch You*, 1940; as by Cornell Woolrich in *Ellery Queen's Mystery Magazine*, November 1951; in *Verdict*, July 1953; in *Ellery Queen's 1966 Mid-Year Anthology*.

For Woolrich, credibility is an elastic band waiting to be stretched to the limits of the author's imagination. "All at Once, No Alice" ventures toward these limits, yet deserves serious attention because it integrates two particular *noir* conventions readily recognized among Woolrich's technical arsenal. For one, the protagonist lives a "waking nightmare": he stumbles through a blurred reality, forced to question what is real and what imagined. The other is the "wholesale conspiracy" premise, where the protagonist is alienated by a society that contradicts his assertions and even seems to be in league against him. Variations on these patterns can be found in works as diverse as "Dark Melody of Madness," "The Boy Cried Murder," "Nightmare," and *The Black Curtain*.

"No Alice" is a prime example of Woolrich's habit of recycling a previous plot, apparent when compared to "You'll Never See Me Again," written the previous year. In both stories, a man's wife vanishes abruptly and he cannot produce evidence or witnesses to substantiate his claims. Key to the conflict and mystery is the wife's personal history, which the husband knows little or nothing about. The befuddled husbands in "No Alice" and "You'll Never" recruit a detective who at first treats their story with skepticism, but once convinced, becomes a resolute ally in unraveling the puzzle. Each story also inserts Woolrich's variation on Poe's premature burial motif to intensify the horror of the crime, and both depend on a substitute corpse to compound the suspense — and complicate the mystery.

In the convoluted plot of Woolrich's "No Alice," a young couple, James Cannon and Alice Brown, get married by a justice of the peace, then have difficulty finding a room for the night. Cannon finally convinces one hotel clerk to let Alice take the last available room by herself, a narrow closet barely large enough for one person, while he spends the night at the local YMCA.

When Cannon returns the next morning, he finds his bride missing. Everyone, including the clerk and bellhop of the previous night, denies that he had seen or heard of her. Cannon raises a ruckus and the police have to take him away.

At police headquarters, Detective Ainslie is assigned Cannon's case. All the witnesses, from the justice of the peace to the hotel employees, insist they never saw her. Cannon remembers that Alice worked as a maid at the Beresford house in Lake City. They phone, but no one heard of her. Ainslie cannot act without proof. Alone and dejected, Cannon tries to commit suicide, scratching his hand as an excuse to purchase a bottle of iodine, which he intends to drink. Ainslie appears in time to stop him. Cannon daubs his scratch, using a handkerchief monogrammed with the letters "A.B.," the tangible evidence Ainslie needs to accept Cannon's story.

The two men follow their lead to the Beresford house where preparations are underway for a funeral service for the dead heiress Alma Beresford. Having sneaked inside, they find Alice's body laid out in the coffin and realize she must really be Alma Beresford. Surprisingly, Ainslie notices that she is still breathing. Mr. Hastings, Alma's guardian and now sole inheritor, discovers their ruse. He and his secretary Mr. Chivers subdue them and tie them up in the basement.

The next morning, Cannon hears the funeral service upstairs. He becomes frantic when he hears the coffin nailed shut. After the mourners leave for the cemetery, a maid faithful to Alma frees Ainslie, who then unties Cannon. They rush to the cemetery with a contingent of police who arrest Hastings and Chivers. Ainslie opens the coffin lid and consoles Cannon with the news that it is a substitute corpse which Hastings must have used to fool the old family doctor into signing the death certificate.

Cannon returns to the Beresford house where he finds Alma sedated but safe. Alma explains how Hastings bribed all the people to hide her existence, then intended to kill her so he could inherit her fortune. Cannon says he still plans to marry her all over again, even if she has to change her name to make it legal. He names Ainslie his best man because he was the only one who believed he was telling the truth.

As in *The Bride Wore Black*, the two lovers, immediately after their marriage, have their dreams of wedded bliss shattered by a devastating calamity. The moment that should have represented the height of their joy is quickly dashed and their happiness turned to despair. Both characters respond with extreme measures—Julie (in *Bride*) becomes an assassin; Cannon seeks solace in suicide. The aborted marriages also mean that consummation has been thwarted, a frequent corollary in a Woolrichian relationship. In Julie's situation, several of her murder weapons have sexual connotations (a tiny closet, an arrow, a shotgun) and symbolize a mock carnal consummation with the men she murders. Jim Cannon accepts no symbolic surrogate for his lost love; he is prepared to kill himself.

Beginning "No Alice" the way he does, Woolrich gets away with not having to reveal too much about Alice and Cannon. The romantic nature of the marriage allows him to gloss over their relationship, to let us accept them as two people who, since they are getting married, must already know each other well enough. Stereotyped as young lovers, they are in a familiar situation that short-circuits any strong curiosity we may have about their past. They seem like ordinary characters engaged in an ordinary event. There are no clues to suggest a dark, secret history behind either of them. Not until later do we learn that it was more like love at first sight, that Cannon knew his bride only from their brief association.

Woolrich manipulates us by making us think of Alice the way Cannon thinks of her, truthful and innocent. Gradually, thanks to Ainslie's persistence, we learn that Alice has a more complex past than she appeared to have and that her peril is the result of her position in the Beresford household—which takes us to one of the story's themes dealing with class conflict: Cannon is a humble clerk who is too self-conscious to marry a woman who has more money than he; Alma pretended she was a maid so that he would accept her on his level. In the end, love becomes the equalizer, enabling Cannon to overcome his prejudice and marry her anyway. In terms of class-consciousness, this situation carries some faint undertones of Woolrich's doomed relationship with Vera Gaffney, only with the male-female roles reversed. Maybe the story acts as a wish fulfillment for him, his ill-fated affair made right through the dream-construct of storytelling.

Another theme in "No Alice" that recurs in numerous variations throughout much of Woolrich's work is that the individual is an impotent, vulnerable entity easily alienated from society by the cruel indifference and casual arbitrariness of fate (or its next of kin: chance, coincidence, fortune, destiny, or providence). Cannon is totally alienated by the people he needs to help him. In his words, it is a "wholesale conspiracy." He has no hope, no court of appeal. Agents more powerful than he have reduced him to a helpless, feeble, abject state. But then fate suddenly extends an unexpected reprieve: enter the observant and insightful detective. Ainslie tails Cannon and keeps him from committing suicide. Coincidentally, there is the discovery of Alice's handkerchief, and from here, Ainslie gradually leads Cannon back into becoming a member of the community. (We see how Woolrich strains logic to achieve his objectives. Cannon did not *have* to scratch his hand to buy the iodine. Woolrich needs him to do this only so he can produce the handkerchief that wins Ainslie to his cause.)

Already noted, Woolrich borrows Poe's motif of the premature burial and turns it into a convention of his own. It can appear as a tangential event, such as in "Dormant Account," or it can be part of the central conflict, such as in "Graves for the Living." The recurrence of this gruesome image suggests that either Woolrich saw it as a simple yet effective device for generating immediate feelings of horror and dread, or he himself possessed some real fears about being buried alive.

Another device Woolrich frequently turns to—to great advantage—is his letting sounds prompt the *idea* of visual description. He does this by describing events from the viewpoint of a character who cannot see what is happening, but can *imagine* what the sounds imply. Cannon, tied up in the basement with Ainslie, hears sounds upstairs that whet his imagination with the horrors of the funereal goings-on.

Nowhere does Woolrich use this technique more effectively than in *Black Alibi* where Teresa Delgado is mauled to death by the jaguar on the step outside her mother's door. As frequently as we encounter this device, it is interesting that it actually appears in Woolrich's first suspense short story "Death Sits in the Dentist's Chair" (1934): the narrator, sitting in a dentist's waiting room, describes what goes on in the adjoining office just from the sounds made by the dentist and his patient. It is a very thought-provoking and emotion-arousing device, not seeing but imagining, mentally visualizing, along with the character, the horror of the unknown on the other side of the impenetrable wall, the terrible truth or illusive impression behind the inscrutable mask.

Film: The Return of the Whistler

1948, Columbia Pictures Corporation. *D:* D. Ross Lederman. *P:* Rudolph C. Flothow. *Cin:* Philip Tannura. *Sc:* Edward Bock, Maurice Tombragel. *Ed:* Dwight Caldwell. *Art Dir:* George Brooks. *Mus:* Mischa Bakaleinikoff ("Whistler Theme"): Wilbur Hatch).

Cast: Michael Duane (Ted Nichols), Lénore Aubert (Alice Duprés Barclay), James Cardwell ("John" Barclay), Ann Shoemaker (Mrs. Barclay), Ann Doran (Sybil Barclay), Trevor Bardette (Arnold Barclay), Richard Lane (Gaylord Traynor), Edgar Dearing (Cpt. Griggs), Wilton Graff (Dr. Grantland), Olin Howlin (Jeff Anderson), Robert Emmett Keane (Hart), Sarah Padden (Mrs. Huiskamp), Eddie Waller (Sam). 61 min.

The Whistler film series was based on the extremely popular radio show of the 1930s and '40s. Eight films comprised the series, produced between 1944 and 1948. The mainstay of the first seven films was Richard Dix, who assumed a variety of roles, everything from harried protagonist to despicable bad guy. A cadre of directors assumed the helm throughout the series, but they all managed to infuse the films with a consistent blend of Gothic moodiness and sinister foreboding. With their hapless characters trapped in repressive settings and facing a dangerous threat, The Whistler films belong entirely to *noir*. Only two of the films were adapted from Woolrich (*The Mark of the Whistler* and *The Return of the Whistler*), but they all contain his *noir*-ish style in tone and plot (wrong man theme, amnesiac killer, and so on).

As a character, The Whistler is a nebulous figure hovering in the shadows, ominous in his presence yet less an active participant in the story than a narrative device (although on occasion he may make his presence *felt*). He comments on events like an omniscient narrator ("I am The Whistler and I know many things."). He intervenes only sporadically to explain a situation or a transition between scenes, but his most effective function is to describe what a character is thinking or feeling, putting into words what the character is internalizing and does not openly express.

In developing his style for the mystery-suspense pulps, Woolrich, either consciously or unconsciously, writes in a vein derivative of Gothic romance, a genre with strong links to *noir*. "All at Once, No Alice" contains elements clearly reminiscent of *Wuthering Heights* and *Jane Eyre*, and *The Return of the Whistler*, taking its cue from Woolrich's story, adopts the classic damsel-in-distress formula in which a female is threatened by a cunning, self-serving villain (a usurper driven by some self-centered obsession, whether avarice, covetousness, lasciviousness, or revenge) before being redeemed by a steadfastly devoted and chivalric lover. Whereas Woolrich's theme works more on the individual, microcosmic level, *The Return of the Whistler* has wider implications for society at large. As a post–World War II film, it modifies Woolrich's story to include relevant meanings for a world struggling through the aftermath of that recent turmoil.

Imitating Woolrich's opening, the film begins with the two lovers, Ted Nichols (Michael Duane) and Alice Duprés (Lénore Aubert), seeking a justice of the peace in a small town outside New York City. In Woolrich's story, Cannon and Alice actually marry, although carnal knowledge is delayed because of the single-room arrangement (and a question of legality). In the film, the JP is away, and so marriage — and consummation — is still postponed. While Ted and his bride-to-be are inside the house talking to the JP's wife, a shadowy figure sneaks up to their car, lifts the hood, and sabotages the engine. When Ted tries to start the car, he detects trouble and they are forced to spend the night in the nearby town.

At the town's one hotel, a cantankerous clerk claims he has no vacancies, but for a fee, squeezes them into a small cubicle. Ted offers Alice the bed and says he will sleep in the chair, a gesture that alerts the clerk to the fact that they are not married. Although avaricious, the clerk's scrupulous prudery remains intact, and he makes Ted leave. Ted tells Alice he will sleep in the shop while the car is being fixed.

What happens next deviates from Woolrich's story in some critical details. Ted returns the next morning to get Alice, but she is gone. Quite unlike Woolrich's character, the hotel clerk does not deny Alice's existence, but merely says that she left in the night. Ted argues with him and is thrown out of the hotel. A private detective, Gaylord Traynor (Richard Lane as the Ainslie character), befriends him, giving Ted the excuse to narrate, in flashback, how he met Alice, incidentally revealing the innocence of their romance and the likability of their characters. Traynor, actually employed by the people who abducted Alice from the hotel, betrays Ted. At Ted's apartment, he knocks him unconscious. He steals photos of Alice and the marriage license signed by her and her first husband, John Barclay, an air force pilot who was killed in action the very night after they were married (another marriage unconsummated. Alice had to retain her virginal innocence for Ted and the censors.). Traynor gives the marriage license to the man he believes is John Barclay (James Cardwell), but who is really a cousin impersonating the dead pilot.

Ted suspects the Barclays of abduction. He confronts the imposter who, claiming to be Alice's husband, says that the false report of his death has left Alice mentally imbalanced. John shows Ted into Alice's bedroom where she admits to him that she is sick and tells him to leave. After he goes, we see that she has been coerced by her dead husband's relatives into substantiating the story so they can inherit the Barclay fortune that legally is hers.

Ted, still suspicious, sneaks back onto the estate and learns from the caretaker that the Barclays are placing Alice in an asylum. Under the pretense of suffering from emotional trauma, he gets himself admitted to the Woodland Sanitarium. He sneaks into Alice's room, frees her from a straitjacket, and starts to lead her out of the building. In the meantime, two things are happening. Traynor, who turns out to be an honest detective after all, has discovered from a photo of Alice and her first husband that the man in the picture is not the one who hired him. He tracks Barclay to the sanitarium. At the same time, Barclay has spotted Ted's car parked outside the sanitarium. He returns to find Ted and Alice trying to escape. Ted knocks him down the stairs. Traynor arrives with the police to arrest Barclay and his scheming cousins. Ted and Alice return to the justice of the peace where they had first tried to get married. They enter his home to complete their vows, while The Whistler delivers a brief epilogue about fate contributing mercifully to a happy ending — at least this time.

Changing the explanation for Alice's disappearance, the film actually deletes one of the *noir* elements from Woolrich's original story. *Noir* often presents contradictory perceptions of reality and then forces an alienated character to cope with those perceptions. These may affect the character's orientation within society, such as in *Street of Chance*, *The Dark Corner*, or *D.O.A.*; or they may affect a character's relationship with other individuals, such as in *Gilda* or *Mildred Pierce*. In Woolrich's story, Alice's disappearance initiates questions about reality and illusion, what a person can know about the real world based on memory and his dependence on others' support of his perceptions. Once it is confirmed that Alice is real, that she does exist (proof from the monogrammed handkerchief), questions arise as to how and why so many people could have been involved in a mass conspiracy aimed at one individual.

In Lederman's film, Alice's existence is never in question. Confronted with her disappearance, the hotel clerk freely admits she was there, but had checked out before Ted's return. The predicament is less baffling for Ted than it is for Cannon: he simply has to find out why she left without him. The mystery begins less as an internal, psychological one than an external, empirical one, subtracting one of the *noir* components that could have added a richer dimension to this competently-made film.

In both the short story and film, the villains' motive for kidnapping Alice is the same: money. But there is also a big difference. Woolrich focuses on an individual's greed. Mr. Hastings needs the help of only one accomplice, Mr. Chivers, to succeed in the conspiracy and fool the doctor that Alice is dead. In the film, the conspiracy involves several family members, a slight detail that affects the theme.

Alice's real husband had told her, if anything happened to him, to visit his father Ed Barclay and he would take care of her. When John was killed, she went to see the elder Barclay, but he got sick and died. By marriage, she became the rightful heir to the Barclay fortune. Instead, greedy relatives saw the opportunity to steal the fortune by falsely accusing the rightful heir of incompetence and unsuitability and then usurping her inheritance for themselves.

The situation suggests a postwar dilemma: the former world order, disrupted by the recent war, is replaced by a new world order groping to establish its own system and policies. Old Edward Barclay is a product of the old world order. He possesses wealth, which according to that system, should pass from him to his son and his son's wife. In the new world order, however, there is no respect for traditions of the old world order or for those who formerly wielded the power. The Barclay cousins feel they have a right to inherit their ancestor's wealth, even if it does not follow the process set up by that previous system. In a world where the new system is still unstable, they try to manipulate things in their favor, taking advantage of post-war uncertainties to achieve their goal (Barclay assumes John's identity to pretend John did not die in the war as was reported.).

The private detective Traynor is representative of the hard-boiled detective, the Spades and Marlowes who cling to principles of an earlier era, but have adapted them to cope with the modern world. Although he mistakenly helps the villains toward achieving their evil designs, he is not in league with them, and once he learns the truth, he reverses his position to help the good defeat the bad. The younger Ted and the older Traynor represent the new and old orders forming an alliance to prevent the unethical, criminal element from triumphing. There is still hope for the new system if the old will serve as "trainers" for the young, teaching them to preserve some of the traditional values (marriage, honesty) so that the new world order will have the strength not to yield to material temptations.

Following the damsel-in-distress formula, *The Return of the Whistler* automatically connects to other films where an odious male antagonist molests an innocent woman until her true love rescues her. Circumstances and motives may change from story to story, but the male antagonist consistently tends to harbor a deep-rooted misogyny. He resorts to a myriad of psychological ploys to dominate the woman, his intention often being to drive her to madness. It is interesting, too, that the hero in these stories is frequently a more insipid, less complex character than the villain who wants to destroy the woman. This last is not true of *The Return of the Whistler*, but it does apply to a number of related films.

Although not an adaptation of Woolrich's "All at Once, No Alice," Mel

Ferrer's 1950 film *The Secret Fury* has many interesting parallels with the short story. On the bright, joyful wedding day of Ellen Ewing (Claudette Colbert) and David McLean (Robert Ryan), a stranger interrupts the ceremony (consummation frustrated once again) to announce that Ellen is already married to a man named Lucian Randall (David Barbour). Along with her guardian-lawyer Gregory Kent (Philip Ober), Ellen and David discover evidence that proves the man's claim is true. Ellen vehemently denies the claim, but gradually grows disoriented as the evidence mounts against her: a marriage license signed by her and Randall; a justice of the peace, his wife, and their housekeeper who recognize her from when she married Randall; a maid (Vivian Vance) at the hotel where Ellen spent the night with her new husband.

David takes Ellen to see this Lucian Randall, who, while talking to Ellen in private, badgers her for abusing him. A gunshot explodes from nowhere and a gun falls to the floor at Ellen's feet. Randall is dead and Ellen is tried for murder. Kent defends her while District Attorney Eric Lowell (Paul Kelly), a suitor before she met David, harasses her relentlessly. She breaks down and Kent has her change her plea from "not guilty" to "not guilty by reason of insanity." Ellen is committed to a sanitarium where she suffers a mental withdrawal from reality.

David never loses faith. He resifts through the evidence and the witnesses, eventually uncovering the plot against her. In the final scenes, Ellen escapes from the sanitarium and confronts Kent for rigging the conspiracy that drove her mad. He confesses his guilt. He reveals that Ellen's father had had him committed some years ago. Although Kent was sane (or at least he claims he was), he spent four years in a sanitarium before the mistake was discovered. Ewing tried to make it up to him by giving him the position of lawyer and executor, but secretly Kent never forgave him. Living among the deranged had affected him. However, Ewing died before Kent could exact revenge, so in an eye-for-an-eye fashion, he avenged himself on Ewing's daughter.

Ellen holds a gun on Kent, but refuses to shoot, knowing he wants her to. She can be exonerated for Randall's death, but she'd be a murderess for killing Kent. Kent is willing to die to secure his revenge, a suicidal act that undermines the credibility of his sanity. (The cause-effect relationship here is ambiguous. We cannot tell if he was insane before he went to the sanitarium, or if, as he claims, living in a sanitarium drove him insane.) Ellen runs into her attic to hide. David returns just in time to foil Kent's attack. They fight. Kent accidentally dislodges a beam that supports a huge upright antique mirror. He screams as the mirror falls on him, his own reflection collapsing on him and crushing him to death.

The freak accident at the end is an ingenious moment in the story, an incredibly amazing image. As the mirror suggests duplicity and vanity, the duplicitous lawyer is killed by his doppelganger, his vain obsession with righteous revenge causing his downfall. The method of Kent's death is not directly borrowed from Woolrich, but it is certainly one that Woolrich would have appreciated. In stories such as "Death Sits in the Dentist's Chair" and "Dark Melody of Madness," Woolrich invented the strangest methods for committing murder; he would have loved this one and might have even been a little jealous that he didn't think of it first. But then there is so much going on in *The Secret Fury* that can be attributed originally to him that he should feel flattered by the imitation.

Although *The Secret Fury* lacks the "disappearing lover" theme, the plot has many other parallels with "All at Once, No Alice": the thwarted consummation of a marriage, the woman's secret past that impinges on events in the present, a self-serving guardian who conspires to create a false reality in order to deprive an heiress her rightful inheritance, and a steadfast, faithful hero who comes to his lover's rescue at the end. In "Alice," guardian Hastings is strictly concerned with retaining control of the money for himself. In *The Secret Fury*, Kent could easily be consumed by the same obsession, but the film gives him a different motive, inserted almost arbitrarily at the last second, perhaps to give him a different objective from Hastings (if "Alice" is indeed the model for this film). Doing so changes the theme of the story. There is the suggestion that insanity is an infection, that the insane can corrupt the sane until the sane degenerates into something less than human. Like many a hapless Woolrichian character, Ellen lives the waking nightmare and suffers from a distorted and unreliable perception of reality.

One of *The Secret Fury*'s most obvious connections to Woolrich is the "wholesale conspiracy" theme. In several of his stories, Woolrich suggests that the wealthy have the power — or in some cases, the illusion of power — to construct an artificial reality to protect themselves or to manipulate others. In "Alice" and *Phantom Lady*, for example, money is used to bribe witnesses and fabricate a phony reality for wicked ends. In *Night Has a Thousand Eyes* and *The Black Path of Fear*, on the other hand, wealthy characters learn that their money cannot make them completely invulnerable to certain formidable forces.

The paranoia inherent in these conspiracy themes reflects the paranoia of the man who wrote these stories. But then, this kind of paranoia is not unique to Woolrich. Consider the many stories of the past, whether novels or films, that exploited fears about conspiracies for the sake of entertainment: *Invasion of the Body Snatchers*, *Serpico*, *The Formula*, *The Pelican Brief*, *The Firm*, *The Net*, *Conspiracy Theory*, *Dark City* (1998), and *The Matrix*, to name a few. Allegorically, Woolrich seems to be saying that there exists, somewhere unseen, a ubiquitous power that can control us, manipulate our reality, determine our future, even decide whether we live or die.

In another prominent film, *Gaslight* (George Cukor, 1944), the male tormentor (Charles Boyer) is obsessed with securing some prized diamonds owned by a once-famous opera diva. He had, in fact, murdered the woman while trying to steal the diamonds, but was scared away before he could complete his quest. The woman's niece (Ingrid Bergman) was living in the house at the time of the murder. Traumatized by the tragedy, she moves to Italy to recover, and years later, unwittingly marries the man who had killed her aunt. His intention is to return to the house and search for the hidden cache of jewels. In the meantime, he takes advantage of his wife's delicate emotional state to fool her into thinking she is forgetful and absentminded and gradually going mad. He hopes to have her committed so he can search the house at his leisure. However, a Scotland Yard officer (Joseph Cotten) was a boyhood admirer of the murdered diva. He sees the resemblance between her and her niece and his interest in the unsolved case is revived. He discovers the villain's tactics and explains away the wife's doubts about herself. He enters the house in time to save the wife from the husband's last attempt to push her over the edge into insanity.

As in "No Alice," a conniving male wants to use marriage to gain an undeserved inheritance, but the loyal admirer spoils the scheme, rescues the threatened damsel, and restores her to her rightful place in society (not to mention that he also reaps intimate fringe benefits for his heroic act).

The following are only a few *noirs* and *neo-noirs* having features related to Woolrich's archetypal story. In *Cause for Alarm* (Tay Garnett, 1951), Loretta Young is tormented by husband Barry Sullivan. In *Dial M for Murder* (Hitchcock, 1954) and its remake, *A Perfect Murder* (Andrew Davis, 1998), the husband hires a killer to eliminate his wife so he can inherit her money and control the purse strings without her. In *Sudden Fear* (David Miller, 1952), Jack Palance finagles his way into Joan Crawford's life and marriage bed for the sake of revenge and money. The post-war thriller *Beware, My Lovely* (Harry Horner, 1952) has Ida Lupino playing balletic mind games with Robert Ryan, trying to distract him and keep him from doing her harm. In *Deceived* (Damian Harris, 1991), Goldie Hawn learns things about her husband she never suspected. And in *Sleeping with the Enemy* (Joseph Ruben, 1991), husband Patrick Bergin becomes a stalker after his own wife, Julia Roberts.

"C-Jag"

Short story in *Black Mask*, October 1940. Reprinted under the title "Cocaine" in *The Pocket Mystery Reader*, edited by Lee Wright, 1942. Distributed as "Cocaine" by King Features Syndicate, 1942. Reprinted under the title "Dream of Death" in *Mystery Digest*, December 1958. Reprinted under the title "Just Enough to Cover a Thumbnail" in *Ellery Queen's Mystery Magazine*, December 1965.

When Woolrich plagiarizes his own work, we can expect to see previous characters, plots, and themes reincarnated in new guises. Amid the glaring similarities, however, differences shine through, most frequently some fresh clever irony in the outcome: if a character's suspicions are contradicted in the original story, they prove justified in the reworked version ("He Looked Like Murder," 1941, versus "Rear Window," 1942); if an act of redemption is successful in the original, it is thwarted or undercut in the reworked version (*Phantom Lady*, 1942, versus *Black Angel*, 1943); if a character saves himself in the original, he plummets to his doom in the reworked version ("From Dusk to Dawn," 1937, versus "Murder Always Gathers Momentum," 1940); and so on.

"C-Jag" has a pivotal position in that it first borrows from an earlier work, then is itself plundered in subsequent hybrids. Pre-dating "C-Jag" is Woolrich's "Murder on My Mind," which appeared in the August 15, 1936, issue of *Detective Fiction Weekly* (and later retitled "Morning After Murder" when included in the short story collection *Bluebeard's Seventh Wife*, 1952). Detective Marquis investigates a baffling murder in which the evidence illogically points to him as the guilty party. Although the apartment where the murder occurred looks familiar to him, it takes some time before he finally realizes that he had lived there as a boy. He discovers in his possession an old key that must have been handed down to him from his parents. He suddenly concludes that he must have committed the murder in his sleep. As a somnambulist, he returned to the building of his childhood, used the key to let himself into the apartment, then killed the tenant, thinking him an intruder.

"Murder on My Mind" is a study of guilt, of what comprises it, of how culpability depends on the doer's full and willful consent. The irony is that Marquis has committed the most heinous of crimes for which he can claim complete innocence without classifying his act as an accident. From the author's viewpoint, the story reads like a psychologically displaced wish-fulfillment. Originally raised Roman Catholic, Woolrich may have known from his catechism that grievous sin depended on the full and willful consent of the doer. Because he flirts with this theme several times, it must be of critical concern to him. He may seek solace in this rationale for something he feels guilty about but hasn't done intentionally. His homosexuality? An issue related to his relationship with his mother or father? Regarding his father, the story has the vague implication that he acts vicariously through his character, returning to his childhood to punish his father with impunity. This situation becomes the basis not only for "C-Jag," but also for two stories of the following year: "Nightmare" (in *Argosy* as "And So to Death," March 1, 1941) and "Marihuana" (in *Detective Fiction Weekly*, May 3, 1941).

Different from "Murder on My Mind" is the dream state in the later stories, which is not a natural phenomenon but one induced artificially by drugs or hypnosis. The man awakens and already has vague inklings that, while in his unconscious condition, he may have actually murdered someone. In "Marihuana," the unfortunate protagonist, like the one in "C-Jag," is wallowing in a mood of self-pity that makes him susceptible to his friends' prompting to take the titled drug. He suffers a temporary confused mental state, after which he is told he had murdered a woman. The murder is a hoax, a sick practical joke, which means that his guilt is totally fabricated, his conscience agitated by the false impression that he committed the deed. "Marihuana" is essentially more like "From Dusk to Dawn" and "Momentum" (originally titled "Murder Always Gathers Momentum") in that the person, guilty or not, believes he will be accused of a crime and is trying to escape. "C-Jag" and "Nightmare" are more alike in that the protagonists fear their possible guilt, yet confront it, hoping to prove their innocence.

Ultimately, what sets the four stories apart from one another is the ironic twist the author gives each ending and the nature of each protagonist's guilt in relation to the murder he supposedly committed. Woolrich deliberately places these protagonists in positions where they are deprived of free will while they perform their crime. As studies in culpability and in whether circumstances should mitigate the crime, all four are excellent *noir* fictions dealing with those extrinsic forces that baffle reason and willpower, causing men to unleash (or think they've unleashed) their darker, repressed impulses. Whether this power represents Fate, Coincidence, or Chance can be argued, but this ingenious plot device is one of the most pure of *noir* conventions because it so precisely epitomizes the idea that some external capricious power determines our actions while we revel in the delusion that we have exclusive control over our own lives. At the same time, Woolrich raises questions about culpability, for if this external power exists, we have to wonder to what extent humans are responsible for their wrongdoings if they act without express direction from their own free wills.

"C-Jag" begins with Tommy Cochrane plunging into the seedy nighttime world of drugs and devious characters. After a hazy, hallucinogenic episode, he returns to his sister Mildred's house where he has been living because he cannot find employment. When he wakes the next day, he recalls having dreamt of locking a dead man in a closet. While dressing, he discovers among his belongings a key, which he cannot fit into any door in his sister's house, and he realizes that he may have actually murdered a man while under the influence of cocaine.

His sister's husband Denny is a detective. Denny takes Tommy along with him while they conduct their search secretly, hoping to find the body before anyone reports its discovery to the police. Denny is not doing this to hide the crime; he just wants to determine whether Tommy is guilty before he makes an official arrest.

Denny prods Tommy to remember what he can of the night before. As vague as his memory is, Tommy is able to recall a few details that give Denny his leads. Trying to follow the leads in their logical progression, they locate and question elevator operator Joe Fraser who took Tommy to the party. From here they go to the Sorrells' apartment where the party was held and where Tommy met a scar-faced man who gave him his first dose of cocaine. Then they find the squalid hotel where the man took Tommy afterward. They discover the sepulchral closet and the dead body of Ben Doyle, a stranger to Tommy. After investigating the area, they discover that a nearby garage is a hideout for gangsters. The boss, Graz, had killed one of his confederates. By chance, he had gone to the party and drugged Tommy, taking him to the hotel room where he planted the body and the murder weapon. He expected Tommy to be discovered the next day and be blamed for the murder. Tommy is cleared of the crime.

The excuse for Tommy's taking cocaine is borne out of the economic desperation of the Great Depression. Tommy tells his brother-in-law Denny that, in his despondency over not being able to find work, he succumbed to momentary temptation. Woolrich often alludes to the Depression as an immoral influence on his characters, and without dwelling extensively or morosely on it, hints that the abnormal economic circumstances forced people to behave in ways they ordinarily would not have. Consider "The Corpse Next Door" or "I Wouldn't Be in Your Shoes" where characters in financial straits behave in selfish, inconsiderate ways that lead to their predicaments. ("Marihuana" is slightly different in that the protagonist is depressed about separating from his wife and goes to a reefer party as a diversion.)

Guilt, Woolrich seems to suggest, becomes qualified under these circumstances. If Tommy had actually killed the man and hid his body in a closet, his cocaine stupor could be blamed as the immediate cause of his unconscious crime. He could plead temporary insanity and be acquitted of murder, even though he is still guilty of unintentional manslaughter and of using illegal drugs. However, the root cause of his two crimes, murder and drugs, goes beyond this to his unemployed status and to the Depression that caused his despondency, affecting his self-esteem, undermining his resolve, and making him vulnerable to the temptation to try cocaine. Taking the drug is a kind of symbolic self-immolation, a pseudo-suicide, a momentary death from which he can return. When he revives, he finds he loves life more than he thought. His quest to discover whether he is guilty of murder is also a quest to reclaim his innocence. This he does.

While the plot of "C-Jag" serves as the same story line for "Nightmare," some of its devices and characters also appear in other Woolrich stories in altered forms. Cochrane's older sister Mildred is the recurring female aegis who time and again supports, defends, and even saves the life of the male. In "Murder in Wax" and "Face Work," other sisters rescue their brothers convicted of murder. In *The Black Angel*, a wife puts her life in jeopardy to rescue her husband who has been jailed for murder. And in *Phantom Lady*, a woman remains loyal to her convicted lover, investigates suspects, and rescues him from pending execution. One cannot help but see these characters as surrogates for Woolrich's mother Claire Attalie Woolrich, whose money supported Woolrich during the Depression, and whose dominant personality buoyed his weaker one.

The sympathetic detective also appears in stories like *Night Has a Thousand Eyes*, *Black Angel*, *Phantom Lady*, "Murder in Wax," and "The Dancing Detective." Another device, the time limit that complicates the quest to prove a character's innocence, recurs in numerous Woolrich stories, *Deadline at Dawn* and *Black Alibi* among them. It's a useful device because it increases the tension and heightens the suspense.

Also in "C-Jag" Woolrich uses a narrative taboo that becomes a convention in many of his stories, the prolonged search for the unidentified witness. Most mystery stories stay focused on the search for the main culprit, whereas Woolrich will often push the central mystery into the background while what should have been a minor consideration becomes the main focus for a segment of the story. Cochrane's search for Joe Fraser, his little known acquaintance who took him to the fateful party, becomes a mystery within the mystery and adds to the suspense of the whole. In *Phantom Lady* and *Black Angel*, Woolrich develops whole episodes around these secondary considerations and momentarily makes them the prime concern of the heroine.

"C-Jag" is a tautly told tale, the questions, doubts, and uncertainties driving us headlong through the story. However, of the three stories based on this identical premise, "Nightmare" works best because the relationship between the protagonist and his brother-in-law is better developed and provides a subtext that adds meaning to the story and enriches the structure and theme. ("Nightmare" is discussed in a subsequent chapter.) "C-Jag" is more linear in its narrative, offering no apparent thematic subtext. However, the telling is typical Woolrich, explicit details making the reader feel as if he is experiencing the same things as the protagonist, thus increasing the dramatic tension and intensifying the emotional turmoil.

Film: Fall Guy

1947, Monogram. *D:* Reginald Le Borg. *P:* Walter Mirisch. *Cin:* Mack Stengler. *Sc:* Jerry Warner, John O'Dea (additional dialogue). *Ed:* William Austin. *Art Dir:* Dave Milton. *Set Dec:* Vin Taylor. *Sound:* Tom Lambert. *F/X:* Augie Lohman. *Mus Dir:* Edward J. Kay. (*Song:* "Tootin' My Own Horn" by Edward J. Kay and Eddie Cherkose).

Cast: Clifford Penn (Tom Cochrane), Robert Armstrong (Mac McClane), Teala Loring (Lois Walters), Elisha Cook, Jr. (Joe Marsello), Douglas Fowley (Inspector Shannon), Harry Strang (Detective Taylor), Charles Arnt (Uncle Jim Grossett), Virginia Dale (Marie), Jack Overman (Mike), Iris Adrian (Mrs. Sindell), John Harmon (Ed Sindell), Christian Rub (Swedish maintenance man), Lou Lubin (Benny the bartender), George Backus (Police physician), John Bleifer (Hotel clerk), Bob Carleton (Pianist at Sindell party), Brother Theodore (Inmate). 64 min.

Arriving at Universal Studios in the late 1930s with a marginal musical background, Reginald Le Borg accepted directorial duties for a sequence of musical shorts before being promoted to feature films. His name is mostly associated with the popular Joe Palooka series churned out in the forties and fifties. Le Borg was also responsible for a few of the less notable Universal horror films (*Calling Dr. Death*, 1943; *Jungle Woman*, 1944; *The Mummy's Ghost*, 1944; among others) before taking on the assignment for Monogram, the *noir* film *Fall Guy*.

In translating the story to film, scenarist Jerry Warner makes several major changes, among them the nature of the protagonist's search for truth. Woolrich's "C-Jag" is more concerned with the blurred line between reality and illusion and with the fate that randomly befalls a person in the wrong place at the wrong time. *Fall Guy* deviates from this, following instead the "conspiracy" formula Woolrich uses in *Phantom Lady* (1942), which was adapted for film three years earlier. The "conspiracy" formula (which also governs the likes of "Face Work" and "All at Once, No Alice") pits the protagonist against a world that seems allied against him or her, stalling him or her from learning the truth. This point is not meant as criticism; any changes an adaptation deploys can work well if done creatively and justifiably. Whatever weaknesses *Fall Guy* has (and it has a few) are not due to this single alteration to the original story.

Fall Guy follows the general arc of Woolrich's story, but changes enough details along the way to produce a different theme. A beat cop finds Cochrane (Clifford Penn) unconscious in an alley with blood on his shirt and a bloody knife at his side. Taken to the police hospital, he escapes before Inspector Shannon (Douglas Fowley) can question him. He returns to his brother-in-law Mac's (Robert Armstrong) apartment where he lives because he can't find a job. He has recently returned from the war and has been acting "moody and restless," which is why girlfriend Lois Walters (Teala Loring) shunned his marriage proposal the night before. He blames her rejection for his predicament, because that is what started the chain of events that led him to murder a girl.

In flashback, he describes how he met a stranger named Joe (Elisha Cook, Jr.) who wanted to cheer him up. Joe steered him to a party where Cochrane became friendly with the female singer (Virginia Dale) because "nothing helps you forget a girl quicker than another girl." She encouraged him to chug a tall glass of liquor, which turned out to be drugged. He lost consciousness and when he woke later, the room was deserted. Outside the window, the partially visible hotel sign glowed with the letters "P-A-L" which made him think of the "pal" who had brought him to the party. He opened a closet door and the dead body of a girl — he wasn't sure if it was the singer or Lois — fell to the ground. He stuffed it back in the closet and left.

Mac and Cochrane run downstairs. From the street, Cochrane glances up at the vertical sign of the Palace Hotel and recalls that the "PAL" fragment had made him think of Joe. Mac realizes that the letters are level with the floor above the Sindells' apartment, and he deduces that, when Cochrane came out of his stupor, he must have been in the room directly over the one where the party took place. They visit the room and discover the body not of the singer but of a girl Cochrane doesn't recognize. Shannon suddenly appears, having followed them. Cochrane escapes, but Mac is arrested.

Alone, Cochrane continues to search for the singer. One night, the girl and her boyfriend Mike (Jack Overman) come to Benny's Place. Cochrane follows them, but Mike spots him. Mike tells Marie to go to her apartment and he will meet her there. He intercepts Cochrane and beats him.

At her apartment, Marie sits at her vanity table when Jim Grossett (Charles Arnt) lets himself in. Grossett is Lois's surrogate uncle who has been acting as her guardian. He had paid Marie to lure Cochrane to the Sindells' party, where she was to get him to drink the drugged cocktail. To accomplish this, Marie paid Joe to lead Cochrane to the party, where she did as Grossett instructed. But Grossett knows that Cochrane is looking for her and may find her, so he strangles her. Mike arrives too late to save Marie, but he scares Grossett who escapes out the window. Cochrane appears in the doorway, having followed Mike there. Cochrane pursues Grossett. They fight, and as Grossett tries to club Cochrane with his cane, Mike wrests it from him and kills him with two violent strokes.

Cochrane explains to Lois what happened. The murdered girl was Patti, a friend of Marie's. She knew of Grossett's shady dealings and was blackmailing him. Grossett, meanwhile, although designated as Lois's guardian, was in love with her. He decided he could get rid of two undesirable people at once, killing his blackmailer and framing Cochrane for her murder to get him out of Lois's life. He was a narcotics user himself and knew from experience that drugs could induce fear and "make you imagine things you hadn't done." Cochrane foiled his plan by coming out of his torpor too soon. The story ends with Lois and Cochrane setting off to get married and Mac joining them now that he is free from prison. Shannon returns to his "Homicide Office" and closes the door, punctuating the film's conclusion.

Fall Guy uses Woolrich's "C-Jag" to lay its structural foundation, then

Fall Guy— Mac McClane (Robert Armstrong, center) looks dourly upon the body of the woman that Tom Cochrane (Clifford Penn) thinks he murdered (Monogram, courtesy William Thailing).

makes its changes and additions to shift the intent of the story and infuse it with a wider variety of typical *noir* themes. For one, Cochrane, rather than playing Woolrich's pathetic loser of the Depression era, is an ex–G.I. This links the film to post-war issues not present in Woolrich's story. Mac alludes to this theme when he diagnoses Cochrane's problem: "I know what's wrong with you. I've seen whole screaming wards full of 'em." In other words, Mac believes that Cochrane suffers from shell shock or some other psychological trauma. Meanwhile, his girlfriend Lois describes him to Uncle Jim as "moody and restless," one who drinks heavily and "can't find the kind of job he wants." It isn't that he can't find employment; he can't find the job that suits him. It may be that he doesn't want to work, so he uses this excuse to avoid this responsibility. Like numerous *noir* characters plagued by residual effects of the war, Cochrane displays the symptoms of returning veterans who have difficulty fitting into society. His situation compares with that of the protagonists in *The Blue Dahlia*, *Cornered*, and *Crack-Up*, and in the non-*noir* drama *The Best Years of Our Lives*.

Lois may seem to fill the requirement of the superficial love interest for the protagonist, but she is much more than that. First of all, she appears more confident and levelheaded than Cochrane — another by-product of the war is that women have become more independent and self-assertive. She rejects his proposal of marriage, suggesting that, for her, marriage is not the cliché be-all-and-end-all in a woman's life. She changes her mind to marry him only because she thinks it may help him become more responsible. Cochrane's confusion and guilt in thinking he may have murdered her suggests that he recognizes the potential in himself to resort to violence when confronted by a defiant, intractable woman.

The second thing that makes her role significant is that Uncle Jim is obsessed with her, that she becomes his motive for framing Cochrane as the "fall guy" for Patti's murder. She is, in effect, an inadvertent *femme fatale*, innocent but liable for the downfall of an obsessive male. As an alternative to the aggressive Spider Woman who deliberately weaves her web and hopes to entrap a gullible man, such as in *The Maltese Falcon* and *The Postman Always Rings Twice*, the inadvertent *femme fatale* shows that the male is susceptible to her influence even when she is passive and makes no seductive overtures. Lois's character is related to the "innocent" or aloof *femmes fatales* in other *films noirs*, such as *Nora Prentiss*, *The Paradine Case*, and *Pitfall*.

Teala Loring as Lois Walters is a stunning beauty, as well as a polished actress, who gives a splendid performance despite the limited material. (Beauty is obviously a genetic trait, for she is the sister of another gorgeous actress, Debra Paget.) She engages our attention right from the time she slides her feet into a pair of slippers and wraps herself in a silk robe. Her buoyant tresses, fabulous figure, and gaunt facial lines qualify her as a Rita Hayworth lookalike who is more than adequate competition for her.

Clifford Penn as Tom Cochrane does an adequate job for his single screen credit. Interestingly, he resembles Al Pacino, not only in looks, but also in the way he delivers his lines, with a bit of brooding deliberation. We will never know what kind of an acting career he may have had.

The main theme of *Fall Guy* focuses on narcotics and alcohol abuse, which appear to be widespread social concerns in the post-war era. Several films of the mid- to late forties deal with drugs or hallucinatory conditions, either centrally or peripherally, literally or symbolically, as a wartime consequence: *The Fallen Sparrow*, *Phantom Lady*, *Murder My Sweet*, *The Big Sleep*, *Crack-Up*, *High Wall*, *The Chase*, *Fear in the Night*, *D.O.A.*, *Panic in the Streets*, and *The Sleeping City*. In *Fall Guy*, Cochrane may take the narcotic unknowingly, but he already has a strong dependence on alcohol, a drug substitute. Lois admits to Uncle Jim that Tom drinks too much. At the Sindells' party, after he finishes one tall cocktail, he shows little hesitation when Marie encourages him ("Aw, c'mon, bottoms up.") and he readily gulps down his second drink, the one laced with a drug. Uncle Jim, however, is supposed to be the real hardcore drug addict. Although his addiction is never shown explicitly or explained adequately, Cochrane's clarification at the end implies that Grossett had extensive experience with drugs, that he had experimented with them and knew which "induced fear" and which "made you imagine things you hadn't done." Cochrane adds, "Under the influence of drugs, he could do almost anything." The statement implies that drugs reduce inhibitions, make a person less likely to obey social proprieties and adhere to law. Conscience is suppressed, guilt negated.

Behind the front desk at the Antoine Hotel hangs a picture of the ruins of the Roman Coliseum. Vaguely suggested is what can happen to a great civilization after its glory is past. It happened to Rome; it can happen in America, its downfall coming from drugs and alcohol. The returning war veterans with their personal problems and feelings of alienation are most susceptible to substance abuse. But it is more widespread than that. At an apartment building where Mac and Tom go to find Joe Marsello, they first talk with a Swedish maintenance man who preaches temperance, but keeps sneaking sips of demon rum from a bottle he hides in his overalls. He tells Mac the story of the milkman who died: "It wasn't the stairs that killed him; it was the bottle." And he warns Mac and Tom to stay away from drink. His hypocrisy reflects that of the general public, drinkers who freely condemn alcohol, then turn around and overindulge whenever they get the opportunity. The Sindells' throwing a party "whenever we hit a longshot" represents the trivial excuse people need to imbibe.

While alcohol has the dubious honor of being "socially acceptable," drugs automatically mark the user an outlaw unfit to function within society. Until Cochrane can prove his innocence, he is a pariah. At the beginning, Detectives Shannon and Taylor (Harry Strang) seem angrier with Cochrane for the condition he is in than for any solid evidence that he killed someone. (They have his bloodied knife and shirt, no body or proof of wrongdoing.) When the police doctor explains that Cochrane has been drugged, they get even more abusive and short-tempered with him. Drugs cannot be tolerated or condoned in any fashion. Cochrane's brother-in-law is ready to turn him in until he is persuaded by Lois to help him. Only after the evidence accumulates in Tom's favor does Mac begin to believe him innocent. Drugs alienate the "shooter" from society and make him or her an outcast.

One flaw in the story is that, at the end, we never learn why Patti is blackmailing Grossett. We can guess that it has something to do with his drug habit, but there aren't enough clues to support this fully. A vague hint here or there may have tied her death to the drug theme more effectively. A few other trivial flaws appear, not hurting the story so much as creating momentary distractions. The silliest is the clumsy set design of the subway entrance. Three subway entrances keep recurring at several different times throughout the film. Obviously, it is the same set adorned with new props (candy bar ad posted on the wall, garbage can, weight scale) placed around the entrance to indicate the alternate site (18th Street, 28th Street, and 50th Street). The entrance is built so low that all the actors descending the stairs, although they try to feign nonchalance, look as if they are performing the limbo, and some of the taller ones risk decapitation.

After Shannon arrests Mac as an accessory to murder, a close-up of a newspaper column covering the story lists Mac's age as 36. Maybe this was inserted to test the audience's suspension of disbelief, but Robert Armstrong, most famous for his role as the ham documentary moviemaker in 1933's *King Kong*, and still looking physically fit and trim, needs more than make-up to give the illusion that he's not on the downward slope of middle age (He is in fact 56.). Another faux pas is Grossett's facial expressions, which are too obvious in marking him as a suspicious character. He broadcasts his sly, slimy villainy from the first moment he walks into Lois's room. The only surprise at the end is not whodunit but whydunit. Also, there is the moment, after Tom discovers the dead body, when he picks up the bloody knife, then wipes his bloody hand on his white shirt — except that there already is a dark blotch on the shirt before he touches it.

John O'Dea was brought in to provide "additional dialogue," so we don't know which lines to attribute to him or Warner — not that there are many verbal gems to claim credit for. "Sparkling" or "crackling" or "original" may not be appropriate descriptives, but most of the lines are passable — primarily because the actors speak their parts with conviction. Even so, a few passages stand out like pepper in a salt cellar. When Detective Taylor learns that Cochrane is under the influence of a drug, he says they should "throw the book at him, the book and the covers and everything in between 'em." The police doctor, nonplussed, responds: "Okay, but the book will only land with a dull thud while he's in this condition." I suppose one character has to play the straight man if another is going to deliver the witty punch line. In another scene, Cochrane takes issue with Lois's explanation of why she wanted to postpone their wedding. Squeezing this dramatic plum for every ounce of sympathy, he struts around, muttering his complaint: "Wait! All we ever do is wait. First, we waited till we were old enough. Then we waited for a war to end. Now we're supposed to wait till Jim is satisfied with me." Good parallel structure, anyway. Cochrane lends the same dramatic intensity to his description of his drugged stupor: "My brain rattled inside like the tongue of a bell." Forced, perhaps, but picturesque.

One example of a change that improves on the original story is the elimination of Woolrich's gangster element. In "C-Jag," the elevator operator who befriends Cochrane takes him to the Sorrells' party where Graz *arbitrarily* fingers him as the patsy for the murder he himself will perpetrate. Graz is, in Woolrich's own words, the *diabolus ex machina*, the fateful, fatal evil that comes out of nowhere to upset or destroy an innocent (or sometimes guilty) character's life. In a Woolrich story, a gangster is usually a stock character, the hardened stereotype associated with corruption, dissolution, evil, and violence, who disrupts or destroys the lives of the people he contacts. Some *films noirs* use gangsters and racketeers effectively in their plots: *This Gun for Hire*, 1942; *Out of the Past*, 1947; *The Racket*, 1951; *Man in the Dark*, 1953); however, it is one of *noir's* trademarks to emphasize domestic crime where common, ordinary people succumb to a sudden temptation (money, love, power) that is too overwhelming for their loosely rooted principles (*Side Street*, *Roadblock*, *Shield for Murder*). In Woolrich, unfortunately, the abrupt appearance of the gangster too often seems plastic and gimmicky, as if his creative powers lapsed into 1930s clichés because he could not invent an original antagonist who had his own distinct motivation or rationale for causing havoc. Note the awkward, incongruous quality of this plot device when it is forced into stories like *The Bride Wore Black*, "Murder in Wax," "Crime on St. Catherine Street," and "Face Work." *Fall Guy* is not the epitome of an adaptation from a Woolrich story, nor is it among *la crème des films noirs*, but it does reduce (somewhat) the contrived nature of Woolrich's denouement by deleting the gangster element and giving the conflict domestic origins.

Other details work very well, such as the comic relief from the Sindells (an episode that comes directly out of Woolrich). At the Bijou movie theater where Mac goes to meet Tom and Lois, a lobby poster advertises one movie, *Don't Gamble with Strangers* and the marquis shows another, *Decoy*. Both titles are clearly associated with Cochrane's situation. Technically, Le Borg and cinematographer Mack Stengler do many of the right things: a sinister black shadow lingers ominously on the wall behind Joe Marsello just before he is pushed into the path of a passing car; the rooftop stairs make a portentous shadow-pattern on the wall as Tom descends them to pursue Grossett. The inky angular shadows draping the rooftops make an acceptable image of the labyrinth that the *noir* hero must often enter to confront the monster and defeat him.

All in all, *Fall Guy* is a satisfying adaptation of a Woolrich story. It shifts the theme and alters or adds some characters, while capturing the mood of desperation and confusion inherent in Woolrich's original work and in the *noir* style in general.

The Bride Wore Black

Novel, first published by Simon & Schuster, December 1940. Subsequent publication by Robert Hale, 1942. First paperback in 1945 by Pocket Books, pbk #271. Reprinted as *Beware the Lady* in 1953 by Pyramid, pbk #80. Various reprints have appeared in hardcover and paperback.

The Bride Wore Black is Woolrich's first attempt at a novel-length suspense-mystery. In the late 1920s and early '30s, he had written and published several realistic mainstream novels born of the Jazz Age and mimicking the work of his idol, F. Scott Fitzgerald. Two were even adapted for film (*Children of the Ritz* and *Manhattan Love Song*), but Woolrich was satisfied with neither the reviews nor the limited success of his output up to this time: "I finally learned to do my job competently in the mid–30s.... It would have been a lot better if everything I'd done until then had been written in invisible ink and the reagent had been thrown away" (*Blues of a Lifetime* 12). That is, not until he started writing his suspense-thrillers for the pulps did he feel some creative satisfaction from his effort. For six years, between 1934 and 1940, he inundated mass market magazines with exercises in the short story, more than a hundred macabre mystery-suspense yarns, some masterfully written, some exceptionally trite, relying most often on intricate, outlandish plot devices and ironic twists a la O. Henry, Maupassant, and Poe. When he finally completed and published *The Bride Wore Black* in December of 1940, it was instantly and enthusiastically received by the reading public. Besides being his first true suspense novel, it also marked the inception of his Black Series, a sequence of six books exploring the inscrutable workings of fate, the desperation of obstructed love, and the tenuous, illogical connection between crime and punishment. Along with *Bride*, these include *The Black Curtain* (1941), *Black Alibi* (1942), *The Black Angel* (1943), *The Black Path of Fear* (1944) — all adapted for film and discussed elsewhere in this volume — and lastly, *Rendezvous in Black* (1948, adapted for television's *Playhouse 90*, October 25, 1956), which, like a bookend to the series, mirrors the first novel in premise, structure, and theme.

Woolrich organizes *The Bride Wore Black* according to a rather rigid format. He divides the novel into five main sections, each entitled with a man's name (Bliss, Mitchell, Moran, Ferguson, and Holmes). The first four sections are further divided into three identical subsections: subsection one, "The Woman," follows the actions of Julie Killeen; subsection two, named for the man she plans to murder, shows how she meets and kills him; subsection three, entitled "Postmortem on —," describes the aftermath of the specific victim's death and how detective Lew Wanger gathers clues in his pursuit of the serial killer. The fifth and final section deviates from the others because events do not go according to Julie's plan: the first two subsections remain intact, but two are added, "Flashback: The Little Casket Around the Corner," to explain Julie's motives for the killings, and "Postmortem on Nick Killeen," to provide an outcome for the story.

The novel begins enigmatically with Julie Killeen saying good-bye to her family in New York and setting off on a railroad trip to Chicago. Without explanation, she gets off at the first stop; we presume she is using the trip as a diversion to deceive her family while she carries out some secret plan close to home. Not until much later in the story do we learn that Julie is on a mission to avenge her husband's untimely death. On her wedding day, just as she and the groom, Nick Killeen, emerge from the church following the nuptial service, a speeding car, wildly out of control, caroms off the church steps, striking the groom and killing him. Julie's love turns to bitter vindictiveness. She seeks out the men riding in the car, finagles her way into their lives and, one by one, murders them.

Only the last is spared because Detective Wanger discovers what the murdered men had in common and why Julie is after them. They had belonged to a group of gambling rebel rousers called the Friday-Night Fiends, who every Friday night took a reckless joyride through neighborhood streets. Theirs was the death car that Julie blames for killing Nick. However, when Wanger intercepts Julie before she can claim her fifth victim, he regretfully explains how she had killed four men needlessly. His investigation revealed that Nick was involved in racketeering with another man, Corey, who was afraid Nick might betray him once he reformed. To protect himself, Corey shot his partner as he and his new bride walked out of the church. The loud backfiring and billowing exhaust smoke from the Fiends' car as they passed the church was merely a coincidental event that obscured the noise of the gunshot. Julie, driven by her hateful resolve to seek revenge, never learned the truth. Now she acknowledges her mistake. She sheds a few tears, accepts her guilt, and prepares to go to prison.

In plotting *The Bride Wore Black*, Woolrich uses an episodic structure, a pattern he will favor for many of his subsequent novels. Here, the central conflict for each of the five episodes is identical, namely the phantom lady's quest to kill her male victims. This commonality connects the episodes and gives unity to the whole.

Throughout the story, Woolrich reinforces Julie's image as a cold, calculating, and malicious monster. First, he maintains a generally objective, omniscient point of view. Other than the brief prologue where she is introduced as a vague, embittered figure, the story is told from outside her perspective. Even in the "Woman" subsections where we are allowed glimpses of her plotting, the narrative occurs outside of her consciousness, so she appears detached, aloof, insensitive. Unable to understand her behavior, we see her as objectified, alienated from our empathy and sympathy. Only at the very end, when we finally learn her motive for the murder, which Woolrich skillfully delays for his ironic purposes, do we feel something for her. For us, the readers, it is almost as if an emotional dam bursts. We have been anxiously waiting to know some reason, some logic, for her doing what she does, and finally, her apparently random, insane acts are explained.

Julie appears all the more monstrous and villainous because we initially learn more about her victims than we do about her; consequently, they are made the more sympathetic characters. A prospective bridegroom, a destitute romantic, a typical husband, a reputed artist — they all seem normal, innocent, maybe even likable, people. We are struck by their apparent innocence, their affability, harmlessness, and vulnerability, so that each time one is killed — and we always know death is coming — we are repulsed by the horror of her cold and callous cruelty. Woolrich does this quite cleverly, convincing us to sympathize with the men until Julie's vengeance is justified and we have to revise our original estimate, jarred suddenly into feeling sorrow and pity for her.

However, guilt and innocence are relative here. Even though the Friday-Night Fiends are innocent of Killeen's death, they are guilty of reckless hell-raising and wanton endangerment of others' lives: they *could* have killed Julie's husband. Despair corrodes Julie's innocence, as she is consumed by a morbid desire for vengeance; she becomes guilty of reckless vigilantism.

Rationalizing her murders as delayed executions, Julie may think of herself as an Avenging Angel, but she is also a prototype of the *noir* Spider Woman. She wriggles her way into men's lives by presenting herself as a sensual object of desire or an ideal helpmate before she teaches them the dangerous, fatal consequences of trusting her.

Her first victim is Kenneth Bliss. She titillates his fancy and momentarily diverts his attention from his fiancée. His brief, innocent flirtation with her is enough to put him in danger. Her pushing him off the balcony achieves Old Testament justice, "an eye for an eye," since she deprives him of the wedded "bliss" she has been denied. In a larger sense, all of the Friday-Night Fiends, having lost their friend, are deprived of "Bliss," a foreshadowing of Julie's taking away any happiness they have attained.

The epigraph that follows the title "Bliss" is an excerpt from the Rodgers and Hart song "Blue Moon." Woolrich often alludes to songs of the times to reflect a mood or reinforce a theme. Here, the words are an apostrophe, a deserted lover calling on the moon to witness his or her despair at a failed romance. In like fashion, Julie's loss causes her collapse into a desperate state, feeling bereft of all possible hope for love and happiness. That the personified blue moon must know what she is feeling suggests a secret, silent compact between her, an incarnation of Hecate, and the mysterious forces of night. In the later flashback section "The Little Casket Around the Corner," we see that after Nick is killed, Julie walks back inside the church "to make a vow. Another vow to Nick." It is a vow of vengeance that she expresses in words and consummates in physical action.

Mitchell, the second victim, is a frustrated romantic, a disillusioned loner who still clings to the dream of meeting the ideal woman. The epigraph from Maupassant at the start of his chapter foreshadows his susceptibility to the innocent pretense masking Julie's predatory designs: "He starts as one who, hearing a deer's tread,/Beholds a panther stealing forth instead." In his absence, Julie previews his room, and from the pictures of various female types on the walls, understands the kind of woman he is looking for. She adapts herself to become that woman. She seduces him by first appealing to his artistic instincts (she sends him a ticket to the theater) and then entering his life as his physical ideal. After she sneaks poison into his drink, he clutches at his chest and exclaims, "...it's being torn apart." What is happening to him physically has already happened to Julie emotionally, her heart torn apart by the loss of her true love. Again she has administered a kind of Old Testament retribution.

The third victim, Moran, is married, a certified member of the conventional establishment. Although his life appears mundane, routine, settled, it is a life Julie must have aspired to with Nick — home, hearth, and children — and it is a life she has been denied. In this respect, her murdering Moran resembles the others as "eye for an eye" justice.

To get Moran's wife out of the way, Julie sends a false telegram that her mother is sick and she should visit her immediately. (We're already acquainted with the ploy of the false telegram in "Face Work"; Woolrich uses it for a similar purpose in "The Boy Cried Murder.") Then she substitutes herself as the ideal wife and mother, attending to all the needs of both the husband and son. After putting the boy Cookie to bed, she tricks Moran into entering a small storage closet which she quickly seals, killing him by suffocation. Deprived of her own family, she deprives Moran's family of their husband and father.

The epigraph for Moran's chapter comes from the introductory verses to Cole Porter's "Night and Day." Like "Blue Moon," this is another song that relates to Julie. The lyrics point to a lover's obsession with a beloved, an image that haunts the lover day and night. Musically, these particular lyrics are sung on a single repetitive note, a kind of driving monotone that echoes the repetitive beat of a drum and ticking of a clock and enhances the feeling of a relentless juggernaut of emotion. This same relentlessness underpins Julie's monomaniacal desire to fulfill her vow of vengeance. In effect, she is an unstoppable instrument of Time and Tide, a fateful and deadly intruder in the lives of her victims.

The fourth victim, Ferguson, is an artist, but one who has subordinated his creative ability to the money he makes from popular drawings for magazine covers and book illustrations. Although likable personally, he has prostituted himself professionally. (This could be a self-reflective comment by a regretful Woolrich. See the discussion on the excerpt from *Into the Night*, pages 12–14.)

The epigraph to this section is another excerpt from Maupassant: "For the portent bade me understand/Some horror was at hand." The words apply less to Julie than they do to Ferguson and Corey. (Corey appeared earlier as a friend of Bliss and re-enters in this section as a friend of Ferguson.) Julie is the "horror" that is at hand. Ferguson, using her as a model, poses her as Diana the Huntress. With her bow poised to shoot her arrow, Julie releases the string and nearly hits Ferguson. This is the portent Ferguson, who is too good natured, overlooks. Meanwhile, Corey sees his friend's early sketches of Julie and even gets to meet her, but cannot recall where he has seen her before. He senses some uneasiness, but cannot define it. The horror is finally realized when Corey remembers too late where he met Julie. He visits Ferguson's studio in the night to warn him, but finds the artist dead, an arrow shot through his heart. Like Mitchell, he sustains his mortal wound in the symbolic seat of love which has been destroyed in Julie.

Holmes, the fifth victim, is also a kind of artist, a successful writer. His case is different, though, because we never learn much about him. To augment the mystery and irony, Woolrich plays a literary trick here. He knows that a writer, in using words, appeals to readers' subjective imaginations, not to empirical objectivity. Therefore, because the reader cannot literally see the characters, a writer can easily disguise them by not identifying them. Presented this way, the character wears a mask and the reader cannot be sure who he or she is until the writer makes it clear. Woolrich creates a bit of misdirection for his readers. His unreliable narrator leads us to believe that an unsuspecting Holmes has placed himself in danger by inviting a strange young lady into his home. There is no evidence enabling us to recognize the familiar Wanger who, setting a trap for Julie, sits in for the unfamiliar Holmes; we can only accept events as they are presented to us, believing that this actually is Holmes. At the same time, we assume that the unidentified young lady, who makes a bet with her girlfriends that she will get her picture taken with the famous author, must be Julie. To create suspense, two women, the young lady and Holmes's typist, are present in Holmes's house. Words have not confirmed the true identity of either, so we are forced to be suspicious of both. Only after Wanger lets his trap fall and he uncovers the identity of the murderer do we realize that the visiting young woman is an entirely new character, while the typist is Julie.

The epigraph to the final section is once again from Maupassant: "It seemed to me behind my chair there stood/A spectre with a cold and cruel smile, lifeless and motionless." The "spectre" is an ambiguous figure, open to interpretation. The most immediate impression is that it is Death, smug and proud, patiently waiting because he knows that all things will eventually come to him. As an Avenging Angel, Julie has already delivered four of the five men to him. At the end, her final words suggest she is contemplating suicide: "Yes,

... it's time for me to go." The terrible thought is that, if the spectre is Death, it waits behind everyone's chair.

Published in *Detective Fiction Weekly* on May 2, 1936, "Johnny on the Spot" does not rank among Woolrich's best short stories, but it contains one ingredient that links it to *Bride*. A woman convinces her man to abandon his life of crime and adopt a conventional American middle-class life style. Reformation, however, proves detrimental for anyone who thinks he can escape his past. The man's criminal cohorts fear his change of heart and refuse to let him reform. Only with the help of his meek wife, who ironically resorts to the criminals' violent methods to rescue him, does he succeed in eluding them, although he must remain a lifetime fugitive.

Most obviously, Johnny's situation parallels Nick Killeen's. A further consideration is the implied theme that a person's past influences the present, that once a life has been corrupted, it can never reclaim its lost innocence. This applies to both Julie and the Friday-Night Fiends. Although innocent of the death of Julie's husband, the Fiends are guilty of other "crimes." And Julie's mistake in blaming the Fiends for her husband's death changes her mission from justice to murder. To say that any of these characters are guilt-free and have died unjustly is to overlook the additional irony that Woolrich implies so subtly.

Because *Rendezvous in Black*, on the surface, so closely resembles *The Bride Wore Black*, a few words need to be said about it. The later novel mirrors the earlier one in several ways. The female Avenging Angel becomes a male avenger (John) pursuing the men he blames for the death of his young fiancée. Julie's villains were freewheeling drunks, a group of card-playing hellions who raced their exhaust-spewing automobile through the streets; John's four adversaries, also drinkers, are a group of hunters riding in an airplane. Thus, both perpetrators are small groups of men, bonded by their desire for male activity (gambling, joyriding, hunting). Almost as if deliberately trying to reverse Hemingway's lofty image of male camaraderie, Woolrich portrays the bonded males as corrupt, irresponsible, and dissolute, inconsiderate toward society and disrespectful of human life.

A slight but important difference between the two novels is the accuracy of the guilt assigned to the group of men. The Fiends are innocent of the crime for which Julie condemns them. They are guilty of other crimes, more ethical than legal, but none is guilty of Nick Killeen's death. The hunting group in *Rendezvous* is not so guilt-free. One of them has thrown the Coke bottle out of the plane that killed John's girlfriend. From this, Woolrich adroitly builds suspense by intertwining three main plot threads: the overriding question of who is the guilty one of the four men; the suspenseful treatment of each episode as we wonder how John will strike and if he will be successful (his object is to deprive the man of his beloved); and finally, the pursuit by the tenacious detective, making us wonder when and if John will get caught before he carries out each of his uniquely planned murders.

Quite a few *films noirs* deal with a character who is jaded by past experiences, but meets another who acts as a redeeming agent. The influence of the past is an obstacle that creates the major conflict for the character. Sometimes, if the redemptive character is stronger than the influence of the corrupt past, the jaded character is saved. In *Kiss of Death*, *Body and Soul*, *Gilda*, and *Party Girl*, the man is rescued by the tenacious love of a good woman. But if the past proves too pervasive and dominant, nothing can save the doomed character. *Out of the Past* is the archetype of this situation.

For Woolrich, characters like Nick Killeen are not only haunted by a past that threatens their destruction; they also corrupt the life of the lover who tries to redeem them. In "Johnny on the Spot," instead of Johnny being reformed into the average, everyday husband by his wife, his wife ironically becomes as much a criminal as the criminals she redeems him from. Similarly, Nick's death inspires Julie's vengeance, which appears justified, except that his death is the consequence of his criminal activity, and Julie's righteousness, based on false assumption, is merely blind faith that corrupts her innocence.

As demonstrated in *The Bride Wore Black* and a number of his other stories, Woolrich insists that a person cannot escape a guilty past, at least not totally; and the guilty person becomes a corruptive influence on those around him or her. It is a notion that recalls a character like Ichabod Crane, who comes to quaint Sleepy Hollow with the stain of education and breeding on him, or Hester Prynne, who is viewed by the Puritans as a dangerous corrupting agent who must be branded and alienated.

The contribution of *The Bride Wore Black* to *film noir* is extremely significant. Published in 1940, it appears just when this new style-genre of film emerges and begins to define itself. As a seminal literary work in this area, *Bride* most importantly prefigures the mysterious and predatory *femme fatale*, a character critical to so many central conflicts in *noir*. In addition, as often occurs in a Woolrich story, it establishes the male characters as weak competitors with the female, susceptible to her wiles and, if not careful, potential victims for her schemes. *Bride* contains other *noir* ingredients as well. The element of pure mystery, the whodunit aspect popular in crime films of the 1930s, is forsaken for an emphasis on the suspense generated from the planning and commission of a crime, like a heist (*The Asphalt Jungle*, *Odds Against Tomorrow*) or murder (*Double Indemnity*, *The Postman Always Rings Twice*), and by leaving the audience wondering if, when, and how the perpetrators will be caught. All this is central to Woolrich's novel and the same conventions become critical in most subsequent *films noirs*.

Film: The Bride Wore Black

Original French title: *La Mariée était en noir*
1967, Les Films du Carrosse/Artistes Associés, Dino De Laurentiis Cinematografica.

The Bride Wore Black (1940) / The Bride Wore Black (1967)

D: François Truffaut. *P:* Marcel Berbert. *Cin:* Raoul Coutard. *Sc:* François Truffaut, Jean-Louis Richard, based on the novel by Cornell Woolrich. *Ed:* Claudine Bouché. *Mus:* Bernard Herrmann. *Asst Dir:* Jean Chayrou. *Art Dir:* Pierre Guffroy.
Cast: Jeanne Moreau (Julie Kohler), Claude Rich (Bliss), Jean-Claude Brialy (Corey), Michel Bouquet (Coral), Michel Lonsdale (Morane), Charles Denner (Fergus), Daniel Boulanger (Delvaux), Christophe Bruno (Cookie), Alexandra Stewart (Mlle Becker), Sylvine Delannoy (Mme Morane), Luce Fabiole (Julie's Mother), Jacques Robiolles (Charlie), Michèle Montfort, Jacqueline Rouillard (Chambermaid), Paul Pavel (Mechanic), Gilles Queant (Examining judge), Serge Rousseau (David Kohler), Van Doude (Inspector Fabri), Elisabeth Rey (Julie as a child), Jean-Pierre Rey (David as a child). 107 min.

It seems fitting that at some point the work of Cornell Woolrich, Alfred Hitchcock, and François Truffaut should intersect. Truffaut, an avid Hitchcock admirer, makes no secret that many of his films have been influenced by the "master of suspense." The fascination which Truffaut and other French critics of the *Cahiers du Cinéma* had with *film noir* makes it no surprise that he should eventually want to adapt a film from a Woolrich novel. Thus, in *The Bride Wore Black*, we have the French director reworking Woolrichian material to produce a Hitchcockian thriller. This is the first of Truffaut's two commendable attempts at adapting a Woolrich novel. The second, *Waltz into Darkness*, filmed as *La Sirène du Mississippi*, is discussed in a later chapter.

Some of Truffaut's earlier work, such as *Shoot the Piano Player*, capture fragments of *noir* tonality and content. However, as one of the initiators of the French New Wave, he infuses his films with the distinct stylistics of that movement (documentary realism from hand-held cameras, numerous long takes, well-lighted scenes). Although developed out of a respect for *noir* and having a kinship with it, his films are hybrids, not strict imitations of that American genre.

Truffaut applies a similar philosophy to what he has learned from the filmmaker he admires most, not so much copying Hitchcock as adapting Hitchcock's style and themes to suit his own vision of filmmaking. Both directors, for one, are more concerned with exploring the paradoxes of human nature than is Woolrich whose stories are generally plot-driven. This is not to say that Woolrich avoids delving into psychology or motivation. He certainly does, as most writers must. However, even he admits that, for him, plot is the hub around which all other story elements revolve:

> ... I came to realize ... that it was far better to be short on words, scantily supplied, poor in them, so long as you could sprinkle the few you had over a damn good basic situation (which could carry you along by itself...), than to be able to work them into a rich weave, make them glitter, make them dance, range them into vivid descriptions and word pictures, and in the end have them covering nothing but a great big hole [*Blues of a Lifetime* 11].

For another thing, Hitchcock is famous for relying on the maguffin, a plot device supposedly vital to the story when all the time it is actually secondary to human relationships and entanglements. The uranium in the wine bottles in Claude Rains's wine cellar (*Notorious*) and Kim Novak's supernatural possession (*Vertigo*) have their place, but ultimately, the stories are less interested in mystery and crime than in the chemistry bubbling between the two lovers. Truffaut gives criminal behavior the illusion of importance in much the same way that Hitchcock handles the maguffin, something apparent in *The Bride Wore Black* and, as we will see later, in *La Sirène du Mississippi*.

True to the novel, Truffaut's film begins with a disturbed, suicidal Julie Kohler (Jeanne Moreau) leaving her family to set off on her own. In a sequence of intermittent flashbacks, we see her, a newlywed bride, emerging from a church with her husband David when a gunshot rings out and he collapses and dies on the church steps. She is consumed by an obsession to avenge his death. She learns of five men who, sharing a common interest in hunting and philandering, had rented an apartment across from the church. While two of them wrestled with a loaded rifle near the open window, the weapon discharged and the unaimed bullet accidentally hit and killed David.

One by one, she tracks down the men and "executes" each in a different way. She pushes Bliss (Claude Rich) off a balcony; she poisons Coral (Michel Bouquet); she locks Morane (Michel Lonsdale) in a narrow closet so he suffocates; and she shoots Fergus (Charles Denner) with an arrow. She attends Fergus's funeral, allowing herself to be arrested, so she can get close to the fifth and final culprit, Delvaux (Daniel Boulanger), a criminal being held in prison. Helping deliver the daily meals to the inmates, Julie takes the opportunity to stab Delvaux with a knife and fulfill her vow of vengeance.

If marriage symbolizes the ideal state of love and happiness, then Woolrich implies that the Friday-Night Fiends deprived Julie Killeen of fulfilling her dream. Stifling of the dream is a *noir* concept which Truffaut incorporates in his film. Julie Kohler, in her flashbacks, reminisces how she and David were perfect lovers, childhood sweethearts whose intimate feelings were born in youthful innocence. They were destined to spend their lives happily together, until the careless prank of five irresponsible men robbed them of their joyful hope. In other words, Truffaut makes David as innocent as she. He omits Woolrich's implication that people like ex-gangster Killeen cannot escape their past and he suggests even more explicitly that reward and punishment in this world do not depend on moral behavior.

Truffaut retains Woolrich's notion that hatred is self-corrosive, that in losing her dream, Julie has allowed her loathing to corrupt her sense of humanity and engender an all-consuming death wish. The relationship Julie has with David acts as a counterpoint to the relationship these men have with women. She is moral and monogamous; they are immoral and promiscuous. Ironically, polluted by her compulsion for vengeance, her moral sensibility degenerates into that of the men she despises; she becomes a predator who uses her powers of seduction to snare her victims. When the painter Fergus dresses her up as Diana the Huntress to model for him, he unwittingly not only places the weapon of his destruction in her hands, but also defines her newly assumed persona.

One key difference between Truffaut's and Woolrich's *Bride* is in the function they assign to the group of men accused of killing David/Nick. Woolrich makes the Friday-Night Fiends a gang of wild delinquents. Truffaut turns them into a pack of male chauvinists bound by their mutual interest in hunting and womanizing, two pastimes that are intrinsically related. In Truffaut's film, Morane tells Julie that he and his friends have lived prodigal lives, but there is no visible indication of this except for their obsession with women. This, not the death of David, may be where their true guilt lies: they are an effrontery to females. Flagrant sexism is their actual crime and Julie represents the feminist avenger.

Also related to Truffaut's and Woolrich's treatments of the accused group is the guilt they attach to the men. Woolrich works with coincidence. The Fiends *happen* to be on one of their riotous escapades at the moment Corey carries out his plot to kill Nick. In a variation of the Wrong Man theme, the Wrong Men are erroneously blamed, pursued, and punished. Julie's error in judgment is central to Woolrich's story, producing the final irony and, moreover, implying the capriciousness of fate and its indiscriminate meting of reward and punishment (particularly punishment). Julie's life was destroyed, unjustly in her eyes, by an external power, and she becomes an instrument of that power, destroying other lives that, despite her righteousness, do not deserve it — or at least do not deserve it for the reason she assumes.

In Truffaut's *Bride*, on the other hand, the stag group undoubtedly is guilty of killing David Kohler, but because of inherent circumstances, the nature of that guilt, not Woolrich's question of whom to blame, begs attention. Julie Kohler may still be considered an instrument of fate, but the fact that the men are actually at fault removes the arbitrariness of their "executions," which are now carried out for a valid reason. Morane tries to explain to Julie: "It was an unfortunate accident.... We all felt guilty, yet also innocent." Their recklessness killed David, but his death certainly was not intentional. Also, some of the men are guiltier than others: Morane loaded the rifle, Delvaux pointed it foolishly at the wedding party, and the two men wrestled with it at the open window. Other members of the group are guilty by association, not by direct involvement, and this mitigates their culpability. However, all the men agree to keep silent, which makes them equally guilty in their complicity. Truffaut, by eliminating the Fiends-Corey complication of the Woolrich story, shifts emphasis from the question of the whodunit to the issue of the degree of culpability and of circumstances affecting our perception of it, thereby prompting broader questions about the nature of guilt than those raised in Woolrich's story.

As if dispensing a poetic justice that befits their sexist behavior, Julie Kohler commits each murder by using methods tinged with sexual connotations. Bliss is engaged to be married; yet he and friend Corey (Jean-Claude

Brialy) still talk of flirting with other women. Julie puts him in a defenseless position outside the railing of the balcony, then pushes him off. Doing so, she reverses their conventional roles as the passive female and the aggressive male. (Of the five men, Bliss is the only one to retain his original name. Truffaut may be using the same pun as Woolrich: the men deprived her of her "bliss," so she deprives them of theirs.)

Coral fantasizes about women, but does not have the skill or confidence to pursue or keep them. Julie seduces him by presenting herself as his fantasized ideal. Then she poisons him by injecting a drug into a bottle of Arak with a syringe, the bottle representing the female, the injection a symbol of phallic penetration. Coral, by his own admission, is nearly a virgin; that is, he is like an inexperienced woman subjected for the first time to the violent throes of intercourse. He is not man enough to cope with the act. When he tastes the "impregnated" liquor, the lethal dose overwhelms and kills him.

Morane appears happily married, but when Julie visits him, his flirtatious conversation and salacious glances suggest that he entertains sexual fantasies about her. Julie tricks him into entering a small, stuffy closet where she locks him in and he suffocates to death. This is the antithesis of abortion: the adult squeezed back into the womb (closet) is an unnatural act which, like the fetus plucked too soon from the womb, must result in death.

After being delayed in her attempt to kill Delvaux, Julie contacts the painter Fergus, who admits unabashedly his insatiable fascination with women. In time, Fergus professes his love for her, but she does not let that deter her resolve. While modeling for him as Diana the Huntress with a bow and arrow as a prop, she takes aim, releases the arrow, and kills him dead. This is Julie's fundamental image, a goddess aloof from the desires of men, shunning them yet besting them at the sport they most identify with.

The fifth victim, treated quite differently from Woolrich's story, is another important factor in Truffaut's film. Delvaux is set apart from the other four men by appearance and character. He is stocky, bald, and repulsive, a striking contrast to the attractive features of the other men. When we first see him in each of the three scenes that involve him, the back of his bald head is toward the camera; he sits or stands rigidly still, as if posed. A delay always occurs before he reveals his face, as if he is marked as a special character, which he is. For one thing, unlike his friends, he never displays a licentious interest in women. While the other men brag about their sexual exploits or show an obsessive taste for sex (even Coral talks of sex, although only as a pathetic discounting of his own virility), it is the reticent Delvaux who is associated with the primary phallic symbol: he is arrogantly pointing the rifle at the wedding guests when Morane tries to wrestle it from him and it goes off. After Julie learns from Morane that Delvaux was the one holding the rifle that killed David, she tries to achieve justice by killing Delvaux with a gun, but the police arrest him before she can shoot him, inadvertently saving him from her.

***The Bride Wore Black*—Femme fatale** Julie Kohler (Jeanne Moreau) seduces her second victim Monsieur Coral (Michel Bouquet) in his pathetically dreary apartment, as she prepares to mete out vigilante justice for an unpunished crime (Lopert Pictures, courtesy William Thailing).

We learn another difference about Delvaux: not only is he most directly responsible for David's death, but he is a local criminal who uses his junkyard as a front for illegal activities. The police raid his business just when Julie is about to confront him. He goes to prison, and Julie, to get to him, allows herself to be arrested at Fergus's funeral. While delivering meals to the inmates, she kills Delvaux with the most blatant phallic symbol, a knife she has stolen from the kitchen. Her revenge is complete.

Because of Delvaux' personality, we perceive his guilt differently from the other men. He appears hardened, ruthless, and remorseless, which seems to make him deserving of the death Julie hands him. The other men appear more personable, more human, more "normal," and this in itself seems to mitigate their guilt and enable us to sympathize with them. Unfortunately for Julie, the one terrible tragedy in her life has transformed her personality, and ironically, she has become like Delvaux, committing murders without compunction. That she is in prison with Delvaux at the end suggests a perverse bond between them. That she stabs him with a knife suggests a consummation of their depraved relationship.

In borrowing Woolrich's ironic plot, Truffaut also borrows some of its flaws, particularly its moments of questionable logic. For instance, if Julie Kohler can discover which men are responsible for her husband's death, the police should have, too. At least in Woolrich's story the police are justified in not connecting the automobile with Nick Killeen's death because they know he died of a gunshot wound, while his bride mistakenly attributes the cause of death to a hit-and-run automobile. In trying to circumvent that preposterous coincidence in Woolrich's story, Truffaut becomes guilty of a different illogic, failing to give the police some credibility.

An aspect of Woolrich's novel that works well and contributes to the suspense is the alternate views of the murders, showing Julie's success with each murder, then showing the detective who is putting the evidence together to pursue her. Truffaut abandons the detective point of view — I'm not sure why. If he likes to adapt Hitchcock's methods, he should see that an alternate perspective on events is a frequent device Hitchcock uses to create tension and contribute to irony and suspense. Consider, for instance, *North by Northwest* (Cary Grant countered with Leo G. Carroll and James Mason) or *Psycho* (Anthony Perkins countered with Janet Leigh, Martin Balsam, and Tom Tryon). Knowing what the opponents are trying to do can add to the suspense as both sides work toward opposing objectives.

Truffaut may have thought that, by getting Hitchcock's definitive coposer, Bernard Herrmann, he achieved the ultimate melding of his style with Hitchcock-like material. Disappointingly, the integration of the musical score with the visual action is awkward, clumsy. The music fails to blend with the scenes and feels as if it were tacked on as an afterthought. Because Truffaut's New Wave style conveys a cinematic realism, his many outdoor locations, shot in bright daylight, lack sinister visual elements. To counter this, the music tries to imply moments of intrigue and great danger and disturbing feelings of malice and hatred. However, Herrmann's dark musical motifs appear incongruous with the brightly lit, mundane scenes. It is possible that Truffaut deliberately wanted this visual-aural dissonance, the realistic sunny scenes contradicted by Herrmann's heavy, brooding chords and passages (All the murders, for instance, take place during the daytime or in well-lighted rooms.). But rather than working in meaningful counterpoint, the music and action appear incompatible, an incongruous clash between sight and sound. It is an unfortunate misapplication of this extraordinary conductor's talents.

The success of Truffaut's film can be debated. The themes, linked to Woolrich and reworked by Truffaut, appear effective. The lush, billowing tonality of Herrmann's emotional score feels strangely misaligned with Truffaut's flat documentary shooting style. Jeanne Moreau will always be regarded as a premier French actress, charismatic and seductive, the epitome of femininity, but her suitability for this part is arguable. As in Woolrich's story, the Spider Woman should have an ideal appearance that immediately charms and captivates the men she is about to kill. At this stage in her career, Moreau does not have the stunning face and svelte figure that Woolrich's *femme fatale* has and needs.

Revenge, as it appears in *The Bride Wore Black*, is an extremely functional tool for bringing out *noir* themes: it suggests the influence of the past on the present; and it usually (but not always) involves erosion of the character's values, transforming him from innocent idealist to bitter fatalist. The character who resorts to revenge often reveals a dark side of human nature, the suppressed wicked vindictiveness that lies within all of us and has the potential to surface and take possession of our actions and our attitudes. In the following *films noirs*, for example, revenge plays either a central or peripheral part while serving different purposes and incurring different consequences: *The Maltese Falcon* (Huston, 1941); *This Gun for Hire* (Tuttle, 1942); *Murder, My Sweet* (Dmytryk, 1944); *Cornered* (Dmytryk, 1945); *Kiss of Death* (Hathaway, 1947); *Ride the Pink Horse* (Montgomery, 1947); *Dead Reckoning* (Cromwell, 1947); *Act of Violence* (Zinneman, 1949); *No Way Out* (Mankiewicz, 1950); *Dark City* (Dieterle, 1950); *Affair in Trinidad* (Sherman, 1952); *The Big Heat* (Lang, 1953); *Kiss Me Deadly* (Aldrich, 1955).

Two films linked to Woolrich's *Bride*, in that the obsession for revenge turns the righteous avenger into a serial killer, are *Sudden Impact* (Clint Eastwood, 1983) and *Fallen Angel* (Marc S. Grenier, 1998). The fourth entry in the Dirty Harry cycle, the Eastwood neo-noir has Sondra Locke eliminating one by one the group of degenerate thugs who raped her and her sister. The frequent excursions through sleazy nighttime labyrinths and the violent encounters with lascivious vermin remind us of the fetid *noir* environment that encroaches on the world of the innocent and infects their lives without due cause. The latter film closely mimics Woolrich's story, but without the chiaroscuro elements necessary to classify it as neo-*noir*, it fits more in the category of a simple mystery-suspense yarn. An introverted high school co-ed (Michelle Johnson) is teased brutally by five male classmates, their ruthless shenanigans resulting in her accidental fall from a bridge. After needing years to recuperate, she seeks out each culprit and lures him to a high place from where she can exact her revenge by having him plummet to his death. Although the actors are seasoned and capable and the story line is sufficiently absorbing (paralleling Woolrich, how can it not be?), the dialogue suffers horribly as mundane gibberish, trite in substance and dull in impact.

Noir, as a style, has the chameleonic ability to cross genre boundaries, lending its look and motifs to other film categories, such as science fiction (*Blade Runner*, the *Matrix* series) or mystery (*Mystic River*). Revenge, besides its prevalence in classic *film noir*, is a useful motive in many westerns, often giving them these transgeneric qualities. In *The Searchers*, *Nevada Smith*, and *The Quick and the Dead*, the vengeful quest, though justified, has a corruptive effect on the avenger. One western in particular not only contains strong *noir* characteristics, but also shares a striking number of parallels with Woolrich's novel (although I hesitate to claim it was inspired by it). That film is *The Bravados* (Henry King, 1958).

Ranch owner Jim Douglas (Gregory Peck) has achieved the idyllic existence Julie hoped to attain with Nick. That life is shattered by an unjust and unprovoked assault. His three-year-old daughter survives, but the brutal death of his wife transforms him (as it does Julie) from a sensitive, loving husband to a vindictive, bloodthirsty avenger. The film retains *Bride*'s idea that the men being pursued are ignorant of their pursuer's motive. Like the Friday-Night Fiends, the Bravados are an unsavory, rebellious bunch, guilty of certain crimes but not of the particular one the protagonist accuses them of, the crime that makes his vengeance just. After killing all but the last one, the protagonist is stalled long enough to learn the truth. The irony is that he could have easily caught and killed the real murderer without his lengthy ordeal, just as Julie Killeen had several opportunities to kill Corey, had she known the truth. This ironic ending, so similar to that of *Bride*, discourages any inclination we may have for the moral justification of revenge and vigilantism and makes us rethink our need to rely on the judicial system.

Another element that links *The Bride Wore Black* closely to *The Bravados* is the interrelated issues of guilt and innocence. In both Woolrich's novel and Truffaut's film, similar scenes occur where Julie confesses her crime, but oddly seeks no forgiveness. In fact, she iterates her murderous intentions, throwing them flagrantly into the face of the priest and the religion he represents. Unlike Woolrich's Julie, who, on learning of her mistake, cries and admits regret at killing the men innocent of her husband's death, Truffaut's Julie displays a total lack of remorse (but then, the men she kills are complicit in the actual crime). *The Bravados* also inserts religion as a reminder of the connection between revenge and conscience. The priest (Andrew Duggan), in a sermon, tries to quell Douglas's vindictiveness, calling for forgiveness and warning of the pitfalls of hate and vengeance. In the end, Douglas returns to the village church where the priest consoles him and grants him absolution for his misguided quest. Except for the protagonist's redemption at the end, *The Bravados* displays more than a few incidental similarities with *The Bride Wore Black* and can easily pass for a western adaptation of Woolrich's material.

"He Looked Like Murder"

Short story in *Detective Fiction Weekly*, February 8, 1941. Reprinted in *The Dancing Detective* as "Two Fellows in a Furnished Room" under the pseudonym William Irish, J.B. Lippincott, 1946. Reprinted in the first paperback edition of *The Dancing Detective*, Popular Library pbk #309, 1951.

"He Looked Like Murder" is based on a recurring premise in the Woolrich canon, one he must have deployed with confidence since he produced a number of effective variations on it. One character, unsure of the guilt or innocence of a second character, gradually uncovers bits of ambiguous evidence that causes him to fluctuate between condemning and exonerating the person suspected of wrongdoing.

"He Looked Like Murder" is told from the first-person viewpoint of Stewart "Red" Carr who shares an apartment with his best friend, John Dixon. One Monday night, Red's usual night to study for school, Dixon asks him to leave so he can have a private conversation with his girlfriend Estelle Mitchell. Under silent protest, Red complies. On his way down the stairs, he briefly encounters Estelle, whom he had never seen before. Outside, he endures several hours of cold, rainy weather before returning to his flat where he finds Dixon anxious and fidgety. Dixon says Estelle just left and that he put her in a cab. Red is ready for bed, but Dixon is too agitated and, although it is after midnight, he steps out for a drink. Before retiring, Red steps on something, a clip from a green raincoat which he surmises had been ripped from the slicker he saw Estelle wearing on the stairs. He sets it aside.

Red's attempt to sleep is disrupted by several phone calls from Estelle's mother, worried because Estelle hasn't come home yet. Since Estelle lives only six blocks away, Red considers that, if Dixon told him the truth, she should have been home long ago. Red, however, deflects Mrs. Mitchell's qualms, trying to protect his friend. Dixon returns and Red confronts him. Dixon admits he lied about putting Estelle in a cab, but claims he heard someone whistle for a cab, and when he went to the window, he saw a woman close the cab door behind her. So he assumed it was she.

The doubts established at this initial stage are compounded by Dixon's suspicious behavior, his half-truths, and the pieces of evidence that fall into Red's hands. For one, after returning from his late nightcap, Dixon refuses to call the Mitchells to inquire about Estelle. Then, looking out the window, Red notices that a detective has pulled up and entered the building. Dixon becomes frantic and asks Red to lie about seeing Estelle get into the cab. Red questions the ethics of such testimony, but when the detective interrogates them, the issue never arises. Red suddenly notices that the raincoat clip has disappeared. Later, Dixon admits that he took it so as not to complicate the matter.

The next night Red visits the bar that Dixon went to. Searching the lavatory, he finds the additional slicker clips lying just outside window. He goes to visit Mrs. Mitchell. While in the lobby of her hotel, he sees two policemen arrive with her daughter's belongings, expecting her to identify them. Red returns home with the news that Estelle is dead. Instead of showing grief or anger, Dixon responds by planning to leave town before the police can arrest him.

At first, Red prevents Dixon from leaving, but then helps him by lending him his hat and coat as a disguise. Detective Hiller and the police arrive shortly after and, suspecting Red of abetting Dixon, take him to headquarters where they show him Estelle's body, her neck broken when the murderer tried to stuff her body down a chute leading to the hotel incinerator. They press him again for what he knows and he tells them the bogus account that Dixon rehearsed with him. But Mrs. Mitchell is also at the precinct with Tremholt, Estelle's fiancée. Red notices how Tremholt's fingernails are bitten down to the quick. The police have Red repeat his story of hearing a woman whistle for a cab just before he saw her close the taxi door. Mrs. Mitchell accuses him of lying because Estelle never knew how to whistle.

The next day, Red attends Estelle's funeral. He notices that, where Tremholt had been sitting, broken matchsticks lay scattered over the ground, a nervous habit like his nail-biting. Red visits the library to get the next book in his series of lessons. At home, he notices a message addressed to him in the margin, obviously from Dixon, who knew what book Red would be borrowing next. At the appointed time, Red goes to meet him, convinced that he is the murderer. He confronts Dixon, accusing him of deceiving him, of not putting Estelle in a cab, of not hearing her whistle, and of taking the raincoat fastener he had found. Dixon offers plausible explanations, but Red won't listen. Frantic, Dixon pulls out a gun and Red disarms him.

Red takes Dixon back to their apartment. Coincidentally, just as he is calling the police, he hears someone outside his window hail a cab with a loud whistle. It is a woman. He intercepts her and learns that she leaves for work at this time every night, doing a bird imitation act at a local club. Red concludes that, despite Dixon's furtive behavior, he must have been telling the truth. He also realizes that Tremholt must be the murderer. He lures Tremholt into a trap, getting him to admit in front of Detective Hiller a minor fact he could not have known unless he saw Estelle the night of her murder.

The murder solved, Red explains that he and Dixon have separated even though Dixon was proved innocent. It is not because Dixon pulled a gun on him, he explains. Rather, it is because they remind each other of a murder.

Nevins calls this kind of plot an "oscillation" story, a "did-he-or-didn't he" conundrum, where one character (along with the reader) fluctuates between doubt and certainty over another character's guilt. As a plot device, it is remarkable how frequently Woolrich relies on it, yet is able to twist it ingeniously into so many different variations. For instance, the complement of "He Looked Like Murder" is "Rear Window": the suspected murderer, innocent in the former, is found guilty in the latter, but before the resolution is reached, evidence points back and forth, making guilt undeterminable. In "The Red Tide" (1940), a woman is plagued by unsubstantiated fears that her husband murdered their boarder for his hoarded wealth. In "Silent as the Grave" (1945), a man confesses to his fiancée that he once murdered a man by accident. She swears to keep his secret, but after they marry, the man's boss is killed and her husband acts suspiciously. Under the strain of great trepidation and doubt, she wrestles with the decision to trust him or to turn him in to the police. In "I Wouldn't Be in Your Shoes" (1938), a man is accused of killing a miser for his money. Although the evidence is circumstantial and contradictory, he is convicted and imprisoned. New evidence proves him innocent and he is released. The man's wife, however, is not so sure of his innocence, and so she leaves him. Fate's indifference leads to a man's punishment even when he may deserve vindication. In the merciless *noir* world, Justice wears a thick blindfold.

The endings of "I Wouldn't Be in Your Shoes" and "He Looked Like Murder" are related in that the dissolution of the Quinns' marriage parallels the dissolution of the friendship between Red and Dixon, the latter an unconventional "divorce" between implied homosexuals. Of course, two men living together does not in itself constitute a homosexual relationship. Unlike "Nightmare," which has a subtext with definite homosexual implications (discussed in the next chapter), "He Looked Like Murder" fails to exploit this notion with any consistent or overt evidence. Woolrich, however, may have intended such a subtext, because he sporadically inserts the faintest of suggestions. Red's anger over Dixon's clandestine meeting with Estelle can be construed as jealousy. Dixon's suspicious behavior continuously riles Red, who curtails his doubts on the pretext of friendship, when perhaps he is disguising his faithfulness as a lover; only after Dixon threatens him with a gun does Red betray him (the phallus rejected) and try to hand him to the police.

Vague homosexual implications aside, a significant element in the story is Red's intermittent critical comments, especially his complaints about Dixon and his self-righteous remarks that compare him to Dixon and make him seem superior in some way. Red is indignant at the beginning, censuring Dixon for his inconsiderateness in making him go out into the rain while he talks with his girl (reminiscent of Woolrich's experience in trying to use his friend Ken's typewriter at Ken's apartment. Whenever his promiscuous friend brought home a willing lady, Woolrich would grant them their privacy and leave. See *Blues of a Lifetime* 19.). Later, Red's criticism for his letting Estelle go home by herself contains the tacit implication that Red would have been more respectful of his own girlfriend. Red also mentions that, if Estelle had been his girlfriend, he would have been more aggressive in finding information about her disappearance, unlike Dixon who seems indifferent toward her. Red begins to see Dixon's behavior as suspicious and admits that, if it were he who was guilty of murder, he would act as secretively as Dixon.

In other words, suspicious behavior indicates guilt. Dixon is the prime suspect on the basis of his behavior. His actions speak louder than his words, so that even when he defends himself, it is difficult to believe him. Like "Rear Window," "He Looked Like Murder" plays with the notion that guilt depends on outward appearances. Woolrich uses both stories to present alternate outcomes: in the one, appearances confirm the person's guilt; in the other, guilty appearances are deceptive. Through themes and allusions Woolrich occasionally shows the influence Shakespeare has on him. In this case, he may be borrowing an idea from *Macbeth* in which King Duncan laments his misperception of the original thane of Cawdor, thinking him honest when in fact he was a traitor: "I thought I knew him well. There is no art to see into a man's heart" (I.ii.47–48). Unfortunately, Duncan never heeds his own insight, for he trusts Macbeth and steps into harm's way, unwittingly producing dire consequences for himself and Scotland.

Guilt pertains to Red in an odd way. Like the narrator of "Rear Window," he is not the perpetrator, and so has no reason to feel guilt connected with the crime. Yet he shows a strange detachment that makes him guilty of something else, lack of compassion and sensitivity toward his fellow man. When Dixon asks Red to lie to the police investigator, the question of ethics becomes an issue. Red relates to us his feelings: "I have a funny conscience, awfully inelastic, practically no give to it at all." If he were that steadfast in his principles, that would be one thing, but he eventually lies about having seen Estelle leave in a cab, and later he helps Dixon elude the police by lending him his coat. His actions prove that he harbors a misconception about the "elasticity" of his scruples.

Such discrepancies between his commentary and his related actions make him an unreliable narrator, in many ways similar to the aloof, detached narrator of "Rear Window." Both men have a condescending attitude, placing themselves in the catbird seat while they evaluate and judge others around them. Yet they have flaws that they fail to recognize. They fail to humble themselves enough to identify with others' hardships and tragedies. This is a trait which gives Red and Jeff (in "Rear Window") wider dimensions, makes them more real and memorable. A nice Woolrichian touch.

The "oscillation" technique is not the only convention Woolrich uses in this story. Estelle's disappearance reminds us of others where a woman disappears without a trace, almost as if she never existed in the first place. Such a situation occurs in *Phantom Lady* and stories we have already discussed: "All at Once, No Alice" and "You'll Never See Me Again." The repetition does not diminish the enjoyment of these stories. It simply shows how Woolrich, gifted with imagination, can form and forge his standard conventions into ever-intriguing, ever-engrossing new stories to captivate and entertain.

Film: The Guilty

1947, Monogram. *D:* John Reinhardt. *P:* Jack Wrather. *Assoc P*: James C. Jordan. *Cin*: Henry Sharp. *Sc:* Robert Presnell, *Sr Ed:* Jodie Caplan, William H. Ziegler. *Mus:* Rudy Schrager. *F/X:* Howard A. Anderson. *Art Dir:* Oscar Yerge. *Set Dec:* Harry Reif.
Cast: Bonita Granville (Estelle Mitchell/Linda Mitchell), Regis Toomey (Detective Heller), Don Castle (Mike Carr), Wally Cassell (Johnny Dixon), John Litel (Alex Tremholt), Thomas E. Jackson (Tim McGinnis), Netta Packer (Mrs. Mitchell), Oliver Blake (Jake the janitor), Caroline Andrews (Leonora Waters). 71 min.

Because its comical elements contradicted what was expected from the "master of suspense," or because its intricate artistic elements were too subtle for the movie-going public to appreciate, or perhaps for yet some other reason, Alfred Hitchcock's *Stage Fright* (1950) received mixed reviews. One device in particular alienated viewers, the opening flashback narrated by a fraud. According to critics, the audience felt duped that the murderer (Richard Todd) had, so early on, deceived the heroine (Jane Wyman) with a total fabrication. The cinematic reconstruction of his narration "proved" his innocence and made him appear a sympathetic character deserving the heroine's trust and love. The audience, embracing conventional but misguided romantic visions, may have preferred to see the pixyish Wyman paired with the dashing Todd rather than with the flaccidly handsome Michael Wilding (Sinyard 73; Spoto, *Art* 181).

A more recent film, *The Usual Suspects* (1997), also uses a phony flashback told by an unreliable narrator. The narrator (Kevin Spacey), even more dangerously devious than Richard Todd's character, concocts his false testimony with the same concern for self-preservation. However, this movie fared much better with a public fascinated by the shrewd character's ingenious talent for invention — although the accompanying graphic violence may have also helped its cause.

The unreliable narrator, then, should not be a criterion for condemning a story. It is not a new or modern concept. Homer's Odysseus captivated audiences with his flair for hyperbole. Shakespeare's Othello won fair Desdemona by embellishing his mythical adventures. Huck Finn, Nick Carroway, and Holden Caulfield may seem truthful and unbiased in their supposedly candid commentaries, but closer examination shows that sincere they may sound, but accurate and totally truthful they are not.

Director John Reinhardt's *The Guilty* fits into this tradition. The narrator at the outset appears likable (he playfully throws a peanut at the bartender to attract his attention), and although clues are strewn here and there to suggest he is not a completely unblemished character, he seems innocent enough until we learn the truth. It may *seem* a cheap trick on the audience, but it could also be more than that. For one, as an adaptation of Woolrich's "He Looked Like Murder," the film has to give the ending a new twist for mystery fans already acquainted with Woolrich's story. Second, the solution to the mystery displays originality, employing irony while deviating from the standard boy-gets-girl formula, an outcome quite in keeping with Woolrich's treatment of fate's vicissitudes. In addition, Reinhardt's film from beginning to end is mired in a depressing, downbeat mood, a prevalent and effective *noir* tonality.

In "He Looked Like Murder," Woolrich's Red Carr relates events chronologically until the very end, where his comments vaguely intimate that he has been reflecting on a past experience, that his story was indeed told in flashback:

> I don't live with Dixon any more. I've moved out since. It's hard to explain just why. He didn't kill her. He did try to kill me, but it isn't that either.
> I run into him now and then, and we're on the best of terms, but we never prolong the encounters, we're never completely at ease.
> There's a self-consciousness between us. You don't want to be reminded of a murder every time you look at a guy [74].

The Guilty takes this hint of a framing device and transforms it into a full-blown frame story, a present situation at the start and close of the film, to book-end Mike Carr's (Don Castle) inset story about the past. In the beginning, the credits roll while the camera follows a lone man meandering up the grungy street of a lower-class neighborhood. The medium-close shot stays tight on the man's back as both man and camera move forward, giving the impression that something or someone is trailing the man very closely. Stores are visible in the periphery of the frame so that his view of the street is also ours. When the credits end, the voiceover (spoken, we presume, by the lone walker) begins: "The old street ... wet, dirty ... reeks of murder.... Why'd they have to be twins?" The man stops before McGinnis's café, pushes open the double doors (an "M" is stenciled on each of the doors' translucent windows), and enters. Bartender Tim McGinnis (Thomas E. Jackson) recognizes his former customer, Mike Carr, whom he hasn't seen in six months, and asks about his roommate Johnny Dixon (Wally Cassell). Carr explains that he left Dixon in an army hospital where they straightened out his "kinks." They run into each other now and again, but don't talk about the tragedy that split them up. (Note how this expands on Red's remark quoted above.) Carr explains how Dixon, a lieutenant, and he, a corporal, were in the war together, how the men disliked Dixon who suffered from shell shock at the Battle of the Bulge. After the war, his infirmity prevented him from holding down a job. He found solace in liquor and women. Not having a place to stay, he appealed to Carr who let him share his apartment with him. The post-war setting reflects the social conflicts of that time, especially the plight of servicemen trying to re-establish themselves in civilian society.

At this point, Carr's story dissolves into the flashback which shows him caring for Dixon who is in bed, crippled by one of his seizures. A girl enters the apartment, Linda Mitchell (Bonita Granville), twin sister of Estelle (also played by Granville). In a series of voiceovers, Carr gradually discloses the complex relationship of the four principles. Linda is the nicer of the two sisters, Estelle the conniver. Estelle used to be Dixon's girlfriend, but they broke up and now he goes with Linda. Estelle has already exposed her duplicity in that, when she was Dixon's girl, she "made a play" for Carr and he capitulated—suggesting his own duplicity by betraying his friend. Carr admits his paradoxical obsession with her: "It was just one of those things when a guy knows it's all wrong, but just can't let go of it." He rationalizes the futility of their relationship, but cannot end it. Meanwhile, although Estelle says she does not love Dixon, she tries to sabotage Linda's relationship with him, continuing to see him secretly. Carr is suspicious, but his obsessive, jealous love prevents him from leaving.

One Monday night, when Carr is studying for his Tuesday class, Dixon asks him to leave so he can have a private talk with Estelle. Carr, surprised, says he thought he and Estelle had parted company. Dixon assures him this is true and that Estelle only wants to talk to him.

Downstairs, Carr runs into Estelle and diverts her from meeting with Dixon. At McGinnis's, she sneaks a phone call to Dixon, then lies to Carr that she called her mother and has to go home. An hour later, Carr returns to his apartment. He admits to Dixon that he has been seeing Estelle ever since the two of them broke up. Dixon says it is all right with him. He goes out for a drink by himself.

In the night, the phone rings, waking Carr. It is Mrs. Mitchell (Netta Packer), upset that Linda never got home. Carr hangs up just as his friend walks in. Dixon confesses that Estelle never showed up that evening, but Linda did. He didn't take her home, although from the balcony, he heard her whistle for a cab and saw her ride away. He asks Carr to back him up with the police. Carr resents having to lie and tries to avoid it, but the next day, when Detective Heller (Regis Toomey) questions him about what he knows, he equivocates, claiming he saw a woman whistle for a cab, but not verifying that it was Linda.

Outside, Dixon, hiding in an alley, stops Carr. Carr convinces him to go with him to Linda's mother to explain things. However, Mrs. Mitchell becomes hysterical, and her longtime boarder, Mr. Alex Tremholt (John Litel), has to console her.

That night, Carr waits for Estelle at McGinnis's. He orders "two beers" and goes to the men's lavatory. Outside the window he discovers a discarded buckle ripped from a woman's raincoat, one that matches another he found in his apartment. Estelle arrives and he takes her home. Carr is aware of her devious nature, for in the hall outside her apartment, he asks her whom she called last night when she said she called her mother. She evades the question.

The Guilty— The policeman reminds us of the law that punishes criminal behavior. The two roommates, Mike Carr (Don Castle, left) and Johnny Dixon (Wally Cassell), are doubles, each potentially the guilty party who committed murder (Monogram, courtesy William Thailing).

"You kind of like me," she says. He answers, "I'd like to break your neck," and kisses her hard and rudely on the lips. Just then, the police arrive with Linda's clothes for Mrs. Mitchell to identify. Carr leaves, declaring in his voiceover, "It made me kind of sick because I knew what it meant."

Carr confronts Dixon in their apartment. Though he accuses Dixon of knowing more than he will admit, he helps him evade the police by having him wear his coat and hat. Heller arrives and has Carr accompany him to the Mitchell apartment where Mrs. Mitchell testifies that the woman who whistled for the cab was not Linda because she did not know how to whistle. Heller takes Carr to the morgue, where he shows him Linda's body and describes in grisly detail how the murderer brutally broke her neck while trying to stuff her into the incinerator chute and then hid her body in a barrel full of gravel.

Three days later, Carr is studying for his Monday class. On the flyleaf of a library book he just borrowed, he finds handwritten instructions from Dixon to wait at McGinnis's for his phone call. Carr meets Estelle there. He again presses her about the phone call of the other night. She finally admits she called Dixon, but that he never showed for their meeting. Dixon's call comes through and he tells Carr to meet him at his new apartment. When Carr arrives, they

The Guilty—(left to right) Detective Heller (Regis Toomey) arrests innocent Mr. Tremholt (John Litel) for the murder of Linda Mitchell, the twin sister of Estelle (Bonita Granville, playing both roles). Carr (Don Castle), the real murderer, hides his culpability for a time, but eventually guilt must reveal itself (Monogram, courtesy William Thailing).

argue and Dixon pulls out a gun. Carr wrestles the gun away from him and makes him go with him back to their original apartment.

The two men find Estelle waiting with Tremholt. Outside, someone whistles for a cab. Carr gives Dixon's gun to Tremholt and runs downstairs to meet the woman (Caroline Andrews) Dixon must have heard that night. A sudden gunshot from inside sends him racing back upstairs. Dixon has taken the gun from Tremholt and runs away. Heller arrives and questions them. Tremholt confesses that he has loved Estelle ever since she was a young girl, that she promised to marry him, but has been running around with younger men, flaunting them in his face. Carr says in the voiceover: "Estelle tied him hand and foot with his own heartstrings." Tremholt is placed in custody and Carr goes to tell Dixon he is no longer a suspect. Dixon has hanged himself, but luckily, Carr is in time to cut him down and save his life.

The flashback ends and the story returns to the present. Carr tells McGinnis of his contradictory feelings for Estelle: "I didn't want her, but I couldn't leave her alone." McGinnis replies, "I know a lot of dipsos who feel that way about the taste of liquor." Carr suffers from the *noir* obsession that usually ends in self-destruction. He was supposed to meet Estelle, but decides to leave without seeing her.

Estelle arrives just then. Outside, Carr speaks gruffly to her. He leads her across the street to his former apartment building where Linda was killed. Estelle slaps him with her handbag, the bag opens, and the contents spill to the ground. Carr leaves her fumbling on the sidewalk and goes inside the building. A police car pulls up to the curb and Heller gets out. He confronts Carr with new evidence proving he is the murderer: Linda's necklace had got caught in the incinerator chute and Carr's fingerprints were on it. Heller suspected Carr and followed him the past six months: "You never stayed in one place for very long. Guilty conscience?" Carr relents without a struggle. They descend the stairs, get into the police car, and drive away. Estelle walks along the sidewalk by herself while Carr's voiceover concludes: "Anyway, who'd want a girl that reminded him of murder?"

Plainly, Woolrich's short story is the schematic for Reinhardt's film. The one major alteration, which in turn instigates so many other differences between the film and its source, is the transformation of the Mitchell girl into twins. Doubling relates to duplicity and, as mainstays of *film noir* in general, both become central motifs in *The Guilty*.

The film is saturated with doubled images to reinforce the doubling of the sisters and the two roommates. The two M's on McGinnis's café doors stand for the two Mitchell girls. The lavatory scene where Carr discovers the discarded coat buckle (the second of two) is furnished with two of everything: sinks, soap dispensers, lighting fixtures, and paper towel dispensers. Several times when Carr orders at McGinnis's, he calls for "*two* beers." (The first time he does this, we also hear a customer off-screen ask for "*two* more of the same.") When Estelle talks with Carr in the café, they stand facing each other; on the wall behind them is a picture of two boxers sparring. Later, Dixon pulls a gun on Carr, and when Carr wrestles him for it, the gun goes off twice. The list grows with many images and verbal references meant to emphasize the duality and duplicity centered on the twin sisters.

Linda and Estelle Mitchell represent the duality of the female, her potential to embody the two extreme moral positions of good and evil. Using this device, *The Guilty* can be classified among the likes of *Street of Chance* (1942), *Murder My Sweet* (1944), *The Strange Love of Martha Ivers* (1946), *Black Angel* (1947), *Out of the Past* (1947), *Pitfall* (1948), *Scene of the Crime* (1949) and many others in which the male protagonist must make a choice between two women, the *femme noire* who will lead him to destruction, or the *femme blanche* who will insure his redemption. Switching from Estelle to Linda, Dixon is able to purge himself of this evil association and win his redemption, although he loses Linda in the process. Not so for Carr. He admits he is obsessed with the wrong kind of woman and he is conscious of his all-consuming jealousy. His possessiveness actually blinds him and inhibits his ability to recognize goodness, for he kills Linda, thinking he is getting his revenge on Estelle.

In *noir*, "doubling" frequently relates to "duplicity," and in *The Guilty*, all the characters enmeshed in their lovers' entanglements (except the virtuous

Linda) are guilty of some form of evasion, equivocation, or deceit. In her first appearance, Estelle stands behind a shower curtain, arguing with her double, Linda. When Linda catches her in a lie, Estelle angrily chases her out of the bathroom, and as she does, her toweled figure is reflected in the mirror. The imagery depicts her duplicity. Like her translucent image, her motives are mysterious, nebulous, ambiguous. Like her mirror image, she is the reverse of her sister, harboring a corrupt, immoral side beneath her superficial beauty. She "makes a play" for Carr while she is going with Dixon (or so Carr says), and after he submits to her charms, she betrays him by continuing to see Dixon, her jealousy driving her to sabotage his relationship with Linda. Estelle tries to make her sister jealous by lying to her that the reason Dixon gave her, Estelle, the bracelet was that he was still more interested in her than in Linda (the gist of the argument in the bathroom).

Dixon, meanwhile, lies to Estelle about Linda and to Linda about Estelle. Besides carelessly giving Estelle the bracelet he had originally intended for Linda, he lies to Estelle that he is in his room alone when she phones him. Actually, Linda is there, weeping on his bed. However, many of Dixon's statements are not outright lies, more like evasions to conceal his guilt. He did not lie about not taking Linda home or about hearing a woman whistle for a cab. His unsupported claims *sound* like lies and make him a strong candidate as the murderer (which is also the case in Woolrich's short story).

Alex Tremholt, the kindly, middle-aged boarder at the Mitchell apartment, has been hiding a secret love for Estelle. Carr's flashback ends with the bulk of suspicion thrust upon him. In Woolrich's story, Tremholt is the murderer, and besides being a jealous suitor, he is a young man. *The Guilty* revises his character so that he is innocent but older. Interestingly, Monogram, who produced *The Guilty*, also produced *Fall Guy* that same year, adapted from another Woolrich story, "C-Jag." *Fall Guy* was revised so that an older man, nurturing a secret love, turns out to be the corrupt and jealous murderer. *The Guilty* seems to have incorporated that motif into its story and varied it so as not to repeat the formula.

Carr, of course, the unreliable narrator, has lied throughout his flashback — or at the least, has left out those details that would point to him as the murderer. He is "the guilty," and when we finally learn this, we can infer from the opening, where he winds his way up the street with the camera following him, that the eyes of Justice — or the Greek Furies — are on him. Heller, who has been dogging Carr's trail, personifies Justice and Conscience: "You never stayed in one place for very long," says the detective. "Guilty conscience?" The answer is certainly "yes."

After relating the entire story to McGinnis, Carr tells Estelle that he just wanted to hear how it sounded. It was, in effect, a qualified confession. He admits a few of his offenses: he lies to Linda that he does not know Estelle and he lies to the police that he heard the girl whistle for a cab. These are minor foibles, however, considering that he is the murderer after all.

The final line of the film is nearly verbatim from the short story (See the excerpt above.) except that "girl" replaces "guy," changing the gender of the person who reminds the narrator of a murder. The film neatly deletes the ambiguous homosexual overtones of Woolrich's story in favor of explicitly heterosexual conventions. Also, whereas the "girl" in Carr's final line must refer only to Estelle, the "guy" in the last line of Woolrich's story refers to both the narrator and Dixon, the two men self-consciously guilty of their association with the murder.

Critics who panned the film were possibly taking issue with its lethargic pacing and sodden, somber atmosphere. Two other weaknesses may have obscured the film's assets. One is lack of character development, of Carr and Dixon, certainly, but more significantly, of Estelle and Linda, whose *femme fatale* roles are the crux of the story and need clearer definition. Linda is the "good" sister simply on the word of the narrator, who is a liar. Saying she is good does not convince us she is good. She is merely a cipher to counter the evil sister, and her death is never felt deeply as a tragedy, even when Heller describes how gruesomely she died. Estelle, also, is not fully realized. In her initial appearance in her bathroom, she wrangles with Linda and shows she has fangs. Again at the end, she adopts a shrewish tone when she talks with Carr. Once or twice, such as when she phones Dixon while she is out with Carr, she exposes her darker side. However, her behavior is inconsistent. In the rooftop scene, when she confesses to Carr her guilt over Linda's death, she sounds sincerely affected by the loss of her more virtuous sister. She is a sympathetic character here, not the evil temptress that Carr makes her out to be. Now, this inconsistency can be the result of Carr's perception of her, his descriptions made within his flashback. However, it is in the final frame story, outside the flashback, that we see her more objectively and she appears rude, haughty, and mean. This would seem to be the real Estelle, but coupled with her fluctuating personality in the flashback, we have difficulty deciding how to code her.

A second shortcoming is the frequent shifts of perspective during Carr's flashback sequence. Several events occur outside of Carr's range of experience and knowledge, events he should not have been able to describe to his auditor, McGinnis. One is the argument that takes place in the Mitchell bathroom between Linda and Estelle. Another is the moment in Estelle's bedroom when, alone, she wakes in the darkness, looks at Linda's empty bed, and realizes the tragic implications. She becomes frantic and unnerved and Mrs. Mitchell has to rush in to console her. Still another shift is the subjective shot from Dixon's point of view when he nearly collapses into one of his spells. From Dixon's perspective, Carr stands in medium full shot but slightly tilted, and his image begins to blur. At this moment, the audience experiences the event through Dixon's eyes, not Carr's.

These shifts in perspective create the effect of objective moments being inserted into a subjective account. Estelle's reaction when she is alone suggests that she can feel some sense of remorse and may not be the cold, heartless woman described by Carr. Dixon's loss of focus proves that he has a very real malady. These shifts may undercut the subjectivity of Carr's flashback, but they also reinforce the two characters' positions as suspects: Estelle may feel genuine remorse for a murder she committed; Dixon, instead of faking his spells, may have committed murder while in one of them.

The Guilty, like many low-budget *noirs*, suffers at times from inane or trite dialogue: "You'll be convicted on circumstantial evidence"; "I wouldn't trust her as far as I could throw a boxcar." However, its sets depicting the entropy of derelict tenements and decrepit neighborhoods enhance the menacing tone of the story and its thematic threads give it sufficient substance as a creditable piece of filmmaking.

The Guilty has other strengths to counter these distracting, and yet interesting, flaws. John Reinhardt is lean on extensive or impressive film credentials, but as an Austrian émigré who directed and wrote screenplays in Europe and America, he shows in *The Guilty* the influence German Expressionism had on him. Stylistically, he and photographer Henry Sharp orchestrate the camera very well, employing an astonishing variety of angles, shots, and movements. One of their most extraordinary shots is the overhead, which occurs twice. The first time is in the lavatory at McGinnis's. The shot underscores the constrictive size and squalid nature of the room, indicating the tight, smutty box into which Carr has squeezed himself. (The shot also anticipates the overheads used by Hitchcock, such as in *Psycho* when Anthony Perkins cleans up the bathroom after killing Janet Leigh.)

The second overhead shot comes at the end. From atop the apartment building where Carr and Dixon lived and Linda was killed, the camera shows Carr get into the police vehicle with Heller and drive away. Alone, Estelle walks along the sidewalk while the camera, outlining a down-turned parabola, follows her as she disappears into the dark street. This shot complements the opening's following shot in several ways. The opening shot occurs at eye-level, causing the spectator to identify with the character because he has the same vantage point as the character. The final overhead, although a following shot, alters our perspective and so alters our impression. The view from above puts us, the spectators, in a superior position, makes us feel aloof from the complications affecting the character. However, the idea of guilt is present in both sequences. The opening shot implies that some mysterious person or thing is doggedly stalking the character (as enhanced by the churning, martial-sounding music). When Heller tells Carr that he had been trailing him the last six months, we realize that that unseen entity is not only Heller but also Carr's restless guilty conscience that prevented him from staying in one place too long. The final shot places the onus of guilt on Estelle. She is the *femme fatale* whose careless behavior provoked a man to murder her sister. The scene where she wakes up and goes into hysterics shows that she has enough sensitivity to experience the torments of a guilty conscience. Her hubris shrinks in the overhead shot; she appears humble and puny in light of the recent misfortune for which she was the primary cause.

Despite those mediocre reviews on its release, *The Guilty* is a respectable *film noir*. It has the typical B-movie trappings of shabby sets, unproven actors, and ludicrous dialogue, which, when first screened, make it look unappealing. Yet these are the very elements that give it the stylistic aura of a bona fide *film noir*—with the added bonus of an intricate, engrossing story line (thanks to Cornell Woolrich).

"Nightmare"

Novelette, first appearing in *Argosy*, March 1, 1941, under the title "And So to Death." Reprinted in the short story collection *I Wouldn't Be in Your Shoes*, J.B. Lippincott, 1943, under the title "Nightmare," as by William Irish. Reprinted in numerous mystery magazines as "Nightmare." Reprinted in paperback as one of three collected stories in *Nightmare*, as by William Irish, The Readers-Choice Library, June 1950.

At the beginning of Shakespeare's *Macbeth*, the three weird sisters, chortling with malicious glee, conspire to play havoc with Macbeth's life. When they appear to him and prophesy that he will first become thane of Cawdor and then one day king, he asks the pivotal question: Will attaining these boons depend on his active pursuit of them, or can he sit idly back and watch them come to him? Having the ability to shape our own fortune (through free will and self-determination) or finding our destiny influenced by some fateful cryptic power (like providence or predestination) is a paradox in *noir*, which Woolrich frequently incorporates in his stories. And nowhere is it more evident than in "Nightmare."

"Nightmare," a direct descendant of his "C-Jag" (and an elaborate improvement on it), is another of Woolrich's ironic excursions into absurd, contrived plotting that still manages to enthrall the reader because of his masterful fusion of style and suspense. At the core of the story is obsessive guilt, an infatuation in so many of his writings, and a character's floundering attempts to deal with it. What makes this story exceptional, though, is how Woolrich constructs the story on two levels at once, the explicit and the implicit, a complex, literal plot masking an ambiguous allegorical subtext. Encapsulating both the explicit and implicit conflicts, the central premise proposes how a man, partaking in a crime, may claim innocence if his actions occur while he is deprived of his free will. The explicit crime in this case is murder; the implicit crime, subtly hinted at, is homosexuality. And although the story has its share of logical flaws, the intricate and intriguing construct that integrates these two distinct ideas makes it easier to indulge the occasionally skewed plotting.

The story begins with a disturbing dream sequence. Vince sees himself in an octagonal mirrored room where a woman's disembodied face floats toward him. He fights with a strange man, and when the woman tries to hand the man an awl, Vince grabs it and stab him with it. The woman runs out of the room while he stuffs the body in a closet. Although the horrible deed seemed an invention of the imagination, when Vince awakes, he finds in his pocket a button and key he saw in the dream, and notices bruises on his neck, all of which suggest that the event must have really happened. Upset by this revelation, he seeks advice from his brother-in-law Cliff Dodge who happens to be a detective. Cliff scoffs at his fears, insisting that "you either dream a thing or you don't dream it, it really happens." But Vince cannot be consoled and spends the night on Cliff's sofa. The next day he runs a classified ad in the newspaper seeking a house with an octagonal mirrored room, but after a week, there is no success.

To distract Vince from his troubles, Cliff invites him on a picnic with him and his wife, Vince's sister Lil. At the site, it starts to rain, and Lil, intensely afraid of lightning, demands they find shelter immediately. Although unfamiliar with the area, Vince displays uncanny knowledge of a nearby vacant mansion where he directs Cliff to take them. He knows where a house key is hidden outside the door and he knows where to find the light switch. He sneaks away upstairs and finds the room where in his dream he murdered a man, an octagonal-shaped room with eight mirrored segments. Cliff walks in, and from what he sees, begins to suspect that Vince committed murder. In the kitchen, Cliff accuses Vince of taking advantage of their close relationship to cover up his crime and he threatens to beat a confession out of him. (Occasionally, Woolrich likes to reveal a policeman's dark side.) A local deputy from Sheriff Waggoner's office walks in and interrupts their fight. He tells Cliff of a recent murder that occurred here and that the mansion belongs to Joel and Dorothy Fleming. The murderer must have been discovered burglarizing the safe in the mirrored room. He killed Dan Ayers and hid his body one of the closets. Mrs. Fleming tried to escape and he ran her down with Ayers's car. She died after giving the police information about the attacker. From the description, it is apparent to Vince and Cliff that Vince must be the murderer.

At Vince's apartment, Cliff gives Vince one chance to escape. He says he will return in half an hour, arrest Vince if he is still here, and then resign from the department. Once Cliff is gone, Vince, driven by guilt and confusion, attempts suicide, slitting his wrists with a razor blade. Cliff returns in time to take Vince to a hospital and save his life. Cliff now believes that there is more to the story. (In the earlier "All at Once, No Alice," detective Ainslie stops Cannon from drinking iodine, a similar incident that serves an identical purpose, supposedly a proof of his innocence, and leads to identical consequences, the loyal assistance of a lawman.) Cliff stays with Vince that night. They talk and Vince relates a story about a neighbor who intruded on him the same night as his nightmare. The coincidence prompts Cliff to make a connection between Vince and this neighbor and their roles in the murder.

Cliff investigates and discovers that the neighbor is actually Joel Fleming, a former hypnotist. Using subtle tactics whenever they met, Fleming tested Vince and found that he was highly impressionable. He hypnotized Vince and directed him to kill his wife and Dan Ayers who, he knew, were having an affair and intended to steal his money and run away together. Vince managed to kill Ayers, but Dorothy fled and Fleming chased her down with Ayers's car. To vindicate Vince, Cliff concocts a plot to trap Fleming. At the mansion, Vince confronts Fleming while Cliff operates a recorder to tape his admission of guilt (another of Woolrich's conventions, tricking the murderer into an overheard confession). The plan goes awry when Fleming hypnotizes Vince a second time and then eludes the police, taking Vince to a lake where he orders him to drown himself. Cliff arrives in time to pull Vince from the water and resuscitate him.

Cliff informs Vince how he, Waggoner, and a deputy shot at Fleming's vehicle while he tried to escape, causing him to lose control. The car flipped over, crashed, and burst into flames, killing the hypnotist. Vince expects to serve time in jail until the arraignment, but he is not worried. The ordeal over and the truth revealed, he should be cleared of criminal charges on the basis of self-defense and not being responsible for his actions. Cliff accompanies Vince into the courthouse and assures him, "I'll be standing up right next to you the whole time."

On its explicit level, Woolrich's story is a study of a man enduring extreme guilt while trying to balance all the confusing contradictions between two realms, between the waking and dreaming states, between reality and imagination. When Vince first wakes from his nightmare, he looks out the window down into the street to see the same buildings, the same diner where he sometimes eats, the same people following their usual bustling routines on the sidewalks. The mundane is countered with the sensational; the common man has experienced a strange, surreal event and, as evidence unfolds, he does not know which existence is the nightmare, which the reality. Guilt for his wrongdoing in that other, unknown world contributes to his unease and confusion, but so does the idea that he does not know what is real anymore, what he can depend on, what he should perceive as fact or fiction.

The explicit text delves into the dilemma facing an innocent man consumed by guilt for a crime he fears he committed, learns that he did commit, and then finally discovers was committed without his consent. The *noir* connection is obvious: an external force deprives a person of his free will, dictates his behavior, and compels him to act contrary to his conscience. Fleming, the external force, represents Fate, which gives rise to the standard questions: What kinds of forces are at work on us at different times, making us do things that we normally would not do? And if these forces compel us to betray our most valued principles, to what extent are we culpable for our wrongdoings? Vince tells Cliff that he doesn't know the answer, that they would have to "ask God — or whoever it is watches over us in the night when we're unconscious."

Perhaps that power is good, like a merciful God, but as an unknown entity, it may be evil, or at best, indifferent. And so a *noir* motif emerges (the same one confronting Macbeth), a paradox about the nature of "God — or whoever it is that watches over us" and tampers with our lives, whether that power tolerates free will or demands strict conformity to its whims, and whether it does so out of benevolence, malevolence, or amusement.

The implicit subtext offers an allegorical motivation behind Vince's troubled conscience: he feels guilty about entertaining homosexual fantasies. This may sound strained, but the symbols and innuendoes are sufficient to suggest that Vince has, or dreams of having, a homosexual encounter. This is especially apparent in the two scenes where he succumbs to Fleming's hypnotic powers and the incident where he blacks out at the constabulary. Fainting and hypnosis are psychological ploys, defense mechanisms, excuses for hiding from the reality he cannot admit that he either has had affairs with men or, at the least, desires a homosexual relationship.

In the first such scene, the introductory sequence that turns out not to be a dream but a hypnotic episode, Vince stabs Ayers with an awl, then hides him in the cramped closet. Despite his locking the door, he sees the doorknob turn and the door begin to open.

The awl is an obvious phallic symbol and the stabbing murder suggests consummation of a sex act between the two men. Hiding the body is Vince's attempt to hide his guilt, but his conscience is too guilt-stricken to think his deed will remain secret. His greatest fear is that the truth of this homosexual encounter will inevitably make its way "out of the closet."

The description of the key he uses to lock Ayers in the closet is blatantly sexual in imagery and homosexual in association. Vince explains:

> It had a head ... a little like a three-leaf clover and the inner rim of each of the three "leaves" was fretted with scrollwork and tracery. It had a stem disproportionately long for the size of its head, and it ended in two odd little teeth bent back on themselves, like a quarter part of a swastika. It was of some yellowish composition, either brass or iron gilded over. A key such as is no longer made or used.
>
> It lay lengthwise in the hollow of my hand, and I kept touching it repeatedly with the thumb of that same hand. That was the only part of me that moved for a long time, that foolish flexing thumb [13–14].

Apparent is the suggestion of masturbation. It is almost as if he is discovering his penis for the first time and is playing with it, mystified by its unusual shape, the stem too long for its head. There is also the suggestion of impotence. Although he holds it in his hand while his thumb plays with it for a long time, it is a "foolish flexing thumb," an exercise in futility. And the key is a defunct instrument, "no longer made or used."

Besides this masturbatory gesture, associations with homosexuality are also present. The scrollwork and tracery paint a picture of something baroque, garish, the stereotypical taste of the homosexual. The bent "teeth" contain the notion of oral sex and the fact that Vince uses the key to lock Ayers in the closet suggests, like the use of the awl, that intercourse between the two men was attempted. But there is also the added question of impotency, which seems a strong likelihood, in that these objects, the awl and key, become substitutes for the organ of the male who desires homosexual consummation but cannot complete it. Murder with a phallic symbol replaces the actual sex act; the key ineffectively locks the door. Thus, his wish fulfillment is stymied, incomplete, and both his homosexual urge and his failure to satisfy that urge leave him feeling frustrated, confused, and guilty — as Vince is.

When Vince shows the key to Cliff, connotations suggest a homosexual relationship between the two men. Vince tells him,

"I've got [the key] right here. I'll show it to you...."
It took me a little while to get it out, my hand was shaking so. It had shaken like that all day, every time I brought it near the thing to feel if it was still on me.... The lining caught around it and I had to free it, but finally I got it out.
He took it from me and examined it, curiously but noncommittally [16–17].

On the literal level, Vince's guilt comes from the fear he committed a murder: the key proves that he executed the action in reality, not merely in a dream. Figuratively, showing the key is like Vince timidly and clumsily exposing himself to Cliff, as either a homosexual overture or a plea for advice on his impotence. Whichever the case, the detective responds indifferently, showing neither rejection nor acceptance.

In the next scene, however, Vince wakes up after sleeping the night on Cliff's couch. Cliff comes downstairs alone. "'How'd it go?' he asked half-secretively. On account of her, I suppose" (23). The question literally refers to whether Vince had a peaceful sleep. Figuratively, Cliff asks whether Vince was able to masturbate successfully, or if he enjoyed the "secretive" sexual encounter they had in the night.

Cliff's is one of a number of statements that suggest bonding between males to the exclusion of the female. For instance, Vince, on his way to consult Cliff rather than Lil, states, "She was my sister, but you don't tell women things like I wanted to tell him.... You tell them the things that you have under control; the things that you're frightened of, you tell other men if you tell anyone" (15). The validity of this philosophy is debatable, but admittedly, it could be the character's chauvinistic ideal, the male's not exposing his flaws to the female. Then again, we see the sexual implications, the man's inability to talk of impotence with a woman, or the man preferring to find solace from another man, not from a woman.

At the Fleming mansion, after Vince and Cliff have discovered the mirrored room, Lil calls out to them. Vince anxiously commands his brother-in-law to stop her from coming upstairs, rationalizing to himself that "you don't want your agonies of soul witnessed by a woman." As in the previous excerpt, Vince wants to hide emotional display, a supposedly feminine trait, in order to perpetuate the stereotypical image of the virile, confident male. He forsakes the female, preferring male companionship and compassion in dealing with his emotional trauma; implicitly, he keeps from the female subjects considered taboo: impotency and/or homosexuality.

Once he has discovered the octagonal mirrored room and the closet with the bloodstained wall, Vince's dream of having murdered a man becomes reality. Cliff's angry outburst in the kitchen supposedly arises from pride, that his brother-in-law was making a fool of him and using him to gain an insanity plea. Once again, though, the row has a homosexual undertone. As Vince's lover, Cliff could view the crime in the mirrored room not as murder, but as infidelity, the symbolic sex act with Ayers suggesting that Vince has had a lover before him. When the deputy sheriff arrives, Cliff takes a seat at the table, turning the chair around and straddling it backward, the back of the chair between him and Vince. He has placed a barrier between him and his lover. Cliff lights up a cigarette and grudgingly throws the pack to Vince, who interprets this gesture to mean, "Whatever there is between us, I'm seeing that it stays just between us.... I'm not ready to give you away to anybody—yet" (39). The close bond between the men enables Vince to comprehend Cliff's action. The action itself, sharing a cigarette, another phallic symbol, signifies Cliff's effort to retain communion between them; despite Vince's unfaithfulness, he jealously wants to hold on to Vince, to preserve their relationship so that Vince does not look elsewhere for a mate. Then, too, Cliff offers the deputy a smoke, which the deputy rejects. Obviously, he is not open to implied homosexual overtures.

Vince blacks out at the police station when he views the repulsive photographs of the dead Ayers and Mrs. Fleming. When he comes to, he is in Cliff's arms, the detective giving him a drink of water and warning him to keep quiet, not to say anything that will incriminate him.

Keenly sensitive, Vince fainted because the photos were so graphically horrid, but in the subtext, he looks at the photo of his former lover, and the shock overwhelms him. On the textual level, Cliff silences Vince to protect him, to keep him from condemning himself. Yet once they return to Vince's apartment, Cliff says he is going to arrest him the next day. If Cliff was sure of Vince's guilt and intended to turn him in, why not let him speak at the police station? On the subtextual level, he was afraid his brother-in-law, not totally coherent, might say something to expose their homosexual relationship.

In the end, Vince again falls under Fleming's hypnotic spell. Coached by Cliff in what to say, Vince gets Fleming to admit his role in murdering his wife and Ayers, while Cliff, in another part of the house, has rigged up recording equipment to tape Fleming's confession. Vince has a gun and thinks he is in control, but Fleming uses his pocket watch as a focal device to hypnotize him once more. Fleming sneaks his hypnotized subject from the house and drives him to a nearby lake where he has Vince undress, write a suicide note, then tie an anchor around his legs and slide into the deep water. The police arrive in time. They shoot at Fleming as he flees, his car crashes, and Fleming dies in the burning wreck.

Cliff and Waggoner pull Vince from the water and administer artificial respiration to revive him. Vince awakens to find himself and Cliff in their underwear, while Waggoner stands nearby, shoeless and coatless. Vince had taken time to undress, but Waggoner jumped into the water clothed. Literally, the two detectives have rescued Vince from drowning; figuratively, they represent a *ménage à trois*: Waggoner may have intended to get into the act before Vince came out of the blackout that conveniently enables him to deny his homosexual experiences.

When the ordeal is over, Vince understands he is not totally innocent, that his role in the crime makes him subject to criminal investigation. But by the next morning, "I didn't mind so much anymore" (72). On their way to the arraignment, Cliff tells him, "You'll be all right.... I'll be standing up right next to you the whole time" (77). Now that he knows his killing was unintentional, Vince can compromise his guilt and find some peace in the knowledge that his crime was not an act of free will. Cliff also accepts his brother-in-law's innocence, and in a warm gesture of male camaraderie, assures Vince he will support him. Figuratively, Vince accepts his homosexual tendencies, intends somehow to live with them. Cliff's loyalty on their way to the constabulary imitates a man's words to his bride-to-be on their way to the altar.

Vince symbolizes Everyman, a good-natured, innocently gullible person, upright and honest and struggling to uphold his moral principles in a corrupt and deceitful world. Honesty is not good enough, for he is vulnerable to the corrupt, insidious, degenerate world that exists beyond his comfortable, familiar neighborhood (the diner where he sometimes eats, the people on the sidewalk, the traffic in the street). Subjected to moral compromise, his keen sense of guilt elicits poignant psychological convulsions. If this is so, the argument, as one criticism of the plot goes, is that he could not have committed murder because a person under hypnosis cannot be made to do something against his will. The counter argument is that, since Vince *did* carry out Fleming's command, he must have already had within him the potential to commit murder. In the *noir* domain, this is a self-destructive trait which often emerges in the most upright of protagonists, suggesting that even good and noble men have inside them the potential to do ill. Many *films noirs* propose this notion. Consider, for example, *Side Street*, *Double Indemnity*, and *The Lady from Shanghai* with Farley Granger, Fred MacMurray, and Orson Welles, respectively, who start out as honest, hard-working stiffs, but succumb to the temptation of money (Granger, MacMurray, Welles) and/or a woman (MacMurray, Welles). The good-man-gone-bad occurs again and again throughout the entire classical period in films like *Scarlet Street* (1945), *Roadblock* (1951), and *Shield for Murder* (1954).

Besides his image as an Everyman, Vince is also a kind of Christ-figure, even if a false or distorted one. To fool the sly Fleming into a confession, he tells him he kept from falling under his hypnotic spell by squeezing tacks into his palms. Although a ruse, the explanation alludes to the stigmata, equating

Vince with Christ and implying that he is merely another innocent victim falling prey to the unscrupulous corrupt forces of the *noir* world.

Film: Fear in the Night

1947, Paramount. *D:* Maxwell Shane. *P:* William H. Pine, William C. Thomas (Pine-Thomas). *Assoc P:* L.B. Merman. *Cin:* Jack Greenhalgh. *Sc:* Maxwell Shane. *Ed:* Howard Smith. *Mus:* Rudy Schrager. *Sound:* Frank Webster. *Art Dir:* F. Paul Sylos. *Set Decor:* Elias H. Reif. *Asst Dir:* Howard Pine.

Cast: Paul Kelly (Cliff Herlihy), DeForest Kelley (Vince Grayson), Ann Doran (Lil Herlihy), Kay Scott (Betty Winters), Robert Emmett Keane (Harry Burg/Lewis Belnap), Jeff Yorke (Deputy Sheriff Torrence), Charles Victor (Capt. Warner), Janet Warren (Mrs. Belnap), Michael Harvey (Bob Clune), John Harmon (Clyde Bilyou), Gladys Blake (Bank clerk), Stanley Farrar (Bank patron), Julia Faye (Mrs. Tracey-Lytton, ad respondent), Dick Keane (Mr. Kern), Joey Ray (Contractor), Chris Drake (Elevator operator), Loyette Thompson (Waitress), Jack Collins (Man on street), Leander De Cordova (Man seated in lobby). 71 min.

A steady contributor to filmmaking from 1937 to 1956, Maxwell Shane accumulated more credits as a writer than as a director. He penned screenplays for nearly 60 films, but sat in the director's chair for only five of them. However, those five films, according to Spencer Selby in his *Dark City: The Film Noir*, can all be classified as *noirs*: *Fear in the Night* (1947), *City Across the River* (1949), *The Glass Wall* (1953), *The Naked Street* (1955), and *Nightmare* (1956, a remake of his own *Fear in the Night*). Evidently, Shane must have appreciated Woolrich's conception for the novelette "Nightmare" because he not only scripted and directed two versions of it, but in adapting it to film, he also retained most of the original material and captured much of the author's atmospheric style and thematic intent.

DeForest Kelley, commendable in his first screen role, plays the confused protagonist, Vince Grayson, who awakes from a disturbing nightmare in which he stabs a man with an awl and stuffs his body in a closet. Although the gory crime seemed an invention of the imagination, Vince finds in his pocket a button and key he saw in the dream, and notices bruises on his neck, all of which suggest that the event really happened. Upset by this revelation, he seeks help from his detective brother-in-law, Cliff Herlihy (Paul Kelly), who scoffs at Vince's imagined fears, but as evidence grows (closely following Woolrich's chain of events), he gradually comes to believe his brother-in-law did commit the murder. After Vince tries to commit suicide by leaping from his hotel room window (not by slitting his wrists as in Woolrich's version), Cliff begins to investigate the facts more minutely. He locates the cuckolded husband Lewis Belnap (Robert Emmett Keane, renamed from the original's Joel Fleming) and guesses how he turned Vince into a hypnotized assassin to murder his wife (Janet Warren) and her lover (Michael Harvey as Bob Clune, replacing Woolrich's Dan Ayers).

"Nightmare" (1941) / *Fear in the Night* (1947) 115

Fear in the Night— Cliff Herlihy (Paul Kelly, right), a police detective, takes offense when he thinks his brother-in-law Vince Grayson (DeForest Kelley) is using him to evade a crime (Paramount, National Screen Service Corp., courtesy of William Thailing).

To clear Vince of murder, Cliff sets a trap for Belnap, wanting him to repeat his ability to place Vince under a hypnotic spell. He sets up recording equipment in the basement and has Vince confront the hypnotist in the mirrored room, where Belnap admits his role in the murders. Belnap succeeds in hypnotizing Vince, but eludes the police, driving Vince to a lake where he orders him to drown himself. Cliff arrives in time to pull Vince from the water while his men pursue Belnap. One cop shoots the tire of the fleeing auto. Belnap loses control and dies in a violent crash.

At his arraignment, Cliff tells Vince that, based on self-defense, he should be cleared of criminal charges. Smiling, Vince walks up the steps of the courthouse with girlfriend Betty (Kay Scott) at his side.

As a faithful adaptation, Shane's film works extremely well for a number of reasons. For one, an able cast delivers convincing performances. DeForest Kelley's portrayal of a meek yet high-strung, emotionally suppressed individual perfectly captures the honest Everyman, who, struggling to uphold his moral principles in a corrupt and deceitful world, suffers psychological upheaval because of his sensitive conscience. (Kelley's emotionally overwrought character battling with ethical questions presages the role he will best be remembered for, the duty-bound and highly excitable Dr. Bones McCoy in the *Star Trek* film and television series.) Imitating his literary counterpart, Grayson also acts like a kind of Christ-figure for the same reasons. Although he fools the clever Belnap into a confession by lying about squeezing tacks into his palms to keep from falling under his hypnotic spell, his "wounds" connect him with Christ, innocents falling prey to society's unscrupulous forces.

Paul Kelly, chisel-faced and square-jawed, gives his reliably convincing depiction of the rough-edged, no-nonsense cop, a role he plays often in his career. Notably, Robert Emmett Keane stands out as the villain. His quietly confident demeanor makes his villainy seem all the more insidious and deadly.

Shane's sequence shooting and Howard Smith's editing retain a logical continuity throughout the film. Shane relies mostly on montage, not only combining close-ups, medium shots, and long shots in nearly every scene but also using a variety of camera angles and camera movements. With few exceptions, the editing successfully blends all of these shots into smooth, natural flowing sequences.

Because he recognizes the effectiveness of Woolrich's style and theme, Shane scripts and directs much of the original story, so that his film captures the essence of Woolrich's vision. Like the novelette, the film operates ambiguously on two planes at once with its text and subtext mirroring the two realms of reality and imagination. Shane retains the two equivocal sources of Grayson's guilt, committing a murder and entertaining homosexual fantasies.

The film's explicit text parallels that of Woolrich's story. A guilt-infected individual is struck nearly impotent with fear because he may have committed a reprehensible murder. And as in Woolrich's story, the same questions emerge as to whether human action is the product of free will or the automatic gestures dictated by some all-controlling external force. Interestingly, when Grayson refers to "the power [that] watches over us when we're unconscious," he changes the original assignation, "God," to "the Almighty." Whether or not the revision is a concession to the censors, it de-emphasizes the Divine, suggesting that the outcome to human endeavor can be held sway by some secular entity.

Shane faithfully adheres to Woolrich's homosexual subtext as the implied reason for Vince's troubled conscience. His relationships with Clune, Herlihy, and Belnap are confusing to his sensitive nature, a psyche stringently molded by social proprieties and religious orthodoxy. The only way he can cope with his "improper" behavior is by suppressing it as fragmented memories from dreams or a hypnotic trance or some black-out state. Under those conditions, he cannot be held accountable for other men having their way with him. Thus, the opening scene with Clune and several scenes with Cliff and Belnap all portray him as an unwitting—and therefore innocent—participant in their illicit sexual liaisons.

After the hypnotic episode in the beginning, Vince suffers unconsciousness a second time when he blacks out at his brother-in-law's house. He knocks over a bottle of nail polish, stains his wrist, and believes it is Bob Clune's blood. Shane uses special effects to distort Vince's image as he collapses. After a fade out and in, we see him lying in bed in the dark, while his voiceover tells us he had a hazy recollection waking and then falling back to sleep until after midnight when "something" woke him. The light goes on and the camera pans Cliff's figure, from his legs to his face, as he stands alongside Vince's bed in a garish robe patterned in circular starbursts.

This blackout, adapted from the novelette where Vince sleeps overnight at Cliff's house, makes it even more evident that Shane is trying to capture Woolrich's homosexual connotations. The opening dream sequence implies a homosexual encounter with Clune and this scene ambiguously presents Cliff as the instigator of another one with him. Throughout the film, Cliff calls Vince "kid," a term of endearment perhaps, but also one male's subtle claim to superiority over another. Woolrich's story handles this a little differently: at one point Cliff tells Vince, "You're 26 years old, you're not a kid" (21), but at the end, when Vince has to go through the legal process for his role in the murder, Cliff asks him, "Are you scared, kid?" ("Kid" evokes the same ambiguities as "gunsel" in *The Maltese Falcon*, where Gutman—Sidney Greenstreet—has an equally equivocal relationship with his gunman Wilmer—Elisha Cook, Jr.—as adopted son and implied lover.) Here, the camera's pan of Cliff presents him as an imposing figure standing at the meek Vince's bedside, the two characters taking the male and female roles respectively. His gaudy robe contrasted with his stern, hard-boiled visage is laughable, but the scene is played seriously, and the insinuation is that Cliff, coming for a romantic tryst, is outfitted to impress the object of his affection. That Vince has a vague memory of waking before again falling asleep complicates the homosexuality motif further, making us wonder if Cliff took advantage of him while he was in a faint.

As in Woolrich's story, the scene between Cliff and Vince in the kitchen of the Belnap mansion is filled with homosexual innuendo. Cliff's anger originates ambiguously from pride (repugnance at being used) and jealousy (possessiveness for his lover). Following this scene, Vince experiences his next blackout at the police station when he is shown the morbid photographs of the two dead bodies. As he goes into a faint, his image becomes distorted like a reflection in a funhouse mirror and black lines fragment his body before he collapses in a fade out. At the fade in, he lies on the floor. Cliff picks him up, cradles him in a pietà-like pose, and administers to him. Vince starts to speak: "It's only since I started—" but Cliff cuts him off so as not to alert the other police of his knowledge of the murders.

Again, the subtextual implication is that Vince faints from the shock of seeing his former lover dead. Cliff seems to silence Vince to keep him from incriminating himself, but once they return to Vince's apartment, Cliff announces he is going to arrest him the next day. If Cliff intended to turn him in, he could have let him confess at the police station. He was afraid his brother-in-law would expose their homosexual relationship, that he might have said he blacks out "only since I started" to have these homosexual affairs.

Fear in the Night — Grayson (Kelley, right), who unconsciously committed murder, confronts the hypnotist, Lewis Belnap (Robert Emmett Keane), the conscious instigator of the crime (Paramount, National Screen Service Corp., courtesy William Thailing).

The film continues to follow Woolrich very closely at the climax. Cliff has set a trap for Belnap with his recording equipment while Vince confronts the hypnotist. Vince brandishes a gun and thinks he's in control, but Belnap distracts him with his pocket watch, reflecting light in his eyes and hypnotizing him once more. Vince's gun is a phallic symbol, and Belnap's request that Vince give "it" to him suggests another homosexual encounter. Hypnotized, Vince is defenseless and vulnerable — that is, the urge to consummate the homosexual sex act is too great to resist. His hypnotic trances and blackouts are excuses, defense mechanisms, to assuage his guilt for submitting to these urges.

We see Vince's face inside the circle of Belnap's watch cover. Black lines criss-cross the image, giving it a shattered, fragmented look. Vince's self-control dwindles into oblivion. Belnap leads his hypnotized subject from the house and drives him to a nearby lake where he suggests that he find peace by drowning himself. Vince slips into the water, the symbol of the unconscious. The police, not far behind, close in. Belnap flees. The police shoot out one tire, causing the car to jump the road and crash, killing the hypnotist. Meanwhile, Cliff, left at the lakeside, has pulled Vince from the water. In administering artificial respiration, he has Vince's inert body prostrate, face down, on the dock while he straddles him. Then he turns him over, and remains straddling him. Vince regains consciousness. Cliff, looking down on him, asks, "Are you all right, kid?" Vince takes his time, but finally smiles and answers, "Yeah ... yeah ... all of a sudden, I'm all right."

This final image of Cliff astride Vince seals the homosexual implications. If, up to now, Vince's fear has been that he is homosexual, this moment suggests that consummation has been an enjoyable experience. "All of a sudden I'm all right" can mean several things, one of which is that submission to and acceptance of his homosexuality has enabled him to feel at peace with himself.

The image of Cliff behind Vince in a front-to-back embrace, the so-called "spoon" position, had occurred earlier when Cliff rescued his brother-in-law from his suicide leap. Before Vince slips from the window ledge, Cliff pulls him inside. They fall backward to the ground with Vince, his back to Cliff, landing on top of him. In itself, the incident does not suggest a homosexual act, but when coupled with the later scene on the dock, it signifies their sexual entanglement.

The ordeal over, true blame for the murder has been determined and Vince is absolved of his guilt. His plunge into the water had a cathartic, cleansing action, a baptism that erased all sins, original and otherwise. At the film's conclusion, the relationship between Betty and Vince is restored to produce the standard happy ending. Significant is that, when she walks with him up the steps of the courthouse, she says, "I'll be right there with you all the time." She usurps the words of Cliff Dodge at the end of Woolrich's story, thus replacing him and what he stands for. The implication is that Vince's "fear in the night," his fear of being homosexual, is over, that his love for a woman redeems him through a "normal" heterosexual relationship.

Besides imitating Woolrich's subtextual theme related to homosexual guilt, Shane retains another important aspect of Woolrich's novel, the conflict and contradiction between the waking and dreaming states, between reality and imagination. When Vince first wakes from his nightmare, he looks out the window down into the street, and like his original counterpart, sees the same buildings, the same diner where he sometimes eats, the same people absorbed their bustling routines on the sidewalks. The ordinary contrasts the sensational; the common man has experienced a strange, surreal event and, as evidence unfolds, he does not know which existence is the nightmare, which the reality. Guilt for his wrongdoing in that other, unknown world contributes to his unease and confusion, but so does the fact that he does not know what is real anymore, what he can depend on, what he should perceive as real or unreal.

Another concern is how the female characters fare in this story, that they are hardly more than props. Invented for the purposes of the film, Betty Winters does not exist in Woolrich's story and appears here to provide a love interest for Vince. His sister Lil (Ann Doran), like her counterpart in the novelette, has a fear of lightning (indicating that hypersensitivity runs in the family), which gives Vince the excuse to rediscover the house where he committed his nightmarish murder. Otherwise, the women fade dutifully into the background when they are not needed. In defense of Woolrich, he wrote many stories where he develops the female character more substantially, such as *The Black Angel*, "Face Work," and *Phantom Lady*. He had a knack for taking on the female persona and telling the story from the woman's viewpoint.

Some films, especially several in the tradition of German Expressionism, use hypnosis as a plot device, where a superior evil genius is able to control innocent victims and make them perform acts against their will. *The Cabinet of Dr. Caligari* (Robert Wiene, 1919), *The Testament of Dr. Mabuse* (Fritz Lang, 1933), *Svengali* (Archie Mayo, 1931; Noel Langley, 1955), and the early Dracula cycle are examples. Their intention of having a weaker mind submit passively to a stronger one relates directly to Woolrich: a superior omnipresent power (Fate? God?), not free will, dictates human action. Free will is an illusion. Thus, in instances where ethical or moral choices are required, humans are not always totally responsible, which makes them less culpable for any immoral, unethical behavior.

Vince's blackouts are reminiscent of the "black pool" into which Philip Marlowe (Dick Powell) intermittently sinks in *Murder, My Sweet* (Edward Dmytryk, 1944). Their purpose appears similar, signifying the protagonist's vulnerability to forces beyond his control. One difference, however, is that Marlowe's "black pool" is always the result of some external physical assault (clobbered on the head, saturated with drugs, etc.). Marlowe is a self-confident, independent thinker, who believes in his ability to act out of self-determination (despite those external forces that try to manipulate him). He has too much internal strength to be attacked from within, so the forces that want to make him conform must attack him from without. (He defeats their attempt to control him with drugs.) In contrast, Vince's blackouts are produced because of his psychological make-up. He does not possess Marlowe's internal fortitude, as evidenced by his susceptibility to hypnotic suggestion and hypersensitivity due to a strong guilt complex.

Although unrelated to *Nightmare* in theme and plot, *The Lady from Shanghai* (1948) bears one striking commonality. The mirrored room, which figures so prominently in Woolrich's story and Shane's movie, is transformed into a clever, elaborate set piece in Welles's film, where the characters have a climactic shoot-out in a hall of mirrors. Executing so complex a scene is commendable in both films. Although undeniably creative, Welles, like any observant artist, was receptive to ideas from other sources and would shape them into intriguing (if oddly baroque) images more in line with his vision for the medium. Since Woolrich's novelette appeared in the March 1, 1941, issue of *Argosy*, it is possible that Welles read it and adapted it for himself, but this is pure conjecture. On the other hand, a few observers have noted that Welles got the idea from Shane. This is not likely, because Welles made his film first, completing it in February 1947 (although release was delayed until the following year). Shane's film was not completed until April of 1947.

Spellbound (Alfred Hitchcock, 1945) is based on the book *The House of Dr. Edwardes* by Francis Beeding, and although the Hitchcock-Hecht screenplay veers far from Beeding's original story of devil worship and the supernatural, the film treats the confusion between dream and reality and the implication of guilt in ways that come very close to those ideas in Woolrich's "Nightmare." The young protagonist (Gregory Peck), a psychiatrist, arrives at a sanitarium to replace the current director (Leo G. Carroll). His paradoxical personality and good looks give him a mysterious quality, making him appear both appealing and menacing. When a recurrent haunting dream harangues his conscience, he turns to a young female psychiatrist (Ingrid Bergman) for help. With her prompting, he discovers the source of his subconscious guilt by recounting the details of a suppressed "nightmare." (The dream sequence is designed by Spanish surrealist Salvador Dalí, who has a penchant for bisecting eyeballs: this image which he uses here is a modified version of the more disturbing one which appears in his and Buñuel's *Un chien andalou*, 1929.) Filled with symbolic imagery and puns, the dream reveals that the retiring director had killed the man who was supposed to replace him and that Peck, an innocent bystander, had assumed blame for the man's death and borrowed his identity to suppress his guilt, keeping the man alive in his own image. As in *Fear in the Night*, the innocent, highly impressionable man assumes the burden of guilt.

The Woman in the Window (Fritz Lang, 1945) has several curious parallels with Woolrich's "Nightmare." First of all, like Vince, who believes he dreams of murdering a man, Richard Wanley (Edward G. Robinson) falls asleep at his private club and dreams he commits a murder. The murder weapon, a pair of scissors, is placed in his hand by a mysterious woman (Joan Bennett as Alice Reed, whom he had just met) in much the same way that the awl was placed in Vince's hand by a mysterious woman, who gave it to him by mistake to defend himself against his assailant.

Just like Vince who has a detective for a close relative, Wanley has a close friend in the police department, Frank Lalor (Raymond Massey), who takes him along while he investigates the very murder that Wanley committed. Wanley gets to follow the case and see whether he will be implicated. Quite ironically, Robinson plays the murderer in *The Woman in the Window*, then plays the detective in Shane's 1956 remake, *Nightmare*, where, in Lalor's role, he starts to unravel the mystery that implicates his panic-stricken brother-in-law as the unintentional murderer.

Despite having a killed a man, Wanley appears in total control of his emotions and the situation. He seems to make all the right decisions to help himself and Alice out of their predicament with the body and later with the blackmailing Heidt (Dan Duryea). (It's his dream, after all — he would naturally inflate his poised demeanor, perceive himself as an unruffled protagonist.) However, guilt cannot be suppressed and, sitting in an armchair beside the photos of his family, he drinks the same poison he intended for Heidt. Since this is his dream, he might have either wakened from it before he took the poison or imagined things ending more favorably. But instead of extricating himself somehow and finding redemption, his guilt is so strong that he actually goes through with the suicide, ending his life out of guilt and shame. Like Woolrich, director Fritz Lang, who single-handedly produced a litany of *films noirs*, often concerns himself with the interrelationships of guilt, innocence, and justice. Also, like many of his fellow German émigrés, he was already delving into *noir* territory even before *noir* became a fashionable term. Among some of his early outstanding attempts to deal with these issues are *M* (1931), his first talkie, and the controversial *Fury* (1936).

Film: Nightmare

1956, United Artists. *D:* Maxwell Shane. *P:* William C. Pine, William C. Thomas (Pine-Thomas-Shane). *Cin:* Joe Biroc. *Sc:* Maxwell Shane. *Ed:* George Gittens. *Mus:* Herschel Burke Gilbert. *Songs:* "What's Your Sad Story?" by Dick Sherman; "The Last I Ever Saw of My Heart" by Herschel Burke Gilbert, lyrics by Doris Houck. *Art Dir:* Frank Sylos. *Set Dec:* Edward Boyle.

Cast: Kevin McCarthy (Stan Grayson), Edward G. Robinson (René Bressard), Connie Russell (Gina), Virginia Christine (Sue Bressard), Rhys Williams (Deputy Sheriff Torrence), Gage Clarke (Harry Britton/Lewis Belnap), Barry Atwater (Captain Warner), Marian Carr (Madge), Billy (Billy May), Meade "Lux" Lewis (Pianist, as himself), Musicians (Billy May and His Orchestra). 89 min.

Nine years after adapting Woolrich's "Nightmare" for his 1947 film *Fear in the Night*, Maxwell Shane directed a remake with the same producers of his earlier film. Although this later film, renamed *Nightmare*, strongly resembles the earlier film, a meticulous analysis shows that, below the surface, they are really two different films.

It may seem odd that a director should remake his own film, but then Shane is not alone. Cecil B. DeMille directed a silent version of *The Ten Commandments* (1923) and remade it as a Technicolor extravaganza, released in 1956. Alfred Hitchcock made two versions of *The Man Who Knew Too Much*, in 1934 and 1956. (That Shane and these two particular directors should christen all their remakes in 1956 is an ironic coincidence that Woolrich himself would have appreciated.) And then there's *Lady for a Day*, which Frank Capra made in 1933 and reproduced 28 years later as *Pocketful of Miracles*. The rationale for a director's remaking his own movie is probably the same for any director who remakes any film: he likes the original material and thinks he can improve on it, reshape it into something better, or if not better, something equally entertaining and creative. Whether he succeeds or not is a question easily answered by comparing the two efforts.

A cursory overview of *Nightmare* shows how strictly Shane's earlier adaptation serves as the blueprint for the remake. Certain sequences are literally taken shot-for-shot from *Fear in the Night*, and the main characters, despite some name changes, are virtually identical. Shane elaborates on a few scenes from the first film, lengthening the second by nearly 20 minutes. He also incorporates into the remake a musical element, which becomes a critical dimension to the story.

Nightmare begins with a similar dream sequence that Shane adapted for *Fear in the Night*. Stan Grayson (Kevin McCarthy), a clarinetist in a New Orleans band, envisions himself in a mirrored room where he encounters a strange woman, then fights with a man and stabs him to death with an awl. After waking, he finds bruises on his neck and pulls from his pocket two items he saw in the dream, a button he had ripped from the man's coat and a key he had used to lock the body in a closet. He seeks help from his detective brother-in-law, René Bressard (Edward G. Robinson), but René attributes Stan's fear to an overactive imagination.

Following the script of *Fear in the Night*, René, several days later, persuades Grayson to go on a picnic with him, his wife Sue (Virginia Christine, the future Mrs. Olsen of Folger coffee commercials), and Gina (Connie Russell, a 1950s pop singer, portraying Grayson's girlfriend and singer in their band). When René asks where they want to go, Grayson impulsively names Bayou Laforche, unaware why he suggested that particular place (Vince suggests Solanda Canyon in *Fear in the Night*.). As in both Woolrich's story and Shane's earlier film, a flash thunderstorm disrupts their picnic and sends them fleeing to their car. When René's windshield wipers fail to work, Sue pleads with him to stop at a house, so she can escape the thunder and lightning. Grayson directs them to a local mansion, unable to explain why it seems familiar to him. He retrieves a hidden key that lets them into the house. While the girls nap, he searches the upstairs and discovers the mirrored room where he murdered the unknown man.

René believes that his brother-in-law was merely using him to establish an insanity plea for murder. He is ready to beat a confession out of him, when the parish deputy sheriff walks in and tells them of the recent murder here. He takes them to the police station and shows them photos of the dead people. Stan faints. When he comes to, René takes him home, but is now convinced of Stan's guilt. He gives him a chance to escape, saying he'll be back in the morning to arrest him if he's still here. Instead, Stan prepares to jump from his window ledge (as Vince does in Shane's first adaptation). René returns in time to stop him. He stays with Stan that night, and during a conversation, Stan talks about his odd neighbor Harry Britton (Gage Clarke), who once persuaded him to drink a rum daiquiri that he didn't want and take a menthol cough drop he had first refused. René recognizes the pattern of one person testing another's will power.

This information leads René to investigate the circumstances of the crime more carefully. He learns the truth, that Britton, alias Belnap, the husband of the murdered woman, had put Stan into a hypnotic trance and ordered him to kill his wife and her lover. René rigs a trap. Stan confronts Belnap in the mirrored room and tricks him into confessing his guilt. Belnap hypnotizes Stan again and leads him outside through an alternate exit. At the edge of the bayou, he orders him into the water "to find peace." René arrives in time to pull Stan from the water. The captain and his deputy chase Belnap on foot and shoot him dead. (The climax of *Fear in the Night* included a car chase. A slight clumsiness in continuity shows Belnap's escape car, a 1940's model, metamorphose into a different 1930's model when it veers off the highway, crashes through the brush, and overturns. Maybe Shane thought the foot chase would reduce the chance of technical error. In any case, the sequence was certainly less expensive to film.)

In the end, Stan and René join Sue at a nightclub where Stan's orchestra is performing. Stan explains that, because he killed the man in self-defense, he will be acquitted at the upcoming inquest. He steps up to the bandstand where Gina is singing. The conductor (Billy May) hands him his clarinet to finish out the song with the group.

Alongside *Fear in the Night*, this plot summary sounds very familiar. It should be expected, since both films are based on the same Woolrich tale of an innocent man tormented by guilt for a crime he fears he committed, and obsessed with substantiating that guilt so he can make peace with his conscience. We still see, on the surface, the *noir* notion of the fated individual deprived of his free will and controlled by an external force that determines his actions.

Despite the retention of so much plot material from the earlier screenplay, this second film diverges in several ways not only from *Fear in the Night* but also from Woolrich's story. Some plot changes are evident, like the renaming of the characters, or New Orleans replacing New York as the setting for the action, or Grayson being a musician instead of a bank clerk. And some differences are tonal. The earlier film has at times a surrealistic quality, true to Woolrich's vision of a murky, drug-infected world defying logical cause-effect relationships. The remake tries to tighten up the logic, make this *noir* world more realistic and perhaps more credible to the audience (which may have been one reason for Shane's remaking the film). But most significant is the thematic difference, due in part from these obvious changes but more so from the cumulative effect of many smaller alterations, the subtle refinements in the *way* Shane shoots his scenes and revises the subtext. What makes the films distinct from each other is how they integrate their subtexts with the main story, an achievement that differs in both content and quality.

While the subtext of *Fear in the Night* points to guilt from suppressed homosexual desires, the subtext of *Nightmare* deals with the internal strife of the creative artist whose sensitive, delicate temperament has difficulty coping with rejection. The subtext of *Fear* has already been discussed at length; the frequent allusions to homosexuality through innuendo and imagery strongly suggest that Vince has a subconscious reason for his guilt, beyond the conscious one of fearing that he killed a man. In *Nightmare*, however, Shane reshapes many of these same scenes to introduce a new subtext through dialogue and imagery. Revisions throughout the film, especially in the four scenes surrounding Vince's fainting spells and hypnotic trances, show that Shane deliberately abandons *Fear's* subtext so he can replace it with another. Because *Nightmare's* opening dream sequence imitates that of *Fear in the Night*, Stan's behavior under hypnosis still carries potential homosexual implications, but events that follow in the rest of the film fail to reinforce this, so that any notion of guilt over homosexual desire evaporates.

Perplexed by his dream, Stan goes to his brother-in-law for help. The first time we meet René Bressard, he is renovating a boat, sanding it with an electrical sander — a more practical, masculine endeavor than Cliff's pastime of making dollhouse furniture in *Fear in the Night*.

After his first fainting spell at René's house, Stan's voiceover narration copies Vince's, but in the bedroom scene that follows, different camera work implies that his relationship with René is different from Vince's with Cliff. When Stan awakes, the camera shoots from his point of view, panning up René's robed figure much as it did Cliff's for Vince. This time, while moving upward, the pan retains an eye-level shot rather than a low angle, suggesting equality between the two men instead of the brother-in-law's dominance over him. Also, René's robe is not garish like Cliff's. Its dark, subdued color is more masculine. In their conversation that follows, Stan stands up and the camera shoots a series of angle-reverse-angle shots as the characters talk. Their parallel positions continue to stress their equality. The separate shots make this a far less intimate scene than the quiet tableau in *Fear* where Cliff sits on the bed, a dominant position above Vince who remains lying under the covers and appears more vulnerable and submissive.

Stan's faint at the police station is not very different from Vince's in the first film, but still lacks the previous homosexual implications. René's administering to Stan in their pietà position seems more literally a concern for Stan's well-being, without the homosexual undercurrent that appears in *Fear*.

This is also true for the end of the film where Stan falls under Belnap's hypnotic trance a second time. The scene is played out very similarly — Stan gives Belnap his gun, the phallic symbol exposed and offered to the homosexual lover, but again, because this is not reinforced with earlier implications, it cannot be interpreted in the same way it is for *Fear*. Instead, Stan shows a more literal submissiveness to the stronger will of another, even to the point where he agrees to kill himself. This, of course, is to find the peace he'd been searching for. His guilt was so strong that he had tried suicide once before, so Belnap has no difficulty suggesting this second attempt.

The significance of the two suicide attempts in *Fear in the Night* is that each is accompanied by an implied homoerotic sex act. The first occurs when

Cliff rescues Vince from his window ledge. He pulls Vince backward into the room so that Vince falls on top of him in the front-to-back position for anal intercourse. The second one occurs when Cliff saves Vince from drowning by pulling him from the water and then straddling him from behind to give him artificial respiration. *Nightmare* nullifies these homoerotic connotations by treating the two events more literally. In Stan's first suicide attempt, René rescues him by dragging him into the room and dropping him to the floor — no homoerotic embrace, no sexual implications. In the second episode, when René saves Stan from drowning, he hoists him onto the pier and sits beside him, again without additional suggestions. Water in both films serves as a figurative purification, so that when Vince and Stan say they feel "all right," they are saying they are cleansed of their guilt. In *Nightmare*, this carries unambiguous meaning, unlike in *Fear*, where the implication is that he accepts his homosexuality and can cope with it.

Shane's astounding feat in shooting *Nightmare* is that, even though he retains much of the plot he had adapted for *Fear in the Night,* he creates an entirely new subtext with an entirely new thematic intent. It is remarkable how he saw in Woolrich's material this potential for chimerical thematic treatment, and still more remarkable that he was able to execute it so effectively.

The new subtext deals with the fragile ego of the artist, his attempt to present his art in progressive, innovative ways, and his difficulty in coping with rejection. The subtext is first implied when, after waking from his dream and discovering physical evidence that it occurred in reality, Stan looks out his window over the city of New Orleans and says in a voiceover: "Out there everything was status quo. The hassle was in here — with me." Different from *Fear*, where Vince sees the same diner, the same people, and the same traffic, Stan's reference to the "status quo" and the "hassle" within himself carries different implications.

It isn't until much later in the story, when Stan tells René in flashback about events on the night of his dream, that the significance of this expression becomes clear. In the flashback, Stan's band has just finished for the night. Stan prepares to leave with Gina when bandleader Billy (Billy May) gives Stan the bad news that, tomorrow at the recording session, they'll record the old charts. When Stan angrily questions him, Billy and several other musicians say that Stan's charts aren't "commercial enough" and are "too far out." Billy adds, "If the public can't hear the melody, you're dead, D-E-D, dead."

What the subtext implies is that Stan is a progressive musician, breaking with traditional approaches to music and trying to offer something new. While Vince in *Fear* represents Everyman, Stan may be said to represent Every Innovative Artist. The "status quo" is the familiar, the comfortably recognizable that we all get used to. The progressive artist introduces change that distorts our familiar world, transforms it, upsets our perspective on it, and forces us to learn all over again how to approach it. Progress is not bad, just disruptive, and it almost always meets with resistance by those who want to cling to the old and the familiar. When Billy and his musicians talk of "commercial" value, this is what they mean, that their music has to appeal to the public by its very familiarity. Music that is "too far out," or "outré," or "avant-garde" will not sell, a consequence already proven by precedence.

Stan, buoyed with artistic energy and anticipating success for his musical creations, is tightly wound up. Artists are, supposedly, by their nature sensitive and emotional and Stan's character is built on this stereotype. His fainting spells (misperceiving nail polish for blood, reacting to the photos of the murdered couple), his swooning (during Deputy Torrence's description of Mrs. Belnap's murder), and his quirky susceptibility to hypnosis indicate a hypersensitized artistic temperament. When René returns to the Belnap mansion for evidence to prove how Belnap manipulated his brother-in-law, one of the books he takes a special interest in is Freud's study on hysteria. Obviously, he knows this applies to Stan.

A six-note musical phrase from the dream continues to haunt Stan. At the Belnap house, when Gina accidentally elbows the speed control on the phonograph and slows down the record, Stan recognizes it as the music from the dream, simply an "old" tune played at a slower speed. This, too, suggests a contrast between conventional and progressive music. To the innovative artist, conventional music is "old" and obsolete; the innovative artist is always stretching the envelope, creating, looking for new ways to express ideas through his medium.

Nightmare's shift in setting from New York City to New Orleans contributes to the subtext, more through association than through any definite imagery or action. Being the reputed birthplace of jazz, it is a symbol of artistic (musical) progressiveness. When Stan makes his rounds through the nighttime city in search of the name of the haunting melody, he is traveling through a labyrinth, seeking an answer that would not help him even if he found it. The name of the tune means nothing; what counts is the context, which is why the revelation at the Belnap house means more than any answer he could have got from one of his musician friends.

The ending of the film carries some ambiguous notions. When he takes his place on the stage behind Gina, he returns happily to playing Billy's "corny" tunes, not the new ones he has written. This suggests that, like the moment on the pier after René saves him and he feels "all right," he has found peace because he returns to the bandstand to "fit in." It is as if the only way one can push the internal "hassle" aside and find serenity is by conforming to convention, joining the "status quo." (Ironically, the very next film that Kevin McCarthy stars in, the science-fiction *noir* thriller *Invasion of the Body Snatchers*, delivers an identical message about conformity and individuality.)

Stan's characterization as a sensitive, innovative artist may be another reason Shane remade *Fear in the Night*. This earlier film received some critical recognition, but may have lacked popular appeal, since it is seldom ever shown, unlike *Nightmare*, which still gets occasional playing time on television. A couple of years after Shane made *Fear in the Night*, *The Fountainhead* (1949) debuted, a collaboration between writer Ayn Rand and director King Vidor. The film isn't *noir*, but does exhibit some *noir* qualities in tone and expressionistic imagery. The story espoused Rand's insistent philosophy about the prerogatives of the creator who contributes more constructively to a society than the milling collective who depend on the creator for breakthroughs and progress in all fields of endeavor, art, medicine, technology, and so on. The subtext in Shane's *Nightmare* indicates he may have been influenced by Rand's philosophy (either having read her book or seen the movie in the meantime). For one thing, the subtext deals with the same material, the progressive artist frustrated by an unimaginative, conventional society. For another thing, Shane may have thought of himself as the frustrated artist. *Fear in the Night* contains some artistically daring shots (a flashback of the dream in the mirrored room matted onto Vince's eye sockets, expressionistic uses of the camera and special effects to imply loss of consciousness, a surrealistic tone to the film) which make it a more "progressive" film than the more conventionally shot *Nightmare*. Perhaps Shane saw himself as Rand's protagonist, Howard Roarke, but then felt the need to tell his story in a way that would give it more popular appeal. This had been done before by more noted directors. Consider Orson Welles, for instance, who discarded his extravagant allegorical style and distinctly personal approach to try to direct a film that would cater to more conventional tastes. The result was *The Stranger* (1946), a satisfactory film but not as intriguing or dynamic as most of his more critically disputed work. (Ironically, Welles, like Shane, relied on the same popular star, Edward G. Robinson, to garner box-office appeal for his "conventional" film.)

Shane's use of the musical motif in *Nightmare* enables him to treat the story from the artist's perspective and so develop his theme around progressiveness versus stasis. This musical element resonates with some of the flavor of Woolrich's "Dark Melody of Madness" (first published in *Dime Mystery*, July 1935, and known widely by its later title "Papa Benjamin") and one wonders if Shane is familiar with it. Woolrich's story deals with a similar issue, a New Orleans musician seeking a new, original kind of sound to market to the public. The overlap is faint but obvious enough to seem more than mere coincidence. Shane employs a few devices to imply the surrealistic world of *noir*, such as the ceiling fan in Stan's room, its blades casting shadows that rotate across the wall and ceiling junctures and appear distorted and broken, like the crooked legs of a menacing spider. But *Fear in the Night* carries a much stronger surrealistic atmosphere, and to differentiate the tone of his new film, Shane tries (not always successfully) to make events appear more logical, make the characters appear more realistic. Stan's artistic temperament gives him a more logical reason for his hypersensitivity instead of it being simply a personality trait as it is for Vince (although it works well enough as a character flaw).

One new scene inserted in the later film is Stan's journey through the nightlife of New Orleans jazz bars. His picking up Madge and taking her home suggests his willingness to cheat on Gina, a kind of "progressive" behavior that ignores the expected convention of faithfulness. However, when he sees the face of Mrs. Belnap in the mirror, he is reminded of the murder and runs away. Guilt and doubt over a murder is too overpowering for him. Yet another implication is that, subconsciously, he may feel guilty for cheating on Gina and cannot go through with it. Still another suggestion is that he cannot have sex with this woman because he is impotent, that he is willing to cheat on Gina, but cannot carry it out. (The notion of homosexuality is too faint to be considered.) Impotence is reinforced in other scenes where he rejects Gina at moments of potential intimacy — on the picnic, or in his flashback, after he indignantly stalks off alone because Billy will not record his charts.

Arguably, *Fear in the Night*, for its more fully developed and coherent subtext and its more interesting ambiguities, is the better film. *Nightmare* is good, and Bob Porfirio, in Silver and Ward's *Film Noir*, considers it superior to *Fear*, but I believe Leonard Maltin's rating is more accurate in that the predecessor just edges out the later work. Even so, *Nightmare* deserves praise for the commendable performances from its ensemble cast and for the imaginative and slick way the director incorporates fresh thematic ideas within the framework of a nearly identical narrative vehicle. Quite a remarkable achievement.

The Black Curtain

Novel, first published by Simon & Schuster, June 1941. Grosset & Dunlap, 1942. Mercury, first digest pbk, #64, 1943. Books, Inc., Midnite Mysteries Series, 1944. Dell, first standard pbk, #208, 1947. Ballantine, pbk, #30490, 1982.

If we have a conscience, we house private demons. Guilt, at its worst, can haunt us like the Erinyes, the Greek Furies disrupting our peace of mind, keeping us from "the innocent sleep, / Sleep that knits up the ravelled sleave of care, /The death of each day's life, ... /Balm of hurt minds..." (*Macbeth* II.ii.35–38). Time may obscure the details, making us uncertain of exactly *how* we sinned, but we forever carry with us the nagging feeling that we *did*. The urge overtakes us to reclaim the past and relive that situation, to learn the truth, to understand our precise role in the illicit act, to see whether we are as culpable as we remember. Our great desire is to discover that we are not as blameworthy as we thought, that our sin is not so heinous, that we are innocent after all and can finally dispel our demons.

The Black Curtain dramatizes this conflict between our fearful guilt that we may have sinned and our compulsive need to know the truth.

The Black Curtain is Woolrich's second suspense novel. His first, *The Bride Wore Black*, had garnered a generous amount of critical acclaim, and Woolrich, perhaps hoping to capitalize on the sudden recognition of his return to writing novels, may have turned out his next work in haste. *The Black Curtain* reads more like a potboiler, not as well crafted as its predecessor. Logic, expendable in many a Woolrich story for the sake of mood, tone, tension, and pacing, suffers frequent lapses here, too many, that make the reader overly conscious of the forced and artificial nature of the narrative. Still, it's a Woolrich creation, and his *noir* style and imaginative, tortuous plot inventions overcome the strained credibility enough to make the story captivating in other ways.

Instead of the episodic structure he used for *Bride*, he chose to write *The Black Curtain* in a more conventional format where a single initial action triggers the subsequent chronological series of events. A young man, Frank Townsend, buried beneath debris that has cracked off from a derelict building, is disinterred by passersby. Having suffered no apparent physical injuries, he is surprised when a boy hands him the hat that had fallen from his head, the headband bearing the unfamiliar initials "D.N." He returns home to find his wife gone and their apartment mysteriously vacant. Mrs. Fromm, the janitor's wife, recognizes the former tenant and directs him to his wife Virginia's new address. ("Fromm" sounds like a possible allusion to Edith Wharton's Ethan Frome, another character who disappears and is believed dead, but who returns after a long hiatus.) Now using her maiden name Morrison, Virginia tells Townsend that he had disappeared suddenly three years ago. Obviously, he had suffered amnesia, perhaps from a blow to the head. His recent accident restored his memories of his former existence without giving him any recollection of the deviant life he lived up until now. This revelation is shocking enough, but when he spies a strange man following him, he infers that, during the years of his dark void, he must have done something criminal.

He returns to his previous job and his mundane routine. He quits, however, when he spies an unknown man relentlessly stalking him. One night, several men, led by the stalker, lay siege to his apartment. Townsend escapes with Virginia, sends her to her mother's for safety, and sets out by himself on a quest to uncover those missing years.

He begins by renting a room on Tillary Street, where the building fragment had fallen on him. He wanders the neighborhood for several days, hoping someone will recognize him. Finally, someone does. When a fire emergency attracts a crowd, Ruth Dillon spots him among the onlookers. Ruth is a maid employed at the Diedrich estate; she knows him from when he worked there as handyman Daniel Nearing. Harry Diedrich was murdered and Nearing became the chief suspect. He escaped to Tillary Street where he was hiding out before the accident erased all memory of his connection to the killing.

Townsend strongly believes he is incapable of murder. He does not tell Ruth the complete truth, but retains his Nearing identity and persuades her to help him return to the scene of the crime so he can discover what actually happened and clear his name. Ruth stows him away in an isolated outbuilding on the estate. She visits him occasionally, bringing with her Emil Diedrich, father of the murdered man. The elder Diedrich, unable to speak and almost totally paralyzed, is wheelchair-bound. Whenever he is in Townsend's presence, he begins to blink frantically and Townsend soon realizes he is trying to communicate via Morse code. The old invalid had witnessed the murder and knows Townsend is innocent. Townsend (who luckily is versed in Morse code) transcribes Emil Diedrich's testimony, which implicates Alma, his son's widow, and William, his younger son, in the murder.

Despite Ruth's precautions, Alma guesses that Townsend is hiding on the premises and she and William lay a trap for him. Townsend discovers their treachery and counters their trap with one of his own. He alerts the police, telling them to arrive at the Diedrich house after he has walked into the trap and the culprits have exposed their guilt (a device that by now has become a convention in Woolrich's repertoire). But his ploy goes awry when William Diedrich overpowers him and prepares to kill him and Ruth. Diedrich wants to arrange it to look as if Townsend killed Ruth and he had to kill Townsend in self-defense. The unforeseen factor is Emil Diedrich, who, to rescue Townsend, sets fire to the house. With smoke filling the room, William flounders about, but manages to shoot and kill Ruth before he collapses from smoke inhalation. The police arrive in time to pull Townsend from the fire but too late for William and Emil Diedrich. Alma is arrested. Expected to testify later, Townsend is allowed to return to his wife and home where he can try to forget his tumultuous past.

With clever subtlety, Woolrich begins his novel not with the shock of a calamitous accident but with the subdued confusion of its aftermath. The result is an understated metaphor for an exhumation. Frank Townsend, after being buried beneath the rubble of a crumbling edifice, undergoes a kind of resurrection. This is quite fitting, the pseudonymous Daniel Nearing rising Phoenix-like from the ashes of decimated memories to the total recollection of his former identity.

Out of this rebirth, Townsend sets out on a quest not only to discover who he was during those blanked-out years but also to prove that he is innocent of any crime. His belief that he is incapable of murder is the premise he works from. In the Woolrich world, where Fate is capricious as a wind current, Townsend may or may not have been innocent. Fortunately for him, it turns out he knows himself well, for he did not commit the murder.

Woolrich establishes a plot pattern we will see time and again in his stories, the quest to verify innocence. Carol Richman in *Phantom Lady*, for example, and Alberta Murray in *The Black Angel* believe their convicted lovers are innocent of wrongdoing; they seek vindication by investigating other possible suspects and uncovering the guilty party. Townsend knows he is morally incapable of murder; his memory blunted, he must investigate his alter ego to prove his innocence to the police and himself. As variations on this theme, other Woolrich's stories explore different degrees of culpability. See "C-Jag" and "Nightmare" where drugs and hypnosis, respectively, are responsible for the protagonists' blackouts during which they may have committed a murder.

Townsend represents the moral man whose overzealous conscience will not let him find peace until he verifies his innocence, even in the face of damning evidence that he committed some grievous sin. Only by investigating his past can he determine the extent of his guilt. Exploring his former identity is like looking at a part of himself he did not know very well, a part that may have strayed from his moral sensibilities, a Hyde set free from the restraints of the upright Jekyll's conscience. Amnesia, like Jekyll's elixir, may have given him an excuse to commit a brutal, immoral transgression. However, what Townsend feels deeply about himself, that he is incapable of murder, proves correct. The implication (at least in this particular novel) is that, while every man has the potential to commit a crime (especially murder), his fundamental moral sense remains constant, intact. The good man and the bad man cannot abandon their core values; they live according to a personal, deeply rooted code that will determine most of their actions, even if the good man occasionally sins, or the bad man occasionally performs a good deed. Townsend replicates the likes of Lee Nugent ("Dormant Account") and Buddy ("The Boy Cried Murder") in that he is basically a good person who strays momentarily, enough to be punished for that indiscretion but deserving redemption in the end.

Yet even though Townsend is not capable of murder, we see also that, suggested in his relationship with Ruth Dillon, he is not a paragon of morality. As Daniel Nearing, he must have had attractive qualities that caused her to fall in love with him. She is a good woman, faithful, devoted, self-sacrificing—who becomes a wife-substitute. In several scenes, it is clear that they sleep together—this after Townsend has his memory back and knows he is married to Virginia. He knows he is committing adultery, yet may reconcile his unfaithfulness by claiming that the ends justify the means. Even so, besides betraying his wife, he is using Ruth unjustly, unethically, even immorally to satisfy his own purpose. Murder may be the greater crime, but Townsend's treatment of her reflects an unconscionable ability to compromise conscience and morals. Although he may appreciate her help in eventually vindicating him, it is at the expense of her life.

Virginia and Ruth, as doubles, signify his association with two alternate life styles. Married to Virginia and following a daily work and married routine, Townsend belongs to a traditional, conventional life style. With Ruth, however, he has an extramarital relationship that is both immoral and unconventional. This alternate life style seems as if it belongs in a dream, the man able to live a deviant life style without being held accountable in the real world. (Again, the Jekyll-and-Hyde theme: the good doctor plotting to keep his social reputation unblemished by assuming an unrecognizable alias that can freely surrender to his basest cravings.)

Amnesia becomes Townsend's excuse for living an alternate life style (reminiscent of the line oft spoken by comedian Flip Wilson when assuming his persona as the promiscuous Geraldine: "The devil made me do it."). Woolrich seems to be shifting the blame for social deviance to some outside source (fate, coincidence, fortune, predetermination, destiny), as if, under certain circumstances, a person can be deprived of free will while he strays from conscience-guided behavior to commit criminal, immoral, or perverted acts. For Woolrich, this becomes a conventional device, the emphasis not so much on *who* committed the crime as on *whether* a person is guilty of wrongdoing. In this respect, *The Black Curtain* bears obvious parallels with "C-Jag," "Morning after Murder," and "Nightmare." In addition, these stories represent Woolrich's way of exorcising his own demons, operating like a kind of cathartic gesture in helping him cope with his guilt, primarily over his homosexuality.

The epigraph Woolrich chooses from a Robert Browning poem sounds as if it were meant to be a favorable prognosis for anyone fearful about suffering from amnesia or some undesirable situation:

> If I stoop
> Into a dark, tremendous sea of cloud,
> It is but for a time.—I shall emerge one day.

The passage is allegorical and highly ambiguous. It contains a hopefulness dependent on faith in a resurrection, but a resurrection from what is unclear. The "dark, tremendous sea of cloud" can refer to ignorance, hardship, disrepute, or any number of obstacles, which the speaker knows can plague him only for a limited time. Eventually, fortune must reverse itself. The notion of a resurrection has religious connotations. Besides its relevance to Christ and Lazarus, it refers obliquely to one of the prominent Old Testament prophets, Daniel, whose name Woolrich gives to his protagonist. Daniel, of course, was an innocent cast into the lions' den, from which he eventually was saved — the same fate endured by Townsend/Nearing. New Jericho also reminds us of one of the oldest of biblical cities, the place where Townsend returns to find the beginnings of his other life and restore his confidence in himself.

With this epigraph (and others, such as at the beginning of *Waltz into Darkness* and at the start of each main section in *The Bride Wore Black*), Woolrich calls attention to his literary background and, perhaps, attempts to connect his writing to a loftier classical literary tradition. Already pointed out are Woolrich's frequent allusions to Shakespeare, particularly *Macbeth* with its nihilistic, fatalistic themes. In *The Black Curtain*, the murder mystery and Townsend's dilemma may resonate with a familiar Shakespearean plot: an ambitious man kills his brother in order to usurp his brother's wife, wealth, and position. Not only do William's murdering Harry and seducing Harry's wife allude to this famous predecessor, but Townsend's constant wrestlings with conscience also make him a kind of Hamlet for the pulp culture.

Film: Street of Chance

1942, Paramount. *D:* Jack Hively. *Assoc P:* Burt Kelly. *Cin:* Theodor Sparkuhl. *Ed:* Arthur Schmidt. *Mus:* David Buttolph. *Art Dir:* Hans Dreier, Haldane Douglas. *Assist D:* Alvin Ganzer.

Cast: Burgess Meredith (Frank Thompson), Claire Trevor (Ruth Dillon), Louise Platt (Virginia Morrison-Thompson), Sheldon Leonard (Joe Marucci), Frieda Inescourt (Alma Diedrich), Jerome Cowan (Bill Diedrich), Adeline deWalt Reynolds (Grandma Diedrich), Arthur Loft (Sheriff Lew Stebbins), Clancy Cooper (Burke), Paul Phillips (Schroeder), Keith Richards (Intern), Cliff Clark (Officer Ryan), Ann Doran (Miss Peabody, secretary), Sonny Boy Williams (Newsboy), Edwin Maxwell (District Attorney Stillwell), Helen MacKellar (Mrs. Webb, landlady), Gladden James (Mr. Clark, Thompson's boss), George Watts (Proprietor of pawnshop), Milton Kibbee (Barber), James C. Morton (Bartender). 74 min.

The Black Curtain (1941) / Street of Chance (1942)

Although Hollywood had adapted several of Woolrich's stories before now (*Children of the Ritz, Manhattan Love Song*, and "Face Work"), *Street of Chance* is his first suspense novel adapted during the classic *film noir* period. As one of the earliest examples of *noir*, it is a respectable effort, establishing trends in motifs, theme, tone, camera angles, and lighting. Its central plot device, amnesia, is especially noteworthy because it becomes an important convention used in subsequent *films noirs*, such as *The Blue Dahlia* (1946), *Somewhere in the Night* (1946), *The Scarf* (1951), and *Man in the Dark* (1953). Most fascinating is how amnesia raises implicit existential questions: a character is automatically forced to search for a lost identity and, usually concomitant with the quest, must determine culpability for his or her actions in that other forgotten existence, which had been independent of, and uncontrolled by, the presently defined self.

Superficially, *Street of Chance* adapts the general thread of Woolrich's original plot. Then, as with many films adapted from mystery novels, it alters the ending so that mystery aficionados who have read the book will be surprised by a new solution to the crime. (Compare, for example, Maurice Tourneur's *The Leopard Man*, adapted from Woolrich's *Black Alibi*.)

Like the novel, the film begins on Tillary Street (the locale inspiring the new title) where Frank Thompson (Burgess Meredith, renamed from Woolrich's Frank Townsend) is knocked down and nearly killed by concrete debris falling from a building under demolition. Thompson goes through a similar ordeal as Townsend. He is confused to learn that his wife Virginia (Louise Platt) has moved from their apartment and reverted to her maiden name, Morrison; he realizes that he has suffered amnesia for over a year (rather than the three-plus years in Woolrich's novel); he escapes pursuit from unknown assailants (who turn out to be the police led by a tenacious Joe Marucci, played by Sheldon Leonard); he sends Virginia off to the safety of her mother's house while he returns to Tillary Street to pick up the trail back to his blank past.

The story begins to tread its own path after Ruth Dillon (iconic *femme noire* Claire Trevor) spots Thompson among the crowd watching a neighborhood fire. Whereas Woolrich's Townsend had ambivalent sentiments for Ruth (he uses her, but feels a sincere attraction to her), the film's Thompson consistently retains his distance, often diverting Ruth's romantic advances.

While Ruth goes out for groceries, Thompson rummages through her bureau drawers and finds newspaper clippings that describe the stabbing murder of Harry Diedrich. He learns that his alias, Daniel Nearing, is suspected of the crime. Without revealing his true identity, he declares to Ruth that he knows himself too well to believe he could murder anyone. He convinces her to return with him to the Diedrich estate to solve the mystery.

At the estate, Thompson meets the paralyzed mute Grandma Diedrich (Adeline deWalt Reynolds, replacing the novel's elderly invalid, Emil Diedrich), whom he learns to communicate with by having her blink yes and no answers to his questions. After several interrupted meetings, he finally gets her to eliminate Diedrich's wife Alma (Frieda Inescourt) and brother William (Jerome Cowan) as suspects. Just when his greatest fear is realized, that he may be the murderer, Ruth walks into the bedroom, and the horror on Grandma Diedrich's face tells him he is confronting the killer. Thompson tells Ruth the truth, that he had been suffering from amnesia and is really married to Virginia Morrison. She goes downstairs and takes a gun out of her purse. Thompson fears she intends to kill herself, until she points it at him. He wrestles with her and the gun goes off, mortally wounding her. Marucci happened to be lurking outside the house all this time. He witnesses the final altercation and overhears Ruth's confession. (Borrowing a page from Woolrich: the cop who just happens to be nearby when the murderer confesses and vindicates the protagonist.) To console her, Thompson tells her that he lied about being married. Ruth dies in his arms and Marucci walks out of the house, no longer interested in arresting Thompson because the case is closed.

Street of Chance toys with the same existential theme as Woolrich's book: if a man is defined by his actions, to what extent is he liable for actions he performs outside his control. Thompson, like his counterpart Townsend, feels confident enough to know that, no matter what his former identity, he was still fundamentally the same person, a person who could not murder. The quest starts out as a search for vindication, but because he cannot be sure of his culpability until he has definite proof, the quest has the essence of a trial by ordeal, the search functioning like a ritual of expiation, a cathartic process.

Although not as meaningful as the book's initial image of Townsend's exhumation, the film's opening accident where Thompson is nearly killed is more dramatic. Both incidents contain the same basic implication: the catastrophe is a catalyst that enables him to make the transition from his amnesiac existence to his former reality. Both events also establish one of the key motifs of the story, the paradox of a living death.

Thompson is reborn from a kind of death, reborn to the life that was dead to him as a result of his amnesia. (We never learn what caused his amnesia in the first place; maybe it isn't necessary, but the circumstances might have contributed substantially to the story.) The film implies this by showing a close-up of Thompson lying unconscious on the ground, then fading to black. A fade-in from a subjective low-angle shot shows a circle of people staring down at Thompson (and us). At first their images are blurred; then they gradually come into focus, signifying Thompson's waking from his stupor. Quickly, a series of incongruities leave him baffled and disoriented because the reality he returns to is not the reality he remembers. His hat bears another man's initials; he finds himself in a part of town foreign to him; his apartment has been vacated; and his wife has not only moved away but is using her maiden name. It is as if he had died, or had never married, or had never existed at all.

Another way of looking at this is that Thompson is born into a world of corruption (the decrepit buildings, the squalid neighborhood). He may at first assume innocence, like a child, but inklings of guilt surface when he notices a complete stranger eyeing him. He runs when the stranger menacingly pursues him. He must be guilty of some wrong to be so aggressively sought. The story then turns into a quest to absolve the self of guilt by returning to that former time and finding proof of innocence.

Marucci appears sinister, behaving more like a criminal than a cop, which misleads us (as Agate Eyes does in Woolrich's novel) to think that Thompson, in his amnesiac state, must have been involved with gangsters in some illegal activity. The nature of that activity never manifests itself and Thompson's three subsequent dream scenes involving Marucci reflect a conscience troubled by vague guilt. While in his office, working on his ledger at his desk, Thompson's mind begins to wander and Marucci's face suddenly appears, superimposed over the ledger, the image moving forward from a medium shot to an extreme close-up, the menacing visage intensified as it closes in on Thompson. When Thompson leaves work, Marucci is waiting. Thompson eludes him in a taxi, but Marucci runs him down. The door is locked, so he pulls out his gun, hammers on the window with the butt end, and cracks the glass. Later at home, while looking out his window, Thompson relives the scene, seeing the event played out on the darkened glass like a movie but with the image reversed. The third dream occurs when, sleeping in bed that night, Thompson tosses fitfully from a nightmare (not shown to us) and wakes up. Fortunately, after waking up, he looks out his window and sees Marucci and his squad about to raid his apartment. Marucci, then, like Agate Eyes (Townsend's term of endearment for the relentless, nameless cop who stalks him), is a surrogate for the Erinyes, the pitiless juggernaut that harasses the conscience and drives the individual to hysteria.

The labyrinth becomes a key image in many a *film noir*, and *Street of Chance* helps establish its significance. When Marucci leads the sortie on his home, Thompson wakes his wife and they escape to the roof. The flight from the security of their familiar surroundings to the foreboding surrealistic, geometrical configurations on the rooftops indicates the desperate measures one will take to escape one's persecuted conscience. (Significantly, the idea is taken directly from Woolrich, although Woolrich has his characters *descend* into a labyrinthine basement for their escape.) Later, Thompson's return to the Diedrich estate suggests that he either enters another labyrinth or perhaps descends into the underworld. If the latter, then mythically, he resembles Ulysses or Aeneas who resorted to the dead for answers to their questions. Grandma Diedrich is like one of the shadows of the underworld. Mute and totally paralyzed, she represents a living corpse, more dead than alive, but able to communicate just enough finally to give Thompson the answer he seeks.

Mirrors become ubiquitous props in *films noirs* to signify duplicity or doubleness in characters or to suggest contradictions between reality and non-reality, truth and deception. *Street of Chance* employs mirrors to serve those purposes in several scenes. When Thompson first reads the newspaper clippings that inform him of Diedrich's death and his implication in the murder, he is facing a mirror. His doubled image suggests that there is a second side to him, the Danny Nearing personality that may be guilty of murder. We eventually learn that, although he has lived a double life, his doppelganger did not commit the crime. The use of the mirror to indicate duplicity is associated with Ruth. Twice while she prepares drinks at the bar, her image is visible in the mirror, suggesting the duplicitous nature of the *femme fatale* who has a side to her other than the innocent one she shows the world. And finally, Grandma Dietrich had witnessed Harry's death by seeing the murder reflected in the mirror near her door. That is, she did not see the murder itself, but the act once removed from reality. The significance of this is not totally clear, unless it relates to the story's doublings which show the difficulty in determining what is real and what is merely perceived as real. Nearing and Thompson as doubles raises questions about which of the two is the real personality. Also, there is the doubling of the two women, Ruth and Virginia, which leads to questions about who has the more legitimate claim on Nearing/Thompson.

Woolrich raises these same issues in his novel, but he defines the women differently from those in the film. In the novel, their difference depends on class, Virginia, middle class, and Ruth, lower class. Otherwise, they appear comparable as honest women sincerely devoted to their man. The film alters this. As a character, Ruth is made more devious, more self-serving — more clearly defined as a prototype of the *femme fatale* that will appear in future *films noirs*. Throughout the period, Claire Trevor will assume this role again and again, becoming the epitome of the good bad girl. After her outstanding performance as pariah-prostitute Dallas in John Ford's *Stagecoach* (1939), she will return to variations on this sympathetic character in later *noirs*, such as *Born to Kill* (1947), *The Velvet Touch* (1948), and *Key Largo* (1948), or reveal herself an outright Spider Woman, such as in *Murder, My Sweet* (1944).

By delineating the ethical/moral differences between the two women, director Hively variates Woolrich's idea and creates a moral dilemma for the male that will occur in future *noirs*: the man must decide between two worlds, one corrupt, one noble, as represented by the two women, the *femme noire* and the *femme blanche*. Both worlds hold a certain appeal, satisfy certain needs, but it is more the male's response to the temptress than to the virtuous, traditional female that determines the outcome. The corrupt or wayward choice is usually weighted with the promise of greater thrills, excitement, and pleasure, and the man either surrenders to it and suffers disastrous consequences, or resists it and wins redemption. Thompson finds redemption here, but there are numerous *films noirs* that incorporate this dilemma with bleaker results. Among some of the prominent ones are *Out of the Past* (1947), *The Paradine Case* (1947), *Pitfall* (1948), *Angel Face* (1953), and the color-*noir Vertigo* (1958) (the last an interesting variation in that the amorous but mundane Judy Barton and the seductive but aloof Madeleine Elster are the same woman with a different persona).

Coincidence is an integral part of most of Woolrich's stories. When

The Black Curtain (1941) / *Street of Chance* (1942)

Street of Chance— Thompson (Burgess Meredith) carries a flashlight to help him negotiate the labyrinth, but he remains in the dark about the motives of the wily female he trusts. Dependably duplicitous Claire Trevor, one of the archetypal femmes fatales, helped define that noir character (Paramount).

treated as an instrument of fate, it works adequately. Too often, though, he inserts it in some outrageous, heavy-handed way that weakens the plot because of its forced, artificial quality. In Silver and Ward's *Film Noir: An Encyclopedic Reference to the American Style*, Robert Porfirio notes that, in another sense, "it is this very weakness that helps develop the whole black and chaotic world that is unique to Woolrich and makes his narratives compatible to film noir" (271). Obtrusive and obnoxious as coincidence may be in a fictional narrative, it is that very element which often interferes with success and happiness in real life.

Street of Chance modifies Woolrich's use of coincidence. In Woolrich's story, Agate Eyes might have seen his quarry, but by stooping to tie a shoelace or happening to spot him first, Townsend manages to avoid him. These events, occurring while he is living with Virginia and carrying out his normal daily routine, are emphasized as coincidental. In the film, variations on these incidents occur while Thompson is scouring Tillary Street for evidence of his past. Coincidence is revealed more objectively, more offhandedly: the audience sees Joe Marucci walking past a striker's placard just as Thompson walks in the other direction on the opposite side of the sign; or Marucci looks in a barber shop for Thompson, just after the barber has lathered Thompson's face, so that neither notices the other. The film treats the motif with far more subtlety than the novel, and the objective nature of the events make them seem more natural, less contrived.

The film's revised title is a good substitute for Woolrich's original one. *Street of Chance* is fitting in that both Tillary Street and Chance are at the root of all the events in the story. Tillary Street is the portal between Thompson's two lives. Here, he *happens* to pass the wrecking site where loosened rubble falls on him and wakens him to his previous existence. And it is here that he returns and *happens* to run into Ruth, who guides him back to his life as Danny Nearing so he can redeem himself. Like Woolrich's story, the film is not concerned with how Thompson became Nearing, only that he lived an alternate existence that left him with inexplicable guilt. Such a revelation might have made the story feel more complete by explaining what chance circumstances could cause a man to lapse temporarily into a dark, clandestine life style that he would later erase from his memory.

Burgess Meredith gives a fine performance as the disoriented Frank Thompson. Already a proven professional with impressive roles in *Winterset* (1936) and *Of Mice and Men* (1939), he gives his character the right touch of sentimentality, perplexity, and desperation. His scenes with deWalt Reynolds reveal his tenderness, yet he can be cold and cruel, too, as he demonstrates by continuously spurning Ruth's romantic pleas. Then again, he reverses his feelings toward her when she is dying in his arms. What might have appeared as inconsistency or contradiction in his character Meredith is able to pass off as natural responses to different situations.

Adeline deWalt Reynolds' performance also deserves mentioning. For a woman who started acting in films in 1941 at the age of 78, she does a remarkable job. Playing the part of a mute paralytic, she is restricted to mouth, eye, and brow movements, yet she is able to express so much emotion that her face continually speaks without words. One haunting aspect of her performance is that it anticipates a similar role the quadriplegic Christopher Reeve will play in the television remake of *Rear Window*. (See the chapter on *Rear Window* for a discussion of this film.) Adeline deWalt Reynolds goes on to play small parts in some outstanding films, including *The Human Comedy* (1943), *Going My Way* (1944), and *A Tree Grows in Brooklyn* (1945). Her last appearance was in *The Ten Commandments* (1956). She died in 1961, one month shy of turning 99.

It is easy to overlook the character actors who appear from film to film and give solid performances every time. Jerome Cowan is one of these, an accomplished veteran of many *noirs*. His specialty is the "dignified scoundrel," the suave gentleman with something despicable hidden just below his refined exterior. Even when he is innocent, as he is in *Street of Chance* or *The Maltese Falcon* (1941), he still exudes a tinge of the detestable. In *Street of Chance*, this characterization suits the purpose of diverting attention away from the real murderer. His extramarital affair with Alma Diedrich, heiress of a quarter of a million dollars from her dead husband's estate, and his telling Marucci to "shoot first" if he sees Danny Nearing, all help to and make us suspect the illicit lovers as conspirators (which they are in Woolrich's story).

It is the outcome of *Street of Chance* that contains its ultimate *noir* essence. Ambiguity in the resolution, with contradictions in tone and outcome, give the film the uneasy, unclear, unsettling qualities that accompany the most interesting *films noirs*. The contradictions in Ruth's character, her devotion to Nearing countered by her selfishness in getting what she wants, make us ambivalent toward her. Although Thompson had just rejected her and declared his love for his wife Virginia, the pietá image of them on the floor, her lying dead in his arms, does not make us feel that the story has been totally resolved. The mystery is solved: Marucci overhears Ruth's confession and Thompson can go free. But he has just wrestled with her for the gun, and although it was an accidental death, he will still have to face some kind of charge in her death. Like Townsend in the novel, he will return to his former life, but it will not be the same. The experience, much like that of Alberta in *The Black Angel*, must change him permanently from the person he was before.

The amnesia motif of *Street of Chance* becomes a useful device in many subsequent *films noirs*. Besides setting up the did-he-or-didn't-he question that compounds the mystery, amnesia temporarily blocks out a past that has some influence on present events. Part of the mystery is finding whether that shrouded segment of a person's life contains a legitimate reason for his feeling guilty or offers the explanation for why he can claim innocence. *Spellbound* (Hitchcock, 1945), for instance, fits this category, where a man (Gregory Peck) suffers amnesia brought on by excessive guilt. He believes he killed a man, but the strain of emotional trauma causes him to banish the event from his memory. (Spellbound is discussed above with *Fear in the Night*.) *Mirage* (Edward Dmytryk, 1965), a post-*noir*, is directed by a German émigré known for his share of *films noirs*, so that this film cannot help but display the dark touches of that genre. Gregory Peck again finds himself in a similar situation as in *Spellbound*, where he believes he killed a man, then shuts out the memory because he cannot accept it. *High Wall* (Curtis Bernhardt, 1947) is a little different in that protagonist Robert Taylor, a former G.I., blacks out just as he is confronting his unfaithful wife and is not sure if he was the one who murdered her. His guilt depends on whether he was still able to act on his dark impulses despite the blackout, or it rendered him unconscious and immobile. The answer to this question becomes his quest.

Similar to *High Wall* in dealing with the post-war G.I. returning home to an unfaithful wife, *The Blue Dahlia* has an amnesiac character possibly guilty of murdering the wife of a cuckolded husband. Like Robert Taylor, Alan Ladd, the wronged husband, struggles to prove his innocence, with the difference that he knows he is innocent. It is his loyal buddy (William Bendix) who, as his alter ego, may have committed the crime, but the head trauma he suffered in the war affects his memory and he cannot remember exactly what happened.

Man in the Dark uses a variation on the amnesia motif in that the amnesia is "scientifically" induced. Edmond O'Brien is a hardened racketeer who undergoes a brain operation that activates his conscience. As a human being suddenly endowed with scruples, he is absolved of his previous crimes and becomes an acceptable member of society. However, his past, personified by his former cronies, comes to haunt him. No longer the ruthless criminal, he undergoes a trial in which he must adhere to his new ability to discriminate between right and wrong or revert to his old illicit life style.

In *The Scarf* (directed in 1951 by E.A. Dupont, an eminent icon from the German silent era), John Barrington (John Ireland) escapes from a mental institution for the criminally insane where he was incarcerated for strangling a woman. He finds refuge in the home of a philosophizing old hermit (Emlyn Williams). The fugitive explains how he had blacked out at the moment of the murder and cannot remember what actually happened (the same convenient alibi offered by the protagonist in *High Wall*); thus, his guilt becomes questionable. With the help of the hermit and an itinerant saloon songstress (Mercedes McCambridge), Barrington discovers that his best friend, the person he trusted most, in fact committed the murder and used Barrington's timely blackout to frame him. (This same antagonistic scheme links *The Scarf* to *The Secret Fury* and *Vertigo*.)

The role that amnesia plays in all of these films suggests how guilt is in some way associated with memory. When the past is revisited or events can be recreated and corroborated, the person may be able to redeem himself. Otherwise, he may have to depend on others' perceptions of his guilt, which may not always be reliable, accurate, or truthful.

"Rear Window"

Short story, originally entitled "It Had to Be Murder," first published in *Dime Detective*, February 1942. Reprinted under the same title in *The Saint Mystery Magazine*, Winter 1953. The title was changed to "Rear Window" for subsequent Woolrich short story collections and mystery anthologies, the first time in *After-Dinner Story* (1944) under the pseudonym William Irish. "Rear Window" appeared in *Ellery Queen's Mystery Magazine*, February 1969, and more recently in *The Cornell Woolrich Omnibus: "Rear Window" and Other Stories* (Penguin, 1998).

When it came to writing what is perhaps the most famous of all his works, Woolrich may have been inspired by a trivial incident in his own life. His autobiography, riddled as it is with unreliable authorial license, refers to an event early in his writing career. He was typing near an open window, and since the day was hot, he had his shirt off. Suddenly, from outside, he heard giggling. He noticed a couple of giddy teenage girls watching him from another window (*Blues of a Lifetime* 21). Francis M. Nevins, Jr., writing a considerably more reliable biographical account, believes that this experience may have given Woolrich the germinal idea for "It Had to Be Murder" (1942, renamed "Rear Window" two years later) (24). He notes also the incident's tenuous ties with another story of voyeurism, "The Boy Cried Murder" (1947). Looking further, we can see that Woolrich wrote a number of stories in which voyeurism plays a major or minor part, among them "Silhouette" (1939), "Momentum" (1940), and "The Light in the Window" (1946). Having a character observe and then interpret what he sees, right or wrong, for good or ill, is a useful device enabling Woolrich to create doubt, conflict, suspense, and irony.

The year before the publication of "It Had to Be Murder," another Woolrich short story appeared in *Detective Fiction Weekly*. "He Looked Like Murder" (1941, later renamed "Two Fellows in a Furnished Room") tells how a man stumbles onto assorted bits of evidence that implicate his roommate in the murder of a young woman. A character's compiling fragmented clues to prove the guilt of a suspect is the same plot device used in "It Had to Be Murder." In fact, before the stories were retitled, their original titles could have been easily interchanged. Woolrich seemed to like the formula of the 1941 story so much that he rewrote it as a variation on that theme, the second time placing the protagonist and suspect in separate rooms and arriving at an opposite conclusion. While "He Looked Like Murder" is a fine Woolrich story, "It Had to Be Murder" is a far superior example of his writing abilities. The narrator's circumspection about human nature, the internal logic of the plot, and the ambiguous ethics of voyeurism make the story an exceptional reading experience.

The Woolrich story line: A man, Hal Jeffries, is confined to his bedroom and takes an interest in the comings and goings of his neighbors. His is one of several houses whose backsides share a quadrangular area, and from his rear window he can glimpse into their windows for brief tableaux of their lives. A shameful voyeuristic pastime, he admits, but a way to pass the hours. Among his specimens-under-glass is a "young jitter-couple," two newlyweds who rush out of their apartment every night of the week looking for entertainment they cannot find at home. Another is a single mother who tucks her daughter into bed each night before going out to seek a less savory sort of pleasure, only to return at dawn, haggard and pathetic. The voyeur quickly dismisses these neighbors, however, to follow the one attracting most of his attention, Lars Thorwald, who, he suspects, has murdered his wife.

While observing Thorwald over several days, Jeffries puts enough scraps of information together to conclude that he must have done away with Mrs. Thorwald. Although he feels definite in his suspicion, Jeffries' argument is based on only partial evidence, and his friend Boyne, a police detective, remains unconvinced. Jeffries decides to force Thorwald to expose his guilt. First, to whet Thorwald's curiosity, Jeffries plays on his guilt by phoning him and telling him he knows what he has done. He sets up a phony meeting to get him out of his apartment. While Thorwald is gone, Jeffries sends his houseman Sam into his flat to disturb a few things, hoping to make the suspect frantic enough to admit his crime. But when Jeffries phones him again later, Thorwald, defensive at first, suddenly realizes which of his neighbors is harassing him. Carrying a gun, he sneaks into Jeffries' house to kill him. Boyne arrives in time to interrupt Thorwald's assault. Thorwald leaps out of Jeffries' open rear window and runs back to his apartment building. He climbs the fire escape to the roof from where he sprays shots at police. One bullet even goes through Jeffries' window. Boyne shoots him and he falls from the roof to the ground.

Boyne explains how he arrived in time: he discovered that Thorwald's wife, who was supposed to be away on a vacation, was actually his lover-accomplice. He was coming to take Thorwald in for questioning. Later, after everyone has left, Sam announces the arrival of Doctor Preston who has come to take the cast off Jeffries' broken leg. This final revelation abruptly explains Jeffries' confinement and his preoccupation with watching life going on outside his rear window.

As *noir* fiction, "Rear Window" depends heavily on the story's primary point of view, a first-person narrator with a cynical, fatalistic attitude, sharing his thoughts in a style that is direct, hard-bitten, and often curt, a tone reflective of most *noirs*. Hal Jeffries makes one statement that is central to his story and to *noir* in general. While looking through his rear window at the routine behavior and predictable idiosyncrasies of his neighbors, he observes: "The chain of little habits that were their lives unreeled themselves. They were all bound in them tighter than the tightest straitjacket any jailer ever devised, though they all thought themselves free" (8).

Stylistically, the word choices connote meanings that reinforce *noir*'s ideology. "Bound," "straitjacket," and "jailer" obviously point to constriction and imprisonment, countering the pretentious belief that humans have free will. Freedom is an illusion, since habits, routines, and customs, monotonous behavior patterns, indicate self-imposed strictures. "Unreeled" contains some subtly profound implications: humans are equated with a lower life form; they adhere to the delusion that they are free, when actually they are hardly more than fish, hooked on a line controlled by some master fisherman who can pay out the line or reel it in whenever he wants. Perhaps, too, the word alludes to the Fates who control the life-threads of every human and can extend or cut them at any time according to their fancy. Life is more fragile and tenuous than we would like to believe.

The tonal quality of *noir* is usually tainted with a cynicism about human nature and life in general. Such a tone permeates "Rear Window" in the narrator's introspective comments about the stagnant, sullen, desperate world around his quadrangle. Jeffries typifies the modern anti-hero, the *noir* protagonist living in the dismally corrupt, industrialized city, who separates himself from the worst of it enough to retain some integrity, but not enough to avoid partial contamination. Like Philip Marlowe and Sam Spade, he interests us as much for his flaws as for his virtues.

Some of that cynicism is reflected in his abrupt dealings with Sam, his houseman. Jeffries may claim he respects him for his long years of service and may show concern when he sends him to trespass on Thorwald's apartment, but he still talks to him condescendingly. His fear of being unable to help Sam if Thorwald finds him burgling his apartment is touching, but the plan is his and putting Sam in harm's way for the sake of proving his point to Boyne seems more self-serving than considerate. At the same time, Thorwald's guilt, up to this point, has not been confirmed. If Thorwald were found innocent, Jeffries' action could be classified as criminally invasive, totally irrational, and even marginally paranoid. He had no right to trespass on his neighbor's domain to verify his own vaguely defined charge.

When Boyne asks him how he acquired his information, Jeffries evades the answer. If he could explain his behavior, if he could be more candid with Boyne about how he arrived at the conclusion that Thorwald killed his wife, he could show that his conscience was guilt-free in the matter. Instead, he knows he is doing something that deserves reprimanding—a consciousness signified by his urge to retire to the shadows of his room when Thorwald scans the quadrangle. There is no real justification for Jeffries' voyeurism; whatever guilt exists is not Thorwald's alone.

This is what gives the Jeffries character some degree of dimension, limited as it is. We may excuse his behavior because we identify with him, wonder along with him whether Thorwald killed his wife — maybe even secretly hope he did, just for the sensationalism of the crime — but it cannot be denied that what he is doing, illicit voyeurism, is wrong. Besides his sneaky way of getting Boyne to look into Thorwald's business, he presses him further, despite their friendship, trying to get him to violate the law by breaking into Thorwald's apartment for incriminating evidence.

However, we can admire Jeffries for his perspicacity. He has exceptional powers in drawing inferences about his neighbors, and especially about Thorwald. The logical train of thought sometimes seems forced, but consider what this means to the story and to our perception of the narrator.

When Thorwald arrives home that first night after the supposed killing of his wife, Jeffries observes:

> He didn't remove his hat. As though there was no one there to remove it for anymore. Instead he pushed it farther to the back of his head by pronging a hand to the roots of his hair. That gesture didn't denote removal of perspiration, I knew. To do that a person makes a sidewise sweep — this was up over his forehead. It indicated some sort of harassment or uncertainty. Besides, if he'd been suffering from excess warmth, the first thing he would have done would be to take off his hat altogether.

Since a person may wipe his forehead with the same gesture for any number of reasons, including an absentminded reflex, Jeffries' conclusion is remarkably naïve. However, so precise and vivid is his description of the gesture, laden too with a barrage of sinister implications, that he gives the mundane act a momentous weight that arrests us and makes us consider the possibilities. The interpretation, then, absurd though it may be, reflects the workings of the narrator's mind. He needs a startling diversion. He wants to discover an outrageous crime. He is a citizen of the city, influenced by its sordidness, and acquainted with its tendencies toward perversity. After all, he is a voyeur himself, and so he looks for someone to justify his perversion, someone with a perversion greater than his own. We may condemn Thorwald for his grievous atrocity, but we should not overlook Jeffries' "venial sin" either.

Jeffries never knew Thorwald or his wife. He even says how odd it is to hear Thorwald's voice for the first time after he has watched him for so long and has already determined his guilt. One irony is that, without knowing him, he cannot fully understand Thorwald's motives. Thorwald's extreme behavior at the end, his attempt to kill Jeffries and his futile shoot-out with the police, suggests a desperation and madness that give his character unfathomable dimensions. His last mad public acts transcend the private act of murdering his wife, and in the end he learns of poetic justice. But is it moral justice?

Although we receive all our information through the narrator, the Hal Jeffries character remains a curiously undefined character. His powers of ratiocination prefigure the likes of Rex Stout's Nero Wolfe, the detective who never (or nearly never) leaves his apartment to solve a case. So we perceive him as a theoretician, a logical, clinically-minded individual. His desire to have Thorwald arrested for his crime seems justified because a murderer should never get away with such a heinous deed. But Jeffries' quest borders on obsession, an almost irrational need to prove himself right in his speculations. He can try to justify his voyeurism as performed in the name of the law, looking to prove the guilt of a murderer, but his "indiscretion" precedes the murder, and if he had not been acting unlawfully in the first place, he would have known nothing of Thorwald's crime.

What Jeffries sees when he visually invades his neighbors' apartments are mere bits and pieces of lives, fragments that suggest how most people are in pursuit of one intangible, elusive goal: happiness. The young jitter-couple and the single mother represent the many people who succumb to the worst side of city dwelling, the pretentious, seductive side that substitutes glamorous veneer for substance. The teen-age newlyweds in the house directly across from him represent the unbridled exuberance of youth; totally free (or thinking they are, as Jeffries declares), they pursue happiness outside their dwelling. Little do they realize, if they cannot find happiness between themselves inside their home, they will not find it in dance halls and nightclubs. Their ritual of forgetting to turn off the lights each time they leave and then having to come back to shut them suggests irresponsibility; however, it is this irresponsibility of youth that is endearing and which most people would tolerate and not criticize. Even Jeffries admits that the newlyweds elicited "an inward chuckle" from him. Only when they move into the next stages of experienced adulthood and then parenthood will they be held accountable.

The single mother, in the house to the left of the jitter-couple, is at that stage. Jeffries feels something poignant when he watches her: "I'd see her put the child to bed, and then bend over and kiss her in a wistful sort of way. She'd shade the light off her and sit there painting her eyes and mouth. Then she'd go out. She'd never come back till the night was nearly spent. Once I was still up, and I looked and she was sitting there motionless with her head buried in her arms ... it used to make me a little sad." The vignette begs interpretation and Jeffries guesses she is a widow, an oddly euphemistic assumption, considering that there are other possibilities: she may be an unwed mother or divorcée. Maybe the poignant situation affects his judgment, but anything he — or we — concludes can only be surmise based on personal experiences and expectations, a highly individual and biased way of looking at the situation, not necessarily a recognition of the reality of it. Although she may be criticized for leaving her little daughter home alone while she goes out, we can only speculate on her motives: Is she simply on the prowl for an ephemeral evening of fun so she can forget her troubles, her loneliness? Or does she have some worthy long-range goal, seeking a husband for herself and a father for her child? Jeffries' "sad" response depends on how he interprets what he sees from a distance.

The lives of these two neighbors directly across from Jeffries become secondary when he shifts his voyeuristic focus onto the life of a third party, one more central to the story. Lars Thorwald lives on the fourth floor of a six-floor apartment building to the left of Jeffries' window and at a right angle to the houses on his street. Jeffries notes that the derelict building is being renovated, the sixth floor already completed and the fifth presently in a state of repair. Watching from his window, he also forms several hypotheses about the characters of the husband and wife and their relationship. Being home most of the time, Thorwald must have been unemployed, which was convenient since his wife appeared to be an invalid who needed his constant attention. Jeffries notes how he must have stayed up all of one night to tend to her, since even with the shades drawn, he could tell that the light was on. That circumstance, coupled with a subsequent one, where Jeffries notices Thorwald smoking a cigarette while giving all the rear windows facing the quadrangle a "peculiar, comprehensive, semicircular stare," starts him on his line of suspicious thinking. Thorwald, like his other two neighbors, seeks his happiness from an outside source, a girlfriend. He takes the most drastic measure of all, killing his wife to attain his notion of what happiness is supposed to be.

Although he describes only three households, Jeffries implies that he can see into more windows, that these three are merely representative of all the others. It is a microcosm of life, particularly city life, and it is a depressing, desperate, lackluster existence. His critical opinions of his neighbors make him appear above their mean existence, when in fact he is not in a position very much different from theirs. While the setting outside his window is highly constricted, Jeffries, inside, is restricted to his one upstairs room and has but a limited view from his bedroom window. That view reflects his narrow perspective: he can see only the rear windows, the less attractive view, the view associated with the unappealing seamy side of life, the secret side of life, the private world that most people want to keep hidden from others' prying eyes. House fronts are literally that, a "front," a protective façade, a pretense to insulate them against criticism and condemnation for what they do in their secret, private lives. (This same idea is well illustrated in Robert Louis Stevenson's *The Strange Case of Dr. Jekyll and Mr. Hyde*. The good doctor, his reputation perceived intact, leaves and enters by his front door; the corrupt Hyde, his hideous deformities signifying his demented soul, must always use the back door.)

Jeffries' vantage point is situated in the physical external setting; his comments, meanwhile, reflect his internal, psychological makeup, the gnarled perceptions of the cynical skeptic. Textually, Jeffries' speculations help sustain the suspense of the story, but they also emphasize the *noir* sensibility of the dark side of life. Jeffries cannot help but interpret Thorwald's actions negatively. He sees them from a tainted viewpoint, insists on emphasizing their criminal implications, even when Boyne counters with a possible positive (or at least neutral) interpretation.

Woolrich sustains suspense by having Jeffries continuously speculate on Thorwald's actions as to whether they reflect the common, everyday habits of an innocent man or the suspicious behavior of a guilty murderer. The narrator's internal debates become ours and we waver between certainty and doubt, his inconclusive inferences infecting us with the same uneasiness and a desire to learn the truth. We know what we know only from what he tells us he sees: he lacks intimate first-hand knowledge of the man and bases his opinions on mere fragments of actions, incomplete scenarios played out in the restricted perimeters of window frames. His inferences are the result of his interpreting gestures as symptoms of human nature. This is not new: Poe's Dupin and Doyle's Holmes have already set early precedents along this line, assembling whole solutions by amassing bits and pieces of evidence. But Woolrich's approach is different, more in reverse. Rather than simply using this method to explain the solution to the crime, the narrator takes us along with him step-by-step, letting events and speculations unfold together so that we feel the tension and doubts, and at times the horror and repulsiveness, as much he does. We are inside his head, a captive audience to his avenue of thought and his sordid conclusions.

Told from the viewpoint of a first-person narrator, the story is able to merge character with theme. The narrator's opinionated observations reveal something about himself (character), while his position as a voyeur is central to thematic implications (the consequences of voyeurism, the right to judge others, the placement of guilt, the question of innocence, etc.).

Hal Jeffries is a voyeur, admittedly so: "Sure, I suppose it *was* a little bit like prying, could even have been mistaken for the fevered concentration of a Peeping Tom. That wasn't my fault, ... my movements were strictly limited just around this time." Although he mitigates his sin by dismissing any perverse intentions, he is nonetheless guilty of a crime, even if a minor one. On this basis, he doubles Thorwald, who commits another, more serious crime. Because he turns out to be right, we may condone Jeffries' voyeurism, but it still raises ethical questions about his actions. His accusations are merely supposition and speculation based on fragments of information garnered from his observations of Thorwald and coupled with his estimate of human nature. To arrive at his conclusion, he would have to have a suspicious and cynical view of human nature to begin with. Such an attitude affects his perception and works Iago-like in his mind, making him accept "oracular proof" as conclusive proof ("It *had* to be murder," the original title) and setting him up for a potential downfall just as Iago did with Othello. Only the fact that his hypotheses turn out to be true saves him from humiliation and criminal charges.

Jeffries is a double of Thorwald; he says as much while watching Thorwald standing at his window and scanning the houses around the quadrangle: "Why is he so interested in other people's windows, I wondered detachedly.

And of course an effective brake to dwell on that thought too lingeringly clamped down almost at once: Look who's talking. What about yourself?" The narrator discounts the unethical aspects of his own voyeurism while assuming that Thorwald is "presumably" guilty of some greater crime. From his window, he plays the role of a judge, making decisions as to guilt or innocence of others without answering to his own culpability.

Through the narrator, we become aware that our limited perception in judging others may lead to awkward, if not outright dangerous consequences. Boyne's investigation initially proves that Thorwald is innocent. If this first finding had proved correct, Jeffries' accusation may have affected the reputations of both Boyne and Thorwald. But then the story takes a turn. Thorwald is guilty after all, a fact that validates Jeffries' voyeuristic intrusion. Yet even with this outcome — that is, the vindication of Jeffries' suspicions — the issue remains that perceptions are subject to personal bias and a limited comprehension of the facts, resulting in distortions of the truth and inaccurate evaluations.

In substance, the narrator's statement, voiced as if by one who stands removed from this kind of trite, repetitive behavior, makes him seem aloof from this "petty pace" of his neighbors. Yet, ironically, with his broken leg in an unwieldy cast, he is totally restricted not only to his room but also in his movements: he is limited to dragging himself from his bed to his chair and back to his bed. Thus, the narrator is no less subject to the vicissitudes of destiny than are his neighbors.

Nowhere is this more evident than near the end when Thorwald assaults and tries to kill Jeffries. Anticipating Thorwald's arrival, Jeffries positions himself in his chair by leaning sideways and situating the bust of some artist or philosopher where his head should be. (That Jeffries cannot identify the bust as that of Rousseau or Montesquieu is one of several hints about his lack of education and his disinterest in it.) It presents a false target for Thorwald who, fooled, shoots and shatters the bust. Jeffries, meanwhile, sidles out of his chair and gets pinned between chair and wall. Thorwald shoots again but misses. The police arrive and he has to flee. Even Jeffries admits he should have been killed several times. However, whether Thorwald was a poor shot, or was completely baffled by Jeffries' ploy, or was pressured by the sudden arrival of Boyne and the police does not make any difference. The outcome is out of Jeffries' hands and rests with Chance or Fate. As Jeffries himself already observed, free will and self-determination are human illusions. Some other agent — Fate, perhaps, or one of its incarnations, Chance, Destiny, or Providence — decides what will or will not be.

Film: Rear Window

1954, Paramount. *D:* Alfred Hitchcock. *P:* Alfred Hitchcock (uncredited). *Cin:* Robert Burks. *Sc:* John Michael Hayes. *Ed:* George Tomasini. *Mus:* Franz Waxman.

F/X: John P. Fulton. *Art Dir:* J. McMillan Johnson, Hal Pereira. *Set Dec:* Sam Comer, Ray Moyer. *Sound:* John Cope. *Costumes:* Edith Head.
Cast: James Stewart (L.B. "Jeff" Jefferies), Grace Kelly (Lisa Carol Fremont), Wendell Corey (Lt. Tom Doyle), Thelma Ritter (Stella), Raymond Burr (Lars Thorwald), Irene Winston (Mrs. Anna Thorwald), Judith Evelyn (Miss Lonelyhearts), Georgine Darcy (Miss Torso), Ross Bagdasarian (Songwriter), Sara Berner (Woman on fire escape), Frank Cady (Man on fire escape), Jesslyn Fax (Sculptress), Rand Harper (Newlywed husband), Havis Davenport (Newlywed wife), Benny Bartlett (Stanley, Miss Torso's boyfriend), Ralph Smiley (Carl the waiter), Iphigenie Castiglioni (Woman with bird), Kathryn Grant (Party girl), Marla English (Party girl), Jerry Antes (Dancer). 115 min.

If Cornell Woolrich has any name recognition with the general public, it is most likely because of Alfred Hitchcock's superb 1954 film adaptation of his 1942 short story "Rear Window." Although the film is a complete make-over of Woolrich's story, his original plot is clearly recognizable: a voyeur, watching the activities of his neighbors, comes to suspect that one of them has murdered his wife; the voyeur tries to trap him, but inadvertently traps himself in a near-fatal confrontation with the killer. Exceptional in its creative blend of suspenseful story, paradoxical characters, and *noir* tonality, the film is indebted to Woolrich for at least one crucial ingredient that makes possible the successful integration of all these other elements, namely an unpretentious yet uniquely conceived plot.

In his biography of Cornell Woolrich, Nevins admits that Hitchcock's adaptation raises Woolrich's story to a higher level with its more elaborately developed plot, characters, and themes. But the story pivots around that one key plot device, the voyeur who sits in judgment of others, confirming their guilt while condoning his own.

Hitchcock, following the schematic of Woolrich's original, develops a story that adheres remarkably close to the classical unities of action, place, and time. While the action involves a number of characters, the central mystery is intently focused on the dynamic created between protagonist L.B. Jefferies (James Stewart as the renamed film character) and suspect Lars Thorwald (Raymond Burr); even Jeff's relationship with Lisa (Grace Kelly), the more important story within the mystery, depends on Jeff's connection to Thorwald. As the conflicts between both Jeff and Thorwald and Jeff and Lisa develop and move toward resolution, so too do the complications in all the other windows within his view. The place, or setting, is confined to Jeff's room and the courtyard outside his window. Retained in the film is Woolrich's five-day, four-night time span, and although the story covers more than a single day (supposedly the ideal duration for unity of time), events progress in a clear, easy-to-follow chronological order that gives the semblance of "real" time. Action, place, and time, so acutely defined and limited, reinforce the confined and constricted nature of Jeff's life style that leads to his predicament.

Studies have already been proposed about the self-reflexive nature of Jeff's voyeurism, how it complements the very nature of movie-going, the audience in effect acting like voyeurs as they watch the actors play their roles, which, in the context of the film, are meant to be private and personal. Another self-reflexive consideration is that the film bears the earmarks of a film in progress. Jeff, sitting in his chair with his eye to a camera, judges the behavior of the "characters" in their "roles." He performs the function of a film director, playing Hitchcock's "alter ego" (Spoto, *Dark Side* 370).

That the film is a fiction contrived by a director manipulating events is further implied in the opening sequence. While the credits roll, the window blinds slowly rise on a view of the courtyard where much of the action will take place. The impression is that a curtain is rising on a stage play, a device Hitchcock used before in *Stage Fright* (1950) where a stage curtain literally rises on the opening scene. (This, of course, is not a Hitchcockian invention. Filmmakers have long used it as a self-reflexive device to telegraph certain themes, such as the difficulty in discerning the ambiguous line between fantasy and reality or the fatalistic notion that "all the world's a stage" and we are the players who "strut and fret" across it according to some manipulative power's pre-scripted plan.) The classical unities themselves lend a static, localized quality to the whole story and further contribute to the aura of a stage play.

The camera work immediately after the credits adds to this impression. The three windows are shown in a full shot. After the credits, the camera tracks in toward the middle window for a closer view of the rear façade of the apartment building directly across the courtyard. A cut to a high angle shot looks directly down from this middle window and shows a cat walking up a stone stairway. The camera follows the cat to the right, where it moves out of the frame. The camera continues its unbroken sweep, from right to left, of the surrounding apartments. We see the glass wall of the Composer's studio apartment; the Thorwald apartment directly across the way; Miss Torso's head and shoulders visible through her bathroom window while she takes a shower; a milkman walking down the alley, left, toward his truck; and the wall of the adjacent apartment building, perpendicular to Jeff's, before the camera comes to rest in a high-angle, extreme close-up of Jeff's face. He is asleep, his face dotted with beads of sweat, and his head situated near the sill of the middle window that just moments ago was empty when the camera dollied forward to begin its maneuver. We can assume that the circular pan operated as a diversion while the lead actor was wheeled into place to begin the story.

The most pronounced difference between Woolrich's short story and Hitchcock's film appears in the number of characters they use. Scenarist John Michael Hayes allows for far more characters, and defines and develops them in a complex network of interrelationships.

We learn more about the character of L.B. Jefferies at the film's outset than we ever learn about Hal Jeffries during the entire short story. The camera's pan of Jeff's apartment (a shot often studied and discussed) reveals many details of his life through wordless cinematic implication. Starting with a close-up of his face, the camera shows him asleep with his head near the open window.

The camera moves down his body to reveal that he sits in a wheelchair, his leg in a solid toe-to-hip plaster cast inscribed with the words, "Here lie the broken bones of L.B. Jefferies." From here, the camera glides left and pauses on a shot of a smashed camera lying on a table and, on the wall behind it, the black-and-white photo of a race car crashing and overturning, one of its tires flying through the air toward the foolhardy photographer. Next, the camera pauses on the framed photographic negative of a young woman, then moves slightly left to the negative's positive counterpart emblazoned on a magazine cover atop one of two stacks of magazines. The scene fades.

Condensed in this brief exposé is a wealth of information. From the inscription on the cast, we learn the main character's name. The damaged camera advertises his profession, and the photo on the wall hints that that flying tire had smashed the camera and was probably the cause of his broken leg. (This is confirmed in a subsequent scene where Jeff talks to Gunnerson, editor of the magazine he works for. He boasts how he risked his life to take that shot on the roadway: "You said you wanted something spectacular.") The young woman who appears in the framed negative and on the magazine cover is not Lisa (we later find out). In the finished photo, we see a beautiful, seductive woman in a black, low-cut evening gown (Lisa will make her entrance in a similar dress.). The two images suggest the duality of Woman, that as a romantic love interest, she has both a negative and positive influence on the object of her affection. (Peter Conrad, in his comprehensive reflections on Hitchcock's oeuvre, catalogs this dual image as a Manichean concept, Hitchcock signifying how the woman embodies the two opposing forces of good and evil.)

As the film progresses, the implications from these images contribute more incisively to the larger story. First, the fact that Jeff is a photographer makes him a voyeur by profession. His interest in the lives of his neighbors may be out of innate human curiosity, but it is also conditioned behavior from years on the job. Voyeurism is, if not a criminal act, then at the least an ethical taboo. As Jeff tells Lisa,

> Much as I hate to give Thomas J. Doyle [Wendell Corey, playing Jeff's detective friend] too much credit, he might have gotten a hold of something when he said that was pretty private stuff going on out there. I wonder if it's ethical to watch a man with binoculars and a long focus lens. Do you suppose it's ethical even if you prove he didn't commit a crime?

Lisa Carol Fremont, as Jeff's love interest, is an inspirational addition to Woolrich's story. She exposes dimensions of Jeff's character not even remotely considered in Hal Jeffries. She acts as a foil for Jeff, getting him to interact intimately with her while revealing paradoxes and flaws that make him a more real, multi-dimensional person than the nebulous Woolrich character.

Lisa's arrival in the story is enhanced by Hitchcock's creative and dynamic shot that highlights her character and conspicuously marks Grace Kelly for star status. (Compare similar high-gloss shots in other films, the close-up of

Claudette Colbert in *It Happened One Night* when she steps around the "Wall of Jericho" and the light creates a soft halo in her hair; or the entrance of John Wayne in *Stagecoach* when the camera zooms in from full shot to close-up after he fires his rifle and signals the stagecoach to stop.) Jeff is asleep in his wheelchair in his dark apartment. His faintly lighted face, in close-up, is darkened by a shadow that moves over him. He opens his eyes, turns his head, and after a brief moment, smiles vaguely. A reverse-angle close-up of Lisa shows her moving forward toward the camera, lips parting. A side view shows the two lovers in profile as she bends to kiss him. Her movements have a choppy, stuttering quality to them, as if affected by a strobe light. The visual effect emphasizes the poignancy of the meeting.

Yet there are paradoxes involved. The shadow hovering over Jeff forebodes something menacing while his smile alerts us that the threat is only illusory, fleeting. Like the framed negative and the magazine photo, the woman epitomizes two contradictory positions: she poses a threat, which, we soon learn, is as a marriage partner who may deprive him of his freedom; but she also satisfies his real need for a companion and lover. The film never resolves this dichotomy, even though the superficial "happy" ending gives the pretense that it does.

Jeff likes Lisa, maybe even loves her, but he wants to keep their relationship "status quo": that is, he wants to remain "friends" without yielding to her desire to marry and "settle down." He justifies his aversion to marriage with what he believes is clear logic: they embrace two extreme, irreconcilable life styles, she a gossamer society woman, an established member of the swank, upper-class Fifth Avenue set, he a rugged, uncouth, nomadic photographer. Beneath his overt rationalization lurk subliminal reasons for his reluctance to marry her. He may associate marriage with imprisonment and he fears being shackled by a permanent commitment or controlled by a woman who may dominate his life once they are bound by oath. He also intimates in his argument that his ego cannot tolerate marrying a woman who has and earns more money than he does. And there are even more serious implications of psychological perversions, like impotence. (His impotence is suggested in repeated ways throughout the film. There is, for instance, his passive position in the wheelchair, his inability to protect Lisa against Thorwald's attack, and his feeble, ineffective attempt to protect himself when Thorwald assaults him.)

Still, Jeff has definite feelings for her. He appears wounded when, after their argument, she gives the impression, while donning gloves and shawl and preparing to walk out the door, that she won't return:

LISA: Good-bye, Jeff.
JEFF: You mean good night.... Couldn't we just keep things status quo?
LISA: Without any future?
JEFF: When am I gonna see you again?
LISA: Not for a long time.... At least not until tomorrow night. (She leaves.)

The importance of Lisa's irate departure is in its timing. Jeff, hurt and confused, swings his chair around toward the window for a view of the blank, lifeless apartments overlooking the courtyard. Only Thorwald's windows are lit, though the shades are drawn. A sudden exclamation, a woman's desperate scream, "Eeee! Don't—!" is cut short with the sound of breaking glass. Jeff scans intently for the source of the outcry, but the only sound comes from the traffic on the other side of the street visible through the alley. Jeff, then, is the only "witness" to what, apparently, turns out to be the precise moment of Mrs. Anna Thorwald's (Irene Winston) murder.

The extensive parallels between the "interior" story of the Jeff-Lisa relationship and the "exterior" stories of the apartment dwellers are what give the film multiple layers of meanings far beyond Woolrich's story which relies on a more linear plot line. Hitchcock and Woolrich give Lars Thorwald a similar priority over the other neighbors; it is, however, in the increased emphasis given the peripheral inhabitants that the film deviates greatly from the short story. Although, outside of the Thorwalds, Woolrich's Jeffries claims he can observe the lives of many neighbors, he accounts for only two of them, the jitter-couple and the single mother, to which he gives but cursory attention. Hitchcock and Hayes, on the other hand, turn the quadrangle into a mosaic of contrasting and complementary life styles.

Rotating counter-clockwise from Jeff's rear window perch, we see to the immediate right a Musician-Composer (Ross Bagdasarian) whose studio apartment has a window-wall that allows full view of his fluctuations between success and failure, between solitariness and social activity. In the building across from Jeff, on the third floor and to the right, lives a married couple, about whom we learn little personally; however, when their frisky dog is killed, it is the wife (Sara Berner), not the husband (Frank Cady), who spews a tirade against the unknown assailant. The woman is obviously the stronger, more dominant personality of the relationship. The Thorwalds live to the left and below the Dog-Couple. Left of the Thorwalds is Miss Torso (Georgine Darcy), a shapely and flexible young dancer who entertains men occasionally, but keeps them at bay, awaiting the return of her true lover, her absent soldier, Stanley (Benny Bartlett). Below the Thorwalds, on the ground floor, is Miss Lonelyhearts (Judith Evelyn in the modified role of Woolrich's despondent single mother), a single woman lamenting her doom as a spinster. Left of Miss Lonelyhearts and below Miss Torso is a Sculptress (Jesslyn Fax), who incurs Thorwald's wrath when she gives him gardening suggestions. One of the sculptures we see her working on is a human silhouette with a hole in its stomach, which she calls, appropriately, "Hunger." (Actually, the stone or clay has a definite phallic shape and looks like the medical symbol for "male.") In the adjacent building to Jeff's immediate left are the newlyweds (a version of Woolrich's jitter-couple), who keep their shade drawn for several days with the implication that they are enjoying a love-fest. All of these people appear intermittently throughout the story to give Jeff (and us) glimpses of their ongoing lives that directly parallel events occurring in Jeff's apartment between him and Lisa.

Lisa's tiff with Jeff and her awkward departure coincide with Thorwald's "solution" for severing the marriage bond between him and his wife. What is more, many of Jeff's neighbors face various "crises" at approximately this same time, most of a romantic nature. Earlier in the evening, before Jeff and Lisa have their argument, Miss Lonelyhearts pantomimes a dinner date with an imaginary suitor; the realization that she is carrying on a charade makes her break down in tears. Later that night, it starts to rain and the Dog-Owner Couple, asleep on the fire escape, have to gather their bedding and push it through the window; the husband trips over the sill and topples head-first behind his mattress. The Composer returns home drunk; he sees his sheet music on the piano, sweeps it to the floor, and falls backward into an armchair. He appears frustrated either because he has reached an impasse with the song he is composing ("Lisa's Theme," played intermittently throughout the film), or he has been rejected in love or a business deal. Miss Torso, who earlier had entertained three men alone in her apartment, returns home after a night out and, at the door, has to fight off one of her aggressive, unwelcome suitors trying to force his way into her apartment.

Such doubling occurs constantly throughout the film and forces us to draw inferences from the comparisons. In the case of these romantic tensions, we see that each reaches a critical stage for different reasons—loneliness, rejection, disinterest, irreconcilable differences. Even though Jeff's speculation that Thorwald murdered his wife finally proves correct, and even though we learn that he had a girlfriend accomplice, there are too many facets to any relationship for us to understand conclusively why he did it.

Hitchcock's doubling is so pervasive, it would be a monumental task to account for it all. Even so, building on the example just given, I would like to touch on a number of the most salient ones that illuminate some of the film's central ideas.

On each of the four nights of Jeff's vigilance, Lisa makes four unique entrances, each time wearing something different. In her initial appearance, she wears a black and white evening gown. The colors signify the duality that, for Jeff, makes her both threatening (associated with the framed negative, she casts a menacing shadow) and desirable (associated with the positive print, she is an image of alluring beauty).

Since Jeff cannot go out to dinner, Lisa brings dinner to him. She has Carl, the waiter from Twenty-One, carry in their food in warming trays. Jeff volunteers to open the champagne and asks Lisa for a corkscrew. When he has trouble with it, Carl handily completes the task with a pocket corkscrew of his own. In what appear to be trite events, Hitchcock subtly combines two motifs he juxtaposes throughout the film: appetite and sex. Appetite can pertain to physical hunger or to psychological or spiritual needs, and Hitchcock deftly links it to sexual desire. Here, Lisa satisfies Jeff's physical hunger (his stomach is "empty as a football"), but he resists her ability to satisfy his sexual needs. The corkscrew incident is another of the impotence images: either he is physically incapable of enjoying sex with her or he is so uncomfortable with her that he has established a barrier that she cannot penetrate.

"Rear Window" (1942) / *Rear Window* (1954)

Rear Window— Jeff (James Stewart) is enticed more by the goings-on outside his window than by the seductive and attainable woman (Grace Kelly) who caters to his appetites (Paramount, courtesy William Thailing).

While Lisa prepares their meals in the kitchen, Jeff watches with fascination at Miss Lonelyhearts's pantomime of entertaining a suitor. When she lifts her glass in an imaginary toast, Jeff playfully returns the salute with his own glass, identifying himself with the phantom suitor. An exchange between Lisa and Jeff follows Miss Lonelyhearts's collapse into tears:

JEFF: At least that's something you'll never have to worry about.
LISA: You can see my apartment from here?
JEFF: No, but remember Miss Torso? She's like the Queen Bee with her pick of the drones. (A long shot shows Miss Torso entertaining three men at once, an ironic contrast with Miss Lonelyhearts who has trouble imagining just one suitor.)
LISA: She's doing a woman's hardest job, juggling wolves.
JEFF: She's picked the most prosperous-looking one. (Miss Torso has walked out onto her balcony with one of the men.)
LISA: She's not in love with him, or any of them.
JEFF: How can you tell that from here?
LISA: You said it resembled my apartment, didn't you?

Jeff responds by giving her an extreme sidelong glance, comprehending her meaning but looking self-consciously guilty. He then shifts his sidelong glance in the other direction, toward the shaded window of the newlyweds, and he looks uncomfortable. When Lisa finally serves the dinner, Jeff oddly comments, "It's perfect — as always." He looks resigned and sounds disappointed, cynically sarcastic.

Jeff is willing to share a toast with Miss Lonelyhearts because he sits at a safe distance away and plays the invisible man; he cannot extend himself so easily with the beautiful woman who is right here in his apartment. Lisa's roundabout way of telling him she loves him, her choosing him over any of the Madison Avenue types she has to wine and dine in her apartment, plus the incessant lovemaking going on in the Newlyweds' apartment, all prompt Jeff's visible discomfort because of his physical or psychological inability to express real love.

Lisa is identified with both Miss Torso and Miss Lonelyhearts. While Miss Lonelyhearts serves a meal for her imaginary lover, Lisa prepares a meal for Jeff, who plays the lover for both women at the same time. Lisa is also Miss Torso, the popular, alluring female who can play the social butterfly, but saves her sincere feelings for her true love. At the end, when Stanley comes home to Miss Torso, he is not the physical or professional ideal we expected, as perhaps Jeff is not the ideal Lisa deserves. After a brief kiss, Stanley's remarks are less than intimate: "Being in the army made me hungry. What've you got in the icebox to eat?" Like Jeff, he uses food — particularly cold food — to displace the passionate fire of sexual appetite. If women can be criticized for their duality, men do not appear totally blameless in sabotaging potential relationships.

Lisa makes her second appearance with her and Jeff in intimate embrace; she is kissing him and whispering playful sexual innuendoes. She wears a black evening gown, as if her "negative" side has completely taken her over so that she now poses the real seductive threat he was afraid might envelop him. But he does not give in to her. Either deliberately or subconsciously, his thoughts are more concerned with Thorwald's activities. He responds to her innuendoes with flippant one-liners and rhetorical questions about Thorwald's behavior:

> LISA: Where does a girl have to go before you'll notice her?
> JEFF: She doesn't have to go anywhere. She just has to *be*.... Don't you ever have any problems?
> LISA: I have one now.
> JEFF: So do I.
> LISA: Tell me about it.
> JEFF: Why would a man leave his apartment three times on a rainy night and come back three times?
> LISA: He likes the way his wife welcomes him home.
> JEFF: Why didn't he go to work today?
> LISA: Homework. It's more interesting.
> JEFF: ... Why hasn't he been in his wife's room all day? ... Lisa, there's something terribly wrong.
> LISA: And I'm afraid it's with me.

Lisa rises and moves to the bed, where she lies down and smokes a cigarette. Across the courtyard, Miss Torso is also reclining on her bed, reading while she eats a snack; she brushes some crumbs from her sweater. Lisa is again identified with Miss Torso as they simultaneously satisfy one appetite (smoking/eating) that substitutes for the sex their "absent" men (mentally/physically) cannot satisfy.

Jeff reaches for the binoculars, positions them to get a better look at Thorwald. Lisa indignantly turns his wheelchair away from the window: "Jeff, if you could only see yourself!" Jeff defends his action: "I just want to find out what's the matter with the salesman's wife." As he says this, he gestures with his right arm, pointing over his left shoulder toward Thorwald's apartment. The importance of the gesture is that it connects Jeff with Thorwald, for Thorwald uses that exact arm movement later when the police arrive at his door and interrupt his assault on Lisa: Thorwald lets them in, and with a baffled look, points with his right arm over his left shoulder at the stranger who has been burgling his apartment.

The gesture has a similar meaning in the two contexts. The men act defensively, trying to justify their actions from someone who raises questions about their behavior. Linked to each other, they have committed a guilty, unethical act, and their gesture becomes an awkward, feeble attempt to point to evidence that is supposed to explain their behavior or make it legitimately justifiable.

After chiding Jeff for his unethical behavior, Lisa seems ready to revel in the triumph of her righteousness until she looks across the courtyard and sees Thorwald tying rope around a large steamer trunk. As in Woolrich's story, our interest is diverted to the trunk, which seems the ideal place for hiding the body and getting it out of the apartment. Lisa is thinking along these lines when she says to Jeff, "Start at the beginning again, Jeff. Tell me everything you saw and what you think it means." His skepticism and suspicion have finally won her over. In *noir* fashion, his getting her to relent to his way of thinking is a Pyrrhic victory: he has corrupted innocence by convincing her to admit the criminal potential in people. She helps him that night by sneaking into the apartment building where Thorwald lives and getting his name and address off the mailbox. She has been recruited and is now a loyal soldier in Jeff's service.

On the third night, the scene opens with a close-up of a cold, meager sandwich on a plate and a glass of milk. Jeff's hand grabs one wedge of the sandwich and brings it to his mouth for a bite. In appearance, the meal is sterile, drab, and unappetizing; that a plain, cold sandwich can satisfy his hunger suggests how base his tastes are, far more elemental and crude than the cultivated, discriminating taste Lisa is capable of satisfying, as she tried to do two nights before with her lobster dinner from Twenty-One. On that night (the first night), they argued, Jeff warning her of living conditions when he goes on assignment for his magazine: "Sometimes the food that you eat is made from things you couldn't even look at when they were alive!" His willingness to eat vermin is supposed to show her how far his world is from hers, how incompatible their life styles are, which at once becomes an excuse for not marrying her and a declaration of independence from her.

Jeff continues his observation of the neighbors. Miss Lonelyhearts wears a solid dark green dress, applies some last-minute make-up, and heads for the local bar, her destination visible through the alley to the left of her apartment building. Later, she will bring home a young man who tries to force himself on her. She will resist, slap his face. He will storm out in anger and she will collapse on her couch in tears.

Before this outburst, though, Lisa enters Jeff's apartment, dressed in a light green, two-piece suit and carrying a black overnight case containing a nightgown and slippers. The green outfits unite the two women: both are at this moment resorting to feminine wiles to seduce a man. However, there is also a contrast. Lisa's green suit, softer and more tasteful, suggests the secure confidence of youth and beauty; Miss Lonelyhearts's dark green dress, more gaudy and brazen, broadcasts her fear of loneliness and spinsterhood and suggests how desperate she is to win a man.

Another implicit parallel occurs in how the male responds to each seductress's tactics. The young man Miss Lonelyhearts brings home destroys her dream of a meaningful romantic relationship when he physically attacks her. Jeff thwarts Lisa but in a less belligerent, more subtle way. Lisa has brought with her a small overnight case, indicating her willingness to compromise her life style by traveling on his terms; and of course, her sexual innuendoes are meant to remind him of the added bonus she brings to their relationship. Inside her case is the temptress's calling card, a provocative nightgown advertising her designs for the night. Jeff, instead of readily acquiescing, assumes the role of a tentative adolescent, responding to her sexual advances with droll sarcasm. He meets every one of her suggestions with an objection, as if, subconsciously, he is looking for an excuse to avoid a sexual interlude with her:

LISA: We have all night.
JEFF We have all what?
LISA: Night. I'm going to stay with you.
JEFF: You'll have to clear that with my landlord.
LISA: I have the whole weekend off.
JEFF: Well, that's very nice, but I just have one bed.
LISA: If you say anything else, I'll stay tomorrow night, too.
JEFF: I won't be able to get into my pajamas.
LISA: I'll trade you — my feminine intuition for a bed for the night.
JEFF: I'll go along with that. (Jeff finally yields when she offers to barter.)

His mock scruples may again be attributed to ambiguous causes, his playfulness disguising impotence or some other deep-seated motive, particularly a fear of female domination or an inability to commit to a relationship.

When Detective Tom Doyle arrives shortly after Lisa, he sees the open overnight case and immediately deduces the nature of their tryst. Before Doyle can speak, Jeff warns him: "Be careful, Tom." Jeff and Lisa are consenting adults and their business is their business. But that is the very point Doyle tries to make as he justifies the inexplicable behavior that has led Jeff to think Thorwald a

Rear Window— An angry Jeff (Stewart, in wheelchair) and a somber Lisa (Kelly) contend with friend Tom Doyle (Wendell Corey) over his reluctance to recognize Thorwald's guilt (Paramount, courtesy of William Thailing).

murderer: "That's a secret, private world you're looking into out there. People do a lot of things in private they couldn't possibly explain in public." Woolrich implies this in his short story as well, that people in their private lives do things, sometimes irrational, even perverted but harmless, acts that they cannot defend or fully explain. Woolrich's protagonist, on the other hand, never discloses to his detective friend Boyne how he acquired the information he has passed on to him. In other words, Hal Jeffries' voyeurism is one of those acts people may do in private but feel foolish admitting to others. Thus, ironically, Jeffries' (and Jeff's) illicit peeping is an example of those guilty pleasures that they would rather not make known to others. And so Hitchcock's Doyle has put into words the same central idea about private idiosyncrasies and perversions that Woolrich implies more subtly.

Shortly after Doyle leaves, Lisa gives Jeff her "preview of coming attractions" by modeling her nightgown for him. Abruptly, a woman's scream from out in the courtyard shatters their prelude to romance. This is the Death of the Dog scene. The sequence is jarring, not only because of the wanton killing of the innocent little dog, but also because, for the first time, the camera moves out of Jeff's apartment and into the courtyard, taking a number of close medium shots of the inquisitive neighbors who gather to investigate the commotion. The wife of the couple who own the dog is screaming, "Which one of you killed my dog? ... You don't know the meaning of the word 'neighbor.' Neighbors like each other, speak to each other, care if anybody lives or dies. But none of you do.... Did ya kill him because he liked ya? Just because he liked ya?" Medium and full shots of Miss Lonelyhearts, Miss Torso, and the Sculptress bring them closer to us and make them more real and personal than they have been up to now. Visually, this is a striking departure from Woolrich's story, which begins with a cryptic observation: "I didn't know their names. I'd never heard their voices. I didn't even know them by sight, strictly speaking, for their faces were too small to fill in with identifiable features at that distance." Other than Thorwald, none of the other neighbors in Woolrich's story becomes so prominent as do these several neighbors in Hitchcock's film. The distance that impersonalizes these people, that makes them ciphers and allows Jeff to label them by one distinguishing trait (only the Thorwalds are identified by name), shrinks when the camera moves closer and we are forced to see these characters as real individuals, real people with real human emotions on their faces.

The significance of the Death of the Dog scene, and particularly of the new camera viewpoint, is not fully evident until the end when it can be compared with Thorwald's attack on Jeff. In that scene, as Thorwald moves vengefully toward his tormentor, Jeff glances out his window toward Thorwald's apartment and sees Doyle, Lisa, and an entourage of police across the way. He yells anxiously, frantically, as Thorwald attacks him. Thorwald manages to throw Jeff on the bed, wrestle him toward the open window, and fling him through it. Jeff clutches the sill with his fingertips, his feet dangling down from his second story window. As in the Death of the Dog scene, quick cuts and an array of dynamic shots within the courtyard contrast the repertoire of lingering, static shots that formerly denoted Jeff's sedentary existence in his apartment. The Thorwald-Jefferies confrontation becomes comparable to the dog's death through visual parallels that link the two events together: the placement of the camera inside the courtyard allows for closer, more intimate shots of the neighbors as they emerge from their isolated cocoons. The two scenes show what it takes — a sensational event that piques human curiosity — to get people to disrupt their routines and converge on a single attraction. On one hand, though, the death of the dog employs a greater variety of shots, with more of them indicating the depth of the tragedy and the emotional reactions of the neighbors. Jeff's encounter occurs at the climax of the film, the tension and suspense heightened by hectic camera movements and rapid cutting. Yet the event has a shorter duration and exhibits a more limited variety of shots, as if the tragedy befalling a human being is, ironically, less poignant than the death of an animal.

At the end of the Death of the Dog scene, Jeff points out to Lisa that of all the neighbors, Thorwald is the only one who has not come to his window to investigate the uproar. Conclusion: He must have killed the dog. Before the scene fades to black, we are left with the final image of his darkened apartment, the only thing discernible being the lighted tip of his cigarette which glows bright when he inhales.

The fade, connoting a lapse of time, is ambiguous enough to suggest that maybe Jeff and Lisa continue with Lisa's plans for the night. However, the death of the dog makes this unlikely, horror and confusion having supplanted any romantic mood. Instead, with the fade, desire and passion slide into limbo. Sexual union has been thwarted, the relationship left unconsummated, like that of the young groom and his bride on Keats's Grecian urn. Jeff's impotence remains untested and intact, literally and figuratively, as the fade leads us abruptly into the fourth and final night and the climactic confrontation between Jeff and Thorwald.

On the fourth evening of his vigil, Jeff is joined by Lisa and Stella (Thelma Ritter as his visiting nurse). Lisa wears a modest print dress, as if attempting to "dress down" and compromise her elegant life style to suit Jeff's more modest ambitions. The scene opens with the camera situated against the back wall of Jeff's apartment and shooting straight out the window for a wide view of the opposite apartment building. This specific shot is significant because it occurs three times in the film: during the credits with no one at the window; as a two-shot of Jeff and Doyle looking directly ahead at Thorwald's apartment, their backs to the camera; and now as a three-shot, Jeff, Lisa, and Stella looking directly ahead at Thorwald's apartment, their backs to the camera. The shot is first of all an establishing shot showing Jeff's perspective on the courtyard and adjacent buildings. The wide angle gives us the configuration of the courtyard apartments and their relative positions to each other. In addition, the three shots show a progressive increase in the number of voyeurs, from none to two to three. It is as if Jeff is gradually infecting those around him, getting them to partake in his guilty pastime.

Up to now, the film has deviated extensively from Woolrich's short story, inventing a more complex narrative so that practically the only original aspect recognizable is the basic premise of a meddling voyeur confined to his room. A few vestiges preserve the connection: Doyle, as the detective character, boasts a more definite history of friendship with Jeff than Boyne has with Jeffries; Lisa and Stella act as mobile go-fers for the housebound Jeff, dividing between them the tasks assigned to Jeffries' houseman Sam. Earlier, Lisa, like Sam, seeks out Thorwald's address for Jeff. Stella performs Sam's function as cook and nurse. As characters, however, Lisa and Stella are more richly drawn, Stella with her droll humor and homespun philosophy ("When a man and a woman ... like each other, they should come together — Wham! — like two taxis on Broadway...") and Lisa with a life style that counterpoints Jeff's. At the same time, both of their running arguments with Jeff highlight a number of concepts for the film and make the two women far more significant contributors to the story than Woolrich's black houseman. They claim a greater stake in the mystery than Sam does, reacting to Jeff's conjectures, first negatively, then positively, even volunteering to help catch the criminal.

On this fourth evening, the film, with expected and necessary modifications, includes many events which come directly out of Woolrich's story: Jeff's letter to Thorwald to intimidate him into exposing his guilt; the letter's delivery and Lisa's nearly getting caught; the phone call to Thorwald to lure him out of the apartment while Lisa and Stella search for evidence in the garden; Lisa's search of Thorwald's apartment; the final confrontation between murderer and accuser; the detective's last minute rescue of his friend.

Lisa's delivering Jeff's letter and almost getting caught is important for its suspenseful nature alone. We watch with Jeff, terrified and helpless (that is, "impotent"), as she evades Thorwald who, like a ravenous Minotaur, pursues her through the labyrinthine corridors of his apartment building. More significant is the aftermath of the event. When she finally returns safely to Jeff's apartment, he turns and looks over the back of his wheelchair, his chin resting on his arm. The extreme close-up shows his face glowing with pride over her achievement. As if having undertaken a trial by fire, she endures the ordeal and survives. She, too, appears exhilarated by the adventure and craves more, which sets up the next stage of the climax.

Stella and Lisa decide to look in the flowerbed for clues to Thorwald's crime. To buy time, Jeff phones Thorwald to set up the phony rendezvous that gets him out of his apartment for awhile. Lisa and Stella sneak into the courtyard garden by walking up the same stairs which the cat climbed at the beginning of the film. Identified with the cat, they are curious and furtive; identified with the dog, they dig in Thorwald's flowerbed. Nothing is uncovered, however, and Lisa climbs the fire escape to Thorwald's apartment. (Hitchcock's notorious use of stairs is subtly inserted here to suggest two planes of knowledge, the known and the unknown, the commonplace and the forbidden.) In Woolrich's story, Jeffries sends Sam to disturb things in Thorwald's apartment, hoping to rattle him enough that he will bare his guilt. Varying that situation, Lisa goes there on her own, much to Jeff's dismay, hoping not simply disrupt the apartment but to find concrete, damaging evidence.

Sam returns to Jeffries' house without mishap. Lisa, however, gets caught because of a complicating coincidence. While Lisa climbs the fire escape, Stella returns to Jeff and tells him, if he sees Thorwald coming, to warn Lisa by ringing Thorwald's telephone. At just that moment, Stella notices Miss Lonelyhearts preparing to take an overdose of pills and she urges Jeff to call the police.

Several things occur simultaneously. In the Composer's apartment are a group of musicians whom the Composer has invited for a run-through of his latest song. (For the film's purposes, the tune is called "Lisa's Theme.") He says, "All right, fellas, let's try it once from the beginning." They start to play. Across the way, Miss Lonelyhearts hears the music and aborts her suicide attempt. She stands up and walks to the window. At the very same moment, in Thorwald's bedroom directly above her, Lisa also stops what she is doing to come to the window and gaze in identical pose toward the source of the music. (This synchronized action may have been inspired by an event in Woolrich's story.

Thorwald in his apartment and the manager in the apartment above him walk in unison from the living room to the kitchen. The parallel action gives Jeffries the clue to finding the corpse of the missing Mrs. Thorwald.) The mirrored movements and reactions of the two women connect them once again, showing their sensitive, artistic dispositions toward things aesthetic even though they are not artistic themselves.

The artist motif has its place in the story since most of Jeff's neighbors whose lives we peek in on are artists of one type or another. Even Jeff, a photographer, belongs to this clique. Of the few neighbors who are not artists, the most prominent is Lars Thorwald. In fact, he is a blatant affront to the art world. He not only fails to contribute anything creative or imaginative, but he sells costume jewelry, making him doubly offensive as a nonproductive member of the artist community and a promoter of false art. (Tongue-in-cheek, this could be considered an even greater crime than what he did to his wife—perhaps the source of his true guilt.) Yet if one is not an artist, displaying a sensitive appreciation of art is the next best thing, and so Lisa and Miss Lonelyhearts merit a place among this select group.

While Jeff is busy on the phone with the police, Thorwald suddenly returns, making it too late for Jeff to warn Lisa. Miss Lonelyhearts now appears out of danger, so Jeff, anticipating what will happen, tells the police that a man is assaulting a woman. Thorwald discovers Lisa, confronts her, shuts off the lights, and attacks her on the couch situated below the living room window. (Although the couch is hidden from sight, we assume one is there because Thorwald earlier stretched out on it for a nap.) While Thorwald attacks his beloved, Jeff can only watch, another indication of the voyeur's impotence, his passive observation a substitute for active participation.

As another connection between Lisa and Miss Lonelyhearts, Thorwald's assault occurs directly above the window in which Miss Lonelyhearts was assaulted previously by the young suitor she had brought home. In addition, while Miss Lonelyhearts was fending off her attacker, the Composer was playing his piano and leading some dinner guests in a chorus of "Mona Lisa," the song's title linking her to Lisa Fremont and foreshadowing Thorwald's present savagery. Furthermore, while Thorwald is having his way with Lisa, the Composer and his musician friends are still playing "Lisa's Theme." The irony is that, like "Mona Lisa," "Lisa's Theme" is a soft, lyrical, romantic melody played contrapuntally to the violent assaults on the two women. In this way, Hitchcock gives romantic under-"tones" to physical attack, creating ambiguity between sexual love and rape.

Both of these assaults foreshadow the final one when Thorwald will assault Jeff on his bed. Jeff's reaction to Thorwald's assault shows more passion, excitement, and enthusiasm than any he has shown for Lisa up to now. The frenzied exhalations and physical exertions carry the implications of a homoerotic encounter, perhaps a fantasy more provocative for the impotent Jeff than the real relationship he has with Lisa.

The police arrive in time. At the door, Thorwald makes that backward-pointing gesture that connects him with Jeff. In all the excitement, Lisa has retrieved Mrs. Thorwald's wedding ring. With her back to the window, she signals to Jeff that she has it by pointing with her right hand to where she wears it on the ring finger of her left hand. Jeff sees the signal, but so does Thorwald, who now locates the vantage point of his nemesis.

The wedding ring creates a complex romantic triangle for Lisa, Jeff, and Thorwald. In a kind of perverted symbolism (reminiscent of *Shadow of a Doubt* where young Charlie is incestuously betrothed to her Uncle Charlie), Lisa becomes Mrs. Thorwald. In this respect, if Jeff wants her, he is coveting another man's wife. Jeff, at the same time, is a double for Thorwald: just as Thorwald, a mild-mannered, soft-spoken man, was driven to commit murder, so too, Jeff has that potential, if he ever marries Lisa.

Although the audience sees most of the courtyard activity from Jeff's perspective, there are a number of times that the camera deviates from that single viewpoint, such as the omniscient shots taken during the Death of the Dog scene and at the end when Jeff is hanging outside his window. Other than these, however, there are three key moments when the audience is privy to information that escapes the protagonist. The first occurs on the night of the murder. Jeff is sleeping when Thorwald leaves his apartment with a mysterious woman dressed in black. (Hitchcock plays a trick here, as he does in *Stage Fright*, allowing us to see something that influences our ability to solve the mystery.) We assume that this is Mrs. Thorwald and Jeff's suspicions, for us, become ironic in that, deprived of this one fragment of knowledge, he insists that Thorwald must be guilty. That is, we are misled about Thorwald's innocence, while Jeff, without this information, is closer to the truth.

The second moment occurs when he fails to see Miss Lonelyhearts preparing to commit suicide. Before this, while observing her, he makes one of his many erroneous inferences: "Stella was wrong about Miss Lonelyhearts." If he was more insightful (and sensitive), he could have alerted the police about her earlier and been better prepared to warn Lisa when Thorwald returned. As it happens, Jeff was not looking when we see her place her suicide note next to the lamp and sit on the bed, preparing herself for her end.

The third omission occurs while Jeff and Stella try to dig up enough money for Lisa's bail. Jeff fails to see Thorwald's contemptuous leer in his direction as he leaves his apartment. He calls Doyle to explain Lisa's arrest and alert him to Thorwald's pulling out, but when he finally gets to look over and see Thorwald's darkened apartment, it is too late. Thorwald is already on his way.

The montage sequence that occurs between Thorwald's anticipated arrival and Jeff's fall from the window is, among comparable sequences in the Hitchcock canon, one of the most minutely drawn and rhythmically precise, as well as one of the most harrowing and suspenseful. Up to now, with brief exceptions, music has pervaded the film, generally from determinable sources; but this entire sequence is shot without music, its sudden absence complementing the tension and the eeriness of the altercation. What begins as a psychological study of a trapped man frantically trying to escape a terrible doom progresses in painstaking increments toward a violent physical confrontation. Jeff knows that the physical distance, the margin of safety, between him and Thorwald is about to be bridged. Like a caged animal, he maneuvers his wheelchair this way and that, shifting from one location to another, even trying vainly to force his unwieldy chair through the bathroom doorway. (Possibly Hitchcock's attempt at a joke as we suddenly wonder, if he can't get into the bathroom now, how did he manage to relieve himself before this. A bedpan?) As Jeff stares intently at his door, we also stare at it, waiting in paralyzed anticipation for the deadly intruder to burst through its dark and inscrutable façade. We hear the sound of the elevator stopping on his floor and the slow shuffle of feet along the corridor, ending just outside his door. We see the abrupt extinguishing of the horizontal sliver of light beneath his door. All these excruciating details create suspense very much in tune with Woolrich's style, as the threat of danger and death moves closer to reality for the protagonist.

When Thorwald comes through the door, he does so, contrary to our expectations, without flourish or dramatics. The subdued entrance belies the simmering tension and it is difficult to predict what will happen next. The subsequent stage of the encounter is an extraordinary demonstration of Hitchcock's use of timing to build suspense. The dialogue is one-sided: Thorwald talks ("What do you want from me? ... A lot of money? I don't have a lot of money.... Say something.... Tell me what you want."); Jeff remains mute. The camera shoots in an angle reverse-angle sequence to depict the two men's perspectives on each other. It is like the prelude to a shoot-out in a Western with the two adversaries sizing up each other for ability and nerves. This encounter, Thorwald the Speaker pitted against Jeff the Auditor, implies how, as doubles, they behave in opposition to each other. They handle their relationships with women differently. Thorwald takes aggressive action to determine his own romantic fate. Jeff, more passive (that is to say, impotent), resorts to words to try to argue his way out of a potential marriage. Both men find themselves cornered, first by women and now by each other. Tension has reached its limits and something has to give way.

Jeff finally breaks his silence when Thorwald asks a question about the ring:

THORWALD: Can you get me that ring back?
JEFF: No.
THORWALD: Tell her to bring it back.
JEFF: I can't. The police have it by now.

What follows is a series of four nearly identical sequences of shots. Thorwald moves toward Jeff; Jeff covers his eyes and shoots off one of his flash bulbs; Thorwald, momentarily blinded by the light, pauses, adjusts his glasses, then moves forward again. This sequence is repeated three times with the same camera shots and angles; the only difference is the camera distance: as Thorwald gets closer, he and Jeff get larger in the their respective shots to indicate their imminent collision.

The implications of Jeff's impotency are further reinforced in this scene. Jeff has no real "weapon," only the illusion of one. The flash bulbs are a feeble substitute for a weapon; they cannot hurt Thorwald or protect Jeff from his attack.

Before Jeff can "fire" a fifth bulb, he sees Doyle and Lisa and a contingent of police at Thorwald's door. He yells across the courtyard; they hear and come running. At this point, Thorwald is obsessed with killing Jeff even if he gets caught. He attacks Jeff, flings him onto the bed (a mock homosexual rape), and upturns his body, tossing it through the window. As in the Death of the Dog scene, the camera's viewpoint shifts to within the courtyard, showing a chaotic variety of shots as neighbors emerge from their apartments to witness the commotion and see Jeff hanging from his window.

Although Thorwald's crime demands greater retribution than Jeff's, Hitchcock's film does not let the voyeur escape unscathed. Jeff, Lisa, Stella, and Doyle have already raised questions about the ethics of voyeurism, a human foible inherent in human nature, an ingrained tendency toward curiosity, envy, and feelings of superiority. In Thorwald's attack on Jeff, a kind of poetic justice is attained. Thorwald uses Jeff's second-story window, the rear window he has been using to commit his indiscretion, as the medium for meting out justice against his nemesis. Simultaneously, as an inversion to Jeff's voyeurism, Jeff becomes the object of exhibition for the neighbors he has been spying on all this time.

Unlike Woolrich's detective Boyne, Doyle does not have to shoot Thorwald. In a conveniently quick and concise wrap-up, Thorwald confesses his crime and tells police where to find the body parts of Mrs. Thorwald scattered around the city. Thorwald's grisly, gory dissecting of his wife's body does not take place in Woolrich's "Rear Window," although it does occur in another of his stories dealing with voyeurism, "The Boy Cried Murder." One wonders if Hitchcock or John Michael Hayes is acquainted with more of Woolrich's work and integrated some of those extraneous ideas in their film.

The final scene offers a brief denouement on the day after Thorwald's climactic arrest. In a reprise of the opening pan of the courtyard apartments, the camera shows a number of resolutions in the romantic lives of the various neighbors. The Composer entertains Miss Lonelyhearts in his apartment, with the suggestion that a budding relationship is taking place. Miss Torso greets her boyfriend at the door: Stanley is home from the army: his first concern is what is in the refrigerator rather than a romantic greeting, another ambiguous intersection of appetite and sex. The Sculptress sleeps on a lawn chair, her hammer and chisel forgotten. In the Newlywed apartment, the shade is up and we can see and hear her complaining that she would not have married him if she had known he was going to quit his job. Here, we see that all romantic resolutions are not happy ones, this last one foreboding the young wife's evolution into the shrewish wife that Thorwald felt obliged to eliminate.

Jeff sleeps in his chair, a dopey smile on his face. He now has two broken legs, an irony that replaces Woolrich's irony. Woolrich does not reveal until the end why Jeffries is confined to his room, that he has a broken leg. The suggestion there is that his confinement is fated, that he would not have been there to discover Thorwald's crime if not for this freak coincidence. Jeff's two broken legs iterate the image of the double. From Jeff's legs, the camera pans over to Lisa's two legs which are clad in jeans, suggestive of her complete transformation to the kind of woman Jeff wants her to be. (A recurring motif in a number of Hitchcock's films, the male's selfish reconstruction of the female identity reaches its ultimate treatment in *Vertigo*.) She feigns interest in an adventure novel, *Beyond the High Himalayas*, but with Jeff asleep, she sets it aside and picks up *Bazaar* magazine. We smile at her ruse, realize her duplicity, that the transformation is merely external, a pretense to appease Jeff. Her taste in literature suggests that she remains the high-brow, high-society woman she has always been. The pun on her magazine title ("bizarre") relates back to her discussion with Jeff about the girl Friday who helps the detective solve the crime, but never gets to marry him: "That's strange," says Jeff. "Weird," says Lisa. It could be that she is planning to revise that predictable formulaic outcome.

Coincidentally, *Witness to Murder* (Roy Rowland, 1954) was released the same year as *Rear Window* and dealt with identical themes of voyeurism and the witness's attempt to prove the guilt of the person who supposedly committed murder. Reminiscent of Hitchcock's film, the voyeur (Barbara Stanwyck) uses binoculars to get a better view of her adversary and lapses into ongoing ethical debates with the detective (Gary Merrill) assigned to the case. Otherwise, the "original" screenplay by Chester Erskine and Nunnally Johnson has less in common with *Rear Window* than it does with *The Window* (based on "The Boy Cried Murder" and discussed at greater length in a separate chapter below). The film works fine as a *noir* entry, but falls considerably short of the aesthetic level of Hitchcock's masterpiece.

Don't Bother to Knock (Roy Baker, 1952), although produced before *Rear Window*, is an ironic complement to Hitchcock's film. Marilyn Monroe plays a young woman who suffered a nervous breakdown after losing her lover in the war and is starving to find someone to fill that void in her life. While working as a babysitter in a hotel room, she exchanges glances with a fellow voyeur (Richard Widmark) looking out his window across the way and he convinces her to invite him over. She is actually Miss Lonelyhearts, and the story, told partially from her viewpoint instead of Jeff's, shows how one may resort to the most bizarre behavior, the most desperate acts, when driven by loneliness and heartache. Nell (Monroe) had already once attempted suicide, just as Miss Lonelyhearts nearly tries it herself, and only love can redeem these alienated outcasts from their cycle of self-pity.

Made-for-Television Movie: Rear Window

1998, Hallmark Entertainment. *D:* Jeff Bleckner. *P:* Sheldon Abend, Robert V. Gaulin, Jeff Bleckner. *Exec P:* Christopher Reeve, Steven Haft, Robert Halmi Sr., David V. Picker. *Cin:* Ken Kelsch. *Teleplay:* Eric Overmyer, Larry Gross. *Ed:* Geoffrey Rowland. *Mus:* David Shire. *Prod Des:* Stephen Hendrickson. *Art Dir:* Randall Richards. *Set Decor:* Beth Kushnick. *Visual F/X:* Sarah Frank.

Cast: Christopher Reeve (Jason Kemp), Daryl Hannah (Claudia Henderson), Robert Forster (Detective Charlie Moore), Ruben Santiago-Hudson (Antonio Fredericks), Anne Twomey (Leila), Ritchie Coster (Julian Thorpe), Allison Mackie (Ilene Thorpe and Ilene's sister), Ali Marsh (Allison Flowers), Max Chalawsky (Writer), Marc Holzman (Gay tenant), David Pittu (Gay roommate), Julie Barker ("Luscious woman"), Maggie Kiley (Professional woman), Peter Giles (Professional man), Monique Cintron (Janet), David Wohl (Dr. Schneider), Kevin O'Rourke (Mason), John Rothman (Parker), Leigh Zimmerman (Business woman), Deedee Lynn Magna (Popoff nurse), Frank Pellegrino (Physical therapist), Gina Colucci-Bradbury (Rehab aide), Tracy Deluca (Rehab aide), Christopher Fontini (Rehab aide), Herbert Karpatkin (Rehab aide), Cathleen Dudley (Violinist, uncredited), Alan Francis (Construction worker, uncredited). 95 min.

Because of the nearly universal critical and popular success of Hitchcock's film, it seems a foregone conclusion that any remake must fall short of the original. Indeed, purists would even consider it blasphemy to tamper with what is esteemed as holy writ. Yet some enterprising apostates came forward and did just that in a made-for-television movie. Part of the thrust for the project came from Christopher Reeve, the most forthright, most recognizable spokesman for the American Paralysis Association, who must have viewed it as an opportunity to educate the public on spinal cord injuries and their ramifications. The credits list Woolrich's tale as the basis for the teleplay, but the film is really more an amalgam of three sources, the short story, the Hitchcock-Hayes film, and the original ideas which Overmyer and Gross incorporate into this new version to satisfy its didactic purpose.

Architect Jason Kemp (Reeve) survives an automobile accident, but suffers a spinal cord injury that leaves him totally paralyzed from the neck down. Refusing to succumb to despair and self-pity, he hires a private nurse, Allison (Ali Marsh), and rehab aide, Antonio (Ruben Santiago-Hudson), and equips his three-floor apartment with the latest computer technology, giving him a degree of mobility and enabling him to continue with his work. Coworker Claudia Henderson (Daryl Hannah) had taken over his last project, but pride and self-confidence prevent him from relinquishing his position so easily and he invites her to work with him to complete the job.

His first night home, Jason looks out his third-floor window into a window across the way, a floor below his, and sees a woman lying on a bed. She returns his gaze, smiles coquettishly at him, and waves. Antonio returns the wave for Jason. The woman turns out to be Ilene Thorpe (Allison Mackie), the wife of sculptor Julian Thorpe (Ritchie Coster), and the eventual object of concern when Jason later believes Thorpe murdered her. Antonio appreciates his employer's voyeuristic need and rigs up a surveillance camera with a zooming device so Jason can observe his neighbors in closer detail.

With their curtains open, the windows of the adjacent apartment building reveal to Jason a collage of life styles and activities. On the top floor, construction workers are renovating several apartments into a single exhibition house for artists, the Spartina Gallery. Another window exposes an affectionate exchange between too men (Marc Holzman, David Pittu), obviously homosexuals. (Jason's face shows understanding and amusement without condescension.) In another, two professional people (Peter Giles, Maggie Kiley) return home after their workday and kiss warmly in a prelude to sex. (Jason's face reflects inward thoughts of regret.) In another window, a woman disrobes behind a filmy curtain and welcomes in a sensual embrace the man who enters her room. (Jason's face beams with the knowledge of experience.) In the Thorpe apartment, Ilene drinks heavily and Thorpe shows himself to be an indifferent, insensitive husband.

One night, Jason witnesses Thorpe assaulting Ilene during an argument. He calls the police and Thorpe is arrested. The next night, Jason is in bed when he is awakened by a woman's scream. He hears banging noises and sees sporadic flashes of light coming from the sculptor's apartment. When he fails to see Ilene in the apartment, he becomes suspicious. A day later, however, Ilene reappears, and even though Detective Moore (Robert Forster) investigates and verifies that it is Ilene, Jason is not convinced. With Claudia's help, he secures Thorpe's email address and sends him a message accusing him of murder. From his darkened apartment, Jason watches Thorpe open his email, read the letter, and become highly agitated. At that moment, Jason's nurse, Allison, enters the room and flicks on the light, making Jason visible to Julian. (While Jason is turned away from the window, we can see Julian in the far background dousing the lights as he exits his apartment. The scene closely imitates Hitchcock in how Jefferies is distracted from his vigil and fails to see Thorwald's foreboding departure from his apartment on his way to confront the nosy voyeur.) Allison leaves and Jason resumes his spying on the Thorpes, but the apartment is dark, until Thorpe's supposed wife strikes a match to light her cigarette. She stares up at Jason and shakes her head menacingly. (The ominous gesture counters the seductive one Thorpe's wife had given him earlier.)

Jason leaves a phone message for Antonio to come as soon as he can. In the meantime, Thorpe sneaks into Jason's apartment, realizes how helpless he is, and demands the password so he can erase Jason's email to him. Jason tells him "Achilles" (suggesting Jason's vulnerability, his Achilles heel) and Thorpe slits the tube on his ventilator. But Jason has learned to breathe on his own, and when Thorpe leaves to examine the files, Jason changes his password to "Icarus" (an allusion to one who suffers for abusing technology, perhaps as Jason has done with his surveillance equipment). Jason evades Thorpe long enough for Antonio and Moore to arrive and save him.

Moore tells Jason that the woman is in fact Ilene's sister who was having an affair with Thorpe. Although Ilene is missing, Thorpe, without a corpse, cannot be tried for murder. Jason had seen Thorpe ship one of his large sculptures in a huge crate (a variation of Thorwald's steamer trunk) and believes Ilene's body is stowed inside that sculpture. Jason and Claudia attend the ribbon-cutting ceremony celebrating their completed project where, ironically, Thorpe's sculpture is unveiled. Jason has Moore x-ray it, but nothing is found.

Claudia returns to Jason's apartment that night to reveal her feelings for him. He is willing to accept her love. While they talk, the camera switches point of view, looking down at the lovers from inside the window of the Spartina Gallery. Jason's curtain slides closed and the camera pans over to one of the large sculptures sitting in the gallery. The signature "Thorpe" is on the thick base of the oversized piece and the ominous music suggests that Jason was not far from wrong about the final resting place of Mrs. Thorpe. (This is a variation on the way Woolrich has Thorwald dispose of his wife's body. However, in Bleckner's film, there is no indication that the body will be discovered and Thorpe prosecuted.)

In borrowing Hitchcock's concept of Woolrich's story, Bleckner automatically inserts some *noir* facets into his version of *Rear Window*: scenes with black angular shadows, music with foreboding tonalities (some passages reminiscent of Hitchcock's favorite composer, Bernard Herrmann), tense situations that cause the characters to fluctuate between doubt and certainty, and a flawed and alienated protagonist with a dangerous obsession that makes him susceptible to personal destruction. These few features give the drama a *noir* flavor, but are not enough to place it in the *noir* category. Claudia is no *femme fatale*. She has the potential to threaten Jason's position in the firm, but this is quickly resolved and she instead becomes a conventional love interest without the ambiguities of Grace Kelley's character. The combination of protagonist Kemp's unassailable position of righteousness and the antagonist Thorpe's remorseless villainy sharply defines the sides of good and evil and prevents us from feeling the ambivalence we have for Hal Jeffries, L.B. Jefferies, and Thorwald. (Despite the limitations of his role, Coster excellently projects his menacing wickedness by his reserved, sadistic iciness rather than with outrageous outbursts, an effective portrayal similar in effect to that of Robert Emmett Keane in Shane's *Fear in the Night*.) The ethical questions related to voyeurism are brought up but never discussed, so that by not contrasting Jason's wrongdoing with Thorpe's commission of a crime, the story fails to address an important facet of *noir*, the contradictions in human nature, the questions of guilt that infest both virtuous and venal characters alike.

Bleckner's *Rear Window* updates certain aspects of the story to have it reflect current social norms, such as modern life styles of gays and unmarried couples and the very real computer technology that enables Jason to function independently at home. The film's success depends on its purpose, which is to entertain the audience while educating them about spinal cord injuries—the impact of paralysis on the victim and the hope that a cure may be attained in the near future—and this it does. We learn of the complications in having to deal with a new way of life and the victim's total dependency on state-of-the-art machinery and competent, unselfish aides. In this, Reeve's character shares similarities with Dalton Trumbo's title character in *Johnny Got His Gun*, both alienated from society by extreme physical limitations. Jason surmounts this with determination and self-confidence, as Reeve had done in real life. Several times in the film, the character voices a firm belief that his condition is temporary, that great strides are being made to reverse the effects of these injuries, and that he expects his current disability to be rectified. As we know, this unyielding prognosis was also Reeve's, who had promised to walk by his fiftieth birthday, but failing this, still made tremendous physical progress until his sad death on October 10, 2004, from heart failure, complications from his paralysis. Unless viewers have hearts made out of old shoe leather, the story *must* inspire in them an identical hope that a cure is possible and imminent.

One of the most moving moments in the film occurs when Jason, after leaving the hospital, returns to his apartment and tells Antonio to open up his closet doors. Lining the walls are racks of suits and shelves of shoes, clothes of a former life style that are now obsolete for the paralyzed architect. The scene is an ironic inverse of parallel moments in Fitzgerald's *The Great Gatsby* and *American Gigolo* (Schrader, 1980) in which an ostentatious display of shirts and clothes shows the characters' ties to materialism and extravagance. Jason, bereft of those once ordinary, everyday concerns, must adapt to a totally new way of life.

Reeve's presence in the lead role gives the film its poignancy and its pitfall. Watching him portray his character hooked up to a ventilator is not like watching Everett Sloane walking stiffly on his two crutches in *The Lady from Shanghai* or Jimmy Stewart waiting for his bones to knit in *Rear Window*. It is more like watching Lionel Barrymore being pushed around in his wheelchair as Mr. Potter in *It's a Wonderful Life*. Sloane and Stewart will stand up on their own when their films are done. Reeve, like Barrymore, will not. We are conscious that this actor is not acting the part of a paralyzed victim. He *is* a victim. It is extremely disconcerting to realize that what he is going through is not all fiction.

At the same time, we must admire this extraordinary performance by a courageous actor dedicated to his profession and to the message he wants to impart. Shooting the film must have made demands on him that incurred real pain and exceptional physical effort. His performance is reminiscent of that of Adeline deWalt Reynolds in *Street of Chance*. Although Reynolds was not actually paralyzed, her acting required that she depend solely on facial expressions to communicate her feelings. Reeve was a gifted professional. He knew his craft and was skillful in manipulating his handsome face in the appropriate ways to convey a wide range of emotions and thoughts, whether sorrow, joy, pain, facetiousness, sarcasm, or whatever else. We must feel awe for this accomplished actor, for his courage in coping with his real-life tragedy and his determination to triumph over it, and this film in its own way is one measure of his heroic stature.

Black Alibi

Novel, Simon & Schuster, April 1942; Robert Hale, 1951; first paperback appeared as an abridged edition, Handibooks, pbk #14, 1943; first unabridged edition, Collier, pbk #02665, 1965; reprints in subsequent paperback editions.

Whenever we read a short story or novel by Cornell Woolrich, we find some evidence of his powers of macabre description, whether it be a large portion of the work or only brief passages. As a sustained journey through a mysterious maze marked by taut suspense and sheer terror, *Black Alibi* ranks among the best of his dark and doom-laden visions. The "unity of effect" borrowed from Poe serves him well as he describes in an unrelenting style the deadly, malevolent netherworld into which his unwary victims descend.

The story begins with enterprising publicity agent Jerry Manning trying to enhance the image of his client, local entertainer Kiki Walker, by having her stroll around the South American city of Ciudad Real, leading a jaguar on a leash. While Kiki and Manning are eating at a restaurant, the jaguar becomes startled. It breaks Kiki's hold on the leash and escapes into an alley. Mysteriously, although both ends of the alley are quickly sealed by the police, the jaguar disappears. The event gives rise to superstitions about the cat's paranormal powers, and rumors grow in the days that follow.

One night, the mother of Teresa Delgado orders her teenage daughter to run an errand. The mother needs coal to keep the fire burning so she can cook her husband's dinner. Fearful from the stories of the jaguar, Teresa refuses to go, but her mother chases her out of the house and locks the door. The nearest store is closed, so Teresa must travel farther, passing under a bridge that spans a dry arroyo bed. She senses something prowling in the dark shadows, but she gets to the store safely enough. On her way back, she must again pass under the bridge, and this time she sees the jaguar. She sprints for home. Inside the Delgado hovel, the mother hears her daughter pleading at the door, but refuses to let her in unless she has the coal. Teresa screams. A loud flurry of noises from the other side of the door change the mother's mind but too late. The lock is rusted and cannot be opened. A thin rivulet of blood courses into the room from under the door.

The investigation team, headed by police captain Robles, infers that this is the work of the jaguar. Manning, however, questions this conclusion. He insists that a jaguar would not behave this way, killing for the sake of killing, and he attributes the crime to a depraved human.

The next victim is young Conchita Contreras. Feigning a dutiful visit to her father's grave, she instead goes to the cemetery to meet her lover Raul. Because she is late, she misses him, but she dawdles, hoping he will appear. The old groundskeeper, thinking all visitors have gone, locks the entrance. Conchita becomes trapped within the high stone walls. Sensing danger lurking in the darkness, she becomes frantic. Her cries attract a stranger who runs to get a ladder. He returns too late: the murderous creature claims its second victim.

Clo-Clo, a poor young girl of the streets, is the next victim. She is an odd moral paradox. She seduces men into thinking she will grant them sexual favors, but at the end of the night, after wheedling a good time and a few pesos out of them, she runs away. She is a kind of virginal vamp, a celibate whore. One night, a wealthy businessman, unmotivated by lustful desire, takes a genuine interest in her fun-loving, mirthful nature. To show his appreciation, he gives her a hundred pesos, enough money to keep her off the streets for a long time.

On her way home, she runs into her fortune-telling friend, La Bruja (The Witch), who tells her her fortune. Black omens and deadly forebodings keep appearing in the cards. Clo-Clo ignores the warning, buoyed by her recent windfall. After arriving home, she discovers her money missing. Frantic, she returns to the streets and retraces her steps. She had tempted fate once and won, but fate does not let her get away a second time. The bloodthirsty beast claims its third victim.

Sally O'Keefe is an American visiting Ciudad Real with her friend Marjorie King. As an American, she exhibits stereotypical traits of independence, fearlessness, and curiosity. This proves her undoing when, even after repeated warnings from the locals, she places her life in jeopardy by visiting a remote nightclub. The jaguar claims its fourth victim.

A grief-stricken Marjorie plans to return to America. However, Manning convinces her to stay and help him trap the murderer who he believes is a mere mortal. He further enlists support from Conchita's boyfriend Raul, knowing that the young man is bitter over the loss of his girlfriend. Even after his thorough preparations for what he thinks is a foolproof way of catching the killer, Manning's plan goes awry. The killer is able to evade the two men and abduct the young girl.

In desperate pursuit, Manning struggles to second-guess where the killer may have taken his victim. He finally deduces the location, the ruins of an old church, and he and Raul interrupt him just as he is about to perform a horrible ritualistic molestation on his quarry. It is Robles who is the sick, sadistic serial killer. He wears the head and claws of the jaguar, a perverted merging of man and beast. Manning shoots him and saves Marjorie. For all its sordid, grisly goings-on, the story ends with a romantic tryst. Manning has become enamored of Marjorie and, although shy with women, is about to make his feelings known.

Woolrich's *Black Alibi* presages in some ways his *Strangler's Serenade* (1951), in which a displaced detective deals with some ghastly strangulation murders while falling in love with a local belle, although the earlier novel is far more dense and consistent in its *noir* tonality. In terms of plot construction, as Nevins points out, *Black Alibi* owes much to *The Bride Wore Black* (1940). Following an overall episodic structure, both begin with a prologue that initiates the action and each of the four middle chapters deals with one of the four victims whose importance in the novel is related like a short story within the framework of the larger narrative. Every chapter ends with a kind of "post mortem" section: Manning and Robles of *Alibi* replace Detective Wanger of *Bride* in exploring the circumstances surrounding the death of each victim. The final chapter of both novels has the dogged pursuer setting a trap for the elusive murderer and the two denouements contain ironic twists in the solution of the crime.

The content, too, is remarkably related and makes the two novels complementary. Most obvious is that both stories deal with a serial killer. Also comparable, by virtue of their contrast, is the nature of the killer and the reason for his/her murders. *Bride* might be called a "whydunit" in that it delays revealing Julie's motive until the very end, when the disclosure alters our perception of her from a mad murderess to a sympathetic figure. *Alibi* more closely follows the standard procedure of a "whodunit," where the identity of the killer is kept secret until the final altercation. Julie's motive is logical and comprehensible and she merits our sympathy; Robles's motive is sadistic and mad and he earns our condemnation.

A central theme in *Alibi* emerges from our ambiguous perception of the jaguar. Its mysterious escape on that first night and its ubiquitous appearances thereafter give rise to beliefs that it has supernatural powers. There is the implication that it has the ability to think with the deliberate cunning and intelligence of a human, which creates discrepancies between the supernatural and the natural: we are not sure what to attribute to paranormal powers and what to explain away with logic and common sense. The superstitions of the townspeople are encouraged by Robles's investigation, even though Manning insists on a natural explanation. Manning represents American practicality that defies hysterical superstitions while it seeks rational causes. Alone against a monolithic myth, his "rugged individualism" finally emerges triumphant over the villain's attempt to perpetuate paranoia.

Possibly drawing from a particular childhood incident at a theater in Mexico when rowdy patrons hissed disparaging anti–American slogans and roused his dormant patriotic fervor (*Blues of a Lifetime* 25), Woolrich includes the American reputation for individualism, tenaciousness, and ingenuity as one of *Alibi*'s themes. This is apparent when Manning, an American, recruits a second American to help him. Not only does Marjorie King display bravery and an exceptional allegiance to her murdered girlfriend, but the fact that two Americans assume the responsibility for solving the mystery indicates that American intervention is necessary to rid the superstition-bound foreign society of its curse. As a setting, Ciudad Real — a "real city" — is anything but real and exemplifies Woolrich's tendency to write allegorically. The superstitions of the people give them a biased, unrealistic impression of the world, as hinted in the city's conflict between tradition and progress, its uncomfortable transition from the old to the new. For example, the automobile, a symbol of technological advancement, contains mixed connotations within the story. Conchita Contreras could have taken a car to the cemetery, but she rejects that mode of transportation and rides in a horse-drawn carriage instead. By traveling via a slower, old-fashioned vehicle, she arrives late and misses her boyfriend, a circumstance that contributes to her death. Or a stranger invites Clo-Clo for a ride in his car, but she refuses because she sees it as an evil omen, her misinterpretation of La Bruja's tarot reading. At the same time, Woolrich's descriptions of places like the arroyo or cemetery contradict realism, tingeing the environment with a surreal quality. Part of Robles's villainy, manifested foremost in his sadistic killings of women, is his exploitation of his people's superstitions and his effort to perpetuate their ignorance. Only the Americans can overcome the obstinacy of old ways of thinking and redeem the city from its paralyzing terror. (The one Latino they convince to help them does so only because he wants revenge, not to solve the mystery.)

Fate is handled very deliberately in *Alibi*, not treated simply as coincidence but as an all-powerful force manipulating both time and circumstance in leading the four women to their dooms. In each case, the woman enters a perilous situation either by her own actions (Conchita, Clo-Clo, Sally) or by force (Teresa). Added to this, however, is the time factor which contributes to fate's domination: not only are the women in the wrong place at the wrong time, but if time could have been manipulated differently, each one might have been saved. Mrs. Delgado needed more time to open her locked door. The man who heard Conchita's cry from outside the cemetery wall needed more time to return with a ladder. Clo-Clo beat fate, returning home before her doom caught up with her, but avarice pushed her out into the streets again, where fate, unable to catch up with her the first time, took advantage. Like Clo-Clo, Sally could have escaped death, but she put herself in danger; she ignored the hints from concerned villagers and, typically American, defied propriety to satisfy personal curiosity.

Related to this is the question of justice. All the women are totally innocent, both in their virginity and in their inexperience with the world. Robles preys, literally, on innocence. His sadistic obsession is an instrument of an indifferent fate that uses and abuses people without regard for deserving. Innocence offers no protection against a cruel and pitiless world. Even the most guiltless of us are not safe from the ravages of evil and corruption, from having our lives ruined by pernicious, destructive elements, even if it is through no real fault of our own.

Black Alibi is an extremely affective novel due to Woolrich's powers of description that make the most of all manner of words and images connoting death and darkness. The passages relating the women's journeys along nighttime paths through the city or cemetery conjure up the image of the labyrinth or a descent into hell. Added to this, the intensity of each situation describing a lone, helpless female left vulnerable to the savage fury of a rapacious beast makes the story an absorbing study in terror.

The one major failing is a standard flaw in many of Woolrich's works: the irrationality of the climactic resolution of the story. For one thing, even if we take the story as an allegory of the American ideology emerging triumphant over an outmoded, obsolete way of thinking, Manning's absurd decision to use Marjorie as bait, not to mention his success in convincing her to do it, pokes holes in the fabric of credibility. Woolrich probably needed the two Americans to work together to emphasize his point about American ingenuity and industriousness—but as usual, in resolving his story, he upsets the logic of it. Also questionable is Manning's choice of Raul as his accomplice in catching the murderer. Woolrich justifies the choice with the supposedly logical explanation that Raul would want to believe the murderer to be a tangible entity (that is, a man, not a mystical monster) on which he could avenge himself. By then, however, the whole city is suspect, even Raul. Woolrich makes some dramatic use of this ambiguity, having it appear that Raul abducted Marjorie at the last second and may have been the murderer after all. This does increase the suspense and sustain the mystery, but logically it is weak. The last-minute rescue is equally absurd, not only because Manning is able to infer in seconds the central hideout of the murderer, but also because he is able to get there in time. In Woolrich's defense, having the hero emerge victorious in his race against time acts as a counterpoint to the earlier tragic episodes where time worked against the victims. Only the American, using industry, creativity, and force of will, is able finally to outwit fate and control his own destiny and that of the woman he saves. If Woolrich is implying anything in this, it may be that fate is not as all-powerful as it appears in some of his other stories. It is superstition that predisposes people to succumb to its control; practical-mindedness enables us to thwart its manipulations and achieve self-determination (or at least the temporary illusion of it).

Film: The Leopard Man

1943, RKO. *D:* Jacques Tourneur. *P:* Val Lewton. *Cin:* Robert de Grasse. *Sc:* Ardel Wray (Additional Dialogue: Edward Dein). *Ed:* Mark Robson. *Mus:* Roy Webb. Art *Dir:* Albert S. D'Agostino, Walter E. Keller. *Set Dec:* Darrell Silvera, Al Fields.

Cast: Dennis O'Keefe (Jerry Manning), Margo (Clo-Clo), Jean Brooks (Kiki Walker), Isabel Jewell (Maria), James Bell (Dr. Galbraith), Margaret Landry (Teresa Delgado), Abner Biberman (Charlie How-Come), Tula Parma (Consuelo Contreras), Ben Bard (Police Chief Robles), Richard Martin (Raul Belmonte). 108 min.

Woolrich's popularity rests generally on his suspenseful crime dramas, and *Black Alibi*, at face, fits that category. However, this particular novel also plunges into the murky waters of the horrific, the sensational, the morbid, and the supernatural, dredging up motifs that give it more complexity than the common detective mystery. A number of Woolrich's earlier stories already veer in this direction ("Graves for the Living," "I'm Dangerous Tonight," "Dark Melody of Madness," "The Screaming Laugh," and even "The Boy Cried Murder" in which the murder victim's body is dismembered), so the terrifying aspects of *Alibi* are not alien to the author. Considering when *Alibi* was written, it is possible that Woolrich, an avid filmgoer, may have been influenced by a whole spate of macabre horror films produced in the early thirties. Films like *The Most Dangerous Game, Dr. X, Island of Lost Souls, Murders in the Rue Morgue, Mystery of the Wax Museum*, and even *King Kong* bear a strong kinship with his story, not in plot but in their gruesome displays of death, murder, and mutilation. Repulsive, gut-churning images are sometimes only implied, but explicit graphic scenes are also viewed in these films made before enactment of the Production Code of 1934 necessitated creative side-stepping of self-regulatory strictures. (Lionel Atwill's sewing up an adversary's mouth at the beginning of *Murders in the Zoo* is not an image one readily forgets.)

In addition, some of these films also share with *Alibi* a subject that, at least up until then, was exploited infrequently, namely the serial killer. It is not that the notion of a serial killer was unheard of. At one point in Woolrich's story, the character Jerry Manning actually lists the precedents well known at the turn of the century: Jack the Ripper, Bluebeard, and "that axe killer — what was his name? — in Germany." (In Tourneur's film, Dr. Galbraith notes the precedents.) Hitchcock had already made a version of The Ripper in 1926 (*The Lodger*) — another of those coincidental connections reinforcing Nevins's claim that Hitchcock is Woolrich's film counterpart — but the distasteful topic, usually kept from mainstream consumption, was confined to a narrow niche of grotesque horror films. Today, films about the gruesome savagery of bloodthirsty killers are not only widely flaunted but, incredibly, welcomed as entertainment. The 1970s spawned several categories of serial killer films, most notably the slasher films, which still thrive today. Known for their unabashed exhibition of gore and mutilation, these whack-'em-hack-'em films supposedly reflect the sick, sadistic, distorted wish fulfillment of a misguided mass culture. *The Silence of the Lambs, Hannibal, Seven, Copycat, Kiss the Girls,* and *8mm* are only a few examples of wretched fare that myopic film critics have touted as "commendable," "engrossing," and "extraordinary" pieces of filmmaking — not to mention the many lesser entries which failed to merit such accolades. The villains, the megalomaniac freaks of these so-called "major" films, can only be exhibiting the twisted but repressed desires of the people who have masterminded their production. Not that they have actually adapted their films from Woolrich's "idea" for a sadistic slice-'n-dice story, but they have made their films in the same vein (pun intended) and increased the number and intensity of the grotesqueries.

As an entry in this genre, *The Leopard Man* may contain many of the same plot devices, yet it certainly handles them with more subtlety and sensitivity. Tourneur is the director, but producer Val Lewton deserves most of the credit, since this is his trademark in many of the films he produced, regardless of who the director was. *The Leopard Man* captures Woolrich's style and tone by retaining the intensity of the terror while not bludgeoning the audience with graphic, sadistic violence. Like most adaptations, the film takes liberties with its source, so that any viewer familiar with Woolrich's original story, can appreciate the adapted story for its new twists, its different outcome. Lewton retains the central idea of innocent victims being stalked by what appears to be a rogue leopard (replacing *Alibi*'s jaguar), and although he alters the identity of the original killer, he still iterates Woolrich's implication that something supernatural is at work here, that the leopard possesses preternatural powers. The film's title dupes the audience into thinking that the leopard is a man who has shape-shifted into a deadly cat creature. Lewton teases us here. Having made *The Cat People* the year before, in which a beautiful young woman (Simone Simon), when under emotional duress, turns into a black panther, he counterbalances any charges of sexism in that film by adapting Woolrich's story so that a male supposedly transforms into the fatal feline. The metamorphosis reminds us of the Wolf man stories, where an innocent man becomes the reluctant medium for a bloodthirsty doppelganger. This hapless individual cannot control the monster springing from his id and he becomes submissive to the overpowering evil, which compels him to commit heinous crimes against society and nature. At the end, Lewton supplies a convention used in several of his films (such as *I Walked with a Zombie*): a character proffers a logical explanation to counter what appeared to be supernatural forces at work, but his argument has just enough ambiguity to leave us with a few pesky doubts and unsettled conclusions.

The Lewton-Tourneur adaptation of *Black Alibi* takes place in a small New Mexico town rather than in the mythical Ciudad Real of Woolrich's South America. The story begins similarly, with publicity agent Jerry Manning (Dennis O'Keefe) bringing a leopard into entertainer Kiki Walker's (Jean Brooks) dressing room and getting her to parade it around town on a leash as a publicity stunt. Because she and Clo-Clo (Margo) harbor a professional rivalry, Kiki consents to using the gimmick in the interest of one-upmanship. That night, she walks the leopard into the nightclub during Clo-Clo's dance routine and diverts attention from the performer. In retaliation, Clo-Clo clicks her castanets at the animal. The cat recoils and Kiki loses her grip on the leash. The cat escapes into the nighttime streets.

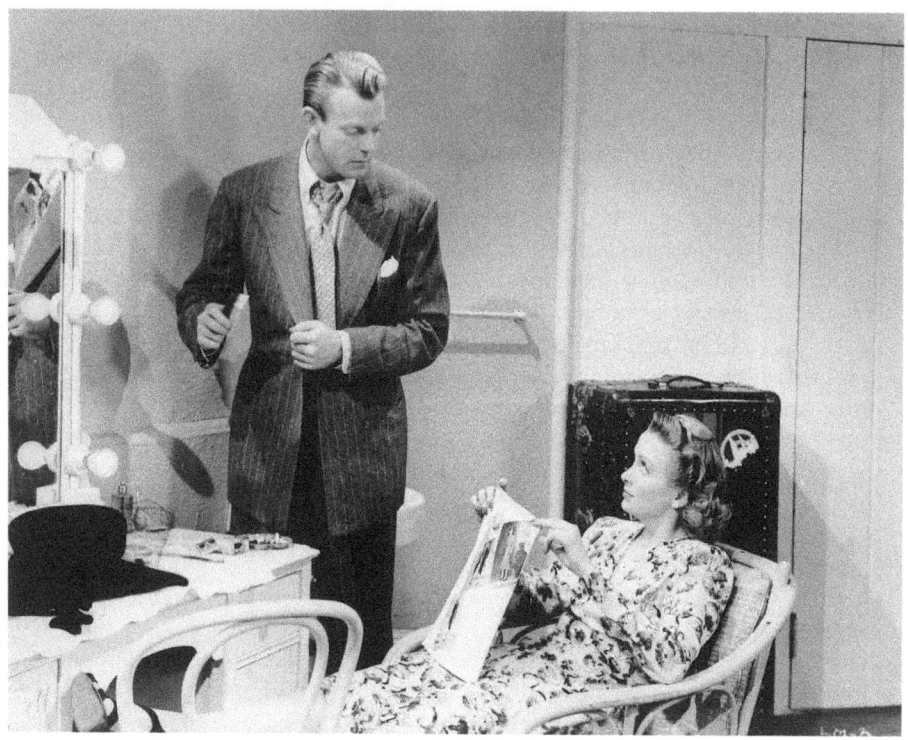

The Leopard Man— In *noir*, guilt often drives the characters' actions. Jerry Manning (Dennis O'Keefe) and Kiki Walker (Jean Brooks) feel responsible for the leopard's terrorizing the village and confer how to solve the dilemma (RKO, courtesy William Thailing).

That night, a mother forces her teenage daughter Teresa Delgado (Margaret Landry) out of the house to get corn meal for her father's dinner. On her way home, she encounters the leopard under a bridge near a dried up arroyo. It chases her and kills her on her doorstep. Two nights later, a rich girl Consuelo Contreras (Tula Parma) goes to meet her lover Raul (Richard Martin) in a cemetery, but accidentally gets locked inside the grounds. Some predator, supposedly the leopard, attacks and kills her. Finally, the entertainer Clo-Clo meets her doom on a village street.

Although the first death seems attributable to the leopard, Manning, like his novel counterpart, believes that the subsequent deaths were committed by a human, a mad but cunning killer using the leopard to cover his despicable crimes. Suspicious of Dr. Galbraith (James Bell), curator of the local museum, he sets a trap with the help of Kiki and Consuelo's grieving boyfriend Raul. Raul, however, is tormented by too much anger and vindictiveness, so that when Glabraith finally confesses his crime, the young man, unable to contain himself, shoots him.

With the murders solved and Manning absolved of guilt, he and Kiki leave the New Mexico town, walking up the dark deserted street toward a brand new life together.

Just as many of Hitchcock's films happen to mirror Woolrich in plot and theme, Lewton parallels the author in tone and story material. Besides *The Leopard Man*, Lewton produced two other films in 1943 that bear some connection to Woolrich. *I Walked with a Zombie* and *The Seventh Victim* are not direct adaptations of any Woolrich work, but they bear striking resemblances to Woolrich's short story "Dark Melody of Madness" in which voodoo and the occult play an important role. (In this respect, Alan Parker's neo-noir *Angel Heart*, 1987, also bears some resemblance.) Woolrich and Lewton both suggest that there are mysterious, inexplicable forces at work that we cannot always account for with our extensive science and knowledge. In this, Woolrich once again connects to Shakespeare, echoing an assertion voiced by the disturbed prince of Denmark who is trying to comprehend the appearance of his father's ghost, "There are more things in heaven and earth, Horatio, than are dreamt of in your philosophy" (*Hamlet*: I.v.165–66).

In *The Leopard Man*, this same notion is indicated as a central theme in the image of the ball that bounces precariously on the apex of the nightclub fountain. It appears several times throughout the film, the first time when Clo-Clo is about to perform her dance routine. Galbraith, talking to Manning the night after Teresa's death, refers to the suspended ball as an analogy for life's unpredictable vicissitudes:

> I've learned one thing about life — we're a good deal like that ball dancing in the fountain. We know as little about the forces that move us — and move the world around us — as that empty ball does, about the water that pushes it into the air, lets it fall, and catches it again.

Galbraith sounds quite fatalistic: by comparing people to a hollow ball, he suggests that they lack substance, and that, subject to an unknown external force, they have no free will. At best, humans are little more than animals, governed only by instinctive motives and base drives. When Galbraith (like Robles in Woolrich's story) plays the leopard, he has symbolically degenerated into a beast, a victim of his own vile animal instincts.

An interesting thing about the above speech is that Galbraith delivers it *before* the death of the second victim, Consuelo Contreras, the woman he murders in the cemetery. (It is determined that the leopard did actually kill the first girl.) That is, he voices this "philosophy," that inexplicable forces constantly motivate and direct our actions, not to justify his crime (which has not yet been committed) but to express a tenet he genuinely believes. Unanswerable is whether the film adopts this attitude toward fate as an objective truth, or whether it simply tries to show how a person's evil perversion predisposes (condemns?) him to act on it when he gets the opportunity. Galbraith seems to think he is not totally culpable. As he explains to Manning and Raul after they trap him:

You don't understand.... You don't know what it means to be tormented this way.... I couldn't sleep. All I could see was Teresa Delgado's body, broken, mangled. I saw it day and night.

[Manning interjects: "And then you found a weapon."]

I didn't want to kill. But I had to. I heard the little girl in the cemetery talking to the man in the auto. When he went away, I thought I was going to help her get over the wall. I can't remember. I looked down. In the darkness I saw her white face, the eyes full of fear. *Fear*, that was it, the little frail body, soft skin, and then she screamed.

[Raul, having listened intently to this narrative, suddenly shoots Galbraith.]

The implications of this speech are varied and ambiguous. For one thing, Galbraith admits that seeing the "broken, mangled" body of Teresa Delgado is what compelled him to mimic the leopard's attack. We know too little about Galbraith to analyze his actions from his personal and psychological history. On the other hand, we might be able to do so if we consider that Teresa's mutilated body represents the horribly grotesque that at once repulses and attracts us. Despite its terrible, gory repugnance, that disfigured corpse spawned an obsession in the curator. It aroused some deep-seated depravity, a latent perversion asleep inside him that needed only this prompting to manifest itself.

Galbraith's abnormality represents the variety of aberrations hidden in us all. It is unsettling, a disturbing notion that all of us could at any time give in to one of those perversions and do serious harm to others. Galbraith begs for mercy, saying that anyone who has not experienced an overwhelming compulsion cannot understand it in those who have. Ironically, Raul shoots Galbraith, putting the degenerate "animal" out of its misery, yet proving Galbraith correct in his observation, that he could expect little sympathy from untested "normal" humans.

Galbraith's assaults, focused on young women, carry much the same symbolism as Robles's attacks on young women in the Woolrich novel. His description of Consuelo's fear and her "little frail body" and "soft skin" connotes complex (and sexual) reasons for his attack, such as male vindictiveness toward the female, the male's violent ambivalence toward virginity, and the male sex drive overwhelming his reason and inspiring a ravenous, animalistic hunger.

Galbraith gives further ironic insights into his motivation when he explains to Manning the temperament of the caged leopard, the animal confined in a small space, repressed and deprived of freedom. This again is Galbraith explaining Galbraith. Like the pent-up leopard, this learned man has considerable potential, yet for some unknown reason ekes out a humble existence in a small isolated town. His uncharacteristic outburst may be a rebellion against the frustrations of his daily life and the repression of his emotions and desires.

After solving the mystery, Manning and Kiki try to reverse the desperate, nihilistic mood created by Galbraith and his heinous crimes. In front of the funeral parlor for the second time (the first time was after Teresa's death), they come to a conclusion about themselves:

The Leopard Man— Consuelo Contreras (Tula Parma) visits the graveyard dressed in black, a fitting foreshadowing of her doom (RKO, courtesy William Thailing).

> KIKI: I hated you that day [at Teresa's funeral], you and your flip talk.
> MANNING: How do you think I felt when you told me not to be soft?
> KIKI: ... I want you to be soft. You *are* soft inside, where it counts. I wanted it that day, too, but I didn't dare tell you.
> MANNING: Galbraith said ... that people were like that ball in the fountain at the hotel, that they got pushed around by things bigger than themselves. That's the way it was with us, only we were too small to see it that way.

Refuting Galbraith's hypothesis, Manning and Kiki walk arm-in-arm up the empty street lit only by a single globed street lamp. They have declared their love and set off deliberately for Chicago, as if they are taking their destiny into their own hands. Their conventional, spiritual love contrasts Galbraith's sadistic, carnal assaults. Even so, the dark, forbidding tonal quality of the film lingers in an after-burn. Free will is suspect; unpredictable forces are like the leopard lurking in the shadows, ready to pounce.

On the positive side, the birth of the relationship between Manning and Kiki is a kind of redemption, foreshadowed in the film's imagery. When Teresa is killed on her front stoop, her blood flows in a vertical line under the door, reaches a crevice, and divides into a horizontal line, forming an inverted "T."

Inside, watching this, her brother holds a log which he dangles above this gory design. The "blood," innocently spilled, and the wood, reminiscent of the "rood," clearly implies that Teresa is a Christ-figure.

The image does not end here. This scene dissolves into a shot of the outside front of the funeral parlor where a window-washer slides his squeegee in vertical strokes down the wet window. The squeegee and his arm form an upright "T," reversing the previous image created by Teresa's blood. The T-shadow falls on the far wall inside the parlor and hovers above Teresa's family who pray before her casket. Meanwhile, Teresa's younger brother, innocently naïve about death, playfully forms a hand-shadow of a leopard's head next to the T-shadow.

The juxtaposition of all these images is suggestive. First of all, the leopard, an animal, cannot be held accountable for any crime: that is, it is naturally "innocent." Galbraith assumes the identity of the leopard, *becomes* the "leopard man," and as he tries to explain, finds himself driven by an obsession he cannot control. He suffers from a kind of "bloodlust," a word that accurately fits his condition in that, metaphorically, his hunger for violence and sex merges. Although accountable for his crimes in a court of law, he is innocent, a victim of forces beyond his control. The argument here is very much the same as that pleaded by an abject Peter Lorre at the end of Fritz Lang's *M* (1931).

In addition, Manning and Kiki appear in the room with the family and then stand in front of the funeral parlor window. They, too, seem associated with the cross image, not necessarily as innocents, but as people redeemed by the events in this small New Mexico town. As Manning says, in a kind of self-effacing confession, he and Kiki were "too small" to admit there *are* forces bigger than they, that they cannot control every phase of their lives. The definition of that ineffable force is left to the audience, who may take it either as indifferent Fate or inscrutable Providence.

Fate and the question of whether there exist the concepts of free will and self-determination are central to the theme of *The Leopard Man*. The film integrates a number of images right from the opening credits, which become important motifs throughout the story.

As the film begins, the opening credits are displayed against the backdrop of an empty village street. Dominating the distinctly Latin music is the rhythmic clicking of castanets. The street scene dissolves to a long shot of a lighted open doorway, the entrance to Clo-Clo's dressing room. The music stops, but the castanets continue to click rapidly and loudly. Clo-Clo glides into the frame of the lighted doorway, dancing and fingering her castanets. The camera pans-right to the open doorway of Kiki's dressing room. Kiki pounds several times on the wall. With her last slap, the loudest, the frenzied clicking stops. Kiki steps around her table and slams her door shut.

That opening street scene serves as a frame for the inset story. The initial deserted street becomes in the end the avenue for two newfound lovers,

Manning and Kiki, who follow it toward a more fulfilling life together. The Latin music creates the sense of an exotic, alien environment, which, when we later learn it is actually still in America, signifies an unfamiliar, foreign enclave embedded within our more familiar environment, the mysterious unknown hidden within the known.

Identified with Clo-Clo are the castanets, their sharp, staccato clicks punctuating the music much as her curt but vivacious personality makes her stand out when she walks along the streets. Related to Clo-Clo are several images that connect her with the deaths of the other two young women. One is the large mirror on her dressing table, visible in the open doorway and reflecting a bit of the dancer who is hidden from direct view. Another is the open doorway itself, which Clo-Clo steps into when she makes her first appearance.

The doorway — and doors in general — become a cornerstone motif in the film. The door is a threshold and symbolizes a gateway between the familiar and the mysterious and between life and death. Our first view of the leopard occurs when it walks through the door to Kiki's dressing room. Danger infiltrates a supposed realm of security; the unknown imposes itself on the known. In both the film and Woolrich's story, the women's deaths are associated with doors. Teresa Delgado is safe in her home until her mother orders her out and locks the door, forcing her to wander the labyrinth of dark streets where looms the ravenous leopard. (When the leopard-man replaces the leopard, he also replaces that other beast-man figure, the Minotaur). The leopard kills her before her mother can reopen the door to safety and security. In the second death, Consuelo Contreras sits on the bench of the cemetery as her image dissolves into one of the great doors being closed by the ancient caretaker. Suddenly, awakened from her romantic reverie, she finds herself locked inside. She follows the winding paths, seeking a way out, but she, like Teresa, becomes a victim of the monster in the labyrinth. The imagery surrounding Clo-Clo's death is linked to theirs. Clo-Clo fearfully wends her way through the labyrinthine streets of her city — and actually arrives safely at her house. However, she has lost the money the kindly old man had given her, and so, goaded by the materialism that has defined her life, she decides of her own free will to return to the labyrinth. Deprived once, Fate does not let her escape the labyrinth a second time.

Kiki is also associated with doors but briefly. When we first see her, it is through the open doorway of her dressing room. She pounds on the wall to silence the frenetic clicking of Clo-Clo's castanets (an obtrusive sound penetrating her sanctuary). Then she walks forward and slams her door shut. Her closing the door signifies the reason she is spared from being ravaged by the roaming monster: she stays inside, keeps herself out of harm's way.

The mirror in Clo-Clo's dressing room is significant for one of its primary associations, vanity. Besides appearing initially as a reflection in a mirror, Clo-Clo is in a number of scenes where her mirror image is prominent. When she dances in the nightclub, we see her reflected in the fountain before we actually see her. On the street walking home, she passes a shop window that sharply reflects her face. Later in her dressing room, her mirror image watches her fortune-telling friend reading the tarot cards. Finally, she has a compact mirror which she uses to primp her face with make-up, just before she is viciously attacked and killed.

Vanity is the basis of the rivalry between Kiki and Clo-Clo, the original sin that jeopardizes the town. Kiki's sole reason for bringing the leopard into the nightclub is to distract the audience from Clo-Clo's performance. Not to be upstaged, Clo-Clo avenges this slight by clicking her castanets in the leopard's face. The cat bolts and escapes, setting up the tragic situation that follows. Although the two women (and Manning) are indirectly responsible for Teresa's death, Clo-Clo is more to blame for creating the circumstances that inspire Galbraith to transform himself into the lecherous leopard man.

Clo-Clo is a product of the city, worldly, ambitious, and materialistic. She might have been spared — after all she did get home safely that night — but she returned to the streets because she was greedy for money. The film character, like the Woolrich character, shows a likable abandon in her flirtatious excursions with men (and even admits she has a boyfriend, Carlos Domingos); however, she is different from her counterpart in that she never confirms her virginity. The film character embodies some interesting facets, but Woolrich gives her more meaningful contradictions.

If guilt and conscience are factors to be considered — as they are in most *noirs*— it is significant that Clo-Clo shows little remorse for what she did, no admission of culpability for the situation she created out of her petty pride. Manning (loosely imitating his counterpart in the novel) and Kiki try to hide their guilt, but they feel it and finally confess it, even to where they risk their lives to rectify their complicity in the matter. Clo-Clo, however, although she admits sorrow for Teresa's death, does not acknowledge her contribution to it. Teresa and Consuelo die while connected to religious imagery, Teresa with the bloody "T," Consuelo with the religious statues and the tree/rood near the wall. Clo-Clo dies on the street while searching for money and applying make-up to her face. In other words, her death comes while she is engrossed in sins of avarice and vanity. Thus, her own death, unlike that of Teresa's and Consuelo's, carries an element of comeuppance, of poetic justice, of divine retribution.

Sheriff Robles assures Manning and the leopard's owner, Charlie How-Come (Abner Biberman), that despite the horror of this tragedy, they shouldn't feel guilty, that it wasn't really their fault. However, admitting guilt becomes a measure of the nobility of character, and assuming responsibility for one's actions can earn exoneration. Charlie, afraid he may have killed while in a drunken stupor, demands he be put in prison rather than kill again. However, the next killing occurs while he is incarcerated and so he is vindicated. Manning and Kiki share in their culpability and try to seek atonement. Both give their paychecks to the grieving Delgado family, and both risk their lives in a plan to trap the suspected murderer. Their success signals their absolution.

During the 1940s, a smattering of films were adapted from Woolrich's works in which a character, plagued by blackouts or a lapse into unconsciousness, was implicated in a crime. Most of these raise questions about the extent of a person's guilt when he commits a crime without complete consent of his will. Some of these films include *Street of Chance* (Thompson's amnesia), *Fall Guy* (Tom's drugged stupor), *The Guilty* (Dixon's spells), *Fear in the Night* (Vince's dream), and *Black Angel* (Marty's drinking). Although not an overriding motif in *The Leopard Man*, Woolrich's theme is inserted obliquely when Galbraith plants the idea in Charlie How-Come that he may have killed Teresa while in a drunken stupor. Charlie becomes fearfully guilt-ridden. Unlike the obsessed Galbraith, he knows the difference between right and wrong and would rather be punished if he were guilty than be allowed to remain free to kill again. (Charlie How-Come is a more developed character than his counterpart in the Woolrich novel.)

Tourneur and Lewton have interwoven fate, obsession, and pretense into a thoroughly intense and engrossing story. The adaptation of Woolrich's *Black Alibi* comes off extremely well and, except for the deletion of the final chapter that sets up the relationship between Manning and Marjorie King, reproduces the original quite faithfully.

"Dormant Account"

Short story, published in *Black Mask*, May 1942; reprinted as "Chance" in *Borrowed Crime*, 1946, under the pseudonym William Irish; reprinted in *Ellery Queen's Mystery Magazine*, May 1953, as "Dormant Account" after *EQMM* purchased *Black Mask* and gained the rights to its previously published stories.

"Dormant Account" begins with narrator George Palmer philosophizing on recent events that have led him to his present situation. His initial comments, then, act as a preamble to the story which is about to be told in flashback, a common *noir* device:

> I often think, what a strange thing Chance is. I often wonder what would have happened if I had picked the name above it, the name below it. Or any of the others. Nothing, probably. But out of all of them, I singled out that one. How? Why? Chance.
> It was in an ad in the paper. The paper was in a waste-bin in the park. And I was in the park on the bum. To make it worse, I was young enough yet to refuse to take it lying down. The old are resigned. I wasn't. I was sore with a burning sense of injustice, bitter about it, and ripe for Chance. And Chance got its devious work in.

Palmer's introspective remarks about Chance and how it impacts on all subsequent events validate why, in a later reprint, the original title was changed to "Chance." At the same time, this introduction implies things about the narrator, which become more apparent as the story develops.

George Palmer is a down-and-out tramp. Having scavenged a newspaper from a trash barrel, he reads an announcement that lists dormant bank accounts waiting to be claimed by their owners. He decides to impersonate one of the delinquent depositors and claim the money as his own. Randomly, he sticks a pin through the back of the advertisement. It pierces the name "Stella Nugent" who holds the account in trust for "Lee Nugent."

Before assuming his new identity, Palmer researches the Nugents' history so as to have answers for questions the bank may ask. Reading back issues of newspapers, he learns that, 18 years ago (1924), the Nugents' apartment building caught fire. The mother and sister died not from burns but from serious throat lacerations they received either when they stuck their heads through the broken windowpanes to call for help, or when they jumped through the window into the safety nets. (Their manner of death serves no meaningful purpose other than to fulfill Woolrich's need to insert something macabre.) Nugent survived and was placed in an orphanage. The apartment building had long since been demolished. Satisfied with this information, Palmer poses as Nugent and succeeds in convincing the bank of his identity. They award him the dormant account, $12,010.

On his way out of the bank, Palmer confronts two news hounds who want the story of his sudden windfall. He tries to flee, but trips over a lame street peddler, Limpy. The photographer takes a picture of Palmer and runs away. Pitying the vendor, Palmer gives him "the odd $10 that came with the $12,010." He has the premonition that the vendor will act as his "mascot, a living good-luck piece, to help ward off the evil that I could feel crowding close behind me."

Palmer plunges into a prodigal life style, spending his illegitimate inheritance with abandon. He demonstrates a lack of moral responsibility, an attitude of entitlement, as if he has the prerogative to exploit the wealth he has not rightfully earned.

Subconscious guilt, however, can surface to harangue the individual. It does so here in one of Woolrich's many personifications of the Erinyes. One night while in a nightclub, sandwiched between a redhead and a blonde, Palmer spies a man tailing him. His unsettled conscience affects his interpretation of the man's motives. He excuses himself and goes to the men's washroom where he pays the attendant $10 to help him elude his stalker. When the other man comes in, the attendant creates a diversion and Palmer slips out.

He takes a cab back to his apartment. On the way, the cab stops under a streetlight where, coincidentally, Limpy is standing. Limpy sees Palmer and warns him of two men who are after him. Palmer suspects that his pursuer is the real Nugent who wants his money. He sends Limpy up to his room for a pair of shoes and a small tin box hidden in his refrigerator. He wants to leave town and tells Limpy to meet him at the train station where he will be hiding behind a newspaper. Palmer knows Limpy must suspect that there is money in the box, about $11,000 of the $12,000 he got a week ago, but he feels he can trust the peddler: "Maybe, I thought shamefacedly, he's not like you, maybe he don't take what don't belong to him." Introspectively, Palmer expresses an awareness of his crime, indicating that he has a conscience. His act of thievery was done out of desperation, not malice or greed.

Limpy shows up with the money and the shoes. Palmer makes a gift of the suits and belongings left in his hotel room. Limpy declines the clothes, afraid they will hamper his ability to peddle his wares if he looks too well-dressed. He says he will hold Palmer's belongings, though, until he can reclaim them. He gives him his address on Pokanoke Street.

Palmer appears to have made a clean escape, but on the train, the police arrest him for a murder that Nugent committed. In the car, Palmer realizes that his captors are not police officers after all. Instead of driving him to the station, they take him to a private mansion where he meets Eddie Donnelly, whose father was the business partner of Lee Nugent's father. Joe Nugent had extorted funds from their company and fled the country, while the elder Donnelly, although innocent, was arrested and sent to prison. Before he died in jail, he made his son vow vengeance on the man who put him there. Joe Nugent died before Eddie could exact his revenge, so he looked to satisfy himself on the son. Palmer protests, confessing his stolen identity. However, he naively reveals facts about Nugent which convince Donnelly he must be the man he is looking for. Donnelly intends to kill him slowly by burying him alive but feeding him air through a small tube to prolong the horror of his death. Palmer admits his trepidation, thinking that "one of the oldest instincts of man is fear of being put into the ground alive." (This is one example of Woolrich's attempt to insert a generalization about human nature. Sometimes the remark is accurate and insightful, but often, such as here, it is suspect as logic or truth.)

On the way to the cemetery, Donnelly's driver takes a wrong turn onto Pokanoke Street, where Limpy lives. Without warning, a truck pulls out and collides with the car. (Extraordinary coincidences abound in this story.) Palmer is able to escape his captors because, he surmises, they confronted death suddenly while he was already facing death and so was better prepared at that moment (another example of a dubious assumption). While running from the car to find sanctuary in Limpy's apartment, he is shot in the arm.

Palmer enters one building, climbs the stairs to the roof, and crosses several roofs to get to Limpy's apartment. He approaches Limpy's door, thinking, "...why do you want to live this bad? ... you have nothing. Just a bench in the park, just a paper out of a bin. Give me that, I breathed, but let me live." (The will to live, the urge to survive — these thoughts reinforce Palmer's statements in the opening paragraphs about youth's durability and persistence, its having the spunk to overcome despair, to fight tenaciously to succeed, and never to accept failure.) Palmer collapses. Limpy appears, helps Palmer to his feet, but hesitates bringing him into his room. Palmer is puzzled, but Limpy asks him, if Palmer were Limpy, would Palmer rescue him, knowing that he himself, as Limpy, is the real Lee Nugent (the ultimate ironic coincidence of the story).

The truck driver from the accident had called the police, who arrive just as Donnelly and his men are breaking down Nugent's door. Donnelly is killed in the fray; the others are arrested. Palmer is sure that both Limpy and he, "the real and the fake," would have been killed if not for this last minute rescue. After spending time in the hospital for his arm, Palmer returns to the park. Fortunately, Nugent, now able to claim his inheritance without hindrance, did not want to press charges. (Another shaky point of logic.) Nugent shows up at the park, dressed in expensive clothes and driving a car. He gives Palmer $10, "completing the circle of events, ending things where they began." Then he invites Palmer to come with him because they have "a lot in common."

Woolrich's relentless use of coincidence in "Dormant Account" iterates the *noir* question of what determines human action and outcomes: whether the course of human lives is dictated externally by Fate or Providence or Chance, or controlled internally by free will and self-determination.

Palmer's experience, from beginning to end, is, as he admits, governed mostly by Chance. Consider the inordinate number of fluke occurrences, accidental intersecting of events without a coherent connection between cause and effect. Chance is responsible for his picking that particular name from the list of dormant accounts. (He sticks a lapel pin randomly into the newspaper to select his alias.) Then, immediately after he uses that name to get his money, he steps out the door of the bank and collides with his alter ego, Nugent himself. Later, when he is returning to his apartment after escaping his pursuer in the nightclub, he *happens* to stop under a light where Limpy (Nugent) *happens* to be stationed to warn him about the men after him. Finally, after Donnelly captures him, Palmer's opportunity to escape depends on the freak convergence of several chance events: Donnelly's driver takes a wrong turn down a street; the street happens to be where Limpy lives; and a truck backs out and hits Donnelly's car.

Woolrich's ending, with Nugent giving Palmer $10 and "completing the circle of events," is a suitably ironic comment on the nature of Chance and the roles the two main characters play. First of all, Palmer and Nugent are inverted doubles. Palmer, a vagrant, comes into the money illegally, until Nugent, his vagrant double, finally inherits the money legitimately. The vagrant who received $10 from the rich man becomes the rich man who now gives $10 to the vagrant who played the rich man. Nugent is a pun for "new gent," which both men become at different times, shedding their vagrant status for a more gentlemanly image.

When Nugent invites Palmer to come with him because they have "a lot in common," the word "lot" is a pun for Fate, which the two men seem to share, from their first collision on the street to their rescue by the police. Their "Chance" encounter means something special to Nugent and he believes they should continue together to insure Fate's intention for them. The story ends before we can learn what that Fate might be, but he appears ready to take Palmer in and help him after his run of bad luck. How their newfound association evolves and what it becomes is arguable. However, whereas in "He Looked Like Murder" and "Nightmare" the male relationships carry strong homosexual overtones, there are no such implications here. To say that theirs is anything other than a fateful friendship is totally speculative.

Woolrich enhances Palmer's character by giving him a mix of noble and negative qualities. His desperate circumstances make him a sympathetic character and his plan to deceive the bank comes partially out of necessity, not wholly out of greed or selfishness. In his opening remarks, when he rails against his "lot" and feels bitter against the injustice of his situation, we feel pity for him and root for his success, unlawful though it be. After he withdraws the money and gives $10 to the vagrant he accidentally knocks down, we see a considerate and sensitive side to his personality. However, within the next week he spends a thousand dollars on riotous living. Vain about going out with two different women every night and his closet already crammed with new suits, he appears to us in a different light. He is extravagant, hedonistic, and unproductive. He is still shiftless, only now he has money to give the illusion that he is someone important, someone with the power and the right to behave this way. At the rate he is going, in 12 weeks he will be back on the park bench.

Our opinion of him changes yet again. When he sends Limpy to his room to get his money, he trusts him, believing him an honorable man, not a thief like himself. Comparing himself to Limpy shows that he is conscious of his wrongdoing and that he appreciates honesty, and we detect a tacit remorse for his crime. Our sympathy for Palmer is further reinforced when Donnelly captures him and sets out to punish him for a crime he did not commit.

At the end of "Dormant Account," Palmer not only manages to escape death at the hands of Nugent's nemesis, but he also avoids a jail sentence because Nugent does not press charges. (A narrative flaw, since Palmer's crimes of fraud and extortion would not need Nugent's blessing to deserve legal accountability, an oversight corrected later in the film adaptation.) He returns to the park bench, his life not much different after the experience. However, Nugent, playing a kind of *deus ex machina*, presents Palmer with a business opportunity that may yet turn Palmer's life around. We can only guess.

Set in a period immediately following the Depression, the story suggests some things about the Haves and Have-Nots, that money may set them apart, but there is no difference in character between a wealthy nabob and a penniless vagrant. Whether people get their money suddenly through profiteering (Palmer exemplifies the *nouveau riche*) or through birth (Nugent inherits), they are two sides of the same coveted coin.

Donnelly's sadistic plan for revenge, giving Palmer (as Nugent) a premature burial and keeping him alive to intensify the horror of that claustrophobic state, is a plot device that surfaces occasionally in Woolrich's works. "Graves for the Living" used it as its central premise. And in *The Bride Wore Black*, one character, Moran, is "interred" alive when Julie locks him in a small closet to die by suffocation. Palmer says that humans instinctively fear being buried alive, but this thought, as gruesome as it may be, is not necessarily a universal truth. It sounds more like Woolrich expressing a personal fear through one of his characters. The macabre influence of Poe once again skims the surface of Woolrich's writing.

When it comes to the guilty party facing punishment for a criminal deed, the standard scenario is to have the villainous character receive his or her just deserts in clear and direct relation to the crime committed. This is the formula Woolrich uses in "Nightmare," *The Black Curtain, Black Alibi,* and *The Black Path of Fear,* where the antagonists get their rightful comeuppance. No irony is present here. It merely substantiates the traditional belief that evil is always punished.

Woolrich, however, also likes to enliven his stories by creating ironic entanglements with guilt, innocence, justice, and punishment. For instance, the position in which Palmer finds himself with Donnelly, after adopting a false identity that places him in jeopardy for something he did not do, is one such ironic situation. In this way, Woolrich demonstrates how fate finagles events to produce dire consequences for indiscreet individuals. Palmer's situation exemplifies one of the more mysterious and elaborate paths that justice can sometimes take. A character, guilty of an infraction or an imprudent decision, finds himself in circumstances where he is punished for a different crime, one for which he is innocent. Woolrich uses a similar approach in "Silent as the Grave," where a husband confides in his wife about a murder he committed many years before. A recent killing occurs and her suspicions are aroused. Under great psychological duress, she reveals his age-old crime to the authorities. He is arrested, and too late she learns her fears were unfounded because he is not guilty of the later murder. This kind of punishment has the quality of poetic justice, where the guilty party cannot escape retribution, even if it is indirectly administered for an unrelated crime.

Another variation on the ironic relationship between crime and punishment occurs in stories where a person's plan to kill another person or triumph over him boomerangs and the perpetrator brings disaster on himself. Some examples of this kind are "Three O'Clock," where a husband's homemade bomb meant for his unfaithful wife becomes a weapon of his own demise, and "The Fountain Pen" where a writing implement, rigged with an explosive, takes a circuitous route back to the vengeful party. "The Corpse Next Door" and "After-Dinner Story" also fit this category in that the murderer's inability to cope with his guilt leads to his self-destruction. "Mind over Murder" contains the double twist in that one conniving character is punished while another more diabolical one gets away with murder.

In a final type of ironic situation, the completely innocent suffer unjust consequences. The point of these stories is that, in a world governed by capricious fate or unpredictable fortune, there is no such thing as poetic or divine justice. The meek will not necessarily inherit the earth. The good, along with the bad, receive no guarantees of success or reward, both equally subject to misfortune. "The Night Reveals," "I Wouldn't Be in Your Shoes," and *Black Alibi* emphasize this pattern of indiscrimination. Examining the scope of Woolrich's work, we see that he entertains a broad scope of possibilities that link guilt and innocence to justice, injustice, punishment, and redemption. Sometimes characters are spared and find happiness (*Phantom Lady*, *Deadline at Dawn*), but any outcome is simply one of *many* possible fates, happy or tragic endings occurring independently of the guilt or innocence of the characters.

"Dormant Account" belongs in that category of Woolrich story called The Living Nightmare, along with other stories like "Nightmare," *Phantom Lady*, or "All at Once, No Alice," where the character gets caught in a surrealistic intrigue that blurs the line between dream and reality, until he or she (and sometimes the reader) is not sure which is which. Despite the cavils about Woolrich's few lapses in logic, "Dormant Account" is still a gem of a story. Such foibles are easily pushed aside in appreciation of the spellbinding suspense and relentless momentum of his plotting.

Film: The Mark of the Whistler

1944, Columbia. *D:* William Castle. *P:* Rudolph C. Flothow. *Cin:* George Meehan. *Sc:* George Bricker (adapted from the Columbia Broadcasting System Program "The Whistler"). *Ed:* Reg Browne. *Art Dir:* John Datu. *Set Dec:* Sidney Clifford. *"Whistler" theme music:* Wilbur Hatch.
    Cast: Richard Dix (Lee Selfridge Nugent), Janis Carter (Patricia Henley), Porter Hall (Joe Sorsby), Paul Guilfoyle (Limpy Smith/Lee Nugent), John Calvert (Ed Donnelly), Howard Freeman (M.K. Simmons), Matt Willis (Perry Donnelly), Willie Best (Shoeshine man), Matt McHugh (Tom), Arthur Space (Sellers, the bell captain), Minerva Urecal (Woman sweeping front stoop). 60 min.

    Between 1944 and 1948, Columbia produced eight films in *The Whistler* series, capitalizing on the popularity of the radio show at that time. None of the films is a cinematic blockbuster, but as mystery-thrillers, all are well written, competently made, and thoroughly entertaining. The series follows the premise of the radio show: The Whistler floats in and out of the story, not so much a participant as a peripheral commentator on events. Although he remains unseen, only his passing shadow visible as it glides over the ground and across walls, the characters react in ways that show they feel his tangible presence. He begins each episode with the words, "I am the Whistler and I know many things." Like his radio contemporary, *The Shadow* ("Who knows what evil lurks in the minds of men?"), he knows what and how people think and so his voiceover, besides filling in some background information, is especially important in relating whatever mental conflicts the main characters are experiencing. Echoing Woolrich's implications about guilt, the Whistler acts like a "voice of conscience," yet he also tends to play a sardonic character, mocking the protagonists' moral dilemmas and imprudent decisions.
    Directed by horror film veteran William Castle, *The Mark of the Whistler* follows the events of Woolrich's "Dormant Account" in a nearly one-to-one correspondence. Otherwise the film's alterations to the original story rectify Woolrich's questionable narrative logic, enlarge the plot, and support a different theme.
    A down-and-out vagrant, Lee Selfridge Nugent (Richard Dix), discovers a list of dormant accounts advertised in a newspaper and impersonates one of the claimants, who coincidentally has his name (minus the pretentious "Selfridge"). He succeeds in deceiving the bank officials and withdraws the amount, $29,010, in cash. Exiting the bank, he is confronted by newspaperwoman Patricia Henley (Janis Carter) and her cameraman. He tries to avoid them and accidentally

The Mark of the Whistler— The collision between the two Lee Nugents (Paul Guilfoyle, left, and Richard Dix, kneeling) shows the strange workings of Fate (Columbia, courtesy William Thailing).

collides with a street peddler, Limpy Smith (Paul Guilfoyle), who befriends him. Later, Eddie Donnelly (John Calvert) sees Nugent's picture in the paper and believes him to be the son of the man who betrayed and ruined his father. He seeks revenge. He abducts Nugent and plans to kill him, but a freak automobile accident enables Nugent to escape. Although shot in the arm, he manages to reach Limpy's apartment to hide. Limpy takes him in, at the same time revealing that he is the real Lee Nugent whom Donnelly is after. While Donnelly and his men are banging down the door, the police arrive. They shoot Donnelly and rescue the two Lee Nugents. At the hospital where the false claimant is recovering, Patricia and Limpy visit him. Limpy tells how he plans to use his newly acquired fortune to fix his lame leg and start a business. Lee Selfridge Nugent will have to go to jail for a brief time, but Limpy promises him a job when he comes out. The Whistler intervenes with the last word, verifying that fate, in the future, will be kinder to the hapless vagrant.

Like Palmer, Lee Selfridge Nugent constructs his false identity carefully and deliberately, but the film inserts some plot devices to make him a more sympathetic character. First, the Whistler introduces him as a businessman who has fallen on hard times. That is, he was once a productive member of society, who through no fault of his own was forced into these desperate circumstances. Palmer also is desperate, but we don't know anything about his past to make us side with him. We follow him with less empathy, more curious about how his story will end than hoping he will succeed.

To prepare for his meeting with the bank official, Nugent buys a suit on credit from a penurious clothier named Sorsby (Porter Hall). Sorsby is so tightfisted, so mean in his miserliness, that we are repelled by his creepy avariciousness (a trait which actor Hall adroitly exudes in many of his screen roles), and by comparison, want to see Nugent prevail and rid himself of this leech. And he does. When he finally gets the money from the bank, instead of buying new clothes from Sorsby, he goes elsewhere.

In terms of conscience and awareness of guilt, Woolrich's George Palmer is almost an amoral character of similar ilk as Hal Jeffries in "Rear Window." In formulating his plan to bilk Nugent out of his inheritance and the bank out of its money, he proceeds with cold, indifferent calculation. After he gets the money, the first thing he does is turn to a life of reckless spending and physical pleasure. He frequents nightclubs, flaunts two different female escorts every evening, and makes friends among the late-night party crowd. This, together with his suite in a posh hotel and the new suits he has bought but not yet worn, shows a vain person wasting his newly gained wealth on frivolity rather than appreciating his being rescued from indigence and using his new money more constructively.

Similarly, Lee Selfridge Nugent rents a suite in a ritzy hotel and eats in an expensive nightclub, but his is a more natural response than Palmer's. Selfridge Nugent eases into his new life style with more reservation, not squandering his money on a hedonistic binge. Plus, the soft-spoken Dix, despite his size, has a face etched with melancholy and vulnerability. His demeanor alone begs our sympathy.

The film deviates from the short story by giving the vagrant the same name as the genuine claimant of the dormant account. Doing so, the film emphasizes the doubling of the two characters, but this is not necessary. As in the short story, the doubling is indicated through other devices, such as both men being vagrants who eventually claim the money, one illegally, the other rightfully. The inclusion of the middle name "Selfridge," however, connotes some new ideas about Dix's character. For one, he once may have been a member of the upper class; the name has the air of wealth. It also confirms his individual identity, separate from Limpy's, as a second Lee Nugent, and it indicates his independence ("self").

Changing one of the two newspapermen into a female gives the film the romantic interest nonexistent in the short story. To its credit, the film does not exaggerate this aspect. It hints at the possibility of a relationship developing between Patricia and Nugent, but it never fully materializes. Only at the end, when she visits him in the hospital and the omniscient Whistler-narrator says that the future will be kinder to Lee Selfridge Nugent do we see the romantic potential looking like a possibility.

The Donnelly character plays a similar role in the film. Although his father is not dead, as in the short story, he has suffered a living death, paralyzed in mind and body. This explains Donnelly's intended eye-for-an-eye vengeance. Woolrich's Donnelly says explicitly that he plans to make Nugent suffer hideously through a premature burial, but the film does not go that far, Donnelly only telling Nugent that he can expect a slow, torturous death. Director Castle is noted for his tongue in cheek horror stories. It is surprising that he did not use more vivid detail to indicate something excruciatingly repulsive.

The conclusion of Woolrich's story reflects the amorality of his protagonist. Although Palmer narrates his story in flashback, he never shows any deep remorse in his endeavor. There is only that one lapse, after he has sent Limpy to his apartment to fetch his money, when he comments: "Maybe, I thought shamefacedly, he's not like you, maybe he don't take what don't belong to him." Palmer's "shamefaced" thought hints at some remorse, but not enough to make him consider returning the money willingly and accepting punishment for his crime. To top it off, even though he failed, he is rewarded. Limpy shows up at the park to invite him to share his fortune in their fateful partnership.

In keeping with Lee Selfridge Nugent's more sympathetic character, the film has him punished for his crime, making amends before he can return to society. Limpy tries to get him off, but the bank has pressed charges— a more logical consideration than Palmer's being able to commit his crime with impunity. Where Chance will take Palmer and Limpy, we do not know. The film offers more definite closure (not necessarily the more desirable ending) with Limpy offering Lee Selfridge Nugent a partnership in his business when he gets out of prison. Since Selfridge Nugent is a businessman who fell out of favor, we see this as a kind of poetic redemption, the individual ruined by society, now saved and invited to rejoin the community. He will serve prison time to erase his social debt and he will return to business to be a productive contributor to society. The idealistic expectation is that he will achieve the American dream, attaining all its promised amenities of money, success, and love.

As a device, the Whistler is effective because he narrates the internal thoughts of the characters, primarily the thoughts of the protagonist. Because the Whistler mimics the voice of conscience, his voiceover deliberates moral questions, weighing decisions that involve right and wrong. We know that Selfridge Nugent is a moral character because, even though he commits a crime, he has feelings of guilt, doubts about what he is doing. In other words, he becomes more convincingly human for us so that we empathize with him even more than if we had to judge him simply by his external actions.

Phantom Lady

Novel, published by The Story Press, a subsidiary of J.B. Lippincott, August 1942; developed from the original Cornell Woolrich short story "Those Who Kill," in *Detective Fiction Weekly*, March 4, 1939, which was expanded into the serial "Phantom Alibi," in *Detective Fiction Weekly*, Parts 1 through 6, May through October 1942, before being revised as *Phantom Lady* under the pseudonym William Irish.

Phantom Lady is the first novel Woolrich authored under the pseudonym William Irish. Why he chose this name is explained in an oft-repeated tale that sounds suspiciously like an attempt to conjure up a colorful myth in a life patently bare of concrete biographical information. In 1942, when editor Whit Burnett at The Story Press decided to publish Woolrich's serial "Phantom Alibi" as the novel *Phantom Lady*, Woolrich, that same year, had already published his third novel *Black Alibi* with Simon & Schuster. Burnett advised him to consider a pseudonym to avoid "overloading his market." Supposedly, this editor suggested a foreign name, something "'Spanish or French or Irish...,' to which Woolrich glibly responded, 'You've just named me—Irish'" (James Nelson, Introduction to *Phantom Lady*. New York: W.W. Norton & Co., 1967). However, this sparks some afterthoughts. In theory, using a pseudonym can be a valid tactic for keeping an author's name from saturating the market, but would a new editor advise a name change to an author who already had popular name recognition? Would he really want to gamble on publishing a book authored by a fresh, unfamiliar name? It is possible that Woolrich's new publisher hoped to capitalize on the author's talents under an identity that separated him from his other affiliations; nevertheless, as presented, the story sounds too trite to be convincing.

Another bit of confusion surrounding Woolrich's alias occurs from the fact that a "William Irish" appears in the credits of several silent films of the late 1920s. This earlier Irish wrote the titles for such indelible classics as *The Haunted House* (1928) and *Seven Footprints to Satan* (1929), both directed by Danish émigré Benjamin Christensen. The question is whether Irish the titlist and Irish the author are one and the same. Understandably, some sources equate the two not only because of the name but because Woolrich had lived in California between 1928 and 1931, just when his first novel, *Children of the Ritz*, was adapted for the screen. It would not be absurd to imagine that some film company at this time recruited him for his writing ability. If true, however, it discredits the Burnett story even more because Woolrich would already have had a pseudonym and not needed one invented spontaneously on an editor's whim. Woolrich's biographer Francis M. Nevins, Jr., hints strongly that Irish the titlist *is* Irish the author, but in his discussion, he raises enough unanswered and unanswerable questions that the discrepancies prohibit conclusiveness. Although Woolrich enthusiasts may take it for granted that both Irishes are the same man, no evidence exists to connect the author with his earlier namesake and Woolrich himself never verified it one way or the other. (In support of Nevins, the Internet Movie Database credits Cornell Woolrich as the titlist of those two silent films. The IMDB also notes a third Christensen film, *House of Horror*, 1929, which Nevins substantiates as another of Irish's handiworks.)

Irish anecdotes aside, *Phantom Lady* is one of Woolrich's most engaging, most suspenseful, and most popular novels. It must have been a very satisfying experience for him, developing it from a short story to a magazine serial and finally to a published novel. It covers a wide spectrum of tonal coloration, from light amusement to dark foreboding, from tender romance to grizzly horror, from playful comedy to serious commentary.

After an unsettling quarrel with his wife, a man stops at a bar, where he picks up a woman he has never seen before and invites her to go with him to a theater show. Her one distinguishing characteristic is the flamboyant orange hat she wears. Other than that, she has a nondescript face and figure. They make a strange pact, agreeing not to divulge their names. From the bar, they go to dinner, take a cab to the theater, and then return to the bar, where he leaves her. He goes back to his apartment and finds his wife Marcella has been murdered. Police are already there. His admission of having had a fight with her and then going out with a nameless woman at the very time she was murdered makes him appear all the more guilty. The corroboration of his mystery date is all he needs, but that's the catch. The police can't find her. In fact, when the husband, Scott Henderson, accompanies them the next day along the route he took, all the witnesses who apparently saw them together will confess only to seeing him alone. The elusive woman becomes the enigmatic Phantom Lady.

Burgess, the police detective who arrested Henderson, has second thoughts about his guilt. He convinces Henderson to ask his good friend John Lombard for help. Lombard is an engineer who recently went to South America, but he returns quickly when summoned. Burgess has also talked with Henderson's girlfriend, Carol Richman, who is intent on finding the woman. While Burgess maintains a low profile, Lombard and Richman act independently, following up the list of witnesses to see if and why they might have lied. Coincidentally, some of these people meet mysterious deaths, by accident or design.

In the end, we learn it is Lombard who murdered Henderson's wife and masterminded the cover-up. He had been having an affair with Marcella. Their plan was to run away to South America and get married. Lombard is standing outside the Henderson apartment when the couple have their boisterous argument. He sees Henderson leave angrily and assumes Marcella had provoked the argument so they can fulfill their rendezvous. Instead, once alone with Lombard, she admits that she had been using him only for her amusement. She belittles him with her shrill, scornful laugh. His vanity bruised, he becomes violently enraged and kills her. He follows Henderson that night, intending to frame him for the murder. With money and threats, he persuades all the witnesses to deny the existence of Henderson's date, thus depriving him of an alibi. When Lombard had returned to New York after receiving Henderson's telegram, it was with the intention of following the trail of witnesses to the one woman who could support Henderson's story. If Lombard could kill her, his safety would have been secure.

Burgess, however, was already suspicious of Lombard, and with Carol's help, he uncovers Lombard's murderous plan and proves his guilt. Lombard confesses to Burgess, who then relates the details of Lombard's intricate scheme to Henderson and Carol. In a finale tinged with romantic overtones, the reunited lovers bid farewell to Burgess and set out with marriage in the offing.

One critical factor in *Phantom Lady* is the narrator's point of view, which, like an uncertain wind, keeps shifting its direction. The story begins from the all-seeing eye of an omniscient narrator, but then segues into a series of limited omniscient points of view divided among Scott Henderson, John Lombard, and Carol Richman. Yet because the narrator seldom, or only superficially, delves into the psyche of the characters, it can be argued that Woolrich is using an objective or dramatic narrator, the speaker generally relating events from outside the characters. Such an approach enables Woolrich to shield the identity and motive of certain characters until the climactic moment, when he lifts the mask to reveal who has been creating the mischief. We already saw this in *The Bride Wore Black*, where in the "Holmes" section he creates an ambiguous situation between two women by making it uncertain which of them is the beautiful but deadly murderess. By delaying this revelation, he can sustain suspense while making use of irony.

From Henderson's point of view, we follow his initial adventure with the woman in the orange hat. We accept the events as real, as actually happening, insofar as Henderson sees and experiences them: a chance meeting in a bar, an impromptu date, a ride in a taxicab, dinner at a restaurant, a theater show. When Henderson returns to his apartment where the police accuse him of killing his wife, we think we know the main complication in the story, that he will have to produce an unidentified woman to corroborate his story and give him an alibi. Instead, when the witnesses from the night before begin to deny having seen a woman accompanying Henderson, the question is not whether he can find her but whether she existed at all. The story becomes an existential exercise in that we suddenly must wonder whether the event, told from

Henderson's viewpoint, was an imagined reality. Even if he did not deliberately formulate it, he might have resorted to a defense mechanism by which his guilty conscience enabled him to deny the murder he really *did* commit. When he tells Burgess to forget looking for the Phantom Lady, that he does not want to look anymore because he is afraid he is going crazy, we understand. Like Henderson, we wonder if she existed in the first place. If she did, how is it that so many witnesses aligned against him? And if she did not, what direction is the story going in after all? If Woolrich is playing with coincidences, he has taken them too far, stacked them so high that they are teetering and ready to topple into a disorderly heap. But no, he is too skillful in this art. He has squeezed us into that tightly compressed state of suspense that longs for some explanation of Henderson's predicament. And so he eventually gives it to us.

Before that resolution is reached, the story shifts to the limited perspectives of the other two characters, Carol Richman and John Lombard. We follow them in their pursuit and questioning of the various witnesses, but we seldom get into their minds to see what they are actually thinking or feeling. Descriptions of the lonely subway station, deserted dark streets, and grungy tenement houses are among the best of Woolrich's *noir* settings and carry special significance for their expressionistic contributions to the story. At the same time, these descriptions are presented as external observations by the narrator or are filtered through the characters as impressions, not as interpretations and opinions. We learn little about either Richman or Lombard, other than that Carol is the woman Henderson wants to marry and Lombard is Henderson's best friend, the kind of friend Burgess urged Henderson to consult if he expected to overturn his conviction. The subsequent coincidental deaths of a string of witnesses create an aura of mystery from several angles. First, we wonder who or what is causing all these deaths: some appear legitimate accidents (the barman, the phony blind man), but some are questionable (the drummer Cliff Milburn). Suspicion falls on both Richman and Lombard. We have to ask whether they are covering something. If not, then a second possibility is that an unknown party is eradicating them to silence them forever. Could it be Burgess? More likely, the Phantom Lady would seem to have a hand in this. After all, the title suggests she has a prominent role in the story, and even though she has dropped out of sight, her presence is continuously felt.

Guilt permeates the story, tainting nearly all the characters in some way. Everyone who accepts Lombard's bribe becomes his accomplice and has something to hide. The bartender, the taxi driver, the headwaiter, and the drummer share his guilt, whereas Lombard is immune to any pangs of conscience. When Carol confronts the bartender and Cliff Milburn, their instinct for self-preservation inspires resistance, but guilt erodes their willpower and justice demands its harsh ultimate sentence, death. (Why Woolrich spares the headwaiter, the table-waiter, and Al Alp from Carol's grilling is unclear. Maybe he felt his novel would have grown to too unwieldy a length.) Lombard, on the other hand, confronts three people he had overlooked or failed to find after the night of the murder. The phony blind beggar, the plagiarizing hat maker, and the woman who purchased the bogus hat are not part of his conspiracy, but their illegal activities stigmatize them with their own private guilt. Madge Peyton, the hat maker, is spared; however, the phony blind beggar and Pierrette Douglas, who bought Mendoza's facsimile, meet their untimely demise. (The chica-chica-boom girl, Estela Mendoza, falls into a vague category of her own. Unexplained is why Lombard, on the night of the murder, had failed to bribe her since, of all the witnesses, she had the greatest reason to remember the Phantom Lady. When Lombard finally visits the singer in her flat, nothing comes of the meeting except that he gets the address of her hatter, Kettisha. What transpires between Lombard and Estela seems intended as a bit of comic relief. It works well enough on its own and demonstrates the breadth of Woolrich's writing abilities, but substantially, it is out of place in the story.)

Although Henderson may be considered The Wrong Man, he is not totally innocent. Married to Marcella, he carries on an affair with Carol. Then on the night of the murder, he betrays both women by going out with a third, the eponymous *femme fatale*. Marcella, meanwhile, is guilty of her insidious scheming with two men. And Carol turns out to be much like her counterpart in *The Black Angel* in that, even though driven by a noble objective, she harasses her prey to the point that she not only disrupts their lives, but worse, drives them to their destruction. The deaths of the bartender and Cliff Milburn are the result of her agitating their already disturbed consciences, complicating their ability to think clearly, and inspiring the desperate behavior that leads to their end. Lombard also harangues his quarries (the phony blind man, Pierrette Douglas), but their deaths are brought about by his deliberate intervention, not from internal duress.

Not immediately apparent is that Lombard and Richman represent a Woolrich convention, a personification of the Greek Erinyes through a character who pursues and badgers others for some wrong they may — or may not — have committed. Sometimes the harassed individuals have our sympathy (*I Married a Dead Man*, "Nightmare," "The Boy Cried Murder") and sometimes not (*Fright*). We see the Erinyes role donned by a plethora of individuals cloaked in various shades of morality: Detective Ames (*The Black Curtain*), Julie Killeen (*The Bride Wore Black*), Stephen Georgesson (*I Married a Dead Man*), Hal Jeffries ("Rear Window"), and Harry Jordan ("The Night Reveals"), to name a diverse few.

In *Phantom Lady*, Lombard and Richman not only assume this role, but also serve functional roles with two contrasting perceptions of how fate operates. Carol forces the guilty characters to look into themselves, so that conscience is a factor in their doom; Lombard, on the other hand, works externally, so that the characters' fate comes to them with or without their cooperation.

The idea that one man, John Lombard, can bribe so many into agreement with him, even to the point of making them commit perjury, requires a few extra cables to support our suspension of disbelief. Although Burgess's final, lengthy explanation describes Lombard's obsession so minutely and painstakingly that Woolrich quite pulls it off, it helps that, on our part, we want to believe the whole ruse is possible. Fortunately, Woolrich tells his story so expertly and engagingly that we accept it in spite of itself.

In many respects, *Phantom Lady* may be considered Woolrich's signature piece, embracing as it does many of the thematic and stylistic elements that infuse his broad body of work. For one thing, by coupling the Wrong Man theme with a woman's adamant love for her falsely convicted lover, he gives his protagonist a strong motive for venturing on her Quest. The Quest, in turn, conveniently enables Woolrich to adopt his preferred plot pattern, the episodic structure, through which he can explore the guilt and innocence of several characters, all implicated by their tangential relationships to the central crime. In other of his works, we find Woolrich experimenting with different combinations of these elements, for example, "Murder in Wax," "Face Work," and *The Black Angel*, as well as in the less directly related "Marihuana," "From Dusk to Dawn," and *The Bride Wore Black*. In what becomes for him a typical *modus operandi*, he strings together a series of blatantly preposterous events, which he justifies in a fusillade of pseudo-rationales, trying to convince us, if not of their possibility, then at least of their plausibility. As is often the case, once we are lured into his world of suspense, we tolerate his wobbly logic as adequate explanation in service of the story.

Film: Phantom Lady

1944, Universal. *D:* Robert Siodmak. *P:* Joan Harrison. *Cin:* Elwood "Woody" Bredell. *Sc:* Bernard C. Schoenfeld. *Ed:* Arthur Hilton. *Mus:* Hans J. Salter. *Art Dir:* Robert Clatworthy, John B. Goodman. *Set Dec:* Russell A. Gausman, L. R. Smith.

Cast: Franchot Tone (Jack Marlow), Ella Raines (Carol "Kansas" Richman), Alan Curtis (Scott Henderson), Aurora (Estela Monteiro), Thomas Gomez (Inspector Burgess), Fay Helm (Ann Terry), Elisha Cook, Jr. (Cliff Milburn), Doris Lloyd (Madame Kettisha), Virginia Brissac (Dr. Chase), Milburn Stone (Voice of District Attorney), Andrew Tombes (Mac, Bartender), Joseph Crehan (Tom, Detective), Regis Toomey (Detective), Harry Cording (Spectator in courtroom, uncredited), Samuel S. Hinds (Voice of Judge, uncredited), Victoria Horne (Payton, uncredited), Joe Kirk (Man in Estela's dressing room, uncredited), Jay Novello (Cab driver, uncredited), Gisela Werbisek (Mama, wife of delicatessen clerk, uncredited), (Max, delicatessen clerk, uncredited). 87 min.

Robert Siodmak is one of those prominent European émigrés (Lang, Wilder, Sparkuhl, Planer, Rozsa, et al.) who came to America in the 1930s (whether to escape the suppressive Nazi regime or to further their careers in a more amenable climate), and with their filmmaking roots grounded in German Expressionism, helped establish the thematic and stylistic essence of *film noir* in the forties. *Phantom Lady* was Siodmak's first in a series of influential *noirs* which he directed, among them *The Suspect* (1944), *The Dark Mirror* (1946), and two outsanding classics, *The Killers* (1946) and *Criss Cross* (1949).

Before adapting *Phantom Lady* to the screen, Siodmak and scenarist Bernard Schoenfeld may have peeked at Woolrich's *The Black Angel* (1943, adapted for film in 1946). Either they deliberately incorporated some elements from that novel (written the year before their film release) or their adaptation of *Phantom Lady* uncannily coincides with material from the earlier work. Jack Marlow, for instance, suffers from megalomania, a disorder different from but reminiscent of Ladd Mason's epileptic seizures. The climax, when Carol Richman becomes trapped in murderer Marlow's apartment where he menaces her at his leisure, mimics the final altercation between Alberta and Ladd. Also, Marlow leaps out the window in a dramatic suicide-escape that parallels Ladd's last gesture after he is "betrayed" by Alberta.

To avoid making a sprawling epic, Schoenfeld reduces Woolrich's cadre of witnesses to a few major ones. Despite this abridgement, and despite his flagrant alterations to the Lombard character, his adaptation still appears recognizable as Woolrich's novel because it retains the general storyline and the main plot device of wholesale bribery, while — most importantly — effectively capturing the pervasive *noir* tonality so integral to Woolrich's story.

Scott Henderson (played notably well by former male model Alan Curtis) meets a woman (Fay Helm) in Anselmo's Bar and invites her to go with him to a current musical revue that everyone has been raving about. She accepts on the condition that they don't give their names. At the theater, the pit drummer (ubiquitous *noir* character actor Elisha Cook, Jr.) ogles her. The star of the revue, lead singer Estela Monteiro (Aurora, real-life sister of Carmen Miranda), sports the same hat as Henderson's date, and when she spots her plagiarized headwear in the audience, she glowers contemptuously at her brazen rival. The date over, Henderson deposits his escort at Anselmo's and returns home.

As in Woolrich's story, Henderson finds several police already waiting for him at his apartment to observe his reaction when told his wife has been murdered. Inspector Burgess (Thomas Gomez) and his two detectives (Joseph Crehan, Regis Toomey) inform him that Marcella has been strangled with one of his ties, the singular tie in his collection that complemented the particular suit he has on. (This same evidence is the incriminating factor in Woolrich's story.) Henderson is convicted. However, his secretary Carol "Kansas" Richman (Ella Raines as the classy *femme blanche*) is in love with him. She takes it on herself to follow first Mac the bartender (Andrew Tombes) and then drummer Cliff, hoping to force them to admit that they lied at the trial and had actually seen the woman in the strange hat, thereby giving Henderson the alibi he needs for vindication.

Driven to the brink of paranoia by Carol's frequent appearance at his bar and her incessant accusatory glare, Mac finally confronts her on the sidewalk. Neighborhood men intervene to defend her and Mac runs into the street and into the path of an oncoming truck. His death can be called an accident, unlike Cliff's, which occurs at the hands of the man who bribed him. To inveigle information from the jive drummer, Carol assumes the role of a tawdry strumpet, flirts with Cliff, and gets him to take her to his apartment. There, he admits to her that he was paid to keep quiet about the woman. However, he discovers Carol's trickery and attacks her, forcing her to flee. Just after she leaves, a mysterious man (Franchot Tone) walks in and strangles Cliff for betraying him. Obviously, this is the real murderer who has paid off the witnesses to keep his secret.

In the next scene, while Carol visits Henderson at Sing Sing, a second visitor arrives. The man who stands in the doorway is the same man who has just killed Cliff Milburn. Henderson shouts, "Jack Marlow!" and we realize that his best friend and the murderer who framed him are one and the same. Carol finally learns who made the infamous hat, and under the pretense of helping her, Marlow accompanies her to Madame Kettisha's (Doris Lloyd) and then to the home of Ann Terry, the Phantom Lady. Ann's fiancé had died just before they were to marry, and afterwards, she plunged into a deep, irremediable depression. Nevertheless, she gives her hat to Carol.

At Marlow's apartment, Carol expects Burgess to arrive, but too late she discovers that Marlow is the murderer. He has locked her inside his apartment, a capacious artist's studio, with sculptures of hands and heads displayed all about. Marlow prepares to strangle her with his bow tie, but Burgess arrives in time. Marlow leaps through the glass of his bedroom window and falls to his death.

Exonerated, Henderson returns to his job. Carol resigns herself to a continuation of their platonic relationship and, on what appears a routine workday, she plays the Dictaphone, expecting to hear her boss's latest business-related instructions. Instead, she hears, to her utter joy, Henderson's playful proposal of marriage.

Although this ending appears to be the obligatory happy one, the film actually toys with some ambiguity. Henderson's Dictaphone message tells Carol he wants dinner with her "tonight, tomorrow night, and every night from now on," which, on the face of it, seems a clear proposal of marriage (and which in 1944 may have been a unanimous interpretation). However, because he does not explicitly mention it, there is no reason to believe that marriage is on his mind. Rather, without benefit of legal contract, he may be willing to commit to a romantic affair that he had been avoiding up to now. Carol's ecstatic reaction tells us that his gesture is exactly what she wanted as her reward, to have him appreciate what she did and why she did it. Whether she interprets his banter as a marriage proposal, or whether he even meant it as one, remains open to debate.

Trite as this point may be, ambiguity reinforces *noir*'s agnostic implications about life, reflects the inscrutable workings of determinant forces that make expectations uncertain and outcomes inconclusive. Carol, for instance, in both the novel and film, strives to rescue the man she loves. Although her quest is noble and she succeeds in saving his life, she is ironically responsible for causing other people's deaths, whether by accident (the bartender), suicide (Woolrich's Milburn), or murder (Sidomak's Milburn). She plays an ambiguous redeemer, a paradoxical Black Angel similar to the character in Woolrich's subsequent novel. She becomes an unwitting instrument of fate.

Another critical aspect of *noir* is its visual tonality, and Siodmak effectively captures some of the most impressive *noir* scenes in Woolrich's writing. In his examination of three *noir* films, Tom Flinn is niggardly with his praise of *Phantom Lady*, both the film and novel, but recognizes at least this one outstanding quality, saying "...Robert Siodmak's mis-en-scène is so exciting that other considerations pale in the face of his inventive direction" (37). He goes on to admit that

> *Phantom Lady* is primarily a work of style, created by the interaction of considerable talent (on the part of the director, producer, and cameraman) with very bland pulp writing (Woolrich's novel). Some of the dialogue is, as James Agee has pointed out, depressingly banal, but the film is redeemed by the originality of the mise-en-scène and by its all-pervading style which represents a considerable advance over the more overtly expressionistic *Stranger on the Third Floor* [40].

Flinn refers to *Stranger on the Third Floor* (Boris Ingster, 1940) because it is one of the three *noirs* he examines and because, predating *Phantom Lady*, it bears a striking resemblance to Sidomak's film. In both, the impotent male protagonists are falsely accused of murder and need rescuing by their plucky female saviors. While the *femme noire* often tries to usurp the male's traditional dominant role either by castrating him and nullifying his virility (Phyllis Dietrichson in *Double Indemnity*), the *femme blanche* performs feats he is incapable of performing himself (Debby Marsh in *The Big Heat*). As the latter, Carol Richman and Jane (Margaret Tallichet in *Stranger*) assume the quest and confront the dangers in place of their men. Important too is the urban milieu as each story's backdrop, a setting of peril and menace which Flinn insists is "a quality that is absolutely de rigueur for any *film noir*" (37). "Absolutely" may be too limiting a word, but there is no question that the city, the modern environment that has changed the course of human endeavors, challenged traditional values, and corroded ethical standards, serves as the arena for most *noir* action. It becomes the labyrinth where the protagonist must face his or her ultimate ordeal, confront the monster in a duel to the death. Taking his cue from Woolrich, Siodmak defines his *noir* vision through such a setting.

The parallels between several key scenes in the novel and film are worth noting. First of all is Carol's persistent hounding of Mac the bartender and her stalking him through the ominously dark and dismally bleak New York City streets. She follows him into a subway station. On the platform, they appear as small, insignificant figures dwarfed by the expansive matte shot of the silhouetted city skyline that hovers behind and over them like a somber, oppressive pall. In the shadows of the platform, their lonely figures shift in a brief cat-and-mouse shuffle, Mac intending to push Carol onto the tracks in front of the incoming train. Only the chance arrival of a black female passenger upsets his plan. Normally quiet and retiring, he was driven by guilt and fear to commit murder.

To get close to Cliff Milburn, Carol later makes herself up as a slovenly tart out for a good time. She succeeds in piquing his interest and he drags her to an all-night, ongoing jam session in the basement of some deserted warehouse (another labyrinth or underworld). This sequence in the small room is shot from an array of oblique angles that create visual disorientation. The blaring jazz music, hot and hysterical as if mimicking some primordial ritual, adds aurally to the feeling of dislocation and otherworldliness. Close-ups of the performers reflect their heady absorption in their playing, while Carol chews gum in sync with the feverish rhythms. She happens to pass a small mirror on the wall and sees her distorted image, her face painted in macabre makeup, not at all reflecting who she really is. A momentary wave of self-pity or self-rebuke crosses her face, but she quickly obliterates it and resumes her façade for the sake of her mission. (Through Carol's behavior, Siodmak has skillfully condensed a scene from the novel where Carol spends a length of time applying her gaudy makeup and, in common Woolrich fashion, mawkishly says to a photograph of Scott Henderson, "Don't look at me, darling.") Elisha Cook effectively imitates a doped-up, strung-out musician beating out a wild, frenetic drum solo, every fiber in his face straining with the wide-eyed glare of a madman. (The bottles of liquor that fill the center table represent more than drink that the musicians are high on.) Solo finished, he cavalierly tosses the sticks aside and leads Carol out the door while the other musicians continue to play, as if they were condemned to a perpetual performance in that underground vault.

After the jam session, Cliff takes Carol to another labyrinth, his apartment. In this squalid lair, he becomes the monster, attacking her after he accidentally uncovers her ruse. However, she escapes. While she runs to a store to call Burgess for help, we learn that there is an even greater monster, a greater threat behind the first. Marlow enters the story for the first time and strangles Cliff for revealing the secret that the Phantom Lady does in fact exist. Before killing him, Marlow gives what appears to be an incongruous speech about the versatility of hands, how they can mold clay or dance through a piano sonata, how they can save a life through surgery—or how they can take life away—and so goodbye, Cliff. Subsequently, we learn that Marlow is a sculptor, which means that his philosophical rumination on hands is not so incongruous after all.

Carol's being trapped in Cliff's apartment is repeated in Marlow's studio, with the difference that the earlier scene occurred in shadows and darkness, while this occurs with the rooms softly lighted. Marlow's world-weary attitude and his lackadaisical approach to killing Carol lend him a quiet menace that makes him appear more sadistically dangerous than the emotional, overreactive Cliff. Some of what Marlow says in his final speech is pertinent to the city and how it can corrupt the human spirit. While lying on his bed, suffering one of his incapacitating headaches, he complains about the noise of the city and how the people here have alienated him for being different. The daily cacophony from the streets and the chaotic activity can upset mental and emotional stability; the bustling, helter-skelter tumult can have an impersonal quality that discourages inclusion and integration of the individual. As an artist, Marlow has a sensitive side to him that is unable to cope with this indifferent, antagonistic element. He admits, at the same time, that he had never let love interfere with his work, and so Marcella's rejection was more than he could tolerate (a similar reaction from Woolrich's Lombard toward Marcella). His artist's ego, inflated beyond normal proportion, and his vanity bruised by a scornful lover, Marlow cannot control his urge to kill. He blames the city, and he may be justified in doing so, at least as far as he is concerned. However, his condemnation does not apply to everyone, as many people function very normally in this environment, working and thriving and content to stay.

Marlow's final diatribe includes an invective against the man who is supposed to be his best friend. Marlow expresses scorn for him, first, by trying to steal his wife, then by framing him for murder. He tells Carol, "What is Scott's life compared to mine?" This Aryan dictum of self-proclaimed superiority is manifested in Marlow's hand fetish and is undercut by the murderer's contradictory nature as a genius with a diseased mind. Marlow's sculpted hands and especially his sculpted heads, their crania bloated to the point of physical distortion, simultaneously signify creative genius (enlarged brains) and the power to exercise that genius (hands). Ironically, Scott, a civil engineer, *also* uses his inventiveness and his hands. The difference is in how each of their professions is perceived.

Siodmak has subtly established the conventional conflict between art and science (an age-old theme that has surfaced in literature of all types over the years). Marlow may think he and his work are more essential to society, but art nurtures only one of humanity's dual needs. Scott's contributions, as they often are with science, have a more utilitarian purpose while the artist's work is more concerned with spiritual and cultural enrichment. Marlow's spirit is warped, though, and so his sculptures are tainted, corrupt, exaggerated images of his distorted perception of himself and his relation to the world. Art wins its share of battles in many stories, but in this scenario, the person making functional contributions to society is the one who benefits society more and deserves the greater reward. (In Woolrich's novel, Henderson works in the "brokerage business," while Lombard is the engineer. These occupations are merely incidental to the story and are never explored for any larger implications.)

There has been some criticism that Franchot Tone, as Jack Marlow (renamed from the insidious Lombard character), enters the film too late, long after the story is underway (47 minutes to be exact, more than halfway through the film). However, this is totally in keeping with Woolrich's story in which

Phantom Lady— Burgess (Thomas Gomez, left) comforts Jack Marlow (Franchot Tone) during one of his debilitating headaches. His headache represents the mental trauma that can plague people who live too long in the *noir* city (Universal).

Lombard does not enter until Carol has already started her own private investigation. The difference is where the main irony is placed. Woolrich saves his for the end. By using the objective/dramatic narrator, he places Lombard in front of us in almost exclusively external terms. Thus, we are restricted in what we learn about his thoughts and feelings or what really motivates his actions. (That is, not to an extent that would expose his secret.) Siodmak chooses to reveal the murderer earlier, forfeiting Woolrich's single-clout irony in his finale and opting instead for an extended series of dramatic ironies that come out of our knowing that Marlow is the murderer. (Like Siodmak, Hitchcock has been criticized for his 1956 *Vertigo*, where he reveals the murderer to the audience well before the end. Interestingly, Hitchcock makes the same trade-off as Siodmak, forgoing the single surprise ending for a succession of dramatic ironies that lend the story more intriguing coruscations. Consider the genius: after being viewed once, the film's outcome is known and the surprise is no more; what endure are the beads of irony strung together throughout the storyline. Woolrich's story works the same way: once read, the ultimate surprise is gone, but the momentary dramatic ironies still remain.)

Marlow's madness has some parallels with that of Ann Terry, the Phantom

Lady. Marlow's megalomania must have been seething for years. His altercation with Marcella merely brought it into the open. It manifests itself in his disgust with people and his compulsion to commit murder to preserve himself and his supposedly more deserving life. Ann's madness is also triggered by a failed relationship, the death of her husband-to-be, but instead of expressing her madness externally, she internalizes it, hurting only herself.

In Woolrich, such a parallel is never explored, even though a similar motif of madness exists between Lombard and the Phantom Lady. Burgess confesses to Carol and Scott that he long ago learned who the Phantom Lady was, but she had gone insane (no explanation given) and could not verify Henderson's claim. Thus, he needed Carol to get his prime suspect, Lombard, to expose and condemn himself. Like Henderson's and Lombard's occupations, the madness motif is more incidental than substantial.

Because of the nature of the written word and how Woolrich sets up his story, the book has the advantage of blurring the line between reality and dream. Although we follow Henderson and his phantom date at the beginning, we are never sure that she really existed until the bodies of the witnesses start to stack up and we realize that so many coincidental deaths, even for Woolrich, must point to something deliberate, such as a conspiracy. In the film, because the woman makes a visual, physical appearance, this question of the elusiveness of reality never enters as an adjunct theme. Woolrich treats it cursorily here, but exploits the motif more thoroughly in such stories as "Nightmare," *Black Alibi*, and "Marihuana."

Eye Witness (Robert Montgomery, 1950) is another film about a phantom witness who can provide a life-saving alibi for the wrongly accused suspect. An American lawyer (Montgomery) reluctantly travels to England to defend his wartime English friend who has been arrested for murder. During his investigation, he uncovers evidence that proves some unknown person must have witnessed the actual killing, and so his quest is to find this person who may be able to save his friend from execution. For this British-made mystery, Montgomery competently directs an able cast with a well-written script and a satisfying story. This material may have given him thoughts of capitalizing on his earlier *The Lady in the Lake* (1946), a *film noir* based on the Chandler novel. However, *Eye Witness* is told with more levity and whimsy and the camerawork itself is more conventional, lacking the stylized and expressionistic techniques associated with an authentic *film noir*.

The Black Angel

Novel, first published by Doubleday Doran, 1943; Robert Hale, 1949; first digest paperback by Avon Murder Mystery Monthly, pbk #27, 1944; first standard paperback by Avon, pbk #96, 1946; followed by various hardcover and paperback reprints.

In structure and plot devices, *The Black Angel* is a close relative of three earlier Woolrich stories, "Murder in Wax" (1935), "Face Work" (1937), and *Phantom Lady* (1942). In all four cases, the central conflict hinges on a woman's loyalty to a man (a husband, brother, or lover) convicted of murder and sentenced to death row; she sets out to find the real murderer and prove her man innocent of the crime. Ironically, the man is, in all these instances, innocent of murder but guilty of another indiscretion: flirting with the wrong kind of woman. The murdered woman in these stories deserves her fate both for her mercenary, immoral character and her posing as an obstacle between the accused man and his loyal lady. The mistaken conviction initiates the faithful woman's quest, which eventually affects, for better or worse, some aspect of the relationship between her and the man she redeems.

Twenty-two-year-old Alberta Murray first suspects her husband of infidelity when he stops calling her by his pet name "Angel Face." After other evidence confirms her suspicions, she visits her rival, Mia Mercer, and finds her dead amid the material splendor of a luxury apartment. As the prime suspect, her husband is tried and convicted and sentenced to execution in three months.

Woolrich uses the "critical deadline" as a convenient device for sustaining suspense by reminding us intermittently of some impending catastrophe for the characters. In *Phantom Lady*, chapter titles provide that reminder, and in *Deadline at Dawn*, each chapter begins with a clock face showing the time moving closer to the climactic hour. In *The Black Angel*, Murray's execution date is mentioned infrequently, but still looms over Alberta's enterprise. Intensity grows out of Alberta's repeated declarations of a love that compels her to endure the ordeal she has undertaken. (Compare this with Carol Richman's self-chastisement when, in search of the Phantom Lady, she makes herself up as a street tart to attract drummer Cliff Milburn.)

Motivated by a blind devotion to her husband, Alberta follows up on a couple of clues. For one, she finds two monogrammed matchbooks in Mia's apartment. The one with a double M would be Mia's. The second, with a single M, she discovers lodged in the door seal and realizes that the murderer must have put it there to enable himself to sneak back into her apartment. Alberta also takes Mia's personal address book, hoping to protect Kirk from suspicion since his name is in it. She uses this telephone book to trace four people whose names start with M.

The first name on the list is, oddly, only a first name, Marty. The vague clue takes her from one hotel to another, a progression that symbolizes a descent in fortune and prestige, until she reaches the penultimate end for social pariahs, the Bowery. Here, she finds Marty Blair, Mia's estranged husband. The promiscuous Mia had severed their relationship, and his obsessive love for her brought on physical and emotional devastation. Over the past two years, despair and misfortune pummeled him into a skid row drunk.

Alberta tries to bait Blair into revealing his guilt; instead, he proves his innocence. Blair runs away and she returns to the Bowery to find him again. When she cannot, she fears that her "test" had distressed him and driven him to suicide: "I remembered what I'd thought ... the first night I'd come in here.... The lower depths, this place was. The lowest depths of all this side of the grave. There was nothing beyond this, nothing further. Nothing came after it except — the river" (112).

She phones the next name on the list, Dr. Mordaunt. His access to narcotics makes him an expedient distributor in an illegal drug operation. Misinterpreting Alberta's reason for seeing him, he hands her four packets of drugs, each of which she delivers to four separate sites representing various descents into the scummy dregs of the urban labyrinth.

During her nocturnal journey, she notices conspicuous individuals hovering near her meeting places. When she makes the last exchange at the Gem Theater, the police converge, alerted by the plainclothesmen who had been following her from Mordaunt's house. All four junkies are caught, but Alberta escapes and returns to Mordaunt's office. Having learned of the drug bust, he angrily attacks her with a syringe filled with poison. The police arrive in time and arrest her along with Mordaunt. Detective Flood, however, knowing who she is, gets her off. (Like Burgess in *Phantom Lady*, he becomes her silent partner.) He informs her that Mordaunt has an alibi: he was in prison serving a six-month sentence and was not released until several days *after* Mercer's murder. (A similar ironclad alibi is given Kosloff in the film version of *I Wouldn't Be in Your Shoes* so that his innocence is unequivocally insured.)

Undeterred, Alberta moves to the next name on the list, Ladd Mason, a playful, easy-going, engaging young man. They meet on a blind date and get along well, having a similar propensity for trading sarcastic quips. He candidly discusses his former relationships, including his second love, unnamed, who was involved in a scandal because she "borrowed" a fur coat she couldn't afford to buy, but wanted to wear to a social event. (The story resembles the one Woolrich tells of Vera in *Blues of a Lifetime*. The question is whether he bases Ladd's romantic history on a real experience, or he resurrects a fiction he used in his specious autobiography.) Ladd's frank sincerity wins her over and she falls in love with him. He invites her to his sister Leila's birthday party. Alberta sees Leila light her cigarette with a match from a blue matchbook with the single monogrammed M like the one she found in Mia's apartment. She suspects Ladd's duplicity and his role in the murder.

Alberta hopes to get the truth out of Ladd. With Flood's help, she has a recording device set up in her apartment (a la "Murder in Wax"). She is supposed to manipulate Ladd into a confession which will be recorded and used as evidence against him. She manages to get his story but not the one she expected. Ladd knew Mia. One time at her apartment, he became "ill" (which we later learn was an epileptic seizure). Mia heard of Leila's engagement to a foreign prince and used Ladd's illness to blackmail him and his sister, promising to inform the prince of this illness that runs in the family. She carried through with her threat, and although the prince was willing to marry her, Leila canceled the wedding. In anger, Ladd planned to kill Mia. He used his monogrammed matchbook to rig the door so he could return later to kill her, but when he got there, she was already dead. Alberta believes his story. Exhausted, he falls asleep on her couch. She packs her few things and abandons her temporary furnished apartment.

The fourth name on the list is Jerome J. McKee, a notorious crime boss and owner of Club Ninety. Although not a dancer, Alberta fakes her way through an audition (already used in both "Face Work" and "Murder in Wax"). She takes an accidental pratfall, which makes McKee laugh, and he hires her for her supposed comic routine. In time, McKee falls in love and, without asking her, throws a party to announce their engagement. She takes advantage of their intimacy to ransack his safe, hoping to find incriminating evidence for the murder of Mia Mercer. However, McKee's henchman catches her. McKee locks her in her room and she overhears him ordering his men to take her out to Long Island and dispose of her. She has enough time to phone Ladd, who sets up an ambush and rescues her.

Alberta and Ladd return to the apartment where she had last seen him sleeping on the couch. (Romantic that he is, Ladd has kept the apartment, waiting for her return.) She tells Ladd she is married and trying to save Kirk from execution. Ladd lapses into a seizure. He confesses he killed Mia because of her betrayal, and now, because she, too, has betrayed him, he attacks Alberta. They bump against the recording console as he tries to strangle her. Suddenly, he stops. The next thing Alberta realizes is that Ladd is hanging to the window frame from outside the window. The police enter and he falls to his death. Fortunately, the recording device was triggered and has recorded Ladd's confession. Kirk is saved.

The story ends with Alberta sleeping with Kirk but dreaming of Ladd. She had found and lost a love greater than the one she has with her husband, a love which, coupled with her reckless ventures into dark, sordid worlds of vice and corruption, has forever tainted her attitude toward life and her feelings for Kirk: "He's cost me dear, but that's the price, and I won't quibble" (300).

In his four stories where a redeeming angel seeks to vindicate her love, Woolrich conveys his *noir* vision through vividly depressing descriptions of a seedy underworld inhabited by the desperate, lost souls of society. The denizens of this underworld are not the guardians of American values or the ideal images for hero worship, and his four female characters infiltrate this unpleasant sphere from slightly different viewpoints. In "Murder in Wax," Angel Face candidly admits that she is no high-minded ingenue. After her visit to rival Bernice Pascal, she frantically tries to stop her husband from leaving. He throws coffee in her face (not "hot enough to scald me") and knocks her down ("I didn't even mind hitting the floor"). This woman does not have to enter the *noir* labyrinth to be transformed by it; she is already one of its casualties. Like her, the heroine in "Face Work," a former striptease, is privy to the seamy underbelly of society. Even so, she is literally branded by the racketeer Militis, a physical scar to signify the psychological scars of her ordeal. Woolrich exposes Carol Richman of *Phantom Lady* to similarly flagitious and depraved experiences, but then tries to offset her contamination by channeling the story into an upbeat romantic ending. In *The Black Angel*, he rectifies his gaffe with an unsettling but necessary conclusion that must result from exposure to a polluted stratum of society.

Woolrich integrates two motifs related to innocence and purity, the child and the angel. A 22-year-old bride endearingly called "Angel Face" by her husband, Alberta is associated with both. She is an angel — that is, a guardian and savior — for her husband, but a "black angel" for the four men whose lives she disrupts. She is the child when she bolsters her resolve by declaring that she is finally growing up and entering the adult world. Associated with youth, she memorizes Mordaunt's instructions like a child learning by rote. Unfortunately, what Alberta's quest ultimately confirms is that the innocence of childhood, exemplified in her child-like ways of thinking and behaving, disintegrates when it collides with the corruptive elements of the urban miasma. Ironically, the idealistic love that motivates her quest becomes a fatality from her psychological and philosophical erosion. Like Buddy in "The Boy Cried Murder," she undergoes a traumatic transition from childhood to adulthood. Occasionally, she reaches dark conclusions, such as "Life is cruel. Death is man's greatest gift." Her loss of innocence and a positive outlook on life suggests that experience, while necessary for maturation, must sadly foster despair and pessimism.

One Woolrichian device that begs credulity is the exaggeration of his characters' powers of ratiocination. A character will plunge into the mystery with no leads, stumble onto the paltriest of clues, and parlay them into concrete evidence pointing to a definite solution or suspect. (Consider what happens in the likes of "All at Once, No Alice" and *The Black Curtain*.) In "Murder in Wax" and *The Black Angel*, the discovery of a monogrammed matchbook serves to initiate the quest. Alberta's ambiguous M implicates several suspects. Angel Face's T.V. initials are more precise, especially after she finds Pascal's personal address book containing the name Thomas Vaillant. (As a short story, the latter work does not have the luxury of a multitude of suspects.)

From the monogrammed matchbook alone, the heroine of "Murder in Wax" is able to delineate the character of its owner:

> ... the cream of the crop don't sport store-bought monogrammed matches— that's tin horn flash. Which meant that this guy, whoever he was, was in quick money of some kind and hadn't caught up with himself yet. Which meant some kind of a racket, legitimate or otherwise. Which meant that maybe she had known a little too much about him and spoken out of turn, or had been about to, and therefore was now sprouting a lot of grass up at Woodlawn. At the same time, as I said before, it didn't necessarily have to mean any of those things, but that was for me to find out [In *Darkness at Dawn*, 82].

So nice of Woolrich to end with that conditional thought, even though it turns out that the narrator's first estimate is right on the mark. Compare this inference with Alberta's conclusion about the two matchbooks with their slightly different monograms. One has a single M on a dark blue cover; the other has a double-lined M on a turquoise cover:

> Why would she [Mia Mercer] go to the trouble of selecting a certain trick monogram — naïve though it was— and then have it scattered around on everything in sight, if she was going to allow a variation of it, a symbol that didn't quite match, to appear on one item? It wouldn't have been in character. To her, monogramming spelt chic, and not to have carried it out identically on everything at once would have been a flaw....
> That initial was somebody else's. It stood for somebody else whose name began with an *M*. And that somebody else had killed her [48–49].

There are arguments galore to counter the points in each train of logic. Yet we accept them, as we do other faulty logic throughout the story, because Woolrich makes them sound so definite, so irrefutable. They offer a starting point, act as a hook for catching our curiosity about the killer and the solution to the mystery. We want to know if the loyal wife's faith in her husband is justified or will be ironically shattered. Her ingenuity in deciphering the little evidence she gathers overwhelms and intrigues us, pointing in the direction Woolrich has staked out for us.

Woolrich does nothing to disguise the similarities between racketeer Tommy Vaillant and his descendant Jerome J. McKee. He not only uses Vaillant as the model for McKee, but also transfers many of the earlier events to the later novel. Angel Face visits Vaillant's Gay Nineties Club and wins him over by sheer beauty alone. Alberta infiltrates McKee's Nineties Club by impersonating a dancer and winning his attention with her looks. Angel Face steals

Vaillant's key to his apartment, where she opens the safe, but finds nothing to connect him to Pascal's murder. Alberta also breaks into her admirer's safe without finding any evidence to link him to Mercer's death.

Among the many plot redundancies in these four related stories is one salient point common to "Murder in Wax," "Face Work," and *The Black Angel*: the seductive power of the *femme noire* is countered by the conspicuous beauty of the *femme blanche*. The sin of the heroine's husband (or brother) is that he fails to appreciate the attractiveness of his wife (or sister) and succumbs to the temptation of a passing vamp. Despite this lapse in affection, the heroine insists on proving the innocence of her man. Ironically, the one who really does recognize her beauty is the racketeer suspected of committing the murder, and in Alberta's case, the murderer himself. Emphasizing the power of a woman's physical charms, Woolrich shows that both the evil siren, who seduces the husband or brother, and the faithful female, who has honorable intentions, possess this identical trait that enables them to get men to do their bidding. The *femme noire* who steals the man from the *femme blanche* uses her seductive powers for selfish, ignoble reasons. Thus, her murder is reparation for her guilt. The *femme blanche*, however, wields her charm for what appears to be a noble cause, so that winning her man's freedom is her reward. At bottom, motive is of little consequence. Whether for good or ill, all females brandish a potent weapon by which they can entice and manipulate the gullible male.

Following his usual episodic format, Woolrich has Alberta infiltrate the life of one suspect at a time, treating each altercation like a discrete short story, with all the stories linked by her ultimate quest, the vindication of her husband. Alberta's four suspects all have a motive for killing Mia Mercer, and all but Mordaunt appear to have had the opportunity to do so. The actual murderer is the least likely of the four suspects. Mordaunt is a seedy physician guilty of drug dealing. McKee is a gangster guilty of various rackets and crimes. Blair is a skid row derelict guilty of stalking his estranged wife. Only the affluent Ladd Mason can genuinely claim to be far aloof from the others' derelict life styles. His guilt for Mia's murder proves that wealth and status do not immunize the upper class against the same social diseases that corrupt the lower classes. Human nature on any social level is susceptible to the same obsessions, temptations, and sins.

The central irony is, of course, in the title. Out to redeem her husband, the self-sacrificing Alberta is a true angel. Yet, under that pretense of that noble quest, she is, for the four other male suspects, a "black angel." She ingratiates herself with them before she leads each to his fateful doom. That each man is culpable for some crime against himself or society seems to justify his downfall. Although subtly glossed over, her husband also shares in their guilt with his own sin, adultery, and we realize, finally, that there is no escape from blame. When Alberta achieves her goal and says it was worth it, the consequences suggest otherwise. All along, the Black Angel has had misgivings about the effect her experiences have had on her and her quarry. When she is trapped in

McKee's apartment, she blurts out that she feels "like a rat in a trap" (279); the figurative association says something about her character. The idealistic woman who set out to rescue her husband has learned to be conniving and duplicitous (Note the *noir* connotation when she sees her mirrored self in Mia Mercer's apartment.), and has brought several men to their ruin. She notes that men like Kittens, Skeeter, and McKee are "no different from other men, except that their moral sense is gone, and you can't see that from the outside" (263). What she fails to see is that she has become "no different" from them. She insidiously bores her way into their lives to entrap them with the hope of implicating them in a murder so she can free her husband. Such an undertaking requires that she deaden her scruples to achieve her ends. (Compare Alberta with Johnny's wife Jean in "Johnny on the Spot.")

That Alberta has trimmed some of her moral fiber is evident when, at the engagement party McKee throws for her, she makes an ambiguous toast: "I raised the champagne high until I could see the ceiling lights turn gold through it. I didn't point it at him. I pointed it upward, through the lights, through the ceiling, toward — whatever it was up there. 'To my husband,' I said in a steady voice" (267). Failing to acknowledge a sympathetic heavenly deity, she instead devotes herself to an earthly mortal, her "husband." The chilling implication is that "husband" applies to her present spouse, Reardon, and to her husband-to-be, McKee. She stands between two worlds, wedded to figures in two extremes of society, the genial, carefree world she was "reared on" and a newly discovered underworld. Rather than straddling the line between heaven and earth, she struggles between two earthly domains. For a person depleted of moral sensibility, God and heaven do not exist.

In the end, Alberta achieves her goal to free her husband, but it proves to be less than satisfying. Experience has taught her that there are other things more desirable than those few she knew in her previously secure, narrowly enclosed existence. More than that, she has exposed herself to the filth, corruption, and evil layering the deep, dark recesses of the city. She comes to realize, "...there *is* such a thing as seeing too much. As seeing too much and too clearly." The sacrifice turns out to be not the time and effort she expended to free her husband but the loss of her child-like innocence.

Film: Black Angel

1946, Universal. *D:* Roy William Neill. *P:* Roy William Neill, Tom McKnight. *Sc:* Roy Chanslor. *Cin:* Paul Ivano. *Ed:* Saul A. Goodkind. *Mus:* Frank Skinner. *Songs:* Edgar Fairchild, Jack Brooks ("I Want to Be Talked About," "Time Will Tell," "Continental Gentleman"). *F/X Photography:* David S. Horsley. *Art Dir:* Jack Otterson, Martin Obzina. *Set Decor:* Russell A. Gausman, Edward R. Robinson.

Cast: Dan Duryea (Martin Blair), June Vincent (Catherine Bennett), Peter Lorre (Marko), Broderick Crawford (Capt. Flood), Constance Dowling (Mavis Marlowe), John Phillips (Kirk Bennett), Wallace Ford (Joe), Hobart Cavanaugh (Jake, the janitor), Freddie Steele (Lucky), Junius Matthews (Dr. Courtney), Ben Bard (Bartender), Michael Branden (George Mitchell), Maurice St. Clair and Vilova (Dance team at Rio's), Robert Williams (Second detective), Mary Field (Mavis's maid), Marion Martin (Millie, girl with the brooch). 83 min.

A prolific and versatile director during the silent era and throughout the 1930s and '40s, Roy William Neill can claim credit for the classic horror film *Frankenstein Meets the Wolfman* (1943) and a fair share of the *noir*-ish Sherlock Holmes entries between 1942 and 1946 in which Basil Rathbone found the perfect vehicle for his exaggerated emoting and brought Arthur Conan Doyle's immortal sleuth uncannily to life. *Black Angel* was Neill's last film before his death in December of 1946.

Although the film strays a considerable distance from its literary source, Nevins praises it highly as one of the best adaptations of a Woolrich novel:

> ... Neill and cinematographer Paul Ivano invest every shot with a visual style that translates Woolrich into film precisely as any novel needs to be translated: with total fidelity to its essence and little if any to its literal text. If a single theatrical feature based on a Woolrich book could be preserved for future generations and all the rest had to be destroyed, *Black Angel* is the one I would opt to keep [463].

I agree that faithfulness to the "essence" of a writer's intentions has greater value than a straightforward regurgitation of the "literal text," but if the "literal text" is altered significantly, or altered even slightly in significant respects, what results can deviate considerably from the thematic core of the original. This is true of *Black Angel*—although this is not to say that altering the source material in essence or plot will necessarily create an inferior product. What Nevins may mean is that *Black Angel* captures Woolrich's *general* literary vision without adhering strictly to the story line of *this* particular source. Before criticizing Nevins' commendation as slightly overzealous, we should consider the operative word "book." Undoubtedly, Hitchcock's *Rear Window* is superior to *Black Angel*; and Tetzlaff's *The Window* surpasses it in claustrophobic intensity—but then both of these are based on short stories. Of the adaptations based on Woolrich's novels, Neill's film ranks among the most competently conceived and produced, even though its plot has only a superficial connection with Woolrich.

In terms of plot, the film is closely linked to Woolrich's story (and several of his other works following the same formula) because they share the same central conflict: an adulterous husband is wrongfully convicted of murdering his lover; his wife believes him innocent of the woman's murder, remains loyal despite his unfaithfulness, and sets out to uncover the real killer. This similarity notwithstanding, scenarist Roy Chanslor transforms most of Woolrich's original material into a whole new narrative.

Woolrich's New York City milieu is transported to Los Angeles and begins with Marty Blair (Dan Duryea) loitering outside the apartment building of his estranged wife Mavis Marlowe (Constance Dowling). To remind her of

The Black Angel (1943) / Black Angel (1946)   221

their anniversary, he sends up a heart-shaped ruby brooch that she receives with scornful disgust. She phones the doorman to prevent Marty's admittance. Marty, waylaid in the lobby, watches another man (Peter Lorre) enter the building and ask for directions to Mavis's apartment. Marty goes on a drinking binge. In a semi-drunk trance, he plays the piano at a bar until he collapses. Friend Joe (Wallace Ford) helps him to his apartment. Joe has the janitor (Hobart Cavanaugh) lock him in his room by bolting the door from the outside. The clock shows it is 10:30 P.M.

At 12:15 A.M., Kirk Bennett (John Phillips) enters Mavis's apartment. Not finding her, he strolls around the room, sees the record "Heartbreak" spinning on the phonograph, and discovers a matchbook with a monogrammed *M* on the cover and a telephone number written inside. A noise from the bedroom attracts his attention. He finds Mavis strangled, around her neck a white scarf emblazoned with a double-*M* monogram. The heart-shaped brooch is pinned to her bodice. He returns to the living room and prepares to make a phone call (to the police?), but a second sound draws him back to the bedroom. He discovers the closet's sliding door open and the brooch gone. Glancing toward the living room, he sees the outside apartment door slowly closing, but when he steps out into the hall, no one is there. The elevator bell rings and startles him and he rushes down the stairs just as Mavis's maid (Mary Field) exits the car in time to recognize him.

Police Captain Flood (Broderick Crawford) catches up with Kirk at his home where his wife Cathy (June Vincent) staunchly defends him. Kirk admits that he had an affair with Mavis long ago, for which she has been blackmailing him. Circumstances are too overwhelming. Kirk is found guilty of murder, and sentenced to death. Cathy's belief in his innocence is firm and unwavering. She is stymied on how to proceed until, at a restaurant, she overhears some people discussing Mavis's ex-husband. Marty Blair becomes her first lead.

The gruff and belligerent Blair seems like a choice suspect until Cathy learns that he had been locked in his room and could not have killed his wife. (This irrefutable alibi is a variation on the classic "locked-room" mystery and parallels Mordaunt's timely excuse.) Cathy pities the slovenly drunk and slides a bill under his door. Too proud to take a handout, he goes to her home to return it. She shows him a framed picture of Kirk and he realizes that this is not the man he saw looking for Mavis's apartment the night of the murder. He offers to help her. When Kirk is moved to death row, his belongings are sent to his wife. Cathy finds the matchbook with the monogrammed *M*, supposedly Mavis's, but Marty, knowing that Mavis used a double-*M*, infers that this must belong to someone else. The anonymous phone number leads them to Rio's, a nightclub whose owner, Mr. Marko (Peter Lorre), turns out to be the stranger Marty saw going up to Mavis's apartment. To find out more about his relationship with Mavis, Marty and Cathy form a piano-vocal duo under the aliases Jack Martin and Cathy Carver and successfully audition for a job at Marko's upscale supper club.

After some time, Marko begins to fall for Cathy. Cathy betrays his affection (as Alberta betrayed McKee's) by waiting until he is out of his office so she can break into his wall safe. (McKee willingly shared the wall-safe combination with his fiancée. Marko, as McKee's counterpart, tests her loyalty by slyly letting her peep over his shoulder while he plies the combination. He has a reputation as a misogynist, so he may have been tempting Pandora, hoping for an excuse to molest her.) Marko returns and catches her at his safe. To satisfy his sadistic streak, he has henchman Lucky (Freddie Steele) apply physical pain. Marty and Captain Flood enter. Marko explains that Mavis had blackmailed him, threatening to make public his criminal past and possibly ruin his daughter's marriage to a prominent socialite. (This motive makes Marko a composite of McKee and Ladd Mason.) In the face of Cathy's vehement accusations, Flood tells her that Marko could not have killed Mavis because he was under surveillance that night and in police custody when she was murdered (another foolproof alibi).

All the suspects accounted for, Marty tries to convince Cathy that her husband must have murdered Mavis, but she refuses. She rebuffs his attempts to console her and he, angry at her rejection, reverts to his former habit of drowning himself in drink. After several days of bingeing, he stumbles upon a woman (Marion Martin) wearing the heart-shaped ruby brooch which, she informs him, he gave her. A brawl ensues and he is knocked out and committed to a sanatorium. Tied to his bed, he dreams how, on the night of the murder, he had bribed the janitor to let him out of his locked room. In a drunken stupor, he returned to Mavis's apartment where he strangled her. He can't convince the doctor (Junius Matthews) to let him go, so he escapes. He hastens to Cathy's house where he shows her and Captain Flood the brooch and tells them what happened. Kirk is saved and Marty willingly accepts his fate.

It is easy to see why Nevins might regard Neill's *Black Angel* as a unique representation of the "essence" of Woolrich's outlook. Even if not strictly faithful to this particular novel, it contains fragments of plots and themes strewn throughout so many of his other works. As in "Murder in Wax" and "Face Work," there are two *femme fatales*, the self-made Spider Woman deliberately bent on destroying men, and the "black angel" who, despite good intentions, inadvertently destroys men who get too close to her. There is Marty's "amnesia," his alcoholic blackout (not occurring in this novel but a Woolrichian device used in stories such as *The Black Curtain* and "Nightmare"), which exemplifies the waking nightmare into which Woolrich's characters frequently stray, enduring a surreal existence hounded by vague guilt and elusive memories.

The deadline device that appears in more than a few Woolrich stories is used tangentially in the film to indicate the strain Cathy feels. Coincidence, too, which Woolrich throws into the mix with the abandon of a confident chef, has its place in the film. That both Marty and Kirk are pianists and that Cathy overhears the movie extras talking about the murder are only a couple of examples of coincidences that move the plot forward. Related to Coincidence is Fate, and the song "Time Will Tell," which Marty writes to express the love he feels for Cathy, signifies the interrelationship of Time and Fate. As Time passes, Fate reveals its designs. Marty eventually runs into the woman to whom he gave Mavis's brooch on the night of the murder. Suddenly, Marty's, Kirk's, and Cathy's fate is all resolved at once. He needed time to find that bar where he finally fulfills his destiny in the dual role of redeemer and sacrificial lamb.

Marty's flashback dream is another common *noir* convention that makes occasional appearances in Woolrich's work. The flashback affects the chronology of the narrative by disrupting the temporal continuum and making time seem "out of joint." Revelation of certain information is delayed by displacement, pulled from its logical temporal position and relocated later in the story. Thus, time possesses a labyrinthine quality that adds to the complexities of the *noir*-scape.

In nearly every one of his stories, Woolrich also sends his characters into a physical labyrinth, a variety of derelict neighborhoods, dilapidated buildings, and contaminated environments fraught with danger and mystery, where they must confront the monster. Alberta enters one each time she pursues another suspect. (In addition, see, for instance, "Marihuana," "The Night Reveals," and "The Boy Cried Murder.") In the film *Black Angel*, the labyrinth is narrowed to Marko's nightclub, ironic in that it is well lighted and appears a cheery, upbeat place — which is appropriate since Marko turns out to be an imaginary monster. The true labyrinth is in Marty's mind, and when he travels through it, he finds the worst possible answer to his quest: he is the real monster.

Of *Black Angel's* other *noir* conventions affiliated with Woolrich's stockpile of devices, one is the doubling of certain characters. Most important is the doubling of the Marty-Mavis and Kirk-Cathy relationships. First of all, both couples started out as pianist-singer duos. This makes it seem more plausible when Marty and Cathy become a pianist-singer duo to find Mavis's killer. In other words, Marty replaces Cathy's husband. He gains free access to her home, entering as he pleases without knocking. He buys her flowers, writes songs for her ("I Want to Be Talked About," "Time Will Tell"), and talks intimately with her while they rehearse. Cathy at the same time replaces Marty's wife. The implication is that their symbolic marriage is more romantic and valid than the one they each had with their legitimate spouse. Mavis separated from Marty for a more luxurious life style and a greater variety of male companions. She turned to blackmailing as a way to sustain her new standard of living. Kirk is an adulterer, albeit a penitent one. However, he does nothing to show he is the exceptional husband-lover that merits her loyalty. She idealizes him in much the same way that Marty had idealized Mavis: both share a blind allegiance to their less-than-admirable partners. When Marty tells Cathy that she owes Kirk nothing, he is probably right. Yet she has brainwashed herself for too long and can only adhere to a relationship that does not deserve her devotion.

This is a variation on Woolrich's conclusion where Alberta suddenly realizes that her ordeal has undermined her innocent optimism and tainted her love for Kirk. When she declares out loud that the price she paid was worth it, that she feels rewarded despite her plunge into the murky vortex of sleaze and venality, we can hardly believe her. Likewise, we probably agree with Marty that Cathy does not owe Kirk the rest of her life.

Duryea's Marty Blair is a composite of Woolrich's Blair and Ladd Mason. Like Blair, Marty becomes a self-pitying skid row alcoholic as a result of his failed marriage. Both earn the nickname Heartbreak, one because unrequited love drove him to his pitiful existence, the other because he wrote a song by that name for his singer-wife. Each is also obsessed with his wife, enough to stand outside her apartment window while she carries on affairs with a string of suitors. Unlike Woolrich's Blair, Marty limits his masochistic self-annihilation to alcoholism, not suicide. Like Ladd Mason, he kills the Spider Woman; only he does it while in an incoherent state of "alcoholic amnesia," an unconscious fit of hate and emotional duress. (Although this psychotic episode echoes Ladd's epilepsy, Ladd killed Mia deliberately while in full control of his faculties.) He then becomes caught between two women, one decidedly evil, the other apparently good, which makes the similarity between Ladd's and Marty's case exceptionally striking because of their relationship with the "black angel." Unrequited love hurts when the beloved is evil; Mia Mercer belittles Ladd and Mavis Marlowe scorns ex-husband Marty, rejecting them for personal, selfish reasons. Their evilness explains their callousness, and the men, hurt as they are, can comprehend the rejection. When the beloved is a good woman like Alberta or Cathy, however, the rejection is more difficult to accept. This is complicated further because the good woman misleads the male into a caring relationship (albeit unintentionally), then makes a heartfelt confession of her conflicted loyalty, leaving the male feeling stranded and hollow. Ladd reacts by attacking Alberta before committing suicide; Marty, less vengeful, forfeits his reclamation and reverts to his alcoholic benders. Naïve because of their romantic turn of mind, both men are easy dupes to feminine extremes, one woman wickedly cunning, the other good-natured but absorbed in her personal quest. The male is ever the victim of the woman, whether she proves a diabolical temptress or a sincere angel.

Marko, the third major character, is more complex than his counterpart McKee in Woolrich's text. His arrival at Mavis's apartment building the night of the murder, his shady behavior and cruelty (having Lucky twist Cathy's arm), and his profession as nightclub owner mark him as a stock villain and likely murderer. Yet when we learn what motivated him in his dealings with Mavis, his special devotion to his daughter and his desire to protect her happiness, he garners a modicum of sympathy from us.

Marko also deserves comparison with Marty in the way they establish a relationship with Cathy. Whereas Marty falls in love without condition, Marko proceeds with caution, tests Cathy by letting her see the combination to his safe,

Black Angel—Pianist Martin Blair (Dan Duryea, left) teams up with Catherine Bennett (June Vincent), hoping to find evidence in Marko's (Peter Lorre) nightclub that will vindicate her husband who has been wrongly convicted of murder (Universal, courtesy William Thailing).

and does not let himself be entirely duped by her pretense. In the scene where Marko gives Cathy a star-shaped brooch, the camera moves in for a medium shot of her standing in her low-cut dress, a forced, uncomfortable smile on her face, while Marko talks about getting to know her better. The scene fades to black with the very subtle implication that she will grant him sexual favors to get closer to him. ("That's the hard way, isn't' it?" Marty warns her sternly when he suspects her intention. His jealousy could have been played up more strongly here.) Cathy's dissembling hurts Marty and Marko just as much as Mavis's selfish machinations. Marty, susceptible to sentiment, suffers pangs of unrequited love, but Marko, more scaly-skinned against feminine wiles, suffers only a bruised ego.

Amnesia has already been discussed as a factor in several Woolrich stories and their film counterparts. It deserves additional mention here. Although amnesia plays no role in Woolrich's *The Black Angel*, director Neill uses it in an appropriately Woolrichian way. The drug-related memory loss in "C-Jag," the hypnotic dream state in "Nightmare," and the physical trauma that erased the character's memory in *The Black Curtain* become in Neill's film a new kind of forgetfulness, "alcoholic amnesia."

As a *noir* convention, the amnesia motif may serve one or more purposes. The loss of memory almost always sets a character on a quest for his or her past. Memory is then closely linked to identity: what we know of what we were is what makes us what we are. The past gives us a context for defining ourselves, and not having that context can create a disturbing feeling, uprooted and disconnected as we are from our personal history.

In the post-war film *Crack-Up* (Irving Reis, 1946), George Steele (Pat O'Brien) suffers a temporary lapse of memory that raises questions about his stability and prompts his dismissal from his position as art critic in an art museum. Dr. Lowell (Ray Collins), a corrupt art museum bureaucrat, is responsible. He had injected Steele with a drug that induced hallucinations and distorted reality. (Drugs that produced narcosynthesis were common properties in many post-war *noirs*. See Dmytryk's *Cornered* and Bernhardt's *High Wall*.) He wants to discredit Steele to protect his own illegal operation of art forgeries and thefts. Steele's quest is to re-establish his credibility (while incidentally uncovering the art theft ring). Steele's memory lapse symbolizes the war years, an hallucinatory gap in reality, and his quest is not so different from the returning G.I.s who have to re-establish their place in society. The film has a consistently depressing, low-key tone to it, reinforced by O'Brien's character whose seething anger is barely contained beneath his soft-spoken, slightly introverted demeanor.

Such a search for identity is also critical in the *neo-noir* science fiction film *Dark City* (Alex Proyas, 1997), a thickly layered, complex existential study that explores the nature of reality and the individual's relation to it. A nearly identical concept is found in the extremely popular *The Matrix* (Andy Wachowski and Larry Wachowski, 1999), also a *neo-noir* sf film.

More often, when amnesia is a factor, the question of identity is complicated by the commission of a crime (usually murder) possibly done by the disoriented protagonist. If so, the story becomes a quest for both identity and, it is hoped, vindication. As a plot device, amnesia links *films noirs* directly to the German expressionist films of the 1920s, in which the theme of good and evil in human nature was prevalent. Amnesia prevents the character from remembering, from knowing whether he or she committed a crime. The implication is that every human has the potential to be evil, to do evil. Even the most noble, most upright, most honorable of society must become suspect because human nature accommodates those moral extremes in every individual. *Film noir* takes the Gothic Jekyll-and-Hyde story and plays with it in a number of variations.

High Wall (Curtis Bernhardt, 1947) is one example of this kind of film. Steve Kenet (Robert Taylor), a returning serviceman, may have strangled his wife after finding her in a love nest waiting for her lover. A war wound, a blood clot in the brain, has affected his temperament and causes a blackout at the moment he starts to strangle her. At first, he is afraid to let doctors inject him with a drug to help him remember, but when he finally gives in, what he remembers gives him confidence that he did not do it after all. His quest is to vindicate himself, personally as well as legally, and find the real culprit.

The Blue Dahlia, directed by George Marshall and released the same year as *Black Angel*, is a special case. According to information provided in Silver and Ward's *Film Noir: An Encyclopedic Reference to the American Style, Dahlia* was not released until April 19, 1946, even though Paramount completed filming on May 22, 1945, virtually a full year before *Angel* was completed on May 17, 1946 (and released in August). Yet besides the amnesia motif, the two films contain an unusual number of coincidental similarities, enough to make one wonder if one work influenced the other. For one, in *Angel*, adulterous husband Kirk is accused of killing his lover; his wife gets help from the dead woman's husband to prove Kirk innocent. In *Dahlia*, husband Alan Ladd is suspected of killing his unfaithful wife Doris Dowling; he sets out to prove his innocence with the help of the woman (Veronica Lake) whose husband (Howard da Silva) was having an affair with Ladd's wife. In other words, both films not only use the innocent man theme, but also have the married couples swap partners, the unfaithful pair doubled with the newly aligned decent pair. *Dahlia* is the more optimistic of the two films: the two unfaithful spouses are killed, the accused husband is found innocent, and he and the faithful wife find their reward in an embrace that predicts their deserved romantic future. This classic Hollywood happy ending is squelched in *Angel*, which, to its credit, offers a darker denouement that preserves something of the disturbing outcome in Woolrich's novel.

Besides the crisscrossing of marriage partners, amnesia plays a role in both films. In *Angel*, the amnesiac Marty never considers his guilt until he realizes he has suppressed the memory of his crime. In *Dahlia*, the amnesiac Buzz Wanchek (William Bendix) actually confesses that he committed the murder, until his memory recalls the truth. As a blustery but faithful Navy buddy of John Morrison (Alan Ladd), Buzz is a sympathetic character whom we prefer to find innocent. But then, the role of Fate in a *noir* scenario is to show no bias either way. *Dahlia* rewards good all around, whereas *Angel* iterates the dark and undesirable outcomes in an unfair universe.

According to Silver and Ward, screenwriter Raymond Chandler intended to make Buzz the murderer, "blinded and desensitized by the brutalizing effects of the war" (37). This sounds like a plausible, though sobering, outcome related to grim post-war *noirs* like *The Guilty* and *Crossfire* (both 1947). Buzz reacts violently to raucous swing music, which suggests that, if music is supposed to "soothe the savage beast," the war has reduced him to less than an animal. His murdering Helen Morrison would have exemplified the extent of his dehumanization. Many post-war films (of World War I as well as of World War II) have dealt with the returning soldier, who, after discovering a different world from the one he left, becomes displaced, disoriented. The U.S. Navy criticized this supposedly negative portrayal of an ex–Navy man and, unfortunately, Paramount bowed to pressure and overrode Chandler's intent to make Buzz the murderer. The result is that the psychological conflict of the returning G.I. becomes secondary to the murder mystery. (Compared to his finely crafted *noir* novels like *The Big Sleep*, *Farewell My Lovely*, and *The Lady in the Lake*, Chandler's *Blue Dahlia* seems uncharacteristically flaccid. Style is of the essence in Chandler's works, and with the emphasis on plot, his biting, edgy language is left unsaid. Outside of the complexly interlaced plot, this does not seem like a Chandler product — compare, for instance, the gritty phrases traded between Barbara Stanwyck and Fred MacMurray in *Double Indemnity*.)

Ladd's initial dilemma represents the same one facing many veterans, such as Zachary Scott in the *noir*-tinged melodrama *The Unfaithful* (Vincent Sherman, 1947): Is the wife of an absent soldier justified in seeking romantic companionship, and should the returning serviceman forgive her for any extramarital indiscretions? *The Unfaithful* ends with Scott struggling to let love overcome his pride and enable him to accept the personal wrong as a forgivable fact of life. Ladd's dilemma is complicated by his wife's responsibility in the tragic death of their boy. Interestingly, that complication simplifies things for him. She appears all the more villainous and he all the more justified in not forgiving her. It also does away with any ambivalence the audience may have felt: we have no difficulty placing blame on the guilty party and deciding which characters to identify with.

Black Angel does not make the sides so clear-cut. We may sympathize with Cathy because, thanks to the camera's objective viewpoint, we saw Kirk at Mavis's apartment and know he is not the murderer. However, Cathy cannot know this. Other than her exceptional loyalty as a wife who believes totally, blindly, in her husband's innocence, she has no definite visible proof that he is not the murderer. At the same time, although we are concerned with Cathy and her quest, the film decentralizes Woolrich's heroine and makes Marty the more empathetic character. He certainly has more interesting facets to him than Cathy, with his psychological complexities, internal conflicts, and paradoxical behavior. The final revelation of his role in the murder, coupled with his selfless sacrifice for moral and romantic reasons, both saddens and inspires us.

In an ironic parallel with Woolrich's use of coincidence, *The Blue Dahlia* contains some coincidences that give it intrinsic connection to Woolrich's novel. The first name of the lover-murderer in *The Black Angel*, Ladd, becomes the last name of the star playing the protagonist in *Dahlia*. A minor actress, Mavis Murray, plays a hatcheck girl in *Dahlia*. Not only does she have the odd first name of the *femme fatale* of Neill's *Black Angel*, but she has the woman's double–*M* initials that appear in both the novel and film. Trivial though these observations may be, they validate in real life the supposedly strained coincidences Woolrich includes in his storytelling.

Another film, *Crossroads* (Jack Conway, 1942), uses a variation on the amnesia motif. The man with amnesia is respected diplomat David Talbot (William Powell). Although he is a law-abiding citizen now, his detractors (Basil Rathbone, Claire Trevor) accuse him of having an unsavory past as criminal Jean Pelletier. Rescued from a train wreck years ago, he shows no awareness of his previous life, making us wonder if his loss of memory changed a criminal mastermind into a morally conscious public figure who contributes to, rather than steals from, society. The question is whether the good side he now shows has completely obliterated the bad side he may have exhibited back then, or whether the good that is in him has always been there, waiting to emerge. (*Crossroads* is a dark treatment of similar story material used in W.S. Van Dyke's 1940 screwball comedy *I Love You Again*. Also starring William Powell, this film is an inversion of the later one, the morally upright character discovering that he was formerly a criminal.)

Man in the Dark (Lew Landers, 1953) has Edmond O'Brien playing an irascible, hardened criminal character until he allows doctors to lobotomize the evil part of his brain. With his evil side extricated, he crosses over to the side of good, overthrows the evil companions of his past, and wins freedom and the girl (Audrey Totter) at the end. (Compare Paul Verhoeven's 1990 science fiction film *Total Recall*, which incorporates a similar dual-personality conflict in Arnold Schwarzenegger's Quaid-Hauser character.) The difference in *Crossroads* and *Man in the Dark* from films like *High Wall* is that they emphasize the present over the past. The past, and consequently memory, has no validity in determining a person's character and credibility if he or she has the ability to function responsibly in society now, no matter what he or she was once before. (This is also true of Powell's reformed character in *I Love You Again*.) The film *Black Angel* uses amnesia to propose a related notion. Marty Blair's memory lapse is meant to show that evil resides within even the most moral of us. Despite his drinking marathons and cantankerous fits, Marty proves he is fundamentally a good person. However, although good dominates, there is an evil fermenting inside, waiting to manifest itself at an unguarded moment.

Black Angel— Blair (Duryea) displays the deranged mental state of the *noir* protagonist confronting the demons in his nightmares (Universal, courtesy William Thailing).

Deadline at Dawn

Novel, first published under the pseudonym William Irish by J.B. Lippincott, 1944; Hutchinson, 1947; first paperback by Armed Services, pbk #878, 1945; various reprints in hardcover and paperback.

The "happy" ending of *Deadline at Dawn* may appeal to readers who need a romantic fillip to satisfy their fantasies. Woolrich's apparent capitulation to sentimentality, however, is counterbalanced with some of his darkest tonalities. After all, when he writes this novel, war still ravages the globe, and although he alludes only obliquely to that international turmoil (with the guilt-ridden ex–G.I.), his characters are condemned to grovel under the pall of a world in despair. A brief excerpt exemplifies the *noir* style that so consistently and effectively pervades the setting, imagery, and atmosphere:

> They came out into the slumbering early-morning desolation, flitted quickly past the brief bleach of the close-at-hand street-light, and were swallowed up again in the darkness on the other side of it....
> It was like walking through a massive, monolithic sepulchre. There was no one abroad, nothing that moved.... The city was a dead thing, over here on its margins, and like a dead thing, it was stark and clammy, it frightened them a little....
> He raised his hat in mock leave-taking, which only imperfectly covered up a very real trepidation. "Goodbye, Manhattan."
> She quickly sealed his mouth for a minute with a sort of superstitious intensity. "Sh, not so loud. Don't tip our hand to it ahead of time. Don't let on to it. It'll cross us sure as you know" [355].

Ubiquitous images of death and squalor, personification of the city as a mummified but calculating monster, feelings of fear, urgency, and desperation — Woolrich relentlessly harps on the bleak, hopeless, depressing circumstances that (like war, like urban blight) stymie his protagonists. Against all odds, they race through the night to beat a morning curfew so they can escape the stifling concrete jungle and start life anew in idyllic Middle America.

Besides occurring within a single night, the whole story virtually takes place in real time. To indicate this, Woolrich inserts at the head of each chapter a clock face designating the current time and reminding the protagonists (and us) how rapidly their deadline to flee the city is nearing and how surely their hope is dwindling. The challenge begins at 12:50 A.M. and ends at 6:15 A.M.

The setting is New York City. At the end of a typical work-night, hard-edged taxi dancer Ruth "Bricky" Coleman meets Quinn Williams, a young man who seems lost and confused. He rescues her from a would-be assailant and she lets him walk her home. Casual discussion divulges their coincidental pasts: they once lived in the same neighborhood on adjacent streets in Glen Falls, Iowa. Nostalgically, they recall their quiet small town and regret having left its comfort and peace for the frustration and despair wrought by the uncompromising city. Bricky confesses how her aspirations to become an actress have collapsed into a hand-to-mouth struggle as a dance hall hostess. Quinn reciprocates with a confession of his own: after he lost his promising job as an electrician's apprentice, destitution drove him to commit a burglary several hours ago. Bricky, smitten by his "boy-next-door" sincerity and appeal, offers to help him return the money before the theft is discovered if he will help her elude New York's invisible tentacles that have kept her from escaping its blighted boundaries. Together, if they hurry, they can rectify Quinn's misadventure and still make the 6 A.M. bus that will take them back home.

Unfortunately, when they reach the fashionable East Side mansion, they find owner Stephen Graves (aptly named) dead in his bedroom. Quinn fears that all the clues point to him and that the police must eventually determine that he was the thief and murderer. Bricky convinces him that he can vindicate himself if he finds the real murderer. From meager evidence at the scene, they conclude that a man and woman were present in the room some time before Graves's death. Bricky follows the trail of the woman and Quinn follows the man's. Both trails start favorably as potential solutions but end as ironic miscues. Quinn catches up with his suspect at a hospital. The man's suspicious manner turns out to be the anxious actions of a stereotypical father-to-be. Bricky's suspect, Helen Kirsch, admits to having shot a man, but in Woolrichian fashion, the bizarre coincidence is that she shot a *different* man, who, she learns, is still alive because she missed. On his journey back to the Graves house, Quinn surveys the nearby bars, and again a shady character gives him false hope before proving to be a mistaken lead. Eccentric behavior that singles out the man as a guilt-ridden fugitive turns out to be the pathetic paroxysms of a physically and psychologically scarred war veteran. (This is a good example of Woolrich's technical ability to protract tension and suspense built on an initial complication.)

Bricky meets Quinn back at the Graves mansion. A timely and revealing phone call from Graves's girlfriend Barbara and the discovery of an overlooked canceled check, overdrawn for lack of funds, set them on new pursuits. Both trails again look promising and Woolrich sustains the suspense by ending each youngster's exploit with a cliffhanger, their lives in danger by two different adversaries, each appearing to be the true murderer. Quinn's suspect is lawyer Arthur Holmes who would have murdered Quinn but for a change of heart.

Bricky's path, however, takes her to the real murderers: sleazy Joan Bristol and her male accomplice Griff were blackmailing Graves, expecting him to pay for suppressing the scandal of her marriage to Graves's younger brother. Bricky is ambushed at the woman's apartment. They take her back to the Graves mansion to find some overlooked evidence they fear may implicate them. Young Quinn fortunately has got there first and gets the upper hand on Griff. He and Bricky tie up the two murderers. Quinn makes a quick phone call to the police before he and Bricky commandeer the murderers' car and race to the bus, catching up with it shortly after it leaves the terminal. The bus driver refuses at first to admit them, but finally relents. Together, Bricky and Quinn return to their roots, redeemed from the Charybdisian maw of the all-consuming metropolis.

Deadline at Dawn is standard fare for Woolrich, true to the personal technique he has honed over the years: the plot follows an episodic pattern; the characters are on a redemptive quest (and in this case, allowed to succeed); and the themes explore various facets of guilt. Without even trying, even the most casual of readers must notice that *Deadline* shares the same genealogy with so many of his previous works, "Nightmare," *Black Alibi*, *Phantom Lady*, and the like. Predictability, however, is not always a shortcoming. Woolrich is such a craftsman at taking his previous plots and motifs and molding them into something new and strange that he makes the hybrid as engrossing as its progenitors.

Thematically, *Deadline* is a modernized version of *Paradise Regained* (although Milton may wish to argue otherwise). At the same time, it explores the paradox of the American dream, how the quest turns into a nightmare when its fulfillment becomes a "dream deferred." The modern city is a hollow El Dorado. People gravitate to an urban center because they expect it to fulfill their dream, when instead, it waylays and crushes their delicate hopes. The city corrodes, erodes, and diverts the aspiring spirit of all the characters, main and minor. Bricky once entertained ambitions of being a Broadway star. Now she struggles for survival in The Jungle, an appropriate name for the dance hall where she works, a microcosm of New York City or any cold, complex environ that obstructs human enterprise. Woolrich made her a taxi dancer, placing her one step away (if that) from being an outright prostitute. She already assumes the image of a saucy-mouthed, hard-bitten tramp, and given time, could probably ripen into another Joan Bristol. Quinn, too, had expectations of finding his life's career in the city—until circumstance spoiled his dream. Desperation clouded his moral sense and his conscience suffered a temporary coma. Helen Kirsch's seething desires drove her to an extramarital fiasco. And Joan Bristol and Griff invested their hopes in a doomed blackmail scheme. With the exception of the father-to-be, all of the characters, including Bricky and Quinn before they rerouted their aspirations, have tried unethical methods to guide their way to the American dream. As Louis Calhern advocates in John Huston's *The Asphalt Jungle*, "...crime is only a left-handed form of human endeavor."

The taxi-dance hall is a useful convention for Woolrich, playing a role in a number of his stories as the microcosm of a shoddy and desperate world, a repository of failed lives, for the patrons as well as the dancers. It represents, "before, a joy proposed; behind, a dream." Bricky very much fits the young dancer's profile outlined by Paul G. Cressey in his study of taxi-dance halls of the 1920s and 1930s. A girl enters the profession for income, or sometimes simply for excitement, but in time, the fascination fades and the money can hardly compensate for the physical and spiritual erosion the life style spawns. Cressey holds out some hope that the taxi dancer's excursion into this underworld is temporary: "The career of a taxi-dancer ends in her late twenties" and is usually a stepping-stone to marriage (84). However, if unable to readapt to conventional ways and mores, a woman may regress into the squalor of this shady existence and never emerge again. Bricky is quite aware of this possible doom as she links her fate to Quinn's so they can strive for mutual redemption.

Deadline is one of the few stories in which Woolrich allows his protagonists to make a mistake and still have the ability to reclaim their lost innocence. This may be why it resonates with much of the tone of *Phantom Lady*, his earlier effort that recognizes the seamy side of life, but skims quickly past the narrative pitfalls in order to produce a light-hearted finale. More often than not, though, Woolrich allows that an innocent's misstep must leave a scar, even if there is redemption and success at the end of the tortuous road. Think of Alberta in *Black Angel* or Bill Scott in *The Black Path of Fear* or Buddy in "The Boy Cried Murder" or Townsend in *The Black Curtain*. Woolrich is not above making frequent forays into romantic — even maudlin — passages, but he does not throw happy endings around liberally to appease the more popular tastes. (See, for example, his 1965 "Too Nice a Day to Die"— a fatalistic flip-side of the woman's weepy *An Affair to Remember*.)

When the two lovers take the bus to Glen Falls after solving the crime and absolving Quinn of blame, they are abandoning the pursuit of the traditional American dream, the dream of success and fame and fortune. They have forfeited these "loftier" ambitions (professional achievement, personal glory) by modifying their expectations to fit a more modest objective. Like Charles Foster Kane who collects artifacts from around the world as a substitute for some other real but unidentifiable need, they use their newfound love as a substitute for their failed original designs. Love, however, is only a fraction of the larger whole and can only offer temporary satisfaction, as they will later learn when other desires (financial security, professional fulfillment), ignored too long, assert themselves.

To intensify the oppressiveness of the malignant city that imprisons and tyrannizes its inhabitants and thwarts the nighttime quest of the two desperate lovers, Woolrich resorts to one of his tried-and-true devices for creating suspense: a time constraint imposed on the protagonist. He adapts that device here, treating time ironically by first establishing a friendly, even intimate relationship between taxi dancer Bricky and the clock gracing the nearby Paramount Building that overlooks her dance hall:

> She had only one friend in all this town. It stayed still, it didn't dance, that was one thing in its favor. And it was always on hand, night after night, seeming to say, "Buck up, kid, you've only got another hour to go...."
> ... It was like a face — all clocks are. It was like the face of a friend. A funny friend for a slim, red-haired girl of 22 to have, but it spelled the difference between endurance and despair.

The clock enables her to tolerate her stint in the dance hall because it tells her when her torture will end. When she meets Quinn and must battle a deadline to save him, time works like an enemy, but it also operates in the same helpful way that it does at the dance hall: it assigns a definite appointed hour when their tribulations will cease. Time pressures her to do what she has to do to vindicate Quinn and when that time elapses, the ordeal is over and the reward is theirs.

In *film noir*, coincidences occur as fatalistic devices showing how human endeavors succeed or fail because of the minutest intersections in time and space. In *The Maltese Falcon*, Miles Archer enters Sam Spade's office just in time to meet Miss Wonderly and wrest the surveillance job from him. Result: Archer gets murdered instead of Spade. In *Double Indemnity*, Mr. Dietrichson suffers a broken leg, a timely accident that enables Walter and Phyllis to carry out their plot to kill him, but also becomes the reason Keyes continues a dogged investigation of his death. *Deadline at Dawn* contains enough coincidences to fill 10 stories, a case of overkill that becomes a travesty of storytelling logic. Yet with a little sleight of hand, Woolrich manages to give the coincidences an iota of plausibility, strained though it be. For one, although these two inexperienced detectives work with the most meager of evidence to reach the most extraordinary of Holmesian deductions, their feisty enthusiasm makes us want to see them succeed. More important, all of their deductions, except one, lead to blind alleys and ironic dead ends that make the coincidences forgivable.

Another recurring device in *noir* is the convoluted labyrinth into which characters descend either to pursue some personal goal or to seek escape from some tenacious hunter, real or imagined, external or internal. In *Deadline at Dawn*, the dominant quest, like that in "Murder in Wax" and its offshoots, is to vindicate the wrongly accused male. The concrete jungle exemplifies the *noir* labyrinth, and each time Bricky and Quinn anxiously follow one of their leads, they must plunge into the roiling maze. Their final bus ride represents their resurfacing from the labyrinth, the departing vehicle taking them from this debilitating underworld to their Elysian fields of home.

Film: Deadline at Dawn

1946, RKO. *D:* Harold Clurman. *P:* Adrian Scott. *Cin:* Nicholas Musuraca. *Sc:* Clifford Odets. *Ed:* Roland Gross. *Mus:* Hanns Eisler. *Art Dir:* Albert D'Agostino, Jack Okey. *Set Decor:* Darrell Silvera. *F/X:* Vernon L. Walker.

Cast: Susan Hayward (June Goth), Paul Lukas (Gus Hoffman), Bill Williams (Alex Winkley), Joseph Calleia (Val Bartelli), Osa Massen (Helen Robinson), Phil Warren (Jerry Robinson), Lola Lane (Edna Bartelli), Marvin Miller (Sleepy Parsons), Steven Geray (Edward Hoenig, gloved man), Jerome Cowan (Lester Brady), Joe Sawyer (Babe Dooley), Constance Worth (Nan Raymond), Joseph Crehan (Lt. Kane), George Tyne (Ray, newsstand attendant), Ralph Dunn (Capt. Dill), Jason Robards, Sr. (Policeman, uncredited), Sammy Blum (Sam, taxi driver, uncredited), Armand "Curly" Wright (Fruit peddler, uncredited), Earle Hodgins (Street barker, uncredited), Larry Thompson (Man shouting in crowd, uncredited). 83 min.

A reputable theatrical director from the 1930s to the 1950s, Harold Clurman directed but one feature film, *Deadline at Dawn*. His only other immediate association with film (although uncredited) was as one of several screenwriters who contributed to Hitchcock's wartime thriller *Foreign Correspondent* (1940). Otherwise, he is probably most famous for co-founding with Lee Strasberg and Cheryl Crawford the Group Theater in 1931. The Group Theater espoused a controversial approach to acting, which became known as The Method, a style adopted by many actors (Marlon Brando, James Dean, Montgomery Clift, Paul Newman, et al.) who gained prominence in Hollywood. After a personal dispute that led to his split with Strasberg, Clurman supervised the Group Theater until it disbanded in 1941.

In a career that ran parallel with Clurman's, scenarist Clifford Odets was a leading playwright from the thirties to the fifties. Thematically, his works center on characters battling the contradictions within themselves, the "existential angst" that haunts so many *noir* protagonists and suits his contribution to *Deadline at Dawn*. Several film adaptations of his dramas made fair *noirs* (*Clash by Night*, 1952; *The Big Knife*, 1955); and besides *Deadline*, he authored a few other *noir* screenplays (*Humoresque*, 1947; *Sweet Smell of Success*, 1957, co written with Ernest Lehman). He was a playwright with the Group Theater (*Waiting for Lefty*, *Till the Day I Die*, both 1935), and this early connection with Clurman prompted their collaboration in adapting the Woolrich novel for the screen. (For further insights into Odets's personality, one can view the 1991 Coen brothers film *Barton Fink*, which supposedly used the writer as a model for the eponymous character.)

In writing his screenplay, Odets makes extensive plot revisions to Woolrich's story. This is standard practice, of course, filmmakers trying to capitalize on a writer's popularity (such as Woolrich had achieved in the 1940s) by attaching his name to the credits and hoping to lure his reading audience into the theaters. However, filmmakers believed it necessary, especially in the case of mysteries, to treat the audience to a plot different from the one in the book (and at the same time tweak the story with a few original ideas of their own). Thus, deviations occur in adaptations like *Phantom Lady*, *Black Angel* and *Deadline at Dawn*, films rewritten to give the Woolrich material a new twist on the mystery and the outcome. Fortunately, although Odets thoroughly redesigns the plot of *Deadline* into a classic whodunit with a gallery of suspects and a surprise ending, two key thematic implications of the original remain fairly intact. One is that the city is an indifferently sinister entity out to entrap its victims and keep them in a permanent state of despair and cynicism. (Hayward's character succinctly describes the ultimate urban black hole: "This is New York, where hello means good-bye.") The other is that love can be the salvation of souls caught in the city's controlling and enervating grip.

Odets also instigates a change that, although not in the original novel, is still in keeping with the spirit of Woolrich's writing. Woolrich's Quinn knows he is guilty of stealing money and he also knows that he did not kill Steven Graves. Odets' Alex, on the other hand, does not remember how he got the money and whether he killed Edna Bartelli. Odets, then, uses a device dear to Woolrich himself, the amnesia motif where the protagonist cannot recall his exact role in a crime, but being implicated, must search to find his degree of guilt in the matter. In this respect, Odets's version of Woolrich's novel is less an adaptation of *Deadline at Dawn* than it is an offshoot of "Nightmare" and *The Black Curtain*.

The film is recognizable as Woolrich's story primarily because it retains the motif of the Fugitive Lovers. Sailor Alex Winkley (Bill Williams, renamed in the Quinn role) meets a street-smart but testy taxi dancer June Goth (a sultry Susan Hayward replacing Bricky) in the dance hall where she works. Later, at her place, he tells her he has to catch a bus at 6 A.M. to get to Norfolk before his ship sails. He confides in her that he unconsciously took a large wad of cash from a mercenary *femme fatale*, Edna Bartelli (Lola Lane), who, after her brother Val (Joseph Calleia) had lured him into a crooked card game and cheated him out of his money, brought him to her apartment to fix her radio. Because she was born and raised in Norfolk, and because her brother is a bellygunner in the Pacific, June feels a kinship with the nice but naïve sailor and decides to help him. She convinces him that, if he replaces the money before the theft is discovered, he cannot be accused of the crime.

They return to the woman's apartment and find her dead. To clear Alex of wrongdoing, they set out to find the murderer based on the few clues they find and the deductions they make. Gradually, a number of people are implicated in the crime: Edna's blind ex-husband Sleepy Parsons (Marvin Miller); theatrical promoter Lester Brady (Jerome Cowan); Nan Raymond (Constance Worth), a married woman having an affair with Brady; taxi cab driver Gus Hoffman (Paul Lukas); a young husband, Jerry Robinson (Phil Warren), being blackmailed by Edna; Jerry's wife, Helen (Osa Massen), seen coming out of Edna's apartment that night; and Val Bartelli, the dead woman's brother. Although all these people are guilty of some wrongdoing or indiscretion and each has a motive for killing Edna, the ironic ending reveals the phlegmatic, philosophizing Gus as the murderer. He killed her because Helen Robinson is his daughter and Edna's blackmailing scheme threatened Helen and Jerry's marriage. Gus, a hopeless romantic, appreciates true love, so he advises June to follow Alex to Norfolk. Alex is cleared of the charges just in time for a police

Deadline at Dawn— Alex Winkley (Bill Williams) brandishes the generous roll of tickets he expects to use on the young taxi dancer June Goth (Susan Hayward) (RKO, National Screen Service Corp., courtesy William Thailing).

car to chauffeur him to the station where he can catch his bus. Riding with him to the station is June. The film ends with a close-up of them kissing, sealing their contract to escape the bleak and disheartening city, he to make his ship and she soon to return "home" to await his return.

Although the film was released in 1946, filming had been completed in 1945 while the war was winding down. In Woolrich's novel, the paranoid soldier is a lone allusion to the ongoing war; Odets sprinkles a few more reminders into the mix. In addition to Alex's military vocation, June's brother is a belly-gunner somewhere over Japan, a significant point because it softens her adamantine heart and disposes her to helping the forlorn sailor. Another reference to the global strife is the presence of the German and Italian émigrés with whom June and Alex become involved in the span of a few hours. It is difficult to tell Odets's motive. On the one hand, he is reinforcing the stereotypes and making buffoons of the axis kindred. Val Bartelli is a repugnant gangster and his sister Edna, who is "no good" and "had the brains, like a man," is an uncouth *femme fatale*. By stealing money from the young navy recruit, Val reveals his contempt, or at least his disregard, for what Alex's uniform represents. Walter Hoenig is a pitiful sort: he has a strange rash that forces him to don gloves so he won't infect the woman he wants most to touch; he has recently become a naturalized citizen, yet instead of being welcomed into the new society, he is repulsed, like a leprous pariah. On the other hand, Gus Hoffman is a tragic and sympathetic character. A taxi driver, he has assimilated successfully into the American mainstream. He comes across as a kindly father figure — a role exemplified in the extreme when he "murdered for love" to protect his daughter's marriage. Most important, when he could have escaped detection and let Alex take the blame for murdering Edna Bartelli, he stepped forward and redeemed the young man. Odets creates some slight ambiguity here. Gus's confession actually occurs immediately after his daughter and son-in-law exchange admissions to committing the crime, Jerry trying to protect Helen and Helen trying to protect her father. It may seem that Gus confesses only because his daughter is in jeopardy. However, in the previous scene, just as Alex was being arrested, he had stepped forward and started to admit his guilt, only to be interrupted by the fiasco caused by his daughter and Jerry in the other office. It is clear enough that Gus was already willing to save Alex without further prompting.

Odets may also be trying to short-circuit xenophobia in the country reputed as a "melting pot" and touted for its diversity and "pluralistic society." Foreigners, immigrants, aliens who come to the United States possess ambitions and expectations quite similar to those entertained by native-born Americans. At the heart of the American experience is the pursuit of the American dream — a good job, money, security, success, happiness, love. All the characters seek these things. Odets, borrowing from Woolrich, undercuts the idealism inherent in that hope by showing how the city has fouled once-hopeful lives and deterred attainment of the dream. Broken marriages, adultery, blackmail, lasciviousness, cheating, stealing, spiritual corruption, abandoned morals, and mindless occupations have drained most of these people of their humanity, driven them into a feral existence governed by Darwinian principles.

Unlike Woolrich's Quinn, who is an ordinary young civilian stumbling toward the American dream, Odets's Alex Winkley is a sailor, an occupation that increases implications for the film. For one thing, more than a simple citizen, he is a patriotic American whose extreme sense of honor sparks self-recrimination when his supposedly shameful behavior defames the uniform. Instead of the pact for mutual redemption made between Bricky and Quinn in the novel, Odets devises a more complex redemption among the three principle characters. Gus redeems Alex by deliberately stepping forward and admitting his guilt in the murder of Edna Bartelli; and he redeems June by convincing her to leave New York and follow Alex to Norfolk. Alex redeems June by accidentally including her in his quest to prove his innocence; his crisis gives her a reason to rise above the tedium and monotony of her pathetic life. And June redeems Alex by buoying him through his ordeal until Gus finally confesses to the crime. For June and Alex, their reward is salvation outside the city. However, what appears a happy ending is not totally free of contradiction.

Deadline at Dawn— Cab Driver Gus Hoffman (Paul Lukas, center) guides June (Hayward) and Alex (Williams) through the *noir* labyrinth during their nighttime ordeal (RKO, National Screen Service Corp., courtesy William Thailing).

Certainly we cheer for Alex and June who find each other and stand at the threshold of achieving the dream the others lost — but it comes at the expense of one of the most likable characters. When Gus says he did it "for love," we respect his motive, but we lament that he had to resort to the most heinous of crimes to preserve one of the most desirable goals in the American dream.

Woolrich sets his story during the nighttime when the claustrophobic grip of the city can be most heavily felt. Clurman's film successfully captures Woolrich's desolate *noir* atmosphere through the chiaroscuro embellishments of veteran cinematographer Nicholas Musuraca and the looming, labyrinthine set designs of Darrell Silvera. To intensify further the oppressiveness of the city and its dehumanizing effect on its inhabitants, Odets adapts Woolrich's funereal descriptions and fills his film, from the very beginning, with allusions to death. Behind the opening credits, Sleepy Parsons, blind pianist, climbs the narrow stairway to Edna's apartment. He knocks on her door and the camera cuts to a close-up of Edna's face, a pasty mask of oblivion frozen in a skewed position, a housefly flitting and landing about her cheeks. Sleepy Parsons, appropriately named, wears a black tuxedo with a carnation in the lapel and represents the apathetic undertaker-priest come for the dead body. He has ascended from the streets, the urban underworld, to claim the corpse. The scavenging fly, an omen, was feeding prematurely — Edna suddenly wakes from her deathlike slumber, but she will be dead before the night is out.

In June's apartment, Alex stuns her with the revelation that his father is an undertaker. His justification: "Somebody's father has to be a mortician, don't he?" June, in turn, speaks despondently of her coffin-sized quarters: "It's all right to live in a cocoon, if you know someday you'll be a butterfly." That is, the city has boxed her inside a furnished casket with no hope of a glorious reincarnation. Later, Alex tells her that he was once declared clinically dead when he was a boy. Both young people have experienced forms of death and are familiar with it. In the end, they are on the verge of a rebirth into a new, happy, contented life that was previously denied them. Yet this is only an illusion. Death, figuratively or literally, is never far away, and others before them who started with inflated romantic dreams — Gus, Edward Hoenig, Jerry and Helen Robinson, Nan Raymond, Lester Brady, and Sleepy Parsons — all suggest that no one is exempt from the tragic complications that must eventually come.

Whatever the event that caused Alex's temporary clinical death, the veiled suggestion is that it has affected his mind and causes his occasional "non compos mentis." Like the Woolrich characters who commit their crimes while under hypnosis or in a drugged stupor, he cannot be held accountable for any sin or wrongdoing performed while in his blackout state. His exaggerated innocence seems unreal, however, especially with his being a sailor. (Even the Gene Kelly and Frank Sinatra sailor films make it clear that their characters are bubbling with unbridled hormones, although these are channeled into vigorous musical numbers.) Gus calls Alex "innocence personified" and he and June often refer to Alex as "a boy" or "the boy," giving the impression that he is a man-child, a perpetual innocent. (As a symbol of American naiveté, he has much in common with Forrest Gump.)

Noted above, Woolrich, in several novels, draws characters plagued by guilt for their uncertain association with a crime they cannot fully recall. In *The Black Curtain*, "Nightmare," "Marihuana," and "C-Jag," some form of amnesia at the time of the crime prevents the character from remembering his degree of culpability, and so he reacts with paranoia, or undertakes a quest to learn the truth, or both. Woolrich does not use this device in *Deadline*; Quinn is fully cognizant that he did not murder Graves, so the murderer he seeks is not he. Odets, however, borrows Woolrich's idea for his screenplay. Woolrich's protagonist usually acts as both the Amnesiac Suspect and the Man in Search of Himself. Odets modifies this role by dividing it between the two characters, Alex and Gus. Alex plays the befuddled blackout victim who is both the Amnesiac Suspect and the Man in Search of Himself (that is, defining his part in Edna's murder). Gus, in pretending to help Alex find the real murderer, is the ironic Man in Search of Himself. This same plot device occurs in Woolrich's "Mind Over Murder" and the film *I Wouldn't Be in Your Shoes* where the murderer and the investigator are one and the same.

The Big Clock (John Farrow, 1948) relates to *Deadline* in a similar way. George Stroud (Ray Milland) is the editor of a crime magazine, one division of a huge publication firm run by the tyrannical Earl Janoth (Charles Laughton). In an extraordinarily complex plot, Stroud, although married, goes out one night with a woman who is Janoth's mistress. Janoth impetuously kills his mistress, thinking she has been cheating on him with Jefferson Randolph, a fictitious name invented in fun by Stroud. To cover himself, Janoth tries to frame Randolph and orders Stroud to muster all his manpower to locate the murderer. From the description, Stroud, like Odets's Gus, realizes that the man he is searching for is himself, so that even while he appears to be working diligently for Janoth, he sabotages his quest at every opportunity. *The Big Clock* is a film rich with *noir* elements and effective performances. The menace of Janoth's bodyguard Bill (Henry Morgan) is heightened by his never speaking a word as he glares and snarls his way around the building. (The massage scene vaguely suggests a homosexual relationship between Bill and Janoth, even if one-sided from Bill's point of view. This scene is reminiscent of a similar one in *In a Lonely Place*, where Gloria Grahame's masseuse tends to her with lesbian zest.)

Its story unfolding as a facsimile of the real passage of time, *Deadline at Dawn* foreshadows an approach used in Robert Wise's *The Set-Up* (1949), which takes place in a single night. The latter story deals with a boxer (Robert Ryan) struggling to uphold his ethical principles and maintain his dignity in the face of strong-arm corruption rampant in the fight-game. Although *The Set Up* is totally different in plot, its thematic implication of moral right battling the oppressive urban forces of moral decay has significant parallels with Woolrich's novel and Odets's film.

The Black Path of Fear

Novel, first published by Doubleday Doran, 1944; first paperback by Avon, pbk #106, 1946; reprints in subsequent paperbacks.

In a 1964 interview, Alfred Hitchcock offered this profound observation on the art of storytelling: "Logic is dull" (*Making Mystery Movies*). Now, Hitchcock was not advocating some lofty Theory of Incoherence in anticipation of remaking *Un chien andalou* as a suspense film. What he meant was that an effective narrative did not depend exclusively on logic, and that, if they expected to corral the audience's attention, filmmakers were actually obliged to stray from time to time into inexplicable areas of irrationality and nonsense. Smart cookie, Hitchcock. The real world limits us with mundane logic; a fictional world feeds our imagination with immeasurable possibilities. The compromise between the rational and irrational is plausibility, a kind of pseudo-logic that tampers with the boundaries of credibility without destroying them, so as to lend a drab narrative a dramatic nuance. At the risk of alienating audience members by making outlandish leaps in his story line, Hitchcock justifies his plausible insertions by merging them with irony, ambiguity, and wit, all of which make the story richer for their presence.

So too with Cornell Woolrich—who shares yet another attribute with the Master of Suspense.

The Black Path of Fear is an excellent example of the extraordinary liberties Woolrich takes with logic and coincidence for the sake of creating a compelling story. Gifted storyteller that he is, he writes with stylistic and allegorical flourishes, like a painter flaunting his artistic skills. Tonal considerations supersede strict narrative logic. However, there are risks. The strained logic works tolerably well most of the time, but when it doesn't, the lapse can be serious enough to detract from the artistic merits of the work. In *Black Path*, unfortunately, this is too often the case. Logical discrepancies overreach their limit until what could have been a minor masterpiece becomes a flawed, although adequate, suspense yarn. We might accept the ethical contradiction in Scott's returning Roman's lost wallet but then stealing his wife. We might accept the surprising reversal in the attitude of the Havana police who badger

Scott for his apparent guilt in Eve's murder and then suddenly show leniency by taking him to the store where he bought the murder weapon, giving him the chance to clear himself. And we might accept Scott's coincidental alliance with the one inhabitant in the whole city who not only is willing and able to shield him from recapture by the police, but who lives next door to an opium addict who provides the very lead he needs to extricate himself from his predicament. We might accept all these things until, for all her supposed street-smarts and common sense, Midnight makes the absurd proposal that Scott place himself in the midst of Eve's murderers so that when the police arrive in the nick of time to rescue him, they will suddenly realize, when they see the murderers trying to kill him, that he must be innocent. The petty dialogue bandied between Midnight and Scott is supposed to establish a rationale for his carrying out her scheme, and when he finally consents to this inanity, we feel that he is even more stupid and unimaginative than he says he is.

Unlike Woolrich's many stories which rely on an episodic format, *The Black Path of Fear* begins *in medias res*. Narrator-protagonist Bill Scott and his lover Eve are in mid-flight from her husband, gangster kingpin Eddie Roman. Six pages into the story Eve is stabbed to death, the murder weapon apparently a knife that Scott recently purchased at a local curio shop. For the rest of the novel Scott scrambles to evade the police, prove his innocence, and avenge his beloved's death. Most of what follows is told in simple chronological order, except for a lengthy middle section which, related in flashback, contributes to the shifting, disjointed temporal structure often found in *noir* film and literature. Having eluded the police, Scott finds temporary refuge in Midnight's squalid apartment and tells her how his ordeal began. Down-and-out in Miami, he found a wallet which belonged to a man named Eddie Roman. He returned it to Roman and was hired on the spot as chauffeur. After a week, he met Mrs. Roman whose routine was to have him drive her to a promontory overlooking the sea. In time, they fell in love. Aware of Roman's penchant for vindictive cruelty, they fled to Havana, where someone in a crowd at Sloppy Joe's nightclub stabbed Eve and framed Scott for the murder.

Midnight helps Scott locate the photographer who took the couple's picture just at the moment of the stabbing, but Scott discovers that he has been kidnapped. Midnight prompts Scott to reveal what he knows about Roman and they eventually conclude that he must earn his wealth from illegal opium trafficking. Next door to Midnight is a Chinese opium addict named Quon. They bribe him to help Scott enter the opium den of the people they suspect responsible for Eve's death. Once inside the derelict den, Scott explores the dark and narrow passages until he finds a secret door leading into the shop of Tio Chin, the Chinese dealer who sold him the alleged knife that killed Eve. Chin and his henchmen nab Scott, tie him up, and hide him in a wardrobe along with the kidnapped photographer, intending to kill them later. Luckily, the police arrive on cue, according to Midnight's plan, and rescue Scott and the photographer.

The photograph shows that a Captain Paulson, who was running opium between Havana and Miami, was Eve's murderer. The captain is a cohort of Chin's, and Scott infers that Chin has been working with Roman in the illegal trafficking of opium. Chin has committed suicide, however, and there is no evidence to substantiate that Roman was responsible for Eve's murder. Free on his own cognizance, Scott slips off to Miami where he sneaks into Roman's oceanside mansion. He attempts to strangle Roman in his bed, when Roman's bodyguard Jordan enters and fires at Scott, but shoots his boss instead. Scott wrestles with Jordan who falls over the balcony railing and has his throat ripped out by the servant's dog Wolf. Scott returns to Havana to give himself up. Police Chief Acosta, aware of Scott's troubles, shrewdly feigns ignorance in order to have legal grounds for letting him go. Scott meets with Midnight once more. They walk together a ways. Midnight leaves him and he enters Sloppy Joe's where he had his last drink with Eve. He muses at the last, "It was lonely standing there by myself at the bar like that."

When Scott begins his narration, it sounds at first as if events are unfolding as he speaks. A number of passing remarks, however, make us realize that the story has already happened and he is reflecting back on it. He says of Eve's appearance just prior to their last moment together, "She was all in white, to fit the climate and the night; satin, I think it was, and I think, too, it must have been sprayed on and then allowed to dry, to be that even all over." We get the impression that he is trying to hold on to his last memory of her before she was murdered, his last image of her as his ideal woman. Then later, when he is running from the police, he has to choose between two doors:

> It was a toss-up. I've often wondered what would have happened if I'd picked the one on the left instead of on the right. Two doorways on a darkened alley; one spelled life and one spelled death [38].

Scott's momentary insertion of the present perfect tense suggests that he is musing on an event that has already happened and he is somewhere else reminiscing what has befallen him and how he has emerged from it. Perhaps he is presently standing at the bar where he winds up at the story's end after he separates from Midnight. His rumination about making the right choice iterates the *noir* theme that human lives are subject to the whims of some indefinable power, whether chance or fate or providence. Foolishly, people believe they can control their destiny; outcomes have no guarantees, no matter what precautions they take. (Compare a similar implication in "Dormant Account" where Palmer reflects on the role Chance plays in his life when he picks an identity.)

By any standard, protagonist Bill Scott falls far short of the stature of Romantic Champion, rescuer of the damsel in distress. Woolrich could have painted him with those paradoxical traits that usually define the ambiguous *noir* anti-hero. Instead, from beginning to end, Scott plays the extreme *noir* victim, a passive seed afloat on the river of fate, completely subject to its undulations and buffeted by its unpredictable currents. He is quite impotent, exerting little influence on the forces affecting him, more manipulated by them than able to take decisive action against them.

A fluke accident initiates Scott's exploit: he finds Roman's wallet on a Miami street. His long, painstaking journey to Roman's house proves unnecessary because Roman is rich enough to overlook this trivial loss. For a moment, Roman becomes frantic thinking that the wallet contained certain incriminating papers, but when he finds them safe in another wallet, the first one is forgotten. The money, then, is a secondary issue. The guilt that motivated Scott to return it and his misjudgment of its importance are foibles that foreshadow his incapability of handling the ordeal ahead.

In Havana, Eve senses Roman's power to exact revenge against her and Scott, but Scott assures her that even Roman cannot reach this far. Minutes later, someone stabs her and she dies in Scott's arms. No sixth sense or powers of prediction has this protagonist.

Scott makes the perfect fall guy. After Eve's murder, he is totally helpless, completely hapless. In his bout with the police, the physical evidence counters all his arguments. His only alternative is to flee. He plunges into the Havana alleyways, a *noir* labyrinth, an abysmally black maze of narrow corridors and frustrating dead ends. He hasn't the power or prowess to succeed by himself. Like many of Woolrich's abject male fugitives, Scott needs the help of a stronger, more resourceful female. To escape the police, he chooses "the door on the right" (that is, the "right" door) and follows the winding halls to the sepulchral, pitch-black hell-hole of an apartment inhabited by a Cuban woman. He asks her name, and she responds: "My real name? I forget it long ago. I've got a dozen of them, one for every place I go.... Around here they call me Media Noche...." She could be one of the hags from *Macbeth*, an anonymous witch given to practicing the grisly "deed without a name." Scott has difficulty pronouncing her name (no linguist, he), so she gives him the English equivalent, Midnight. His shying away from speaking her name aloud is like refusing to invoke the name of the devil. He makes a momentary pact with this underworld figure, hoping for a reprieve from his distress, but unlike Faust, he does not expect the contract to be permanently binding.

To help him escape the police, Midnight invents the smallpox ruse: she paints red dots on his back to make the officers think he has the disease. Smallpox is symbolic of his outcast state: he is quarantined from society, a pariah, abetted by a woman who does it not for his sake but for "flowers on a grave," an homage to the memory of her lover who was wronged by the law. Midnight, not Scott, puts herself in danger by seeking out the name of the photographer, while he waits in safety in her apartment. She, not Scott, devises the plan for him to enter the opium den and expose the whereabouts of the men who framed him and killed his girl. She, not Scott, braves the repulsive task of bringing the emaciated Quon out of his opiate stupor and persuades him to lead Scott into the opium den. And she, not Scott, calls the police to rescue him just before the drug runners are about to kill him. Scott has all along been admitting that he is unimaginative, and by gosh, he is right. He does little to help his own cause until he tries to take revenge into his own hands. His acquiescence to Midnight's scheme signifies his inability to think for himself. The scheme itself requires that he submit to her questionable logic and to the mercy of pure luck: once he places himself in harm's way, he can only wait for the police to arrive in time to save him. Drugged by his captors, he inadvertently knocks over the large wardrobe he's concealed in, attracting the attention of Acosta's officers who are in the process of leaving after their unsuccessful raid on the opium den.

Declared innocent of Eve's murder, Scott returns to Miami to kill Roman. He tries to choke the gangster to death, but he is deprived even of this satisfaction when Jordan breaks in and accidentally shoots the wrong man. Scott is an ironic double of Roman: each gained revenge on the other for taking Eve away and each had their murders committed by proxy.

Woolrich frames *The Black Path of Fear* with contrapuntal sexual implications related to the story and to himself. The phallic knife that Roman's surrogate uses to stab Eve suggests a symbolic consummation of Roman's relationship with her that simultaneously deprives Scott of experiencing literal sex with her. The knife, a substitute for the phallus, also implies that Roman may have been impotent; after all, he and Eve were in an asexual relationship, sleeping in separate bedrooms. Likewise, Eve and Scott had separate quarters on the ship, another parallel between Scott and Roman suggesting that Scott, too, may have been impotent. Eve had invited him to share her stateroom because she was afraid, and intercourse might have occurred, but Scott overtly denies this. He would like us to believe that, despite the heat and bloom of their passion, they practiced platonic celibacy. On the other hand, she may have trusted him because she knew he was impotent or she may have rejected his outright advances. Worth noting is that, before Eve is killed, she insists on wearing all the jewelry Roman gave her. Scott interprets this as her ritualistic way of severing ties with her husband, when it may be that she cannot part with the literal wealth she has amassed. He holds her up as his ideal, whereas she may be the classic *femme fatale* who has used him to help her flee an unpleasant situation and plans to leave him at the first opportunity.

Complementing the sexually related imagery of the beginning, the ending suggests a homoerotic encounter when Roman and Scott wrestle in violent embrace on the bed. Here, too, Scott is deprived of symbolic sexual union because Jordan kills Roman before the murder is consummated. Earlier, at the opium den, Quon appears to be climbing into the crib with Scott. Scott angrily starts to repel him, a gesture that might suggest either homophobia or xenophobia. Yet in the end, he willingly crawls into bed with Roman, driven by his urge for violence. He has overcome his homophobia only to face frustration in that overture as he had in his heterosexual relationship with Eve. He remains stranded between the two polar worlds of sexual orientation. When he enters Sloppy Joe's for the last time and says he realizes how alone he is, the implication is that in failing to consummate a relationship with either sex, he is now alienated sexually from both. (Scott's situation is remarkably similar to that of L.B. Jefferies in Hitchcock's *Rear Window* where Thorwald has his way with him on Jeff's bed.)

Scott's thwarted bisexual ventures are mirrored in his relationship with Midnight, a dual male-female figure. Midnight is described as a voluptuous, lusty woman, yet she smokes cigars, lights them with a masculine flair, and has the temperament and bearing of a man. She lets Scott spend time in her apartment with the stipulation that he respect their asexual collaboration; that is, he is forbidden to satisfy any sexual desires with either of the genders she represents.

Like Scott, Woolrich himself was alienated from society, although apparently more by choice. He adopted a reclusive life style, motivated partially by the demands of the writer's profession, partially by his strange sense of responsibility for and dependence on his mother Claire, and partially by his failure to find satisfaction in any sexual relationship. His disastrous experiment with marriage and his secret homosexual affairs are allegorized in Scott's symbolic impotence, his inability to consummate a union with either men (Quon, Roman) or women (Eve, Midnight). One can easily see how Woolrich may have identified strongly with this particular character.

Bill Scott fits into a category that defines many of Woolrich's male protagonists, namely, the ill-fated, slow-thinking man who becomes indebted to a stronger, smarter woman. Eve is a *femme fatale* (debatably an inadvertent one) who leads the gullible Scott into danger. Scott interprets her behavior as sincere, but his descriptions hint at the possibility of duplicity. He mentions her attachment to the jewelry given her by Roman, but he dismisses it as her way of snubbing her husband. However, she seems to have an obsession with it that Scott fails to notice. Even though he believes she would have thrown it into the water, there is no proof that she would have carried out this manipulative threat. Then there is his association with Midnight. Connected with the underworld, Midnight is an ambiguous devil-figure, a teasing succubus who enters Scott's nightmare, but offers no promise of sexual fulfillment. She is tough, bitter, trial-hardened, and streetwise, her callousness a defensive weapon for confronting the ruthless realities of an indifferent, Darwinian world. She is an extreme version of Bricky in *Deadline at Dawn*, and belongs among the women of *Phantom Lady*, *The Black Angel*, and "Angel Face" who assume the more assertive, efficient roles of private investigators when the police are derelict in their duties and their male ward is victimized to the point of impotence.

Bill Scott may be the protagonist, but he deserves less recognition than an anti-hero. The traditional anti-hero, because of some redeeming virtue (integrity, perseverance, self-sacrifice), earns our admiration in spite of his moral flaws and social improprieties. However, this particular Woolrichian protagonist lacks any outstanding redeeming trait to set him above his fellow humans. Bill Scott, for instance, never does anything to win our admiration or give him the status of hero. His escape from the police? Desperation, not heroism. His infiltration of the opium den? Stupidity, not heroism. The one act that approximates gallantry is his return to Miami to avenge Eve's murder. To choke Roman to death, although vigilantism, is at least his attempt to take justice and fate, literally, into his own hands. However, even this is undermined when Jordan does the job for him. Chance hovers around Scott, makes him a part of its machinations, brings about events without his ability to influence them for his own designs.

Associated with Scott's impotence are the knives with their jade handles carved with the figures of the three monkeys that see-no-evil, hear-no-evil, and speak-no-evil. Much is made of the elaborate switch from the hear-no-evil knife that Scott bought to the see-no-evil knife that becomes the murder weapon. Of the three knives, these two are both related to passivity: sights and sounds can assault a person without his consent. The third knife, speak-no-evil, is the only one of the three that requires active participation by the individual. Woolrich is very shrewd in the way he treats the knife as a phallic symbol. To indicate Scott's impotence, it is crucial that the knife not belong to him, and so the switch is made. The murder weapon is identified with Roman, but because he hires an assassin, even the crime boss is not directly related to the knife. Both men are identified with these two particular knives and the passivity of the monkey figures on either signifies the questionability of their virility.

Woolrich uses marginal characters like Scott deliberately. From story to story, they share traits that leave them weak or useless against an adversary or obstacle. Part of this has to do with the idea that fatalism, not self-determination, controls outcomes. Subject to the power of fate, humans are merely motes of dust caught in a giant windstorm; no matter how much they may resist at first, they must ultimately surrender to fate's temporal and directorial forces. Bill Scott is trapped in this irresistible vortex when he is framed for Eve's murder. Roman, as a fatalistic agent, possesses the power to tamper with a man's life and keep him from controlling his circumstances. In the end, Roman becomes an ironic victim of fate's fickle vicissitudes when his bodyguard, the man supposed to protect him, kills him.

This is true of the many anti-heroes in literature and film. The difference is that when the anti-hero resists the evil forces, he can still emerge with a modicum of victory. Philip Marlowe and Sam Spade may not be in complete control of events from beginning to end — they may endanger themselves and others along the way — but when the riddle unravels, they can walk away with some sense of accomplishment, even if a guilty party escapes legal justice (such as in *The Big Sleep*). Not always so with Woolrich. Bill Scott has done nothing to deserve Eve in the first place. His attempt to expose the real culprits ends with his being captured by them; he is saved by the police, not by his own efforts. He is deprived of dictating his revenge against his enemies: Chin commits suicide; Jordan shoots Roman; Job's dog kills Jordan. No wonder, when he steps into the cantina for a final good-bye to Eve's ghost, Midnight keeps walking and does not bother to spend any more time with him.

Film: The Chase

1946, Universal. *D:* Arthur D. Ripley. *P:* Seymour Nebenzal (Nero Producers). *Assoc P:* Eugene Frenke. *Cin:* Franz F. Planer. *Sc:* Philip Yordan. *Ed:* Edward Mann. *Mus:* Michel Michelet. *F/X:* Ray O. Binger. *Art Dir:* Robert Usher. *Set Dec:* Victor A. Gangelin.
Cast: Robert Cummings (Chuck Scott), Michele Morgan (Lorna), Peter Lorre (Gino), Steve Cochran (Eddie Roman), Lloyd Corrigan (Emmerrich Johnson), Jack Holt (Commander Davidson), Don Wilson (Fats), Alexis Minotis (Police Lt. Acosta), Nina Koschetz (Madame Chin), Yolanda Lacca (Midnight), James Westerfield (Job), Jimmy Ames (Eve's assassin), Shirley O'Hara (Manicurist), Florence Auer (Barber, uncredited), Martin Garralaga (Carriage driver, uncredited), Alex Montoya (Detective, uncredited). 86 min.

If ever a film deserved more recognition than it has received, Arthur D. Ripley's *The Chase* is that film. It is not that critics have panned it or, worse, ignored it. In fact the opposite is true: most critics (that is, most who got around to seeing the film) rate it very highly. Bob Porfirio finds in it "those qualities that Borde and Chaumeton ... see as quintessentially *noir*: its oneirism...; its eroticism...; its unprecedented elements, such as the dreamed death of the hero; and its aspects of cruelty and ambivalence..." (In Silver and Ward 55). Lee Server conspicuously includes it as an entry in his "Black List: Essential Film Noir" and declares that "Arthur Ripley directs with a real flair for Cornell's paranoid lyricism and nutty logic" (In *The Big Book of Noir* 154). Spencer Selby calls the film "Woolrich's paranoid nightmare ... reconceived as a dark, hypnotic coalescence of dream and reality" (135). Nevertheless, *The Chase* is confined to the darkest recesses of oblivion, a *noir* film ironically condemned to the shadow existence from which it was born, seldom requested and seldom shown.

More prolific as a screenwriter than a director, Arthur D. Ripley spent his 40-plus years in filmmaking getting hands-on experience in the most creative aspects of the art form. In 1914, he broke into the silents as a cinematographer, sitting behind the camera for eight films over a two-year period. He worked as an editor on a couple of films, including Erich von Stroheim's *Foolish Wives* (1922). Between 1920 and 1944, he wrote two-and-a-half dozen screenplays. His directorial output was less, only 18 films, none of which created waves of popular acclaim, although his last film, *Thunder Road* (1958), gained some notoriety because its star, Robert Mitchum, had written it and also contributed as producer and songwriter. (Songwriter? Talk about hidden talents.) Despite the 12 years that separate them, *Thunder Road* and *The Chase* are not very far removed from each other. In both, the protagonists are scarred war veterans (Cummings from World War II; Mitchum, the Korean War) who become enmeshed in circumstances that affect their decisions and their actions. In an interview with Peter Bogdanovich, director Edgar Ulmer reminisced briefly about his cursory acquaintance with Ripley at PRC (Producers Releasing Corporation), attributing his scanty output to both mental and physical infirmities. Interestingly, although he recognizes Ripley as a better editor, Ulmer praises one particular film he wrote and directed, *Voice in the Wind* (1944) (in McCarthy and Flynn 377–409).

Ripley's *The Chase* dispenses with Woolrich's lengthy flashback, and instead, incorporates it into the beginning so that the story can be told in chronological order. The first shots of the film are taken from inside a restaurant, at a slightly high angle, showing a short order cook lining up bacon and pancakes on his grill while a mesmerized Chuck Scott (Robert Cummings) stands outside the window, gulping his saliva because he cannot afford breakfast. The image of the lone figure on the outside looking in symbolizes Chuck's role as the quintessential *noir* victim, the totally alienated individual, the pariah who can never be a viable part of the community no matter how hard he tries. In this respect, Chuck faithfully mirrors Bill Scott, an insipid, powerless character, subject to the whims of fate, manipulated by circumstances rather then able to dictate decisive actions for himself.

Unable to afford the luxury of a breakfast, Chuck pulls out a bottle of pills from his pocket and pops one into his mouth. We later learn that the pills are prescribed medication. A psychological casualty of war, he suffers from a post-traumatic disorder. Ripley inserts this new twist to imply a reason for Chuck's vulnerability, fragility, and brittleness. Woolrich isn't concerned with establishing a rationale for Scott's impotence; it is enough for him that Scott has these passive qualities. Ripley's post-war circumstance links *The Chase* with many other films that deal with the changed men who return to a changed society and have to learn to cope with it or face damaging consequences. Although *noir* is the perfect vehicle for confronting these issues (*High Wall*, *Crack-Up*, *I Walk Alone*, *The Unfaithful*), non-*noir* films, like *The Best Years of Our Lives*, also deal with them.

Repeating the actions of his counterpart in Woolrich's novel, Chuck finds Eddie Roman's wallet and extracts a small portion of the contents before he returns the wallet to its owner. Roman (Steve Cochran, understating his menace to make it all the more chilling) verbally abuses his female barber, then physically assaults his manicurist for accidentally hurting him. The scene, as in Woolrich, exposes his sadistic streak. Ripley's alteration of the barber's gender, though, is a nifty touch. A female cutting a male's hair makes an oblique allusion to Samson and Delilah. Roman, with his bloated chauvinistic male ego, refuses to acknowledge the female's power. It is ironic that Chuck arrives at this moment, for Roman will hire him as his chauffeur, only to have him run away with Mrs. Roman (Michele Morgan), forcing him into a pursuit that, driven by his possessiveness for the female, leads to his destruction.

Roman teases Chuck for his honesty, telling his henchman Gino (Peter

The Black Path of Fear (1944) / *The Chase* (1946)   251

The Chase— The vain and lethal Eddie Roman (Steve Cochran) sits poised between the masculine female barber (Florence Auer) and the feminine manicurist (Shirley O'Hara) while his lackey (Peter Lorre) looks on (United Artists, courtesy William Thailing).

Lorre) that the Good Samaritan ought to get a medal. Chuck answers, "No, thanks. I've already got a medal." He is a decorated navy veteran, a hero, who, having returned to the society he fought for, finds it indifferent to his difficulty in getting work. Roman asks why he returned the wallet. "Just a sucker, I guess," says Chuck, and Roman responds, "I like that, too." Roman's remark sounds sincere, but it may be that he likes Chuck as an easy mark, a dupe he can control and who, grateful for the job, should be most loyal. He hires him on the spot as his chauffeur.

Next, Ripley's film introduces a twist to Woolrich's novel. While Chuck is driving, his employer tests his chauffeuring abilities. In the back seat, Roman has a device that lets him control all aspects of the driving except the steering. He becomes a literal back-seat driver as he accelerates the car beyond the 110-mile-per-hour limit on Chuck's speedometer. With Gino fearfully quiet alongside him, Roman races toward a railroad crossing, planning to beat the locomotive, but as he gets there and the train clears the crossing, a second train passes from the opposite direction, cutting them off. Roman slams on the brake, stopping barely in time. Ripley's insertion is an inventive addition to the story. For one, as a plot device, the scene foreshadows the climax when Roman once again races with a locomotive, but fails to brake in time, and he and Gino die in a fiery crash. The back-seat accelerator demonstrates Roman's obsession with power and control (similar obsessions apparent in Woolrich's gangster), and his demise shows that such traits are vain and illusory. When Roman races the first locomotive and nearly hits the unexpected second train at the crossing, the near-collision suggests that no one can predict the unforeseen obstacles that always arise, the dangers and dilemmas that frequently block our way despite our confidence that we are in control. In this respect, Chuck is the antithesis of Roman: he is the passive, cautious outcast working for the ambitious, self-made egotist.

The dog that kills Jordan at the end of *Black Path* plays a different role in *The Chase*. Roman, not the servant Job, owns the dog, a large mastiff named Tony. When dinner guest Emmerrich Johnson (Lloyd Corrigan) refuses to sell his shipping concern, Roman invites him into his wine cellar where he lets Tony loose on the entrepreneur. Ripley executes the scene in the Val Lewton tradition, letting sounds rather than images roil the viewer's imagination. We never see the dog; we only hear its low growls while Johnson fearfully retreats from its approach. At the moment the dog pounces, Johnson covers his face and drops a bottle of Napoleon brandy that shatters on the floor. While the man screams and the dog barks and snarls, we watch the wine run along the ground, symbolic of Johnson's bloodletting. (The image is strikingly comparable to that in *The Leopard Man* when Teresa Delgado is attacked on her doorstep and her blood flows under the door.) The grisly scene impresses on us Roman's horrifically sadistic nature.

Chuck meets Lorna for the first time when he chauffeurs her out to a promontory overlooking the ocean. In her white dress, standing and staring out at the turbulent waves, she looks like a woman resigned to being a sacrificial offering for some indifferent god. With her back to Chuck, she responds to his desire to help: " Yes, make it four years ago.... If you can't do that, just look the other way." Obviously, she would like to erase her years with Roman.

A montage sequence of superimposed shots follows, suggesting the passage of time and many visits to this promontory where Chuck gets to know Lorna better. To Lorna's question about what is out there beyond the horizon, Chuck answers, "Havana." Lorna offers him a thousand dollars to take her there. "Why me?" he says. "I trust you," she answers, to which he adds, "And I look like I need a thousand dollars." Her offer is based on her need to escape her ruthless husband, not on any attraction for Chuck. Although he hints that he would consider helping her for something other than the money, their exchange at this point does not touch on reciprocal feelings of love. He purchases two tickets to Havana.

The next scene becomes pivotal to the film for both its plot machinations and its thematic implications. Chuck, in his room, packs his bag for the Havana voyage. He stretches out on his bed to read the newspaper while awaiting

Lorna's phone call to take her for a supposed drive. The scene fades to black and when the next one fades in, the story resembles an abridged and altered version of *The Black Path of Fear*.

Gino discovers Chuck's room deserted, but a brochure tells where he and Lorna have gone. When he tells his boss, Roman remains unflustered, lying on his couch and listening to a piano concerto playing on his phonograph. His calm, self-contained indifference belies his seething anger and bodes his ability to seek vengeance in his own time and on his own terms. Aboard the *Cuba*, Chuck plays piano in Lorna's stateroom. She offers him the thousand dollars, but he shuns it. Here, director Ripley injects an exquisite device, a purely *noir* artifice, to close the scene. The shot is taken from outside the porthole, Lorna framed like a cameo just inside it, Chuck in the background. As an inversion of the film's opening shot, Chuck now enjoys a reversal of fortune by being on the inside where he can feel as if he "belongs" to something. The wall surrounding the porthole is lighted, but the ship lists and a dark shadow slowly descends like a curtain over the porthole wall, blackening it. Visible through the lighted porthole, Chuck steps past Lorna and drops the shade over the porthole, blotting out the light and completing the fade out. The fade is a classic convention in romantic scenes during the Production Code years, the abbreviated trysts between Bogart and Bergman or Heflin and Stanwyck (in *Casablanca* and *The Strange Love of Martha Ivers*, respectively), where heightened passion was visually castrated and the viewer's whetted expectations were left unconfirmed. Later, when we learn that this segment was something Chuck dreamt, the implication is that the dream may be his wish fulfillment for sexual potency.

In Havana, Chuck goes through the same ordeal as Woolrich's Bill Scott. While in the nightclub La Habana, Lorna is stabbed. Chuck has difficulty defending himself before Detective Lieutenant Acosta (Alexis Minotis) because he cannot explain how the murder weapon resembles a knife he so recently purchased, except that his had a handle with a carved monkey holding its ears, while this one has the monkey covering its eyes. (The knives carry the same implications as in Woolrich's novel: the images of the two monkeys' trying to shut out offensive sounds and sights are the passive gestures of an introvert and suggest the impotence that Chuck brings to his relationship with Lorna.) Acosta allows Chuck to lead police to the local store where he says he had bought the knife. Madame Chin (Nina Koschetz) is the proprietor, who, like Roman's barber, differs from Woolrich's character by having undergone a sex change. She refutes Chuck's claim about which knife he bought, and Chuck is forced to attempt an escape from the police to clear himself.

By disconnecting a light cord and plunging the shop into darkness (repeating his blocking out the light of the porthole), Chuck is able to elude his captors. He wends his way through the dark labyrinth of alleyways and an apartment complex where an impoverished female tenant, Midnight (Yolanda Lacca), diverts Acosta and his men away from him. Unlike Woolrich's Midnight who has an extended and critical relationship with Scott, Ripley's Midnight has only this narrow role. Her only other trivial function is to direct Chuck to the photographer who took pictures at La Habana and, Chuck wonders, may have taken an incriminating shot of the man who murdered Lorna. At the photographer's, Chuck finds the man dead, drowned horribly in his sink (unlike in *Black Path* where the photographer was kidnapped). Chuck notices a cord festooned from one wall to another, acting as a drying line for the photographer's pictures. A close-up shows where a clip holds a shard of a negative that had apparently been ripped from the line.

The scene dissolves into a close-up of the complete negative that had been stolen. The hand holding the negative compares it to the positive print, which shows a man at La Habana about to throw a knife. Chuck was right about the picture's importance. The hand moves the negative into the flame to burn it and the camera tracks back to reveal Gino, who has come to Havana to carry out Roman's vengeance against Lorna and Chuck. Gino is in Madame Chin's establishment. He and Chin exchange hostile words which reveal that Chin and Roman run a drug smuggling operation. Chin claims she takes all the risks and deserves a greater percentage of the profits: "We run the stuff across, not you. All you have to do is wear out that seat, which you do." Gino, ever conscious of trimming unnecessary overhead, kills her. Chuck, meanwhile, has worked his way back to Madame Chin's. He is hiding in the attic when he witnesses Chin's murder. Gino comes upstairs, finds Chuck behind a curtain, and shoots him. He drags the body to the trapdoor in the attic floor and slides it down the ladder.

The image of Chuck's crumpled body fades out and a fade-in returns us to Chuck asleep on his bed in his room in Roman's mansion: this pivotal moment acts as an interface between dream and reality. The phone is ringing, but Chuck wakes too slowly to answer it. He appears confused, disoriented. He swallows more pills and phones his navy psychologist for an appointment. Commander Davidson (Jack Holt) takes him to the Florida Club to discuss his case. Chuck suffers from amnesia, which, although not a factor in *Black Path*, is perfectly congruent with Woolrichian situations. To justify it scientifically, Davidson calls it "anxiety neurosis." (We have already discussed how other film adaptations incorporate the amnesia motif even when Woolrich's original story does not. See Clurman's *Deadline at Dawn*, Tourneur's *The Leopard Man*, Neill's *Black Angel*, and Reinhardt's *The Guilty*.)

By coincidence (another device *The Chase* borrows from *Black Path*), Roman comes to the Florida Club with Gino. They take a seat near a wall that separates them from the bar area where Chuck sits with the psychologist. While Davidson leaves to make a telephone call, Chuck finds inside his coat pocket the two tickets to Havana and he remembers Lorna. He returns to the mansion, slugs Job, and frees Lorna from her locked room. Instead of the *Cuba*, they take a second ship, the *Cristola*, sailing for Havana, but a delay keeps them in the harbor.

At the Florida Club, Roman talks with Fats (Don Wilson) who happened to see Chuck buy the two tickets for Havana and innocently mentions the incident to his host. The vindictive Roman realizes he has been betrayed and goes after his wife and Chuck. Racing toward the harbor, Roman uses his back-seat control device while Gino steers. Again, a train runs on the track parallel to the road, and again, Roman pits the speed of his car against the speed of the locomotive. This time, however, he cannot beat the train to the crossing and he and Gino crash and burn. Obsession drives humans to take extreme risks and Fate is ever willing to challenge their false conviction that they control their own destinies.

Chuck enters Lorna's stateroom with a telegram that announces Roman's death, so he knows he and Lorna are safe. (Where the telegram came from is left unexplained.) In Havana, Chuck and Lorna are in front of La Habana, sitting in the identical carriage that appeared in his dream. In an extreme, intimate close-up, they exchange words of love:

CHUCK: I love you.
LORNA: I want you to keep telling me that as long as we're together.
CHUCK: That'll be forever.
(They kiss.)

"Forever" is pabulum for the romantic; it is too questionable an absolute. Lorna's conditional remark, "as long as we're together," if taken ironically, sounds more credible. In front of La Habana, they have arrived at the precise moment that preceded Chuck's dreaming of Lorna's death. Once they leave the carriage, their relationship will be susceptible to all those variables that make life an unpredictable journey. Chuck is perhaps too romantic to see this, but the *femme fatale*, more practical, is not.

The *noir* "oneirism" praised by Porfirio refers to the whole of Ripley's film. From beginning to end, the story has a surrealistic quality, some of its dreamy effect created through the editing, which relies frequently on soft dissolves rather than abrupt cuts. In terms of narrative, the dream sequence acts as the cornerstone of Ripley's intentions. As the point of departure between dream and reality, it initially suggests that Chuck, safely asleep in his bed, has dreamt of his and Lorna's deaths, and that when he awakens in bed afterwards, he has returned to reality. Woolrich's novel does not include this device. Instead, as in most of Woolrich's stories of this type, the nightmare *is* the reality. Bill Scott does not wake from a dream to find his fragmented world suddenly and benignly intact. Neither do the protagonists in *The Black Curtain*, "Nightmare," and "C-Jag."

The dream sequence in *The Chase* may deviate from the plot in *Black Path*, but it is not something irreconcilable with Woolrich's ideas about the nightmares that infringe on reality. Ripley offers us two endings: our predisposition determines which one we believe is the reality and which the dream.

The way the film is constructed, the first ending, the story of Chuck's and Lorna's deaths, appears to be the dream sandwiched between the continuum of the real life narrative. While waiting for Lorna's call, Chuck falls asleep.

The Chase— During his ambiguous dream sequence, Chuck Scott (Robert Cummings) acts with uncharacteristic self-confidence by helping Lorna (Michele Morgan) escape Roman's sadistic clutches (United Artists, courtesy William Thailing).

What follows is his dream of their flight to Havana, where Roman's far-reaching vengeance catches up to them. Taken as a dream, Chuck's vision of his and Lorna's deaths can be the result of his guilt. Like Woolrich's Bill Scott, he presents himself as honest to a fault, yet in a kind of perverse barter, he returns the man's wallet, then steals his wife. The episode where Chuck lowers the porthole shade as a prelude to a secretive sexual encounter is the wish fulfillment of a carnal desire. Yet legally and morally, it is also adultery, and poetic justice is served when Roman's agents kill Lorna and him with weapons symbolic of phallic violence (knife, gun). Unable to envision his actual murder, Chuck imagines it taking place behind a curtain. For his betrayal of his employer, his body is further desecrated, thrown from a height (attic) to a lower level (Chin's shop). Figuratively, he sees himself condemned to hell, his own body lumped with that of the criminal who was killed just before him.

When Chuck awakens from this dream, he supposedly returns to reality, yet he suffers from amnesia, another kind of dream state that divorces the psyche from reality, and so his cognitive connection to the world is delayed. The timely discovery of the two tickets in his coat pocket triggers his remembrance of his plan to run away with Lorna. Roman learns of their plan and, in his rashness, drives himself and Gino to their destruction. Chuck and Lorna can continue their life together without fear of reprisal from Roman.

For the romantic-minded, this is the more desirable ending. However, Ripley has created a complex paradox: although either ending can be the dream or the reality, both can also be dreams. When Chuck falls asleep and dreams the first dream, it is possible that, dissatisfied with the ending of that dream, he remains on his bed and dreams a second, more acceptable outcome to his relationship with Lorna. In this respect, he resembles Scotty Ferguson (James Stewart as another bewitched "Scott") who may still be hanging from the gutter above the alley when *Vertigo* ends, his relationship with the dual Madeleine-Judy an imaginative mental distraction while he awaits rescue. Chuck, like Scotty Ferguson, finds the romantic entanglement appealing and may be inventing two possible scenarios in which he satisfies his ego by including himself as one of her reasons for leaving Roman. Therefore, in *The Chase*, both film endings may be dreams and Chuck's relationship with Lorna a mere fantasy of his own creation. In the first part of the film, unconditionally accepted as reality, Lorna never gives any indication of romantic feelings for him. Her motives appear naturally self-serving; she trusts Chuck and is willing to pay him, but she does not try to seduce him. She bargains with her money, not with her body.

As a third possibility, the first ending may be the reality and the second ending the dream. When Chuck stretches out on his bed, a piano concerto is playing (asynchronous music, the source initially undefined). After a fade, the bed is empty and Gino enters the room looking for him. The piano concerto, uninterrupted through the transition, is still playing. A cut to Roman's living room shows him lying on his couch, listening to his phonograph, the source of the piano music. (That both men are lying down is one of many doubled images occurring throughout the film. Most of the doubled imagery suggests this dual relationship between them.) The music continues unbroken from the pre-dream sequence into the supposed dream sequence, suggesting that this is not a dream at all, but a continuation of the reality. What immediately follows, then, may be the actual outcome of Chuck's flight with Lorna, she knifed, and he shot to death. After being shot, his last vision before he dies may have been an alternate outcome for his flight to Havana, a situation very similar to that of the doomed Farquar in Ambrose Bierce's "An Occurrence at Owl Creek Bridge." What Chuck imagines within the span of milliseconds is a successful escape with his lover and the death of her husband, so that their relationship can continue without guilt.

The Chase bears similarities with other films on the basis of two primary aspects in the premise. One is the devastation that befalls a decent man who succumbs to temptation and falls helplessly in love with another man's wife (or girlfriend). The other is the nature of the protagonist, a basically good but gullible character who moves to and fro according to the whims of the forces that steer him.

Vertigo, in addition to what has already been mentioned, shares a number of additional parallels with *The Chase*. Gavin Elster (Tom Helmore) hires old friend Scotty Ferguson to follow his wife Madeleine (Kim Novak) because she seems possessed with the spirit of a long dead relative. While following her, Scotty falls in love with her and she with him. During their visit to an old Spanish mission, she runs away from him and up the staircase of the highest tower. He tries to follow, but vertigo prevents him from reaching the top floor. She commits suicide by leaping from the tower while he can only witness her body falling past the window. Afterwards, he becomes deranged, nearly catatonic. His shattered psyche appears the direct result of losing a loved one, but it may also be from guilt, the guilt that he could not prevent her death — or less likely, the guilt that he betrayed a friend by having lustful designs on Elster's wife. Like *The Chase*, *Vertigo* offers two possible endings. Wandering the streets of San Francisco, Scotty spies a woman who looks like Madeleine (Kim Novak doubling herself). Judy Barton is her name. As he gets to know her, he gradually transforms her into the woman he lost. In recreating his beloved, he can restore the loss and absolve himself from guilt. This is similar to the rationale which Bricky and Quinn apply to their situation in *Deadline at Dawn*: if given a second chance to return to the lives they led before they made their mistakes, they can reconcile their guilt and recover their innocence. Woolrich gives Bricky and Quin the chance to realize that hope; Ferguson finds such a turnabout more difficult. The film ends with his very questionable triumph. Likewise, Chuck may have constructed an alternate ending, recreating events until they offered a more pleasing outcome for himself.

Another film connected to *The Chase* is the seminal *noir* thriller *Out of the Past* (1947). Hired by gangster Kirk Douglas to locate mischievous runaway girlfriend Jane Greer, Robert Mitchum falls helplessly in love with his quarry. They evade Douglas for a time, but Mitchum's ex-partner locates them. Greer shoots the partner and runs back to her old boyfriend. Douglas is cut from the same cloth as Eddie Roman and does not like to dismiss private wrongs with impunity. With Greer's help, he tries to trap Mitchum in an elaborate frame, but it leads to the ironic demise of all. Mitchum knows what he is doing when he surrenders to Greer's charms the first time. He even enters the frame with open eyes, a masochistic gesture, a kind of self-flagellation as if attempting to purge himself of the wrong he has done. (In burying his partner's body to protect Greer, he not only implicates himself in the killing, but also defiles the code of the private detective as espoused by Sam Spade in *The Maltese Falcon*.) A remake of *Out of the Past*, the neo-*noir Against All Odds* follows the original film closely (while echoing the title of one of the last classic *noir* films, *Odds Against Tomorrow*) and ends in a more hopeful spirit (which counters the *noir* qualities it tries to replicate).

Vaguely reminiscent of *The Chase* is *Where Danger Lives* (1950), in which Robert Mitchum again plays the naïve patsy of the *femme fatale* (foreshadowing a similar role he takes in the 1953 *Angel Face* with Jean Simmons as the deadly Spider Woman). A doctor who should know better, he has Maureen O'Sullivan for a stalwart, steady girlfriend (a sure reason for a *noir* male's apathy), yet finds himself attracted to the more sensually exciting Faith Domergue. When he abruptly learns that she is married to an older man (Claude Rains), he tries to walk out, but she finagles him into a brawl with her husband. Mitchum sustains a concussion and Rains receives a fatal blow from his poker-wielding wife. Domergue convinces Mitchum to flee with her and for the rest of the film they evade the police and try to find sanctuary in Mexico. Domergue does not exude the vulnerability of Michele Morgan in *The Chase*. It is interesting that the two men, both basically moral and upright, are attracted to women who represent polar opposites in their moral makeup. The female, noble or not, symbolizes or possesses something the male wants but cannot cannot define, whether it is excitement or sex or some other inexplicable commodity. For the *noir* male, the pursuit of the forbidden article (the married women in *The Chase* or *Double Indemnity* or the siren in *Pitfall*) promises untold rewards and pleasures, but usually leads to humiliation, unfathomable guilt, and self-destruction.

Chuck Scott, as the gullible, impressionable *noir* male who lacks clear self-identity, firm determination, and unshakable self-confidence, has a counterpart played by Joseph Cotten in *Journey into Fear* (Norman Foster, 1942) and *The Third Man* (Carol Reed, 1949).

In *Journey into Fear*, Joseph Cotton's character of Howard Graham sets a precedent for Chuck Scott. Based on the Eric Ambler novel, the story relates Graham's adventures as an arms dealer in Turkey at the outset of World War II. Underground German agents are out to kill him to delay the shipment of armaments that could interfere with their cause. Colonel Haki (Orson Welles) of the Turkish secret police tries to protect Graham, while Graham is intimidated by the German agents, cowering into corners from his own fears. In the end, he appears to take a stand by confronting his assailants, but when he survives, it is by luck. Graham pursues his would-be assassin on the outside ledge of a building. The assassin prepares to ambush him, but slips and falls to his death. Graham made an effort to control his destiny, but fate (accident) affected the outcome. In *The Chase*, Chuck Scott appears to be taking definite action against Roman (punching Job to get to Lorna, fleeing with her aboard the *Cristola*), but if the second ending is accepted as the reality, Roman's death occurs because of his own rash efforts, not Chuck's.

In *The Third Man*, Cotten plays Holly Martins, writer of pulp westerns. An outsider in Vienna after the war, he came to visit his friend Harry Lime (Welles again), but learns that Lime was killed in an automobile accident just prior to his arrival. Clues fall coincidentally into his path and he concludes that Lime was actually murdered. All along the way he misjudges people and evidence and makes the wrong inferences. His biggest mistake is in falling in love with Lime's girlfriend (Valli). Offended by Martins's helping the new postwar world order triumph over obsolete (or imagined) romantic ideals, Anna

Schmidt in the end leaves him standing alone on the tree-lined promenade. She walks away, fully aware of his powerlessness and ineptitude, a thoroughly impotent figure. This image closely parallels the ending of *The Black Path of Fear* when Midnight deserts Scott and leaves him to himself. *The Chase* does not portray Chuck Scott this way when the story ends, but up until then, his gulping pills, suffering from momentary amnesia, and being unable to protect Lorna or himself from Roman — whether events occur in reality or dream — suggest a weak, impotent character. Although this theme appeared in other eras as well, it was in the post-war period especially that the *noir* male had lost his virility, potency, and masculinity. Films like *The Chase* show his dilemma, his personal struggle to recapture and redefine that image, sometimes successfully, sometimes not.

Night Has a Thousand Eyes

Novel, first published under the pseudonym George Hopley by Farrar & Rinehart, 1945. Grosset & Dunlap, 1945. First paperback, Penguin (London), pbk #660, 1949. First American paperback, as by William Irish, Dell, pbk #679, 1953.

Writing his Sherlock Holmes series, Sir Arthur Conan Doyle ingeniously tantalized his audience by beginning his detective's adventures with a distressed client narrating an experience tied to what seemed an inexplicable, paranormal phenomenon. Holmes's quest, therefore, became not only to solve the crime but also to give mysterious events a rational, natural explanation. In a more modern example, Tony Hillerman's mysteries about Navajos Jim Chee and Lieutenant Joe Leaphorn often begin in a similar way with a similar effect: the line between the natural and supernatural is blurred, so that we read the stories, intent not only on uncovering the culprit of the crime but also learning the logical reason for the eerie occurrences.

This discrepancy between the real and the fantastic is something Woolrich incorporates in a number of his occult stories, such as "Dark Melody of Madness." However, when his stories end, the outcomes, unlike those of Doyle and Hillerman, usually raise more questions than they resolve, underscoring the inscrutable nature of the events rather than offering a satisfying clarification of what just took place. In Woolrich's world of *pulp noir*, the ambiguity affirms the notion that some ineffable force is ever at work, manipulating lives toward its own mysteriously determined ends. In *Night Has a Thousand Eyes*, Woolrich treats the supernatural paradoxically, countering plausible rationales for the clairvoyant's foreknowledge with outrageous coincidences that cannot be logically explained.

Detective Tom Shawn, walking home from his precinct one evening, stumbles onto a young lady, Jean Reid, attempting a suicide leap into a river. He stops her and takes her to a restaurant to talk. In a lengthy flashback sequence, she tells him about her widower father, Harlan Reid, and their previous encounters with a psychic, Jeremiah Tompkins. Most recently, Tompkins has told her father that, in three weeks, "you will meet your death at the jaws of a lion." The highly impressionable Reid begins to wither away physically and his daughter loses all hope for his recovery. Despair had compelled her to attempt suicide, until Shawn intervened.

The remainder of the story moves along chronologically in the present. Shawn becomes romantically attracted to Jean and volunteers personally to help her and her father. He reports her story to his superior, McManus. Although the general consensus is that Tompkins is a phony using Reid's gullibility to extort money from him, the police launch an elaborate investigative campaign to protect Reid and his daughter. Two investigators, after bugging Tompkins's apartment, overhear a conversation between him and Walter Myers, Reid's financial broker, who is coercing Tompkins to use his psychic power to influence Reid and make him believe in his imminent death. Coincidentally, an escaped circus lion lends some credence to the prophecy.

The suspense is too much for Reid. Obsessed with his inevitable doom, he finally goes berserk. He runs wildly through his house until he crashes headlong into a stained-glass window, impaling his neck on the spiked shards of glass and slicing his jugular vein. A picture of a lion is painted on the window in such a way that it looks as if Reid has plunged his head into the open maw of the animal, thereby validating Tompkins's prophecy. Tompkins, meanwhile, has surrendered to the police. He commits suicide in his cell, cutting his throat with a jagged coat button. McManus surmises that he was tormented by guilt for working with Walter Myers to delude Reid and drive him to his death. Jean is spared, however, and Shawn remains with her to comfort her through her difficult time.

This synopsis cannot do justice to Woolrich's captivating story, how he treats tension and suspense with superb mastery, intensifying the conflict in miniscule increments until Reid flies toward death in a shrieking crescendo. The pacing throughout the story, from tension to release, tension to release, is handled exquisitely. After the opening hooks the reader with Jean's curious reason for attempting suicide (to escape being scrutinized by the stars), the narrative moves into Jean's lengthy flashback, which begins quietly, then gradually grows in stress and strain as a series of mysterious events complicate the narrative. Tompkins's prophecies seem credible and incredible at the same time. Reid believes them, as they enable him to invest confidently and make hefty profits. The results also make a believer of the reader. Finally, the climax comes when Tompkins's portent of Reid's death nears consummation. For whatever reason, because of an inability to shed a lifetime of materialistic bondage, or simply because he is deathly afraid of death, Reid succumbs to a fatalistic compulsion and goes on a frenzied rampage through his house, causing his own destruction and fulfilling the prophecy. His is the same ironic urge that occurs in Maupassant's short story "The Coward," in which a man challenged to a duel becomes so overwhelmed and overwrought by the fear of dying that he commits suicide.

McManus plays the role of guardian of sanity—he is here to remind us that, in a sane, rational world, Tompkins is a charlatan. McManus deploys logic and determination to disprove all that Tompkins has foretold. He sends out a team of investigators to undermine Tompkins's prophecies, yet in the end, with all the precautions taken to insure Reid's safety, Reid still manages to kill himself in the very way that Tompkins predicted, "in the jaws of a lion." The contradictions that exist between predestination and self-determination remain intact. No amount of debate, no lengthy study of events and outcomes, can resolve this paradox.

This theme appears in many stories with which Woolrich could have been familiar, since it is as old as literature itself, of prominent concern in Homer's *Iliad* and *Odyssey* and in Sophocles' *Oedipus Rex*. The debate over whether humans control their fate or fate controls them appears in many variations; to illustrate, we can look at three examples of stories that use three different methods to reconcile behavior with foreknowledge. Dickens's *A Christmas Carol* enables the miserly Scrooge to witness his future in a *dream*. He sees that, after his death, he is remembered with disdain and acrimony. He asks the Ghost of Christmas Future if this is the shadow of things that must be or might be. Although he never receives a definite answer, he awakes in the morning with a new attitude on life. Supposedly, altering thinking and behavior will alter predicted outcome, and we joyfully assume that his moral transformation will redeem him from the ghost's dreary portent. In H.G. Wells's *The Time Machine*, the Time Traveller *physically* visits a bleak and demoralizing future, where he witnesses the devolution of humanity and finally its obliteration. The Time Traveller's friend, however, advises that even if this were true, people must live as if it were not so. That is, even with foreknowledge of inevitable doom, we must not alter our behavior or we will surrender to despair. (Wells varies this theme in his subsequent novel, *The Island of Doctor Moreau*, by addressing the current relationship between God and humanity.)

The third approach deals with this theme examined in relation to *supernatural forces*. It has already been noted how Woolrich resorts to Shakespeare for a number of plot and thematic devices and *Night Has a Thousand Eyes* is rife with allusions to the Bard. For one thing, there are many passages that paraphrase the poet's own words:

"...what else is there you can do if you're to be honest with yourself"[35]: "To thine own self be true" [*Hamlet*]
"...keep those thoughts out. There's madness at the end of them": "That way madness lies" [*King Lear*]
"And, oh, what fools we two would be—!" [109]: "What fools these mortals be" [*A Midsummer Night's Dream*]

More significant than these brief allusions, however, is the morbid kinship that Woolrich's novel has with *Macbeth*, a play whose dark tonality and gruesome themes seem to infect much of Woolrich's work. The way Tompkins ensnares Reid with his fortune telling abilities parallels how the three weird sisters suborned Macbeth, first promising him good fortune, then capsizing his world with vague equivocations about his impending death. One witch tells her cronies of a sailor whose return home she has impeded, but whom she must eventually allow to reach his destination (an Odysseus figure, obviously). Thus, she can fiddle with the means, but she cannot affect the ends—which raises paradoxes about Macbeth's situation: did he act out of free will (with some spousal prompting) or was he destined to kill King Duncan and become a tyrant in spite of himself; do the witches manipulate him with their magic or does he act on his own once they have planted in him the vile seeds of obsessive ambition? These questions receive the same go-rounds in *Night Has a Thousand Eyes*, as we wonder whether Reid has the option to change Tompkins's dreadful prophecy or can only wait for its fulfillment. The event occurs as predicted and the latter outcome seems the fatalistic conclusion.

While relating in flashback to Shawn the events that led her to this point (Chapter 2, "The Telling"), Jean Reid mentions one memory she has of her father closing his briefcase and fastening the chromium latch, which

> was oblong, and bright as a mirror. I remember noticing how it clouded, as his thumb left it, to clear again, as a mirror does when you breathe upon it. Sometimes I think that's all the impress we make upon life, a misted, evanescent finger mark like that, that evaporates again even as our touch is removed from it.

This is pure Woolrich—a metaphor that so aptly epitomizes the fatalistic philosophy pervading the majority of his writings. (The passage expands on the aphorism *First You Dream, Then You Die*, a title he formulated but never used, and which Nevins niftily appropriated for his Woolrich biography.) Yet again, the roots of this cynical outlook are grounded in Shakespeare. Prospero says that "we are such stuff/As dreams are made on, and our little life/Is rounded with a sleep" (*The Tempest*, IV.i.156–58). And Jaques in *As You Like It* tells his merry company that "all the world's a stage," that men and women pass through a doleful "seven ages," starting life as a "mewling and puking" baby and ending it in a second childhood highlighted by "mere oblivion" (II.vii.139–66). And we return once again to *Macbeth* where the tyrant's most despairing thoughts are elicited by the death of his wife:

> Life's but a walking shadow; a poor player
> That struts and frets his hour upon the stage
> And then is heard no more. It is a tale
> Told by an idiot, full of sound and fury,
> Signifying nothing [V.v.24–28].

In addition to the theme of despair that arises from the paradoxical relationship between self-determination and predetermination, class structure becomes important to the story. Having written his novel in 1945, Woolrich still lives with the scars of the Great Depression that stratified society into extremes, the impervious rich and the destitute poor, while the middle class became an endangered species. It is significant that, while the Reids are insulated by inherited wealth, Tompkins and his ilk live in a modest apartment house "where upper lower class meets lower middle class."

The story begins with Jean Reid's symbolic rejection of her wealth—her purse overturned so that the paper money is scattered to the winds, her perfume bottle smashed, and her watch broken. Jean has become disenchanted with her and her father's materialism that has no power to save them and may have actually contributed to their present woes. The Reids' wealth is contrasted with Tompkins's penury, yet Tompkins is the one whose power, both paranormal and authoritarian, makes Reid dependent on him for advice to sate his materialistic needs. When Jean visits Eileen, the maid she fired, to learn more about her father, they pause on the stairs: "She [Eileen] was above me, because of the difference the steps made." In this image, Eileen holds the position of power because she may be able to give Jean information about Harlan; at the same time, feeling guilty because she fired Eileen for a petty reason, Jean feels inferior to the lower class woman. Socially defined boundaries exist between these classes, but they are now crossed freely, the question of superiority relative to the personal relationship, not to the show of wealth. When Reid finally succumbs to his fear, he impales himself on the stained glass windows he imported from Italy and reconstructed in his parlor strictly for show, not for practical use. At a dear cost to himself, he shatters this façade of pretension. Coincidentally, Woolrich's novel again relates to Wells's *The Time Machine* in which class is a primary issue. In the world of the future, the Time Traveller discovers that the reins of power are reversed, as the Eloi, descendents of the once elite potentates of industry, become fodder for the Morlocks, descendents of the working class. The irony in Woolrich's story is that Jean is redeemed at the end, not by anything Shawn does, but by the simple fact that she will lose most of her family fortune. Wealth is a curse that prevents her from connecting to the world; a more moderate life style gives her a reason to find common ground with others.

Jean's association with her father creates some unsettling insinuations. Their displays of affection exceed the innocent feelings of a daughter for her father and suggest an unwholesome relationship. Extremely close and dependent on one another, his fears become her fears and his obsession with death affects her until she nearly takes her own life. In describing their relationship, Jean speaks in terms of two lovers; that is, their relationship borders on incest. When Tom Shawn rescues her from suicide, his intervention has secondary consequences. His arrival gives her an excuse to channel her feelings away from her father, making Shawn responsible for her redemption on a subtextual level. Consciously or unconsciously, Woolrich has depicted a parallel to his own relationship with his mother. He was aware of people's perception of that relationship, and although he affirmed that it was simply a loving concern of a son for his mother, the intensity of that bond and the duration of their private existence in their hotel retreat cannot help but give rise to wry speculations.

When it comes to guilt, Myers can be blamed for the overt criminal acts of bribery, coercion, and embezzlement, and for Reid's eventual inadvertent suicide. However, guilt also infuses the story in many other ways, linked subtly with moral questions tied to class division. The maid Eileen McGuire becomes a pawn in bringing the Reids to Tompkins. Her absentminded bus ride on her way to committing suicide shows that she suffered pangs of conscience and could not contain her guilt any longer, so she punished herself for her complicity. Tompkins, too, did not have a habit of using his prophetic powers indiscriminately, and was fundamentally a simpleminded, honest man with a talent he sincerely could not understand. Jean's estimate of him on their first meeting is probably accurate: "Just a farm boy, a lifelong misfit, embittered by the burden of something he wasn't equipped to cope with" (89). The strain from Tompkins's power isn't totally clear, although McManus tries to explain his impression to Shawn:

> He was just a poor tormented soul, cursed from the day he was born; caught in the middle of something that he probably couldn't understand himself. Wriggling all the time to get free, like a blind worm under a stone. A farm boy, with a flash of searing fire between his eyes.

That the rustic prophet was as much an innocent victim as Reid, both expendable figures in fate's game of life, is suggested in the scene where Tompkins sits in a diner contemplating calling the police and surrendering himself to them. He is immersed in an environment saturated with whiteness, the color associated with innocence and purity. He stares into his coffee cup: "...the milk in it had separated from the coffee, drifted to the sides, forming a hollow white ring. In the middle of it, the coffee was back almost to its original blackness. A spoon handle thrust up through the center of this like a submerged spear." Whatever innocence he claimed to possess was forfeited once he agreed to help Myers—the black center, his guilt, pushes aside the "milk of human kindness," his compassion and his purity. (One just can't escape those Shakespearean allusions.) Committing suicide by slitting his throat becomes an ironic complement to Reid's death.

Harlan Reid's death came about because of fear, not guilt, a significant difference that separates his kind from the lower classes. The wealthy, like Reid, have forfeited God for Manon, so that if they are driven to commit suicide, it is more likely from distress over losing their possessions, not grief over unethical behavior. Given over to materialism, they base their life-decisions on physical gain (luxuries, profits) without considering moral consequences. Even Jean's suicide attempt at the beginning of the story is connected to her fear of losing a "possession," her father, not a moral question at all. On the other hand, the suicides of McGuire and Tompkins are motivated by moral anguish, discouragement over failing to do right. As members of the lower class, they live with a consciousness of conscience. Jean's decline in fortune, therefore, becomes a hopeful sign that she may yet be saved.

Film: Night Has a Thousand Eyes

1948, Paramount. *D:* John Farrow. *P:* Endre Bohem (Paramount). *Cin:* John F. Seitz. *Sc:* Barré Lyndon, Jonathan Latimer. *Ed:* Eda Warren. *Process Photog:* Farciot Edouart.

Mus: Victor Young. *Art Dir:* Hans Dreier, Franz Bachelin. *Set Decor:* Sam Comer, Ray Moyer.
Cast: Edward G. Robinson (John Triton), Gail Russell (Jean Courtland), John Lund (Elliott Carson), Virginia Bruce (Jenny), Jerome Cowan (Whitney Courtland), William Demarest (Det. Lt. Shawn), Richard Webb (Peter Vinson), John Alexander (Mr. Gilman), Luis van Rooten (Mr. Myers), Roman Bohnen (Melville Weston, Special Prosecutor), Onslow Stevenson (Dr. Walters), Douglas Spencer (Dr. Ramsdell), Bob Stephenson (Det. Gowan), Artarne Wong (Waiter), Henry Guffman (Butler), Mary Adams (Miss Hendricks, housekeeper), Georgie Nokes (Newsboy). 81 min.

Known primarily as a director (and, perhaps, as the father of Mia), John Farrow also displayed artistic versatility as a writer, producer, and actor. After attending the Royal Naval Academy in the early 1920s, he served a four-year stint in the British navy, where he devoted some time to writing short stories and plays. When World War II erupted, he again joined the Royal Navy, this time as a Lieutenant Commander. He was wounded, and shortly after the war, converted to Catholicism. He subsequently wrote two books, a biography of Sir Thomas More and a history of the Papacy, suggesting that he had an elevated religious consciousness, something that is evident, though subtly so, in a number of his films.

Of the films he directed, he made five which, according to surveys in Silver and Ward's *Film Noir* and Selby's *Dark City*, can be classified as *noirs*: *Calcutta* (1947), *Night Has a Thousand Eyes* (1948), *The Big Clock* (1948), *Where Danger Lives* (1950), and *His Kind of Woman* (1951). The plots of all five films share a common central theme: if a man finds himself the pawn of some external force trying to subdue and control him, he must resist and fight to redeem his integrity and independence. *Calcutta* and *Where Danger Lives* appear complementary in that their male protagonists fall under the fatal charm of a duplicitous woman: in the former, his wariness and misogynistic reservations save him; in the latter, foolish blind trust leads him nearly to self-destruction. In *The Big Clock*, a man struggles against constrictions of time and space, fighting to clear himself of a crime he did not commit. In *His Kind of Woman*, the man, tempted by money, is nearly duped by a deported thug, but with the help of "his kind of woman," battles to save himself. In *Night Has a Thousand Eyes*, a stage-show psychic acquires the genuine ability to foretell disasters, and even when he knows he cannot do anything to avert these tragedies, he tries anyway. In *noir* terms, Farrow's male characters are defying fate, ignoring the odds against them, battling forces bigger than themselves. Win or lose, this is a redemptive struggle, which, like their prototypes in Greek tragedies, makes them heroes.

In adapting *Night Has a Thousand Eyes* to film, Farrow makes major changes to Woolrich's story to extract this theme of redemptive struggle, a notion that may be affiliated with his own religious awareness. Other than revisions in plot, character, and theme, the primary alteration is to the narrative point of view. By shifting the novel's point of view from that of the three main characters affected by the clairvoyant's fatal prophecy to that of the clairvoyant himself (Edward G. Robinson as psychic John Triton), Farrow creates a sympathetic character who merits our admiration. Triton, imitating Tompkins, despises his psychic "gift." He models John the Baptist and Christ by exiling himself to a period of purgation in the desert. More than that, like Christ, he foresees his own death, yet ignores that knowledge to redeem the life of another.

As in the novel, the film begins *in medias res* with a young woman attempting suicide. Jean Courtland (Gail Russell) prepares to throw herself from a bridge into the path of an oncoming locomotive, but Elliott Carson (John Lund, her boyfriend, instead of the detective-stranger Tom Shawn) rescues her at the last second. She says something cryptic about the stars watching, "like a thousand eyes." Her fear of the stars is similar to that of her counterpart Jean Reid. The stars, for Jean Courtland, are tied to her doom; Triton has already told her he envisioned her death under the stars, so she has a reason to dread them. This isn't so in Woolrich's novel, where stars are connected to fate and time in a tenuous, incidental way. After Jean Reid's initial outburst, the role of the stars, except for a few cursory references, is all but forgotten.

Carson takes Jean to a restaurant where John Triton awaits them. Carson explains to her that he found her because Triton told him where to look. Triton's powers of clairvoyance are immediately established and his story, more than Jean's, becomes the focus of interest.

In a lengthy flashback sequence, Triton narrates his personal history and how he came to possess this "power" to prognosticate. Billed as "John Triton, the Mental Wizard," he once worked in a stage act with two friends, his fiancée Jenny (Virginia Bruce) and Whitney "Court" Courtland (Jerome Cowan). Their act was an entertaining scam, until a series of small authentic predictions finally led to a climactic life-saving one. From then on, visions regularly came to him, some beneficial (Court profited from Triton's investment hunches), but most foreboding tragedy. When he foresaw that Jenny would die in childbirth, he ran away, hoping his desertion would alter her fate. Instead, she married Court, and died anyway when giving birth to Jean. His predictions, then, could not be avoided, no matter what precautions he took. Fate or destiny insists on its predetermined consequences.

From Triton's stock and investment predictions, Court became a wealthy and prominent citizen. Triton learned that his friend was settling in Los Angeles, so after living in seclusion for 20 years, he decided to move there to be close to him and his daughter. At Jean's celebrated debut, Triton, hidden in the crowd, had a foreboding of a plane crash in which Court was killed. He visited the Courtland mansion to warn Jean that her father, already making his transcontinental flight, should abort the attempt. But he was too late. The plane crashed and Court and his pilot were killed. Jean and Carson visited Triton at his apartment, and he hinted that he also saw Jean's imminent death "under the stars." Psychologically stressed, she attempted suicide—the event

***Night Has a Thousand Eyes*—** Triton (Edward G. Robinson, right) has the name of a minor Greek deity, suggesting that, yes, he may have supernatural powers, but he is subject to the same greater force that all humans are. He thinks he foresees disaster for Jean Courtland (Gail Russell), while the Chinese dragon behind her, a symbol of good fortune, contradicts him (Paramount, courtesy William Thailing).

returning us to the present moment. From here, the rest of the story unfolds chronologically in present time.

Convinced that Triton is a charlatan trying to defraud Jean of her inheritance, Carson turns to the police. Special Prosecutor Weston (Roman Bohnen) assigns Lieutenant Shawn (William Demarest, not quite the handsome leading man of Woolrich's story) and several men to protect Jean. At the Courtland mansion, several of Court's business associates are trying to close a deal he started before he died. Oil company president Gilman (John Alexander), estate lawyer Myers (Luis Van Rooten), and Courtland's secretary Peter Vinson (Richard Webb) are working with Jean to complete a merger. After an attempt that night is made on her life, they each become suspected as Triton's accomplice in an extortion racket.

Confined to his room in the mansion, Triton looks into a mirror and foresees his own doom, along with a sequence of occurrences leading up to Jean's death: a flower crushed under a heel, a sudden wind, a shattered vase, someone saying "It's all right now," and Jean lying on the ground at the feet of a lion. Her death is to take place the next night at the stroke of 11:00. Shawn oversees precautions until then. One by one, Triton's predictions come to pass. Then, with 20 minutes to go, an anonymous hand pokes from behind a window curtain and moves the hand of the grandfather clock six minutes ahead. When the clock strikes 11:00, the vigilant protectors drop their guard. Jean, relieved, asks Carson to let her stroll in the garden by herself.

Meanwhile, Triton, held by the police, has to convince them with another prophecy that his power is legitimate. (He correctly predicts that a distraught inmate will hang himself.) He believes his fate is linked to Jean's and he wants to return to the mansion to save her. The police concede and he enters the mansion while Jean is alone in her garden, gazing over a parapet toward the lights of Los Angeles. A mysterious hand pushes aside some ferns, revealing the statue of a sitting lion. It is Gilman, the oilman. He tells Jean, "There's no danger now," and she realizes he is her murderer. As he attacks her, Triton enters, grabs a chair, and clubs him with it. Police detective Gowan (Bob Stephenson) thinks Triton is attacking the woman and shoots him. Triton falls dead "at the feet of the lion."

A letter addressed to Carson has fallen from Triton's pocket. Carson reads Triton's accurate description of the event which just happened, his death from Gowan's gun. In a voiceover, Triton finishes "reading" the letter, calling for more respect for life's dark secrets that we know so little about.

Night Has a Thousand Eyes emphasizes one particular *film noir* component, the inescapable inevitability of Fate (or from a more religious angle, Providence). That some form of predestination rather than self-determination governs our lives is exemplified in the contradictory power of John Triton, a clairvoyant able to foretell the future but unable to alter or influence outcomes. Triton raises this question himself when he desperately asks the two psychiatrists, "Why was this gift given to me, and why was this other power withheld, this power to turn evil into good?" Other than his few predictions about horse races and investments that enable his friend Court to become a millionaire, his prophecies generally foretell tragedy. This dilemma gives rise to his guilt, for Triton believes that foreseeing is somehow linked to cause, as if he were the catalyst for these catastrophes. Even after he realizes he is powerless to change the future, he nonetheless feels responsible for the disasters that befall his fellow humans. Thus, he retreats into desert seclusion for 20 years to avoid people, the stimuli for his visions.

Similarly, in Woolrich's novel, the clairvoyant Jeremiah Tompkins is a semi-recluse, seldom associating with fellow tenants. He also appears an ambiguous figure, his psychic abilities apparently genuine but open to suspicion. When he finally informs the police about Walter Myers's plot against Harlan Reid, it isn't clear what prompted him. We never enter Tompkins's mind to understand his thoughts or feelings. Even the scene in the diner, the closest we get to "reading" him, is told entirely from an objective viewpoint. His suicide appears motivated by guilt, but its exact nature is only surmised later by Police Chief McManus. Tompkins may have regretted his role in the conspiracy to defraud and ruin Reid, or he may have grown weary of this gift to foretell the future, a cursed blessing if he has to foresee many tragic incidents befalling his neighbors. Although Woolrich speculates on Tompkins's guilt at the end, Farrow exploits Triton's guilt more deliberately by making it a basic motivation behind his character.

Carson alludes to fatalism when, in the garden, he tells Jean, "I hate this terrible resignation, as though you were half dead already, like an automaton playing a part." She answers, "An automaton wound up for 48 hours." Surrendering to fatalism is to live life mechanically, robotically, responding to programmed commands. Carson is pushing her to resist, to fight the urge to become, in Macbeth's desperately fatalistic metaphor, "a player that struts and frets his hour upon the stage and then is heard no more." Fate may be a very real force, but we must live our lives as if it does not have that kind of control over us. Otherwise, we act "half dead already."

For both the novel and film, the primary symbol of Fate is, of course, night's "thousand eyes," the stars that, as components of astrological signs, traditionally hold the secrets to each person's destiny. So when Jean (both Courtland and Reid) expresses her paranoia at being watched by them, she implies that she cannot tolerate their knowing her future and dictating her actions. Jean Courtland does not exhibit the degree of hysteria that Jean Reid shows in the novel, which makes it easier for us to sympathize with her. However, the situations of the two Jeans are different. While Jean Courtland attempts suicide because she cannot endure the tension of knowing she will die soon (a response similar to Harlan Reid's), Jean Reid attempts suicide because of her despair over losing her father.

Woolrich calls attention to the stars mainly at the beginning and end of his story. The "distant inscrutable pin points of brilliance" are meant to carry the implication of preordained events for humankind. Farrow, however, refers to the stars several times throughout, either verbally or through imagery. The imagery carries some imaginative implications.

Besides the literal stars shown at the start and close of the film, there is in Triton's room a single star on a pedestal, which he carries from one side of the room to the other just before Jean arrives to ask him if he has foreseen her death. Triton's ability to move this "star" affiliates him with the stars that control destiny and also suggests that he has control over them, can maneuver them to suit his purpose. This latter implication, however, lacks substantiation, unless it is meant to hint at some duplicity on Triton's part, but such evidence never materializes. More likely, this ornamental star adds to a subtle foreshadowing of Triton's erroneous conclusion about Jean's death "under the stars." When he admits to her that he pictured her lying dead under the stars, she faints—and there behind Triton is the star he just moved. That is, at this moment she lies "under a star," yet is not dead — which is what happens at the end. The irony is that, while Triton foresees her prostrate on the ground, apparently dead, he himself dies (as he will also foresee) and so fails to glimpse her rising again afterward, still alive. Perhaps this bears some relationship with her initials, J.C., an implication, albeit a flimsy one, that she is a Christ-figure.

Triton is the truer Christ-figure, redeeming her at the expense of his own life. This is reinforced by the subtle connotation in his initials. Although the name of Farrow's psychic differs from that in the book, Triton retains the same initials. "Jeremiah" gives Tompkins an Old Testament connection, while "John" links Triton to the New. The "J" in both names has a vague connection to "Jesus" and the "T" stands for the holy rood, an ironic foreboding of both of their destinies. "Triton," in Greek mythology, is a minor sea deity, half man, half dolphin. That is, Triton has amphibious/ambiguous qualities which, like Christ, connect him with two worlds at once, the natural and the supernatural.

Another interesting implication relates to the two scenes where Triton (in his room in the Courtland mansion) and then Jean (at the parapet in her garden) look out over the nighttime cityscape of Los Angeles. The sprinkling of city lights in the valley could be the "thousand eyes" of the title. As a *noir* convention, the city generally corrupts those unfortunate enough to live within its jurisdiction. (Compare *Deadline at Dawn*, for instance, which does not equivocate about the city as a noxious quagmire, poisoning the spirit while dulling the will to escape.) Here, then, by dint of its identification with the stars, the city appears as Fate's agent for controlling destinies and jading lives.

Another difference between novel and film is in the degree of ambiguity they lend to the psychic's power. All the while that Woolrich's characters are immersed in their quandary, unsure whether something supernatural is determining their fate, the reader is forced to question the credibility of supernatural phenomena. By the end of the novel, there remains a blurred line between coincidence and clairvoyance that leaves both the characters and the reader wondering what to believe. Not so in the film. Although all the characters except Jean are skeptical of Triton and try to rationalize his prognostications, the audience never doubts the validity of his prophecies, which are offered spontaneously and sincerely. (The eerie Theramin music in the background helps to verify this authenticity.) Thus, unlike Tompkins, who stands as an ambiguous figure for both the characters and readers, Triton never appears ambiguous to the film audience, only to the characters in the story, at least until the end. In *film noir*, ambiguity is a critical ingredient related to moral dilemmas and fateful outcomes. By disregarding this, Farrow diminishes the tension and suspense maintained so masterfully in Woolrich's novel, a revision not serious enough to condemn the movie (although critics found other reasons to pan it when it debuted).

As far as flaws are concerned, the ones in Farrow's film differ from those in Woolrich's novel. The Woolrich style, as often happens with him, can work both for and against the story. Most of the time, tone, word choices, and descriptions meld marvelously and admirably with the narrative, creating gripping, heart-pounding effects. Occasionally, however, Woolrich strays into the maudlin, overplaying the melodramatic and making us self-conscious of reading a story. Observe, for instance, how Jean and Harlan turn into ridiculous caricatures after Tompkins discloses his fatal portent and they sit paralyzed in their car. Or consider the trite, childish behavior of Shawn, Jean, and Harlan during their drawn out death-wait. The narrative logic of Woolrich's novel is not without discrepancies, but he handles it well enough, something difficult to do when imposing the fantastic on a realistic world.

Farrow's blunders occur more in this area of narrative logic. As is often the case with film adaptations of mysteries, a new culprit and outcome are inserted to create a surprise ending for anyone familiar with the original story. In changing the ending, however, some distracting incongruities are forced on the film. Because Triton quickly wins our confidence as an innocent participant, three other suspects are elected to contribute to the mystery: Mr. Myers, Mr. Gilman, and Peter Vinson. When the three ask to remain in the house "to protect Miss Courtland," Lt. Shawn readily consents, even though these men are strangers to him and he isn't sure from what direction danger may attack the young woman.

Vinson is Courtland's male secretary. He declares himself Carson's rival for Jean's love, but he has entered the story too late and plays too peripheral a role to be taken seriously. He is simply there to add to the number of suspects. The same with Myers. Blamed for Reid's mental and physical disintegration, Myers, a broker in the novel, is transformed into Courtland's innocent lawyer. Ironically, he has the honor of pointing the finger of guilt at the real villain, Mr. Gilman. Gilman, president of Midside Oil, is cast as the new murderer (already responsible for the crash of Court's plane) and contributes to a series of narrative faux pas. Hiding unseen behind the window curtain, he pokes clumsily at it as he sidles toward the grandfather clock. Such extraordinary stealth goes unnoticed by the throng of police traipsing willy-nilly through the room. Destination achieved, he sticks out his arm and, in full view, moves the hand of the clock ahead seven minutes. When the clock later chimes 11:00, Jean requests to take a walk in her garden — ALONE. No one displays the normal impulse to glance at his watch and see if it tallies with the chimes— even though, minutes before, they stood around comparing and synchronizing their watches. To allow for a margin of error in Triton's prediction, at least one of Jean's protectors might have cautioned her to give it more time.

On the plus side of Farrow's direction is his imaginative handling of the long take for meaning and effect. There are seven long takes in particular, each striking in duration and camera movement and each involving the image of a doorway. The seven examples are as follows:

1. A man walks past a caricature of Triton's bloated face advertised on a sandwich board in a theater lobby and buys a ticket to see "Triton the Mental Wizard." The ticket-taker pulls back a curtain and the camera follows the patron in a left-to-right pan shot (as if there were no wall on this side of the

entrance), and without a break, sweeps slowly over the crowd until it stops on Triton, standing on stage and delivering his spiel.

2. Inside his hotel room, Triton sees Court and Jenny to the door and tells them to go ahead to dinner and he'll join them shortly. After they leave, he steps out of the frame, left, and the camera tracks back from the empty room while his voiceover explains that he has decided to run away because he foresaw his fiancée die in childbirth. As the camera passes under the arch that leads to the bedroom area, he reenters from the left with a suitcase and takes some clothes out of his bureau.

3. A Los Angeles trolley grinds up a slope while Triton, in the extreme background, descends a stairway. He buys a newspaper, crosses the street, and climbs the stairs to the porch of his apartment house. He opens the door to his private sanctuary and the camera pans his entrance into the room (left-to-right, as it did with the patron at the tent show, ignoring the wall this side of the door) and lingers on him as he strolls to the background near his picture window.

4. Intending to warn Jean that her father's airplane is going to crash, Triton visits the Courtland mansion. He enters the front door and disappears inside. The patient camera pans across the façade of the house to rest on an upper terrace where Triton emerges through another door and stands amid the guests of an ongoing party. His voiceover says that he failed to find Jean there, and so he descended to the lower terrace. (After Triton comes face to face with Jean and Carson, a series of cuts follow.) He tells her of her father's imminent death and she agrees to try to reach him. (The next long take is a continuation of this scene.)

5. They walk toward the house and through the terrace entrance (again, a left-to-right pan through the wall). Jean telephones Wichita to warn her father, but she is too late; he has already left. (Court's fated flight is a variation of Reid's flight in Woolrich's novel; Reid, fortunately, fails to board his doomed aircraft and so survives.) In the foreground, Carson, who has been accusing Triton of treachery, walks toward Jean in the background, while Triton melts out of the frame to the left. When they turn around, Triton has disappeared. They leave the room and Triton steps into the hall doorway. A cut to a low-angle shot shows him looming large in the threshold.

6. Moving left to right, a secretary opens the door to the offices of "Special Prosecutor M. Weston" and the camera follows her in a pan (again ignoring the wall). She passes three desks where loud legal complaints are taking place. At the first desk, a woman protests having to install "two lights" to get a building permit. (The reference reinforces the doubling related to Triton's character.) At the second desk, a policeman dictates his findings after raiding an illegal gambling operation. (The covert action of criminals reminds us that Triton, too, may be doing something illegal; at the same time, there is the suggestion that truth, not always apparent, lies deeper beneath the surface of things.) At the third desk, an irate receptionist complains into her phone about corporation papers for the "Triton novelty company": "I've given you the name

twice now." (The coincidental company name trivializes Triton's claims with the subtle suggestion that his is a "novelty" act; that his name is said "twice" reminds us again of doubling, either of his duplicity or his duple-ness as the dolphin-man living in two realms.) The secretary opens a second door marked "private" and the camera pans into the room, left to right, without a break, following her to Weston's desk where the special prosecutor sits, reviewing Carson's case against Triton.

7. The last related long shot takes place at the Courtland mansion. Triton and Shawn have a brief altercation in the study. Triton turns and walks through the doorway. The camera cuts quickly to the foyer and stays on Shawn, then tracks back until its view encompasses the whole foyer and the winding stairway, a low-angle shot showing Triton making his way to the second floor where Jean has provided him with a room. (As in the low-angle shot at the Courtland mansion, Triton appears a dominant figure rising above his detractors.)

The scenes where Triton moves from foreground to background, from upper to lower terrace, from a place of prominence to a position of inconsequence, relate to his fluctuations between uniqueness and ordinariness. His gift makes him an exceptional human being, but other than that, he has no marks to set him apart, to make him seem more than Everyman. (This is also true of Tompkins in Woolrich's novel.) The importance of doors is that they are thresholds between two locales. One side is the natural world where all appears normal; the other side represents the supernatural world where paranormal events are not so easily explained. Triton stands at this threshold, moving back and forth between the two milieus. Noted already, Woolrich's novel points to the paradox between predestination and self-determination without offering any way to reconcile them. Farrow's story is different: Triton's power of prophecy does not so much raise the argument of predestination versus self determination as it reminds us of the ineffable, unfathomable workings of some supernatural power in our world. The character's final message bids us open our minds to this mysterious power and work with it, very likely reflecting the views of the religious convert Farrow.

Interestingly, Edward G. Robinson had earlier starred in similar films dealing with the supernatural, *Tales of Manhattan* (1942) and *Flesh and Fantasy* (1943). (In the latter film, Robinson's segment was adapted from Oscar Wilde's "Lord Arthur Saville's Crime.") Another film, closer in tone and plot to *Night Has a Thousand Eyes*, is the British *Dead of Night* (1945), which, like *Tales* and *Flesh*, has an episodic structure, each episode dealing with a different individual who experiences a brush with the supernatural. All have themes related to *Night Has a Thousand Eyes*, showing us that our lives intersect with occult powers, ineffable forces out of our control yet affecting what we do, what we achieve. These films were released before the publication of Woolrich's book. A habitual moviegoer, Woolrich may have seen *Tales of Manhattan* and *Flesh and Fantasy* before he wrote *Night Has a Thousand Eyes*. If so, this would not be the only time that film inspired him with ideas for his writing.

Waltz into Darkness

Novel, first published by J.B. Lippincott under Woolrich's pseudonym William Irish, 1947; Hutchinson, 1948; first paperback (abridged) by Ace, pbk #D-40, 1954; first unabridged paperback by Ballantine, pbk #30669, 1983; reprinted in *The Cornell Woolrich Omnibus*, Penguin, 1994.

By the end of the 1940s, with *noir* style and themes well established, film is as much an inspiration to Woolrich as are his works to filmmakers. He can borrow from the medium that has developed the very *noir* conventions he instigated. The *femme fatale*, the descent into the labyrinth, the relentless power of fate, the ironies of coincidence, and so on, originally among his armory of motifs, are important components of the films he now watches.

Waltz into Darkness and *I Married a Dead Man*, among the final works discussed in this study, represent a kind of retro-writing for Woolrich in that he combines the dramatic realism of his earliest work (*Cover Charge, Children of the Ritz, Manhattan Love Song*) with the suspense-thriller genre that made him famous. In many ways, these novels are two of the best samples of his creative abilities.

Waltz into Darkness begins with a different tone and tempo from most other works in the Woolrich canon. One reason may be the story's historical setting, 19th century New Orleans and the Gulf coastal region, which lends it, if only at the start, a more romantic mood than his stories set in modern day cities. The life style of a bygone era, captured eloquently in Woolrich's language and descriptions, seems less subject to unforeseen menace than that of modern city dwellers who may find daily living a frantic clawing for survival. However, after the two main characters establish their relationship, the story moves quickly into the dark, morbid existence that characterizes most of the author's work.

Traumatized in his youth by his fiancée's premature death, Louis Durand shunned any kind of romantic relationship. Fifteen years later, at 37, he proposes marriage to a woman he knows only through their exchange of letters. When Julia Russell arrives in New Orleans by steamboat, she is not the woman in the photo she had sent the expectant bachelor. She is petite and much more beautiful, an enchantress, and Durand falls immediately in deepest love with her. Small discrepancies hint that this Julia may not be the Julia of the letters, and when one day she absconds with nearly all of his bank assets, $50,000, he realizes the truth.

Durand becomes obsessed with finding and killing her. Concerned about what happened to the real Julia, he visits her sister Bertha in St. Louis and together they hire a private detective, Walter Downs. Shortly after, Durand, on one of his business trips, runs into the false Julia (one of Woolrich's typically flagrant coincidences). He confronts her, but cannot harm her. She tells him her "real" name, Bonny Castle. She had been working with a male confederate who killed the real Julia on the steamboat and made her take the woman's place in order to swindle Durand out of his money. Despite this confession, and even though he suspects that her genteel beauty belies a corruption deeply ingrained in her, Durand cannot help but love her madly.

Durand and Bonny reunite as husband and wife and become fugitives. They settle in Mobile for a time, living first in a hotel suite, then in a house. Downs catches up with Durand and guesses what he is up to. To protect his wife, Durand shoots him. Conscience, however, paralyzes him in thought and action, but Bonny, oblivious to any moral implications, takes control and has him bury Downs's body in the cellar (shades of Lady Macbeth's domineering influence over her husband). They sell the house and flee the city.

The fugitive couple takes up residence in a hotel room until they run short of money. Durand risks exposure and capture by returning to New Orleans and getting money from selling his coffee business to his friend Jardine. Shortly after, Durand reads in a Mobile newspaper that Downs's body has been discovered and the murder is being investigated.

He and Bonny flee to Pensacola where they buy another house. When money runs low again, Bonny teaches Durand how to cheat at cards. Their first and only attempt to cheat a group of gamblers fails, and Bonny, worried for herself, corresponds with her old crony, Billy, the man who allegedly killed Julia. Bonny gradually administers poison to Durand until he is almost too sick to move by himself. Once, he is able to escape the house and get to a doctor's office, but Julia finds him. She tells him she loves him. He so desperately wants to believe this that he lets her take him home, even though he now knows she is poisoning him. This unusual declaration of love, his unconditional sacrifice of self for her sake, suddenly inspires her with the sincere love Durand has longed for but which she had been unable to give.

Her epiphany and transformation have come too late, however. Her accomplice is at the front door. She sneaks Durand out the back way and guides him to a hotel where they hope to hide until they can take a train out of town. But the end has come for Durand and he is ironically content, for even as he dies, he accepts her admission of love as his reward for persisting with her for so long. At the door are the police, and Bonny realizes that Durand's heaven is her hell, for she has learned to love him only at the moment she has lost him.

Waltz into Darkness begins with an epigraph, a single stanza excerpted from the poem "Faustine" by Algernon Charles Swinburne:

> If one should love you with real love
> (Such things have been,
> Things your fair face knows nothing of
> It seems, Faustine)...."

Taken as a whole, the poem has more than a cursory impact on Woolrich's novel. For one, Swinburne, an English poet of the late 19th century, describes the devilish Faustine in terms that accurately foreshadowed the nature of the *femme fatale* of *film noir*. Structured as a series of quatrains, the poem explains how God and the devil rolled dice to decide who would possess this beautiful woman; the devil won. Consequently, Faustine, identified with malignant scorpions and the sinful Mary Magdalene (Mary, like Bonny, converts after realizing the error of her ways.), enjoys watching men engage in games of death and destruction. Bonny, a central, inextricable part of Durand's life, is the uncontrollable, fatal obsession—*noir's femme fatale* that always proves disastrous for the enrapt male.

The lengthy poem ends with four stanzas, the one above leading into the following:

> That clear hair heavily bound back,
> The lights wherein
> Shift from dead blue to burnt-up black
> Your throat, Faustine,
>
> Strong, heavy, throwing out the face
> And hard bright chin
> And shameful scornful lips that grace
> Their shame, Faustine,
>
> Curled lips, long since half kissed away,
> Still sweet and keen;
> You'd give him — poison shall we say?
> Or what, Faustine?

The poem's speaker could easily be Durand telling Bonny that any rejection in her early life should not impede her from opening her heart to him who tried to show her the "real love" she failed to find before.

In one stanza, the poem notes that Faustine has "Wine and rank poison, milk and blood,/Being mixed therein," a nature composed of contradictions, good and evil, wholesomeness and harm, sustenance and sin. This, too, is Bonny, as well as many other *femmes fatales*— Brigid O'Shaughnessy, Elsa Bannister, and Phyllis Dietrichson—who understudied Lady Macbeth. Durand senses that she embodies something noble and worthy and it is this he clings to despite the damaging consequences from her evil side.

Earlier in the poem, the speaker alludes to Faustine's "flower-like lips dashed with dew" from the wine-god Bacchus's own lips. As a physical feature, her lips resolve into another contradiction: their pleasant appeal as flowers become, in these final lines, a sign of shame and scorn. Woolrich picks up on this image with frequent references to Bonny's "crumpled rose petal of a mouth." Hers is a small mouth, one of her most salient attributes, at once attractive yet deficient.

The poison mentioned in the last stanza has a dual implication in that Faustine destroys her men not only physically but also spiritually. Her *modus operandi* is foreshadowed by earlier references to "scorpion" and "rank poison." In *Waltz*, Durand is Bonny's victim; he could not resist the lethal charm of the temptress. Whatever she possessed that attracted him consumed him in an obsession that dominated his will, until in the end, she administered the literal poison that gradually destroyed his physical life. (Compare Hitchcock's *Suspicion* where the male and female roles are reversed.)

Waltz contains many elements that give it the bleak, doomed, and desperate quality of the *noir* conflict. Fate, always a factor, often takes the guise of coincidence in Woolrich's novels and *Waltz into Darkness* is a succession of coincidences that culminate in Durand's destruction. He admits that his friend Jasmine has luck on his side, but that he, Durand, is the kind of person who does not. As evidence, he selects a specific kind of detective, a persistent, tenacious hunter, who is, as Downs himself tells him, a one-in-a-hundred chance. That tenacity (a form of obsession) seals both Downs's and Durand's doom, for in murdering the detective to protect his wife, Durand crosses his point of no return. Durand's reading the particular Mobile newspaper that reports the fluke discovery of Downs's body appears as mere happenstance, but such an accident is not totally random. More likely it is the hand of fate shaping events to turn out a specific way for specific people. Durand is manipulated by that hand.

Woolrich further exaggerates the role of fate by using a dramatic convention to introduce his story. In a parody of the Dramatis Personae, he lists "Characters That Appear in the Story" and a "Character That Does Not Appear in the Story," and he opens and closes the novel with the semblance of stage directions. At the beginning, "soundless music" plays for the dancers who enter waltzing. At the end, "soundless music stops" and the dancers collapse at the completion of their waltz. Such "directions" iterate the novel's dancing motif. What starts as a literal description, when Durand and Bonny waltz at their wedding, yields gradually to a series of figurative images implying that Durand is following the alluring song of the Siren down a path to destruction.

These dramatic devices give the impression that the novel operates like a stage play, and since, in a play, characters must act according to a script and follow the director's commands, the characters are "fated" to act their parts, in predetermined roles with predestined ends. One cannot help but recall here the words of Shakespeare's doomed and despondent protagonist in *Macbeth*:

> Out, out, brief candle!
> Life's but a walking shadow, a poor player
> That struts and frets his hour upon the stage
> And then is heard no more. It is a tale

> Told by an idiot, full of sound and fury,
> Signifying nothing.

As an evaluation of human endeavor, this bleak and pessimistic rumination denies the existence of free will and admits that Fate predetermines all human actions, our dreams in the end amounting to "nothing," controlled as they are by this amoral and apathetic power. This is the ultimate statement on nihilism and despair as applied to *noir*.

Cynicism, a typical *noir* attitude recurring in most Woolrich stories, is strongly evident here. Its insistence in the love-hate relationship between Durand and Bonny gives it the quality of a motif. The story might have alleviated some of the cynicism if a morally upright figure emerged to counterbalance the constrictive corruption of the diseased relationship and offered some hopeful alternatives, but *Waltz* is relentless in excluding hope as a meliorating virtue. There appear no major characters to remind us that good exists in the world. Durand's amusing servant, Aunt Sarah, may have stood for something of goodness until she exits the story with a cartload of Durand's belongings. Granted, he gave them to her, but she hastens away, afraid that Durand may reverse his decision and reclaim his generous gifts. She has a bit of avarice in her, different from Bonny's only in degree. Even Durand's original fiancée, Julia Russell, had hired a private detective to investigate his assets before she committed herself to marriage. By the end of the story, goodness is determined by whether Bonny can sincerely return Durand's love and openly admit it to him. It is not a moral issue. He knows what she is, an amoral creature who has learned to survive in a hostile world. Her harsh beginnings, if she is to be believed, excuse her in Durand's eyes. He may have hoped to teach her to think differently, but instead, she is the one who teaches him how to adapt to a new way of life, the life of a fugitive. He stands by her, and when the end comes, she does not change, at least fundamentally. Her personality remains the same. What does change, though, is the thing most important to Durand, her attitude toward him. His willingness to die at her hands proves a love that finally penetrates her emotional, psychological barrier, but too late. She will now be alone without the love she has admitted into her life. That is her punishment.

A significant aspect to Bonny's character is that she is not blatantly evil. She more closely resembles female opportunists like Martha Ivers (Barbara Stanwyck) in *The Strange Love of Martha Ivers* and Joan Fontaine's character in *Born to Be Bad* than overtly destructive Spider Women like Elsa Bannister (Rita Hayworth) in *The Lady from Shanghai* or Phyllis Dietrichson (Barbara Stanwyck again) in *Double Indemnity*. As Durand comes to learn, Bonny, due to the hard lessons of her early life, lacks "moral sense"; that is, she is amoral. Her small size gives her a childlike stature that reflects a qualified innocence, an arrested stage of development in conscience: like a child, she cannot clearly discern right and wrong. She makes her choices on the basis of desire and practical need without consideration of others' feelings or deserts. In this, she parallels Jeanne Simmons' devious character in *Angel Face* but without the vicious conceit. Yet she is still responsible for the male's downfall. She knows men better than they know themselves and she has learned to use the susceptible males, like Louis Durand, to serve her selfish designs. She has a plethora of sisters in the *noir* cycle—Kathie Moffat in *Out of the Past*, Kitty Collins in *The Killers*—women who flatter their men by spending some "quality time" with them before throwing them away. Bonny stays with Durand for several years until his paranoid behavior begins to wear on her and she plans to sever their ties, permanently. In some respects, she strongly resembles the title character in *Nora Prentiss*, acting as a loyal helpmate, playing the role of dutiful wife for a time. Finally, though, like all *femmes fatales,* she tolerates the man's obsession with her only until she sees fit to lead him lemming-like to his ruin.

Very often, the *noir* protagonist forsakes his/her integrity or, worse, abandons all moral scruples to purchase a one-way ticket to hell and destruction. The Swede (Burt Lancaster) in *The Killers*, Jeff Markham (Robert Mitchum) in *Out of the Past*, and Michael O'Hara (Orson Welles) in *The Lady from Shanghai* are a few representative examples of the many who make the one mistake that puts their careers and their lives in jeopardy. In *Waltz*, Durand makes his fatal decision when, inadvertently or not, he kills Downs to protect Bonny from being arrested. Up to that moment, before murdering the detective, he has the chance to return to his normal life; after that, all choices are taken away. He loses his integrity along with his clear conscience and forfeits his membership in the human community. He is forced to adopt the life of the fugitive, the pariah.

The role that morals play in the story may be a reflection of Woolrich's own attitude toward religion. As Nevins notes in his biography of the writer, Woolrich confesses that, although his father was Catholic, he himself had no affinity for religion and never set foot in a church (6). Yet Woolrich's stories often contain religious allusions, suggesting that religion has some influence on his writing.

A symbol that Woolrich uses in several of his stories, significant, perhaps, because it was something he did not own in real life, is the house. In *Waltz*, the house represents a place where the occupants can settle and become a viable part of the community, while the hotel room, Woolrich's actual home, suggests a life of transience and instability. Durand's several efforts to settle in a house are contrasted with the number of hotel rooms the fugitive couple must lodge in from time to time.

In Chapter 2, for instance, the elaborate description of the house Durand is building for his bride-to-be reflects the pride of ownership and his standing in the community. Ironically, Durand, whose first name is Louis, builds his house on St. Louis Street, which suggests a kinship between the man and his domicile. Later, overcome by Bonny's treachery, he closes the house for the last time, and we are told: "The death of a man is a sad enough thing to watch, but he goes by himself, taking nothing else with him. The death of a house is a sadder thing by far to watch. For so much more goes with it ... yet, he realized, he was not so much leaving this place as leaving a part of himself behind in a common grave with it" (Chapter 30). After Durand reunites with Bonny, they live in a hotel suite in Mobile until Bonny convinces him to rent a house, which represents the fulfillment of a secret aspiration: "...a house of one's own; ...an expression of *legitimate* wealth; ...the ultimate in stability, in *belonging*, in caste... [Chapter 43]."

Evident is the house as a symbol of prestige in a community. It advertises one's right to share in communal activities. It creates roots and nurtures feelings of self-esteem and self-satisfaction. Bonny ruined Durand at first, took away his pride and his sense of place in the community. Here, in Mobile, for a short time, she restores that ideal life style for him — and for herself. Then Durand kills Downs and the series of hotel rooms they must return to marks the end of that tranquil existence.

Durand manages to purchase one more house in Pensacola, but guilt and fear have replaced any illusions of happiness in this world. Afraid of being recognized, he chooses a house isolated from the rest of the village. This is the house where Bonny poisons him and from where they flee to take their last hotel room before being overtaken by the police. It is fitting that they are caught in the hotel room, the symbol of the unsettled, unconnected itinerant. Ever since he murdered Downs, Durand found his mental and physical worlds turned inside out. He suffered from an inconsolable conscience and dwelt on the fringe of the community. The hotel room represents this realm where the outcast spends his last moments.

Another key *noir* image in *Waltz into Darkness* is the labyrinth, the inescapable maze into which the protagonist descends, full of wrong turns and wrong decisions, instilling fear, frustration, despair. A kind of hell on earth, it seldom allows its prisoners to escape, but if they do, Woolrich's characters are often scarred by a loss of innocence and a less idealistic, more cynical attitude toward life.

After Bonny deserts him, taking all but a pittance of his savings with her, Durand, during Mardi Gras, thinks he spies her in costume among the revelers. Woolrich's word choices describing the winding New Orleans streets through which the possessed Durand pursues the female figure he mistakes for Julia indicates his initiation into his private, hellish labyrinth:

... A city gone mad....
... The street lighted up again, as though it had caught fire. Wavering giant-size shadows slithered across the orange faces of the buildings....
Just then her hood was dislodged ... he had glimpsed the golden hair....
He plunged into the maelstrom, and like a drowning man trying to keep his head above water, was engulfed....
... she ... darted down a dimly lighted alley.
He reached its mouth ... and could still see the paleness of her light blue garb running ahead in the gloom [Chapter 23].

The fires and demons of hell abound in this "city gone mad." The "maelstrom" suggests Durand's vertiginous descent into a netherworld where free will is lost and he is controlled by demonic forces. He is swallowed up in its "mouth"— an oblique reference to Julia's mouth, a prominent feature that once pleased him, but now consumes him utterly so that he is obsessed with destroying the woman who destroyed him.

Durand is marked as a tragic *noir* figure because of the extreme obsession that pushes him beyond the bounds of rational thinking. Bonny's betrayal first fills him with an insatiable hate that seeks her death. On seeing her again, however, he realizes that his desire to possess her supersedes his hate and he gives up his previous respectable life just to be with her. In the end, that obsession permits self-sacrifice, as he is willing to let her destroy his body as she already has his soul.

Durand's obvious obsession with the amoral seductress predetermines his actions and his ultimate self-destruction. But obsession is not limited to Durand, as it infects some of the other characters. When Bertha Russell, sister of the missing Julia, takes the wronged husband to Downs's tenement office, Durand can see that she is even more resolute and zealous than he is. Despite Durand's protest, she insists on sharing the expense of the detective.

The hired detective is no less obsessive about his cases. The two clients tell Downs they want proof of Julia's murder and punishment for the murderer. He tells them that he cannot promise success, but will persevere until he finds all the answers. Downs explains to Durand that his quest will take time, maybe months, maybe years. No apathetic, disinterested detective, he. Rather, he is a fanatic, a pit bull that, once his teeth are clamped onto his victim, will not let go for love or money.

When Downs finally catches up to Durand and Bonny in Mobile after their reconciliation, Durand cannot get him to drop the case, even if he resigns as a client. Ironically, Downs tells him he does not need him anymore: "I'm working for my own conscience" (Chapter 45). Thus, he professes a loyalty to the detective's code similar to that which Sam Spade (*The Maltese Falcon*) exhibits for his dead partner when he hands Brigid O'Shaughnessy over to the police. His obsession is based on personal and professional integrity. By attributing his motivation to conscience, he identifies with the Erinyes or Furies, the relentless haranguers of wrongdoers. Durand reacts rashly to this threat of upright persistence: he shoots the detective dead. Instead of "scotching the snake," however, this merely gives rise to new problems, and as if from the grave, Downs haunts Durand to the end.

These three characters, Durand, Bertha, and Downs, form a trio of obsessive characters. They come together in Downs's office as a group with a single motive, a single mind toward reaching their goal. Bertha disappears from the story, but we see in the two men a dualism, one choosing a noble path, the other a corrupt one. Ironically, both paths are extreme and lead to destruction, as if any obsession is self-destructive. An obsession blinds a person to logic and common sense. There was no "reasoning" with Downs, who, if he had been more flexible, might have seen how Durand's desperation put his own life in jeopardy. Durand, on the other hand, seems to understand his position, but cannot do anything about it. As he confesses to his friend Jasmine, his very nature compels him to do what he does (Chapter 53).

Obsession is a critical motivator in most *films noirs*. If it is not the man's obsessive desire for a woman (*Double Indemnity, The Lady from Shanghai, Laura*) or a woman's for a man (*Possessed, The Strange Love of Martha Ivers*), then it is the avaricious pursuit of money (*The Killing, The Asphalt Jungle*) or power (*The Big Clock, Touch of Evil*). In general, an obsession is an unhealthy condition that sets up one or more characters for a tragic end.

Generically, American *film noir* is a descendent of 1920s German Expressionism. Woolrich's literary style, while necessarily influenced by other authors, bears a remarkably close relationship with this German film movement. It is the overall tone of a Woolrich story that gives it its Expressionist flavor: his moody descriptions of settings and images convey not only the internal psychological struggles and moral dilemmas of his characters but also the pervasive desolation underlying a whole world built on corruption, evil, and death. His language, especially, dictates these strong associations with the dark side of world gone wrong. Consider a brief description of the interior of the Dryades German Methodist Church where, at the very moment the sun is setting, Durand prepares to marry the false Julia:

> Fulminating orange haze from without blurring its leaded windows into swollen shapelessness; its arched apse disappearing upward into cobwebby blue twilight. Grave, peaceful, empty... [Chapter 4].

The occasion should elicit joy and excitement. Instead, the unpleasant connotations in words like "fulminating," "blurring," "swollen shapelessness," and "cobwebby" forebode catastrophe. The images reinforce this: the German Methodist Church (its strict, somber puritanical roots); the (heavy, gray) leaded windows "chastised" into distortion by a setting (or dying) sun; and the "grave" air and paltry party make the affair appear more funereal than celebratory. In addition, the sentence structures, all fragments, encapsulate the whole scene in a hastened description, making it feel rushed, scanty, incomplete.

True to Expressionism, images perceived through the eyes of a character are described in surreal, dreamlike terms that reflect his psychological turmoil. A few days after Bonny begins administering poison to Durand, he views his room in images that reflect his now murky and distorted state of mind:

> ... in the far corner, miles away, stood a chair with his clothes upon it....
> ... he looked longingly across the miles, the immeasurable distance ... from death to life.
> ... the rest of the room seemed to fog out, and narrowing concentric circles of clarity seemed just to focus on that chair alone, so that it stood as in the center of a bright disk, a bull's-eye, and all the rest was a blur [Chapter 62].

After Bonny recants her pact with her accomplice to kill Durand, she helps Durand escape. They quit their house and head for the train station, but

Durand collapses on the ground. She rents a room at a nearby hotel where the manager helps her carry her ill husband inside. Durand, practically unconscious, feverish, and nearly blind, has a limited perception of his surroundings:

> The black sky..., pocked with stars, eddied about this way and that.... Then it changed to gaslight pallor on a plaster ceiling. Then this slanted off upward, gradually dimming....

Again, mental state is implied in the description of events unfolding from the perception of the character. It is not simply a matter of seeing through the subjective eye of the character, but of experiencing the distortions that signal the agitated and imbalanced vision of an irrational or unstable mind that may be ours. In much of Woolrich, as in many *noirs*, the desperate, wretched, and unconscionable side of human nature is exposed.

Film: Mississippi Mermaid

Original French title: *La Sirène du Mississippi*
1969, Les Films du Carrosse/Artistes Associés/Produzioni Associate Delphos. *D:* François Truffaut. *P:* Marcel Berbert. *Cin:* Denys Clerval. *Sc:* François Truffaut. *Ed:* Agnès Guillemot. *Mus:* Antoine Duhamel. *Set Decor:* Claude Pignot.
Cast: Jean-Paul Belmondo (Louis Mahé), Catherine Deneuve (Julie Roussel/Marion Vergano), Michel Bouquet (Comolli), Marcel Berbert (Jardine), Nelly Borgeaud (Berthe Roussel), Martine Ferrière (Landlady), Yves Drouhet (Detective), Roland Thénot (Richard). 123 min.

Structurally, Cornell Woolrich's *Waltz into Darkness* is divided into two parts. In the first part, Durand finds his ideal love, only to lose her. Julia is not the ideal woman he supposed her to be, and his total trust in her and his absorption in the affair make him vulnerable to an emotional collapse. In the second part, he recovers his lost love under her new identity, Bonny Castle, and they renew their relationship until fate and complicating factors doom them to a tragic end. Fundamentally, this is the story of Alfred Hitchcock's *Vertigo*. François Truffaut, noting the resemblance, may have been attracted to the idea of translating *Waltz* into a film that paid homage to one of his idols; it gave him the chance to "remake" a masterpiece on his own terms without committing sacrilege by tampering with a revered icon.

As he did with his 1967 adaptation of Woolrich's *The Bride Wore Black*, Truffaut combines the author's *noir* material with motifs from a number of Hitchcock films. In its narrative thread, *Mississippi Mermaid* is a close adaptation of *Waltz into Darkness*, the parallels clearly recognizable until the ending, which, although appropriate, is disappointing, not because it deviates from the novel but because it is saccharine, flat, and ineffective. Another matter is the texture of *Mermaid*. Although Truffaut mines the pulp fiction of an author known for some of the grittiest, grisliest stories in the hard-core *noir* tradition, he avoids the expressionist chiaroscuro so vital to the film counterparts of Woolrich's dark novels. Shot with consistent high-key lighting and mostly daytime scenes, the film would not be considered *noir* on the basis of its "look." And as far as its connections to Hitchcock, particularly *Vertigo*, the allusions are more conceptual than stylistic. Ideas are emphasized over mood and tone.

One popular perception of a film adaptation is that its success depends on its faithfulness to its source. According to this notion, the artistic merit of *Mississippi Mermaid* is proportional to the extent to which Truffaut captures the story, tone, character, and theme of Woolrich's novel. This is not the position of Truffaut who, on the contrary, would agree with his aegis André Bazin that a literary source is no more than raw material subject to a filmmaker's own interpretations and capable of leading to a totally new creation. Thus, Truffaut can claim license to mold Woolrich's story into anything he chooses. Rather than measuring a film on the basis of "faithfulness," then, we might judge it on cinematic terms, determine its artistic integrity by examining film techniques (camera movement, editing) and story elements (character development, plot devices). Truffaut's film, not quite a commercial blockbuster, achieves this artistic integrity. We may question whether its tone and style correspond with its subject matter, or whether it strays from Woolrich's thematic issues, or even whether Hitchcock might have given this topic more effective treatment. However, regardless of its not remaining completely "faithful" to Woolrich, deviating as it does from the writer's tone and outcome, the film is totally consistent with Truffaut's own personal style already evident in his New Wave precedents.

Except for its modern setting and the necessary elliptical treatment of scenes from the novel, the plot line of *Mississippi Mermaid* appears nearly identical to *Waltz into Darkness* and, until the altered ending, is quite comparable to its source. Because Woolrich's plot is tightly written and works as well as it does, Truffaut is wise to retain the same chronology of scenes and a similar dynamic between the two main characters. In adapting the novel, Truffaut uses subtle visual and aural devices to replace the more obvious denotative descriptions in the written source. He inserts into many scenes symbols and connotative imagery that fill the story with layers of implied meaning. This approach may work for and against the story: it gives the film intellectual appeal, but deprives it of emotional empathy. In the long run, we appreciate the filmmaker's artistry, even if we feel disengaged from the characters.

While the original setting, New Orleans and the American South of the late 1800s, is transported to a modern-day locale, first, on the island of Réunion in the Indian Ocean and, later, in the south of France, the film, chronologically and substantially, strings together all the main scenes of Woolrich's plot. Plantation owner Louis Mahé (Jean-Paul Belmondo) marries a woman, Julie Roussel (Catherine Deneuve), whom he knows strictly through their exchange of letters, only to find she is an imposter, her real name Marion Vergano. She withdraws most of his money from the bank and then flees. He and the sister of the missing fiancée suspect foul play, so they hire a private detective, M. Comolli (Michel Bouquet), to bring the imposter to justice. However, the betrayed husband accidentally meets up with his estranged wife, and instead of killing her as he intended, forgives her. They reconcile and rent a house as a hideout in Aix en Provence; unfortunately, the detective catches up with them. To protect his wife, Mahé shoots Comolli and buries his body in the cellar. The couple moves to Lyons, but they later learn that a flood in Aix has resurrected the detective's body and they must flee again. They settle for a time in an abandoned cabin in Switzerland. Planning to go on without him, Marion slowly poisons her husband. Mahé realizes what she is doing, and declares his acceptance of this fate to prove his love. This act of sacrificial submission causes Marion to repent her murderous deed and she suddenly experiences a reciprocal love for him she had not felt before. She nurses him back to health. On a snowy overcast day, they leave the cabin, heading on foot for no place in particular.

Except for the outcome, this skeletal synopsis is identical to the original story and the film offers numerous examples of Truffaut's imagery complementing Woolrich's writing. In the early part of their relationship, for instance, Mahé and Julie eat on the veranda. Beyond them, in the background, is a road that trails into the distance across the plantation, perpendicular to the horizon. The road is the entrance to the labyrinth they will soon travel together by car. Julie's traveling trunk, true to the novel, is the mask which Mahé/Durand penetrates to discover the truth about the imposter. After he learns that she has run away and stolen his money, he takes her undergarments, rips them to shreds, and burns them in the fireplace. Earlier, he told her he liked her lacy things. Symbolically, then, he is destroying her, violently assaulting or raping her and casting her into the flames of perdition. A closer glimpse shows in what ways the film refines the novel to accommodate the visual medium and new thematic implications. The result is a *film noir* rendered in New Wave style with a smattering of Hitchcockian allusions.

The opening credits overlap a background of printed classified ads, while a woman's voice alternates with a man's in reading the content of the different advertisements. The two voices state their personal statistics and interests, then note the traits they seek in a partner. Gradually, the voices overlap into a cacophony of inarticulate babble. One implication is that

> the credit sequence is ... an integral component of the film's theme and texture. We see the personal column of a newspaper, indicative of men and women seeking companionship and placing us in the Truffautesque universe where the search for love is the point of all departures... [Insdorf 62–63].

This clearly suggests that Truffaut changed Woolrich's ending to complement his vision for the story. First, he "advertises" everyone's search for some vague,

Mississippi Mermaid—The unwary protagonist (Jean-Paul Belmondo) enjoys a quiet moment in love before the *femme fatale* (Catherine Deneuve) unleashes her latent wickedness (Les Films du Carrosse, courtesy William Thailing).

general idea of love; later, he defines that love in more specific terms as the mutual dependency two people must share before their love can be deeply authentic.

In this beginning is also a very subtle Hitchcockian allusion to *Rear Window*. The "lonely hearts" column recalls the character Miss Lonelyhearts and her desperate desire for a man, for a love of her own. ("Maybe someday she'll find happiness," says Thelma Ritter's Stella. Translation: Maybe one day she'll find a man she loves enough to marry.) Miss Lonelyhearts's plight is symptomatic of all the main characters in Hitchcock's story: Thorwald, Miss Torso, the composer, and even Jeff. All in their confined private cubicles seek a companion they can love and who will love them on the terms they want to be loved. (Charles Foster Kane makes a similar pronouncement to Jed Leland in *Citizen Kane*.) Truffaut is very aware of the love motif in *Rear Window* (Truffaut 216) and may have wanted to reflect that theme in Hitchcock's terms rather than with the elusive, ill-fated quality Woolrich gives it in *Waltz into Darkness*.

Much later in *Mississippi Mermaid*, Mahé explains to Marion the self-deceptive nature of the people who place those ads and the ramifications of her having impersonated Julie Roussel:

> People who use want ads are idealists. They try to change their lives in five lines which they spend hours composing and to put into a few words all their hopes, their dreams, their ideas of what life should be.... Julie's letters were beautiful. They were full of hope. In our letters, we tried to create something permanent. But you came instead. What you brought was ephemeral. Before I met you, life seemed simple. Now I know it isn't. You fouled it all up. In a way, it's too bad.

In the same way that Bonny shattered Durand's faith in his simple, secure, sedate existence, Marion has destroyed Mahé's illusion of that same kind of life. However, Mahé's words, "it's too bad," carry ironic implications. The quiet life, simple yet static, content yet shallow, lacks the profound range of emotions and experiences available in that other reckless but more fulfilling existence. Julia/Julie, in the novel and film, is mythologized as the ideal because she is an unreal figure. She reinforces Durand/Mahé's concept of the ideal life, contented but emotionally stagnant, while Bonny/Marion introduced him to the extremes of pain and pleasure, anger and joy, panic and exhilaration, in a passionately charged affair.

After the opening credits, Truffaut presents a brief frame story in pseudo-documentary fashion about how the island of Bourbon in the Indian Ocean was renamed "Réunion" when two opposing French military factions avoided bloodshed by laying down their weapons and embracing each other, thus ending their conflict with a symbolic "reunion" of a divided nation. The event seems an anomalous historical footnote, until we later see that the reunion of a man and a woman, their putting aside animosity for the sake of mutual consideration and accord, is what the film is about.

Following the historical allusion, the modern-day story begins with Jardine (Marcel Berbert) in a car winding through the city streets of St. Denis on his way to pick up Mahé at his hotel. The camera is in a fixed position behind him, so that as he drives forward or turns left or right, he remains in one constant position while the street scenes ahead keep changing in a series of abrupt jump-cuts. This sequence of following shots recalls the opening of Rudolph Maté's *D.O.A.* (1950) where the camera tags behind the doomed Frank Bigelow down several endless corridors to the office of the homicide bureau. More likely, though, Truffaut is deliberately alluding to Hitchcock, imitating the sequences in *Vertigo* where Scotty follows Madeleine Elster through the streets of San Francisco. All connote the same thing, the journey through the labyrinth, but the image in *Mermaid* offers something a little different for its protagonist.

Bigelow's walk through the labyrinth ends at the homicide bureau where he recounts in flashback how he got here, how he had lost his way and stumbled into this inescapable maze and his tragic doom. Because Madeleine leads

Scotty into the labyrinth, she represents the Siren/Monster who seduces and then destroys the unsuspecting detective gullible enough to swoon over her song of enchantment. But Mahé is already in the labyrinth without the conniving of any *femme fatale*. How did he get here? He has been a bachelor all his life, devoted only to his work. His labyrinth is a self-made prison, a life without love and emotional connection. Later he asks his wife, the false Julie, what day it is. She answers, "Thursday," and he says that he used to live for the weekdays and now, married to her, he lives for the weekends. That is, he has learned what love is and it has changed him, reversed his priorities, made him a new man. Julie plays an ambiguous *femme noire*: she is duplicitous, will be the cause of his emotional and financial setback; but she is also an inadvertent, benevolent *femme blanche*, teaching him what love is, playing the obliging Ariadne who helps him out of his labyrinth. At first, on Réunion, she has not been honest with him, and so their relationship is based on pretense, not truth. When she abandons him and takes his money, he remains in the labyrinth, feeling worse off than before because now he must also bear the pain of knowing what love felt like until he lost it.

A critical sequence where Truffaut intersects with Hitchcock and Woolrich in a unique way is in the aftermath of Julie's departure, when Mahé suffers an emotional breakdown. After his wife betrays him, he closes up his house and takes a trip to the south of France, a decision that moves him physically out of his self-made labyrinth and prepares him for entry into another, the labyrinth of the relationship. He falls ill on the plane. Although the nature of the illness is unexplained, the implication is that it is an emotional trauma, a side effect of his physical and psychological upheaval. Loss of love has affected him with an intense psychosomatic illness, a period of mental and physical paralysis. Mimicking Hitchcock's sequence in *Vertigo* where Scotty plunges into a phantasmagoric nightmare, Truffaut begins his bedroom scene with an overhead medium shot of the tormented Mahé, his head on a pillow, stirring in fitful sleep. Suddenly, superimposed shots of railroad tracks crisscross his face, unseen trains seeming to speed over the rails. Alternating with this is the image of sky and treetops sweeping by, as if one were racing along a highway in a convertible, looking up and watching the scenery stream past. The impression is that of a restless and agitated state, a frenzied mind confined behind imprisoning bars.

At the same time that he imitates Hitchcock's conception of the protagonist's disturbed mental condition, Truffaut actually adapts Woolrich's identical implications for Durand. In the novel, after Julia's flight, Woolrich uses his powers of description to depict Durand's unbalanced faculties:

> The room was a still life.... A window haloed by setting sunlight, as if there were a brush fire burning just outside.... Dank bed, that had once made a bridegroom blush;.... Graying linen receding from its skeleton on one side.... And on the table three immobile things. A reeking tumbler, mucous with endless refilling, and a bottle of brandy, and an inert head, crown-side up, matted hair bristling from it [Chapter 20].

When it comes to rendering *noir* imagery in words, Woolrich is the master. All that is bleak, baleful, despairing, disheartening, and gloomy he can connote in his poignantly depressing descriptions. Durand, linked to his setting, shares with Mahé and Scotty the confused, frustrated, and desperate emotions of the spurned lover who trusted unconditionally and loved too strongly for the first time in his life. Subsequently, he searches for Julia among prostitutes in a bordello (the implication is that he believes she came from there or may have resorted to that life style) and stalks a Mardi Gras reveler he thinks is his estranged wife (a symbolic pursuit of the real woman behind the mask). Truffaut's treatment of Mahé's distress may differ from Durand's in specifics but not in substance. In the aftermath of a love-gone-wrong, Durand and Mahé (as well as Scotty) undergo an emotional crisis, a cathartic ordeal that takes them to a new level of the relationship with their beloved.

Durand, in Woolrich's novel, descends into a netherworld quite different from the respectful, open existence he led in New Orleans. Later, after he reunites with Julia, their flight is always to a city. As Nicholas Christopher maintains in his reflection on *noir*:

> However one tries to define or explain noir, the common denominator must always be the city. The two are inseparable. The great, sprawling American city, endlessly in flux, both spectacular and sordid, with all its amazing permutations of human and topographical growths, with its deeply textured nocturnal life that can be a seductive, almost otherworldly, labyrinth of dreams or a tawdry bazaar of lost souls: the city is the seedbed of noir [37].

The city *is* the labyrinth and Durand plunges physically and emotionally into this dauntingly tortuous realm. Mahé's experience is quite similar. Although he avoids Paris, he, like Durand, relocates with Julie/Marion in a series of cities. But Truffaut further exploits the image of the labyrinth in another way.

From the very beginning, with Jardine driving through town, the automobile is associated with the labyrinth. It is the vehicle that takes the characters through the corridors (roads) of the winding maze. In the many scenes where the two characters are in cars, whether on a relaxed drive or in hasty flight, there is always a sense of confinement, isolation, impersonality. Mahé takes Julie around the plantation to meet his staff, but they tour by car, an aloof, impersonal approach that prevents close contact with the workers. After Mahé, suspecting Julie's duplicity, opens her trunk and realizes the clothes are not hers, he drives back to the city to find out from the bank manager what happened. The camera shoots him in close profile behind the wheel as he races along a country road, while a voiceover, anticipating the conversation between him and the bank manager, reveals how Julie withdrew his savings and disappeared. The restrained fury on Mahé's face, the vibrations caused by the speeding of the car, the harsh fluctuating drone of the engine as Mahé changes gears, the setting sun in the horizon beyond, all contribute to the tension in the scene, to the dire state that Mahé has been put in. The automobile shares in this.

Mahé meets up with Julie at her hotel, the Monorail. Related to the car as a mode of travel, the "monorail" is also linked to the train rails that appear in Mahé's nightmare. The rails are associated with Julie, the Spider Woman who has ensnared Mahé in a labyrinthine network of intersecting complications.

Their first act together after reuniting is to buy a car. Mahé wants a gray one because it is less flashy, less prominent. Marion wants a red one. They buy the red one. (In a related way, Marion wants to go to Paris, a city where there is more excitement but less privacy. Mahé relents to the car, but succeeds in diverting her from Paris.) This is the car they will use for flight; that is, it is the vehicle for leading them along the labyrinth of roads to nowhere. It is not until the end, when they sell it, that they can think more about their relationship and less about escape.

Whenever they are at a crossroads in their relationship, Mahé and Marion stop the car and discuss their options while sitting in the vehicle. In these scenes, the camera coldly, aloofly shoots them through the windshield. The climax to these discussions occurs when they reach Switzerland and, in anger, Mahé orders her out of the car. He changes his mind, gets out, and brings her back, but while out of the car and on foot, they notice the deserted cabin that will become their final retreat.

After settling in the shack, Marion and Mahé argue and she threatens to leave with the car. From then on, he keeps the keys tethered around his neck. The car is a symbol of power and independence for whoever possesses it. While Mahé sleeps, Marion tries to steal the keys. He awakens and she covers her treachery by shouting that she saw a rat. She now has an excuse to buy the rat poison which she secretly sprinkles on his food. We are made to understand that the car has been sold because at one point, when she goes to the pharmacy for medicine, she returns after hitchhiking a ride on a truck. Then at the very end, when the two lovers have reconciled with a newly discovered love for each other, they set off on foot. Without a car, they are no longer wandering mechanically in the labyrinth, and inconvenient as it is, this new life style indicates the redemption of their relationship.

Associating the automobile and highway with the labyrinth is one way Truffaut incorporates *noir* iconography into his film, but adapts it to his own style. These episodes are shot always in daylight, without the dark and distorted nighttime shadows of conventional *noir*. The labyrinth is present in concept but not in tonality. Again, this validates Truffaut's individual approach to filmmaking, retaining the documentary style of the New Wave and distancing himself from traditional genre methods.

Another noteworthy comparison between Woolrich's novel and Truffaut's adaptation concerns the scenes where Durand/Mahé accidentally catches up with his estranged wife and confronts her for her thievery and desertion. In adapting this incident, Truffaut signals the protagonist's transformation in a more obvious, less suspenseful way than Woolrich.

Durand spots Bonny on the street in the company of another man. He discovers where she lives, and before facing her, hides in her hotel room and awaits her return. We follow events from Durand's point of view. His thoughts are inflamed with odious plans for revenge; we expect the meeting to have a violent outcome, possibly death. Given that we sympathize with Durand for the wrong done him, we want to see justice done and Bonny punished. The rising tension and delayed denouement is a showcase of Woolrich's mastery in handling suspense. When Bonny arrives and tells her woeful tale, something of an Oliver Twist story about being an orphan taught to steal when she was young, revelation of her hard life wins Durand's pity and forgiveness. Yet questions persist: How can he protect her, since she was an accomplice to murder? Will they escape the persistent detective Downs, whom Durand ironically hired to find her? These uncertainties generate the suspense that propels us into the story's new direction.

Truffaut sets up the hotel confrontation differently. Mahé, hospitalized after his mental breakdown, is watching television when he sees a news story about the opening of a new Antibes nightclub called the Phoenix. The camera scans the revelers and Mahé spots Julie, one of the "hostesses," dancing with a customer. Julie is a modernized version of the taxi dancer who frequently appears in Woolrich's stories as a denizen of the city's sordid counterculture. Named for the mythical Egyptian bird that dies in a fiery crash so that a new bird can rise from its ashes, the "Phoenix" obviously announces Julie's resurrection: she re-enters Durand's life as Marion Vergano. Once again, Truffaut is indebted to Hitchcock's *Vertigo*. The names of Marion's nightclub and hotel (the Monorail) connect her with Durand, just as Judy Barton's hotel, the Empire, associates her with height (Empire State Building) and links her to Scotty's phobia. In addition, Truffaut insinuates a tongue-in-cheek irony when he has Mahé climb the façade of Julie's hotel to get to her room. Belmondo, with a reputation for doing his own stunts, performs the scene in a long take, allowing him to exhibit his versatility (minus the tiny slip when he reaches the top balcony) and mock Scotty whose acrophobia prevents him from making such an ascent.

The confrontation in the hotel room between Marion and Mahé differs greatly in tone from that between Bonny and Durand. Because Woolrich makes us privy to her attitude and motivations during this exchange, Bonny wears a transparent mask and appears a devious Spider Woman, who even now, cleverly tries to finesse Durand with her sob story. She is pleading for her life, so her account sounds contrived despite its carrying tinges of sincerity. We wonder, while she talks, if her story deserves believing. Tension hinges on our uncertainty of what Durand will do. Will he think she is duping him again? Will facts come out later to show she was lying? This all contributes to the suspense now and for the rest of the story, as we are never quite convinced of her commitment to their relationship.

Film, a visual medium presented in predominantly objective terms, still manages to convey internal thoughts and feelings through various means, such

Singapore— Mr. Mauribus (Thomas Gomez, right) confers with Chief Inspector Hewitt (Richard Haydn). Woolrich and film have a symbiotic relationship in that his works inspired a plethora of film stories, while many films in turn inspired his creativity. In *Singapore* (John Brahm, 1947), a man loses his fiancée, but then runs into her years later. The gist of the plot sounds coincidentally like Woolrich's *Waltz into Darkness*, which happened to appear that same year (Universal-International).

as voiceovers, superimposed shots (like Mahé's dream), flashbacks, facial expressions, and other devices. Truffaut, the consummate New Wave stylist, adheres to the impersonal documentary style, which minimizes revelation of internal, subjective feelings. He shoots much of the scene in Marion's hotel room as a long take, the camera locked on her pacing figure as she spews her tragic life's story. The event is more a transitional device for getting her and Mahé back together than it is the psychological confrontation in *Waltz into Darkness*. Marion's story is never in doubt. She sounds sincere, Mahé believes her, and in the next scene they are together buying the automobile that will take them through the labyrinth to their final fate.

Another convention of New Wave is to allude to American films, often to westerns. Truffaut does this twice. In Aix en Provence, while Marion goes off to buy clothes, Mahé tells her he is going to a movie to see *Arizona Jim*. (Truffaut appears to have invented this title for his own purposes.) However, Mahé never gets there. He runs into Comolli, which leads to the scene where Mahé shoots him. Later, after they have fled to Lyons, Mahé takes Marion to see *Johnny Guitar*, a highly symbolic film about political and social pressure to force conformity on the individual. (The film is a thinly disguised diatribe against communism and the McCarthyism that was supposed to be combating it).

Arizona Jim suggests some general conventions about the American western, perhaps the lone cowboy fighting against insurmountable odds, forced into a shoot-out at the end to uphold righteousness. Ironically, Mahé has a shoot-out with Comolli, but in killing the detective in a crime of passion, he becomes the outlaw. After burying the detective in the cellar, he and Marion must become fugitives again.

Johnny Guitar also contains some of the western's conventions that were important to New Wave. The individual against society, for one, becomes the plight of the two lovers. As another irony, Mahé is the criminal who, although justified personally, has committed an act against society. He justly deserves legal punishment. His crime is too heinous to go unpunished.

In the cabin, the death Marion nearly metes out to him might be considered a just, if ironic, punishment: he killed for her and now she is the instrument of his execution. This is the scenario played out in Woolrich's novel. Durand chose to live with Bonny, to protect her and kill for her. She poisons him to where the effects are irreversible, and he dies. Truffaut, however, turns the event into a successful love story. Mahé not only survives and gets to keep the greatest love he has ever known, but he has convinced Marion to love him sincerely, completely. In the final scene, they walk off together into a light, misty snowfall, suggesting that their future is not clear, but at least they are together and he is still free. Love may be a passion of the highest order, but can it justify a murder, the taking of another human life, particularly a killing done under circumstances where the righteous murderer is legally in the wrong? Yet Mahé escapes prosecution, compensated with the only thing he desires. We are left with the question of whether the couple can sustain their happiness or whether their fugitive life is itself a kind of condemnation, their banishment from society.

Film: Original Sin

French title: *Péché originel*
2001, Metro-Goldwyn-Mayer Pictures in association with Hyde Park Entertainment; Via Rosa/DiNovi Pictures Production, and Intermedia/UGC International. *D:* Michael Cristofer. *P:* Denise Di Novi, Kate Guinzburg, Carol Lees, Michael S. Glick (line prod), Edward L. McDonnell (co-prod). *Exec P:* Sheldon Abend, Ashok Amritraj, David Hoberman. *Cin:* Rodrigo Prieto. *Sc:* Michael Cristofer. *Ed:* Eric A. Sears. *Mus:* Terence Blanchard. *Prod Des:* David J. Bomba. *Art Dir:* John R. Jensen, Jorge Sainz. *Set Decor:* Beth A. Rubino. *F/X:* Adrián Durán, Fermín Durán, Jesús "Chuco" Durán, Jamie Baxter (uncredited), Franklin Cofod, Charles Darby, Victor DiMichina, Kevin Fisher, Patrick Flanagan, Tyler Foell, Jim Gorman, Nathan

Haggard, Kim Lavery, Gregory D. Liegey, Ray McIntyre, Jr., Patrick Murphy, Geordie Spradling, Todd Vaziri.

Cast: Antonio Banderas (Luis Antonio Vargas), Angelina Jolie (Julia Russell/ Bonny Castle), Thomas Jane (Billy/Walter Downs/Mephisto), Jack Thompson (Alan Jordan), Gregory Itzin (Colonel Worth), Allison Mackie (Augusta Jordan), Joan Pringle (Sara), Cordelia Richards (Emily Russell), James Haven (Faust on stage), Pedro Armendáriz (Jorge Cortés), Mario Iván Martínez (Julia's confessor), Harry Porter (Stage manager), Fernando Torre Laphame (Wedding priest), Shaula Vega (Dressmaker girl), Lisa Owen (Margareta on stage), Daniel Martínez (Rafael), Farnesio de Bernal (Bank clerk), Nitzi Arellano (Prostitute), Roger Cudney (Ship's captain), Adrian Makala (Ship's waiter), Francis Laboriel (Ship's stewardess), Patricio Castillo (French dining steward), Derek Rojo (Bell boy), Abraham Stavans (Mr. Gutiérrez), Roberto Medina (Card player), Julian Sedgwick (Card player), Alejandro Corp (Card player), Alejandro Reza (Man at train station), Guy De Saint Cyr (Chief jailer), Julio Bracho (Guard), George Belanger (Moroccan gentleman), Osami Kawano (Moroccan gentleman). 112 min.

Before his plunge into *Original Sin*, Michael Cristofer had skinny-dipped in the waters of filmmaking as an actor, director, and screenwriter. He played a few roles on television and the big screen and wrote some half dozen teleplays and screenplays, including *The Witches of Eastwick* (1987) and *The Bonfire of the Vanities* (1990). In 1998, he wrote and directed the made-for-television film *Gia*, based on the tragic life of supermodel Gia Marie Curangi (played by Angelina Jolie), which perhaps prepared him for the writing-directing responsibilities of this Woolrich adaptation. Despite his limited pedigree, he had enough experience to qualify for the venture. The final product, however, is an odd mix of inventiveness, intrigue, inconsistency, and repugnance, which makes the viewing an uneven, uncomfortable experience.

As author of the adapted screenplay, Cristofer must be commended for developing his film from the original novel rather than basing his remake on Truffaut's film. Doing so, he follows Woolrich very closely, and any alterations he makes appear more as his own invention than a superficial reworking of *Mississippi Mermaid*. Although his interpretations have some connection with his source's intent, the method of the telling moves the story away from its *noir* roots and into the realm of the erotic and bizarre. As director, he works competently with his cinematographer to fill the film with a wide array of camera techniques—extreme close-ups, dizzying overheads, oblique angles, choreographed long takes, and so on. With his editor, he uses a variety of striking transitions between scenes, although one device taken to the point of tedium is the jump-cut, which crops up more frequently than a weed. For all of these camera and editing calisthenics, however, there is not much substantial development. The popular film pundit Roger Ebert slants his comments favorably, yet admits he is not sure whether he recommends the picture:

> The movie is not intended to be subtle. It is sweaty, candle-lit melodrama, joyously trashy, and its photography wallows in sumptuous decadence. The ending is hilariously contrived and sensationally unlikely, as the movie audaciously shows

an unrevocable [sic] action and then revokes it. I don't know whether to recommend "Original Sin" or not. It's an exuberant example of what it is—a bodice-ripping murder "meller"—and at that it gets a passing grade. Maybe if it had tried to be more it would have simply been watering the soup.

I believe Ebert's indecisiveness has to do with the contradiction between the film's deceptive air of significance—its glossy trappings wound around an extremely intriguing Woolrichian plot—and the story as a whole, fraught with an offensiveness that disturbs us and makes us question whether the film really has any redeeming value or substantial import. I appreciate Ebert's waffling between recommendation and condemnation, but I have a more definite opinion of the movie.

Original Sin opens on a map of the Caribbean region. The camera isolates Cuba, then zooms in and focuses on the city of Santiago. Colorfully and artistically drawn, the map designates the location of the city with an image of a two-paneled wrought-iron gate, a portal into the city and into the story. As the camera tracks in, a dissolve reveals a blurred close-up of a figure moving behind this gate, someone wearing a death's-head mask. A second dissolve shows a black screen framing an extreme close-up of a woman's pouty lips grossly inflated like two puff pastries. The two fleshy labia open to emit the first words, "You cannot walk away from love." (The line serves double-duty as a motif and as the title of a Gloria Estefan song for the film, one of the marketable tie ins the producers hoped to capitalize on.) The camera tracks back and we see the face of Julia Russell (Angelina Jolie) peering at us through what look like the bars in a prison door. (We are not sure of this until we are granted a subsequent return to her cell. She seems at first to be speaking aloud to us, but we learn later that she actually narrates her story to a father confessor who dotes gullibly and salaciously on her every word.)

The death's-head mask complements the very end of the film when Julia signals to card-playing Luis Vargas (Antonio Banderas as Woolrich's Louis Durand character) what the other gamblers are holding in their hands. She slides her finger across her neck in the manner of the cutthroat: "This means they have nothing," she says in her voiceover. The film story, then, is framed between two images suggesting death, nicely drawn, but exactly to whom or what they pertain is never made apparent (To unwary ordinary people in general?). We see in this denouement that Luis Vargas has survived her poisoning and, although she has exhibited traits of the Black Widow, the two of them appear reconciled and totally compatible with one another. Their friendly alliance is an ironic inversion of a similar relationship that results in the neo-noir *Basic Instinct* (1992): the detective (Michael Douglas) willingly surrenders to a precarious co-existence with the Black Widow (Sharon Stone), for as they lie in bed, she keeps an ice pick always within reach, thus posing a perpetual and unpredictable threat to him.

Cristofer strays from the beginning of *Waltz into Darkness* by taking a page from Woolrich's previous novel *I Married a Dead Man*: he opens with a framing device that, like Patrice's monologue, hints at a tragic outcome and makes us wonder what events have led Julia to this situation. More important is that the frame indicates how the story will be told from Julia's perspective. Ironically (illogically?), once the story begins, most events occur from the limited vantage of Luis Vargas, which creates a discrepancy between what she knows but fails to reveal, and what she could not know yet makes manifest. This is not the slight momentary lapse in a narrator's voiceover, such as occurs in *Mildred Pierce* or *Sunset Boulevard*, where the character narrates some passing details that he or she could not have been privy to. In *Original Sin*, Cristofer doesn't "play fair." He manipulates us, slipping into Vargas's limited omniscient viewpoint whenever it serves him to keep Julia's motives a mystery. For example, when Vargas and Julia go to the theater, she sidles out of their box during intermission. The camera follows Vargas as he follows her. He watches from a distance while she talks to the actor who played Mephisto (Thomas Jane). The scene is told from Vargas's perspective, not the narrator Julia's, in order to make her relationship with the actor appear suspicious.

While Vargas combs the docks for his new bride who was supposed to have arrived that morning, Julia's voice again intervenes: "No, this is not a love story, but it is a story about love and the power it has over a life, the power to heal or destroy.... And this is where the story begins." A melodramatic portent, yes, but the distinction between "a love story" and "a story about love" is enigmatic, if not ambiguous, and begs a clarification that never comes. The practical-minded Vargas does not expect a woman who is beautiful but who "is made to be kind and true and to bear children." He refutes the counsel of his friend Alan Jordan (Jack Thompson), saying, "Love is not for me, Alan. Love is for people who believe in it." His flippant remark ironically presages the quicksand into which he is about to slide, what is supposedly "a story about love" and not "a love story."

After the wedding, Vargas, all gallantry and propriety, tells his bride they do not have to sleep together until she feels "ready" for him; he retires stoically to his own bedroom. Several days later, she is "ready." They set about roiling over, under, and around the sheets of their connubial bed with limbs and torsos twisted into images that rival the kama sutra. His sexual appetite appeased like never before (Up to now, he was not averse to recruiting sportive ladies from the red-light district.), Vargas becomes obsessed with their carnal romps. Vargas's friend raises questions about the exact nature of this relationship:

> JORDAN: So, Luis, is it love after all or is it just lust?
> VARGAS: Is there a difference?
> JORDAN: Oh yeah, to love someone is to give and then want to give more.... Lust is to take and then take more, to devour, to consume, no logic, no reason.... So which is it?
> VARGAS: Both. I want to give her everything and I want to take everything from her.
> JORDAN: Oh, Luis, thou art a lost man.

Thus, one theme of the film emerges regarding the nature of love, that it contains a spiritual and corporal dichotomy. Vargas's answer attempts to resolve the ambiguity, claiming that, for him, love is a merging of psychological and physical aspects. As a theory, this is certainly open to argument. However, for the purposes of the film, it suggests that Vargas has been "consumed" by Julia, body and soul.

Although Cristofer handles this differently from Woolrich, he simply and neatly translates a similar notion that appears in *Waltz into Darkness* where the death of a house is compared to the death of a man: the impregnable *femme fatale* has the power to destroy her lover completely, devastate him internally and externally. The question that arises is whether there exists a point where love overreaches itself and turns into an unhealthy, self-destructive, self-centered obsession. That is, love evolves into lust. Vargas, like Durand, believes he has to prove his love by willingly ingesting the poison she offers him. This is not love; this is a masochistic death wish or a warped sense of self-sacrifice. Love that is unilateral must shrivel and die, for it can only replenish itself when nurtured by requited love. Since this woman with her heart of adamant clearly does not need him, Vargas's (and Durand's) resolute faithfulness suggests that he is satisfying some need, some emptiness, in himself. Vargas's answer to Jordan, that his relationship with Julia is both love and lust, may be a truism at the moment he utters it, but by the end of the film, that relationship has become neither love nor lust but something else entirely — something erotic, vile, and repulsive.

For all his faithfulness to Woolrich's story line, Cristofer deviates in three particular areas that create a new story and make the film at times painful to watch. The first is Thomas Jane's character. Jane plays Julia's boyfriend Billy, who was acting in the traveling troupe and wearing the guise of Mephisto, a signification of his treacherous role in the story. He approaches Vargas, unsolicited, as private detective Walter Downs, thereby embodying two characters from Woolrich's story. This deviation from the original is a clever innovation that enhances the intrigue in Cristofer's story. The flaw, though, is not in the deviation but in Billy's deviance. His character appears to be another idea borrowed from *I Married a Dead Man*: like Steve Georgesson, his malevolence makes him so thoroughly despicable that he becomes a one-dimensional figure, a caricature of the stereotypical villain. Billy embellishes his evil with various perversions. Besides reveling in murder, extortion, and deception, he is a sadist. While making love to Bonny (Julia's real name), he uses a knife to cut thin slits across her back; then he sucks her blood. As if that were not enough to satisfy his perverseness, he sodomizes her.

The graphic sex that appears here and elsewhere in the film is a second major divergence from Woolrich's story. Filmmakers often feel obliged to use their medium to display explicitly what may have been discreetly implied in the written source. Such appears to be the case here. The visual stimulation is gratuitous, however, in that the same heated infatuation could have been depicted without high-angle shots of Banderas's buttocks and close-ups of Jolie's oscillating breasts. In *Vertigo*, for instance, the two key scenes in which Scotty and Madeleine kiss are accompanied by Herrmann's swirling musical crescendos and Hitchcock's dynamic camera shots, effects enough to depict the intense passion between them. Hinted thoughts and actions inspire imaginative interpretations and unlimited personal fantasies; graphic depictions expose all of the secret nuances and deprive the imagination of exploring the wonderful possibilities.

Actors may sometimes play a role that asks them to do the unthinkable, to perform in an undignified, disgusting, and degrading manner. Mistaking the humiliating act as a devotion to their "art," they accept the role. However, when actors are compelled to do extremely outrageous things, it isn't always for their art that they do them but to satisfy the private perversions of the director. This is no astounding revelation; it has been going on for as long as movies have been made. There is the story of how Michael Curtiz endangered the lives of his extras during the thrilling but hazardous flood scenes of 1929's *Noah's Ark*. Another anecdote tells of how Otto Preminger, while directing *Angel Face* in 1952, kept urging Robert Mitchum to slap Jean Simmons harder and harder across the face until Mitchum threatened to slap *his* face.

A third major deviation is the ending, which rather than following Woolrich, imitates *Mississippi Mermaid*: the lovers conveniently and unconscionably discount their previous crimes and settle into a comfortable, mutually agreeable life style. This is a far cry from the ironic justice in "The Corpse Next Door" or *The Bride Wore Black*, and herein lies a disturbing trend in many modern films that flirt with *noir* techniques and supposedly claim to recapture the themes of their earlier prototypes.

Let's be clear that the perversity, depravity, degeneracy, inhumanity, and corruption found in Cristofer's film are no less a part of Woolrich's *noir* world, usually more understated by the author (even if grimly described), yet always evident. That world is a cesspool, and Woolrich's characters may wallow in it, such as Durand, who forfeits luxury to live a fugitive life with his beloved, or such as those who take drugs ("C-Jag," "Marihuana") or are dragged by desperation into the seamy, soiled environs of criminals and degenerates (*Deadline at Dawn*, *The Black Path of Fear*, *Black Angel*)—but Woolrich always depicts that world as odious, repugnant, and vile, so that it carries the stigma of unsavoriness and disgust. *Original Sin*, while not ignoring this implication entirely, circumvents its distasteful qualities in the final message. Like Truffaut's *Mississippi Mermaid* and Davis's *J'ai épousé une ombre*, *Original Sin* adopts a modern concept of the *noir* ending, disregarding guilt and suggesting that "love" justifies whatever means, criminal or otherwise, two people must do to stay together. Gone is the character's remorse that comes from a consciousness of wrongdoing. Thus, Vargas can ignore Julia's complicity in the death of the real Julia Russell; Julia can kill Billy with impunity; Julia can seduce her naive confessor into helping her escape from prison (Did she bribe him with a sexual favor?); and Julia and Vargas can resume their life together cheating gamblers at cards, all without legal, moral, or psychological ramifications.

Although the evildoer in the classic *film noir* eventually faces a deserved punishment, the viewer often feels that a sense of tragedy accompanies the justice. Ambivalence causes a conflict between understanding and regret: one can appreciate the necessity of punishment for the crime, but one feels apprehensive when characters meet their doom this way. *Shield for Murder, Out of the Past, Roadblock,* and *The Postman Always Rings Twice* are examples of films that arouse sympathy for the ill-fated protagonist. On the other hand, since a happy ending depends on the two lovers reuniting, some neo-*noirs* insist that the lovers, by golly, no matter what sins they've committed against themselves or humanity, must come together, even if it contradicts narrative logic or legal and moral justice. *Original Sin* fits into this category along with Truffaut's and Davis's films, which place love (or some vague semblance of it) above justice.

This is not true of all neo-*noirs* that depart from the classic formula. In *The Silence of the Lambs* (Jonathan Demme, 1991), F.B.I. agent Clarice Starling (Jodie Foster) defeats one evil while another evil, Hannibal Lecter (Anthony Hopkins), escapes into society. In Lawrence Kasdan's *Body Heat* (1981), an effectively unabashed remake of *Double Indemnity*, the *femme fatale* (Kathleen Turner) winds up on a tropical beach while her emasculated accomplice (William Hurt) faces murder charges in prison. These particular films play with allegorical devices, suggesting symbolically that certain evils cannot be contained, that they infect lives, lead them to ruin or triumph, and then set out again to roam the world at will. Interestingly, this is frequently an unstated premise in classic *films noirs*; neo-*noirs*, however, may offer the pretense of narrative closure while teasing us with contrived ambiguous implications.

With the two men, Julia has a split identity: she is Julia with Vargas but Bonny with Billy. As she tells her confessor when he asks if she is afraid of being executed on the garroting machine, "Julia is not afraid, but Bonny is." That is, Julia, nurtured on Vargas's love, has a conscience which admits to her guilt and sees the penalty as justified, while Bonny, incorrigible and self-centered, clings to life in spite of deserved punishment. Whereas Julia is in this one character both the *femme noire* and the *femme blanche*, most *films noirs* who play with this notion will position a man between two separate women, the one a vivacious woman of the world who promises thrills and excitement and unprecedented passion; the other a steady, reliable helpmate who promises a life that is constant, stable, and secure but imperturbably dull. In some cases, the man succumbs to the lure of the temptress, forfeiting his secure life (home, family, steady job) and treading the downhill path to perdition: *Out of the Past, Conflict, The File on Thelma Jordan, Nora Prentiss, Angel Face, Beyond a Reasonable Doubt,* and *Where Danger Lives*. In another film, *Born to Kill*, Claire Trevor appears to be a harbinger of Jolie's character. Reversing the idea of the male caught between two women, she finds herself torn between two men. Conscious of the difference between right and wrong, she guiltily forsakes her benevolent fiancé for a handsome, virile murderer (Lawrence Tierney) who fascinates her as a figure of physical and psychological menace. The choice, as she knows all along, will lead to her doom. Offering a contrast to this is *Clash by Night* where Barbara Stanwyck finds herself caught in Claire Trevor's predicament, but unlike her, abandons the more stimulating and attractive lover for a conventional life style, which should guarantee a longer, if more monotonous, life with her stolid, lackluster husband. In other films where the protagonist faces the ethical dilemma of choosing between two women, he may make the wrong choice and become scarred by the experience, but in the end, will find some vague and ambiguous form of redemption: *Pitfall, The Paradine Case,* and *Sunset Boulevard*. In *Original Sin*, after the two characters somehow reconcile their differences, the irony is that Julie has not had to make any concessions at all; she still cavorts in the life style she has always known. It is the man who has changed, has become more like her, content to live a corrupt life of gambling, deception, and dissipation as long as he has her. Is this a sacrifice for love or lust — or something else?

"The Boy Cried Murder"

Short story, first published in *Mystery Book Magazine* March 1947; reprinted under the title "Fire Escape" as by William Irish in the short story collection *Dead Man Blues*, J.B. Lippincott, 1947; reprinted under original title in *The Saint Mystery Magazine*, September 1954; reprinted as "Fire Escape" in *Child's Ploy*, eds. Marcia Muller and Bill Pronzini, 1984; reprinted under original title in *Murder in the First Reel*, eds. Bill Pronzini, Charles G. Waugh, and Martin H. Greenberg, 1985.

For one of his best short stories, Woolrich uses a title that alludes to an Aesop's fable, "The Boy Who Cried Wolf." Most of us are familiar with it. A shepherd boy amuses himself by yelling "Wolf!" to scare his neighbors even though no ravenous predator is in sight. When he really does see a wolf, he shouts for help, but his neighbors, already twice fooled, ignore his cry. The wolf kills not only the sheep but also the boy. Moral: If you want people to believe you, avoid a reputation as a liar.

In "The Boy Cried Murder," Buddy, a modern-day counterpart of the shepherd, is a 12-year-old prone to exaggeration and lies. One hot, stifling summer night, he sleeps on the fire escape outside his fifth-floor window. The air is stagnant, so he climbs up to the next level. He falls asleep, but wakes when a shaft of light, seeping from beneath the apartment's partially drawn window shade, hits his face. Through the narrow slit between shade and sill he sees the Kellermans, the married couple from upstairs, steal money from a man and then murder him. While Buddy slinks down the fire escape ladder in fear, he overhears Joe Kellerman tell his wife he intends to cut up the body with a straight razor and pack it in two valises. Buddy remains awake all night, disturbed by the creaking sounds above.

In the morning, his father, who works nights, arrives home in time for breakfast. Buddy tries to tell him what he saw, but his penchant for extravagant storytelling prevents his father from believing him. Instead the father beats him for lying, then locks him in his room. Buddy sneaks out through his window and goes to the police. Captain Brundage doubts his story, but sends Detective Ross to investigate.

Ross returns without finding anything suspicious. He attributes Buddy's fantasy to a particularly gruesome radio program Mrs. Kellerman says she listened to, which Buddy must have heard in his bedroom below. (Of course, when Woolrich wrote his short story in 1947, just before the television boom, radio was a primary source of news and entertainment.) A policeman takes Buddy home. On the landing in front of Buddy's apartment, the policeman explains to Buddy's mother what happened. Mrs. Kellerman passes by just then and inquires if anything is wrong. Although the mother does not explicitly say what happened, she tries to force Buddy to apologize to Mrs. Kellerman, which alerts the woman to Buddy's knowledge of the murder. Buddy now fears for his life because his well-intentioned mother has deprived him of his protective anonymity.

    The mother relocks Buddy in his bedroom and leaves for work. The father sleeps during the day, so Buddy feels safe for the moment. After his father leaves, however, the Kellermans enter the apartment. Before they can open the bedroom door, Buddy uses a chair to smash his window and escape. The Kellermans pursue Buddy and catch him hiding on a trolley. While being dragged down the street, Buddy calls to two men and a policeman for help, but each time, the Kellermans pretend they are his parents. The adults see the boy as rebellious, deserving of the beating his supposed father says he intends to give him. In a cab, Kellerman even punches Buddy on the jaw to keep him under control. He has the cabbie take them to a deserted building where he intends to kill the boy.

    Kellerman tries to strangle Buddy, but the boy lashes back and suddenly the whole floor gives way. Kellerman and his wife plummet through the five floors and Buddy becomes stranded on a narrow ledge. The police arrive. One directs Buddy to jump into a safety net they have spread, but it is a blind leap, since Buddy cannot see his target in the darkness. The man counts to three and Buddy jumps.

    Detective Ross greets Buddy, having just deduced that the Kellermans were guilty after all. He liked Mrs. Kellerman's description of the radio program so much that he tuned in tonight to see what it was about and heard an announcement that last night's show had been canceled. He returned to their apartment where he found a well-worn razor strop. He followed their trail and would have caught up with them, although he would have arrived too late to save Buddy. He commends the boy on saving himself.

    Ross returns Buddy to his apartment. The father is angry because Buddy had stayed out all night. He is ready to strike him, but Ross grabs his arm and tells him that nobody should "swat a member of the Detective Bureau.... Even an auxiliary, junior grade."

    The theme of Woolrich's story does not stray far from the obvious moral of Aesop's fable, and even though Buddy emerges from his ordeal basically unchanged and unenlightened from the experience (unlike the boy in Tetzlaff's superb 1949 film), the reader understands the lesson he was supposed to learn. Of greater importance is that Woolrich's narrative, more complex than the simple fable, shows how a child's world does not coincide with that of the adults. Adults treat children as inferior to themselves, giving them little respect and credibility.

Besides being reprimanded and punished by his parents, Buddy is ignored and chastised by various authority figures. The police, for one, do not believe him. When Detective Ross leaves to investigate Buddy's outrageous claim, he does so out of duty and with the assumption that it is merely a childish fantasy, not a plausible report. The murderers easily convince the policeman that the boy imagined it, the one adult willing to accept the explanation of other adults. Later, when the Kellermans abduct Buddy in a cab, he screams to a passing policeman who sees little urgency in the plea: "A kid's cry for help, that wasn't the same as a grownup's cry for help, that wasn't as immediate, as crucial." The cop treats the situation as typical of a parent-child relationship and is easily duped into believing the killers are Buddy's parents.

Other adults who ignore Buddy are the drunk and the two men he solicits for help while running from the Kellermans. The drunk is an oblivious, impotent authority figure. The two men believe the Kellermans rather than Buddy, demonstrating how adults relate to adults, becoming automatic allies against the child and his accusations. Denied help from his real parents, police, and strangers, Buddy asks (indirectly through the narrator), "Wasn't there anyone in the whole grown-up world believed you? Did you have to be grownup yourself before anyone would believe you, stop you from being murdered?" Buddy now finds himself under the control of corrupt, dangerous adults and totally alienated from authority figures who are supposed to protect him.

The Kellermans act as doubles of Buddy's real mother and father. The irony is that his natural parents do not believe him, while his "surrogate" parents do. Besides their contrasting credulousness, the most salient quality of both sets of parents is their disciplinary methods. One might expect the real parents to be nurturing and loving and the evil ones to be abusive and odious, but Woolrich blurs that distinction. Instead, both sets of parents appear as disciplinarians, the harshness of their reprimands separated only by degree. Buddy's real parents discipline him with what may be considered traditional expectations of strict punishment: physical thrashings, sent to bed without supper, confinement in his room. The Kellermans, like evil stepparents out of a fairy tale, escalate physical punishment to outright life-threatening abuse: the physical thrashing becomes a punch on the jaw, then strangulation, and finally execution. The brutal callousness of Buddy's father suggests that he possesses a latent viciousness approaching that of Joe Kellerman. He is not very likable, even at the end, where he is prepared to strike his boy without waiting for an explanation.

A question arises from this: Could Woolrich be implying that there is little difference between an abusive child-beater and a strict parent who uses physical punishment to discipline his children? There is no evidence that Woolrich's father meted out physical punishment to him, but maybe Woolrich had given this matter some thought and was commenting on it. If so, he makes a statement about evaluating a child's guilt and innocence. Any physical punishment may be unfairly abusive because the child does not perceive the world in the same terms as the adult; he associates with it differently and so interprets it according to different standards. The adult must recognize and appreciate this difference and not deal with the child's behavior so harshly and imperiously.

The story plays with a self-reflexive irony that comes out of the ambiguous moment when Buddy falls asleep on the fire escape. We can assume that the story begins in reality with the boy chastised by his parents for being a notorious yarn-spinner and then having trouble that night sleeping in his stuffy bedroom. However, when he climbs up to the Kellermans' fire escape, falls asleep, and then wakes to witness the murder of the merchant seaman, the question is whether the rest of the story is reality or a dream concocted by the boy who may still be sleeping outside the Kellermans' window. The irony is that this reality-fantasy ambiguity is the same conflict Buddy faces when he tries to convince the adults that he witnessed a murder. When the storyteller (Buddy/Woolrich) relates his tale, how much of it should the audience (Buddy's adult auditors/we) accept as real, how much as fantasy?

Maybe it does not make any difference. In the end, the story comes out in Buddy's favor, either because of the logical culmination of events (reality) or because it meets Buddy's wish fulfillment (dream). He has finally convinced the police, the ultimate authority figures, and he outmaneuvers the disbelieving parent by earning an authoritative title ("auxiliary, junior grade" detective) that is supposed to protect him from future beatings.

"The Boy Cried Murder" is one of several Woolrich stories told from a boy's perspective where the father-son relationship is at issue. Whereas Buddy's belligerent father needs chiding from the police so he will be more tolerant toward his son in future, two other *noir* stories deal with a father and son who enjoy an amiable association that gives the boy a reason for helping him through a predicament. In "The Corpse and the Kid" (1935), a husband kills his philandering wife, while the son, a young man, accepts his stepmother's death as justified and loyally protects his father by framing the woman's lover. Carrying the body around town in a rolled up carpet prefigures the drolly macabre situation in Hitchcock's *The Trouble with Harry* (1956). "Through a Dead Man's Eye" (1939) deals with a 12-year-old boy hoping to restore his detective father to his position on the police force by steering him toward some crime he can solve to impress his superiors. In a swap with a friend, little Frankie acquires a discarded glass eye which becomes the first in a series of clues that lead him — and coincidentally his father — to capturing a murderer. In these two early stories, the sons go on a quest to redeem their fathers from disgrace, one for a crime, the other for a demotion.

As wish fulfillments of the author, both suggest that Woolrich the Child intervenes to rescue his father from some crisis he cannot handle by himself.

The later story, "The Boy Cried Murder," shifts the emphasis to the redemption of the son. Buddy, a "storyteller" of sorts, could be Woolrich's alter ego, so that some 10 years after the other stories, he redefines his perception of his relationship with his father.

Film: The Window

1949, RKO. *D:* Ted Tetzlaff. *P:* Dore Schary, Frederic Ullman, Jr. *Sc:* Mel Dinelli. *Cin:* William Steiner, Robert De Grasse. *Ed:* Frederic Knudtson. *Mus:* Roy Webb. Art *Dir:* Sam Corso, Albert D'Agostino, Walter E. Keller. *Set Dec:* Harley Miller, Darrell Silvera. *F/X:* Russell A. Cully.
Cast: Bobby Driscoll (Tommy Woodry), Barbara Hale (Mrs. Woodry), Arthur Kennedy (Ed Woodry), Ruth Roman (Jean Kellerson), Paul Stewart (Joe Kellerson), Richard Benedict (Merchant seaman, uncredited), Anthony Ross (Det. Ross, uncredited), Lloyd Dawson (Police officer, uncredited), Carl Faulkner (Police officer, uncredited), Budd Fine (Police officer, uncredited), Charles Flynn (Police officer, uncredited), Eric Mack (Police officer, uncredited), Lee Phelps (Police officer, uncredited), Carl Saxe (Police officer, uncredited). 71 min.

In the late 1940s and early 1950s, Ted Tetzlaff directed several respectable *films noirs*. Even if the titles are not memorable, they included some of the most prominent actors of the era: *The Window* (1949) with Arthur Kennedy, Paul Stewart, Ruth Roman, Barbara Hale, and child actor Bobby Driscoll; *A Dangerous Profession* (1949) with George Raft, Ella Raines, Pat O'Brien, Bill Williams, and Jim Backus; *Under the Gun* (1950) with Richard Conte, Sam Jaffe, and Audrey Totter; *Gambling House* (1951) with Victor Mature, Terry Moore, and William Bendix.

Before directing these productions, he could claim credit as cinematographer for Hitchcock's *Notorious* (1946), in which his imaginative use of lighting and camera angles for expressionistic effect confirmed his expertise in handling *noir* stylistics. The crane shot that dwindles from a wide, high-angle establishing shot of a crowd of people to an extreme close-up of a latch key in Alicia's (Ingrid Bergman) hand is one of the classic shots in cinema. And the sequence of angled shots in which the greatly oversized cup of poison in the foreground overwhelms the shrunken image of the drugged Alicia in the background captures both external and internal implications for the character. No wonder Tetzlaff is later able to turn Woolrich's compelling suspense story into a *noir* study of the child who must, like Everyman (and Everywoman), make the traumatic and disconcerting transition to adulthood.

An admirer of Fritz Lang and a dabbler in the practices of German Expressionism (the movement that so profoundly influenced American *noir*), Alfred Hitchcock was already incorporating *noir* themes and techniques into his films before the "official" date of *noir*'s inception, 1941. So it is debatable how much Tetzlaff brings of his own to *Notorious* and how much belongs to Hitchcock (According to most sources, it is Hitchcock who ordered the coffee cup to be enlarged to several times its normal size.). However, Tetzlaff in turn may have influenced Hitchcock. For instance, in *The Window*, the climactic chase over the tenement rooftops bears a marked resemblance to the rooftop chase at the beginning of Hitchcock's *Vertigo* (1958). More important, the voyeurism that instigates the conflict in Tetzlaff's film becomes a major theme in Hitchcock's masterpiece, *Rear Window* (1954), which "just happened" to be adapted from another Woolrich story. One wonders if *The Window* inspired Hitchcock to look more closely at Woolrich's work. As evidence of this, Woolrich does *not* include a grisly dissection of the victim's body in his short story "Rear Window," whereas Hitchcock does so in his film version. The filmmaker could have got the idea from "The Boy Cried Murder," in which the Kellermans dispose of the body in that way (and Tetzlaff's film, conversely, omits the gory deed in deference to viewer sensibility).

The Window is too restricted in scope and thematic implications to merit status as an indisputably great film. However, judged within its limitations, it is a minor masterpiece. I saw the film in the mid–1950s when I was about seven years old and I was totally absorbed in it, perhaps because of its being told from the viewpoint of the young protagonist and his dilemma of not being believed or taken seriously by his parents. (That and the fact that the boy's name is Tommy.) Yet 50 years later I can watch it and still feel much of that original impact. The suspense is still there, driven by the child's real fear of some external menace waiting to hurt him; also still evident is the empathy for the child who, virtually abandoned by his parents, is left to solve his predicament on his own. Who of us growing up has not at some time felt this alienation, that we were misunderstood, unappreciated, overruled because our youthful opinion did not matter as much as an adult's? (This is very much in line with Woolrich's theme.) At the end of the film, with the restoration of the family, we feel relief and joy but with some reservation because the crisis has changed the dynamics of the relationships. True, there are more than a few flaws visible to me now that were not obvious then, but they are willfully dismissed in the desire to preserve the blissful suspension of disbelief.

Except for a few changes to accommodate the visual medium and give the characters fuller dimension, the film is a very close transcription of Woolrich's short story. Nine-year-old Tommy Woodry (Bobby Driscoll), sleeping on his upstairs neighbors' fire escape, awakes and sees the Kellersons murder a man in their apartment. His reputation for extravagant lies prevents parents (Arthur Kennedy, Barbara Hale) and police from believing him. To them, such a horrific crime is beyond the ken and experience of a child; they attribute his accusation to nightmares and an overactive imagination. The Kellersons (Paul Stewart, Ruth Roman) learn that he is privy to their secret and they kidnap him while he is home alone.

Tommy escapes briefly, but the Kellersons catch him again and drag him into a cab. Unable to control the boy, Joe Kellerson punches him on the jaw and knocks him out. He carries Tommy up to his apartment where he props him on the railing of his fire escape, expecting his fall to look like an accident. Tommy is feigning unconsciousness, however, and just as Jean Kellerson, jolted by a sudden pang of remorse, intervenes to save him, Tommy breaks away. He climbs up to the roof and runs across to the adjacent deserted tenement building. He evades capture until he climbs out on some creaky rafters and becomes trapped when he reaches a dead end. Joe follows, balancing himself along one wobbly beam. When he gets too close, Tommy kicks the beam free and his stalker falls to his death. Tommy is stranded precariously on a projecting joist until the fire department rescue team arrives and spreads a safety net. The boy slides off his perch and is caught safely below. He reconciles with his parents, they promising to believe him from now on and he vowing never again to tell a lie.

Structurally, the film story is enclosed by a framing device, the end mirroring the beginning in a number of ways. For one thing, the film opens and closes with what is a conventional establishing shot for many *films noirs*, namely, a cityscape, a panoramic glimpse of the modern symbol of corruption, desperation, and decay. *Noir* characters commonly face their destinies in this concrete jungle of hulking skyscrapers, monuments to progress that create the illusion of success and affluence, while the deleterious and enervating environment stymies dreams even before they are dreamt. New York City, perhaps the most exploited setting for *noir*, is the city of *The Window* but with this variation: the New York skyline stands upright in the background, hovering over a sprawling, decrepit tenement district that dominates the lower foreground. This latter area is where Tommy Woodry and his family live and where the story takes place. The opening cityscape appears under the bright sun of daytime; the closing cityscape is hazily lit with the murky glow of dawn. Meanings are attached to this as the bright days of carefree childhood are forsaken when the boy's adventure initiates him into his new consciousness as a young man.

After the opening establishing shot, a series of dissolves narrows our perspective from a general overview of the neighborhood to a single moldering building. The camera tracks in for a close-up of one side of the deserted structure, its windows and doors partially boarded up, and finally rests on the gaping black maw of a paneless window frame on the second floor. The building is the labyrinth of *noir*, the place into which the protagonist descends to complete his ordeal, either to succeed or fail.

A dissolve takes us through the window and into the building's squalid interior of Tommy's world. The music, quietly tense, portends some ominous incident as the camera tracks through a barren room, its latticework stripped of plaster. The camera peers through a doorway where lying in the straw on the floor is a handgun. The camera continues to move forward, reveals a child's arm and finally the child himself, Tommy, lying prostrate on the floor as if crying or sleeping—or even dead. He rouses himself and acts as if he is hurt or wounded. He reaches for the gun and creeps stealthily to an interior opening overlooking a group of boys playing marbles on the dirt floor inside the condemned building. From his lofty second-floor roost, he aims his gun and shoots at them. Only now does it become evident that his gun is a cap pistol and he is playing. He admonishes his friends for not dying on cue, but they ignore him.

After shooting at his friends, Tommy runs up the stairs to the roof, runs across the rooftops, and descends the fire escape ladder. As he passes the Kellersons' window, he shouts good morning to Mrs. Kellerson, who, unseen through the curtains, returns an audible greeting that shows she knows him. Tommy reaches the next landing, his apartment, enters the window, scurries through his apartment (with a quick hello to his unseen mother), and hurries downstairs to reach his friends at their game of marbles. The sureness and speed with which he makes this journey show he has done it before. He belongs here, knows the layout intimately, is totally comfortable.

At the end, Tommy makes the same journey in reverse when he runs from Joe Kellerson who is trying to kill him. He climbs up the fire escape ladder, runs across the rooftops, and finds hiding places inside the derelict tenement. This is the domain of the child, not the adult. Tommy can scramble and elude his older pursuer almost indefinitely. At first, the adult may seem the monster, the Minotaur, who viciously intends to murder the boy, but he is no match for the child who knows this world better than he does. When Tommy kicks aside the loose rafter and sends Kellerson to his death, he inherits the title of monster, and after this experience, he can no longer claim innocence. The child is trapped on the rafter and must make the leap into the void, return to earth and the realm of the adults where he now will be accepted as their equal (They finally accept his accusation as truth.). In the cab with his parents, he promises never to tell lies again, at least not the lies associated with childish exaggeration.

Tetzlaff's use of irony in the beginning may seem trite, but it in fact reflects his craftsmanship, for the simplicity belies its important implications for what will happen at the end. From the start, the main theme is subtly implied in the ambiguity between fantasy and reality: the boy playing with a cap pistol is about to make the passage from childhood to adulthood, will forsake childlike ways for the attitude of the mature adult.

The "window" of the title would seem to refer to the window Tommy looks through when he sees the Kellersons murder their victim. This may be the most critical window, leading as it does to the central conflict of the story, but it turns out that there are many other windows in the story, and related to the windows are doors, some opened, some closed, most suggesting the threshold between the world of the child and the world of the adult.

This is true, for example, of the first window we see. Through this dark opening we move from the normal boisterous activity outside on the streets to the child's make-believe world inside the building. The building is condemned, which means it is unsafe, off limits—but not for the child. The deserted tenement is Tommy's playground, the place where his imagination

The Window—The evil surrogate father (Paul Stewart) pursues Tommy (Bobby Driscoll) and endangers their lives (RKO, courtesy William Thailing).

is free to wander at will, to behave as wildly and illogically as it wants. In the irony (the music codes our entrance into this realm of play as ominous, the visuals indicate a grim situation), there is a blurred line between the imaginary world of the child and the real world of the adult. Tommy can pretend to be hurt and to shoot his friends, but in the real world, the world of adults, these are things that happen for real. The Kellersons, after trying to cheat a man out of his money, are forced to kill him. Then they go after Tommy who they realize witnessed the murder. The adult world invades the world of the child, supplants his imaginary one with a real and dangerous one. And all through the film, his parents and the police (no dearth of skeptical authority figures) refuse to believe him because they cannot accept that children (innocent inhabitants of an imaginary realm) could be privy to the goings-on of adults (vain champions of reality).

In another irony, it is the adults, the authority figures, who jeopardize Tommy. If they had believed his story and responded to his misgivings, his life would not have been endangered. Given his reputation for exaggeration and lies, it is understandable that his parents refuse to believe him. However, when his mother takes him up to the Kellersons' apartment to apologize, she,

The Window—Tommy Woodry (Driscol) and Ed Woodry (Arthur Kennedy) depict the complex father-son relationship that faces the critical moment when the son must learn to stop looking up to his father as his ultimate hero (RKO, courtesy William Thailing).

like her counterpart in Woolrich's story, inadvertently exposes him to danger by revealing his possession of that forbidden knowledge. When the father later nails the window shut and locks the bedroom door, he also thinks he is doing good, but ironically makes his son easy prey for the Kellersons. In all this, the adults are alienating the child, forcing him to think for himself, to decide and act on his own. This is part of the process known as maturation: the child's transition from childhood to adulthood can be a lonely, self-determined path. Adults can care for the child, but when the child is ready to become an adult, he does so on his own.

Woolrich gave his antagonists the name Kellerman, which connotes a "man killer." And they are that when they murder their guest. In changing the name Kellerman to Kellerson, Tetzlaff suggests a "son killer," a small alteration that, already hinted at in Woolrich's story, makes the doubling of the boy's parents more salient. Like the fairy tales in which an evil stepmother replaces the benevolent but dead or missing real mother, the film presents the Kellersons as Tommy's alternative parents, an evil mother and father unsuitable for raising a healthy, well-adjusted child.

In Woolrich's story, Buddy's father is a disciplinarian who beats him as punishment when he disobeys or fails to meet the father's expectations. This contrasts with Ed Woodry, who, like a model father, tries to discuss things, to rationalize with his son, respecting his ability to understand and obey because he is persuaded by reason. Joe Kellerson is more like the strict father in the original story. While impersonating Tommy's father, he tells the policeman that he plans on giving the boy a "shellacking" when they get home. What appears a ruse becomes reality when he punches Tommy on the jaw to knock him unconscious; the "strict father" has gone to extremes. At his apartment, he balances Tommy on the railing of the fire escape, a symbolic gesture of the father putting the child in harm's way, of jeopardizing the life of "his" child to suit his own selfish purposes.

Ed Woodry goes to extremes when he nails shut Tommy's window and locks him in his room. Looked at literally, this probably did not seem abusive in 1949 because Woodry does not physically hurt the boy. Symbolically, however, by nailing shut the window, Woodry denies Tommy access to an escape route, both a physical and imaginative one. He now must seek an exit through the door, and this is where he comes face to face with his surrogate father, Kellerson, in the real world of fear and danger. Later, when Tommy kicks away the loose rafter that results in Kellerson's fatal fall, he rids himself of his evil father, the mean disciplinarian, and makes it possible to restore his relationship with his kinder real father.

The mother is important, too, but in a limited way. Mrs. Woodry also prefers dialogue to physical punishment in teaching her son right from wrong. But her motives are rooted in her desire to please her husband: she tries to rankle Tommy's conscience by appealing to him to stop his lying for his father's sake more than for any outright ethical reason. Jean Kellerson goes along with her husband in much the same way as Mrs. Woodry goes along with hers, but when the boy's life is endangered, her maternal instinct is aroused. It is in that split second when she rebels against Joe's design and tries to rescue Tommy that Tommy is able to escape. The fathers, then, are the more dominant figures in the parents' relationship with the boy.

The boy's harrowing experience coupled with the outcome shows the fragility of childhood and the inevitability of the loss of innocence. When Tommy is stranded on the ceiling beam, his parents arrive and Ed, possibly fearing that Tommy's seeing them may upset him and complicate the situation, whispers to his wife, "Don't let him see us." This means, however, that the child is now on his own, making his decision without his parents to guide or advise him. He is "out on a limb," suspended in the middle of nowhere with only his wits and intelligence to depend on. A policeman, another of the many parent-figures in the film, directs Tommy to jump on the count of three. But Tommy does not jump. It is not that he hesitates out of fear since he is clearly moving into position to jump. Rather, he is deciding for himself the exact moment to make the leap, not heeding the command of one of the authority figures who were supposed to protect and guide him through the adversity he was left to face on his own. When he makes that leap, it is a defining moment in his life, a step across the threshold (passage through another window) from childhood to adulthood.

Reunited with his parents and riding down to the station in a police car, Tommy says, "I know one thing. I'm never gonna be a fireman. I don't like jumping into those nets." We smile at the irony, knowing he survived a far greater danger than the jump. In the declaration, though, he renounces one of those common childhood dreams, to become a fireman when he grows up. It is as if he were cleansing his mind of all childish whims.

In this last scene, too, Tommy vows that he will "never make up another story," and Mrs. Woodry says, "That'll make us all happy." His promise reflects what is supposedly the desirable notion that he is grown up enough to realize he should not tell untruths in the adult world. However, there is a hidden negative consequence. Adults too often concern themselves with reality to the detriment of the imagination, and here, the loss of childhood is equated with the forsaking of imagination. When Tommy promises he will never lie again, he means he will now abide by the code of adults, to tell the truth — that is, conform to reality. He can no longer be the imaginative child at the beginning when he played a wounded cowboy who sneaks up on his friends and shoots them from his hiding place, who impresses and entertains them by disrupting their mundane life in their tenement neighborhood with fantastic, imaginative stories. Maybe Tetzlaff implies this more as a caveat than a certainty, that adults do not have to abandon their imagination totally to claim their role as adults. After all, if Tommy's parents had used their imagination, they may have been better prepared to deal with the threat from the Kellersons.

Also while taking this final ride in the police car, Ed Woodry tells his son, "I bet when we get down to the station, a lot of guys are gonna point at me and say, 'There goes Tommy Woodry's father.'" Earlier, he had defined this as his greatest wish, as if it were the ultimate validation of Tommy's maturity and progress, the imprimatur of his growth into genuine manhood. The irony is that the father measures success and pride through whatever glory his son attains rather than through his own achievements. He sounds nurturing and sincere when he says it, but in its inspiration of guilt, it is a terrible strategy for getting a conscientious child to conform to the adult's rules for living. It can place an enormous burden on the child, create the stress of having to live up to unclear codes and undefined values. All the harsh physical "disciplinary" methods of the Kellersons could never be as insidiously manipulative as the psychological ploys of the tenderhearted parent. The smiles on all the Woodrys' faces suggest that they are content, the parents that their son has consented to their wishes and the son that he has learned to conform to their way of thinking. It is not a consoling thought, and like many *films noirs*, *The Window* ends with the pretense of closure while a subtext suggests ideas that keep us uncertain and unsettled.

Ironically, Tommy's real-life adventure is more outrageous than anything he has ever made up. Because he falls asleep on the fire escape before witnessing the murder and experiencing the subsequent events, it could be argued that the entire adventure is Tommy's dream (an idea more strongly implied in Woolrich's story). The final shot of the New York skyline and the sprawling tenements shows the sunrise (a reprise of the opening establishing shot), which could be the new dawn after his long and convoluted nightmare. Whichever way this is interpreted, it does not change the main thrust of the story, that adulthood and childhood are separated by the degree to which either has the ability to use the imagination. This is also apparent in Woolrich's story, a point made obvious when he refers to Buddy's two worlds, the real world inside his cramped apartment and the boundless imaginary one inside his head.

That the reality of Tommy's story is ambiguous, that we can interpret it as an actual experience or a concoction of his own imagination, is not a new device. In the silent era, many early films used it to justify sudden fantastical occurrences. A film would begin in reality, then collapse into unreality when the main character fell asleep and witnessed various surrealistic visions (appearances and disappearances of people and objects, autonomous movement by normally inanimate objects, the materialization of fairies and monsters. See especially the films of Georges Méliès.). The character eventually awoke and mundane reality was restored. In *noir*, however, this ambiguous dream device has a different function. It is a deliberate attempt to add to the confusion of the labyrinth in the *noir* world, to complicate the dilemma of the protagonist by making it difficult to differentiate between reality and non-reality, between actuality and perception, and to emphasize the futility of dealing with capricious fate and an unjust society that ignores any logical, equitable system of reward and punishment.

Although the boundary between waking and sleeping appears obvious in *The Window*, Tommy's falling asleep on the fire escape and waking to witness the murder still bears a hint of ambiguity. We see this same thing in *Laura* (Preminger, 1944). The film greatly simplifies the structure of Caspary's novel where, as in Faulkner's *As I Lay Dying*, or Welles's *Citizen Kane*, or Siodmak's *The Killers*, descriptions of events are divided among several first-person narrators. Thus, the narrative is fragmented and truth is muddled; perspective equals perception and reality becomes relative to the observer. In the film, the narrative is divided between only two characters. The first half, much of it narrated in flashback by Waldo Lydecker (Clifton Webb), appears real enough; but when Detective Mark McPherson (Dana Andrews) falls asleep in front of Laura's (Gene Tierney) portrait and then assumes the central role in the remainder of the story, we may wonder whether what we see is his wish fulfillment of how he would like things to turn out. The "girl of his dreams" (he has fallen in love with the woman in the portrait) materializes as he wakens; he takes control of events from here on, eventually becoming the hero by rescuing his beloved at the last moment. Ironically, while the ambiguous dream of the young detective looks forward to an enjoyable future with his female paragon, the dream of the elderly Waldo (his lengthy flashback is a memory of how his relationship with Laura evolved) reverts to an unrecoverable past.

The Woman in the Window (Fritz Lang, 1945) uses the dream device more overtly. Like McPherson, the protagonist (E.G. Robinson) has let a woman's portrait pique his romantic fantasies. Coincidentally, he meets the very *femme noire* in the painting, a fatal encounter that triggers his involvement in a murder intrigue — until he finally wakens in the armchair at his club and realizes his adventure was all a dream. Confusion between the real and non-real momentarily evaporates, but then the man steps outside and comes face to face with a woman as he had in his dream. He abruptly runs away, afraid his dream can come true. Ambiguity, playfully and implicitly, is restored.

Even the so-called "first" *noir* film, *The Maltese Falcon* (John Huston, 1941) plays with this paradox. The story begins with Miss Wonderly (Mary Astor) hiring Sam Spade (Humphrey Bogart) to do a job. Spade's partner, Miles Archer (Jerome Cowan), smitten by the *femme fatale*, steps in to volunteer his services before Spade does. Later, Spade is wakened from his sleep by a phone call from the police who tell him his partner Archer has been shot. And so begins the adventure. Events result in Spade's favor, as they did for McPherson, but we have to wonder if it is not because the character is still lying in bed, fabricating the story in his imagination and controlling the outcome through wish fulfillment.

This same idea has already been discussed in regard to Hitchcock's *Vertigo*. After the rooftop chase sequence at the beginning and the policeman's fall to his death, Scotty hangs from a sagging rain gutter. We never see how he is saved. For all we know, he may be imagining the rest of the story while still dangling from that drain duct, so that the end, a shot of his triumph over vertigo, is his mind playing tricks to assuage his guilt over the death of the policeman.

This dream device is a variation of the narrated flashback that occurs in many *films noirs*, such as *Double Indemnity* (Billy Wilder, 1944), *Murder, My Sweet* (Edward Dmytryk, 1944), *The Postman Always Rings Twice* (Tay Garnett, 1946), and *The Lady from Shanghai* (Orson Welles, 1948). Here, too, events unfold according to the narrator's desires, so that what we see on the screen may or may not have happened as the narrator says they did. In this capricious world where fate controls our destiny regardless of divine or human justice, at least the story can be controlled by the narrator who wants to see events proceed in a certain direction and end, if not in his favor, then on his terms.

Another coming-of-age story having some incidental parallels with "The Boy Cried Murder" is *Talk About a Stranger* (David Bradley, 1952), based on "The Enemy" by mystery writer Charlotte Armstrong. A young boy, Bud Fontaine (Billy Gray), an irascible loner, befriends a stray dog. A day later, the dog dies after eating poisoned meat. Although he lacks tangible proof, Bud suspects his new neighbor, Matlock (Kurt Kasznar), a reclusive stranger, whom he vociferously accuses of the deed. No one believes Bud, and Matlock's aloofness makes him appear threatening, but in time, the stranger's mystery is exposed and Bud learns the dangers of spreading malicious slander.

In one respect, *Talk About a Stranger* is the inverse of *The Window*. Both deal with a boy's initiation into adulthood by learning to shed a childish trait, but each treats this critical transition in a different way. Bud and Tommy accuse a neighbor of wrongdoing and they are ignored because of their youth. They must rely on their own ingenuity to prove to others that they are right. Tommy endures an ordeal partially brought on by himself: his lying has conditioned people not to believe him. Bud, on the other hand, is a very serious individual; yet, even more than Tommy, he is responsible for the crises that arise because of his vindictiveness. For Tommy, the adventure awakens him to the very real dangers brought on by lying, a habit he must curb in future; Bud's transition depends on his ability to discern truth from biased inferences, an important step in mature thinking. Both films show that, as a mythical experience, the passage into adulthood can be traumatic, violent, and costly.

Like Tommy in *The Window*, Cheryl Draper (Barbara Stanwyck) in *Witness to Murder* (1954) is an inadvertent voyeur who sees a murder, but cannot convince authorities that a crime occurred. While closing her bedroom window, Cheryl witnesses a strangulation murder committed by her across-the-street neighbor, Albert Richter (George Sanders). Richter manages to hide the body and conceal incriminating evidence (as the Kellersons neatly did), so that the police investigation, headed by Detective Lawrence Mathews (Gary Merrill) is stymied. Richter learns that Cheryl is his accuser and he manages to finagle false evidence against her so she appears an hallucinatory psychotic. She is committed for a time, but when released, confronts her nemesis. Richter readily admits his guilt, but displays no remorse. For him, murder can be a necessary, practical act. As a neo–Nazi, he espouses an obsolete superior-race theory that justified his killing his mistress before she upset his plans to marry a prominent wealthy socialite. He has brainwashed himself with a barbaric, sadistic philosophy that makes him a man without a conscience. At the end, when he fights with Mathews atop a building under construction and falls to his death, the unconscionable egotist is brought down to earth for his monstrous and inhumane conviction that there exist superior beings who have the right to take the lives of those they believe inferior to themselves.

This theme may have had some currency in the 1950s, especially as a remnant of the recently suppressed Nazi threat. Related to the Aryan demagoguery were the implications that came out of the 1924 murder trial of Nathan Leopold and Richard Loeb, and two movies, based on the thrill-murder by the two young men, appeared at this time: *Rope* (Hitchcock, 1948) and *Compulsion* (Richard Fleischer, 1959). It could be argued whether these two films belong in the *noir* catalogue, *Rope* filmed in color and *Compulsion* released after the prescribed limit of the original classic *noir* cycle (1958). However, both contain *noir* characters who suffer the consequences of their actions and existential beliefs, and both address *noir* themes of guilt and the contradictions between fate and self-determination.

Film: The Boy Cried Murder

Alternate titles: *Decak vikao ubistvo* and *Junge schrie Mord, Ein* (UK/West Germany/Yugoslavia)
1966, CCC-Carlos Film Production in association with Bernard Luber. *D:* George P. Breakston. *P:* Philip N. Krasne. *Ph:* Milorad Markovic. *Sc:* Robin Estridge. *Ed:* Milanka Nanovic. *Mus:* Martin Slavin.
Cast: Fraser "Fiz" MacIntosh (Jonathan "Jonno" Durrant), Veronica Hurst (Claire Durrant), Phil Brown (Tom Durrant), Tim Barrett (Mike), Beba Loncar (Susie), Edward Steel (Col. Hugo Wetherall), Anita Bolster (Mrs. Wetherall), Yorda Hlepsa (Marianne), Alex MacIntosh (Police sergeant), Vuka Dundzerovic (Mrs. Bosnic), (Nadia, Jonno's girlfriend, uncredited), (Laura, Mike's accomplice, uncredited). 85 min.

Born in Paris, France, in 1920, George Breakston made his first inroads into film as an actor. He landed early roles in the 1934 productions of *It Happened One Night* (as the boy whose mother faints from hunger) and *Great Expectations* (as young Pip), and his path to stardom may have seemed paved. However, it was not to be. Toward the end of his acting career, he was still manning the minor roles, playing such characters as Beezy Anderson, a regular fixture in the popular Andy Hardy series of the 1930s and '40s, which starred Mickey Rooney. His first directorial assignment came in 1948 with *Urubu* (which he also scripted). *The Boy Cried Murder* is one of his last film projects before his untimely death in 1973.

The Boy Cried Murder is more a remake of Tetzlaff's *The Window* than it is an adaptation of Woolrich's short story. The filmmakers must have liked the material enough to reshape it into a subtle statement about the social and attitudinal upheavals of the 1960s, alluding to the moral deviations of that contentious period.

The story begins on a cruise ship in the Mediterranean with a man falling overboard and the crew having to scour the water for him. Young Jonno (Fraser MacIntosh) tells a nearby elderly couple (Edward Steel and Anita Bolster) that he saw someone push the victim, but when the crew finally recovers the man, he admits that he was drunk and had jumped overboard on his own. We soon realize that Jonno's penchant for lying is his way of manipulating his mother (Veronica Hurst) for marrying second husband Tom Durrant (Phil Brown) after his real father had died. Jonno will play other tricks as well, such as faking an illness to keep his mother from going out with Tom and releasing a captive bear to disrupt the enjoyable time his parents are having together.

The ship docks at Budva, a resort on the Adriatic coast of Montenegro, and the tourists disembark for several days of vacationing. Awaiting the tourists is a professional thief named Mike (Tim Barrett), who with his girlfriend Susie

(Beba Loncar) plans to extort money from the list of well-to-do tourists. Mike's previous accomplice, Marianne (Yorda Hlepsa), suddenly appears and, angry at him for deserting her, threatens to go to the police. He tries to placate her, walking and pleading with her through the streets of Budva, but she remains smugly intractable. Jonno sees them pass by and he playfully follows them, hiding in the shadows along the way. From the stairs, Susie notices Jonno, but disregards his appearance as unimportant. Jonno loses the twosome until he reaches the docks and stumbles onto Marianne's body. He knows Mike has killed her and tries to tell his parents, but they won't believe him.

Ignoring his pleas, they go on an evening's excursion with the other tourists. While they are gone, Jonno goes to the police, but after the bear incident, they won't believe him. The sergeant (Alex MacIntosh) takes him back home. Mike, aware by now that Jonno knows of his crime, sneaks into Jonno's room to kill him. However, Jonno escapes and leads Mike on an all-night chase through the town.

Mike finally catches up to Jonno at the ruins of an ancient fort in the center of town. He knocks Jonno out to silence him, then carries him to the precipice of the tower that overlooks the main street. Tom Durrant makes his way up to the precipice and pleads with Mike to spare the boy. With a change of heart, Mike hands him the inert body just before he loses his footing and falls to his death.

Later that day, Jonno and his parents try to forget their ordeal by swimming on the beach and then setting out on a sailboat excursion. Jonno calls Tom "dad," suggesting that he has finally accepted him as his father.

Reminiscent of *The Window* are the murderer's attack on the boy while the parents are absent, the boy's inability to convince two representatives of authority (parents and police) of the truth, and the boy's short note to his parents that becomes a means for the murderer to protect himself. Susie is clearly a substitute for Mrs. Kellerson (Ruth Roman): their maternal (or humane) instincts cause them to interfere with their man's objective to kill the boy, ultimately effecting the boy's rescue and the murderer's demise.

Even with these corresponding elements, Breakston's film comes about as close to Tetzlaff's film as glass comes to diamond. Nevertheless, it has its merits, if we don't try to glean more from it than it has to offer. For a suspenseful potboiler, *The Boy Cried Murder* is competently made and well acted, although Jonno, unlike Tommy Woodry (Bobby Driscoll), is far too precocious, spoiled, and vindictive to win our sympathy. Watching his journey through the labyrinthine streets of the town, we hope he will elude Mike, more out of an instinctive desire to see the child escape the clutches of the malevolent monster than out of some basic identification with the character or an empathetic need to see him evade unjust punishment.

On the other hand, the father-son conflict in Breakston's film is an imaginative variation on the parallel tensions in Woolrich's story and Tetzlaff's film. In each case, the father's temperament determines the kind of relationship

The Boy Cried Murder— Jonno (Fraser MacIntosh, left) enters the labyrinth and tries to elude the evil "Minotaur" (Tim Barrett) (United International, courtesy William Thailing).

forged with the child. Woolrich's father is cruel and domineering; Tetzlaff's father is hard working and devoted. Breakston's stepfather is different still. He tries to be reasonable and tolerant, fully aware of the truth his wife keeps ignoring, that Jonno is a manipulative brat. Durrant truly loves Claire and Jonno. His strength is his commitment, his determination to replace the lost husband and father and restore integrity to the shattered family.

Tom Durrant's modest ambition contrasts with what the film suggests is happening to the world at large. Society has lost its guiding values, its ethical guardrails, and has degenerated into pockets of hedonism, crime, lust, drunkenness, and murder. The story begins with a drunken passenger willfully falling off the ship. Mike and Susie make their entrance after just concluding an illicit sexual episode. Mike makes a living out of extorting money from innocent tourists. Later, when Jonno flees from Mike through the streets of Budva, he bangs on the door of a house where all-night revelers are too engrossed in their party (a symbol of hedonism?) to hear his cries. He moves on and interrupts two (unmarried?) people about to make love. He is even evicted from a church where he sought sanctuary; the holy house of worship, once a haven for outcasts, does not provide that kind of service anymore. When Durrant reaches his breaking point and administers the traditional spanking to the boy, he upsets the mother, but he is at least exercising a disciplinary method that recalls a past where such recalcitrant behavior was not tolerated or condoned. Yet we are forced to question even these well-intentioned parents, for they consider giving Jonno a sedative to help him sleep (the new pill-popping generation that believes there is a panacea for every ill) and they discuss the possibility of his seeing a psychiatrist (the modern way to deal with guilt, the psychiatrist as secular confessor).

A noticeable parallel between Jonno and Mike is that they have the same kind of wispy peroxide-blond hair. Although this immediately establishes a duality between the hunter and the hunted, the film lacks any definitive evidence to suggest why these two characters are doubled. One may speculate that Mike is the adult Jonno could become if he continues with his self-centered and obstinate behavior. In the end, Mike seems to have attained an epiphany. He appears a defeated man, pitiful and repentant. His gesture of returning Jonno to his father may be an act of redemption and his fall to his death, although unintentional, can be interpreted as self-sacrifice. However, as noted above, it is difficult to take this too far because the film does not lend itself to profound or extensive analysis.

Another film, *Domestic Disturbance* (Harold Becker, 2001), does not credit Woolrich as its source, yet it contains many superficial comparisons. If looked at as an adaptation, Becker's film takes the same tact as Breakston's, modernizing the social situations and the relationships among the characters. In a way, *Domestic Disturbance* exemplifies the standard progression of adaptations as they move further and further from the original concept. Although the actors give capable and even outstanding performances, the film is too predictable and imitative to merit endorsement.

Like Jonno, 11-year-old Danny Morrison (Matthew O'Leary) is a disturbed child, the backlash from losing his intact family. Whereas Jonno's father has died and he must cope with his mother's choosing a new husband, Danny sees his parents divorce and his mother remarry. In other words, Becker substitutes a more modern circumstance to explain the splintering of the cohesive family. At each critical moment in his parents' lives, when they divorce, when his mother starts dating a new man, and when his mother remarries, Danny rebels with irrational and irresponsible behavior. He witnesses his stepfather Rick (Vince Vaughn) stab Ray (Steve Buscemi) with an ice pick, but because of his previous behavior, no one believes him. In *The Window*, the stabbing is not shown and Tommy only knows that scissors are the weapon because they fall blood-stained to the floor. Breakston never even shows Mike kill Marianne. Becker, however, does not have to worry about the sensibility of his modern audience: he explicitly depicts Ray's horrified, contorted expression when Rick plunges the ice pick into his back.

Like all previous versions of the story, *Domestic Disturbance* focuses on the father-son relationship. Luckily for Danny, his father Frank Morrison (John

Travolta) realizes that, although his son may have lied to many people, "he's never lied to me." Driven by that unwavering confidence, Frank does some private investigating, uncovers Rick's hidden criminal past, and rescues his son and ex-wife at the 11th hour. The film tries to show that no matter what damage is done to the family structure, certain bonds, particularly the father-son bond, can continue.

Domestic Disturbance contains some *noir* conventions suggesting its aspirations for neo-*noir* status. The dark intruder who is welcomed into the home and then poses a threat to the occupants has its origins in films such as *He Ran All the Way* (John Berry, 1951), *Beware, My Lovely* (Harry Horner, 1952) and *Sudden Fear* (David Miller, 1952). Another *noir* motif is the character's guilty past returning to haunt him. Ray, who had spent time in prison with Rick, comes to town to claim some money from a job they had done together before they went to prison. Ray's appearance threatens Rick's new status of respectability. This could work well if Rick were not so one-dimensional: he is too thoroughly evil. He shows some tenderness toward his new wife, but not enough to offset the maliciousness that looms beneath his pretentious façade. His character is presented totally from an objective viewpoint; the story is more Frank's than his. His failure to show some remorse or to question his guilt diminishes the film's connection to *noir*.

Film: Cloak & Dagger

1984. *D:* Richard Franklin. *P:* Allan Carr. *Cin:* Victor J. Kemper. *Sc:* Nancy Dowd (uncredited), Tom Holland. *Ed:* Andrew London. *Mus:* Brian May. *Prod Des:* George Trimmer, William H. Tuntke. *Art Dir:* Todd Hallowell. *Set Dec:* Hal Gausman. *F/X:* Robert G. Willard.
Cast: Henry Thomas (Davey Osborne), Dabney Coleman (Hal Osborne/Jack Flack), Michael Murphy (Rice), Christina Nigra (Kim Gardener), John McIntire (George MacCready), Jeanette Nolan (Eunice MacCready), Eloy Casados (Alvarez), Tim Rossovich (Haverman), William Forsythe (Morris), Robert DoQui (Lt. Fleming), Shelby Leverington (Marilyn Gardener), Robert Curtin (Murdoch), Linden Chiles (Chief of Security), William Marquez (Guard #1), Wendell Wright (Guard #2), Doris Hargrave (Woman in café), Gary Moody (Man in café), Eleese Lester (Woman on boat), John R. Edson (First man on boat), Corey Rand (Building guard), Nicholas Guest (Taxi driver), Karen Leigh Hopkins (Receptionist), Tammy Hyler (Clerk), Charles Beall (Alamo Guardian #1), Stuart MacGregor (Alamo Guardian #2), Alvaro Rojas, Jr. (Boat Captain), Robert Traynor (Ticket clerk), Steve Fromholtz (Second man on boat), Berkley Garrett (Bus driver), Gene Robb (Second bus driver), Louie Anderson (Second taxi driver), Earl Houston Bullock (Navigator), Al Gomez (Ship crewman). 101 min.

Another remake of *The Window*, not at first obvious, is Richard Franklin's juvenile but sufficiently entertaining *Cloak & Dagger*. Although the film is neither *noir* nor *neo-noir*, its title and its story of espionage allude to Lang's 1946 *noir* spy thriller, and its "boy-who-cried- murder" premise links it to the dark Woolrich-Tetzlaff material. A boy, Davey Osborne (Henry Thomas, formerly in Spielberg's popular *E.T.*), an avid player of computer games, witnesses the murder of a lab technician who, just before he dies, hands him the game cartridge called "Cloak & Dagger." The boy's adult friend, Morris (William Forsythe), is a computer game expert, who cracks the code and finds that the cartridge contains classified government secrets about a fighter plane. Three thieves pursue the boy, seeking the cartridge for some international spies. Davey's father Hal Osborne (Dabney Coleman) does not believe his story, thinking his overactive imagination has been influenced by his obsession with games. The boy has an imaginary friend, Jack Flack, the hero in one his games, who resembles his father (Coleman in a dual role) and appears to him at critical moments to give him advice on eluding the thieves and dealing with the spies. Davey defeats the thieves, but because Flack had urged him to resort to violence to kill the last of his pursuers, the boy loses faith in him, and the imaginary hero disappears. In a frenzied climax, the spies abduct Davey and take him aboard a plane. Hal Osborne arrives in time to rescue his son. Just before the plane explodes on the runway with the spies on board, Osborne escapes and is reunited with his boy.

The plot of *Cloak & Dagger* intersects *The Window* at several points, enough to verify that the former is a remake of the latter. Among the key thematic points are the boy's fusion of imagination with reality and the exploration of the parent-child relationship. Like Tommy Woodry who lets his imagination run wild with exaggerated storytelling, Davey is influenced by modern computer games, which inspire his imagination to construct an illusory playmate-counselor. Ironically, he imagines this playmate in the image of his father, which suggests who his real hero is and that in his mind he is fusing the real world (of Hal Osborne) with an imaginary one (of Jack Flack). When Davey abandons Flack, he is letting go of his childhood and accepting adolescence in a symbolically similar way that Tommy does when he leaps from the rafter without benefit of parental support or guidance. When his father, not Flack, rescues him, reality replaces imagination; there is no longer a need for a fictitious friend to fulfill childhood desires.

This same point has more paradoxical implications in Tetzlaff's film than in Franklin's. However, at the risk of reading too much into it, I believe the last shot of *Cloak & Dagger* contains some possible parallel ideas. The father and son are hugging in the foreground with fiery explosions raging in the distant background, framing them in a billowing, blazing cloud of fire. The catastrophe that took the lives of the two elderly spies and almost killed the father and son suggests how traumatic can be the transition from the child's imaginary world to the adult's real world. It is not a simple stage in a person's development and the trade-offs are not all acceptable or desirable.

I Married a Dead Man

Novel, published under the pseudonym William Irish for the J.B. Lippincott Company, 1948; Hutchinson, 1950; first paperback by Avon, pbk #220, 1949; reprinted in various paperback editions.

Few would dispute that Cornell Woolrich invents some of the most bizarre and original plot twists to captivate, amaze, and mystify his readers. However, as narratives that often test — and even defy — logic, their sensational nature sometimes makes them more suitable for the short story form. In a short story, the illogic, offered in small dosages, is more digestible and Woolrich can compensate for the coincidences and the absurdities with his skillful handling of style and suspense. Over a longer duration, the lapses in logic are more difficult to ingest because they keep recurring and gradually undermine the "suspension of disbelief." In addition, Woolrich's flair for ironic plot twists makes the stories more plot-centered than character-driven, so that character empathy tends to wane in a longer work. We may make more allowances for, say, a Hal Jeffries in "Rear Window" than for a Bill Scott in *The Black Path of Fear*, even though both protagonists are equally flat two-dimensional figures.

I Married a Dead Man, a perfect example of Woolrich's emphasis on plot over character, is one of the few exceptions to this rule. In spite of a few typical Woolrichian flaws in logic and character, the novel, tightly crafted, manages to be convincing because of the author's tactful manipulation of suspense. The protagonist is never fully developed as a character, but Woolrich makes her very sympathetic, instilling her with noble, stoic qualities while continuously placing her in precarious positions between certainty and doubt, security and ruin, happiness and despair. Able successfully to write a number of novels and stories from the woman's point of view, Woolrich inserts into this story a considerable measure of the gothic romance, which, perhaps, makes this work a precursor to that modern genre.

The novel contains a Prologue and Epilogue voiced by the protagonist herself, subjective first-person narratives that frame the inset story told in the third person. The Prologue draws us immediately into the story by describing in vague terms a paradoxical intrigue. The simplicity and sincerity of

Patrice's language make us sympathetic to her dilemma; her half-revelations arouse our curiosity and lead us into the story wondering what, why, and who.

Patrice tells us that she has something to hide, something so serious that, despite the idyllic atmosphere of Caulfield, she can never be happy here. The description of peaceful Caulfield contrasted with her emotional wretchedness and agitation makes us wonder what could have been so devastating that it disrupted her and her family's lives. What that something is, she confesses plainly enough, is murder, but we don't know who was killed or why. She leaves the details vague, yet hints that either she or her husband Bill is guilty. Their strange dilemma stirs our sympathy. The understated, melancholy tone of her voice sounds sincere and makes her likable. We question whether it is possible that one of them actually did kill someone, and if she is mistaken, how she could have gotten this wrong impression. We wonder what events led her to this crisis, and we may even believe that, in the unfolding of the story, we will finally learn that neither Patrice nor Bill murdered anyone and that they are entitled to happiness after all.

The significant merits of the story lie in their adherence to the laws of the *noir* universe. Neat, tidy resolutions are anathema. Like Patrice, we emerge from the story just as baffled by events (Who actually murdered Stephen?), just as uncertain of the ultimate outcome (What will come of her relationship with Bill?), and just as frustrated (Can the mystery be resolved so the characters can get on with their lives?).

After the Prologue, we learn in flashback Patrice's story. Patrice is originally Helen Georgesson, unwed but pregnant with child. Outcast, despondent, and poor, she takes a train to seek a better life outside of New York City. On the journey she meets the Hazzards, Patrice and Hugh. Patrice is pregnant with their first child and the common condition establishes an immediate bond between the two women. Without warning, he train crashes and the Hazzards are killed. In a case of mistaken identity, the Hazzard family, never having seen their son's bride, assumes that Helen is their daughter-in-law who has survived the tragic accident. They care for her, nurse her back to health.

Because the inset story is related not by Helen but by an "impartial" third-person speaker, we develop our opinions of her without the bias of her subjective viewpoint. The objective narrator seems more reliable and we are compelled to believe that she really is a sensitive, sincere, and well-intentioned woman, traits that make her a sympathetic character. She intends to tell the Hazzards of their mistake, but then sees how their status and wealth can insure the security and success of her own child. Motivated by concern for him, not for herself (so she says), she vows to spare little Hugh from having to wallow in the depressing squalor she endured and could not surmount. She remains mute and accepts her new identity as "Patrice." In time, she develops a close relationship with Bill Hazzard, the Hazzards' second son.

Patrice, however, cannot escape her disreputable past. Stephen Georgesson, the callous ne'er-do-well who fathered her child and then deserted her, discovers Patrice's new home and blackmails her into secretly marrying him so he can be a legitimate heir to the Hazzard estate. Patrice takes father Hazzard's gun and sets off to confront Stephen in his hotel room. She finds him sprawled on his bed in a darkened room. She aims the gun and shoots, but just as she does, she is filled with a sudden yet vague impression that he was already dead.

Bill arrives. He has been following her and knows about the forced marriage and Stephen's blackmail scheme. He instructs her to help him dispose of the body. Later, the police question Bill about Georgesson's death. Bill admits that he knew Stephen as a gambler who extorted money from his brother Hugh. The upshot of the police investigation is that some disgruntled gamblers must have got revenge by murdering him.

Complicating this, Mrs. Hazzard dies and leaves two letters, one addressed to Patrice for "when you most need help," and a second for both Bill and Patrice. The first letter is a confession that she killed Stephen, which Patrice is supposed to use in the event of one of their arrests. Patrice does not have to use this letter because Bill's story receives corroboration and appears to be true. The second letter, however, rescinds the confession, Mrs. Hazzard admitting that she could not commit murder. The question then is, if she did not kill Georgesson, who did. Although Patrice shot him, he may have already been dead. If he was not dead, either asleep or only wounded, was hers the fatal blow? Then again, if he was dead and Mrs. Hazzard did not kill him, Bill might be guilty—unless his story about the vengeful gamblers was true. There are several suspects with clues pointing to all of them (including Mrs. Hazzard, whose reversal could be a lie). But with Bill and Patrice suspecting each other as the murderer, and neither seeming sure if he or she was the guilty one, their relationship has begun to deteriorate. Patrice knows that, in time, their relationship must crumble like dry, stale bread, that either Bill will leave or she will.

Security and happiness, then, are illusive quests. They may be enjoyed occasionally and temporarily but not permanently. Conscience intervenes and slices through contentment with a double-edged razor of guilt and suspicion. Like Chris Cross in Fritz Lang's *Scarlet Street*, we become victims of our own psychological projections, uncomfortable with ourselves because of our personal faults and secret guilt, uncomfortable with others because we know they are no different from our flawed selves.

One of the main themes in *I Married a Dead Man* concerns how literal and figurative births become a prime determinant in a person's destiny. Born into poverty and squalor, Helen faces a life with few opportunities and expectations. She meets Steve Georgesson, a violent, insensitive product of the slums, develops a relationship with him, and becomes pregnant with his child, all a matter of course in this environment.

However, Fate can influence events, and does. Under the guise (or literary device) of coincidence, it steers Helen onto the train where she meets her pregnant counterpart Patrice Hazzard. It then finagles Patrice into giving Helen her wedding band to wear just before the train wreck. After the tragedy, the dual coincidence of pregnancy and wedding ring ironically enable Helen to be reborn as Patrice into a life of luxury and affluence. At the same time, her baby, Hugh, is born into wealth with all the security and promise that attends such a birth. By becoming Patrice, Helen enables her son to play the changeling who usurps all the rights and riches of the true heir.

As Helen knows, she is not Patrice, and so her "rebirth" is accompanied by guilt and fear. Fate has provided an opportunity for her son to live a life he never could have had as the son of Helen Georgesson, but her scrupulous nature cannot let her accept this opportunity without guilt. Helen has to live a lie if her son is to take advantage of this new life of promise.

A kind of original sin taints these births. Instead of being able to enjoy and appreciate her good fortune at being "born" into the Garden of Eden (Helen's description of Caulfield as all beauty and peace suggests this parallel), she can only anticipate ruin. Heaven on Earth cannot exist, especially for one already stigmatized by a lowly birth. She lives in fear of the day when she must be expelled from the Garden, and she cannot enjoy the golden fruits of her surroundings. The despair comes in the knowledge that all things earthly are transient and mortal.

Related to this, her 17 cents is a symbol of the paradox of the American dream, its inclusive and exclusive qualities. The images imprinted on the coins — Indian-head penny, Lincoln-head penny, buffalo nickel, Liberty-head dime — are associated with American heritage, the mythical pioneer spirit and the American dream. Yet two pennies, a nickel, and a dime are in themselves no great accumulation of wealth and represent the powerlessness of poverty despite the noble values connoted in the inscribed images. Helen comes from a segment of society denied easy access to the American dream. Lack of money means the lack of power and opportunity, so that her only chance to surmount the insurmountable is to get lucky — which she does. Fate manipulates events so she can cross that barrier between poverty and wealth.

Unfortunately, she has a conscience. Integrated into the Hazzard family, she has achieved a large share of the American dream, with wealth, status, and security. But she is uneasy because her good fortune is undeserved — she has not *earned* it through talent or industry. She decides reluctantly to accept it only to insure the future for her son and to comfort her sickly mother-in-law. When the serpent Georgesson enters the Garden called Caulfield, she is prepared, first, to leave, then to defend herself against him. Helen, like Satan in Milton's *Paradise Lost*, finds her Heaven turned into a Hell. This, most revealingly, is the disturbing, unsettling condition of the Woolrich world: happiness is elusive even to one who seems to have it all. Despite the Elysian appearance of Caulfield, despite the Hazzard wealth being extended to Helen and her son, there is an undercurrent of insecurity and sorrow, emotional obstacles to the American dream. Thus, even for Haves like the Hazzards, of whom Helen is now one, that ultimate Heaven on Earth remains an unattainable myth.

Film: No Man of Her Own

1950, Paramount. *D:* Mitchell Leisen. *P:* Richard Maibaum. *Cin:* Daniel L. Fapp. *Sc:* Sally Bensen, Catherine Turney, Mitchell Leisen (uncredited). *Ed:* Alma Macrorie. *Mus:* Hugo Friedhofer. *Prod Des:* Hans Dreier, Henry Bumstead. *Set Des:* Sam Comer, Ray Moyer. *F/X:* Gordon Jennings.

Cast: Barbara Stanwyck (Helen Ferguson/Patrice Harkness), John Lund (Bill Harkness), Jane Cowl (Grace Harkness), Henry O'Neill (Donald Harkness), Richard Denning (Hugh Harkness), Phyllis Thaxter (Patrice Harkness), Lyle Bettger (Stephen Morley), Griff Barnett (Dr. Parker), Milburn Stone (Plainclothes detective), Esther Dale (Josie), Harry Antrim (Ty Winthrop), Catherine Craig (Rosalie Baker), Dooley Wilson (Waiter on train, uncredited), Gordon Nelson (A.J. Finkle, Justice of the Peace), Carole Mathews (Blonde). 98 min.

Mitchell Leisen (1898–1972) was a steady and reliable contributor to the Paramount studio system. Although he worked well into the 1960s, his finest accomplishments came in the 1930s, '40s, and '50s. His directorial output is eclectic, including screwball and romantic comedies (*Easy Living*, 1937; *Midnight*, 1940; *Take a Letter, Darling*, 1943; *The Mating Season*, 1951), musicals (*Swing High, Swing Low*, 1937), costume dramas (*Frenchman's Creek*, 1944), and women's romances (*Death Takes a Holiday*, 1934; *Hold Back the Dawn*, 1941; *Kitty*, 1945). At the callow age of 21, he started his career in film as a costume designer, working with Cecil B. DeMille (*Male and Female*, 1919) and Douglas Fairbanks (*Robin Hood*, 1922; *The Thief of Bagdad*, 1924). Before that, he had studied architectural design, a field which prepared him for his job as art director on all of DeMille's projects between 1925 and 1933, including *The Road to Yesterday* (1925), *The King of Kings* (1927), *The Squaw Man* (1931), and *The Sign of the Cross* (1932). For Leisen, set design became so integral a part of a production that, when he assumed the role of director in 1933, the ambience or "look" of a film became one of his prominent trademarks. His movies consistently shimmered with the sumptuous and sophisticated glamour that epitomized the classic Paramount style.

No Man of Her Own is no exception. At the film's beginning, the well-manicured properties and pleasant, peaceful thoroughfares of neighborhood streets are shot in soft, muted grays and whites that foster an atmosphere of harmony and serenity. Under Leisen's direction, Woolrich's idyllic American city is reconstructed in comparable visual terms.

In the opening of Woolrich's novel, Helen introduces Caulfield as some gloriously tranquil retreat where all the residents are sincere and considerate to the point of exaggerated perfection. Everyone treats each other with generosity and kindness, and Helen, although a pariah in New York City, actually belongs in Caulfield because she possesses these same virtues. However, an Edenic community must have a serpent: enter Stephen, who disrupts everyone's life and then leaves (albeit involuntarily), but not without contaminating their purity and their innocence so they can never reclaim what they once were.

This is Woolrich's story, totally *noir* in the bleakness of its outcome, in how it truncates hope and happiness, in its finale of despair and damnation. But this is not Leisen's story. For the most part, Leisen's film, the first of several adaptations of *I Married a Dead Man*, is extraordinarily tenacious in adhering to the Woolrich story line. Yet in inimitable Hollywood style, it reverses the novel's final collapse into utter despair and caters to popular demand for the happy ending, Despite this, and despite its presenting itself as a woman's "weepy"—the sort of melodrama Leisen was noted for and which could very fittingly serve as a classification for this particular Woolrich novel—the film faithfully renders much of Woolrich's *noir*-ish mood and intent throughout most of the telling.

Leisen uses a similar framing device. As in the novel, Patrice (Barbara Stanwyck as the usurper) narrates the opening scenes, first describing Caulfield with dreamy sentiment, then countering her peaceful ruminations with the refrain, "But not for us ... not for us." She blurts out the catchword "murder," arousing our curiosity. We enter the story apprehensively, uncertainly, knowing we are in the middle of a crisis, but unable to comprehend it. We can tell that the two characters Patrice and Bill (John Lund) love each other, yet we cannot see any reason for this tension, or how murder could fit into this paradisiacal setting.

The phone rings and Bill answers it. He tells Patrice the police are on their way. She calmly puts the baby to bed. The camera holds a medium close-up on her face until it dissolves into a close-up of a Manhattan phone directory, taking us into the flashback that will reveal her past and how she came to her present situation.

Before becoming the wealthy and sophisticated Patrice, the narrator is the destitute Helen Ferguson. She is with child, yet unwed and rejected by her lover Stephen Morley (Lyle Bettger). She tries to telephone, but he doesn't answer. She goes to his apartment and weeps outside his door, sobbing that she doesn't know anyone in New York. Inside, we see a blonde woman (Carole Mathews) furtively lock the door and call to Steve. Steve, minutely remorseful, puts five dollars and a train ticket to San Francisco inside an envelope, which he slides under the door. From this, and from information we learn later, we can infer that Helen is originally from San Francisco, met Steve there, and came to New York with him. Now he is sending her back. She opens the envelope, and the five dollar bill, unnoticed, falls to the floor. She steals pathetically away.

On the train she is befriended by another expectant mother, Patrice Harkness (Phyllis Thaxter), and her husband Hugh (Richard Denning). As in Woolrich's novel, the two women retire to the ladies' room where Patrice tells Helen to try on her ring. "Isn't that supposed to be bad luck?" says Helen. "Oh, nothing bad could happen to me," answers Patrice ironically, seconds before the train crashes. Patrice dies, but Helen survives. In the hospital, doctors perform an emergency cesarean operation to save her baby boy. While recovering, Helen

No Man of Her Own— Patrice (Phyllis Thaxter, left) and Hugh (Richard Denning, far left) invite Helen (Barbara Stanwyck) into a world to which she is not entitled (Paramount, courtesy William Thailing).

learns, because of the wedding ring she wears, that all mistake her for Patrice. She tries to correct them, until she realizes that her private room and her baby's gifts are the result of her being the wife of her dead husband Hugh. She chooses to go along with the charade.

Out of the hospital, she travels to Caulfield where the Harknesses welcome her warmly and treat her and her baby like true family members. When the baby is christened Hugh Donald, the religious ritual sanctions that relationship.

Just when Helen settles into a comfortable routine with her adopted family, she receives a telegram with the questions "Who are you? What are you doing here?" She fears that someone knows her secret. She prepares to leave, but that night Mother Harkness (Jane Cowl) suffers a seizure and Helen stays, knowing how comforting baby Hugh's presence is to her.

Bill takes Helen to a club social where Stephen Morley appears and sets her up for his blackmailing scheme. Later, he coerces her into marriage so that he will be eligible for the money she will inherit when the Harknesses die. Like Woolrich's antagonist, Morley is a consummate villain, purely evil, inexorably selfish and unpitying.

Helen relents, but her contempt for Morley is evident in her face, and during the marriage ceremony, when she mulls over the words, "till death do us part," she intimates that murder is already in her heart. (As a gifted actress, Stanwyck has the incredible ability to produce a blank stare that paradoxically conveys an impassive exterior while telegraphing a dark, turbulent malevolence roiling behind the mask.) After the service, Helen returns home only long enough to get a gun and call a cab. She leaves just as Mother Harkness comes downstairs to find the gun gone and the bullets strewn on the desk.

Helen confronts Steve at the office where he lives. He is lying on the bed, eyes open. She is suspicious that something is wrong, but the gun accidentally goes off in her hand. Bill suddenly appears at the door. She helps him take the body to the railroad yard, where he drops the body from a bridge onto a passing train: "[Steve] stayed on the catwalk — or whatever it's called. His hat didn't. It came off." In other words, Steve has been eliminated, but he has left something behind. No matter how much they try to reverse his corruptive influence and return things to normal, his kind always leaves behind some despicable remnant to taint lives forever and remind them of the black event.

When they arrive home, they find that Mother Harkness has died. The question posed is similar to that in the novel: Who killed Stephen? He already looked dead before Helen fired the gun, so her bullet may have been meaningless. Bill's coincidental arrival suggests he may have been there before Helen. Neither can be sure who did the deed.

However, Leisen does not play with ambiguities very long. Unlike Woolrich, who prevents closure by condemning Helen and Bill to paroxysms of doubt and guilt about themselves and each other, Leisen shows Helen and Bill in tacit agreement that she killed Morley. In the closing frame story, Helen's arrest is pending. She expects to admit her guilt to the police, but the maid Josie (Esther Dale) steps forward with a signed confession from Mother Harkness that she killed Morley. Although the letter is farfetched, Bill is willing to let his mother take the blame; Helen, truthful and noble, won't allow it. When the police arrive, she confesses. However, the detective (Milburn Stone) explains that the bullet from Helen's gun was found in the mattress. Morley was shot with a gun of a different caliber, and in fact, they have the suspect already in custody. In the police car, we see that the murderer is the blonde from Morley's New York apartment, who had warned him he could not get rid of her as easily as he did Helen.

In the final voiceover, Helen as Patrice expresses her belief that happiness has been attained and she and Bill can truly become a part of idyllic Caulfield.

Structurally, Leisen's film is very much akin to Woolrich's novel. The opening frame stories, narrated in the present tense, carry the same ethereal tone with Helen/Patrice describing Caulfield as a kind of small-town utopia. Disrupting the harmony is some unsettling guilt, which prevents the speaker and her family from attaining happiness. Following the introductory frame is the inset story, the bulk of the film told in flashback. Mimicking Woolrich's episodic structure, the film segments Helen's story into a sequence of set scenes, each scene ending with a fade-to-black. In effect, Helen remembers her story in a series of isolated incidents rather than as a smooth transition from one event to the next, even though these isolated incidents are retained in chronological order.

The inset story ends and the closing frame story returns us to the present, Helen and Bill tense as they await the outcome. Leisen makes the greatest deviation from Woolrich here, retaining Woolrich's winding plot twists (the mother's delayed letter, Steve's association with criminals), but revising them so he can opt for the one that offers the most hopeful romantic end. For Leisen's characters, a good heart merits redemption; for Woolrich's characters, regardless of nobleness of purpose, absolution is impossible. The guilt that continues to thrive after Woolrich's story ends is, in the film, removed when Helen, in her final words, declares paradise regained.

Woolrich's title, *I Married a Dead Man*, has both literal and figurative relevance. Most obviously, it refers to Helen's pretending to be the wife of Hugh Hazzard, the victim of a train accident, so that she is, in effect, married to a dead man. The title has wider implications, however, when applied to the other two men in her life. After being blackmailed into marrying Stephen, she literally becomes his widow when he is killed. Then, too, after she marries Bill, their relationship becomes strained with doubt because of Stephen's mysterious death. Bill thought his love would surmount this crisis, but the circumstances are too overwhelming, too relentless, so that emotionally he is a dead man.

Not so in *No Man of Her Own*, which shifts emphasis. In her two incarnations, first as Helen Ferguson and then as Patrice Harkness, Helen fails to establish a lasting relationship with a man. She has had to share two men with other women, and her implicit quest becomes to find a "man of her own." In New York, she loses Steve Morley to a blonde gold-digger. When Morley reappears and she marries him, it is, as he tells her, to salve his mercenary ambitions, not to appease her romantic dreams. At the same time, pretending to be Mrs. Patrice Harkness, she shares the title with the true claimant, so the dead husband is not "her own." With Bill, however, she finally does find a "man of her own" and her quest ends in success and happiness.

The guilt that figures so crucially in Woolrich's *I Married a Dead Man* is retained in *No Man of Her Own*. Guilt is what makes Helen the sympathetic character she is, in both Woolrich's novel and Leisen's film. Helen commits a series of indiscretions, which eventually culminate in the reason for her greatest guilt, murder. First, as an unwed mother, she commits both a moral and social transgression. If Morley would have remained true to their relationship, she may have been able to displace the guilt. His rejection is what turns her into a withdrawn pathetic figure. Pregnancy out of wedlock is a social disgrace and she knows that she cannot expect sympathy from her fellow humans.

Instead, she meets Patrice and Hugh Harkness. Their kindness is an anomaly for a woman in her condition. Although the Harknesses are not aware of her unwed mother status, once we see their generous nature, we realize Helen's predicament would probably not have made a difference anyway. Patrice's aggressive samaritanism creates the circumstances that enable Helen to commit the next indiscretion. Wearing Patrice's ring, she is mistaken for Hugh's wife after the train wreck. She accepts the mistaken identity reluctantly, compromising her honest nature in order to provide her son with greater opportunities to succeed. Her former life style, without hope for betterment, has predetermined her decision.

Later, her guilt over her dishonesty affects her ability to develop a relationship with Bill. She is living a lie, and therefore she feels she is less than the person he thinks her to be. Guilt hampers her desire to fall in love with him and let him fall in love with her, stalls her ability to surrender to happiness in a loving relationship that can lead to marriage.

Finally, when she thinks she has murdered Morley, her guilt creates the greatest complications for her, her child, and the Harknesses who have treated her so selflessly and lovingly. Helen and Bill are able to marry and live together because of their love, but the threat of Morley's death being solved presents an obstacle to their happiness.

Woolrich does not let Helen escape her guilt. She is responsible for all her choices. She chose badly when she chose Steve Georgesson, and everything that follows is the result of that first indiscretion. Even if her choices were influenced by her love for her baby, that does not make them right. In *noir* fashion, Woolrich leaves her in a moral and emotional limbo. She and Bill will only learn what effect her mottled past has on them as time evolves.

Leisen, however, leans toward redemption. Despite her birthing another man's bastard child, despite her imposture, and despite her committing murder, Bill has a love for her which enables him to forgive her and protect her, even to the point of besmirching his mother's good name for the sake of keeping her free. Helen, conscious of her guilt, is too morally upright to stoop that low. She confesses to the plainclothes policeman, and her reward is that the evidence shows her bullet could not have killed Morley. At the moment that she retains her integrity, she receives her reward. The final voiceover explains that at last she has found happiness, that she can openly declare that she belongs in Edenic Caulfield with all the other happy families.

Thematically, Leisen's *No Man of Her Own* is concerned with the same issues as *I Married a Dead Man*, how a fateful power influences life and how wealth and status are the necessary determinants of a person's mobility and freedom in society. Helen and her child are products of the underprivileged society: they have no money, no status, and no prospects. As an unwed mother, she is economically and socially destitute. Bill tells her she was not born until she came to Caulfield, and figuratively this is true. She and her baby are born to a new life of opportunity and security that would have evaded them if not for fate's intervention. Leisen retains Woolrich's string of coincidences that represent fate's manipulating Helen until she comes full-circle, face to face with her abuser, and metes justice on him. Fate's arbitrary control of her life seems to fade when we learn that Helen and Bill despaired needlessly. All the time she was innocent because another had committed the crime.

The predetermined fate that Woolrich imposes on Helen is handled differently in Leisen's film. Leisen retains the image of the 17 cents, shown when Helen takes her unspent nickel out of the phone and places it in her open palm alongside the dime, nickel, and two pennies. However, Leisen is not as complexly descriptive as Woolrich — the only image discernible is the Liberty-head dime, suggesting a link between poverty and freedom, unlike Woolrich's more intricate connotations. This places Helen at the lowest social level, a lone, outcast pregnant woman trapped in extreme poverty. Her experience with the Harknesses helps her to appreciate even more the value of money, the opportunities it opens up, the freedom it offers the possessor who can buy without restraint, declare ownership, and claim status.

Woolrich more logically follows Helen to her bitter end: she does not deserve her claim to the Hazzard fortune despite her kind heart, good will, and uneasy conscience. Leisen feels otherwise. Perhaps he feels Helen's moral sense and selflessness for her child give her a right to some happiness. Though it appears that the Harknesses redeem Helen, it is also true that Helen redeems the Harknesses. By bringing baby Hugh into their household, she fills the void resulting from their tragic loss and keeps them from falling into utter despair. She and her baby give Mother Harkness some tangible reason to live. (Mother Harkness's name is Grace, meaning that Helen redeems "grace" for the family.) This entitles her to some reward. When the police finally visit her, she bravely assumes blame for the crime in order to preserve the reputation of Mother Harkness, that is, of good "grace." Confession makes her worthy of salvation.

There is a sharp contrast between the two outsiders who come to Caulfield. If Helen is a redeemer, Morley is a serpent. He is a totally despicable character without any saving virtues. His name, changed from Georgesson, vaguely links him to Jacob *Marley* from Dickens's *A Christmas Carol*, the business partner and fellow miser of Ebenezer Scrooge, whose main goal in life was material wealth, even if gained at the expense of his neighbors and his own humanity. Such an attitude infects Stephen Morley's personality. When he isn't gloating over his domineering position, he is violently angry over not getting his way. His takeover of the office of Superior Investments symbolizes his "superior" attitude. When Bill peels the handwritten "Stephen Morley" from the door and reveals the original Superior sign beneath it, his gesture suggests how pride ("superiority") brings about its own final and self-obliterating destruction.

One of the remarkable things about Woolrich's *I Married a Dead Man* is how he weaves together three distinct plot patterns into a single *noir* fabric.

No Man of Her Own— Bill (John Lund) and Helen (Stanwyck) hear someone at their door and assume that Fate has caught up with them (Paramount, courtesy William Thailing).

Each of these three patterns can serve as the central conflict for a single story or film, and consequently, an extraordinary number of *films noirs*, adopting one or another of these patterns appear related, if only tangentially, to *I Married a Dead Man*.

The first of these patterns is the "mistaken identity" motif. The issue of identity serves as one of the keystones in *noir*, since every (or nearly every) *noir* includes existential questions about individuality, humanness, and conscience, particularly as related to reasoning, motive, and guilt. Identity or personality is often explored by doubling the protagonist with another character to force comparisons between them that will lead to conclusions about human nature and thematic concepts important to the story. In *Rear Window*, for instance, Thorwald doubles Jeffries and enables us to infer ideas about gender roles in love and marriage. A special category of mistaken identity, and one of the most common, is the Wrong Man theme. In this scenario, the doubling creates confusion between two characters either because they look very much alike, or because something happens, accidentally or intentionally, to cause people to think one character is the other (as it does in the Woolrich and Leisen stories). Hitchcock's *The Wrong Man* (1956), by its very title, serves as one of the seminal works on the issue of mistaken identity. Other examples of films (among which are several adapted directly from Woolrich) include *Phantom Lady* (1944), *Dark Passage* (1947), *The Black Angel* (1947), *Call Northside 777* (1948), *The Big Clock* (1948), *In a Lonely Place* (1950), and *Beyond a Reasonable Doubt* (1956). Generally, the innocent protagonist is blamed for a crime committed by another, the guilty double, but we can see how many of these films try to create variations on this situation. *I Married a Dead* (and *No Man of Her Own*), for instance, receive a fresh twist to the mistaken identity formula in that the innocent Patrice is replaced by an imposter who herself is an innocent victim of circumstance. Woolrich's story foreshadows the well-made French non-*noir Le Retour de Martin Guerre* (1982) — and its remake *Sommersby* (1993) — in which circumstances confuse identities and place the life of the well-meaning double in jeopardy.

In the second pattern, a character's guilty past resurfaces to upset his or her established and successful life in the present. Even more pervasive than "mistaken identity," this is a theme that is extremely critical to most *noirs*, the notion that one cannot escape one's past, that guilt must be punished or that redemption, if attainable at all, requires ordeal and catharsis. *Films noirs* incorporate this pattern especially because it emphasizes guilt as an essential component of human nature. In these stories, a character, already burdened by guilt, has struggled successfully to conceal it, but then another character, personifying conscience or vengeance (or the Erinyes), exposes the truth, and the revelation leads either to tragic consequences or to a chance for redemption. The lengthy list includes films laced with dark cynicism and portentous doom: *Murder My Sweet* (1944), *The Dark Corner* (1946), *The Killers* (1946), *Kiss of Death* (1947), *Out of the Past* (1947), *All My Sons* (1948), *I Walk Alone* (1948), *Criss Cross* (1949), *Act of Violence* (1949), and more recently, *Chinatown* (1974), *Cape Fear* (1991, and the 1962 original), and *Memento* (2000). In *No Man of Her Own*, Helen thinks she can obliterate all memory of her previous sordid existence and assimilate into the splendid life style of the Harknesses, but a despicable figure from that former life intrudes on her dream. The film reverses Woolrich's nihilistic ending and restores hope that Patrice and Bill will find happiness together.

In the third pattern, some disruptive agent infiltrates a secure and stable, if not ideal, community (town, family, institution, organization), upsets the status quo, and forever alters the attitudes of the members (sometimes innocent, sometimes blameworthy) who, their consciences at peace, had been living in blissful ignorance or contented denial. This story is as old as the story of Eden. In American literature, Washington Irving created a variation of it in "The Legend of Sleepy Hollow" and Mark Twain exploited it mercilessly in "The Man Who Corrupted Hadleyburg." Again, the list of *noirs* that employ this plot pattern in various forms and degrees is quite long, among them, *Citizen Kane* (1941), *The Maltese Falcon* (1941), *This Gun for Hire* (1942), *Shadow of a Doubt* (1943), *Gilda* (1946), *The Strange Love of Martha Ivers* (1946), *Nora Prentiss*

(1947), *Pitfall* (1948), *The File on Thelma Jordan* (1949), *Vertigo* (1958), *Cape Fear* (1962), *The Naked Kiss* (1964), and *Mississippi Mermaid* (1969).

It seems very fitting that one of the last of Woolrich's best works should be so rich in its narrative structure as to encompass the central motifs of so many *films noirs*. It suggests not only the influence he had on *noir*, but also the influence that *noir* had on him.

Film: J'ai épousé une ombre

English titles: *I Married a Shadow* and *I Married a Dead Man*
Sara-Films/T.F.1 Films Production (1982). D: Robin Davis. P: Alain Sarde. Cin: Bernard Zitzermann. Sc: Patrick Laurent, Robin Davis. Ed: Marie Castro Vazquez. Mus: Philippe Sarde. Sound: Michel Laurent. Prod Design: Ivan Maussion.
Cast: Nathalie Baye (Hélène Georges/Patricia Meyrand), Francis Huster (Pierre Meyrand), Richard Bohringer (Frank Balit), Madeleine Robinson (Léna Meyrand), Guy Tréjan (Mathieu Meyrand), Victoria Abril (Fifo Pessac), Véronique Genest (Patricia Meyrand), Humbert Balsan (Bertrand Meyrand), Solenn Jarniou (Nelly), Marcel Roche (Pessac), Maurice Jacquemont (Basso, Attorney for the Meyrands), Jean-Henri Chambois (Meyrand family doctor), Christine Paolini (Sick woman), Arlette Gilbert (Wise lady), André Thorent, Nella Barbier, Philippe Guegan, Fernand Guiot, Los Reyes (Musical group). 110 min.

This French version of Woolrich's *I Married a Dead Man* exhibits very high production values that, visually, place it on a par with Leisen's film. The sets and locations are rich and ostentatious; the train wreck is handled with satisfactory special effects; and the actors are all capable and convincing. Unlike Leisen's film, however, which retains most of Woolrich's darker implications, Davis's film is stripped of its *noir* tonalities and themes and treated more like a modern soap opera. Even so, a few points merit comparison.

Woolrich's frame device that sets up the inset story may seem like a simple gimmick, but it is in fact critical for creating a tension that stays with the story until its conclusion. The incongruity between the melancholy tone of Patrice's voice and her idyllic description of Caulfield, and between her insistent love for Bill and her speculation that their love will not endure, infuses the narrative with an apprehension and mystery that beg the reader to pursue events to the end in order to resolve these contradictions. Davis's film, on the other hand, omits this flashback. The story begins at the beginning — that is, with the relationship going sour between the pregnant Hélène (Nathalie Baye, who this same year played Gérard Depardieu's wife in *Le Retour de Martin Guerre*) and her boyfriend Frank Balit (Richard Bohringer) — and events unfold chronologically, in general following the construct of Woolrich's inset story. Davis's film moves soporifically through a linear, superficial plot, unlike Woolrich's story, which is thickly layered with mystery, suspense, and anxiety. Although Hélène's predicament may prompt our sympathy and interest (as it does in Woolrich's novel), without the frame story hinting at murder and lost love, the film lacks the *noir* subtext to suggest that all the characters' actions are predetermined to end in a catastrophic fate. In defense of Leisen's film, although chance redeems his characters at the last moment, the whole of the story feels the burden of doom Patrice had predicted at the start.

Events that steer Hélène's life closely parallel those that guide Helen Georgesson and differ only slightly in content. Both are unwed mothers whose relationship with a scoundrel culminates in an eviction and train ride to a better life. Ironically, that better life was meant for another, but circumstance (the family never knew the pregnant wife) and mistaken identities allow them to live that life for the sake of their newborn child.

Part of the phony daughter-in-law's ability to succeed in her charade rests with the mother-in-law. Like her counterpart in the novel, Mother Léna Meynard (Madeleine Robinson) is an overly sentimental figure. She suffers from some unspecified illness, and the presence of Hélène and her baby becomes therapeutic for her physical and psychological well-being. The film follows the novel in retaining her untimely death and her self-sacrificial confession as important contributions to the suspenseful yet emotional denouement.

Besides omitting the flashback, a convention in most *films noirs*, Davis's film sidesteps all the *noir* techniques related to camerawork and lighting. High-key lighting eliminates all moody, expressionistic shadows, and standard eye-level shots avoid any distortion or disorientation for the viewer. In addition, this adaptation greatly refines the complexities of Woolrich's plot and concentrates on a straightforward plot with nary a twist or turn to hinder the story's reaching its inevitable romantic end. As one example, Hélène is falling in love with Pierre Meynard (Francis Huster). Pierre has a jealous lover, Fifo (Victoria Abril), who tries to discourage Patricia by claiming that Pierre has a good laugh with everyone over Patricia's infatuation. Instead of prolonging this complication and letting it lead to other ironic situations, Davis resolves it in the very next scene. Patricia throws a tirade at Pierre, but he quells her and restores their relationship to romantic equilibrium. And when Frank Balit finally appears, he barely has time to pose a threat to the peace and stability of the Maynard home before he is swiftly and expeditiously eradicated.

This last episode, the death of the prodigal rogue, is pivotal in all versions of *I Married a Dead Man*. In every case, the pretender sets out to kill the vermin who would disrupt the lives of the family she has grown to love. Clearly, she does not do it solely for her own sake or for the sake of her son. She reveres the sanctity of the family and makes a cool, rational decision to kill the evil blackguard who profanes it.

One significant difference, however, between Davis's film and the Woolrich and Leisen versions is that it leaves no doubt that Hélène kills her blackmailing ex-boyfriend. Woolrich offers a plethora of possible conclusions, then selects the one most inconclusive, the outrageous notion that no one knows who killed the offender. This raw *noir* ending is filled with ambiguity that prevents peace of mind in those most susceptible to guilt, those who, if there were a divine justice, should have found some peace and happiness after their ordeal. Leisen invents a happier outcome derived from a circumstance provided in Woolrich's novel: the prodigal rogue has taken up with a proud, vengeful woman who foreshadows the outcome by warning him not to discard her as he did Helen; he fails to heed the warning and she carries out her threat. (This is the same out Richard Benjamin uses to produce a happy ending in his 1996 adaptation, Mrs. Winterbourne.)

Davis opts for one of Woolrich's other optimistic alternatives: Léna Meyrand signs a false confession which removes the guilt from Patricia and Pierre. However, unlike in Woolrich and Leisen, Patricia is unequivocally culpable for Balit's death. She rendezvous with him in a dark wood and stabs him with a knife. Pierre happens along — how he happens to find her in that desolate location is left unexplained — and helps her dispose of the body. The two lovers are complicit in the murder, then, and contrary to Barbara Stanwyck's staunch scruples, they willingly accept Léna's magnanimous gesture to protect their relationship at the expense of her good name.

The film ends with Patricia strolling out to the vineyard to join Pierre who stands there holding her child and looking out over the golden-green fields. Pierre's final comment about little Bertrand suggests the direction of their future: "I think he'll love the vineyards as I do." A general theme in *noir* is that people can never escape their past: either guilt catches up with them and destroys them (*Act of Violence*, 1949) or they have to live the rest of their lives haunted by their crime (*Scarlet Street*, 1945). There may be exceptions, but most films, even *No Man of Her Own*, will advocate that some form of punishment must accompany guilt.

Davis's film suggests that people can escape the sins of their past. If this is a more optimistic statement, breaking with the traditional credo that "crime doesn't pay," then it is also less moralistic. In Woolrich, although she is possibly innocent in Stephen's death, Patrice has committed other "crimes" (premarital sex, illegitimate pregnancy, deceit) that demand retribution. In Leisen's film, the potential for disaster looms as a warning until the very end, when the two lovers and their relationship are redeemed because of some deserving qualities — and a little bit of luck that the real culprit was caught. Davis's film, however, allows Patricia to defy both social and moral standards and still thrive in the end.

In an ironic way, the outcome is not so remote from *noir*, if we consider poetic justice or divine retribution a figment of the imagination. When characters like Jeff Bailey (*Out of the Past*) and Barbara Graham (*I Want to Live!*) are condemned for past mistakes even after they try to reform, or when the innocent are punished for upholding their values (the Bradford Galt character in *The Dark Corner*), why shouldn't the ignoble achieve success after flagrantly transgressing against standards of propriety and morality. At bottom, all these approaches prove the arbitrary nature of fate: if good is not always rewarded, then evil does not always have to be punished.

Film: Mrs. Winterbourne

TriStar Pictures/A&M Films (1996). *D:* Richard Benjamin. *P:* Dale Pollock, Ross Canter, Oren Koules. *Exec P:* Patrick Palmer. *Cin:* Alex Nepomniaschy. *Sc:* Lisa-Maria Radano, Phoef Sutton. *Ed:* Jacqueline Cambas, William Fletcher. *Mus:* Patrick Doyle. *Prod Design:* Evelyn Sakash. *Art Dir:* Dennis Davenport. *Set Decor:* Casey Hallenbeck. *F/X:* Warren Appleby, Tim Good, Michael Kavanaugh, Brian Ricci.

Cast: Ricki Lake (Connie Doyle/Patricia Winterbourne), Shirley MacLaine (Grace Winterbourne), Brendan Fraser (Hugh/Bill Winterbourne), Miguel Sandoval (Paco), Loren Dean (Steve DeCunzo), Susan Haskell (Patricia Winterbourne), Paula Prentiss (Nurse), Peter Gerety (Father Brian), Jane Krakowski (Christine), Cathryn de Prume (Renée), Debra Monk (Detective Lt. Ambrose), Craig Eldridge (Ambrose's partner), Kate Hennig (Sophie), Victor A. Young (Dr. Hopley), Jennifer Irwin (Susan), Justin Van Lieshout and Alec Thomlison (Baby Hughie), Bertha Leveron (Vera), Nesbitt Blaisdell (Homeless man), David Lipman and Jim Feather (Conductors), Irene Pauzer (Woman on train), Thomas Joyce (Jeweler), Johnie Chase (Detective who visits Steve), Tony Munch, Jack Mosshammer, Santino Buda, and Marco Kyris (Steves's loathsome friends), Tom Harvey (Ty Winthrop), Caroline Yli-Loumi (Florist), Peter Fleming (Wedding planner). 105 min.

Richard Benjamin is probably more widely known for his comedic roles (*Good-bye Columbus, Catch-22, The Last Married Couple in America*), but he also has a dozen and a half directorial credits, a few of them outstanding (*My Favorite Year*, 1982; *Racing with the Moon*, 1984; *Mermaids*, 1990). In directing *Mrs. Winterbourne*, he obviously saw how the premise easily disposes itself to ironic comedy and this he exploits freely. Tonally, then, his film lacks any *noir* ambience and strays considerably from Woolrich's nihilistic message. Yet although not a *film noir* and despite the occasional clash between the humor and the more serious moments, the effort is, on the whole, a worthy accomplishment that deserves mention here.

Benjamin follows Woolrich by employing a frame device, but one that greatly deviates from the original in form and concept. The camera pans the dingy motel room of Steve DeCunzo (Loren Dean as Patrica's tormentor). He lies prostrate on his bed, staring vacantly at an Anthony Robbins infomercial on television. Robbins discusses the importance of taking control of one's future, something that no longer applies to Steve, for the camera moves in closer to reveal two small bullet holes in his chest. From this sordid scene, the camera cuts abruptly to bright daylight in front of a church where a wedding is about to take place between Patricia Winterbourne (Ricki Lake in the dual role) and Bill Winterbourne (Brendan Fraser). Grace Winterbourne (Shirley MacLaine) and Father Brian (Peter Gerety) are conversing when a police detective, Lt. Ambrose (Debra Monk), walks up and requests to see Mrs. Winterbourne. Grace acknowledges the title, but Ambrose clarifies that she wants to see Patricia. Ambrose announces that this has to do with the murder of Steve DeCunzo, and Grace readily confesses that she is the murderer. Grace's oral confession emulates the written confession of Mother Hazzard, but unlike

Woolrich's character, Grace does not die before the mystery is solved. This, of course, is important to keep events in line with the more upbeat ending.

From here, the story moves into a flashback intermittently narrated by Connie Doyle (Lake's initial identity). She tells how she leaves Hoboken (versus Woolrich's San Francisco) for New York City to find her destiny. There, she meets Steve and moves in with him until she becomes pregnant and he evicts her. While trying to board the subway, she gets swept by the commuting crowd onto a train bound for Boston. She meets Hugh and Patricia Winterbourne, the young lady pregnant like herself. Tragedy strikes when the train derails. Patricia and Hugh are killed. Connie, wearing Hugh's wedding ring because Patricia told her to try it on, wakes in a hospital where she discovers her baby has been born and she has been cared for by the Winterbournes who have mistaken her for Hugh's wife.

Much of Woolrich's story is intact here. Connie tries to rectify the mistake, but concern for Hugh and a liking for the feeble but feisty Grace keep her from telling the truth. One difference is that Bill is Hugh's identical twin. He is suspicious of Connie, and after he sees her accidentally sign her true name on a check, he is ready to expose her. (The writing gambit is used in all versions of the story.) The turning point for Bill (as in all the versions) comes when Grace declares she will name Connie and baby Hugh beneficiaries in her will, but Connie protests vehemently, thereby convincing Bill that she is not after their money. His attitude toward her changes, and he actually falls in love with her.

Like the pond-scum vermin of Woolrich's novel and subsequent adaptations, Steve DeCunzo, evil incarnate, turns up and foists a malicious blackmail scheme on her. (Unlike in previous versions, he does not force her into marriage to give himself legal claims on the estate that will one day come to her.) When Connie confronts him at gunpoint in his motel room, we can see he is already dead. She realizes it, too, but she trips on a toy and fires the gun into the ceiling. Bill, happening to be nearby, rushes into the room. Meanwhile, Paco (Miguel Sandoval as the gay chauffeur) is outside the motel, sitting by himself in the family Rolls Royce and spying on DeCunzo. The narrative returns to the frame story, the Winterbourne wedding day, where Grace has just confessed to Ambrose that she is the murderer. Her three family members step forward and blurt out their guilt, each trying to protect the other. We are fairly sure that Patricia is innocent, but Bill, Paco, and Grace have no clear alibi and, at this point, either of them could very well be the murderer. (Benjamin plays with the ambiguity humorously and touchingly, a variation on the Woolrich ending where multiple suspects and several possible solutions create confusion that leads to his more tragic consequences.)

The denouement reveals that Steve's second pregnant girlfriend is the confessed killer. (Benjamin borrows the ending invented for Leisen's film.) Connie tells Grace the truth, which she accepts, and all parties return to the church where Connie marries Bill under her real name, thus restoring her original identity, legitimizing the marriage, and putting an end to the charade.

One fresh idea incorporated into *Mrs. Winterbourne*, which appears to be a logical deviation from Woolrich's initial conception, is not simply to present Connie as an uncouth street urchin, as Helen Georgesson is, but to make this woman, who is not to the manor born, ignorant of certain upper-class proprieties. Benjamin uses her lack of social grace for humorous effect, having her stumble with gaffs and blunders, groping for the proper behavior. Sometimes this succeeds; at other times, it approaches silliness (her clothes taken from the dead Patricia's wardrobe fit her like a rug; she drags her cuff through the gravy dish; she battles with the servant over serving the food; and so on).

The name Winterboune in the title is ambiguous in that it refers to four women: Grace's mother-in-law, already dead but referred to as a staunch repository of stiff family tradition; Grace herself, who knows how Connie must feel in her unfamiliar environment and tries to make her comfortable; Patricia, the legitimate wife of Hugh; and Connie Doyle, the fraud. When Connie stands with Bill before the marriage altar and the priest asks her, "Patricia, will you take this man?," she answers no, then sets the record straight by saying, "I, Connie Doyle, will take this man." She takes the name legitimately as the fourth Mrs. Winterbourne.

The name Winterbourne is also a pun. If winter is associated with death, then all the Mrs. Winterbournes are ironically "born" to death in some way. Grandmother Winterbourne is already dead. Grace Winterbourne has a chronic condition that keeps her at the brink of death. Patricia Winterbourne dies in the train wreck. And Connie, in using her name, dies to her old way of life. When Connie meets the woman who murdered Steve, the woman says, "I thought you died." Connie answers, "I did." She did die, metaphorically, and is born to a whole new existence. This connects in a way to one of the main ideas in Woolrich's story, how fate is often linked to birth, particularly in respect to class status. However, the film reverses the outcome faced by Woolrich's heroine. Connie has no guilt or fear or dread of the future, only expectations of happiness with the man of her dreams in a new life of wealth and leisure.

Benjamin's frame story reduces Helen Georgesson's cheerless prologue to one key issue. Steve lies murdered on his motel bed while the television blares with psychic guru Anthony Robbins pandering his pseudo-philosophy about controlling one's *destiny*. (Connie quotes her mother's advice: "Destiny is waiting for you. You just gotta find it.") The irony, of course, is that the dead man "watching" the show is proof to the contrary, that our destiny is out of our hands. Connie gets on the same train as the Winterbournes by *accident*: she gets dragged along by a throng of people who set her on the wrong "track." Everything that follows is the result of the train *accident*. Chance and accident depict fate's arbitrariness. Patricia lets Connie try on her wedding band and dispels her fear that letting another wear it can bring bad luck. With faith in her health, her happiness, and her prospects for the future, she declares: "I couldn't have bad luck." Connie slips the ring on her finger, and seconds later, the train crashes. Hugh and Patricia are killed; Connie survives. There is no divine judge to mete out the proper deserts to the likes of Steve DeCunzo and Hugh and Patricia Winterbourne. All people, good and evil, suffer pain and joy. Connie had to endure both extremes, for tragedy and triumph come to the righteous and the sinful without discrimination. *Mrs. Winterbourne* is not a *noir* film, but it does emphasize that one *noir* concept.

Made-for-Television Movie: She's No Angel

2001, Lifetime Network. *D:* Rachel Feldman. *P:* Pierre David, David DeCrane, Rick Eyler, Anita Gershman, Larry Gershman, Tracey Gold, Ken Sanders, Chris H. Ulrich, Noel A. Zanitsch. *Cin:* Steve Adcock. *Sc:* Rachel Feldman. *Ed:* Frederick Wardell. *Orig Mus:* Richard Bowers, Steve Pierson. *Set Dec:* Jennifer Knepshield.

Cast: Tracey Gold (Liddy Carlyle), Kevin Dobson (Donald Shawnessy), Dee Wallace-Stone (Maureen Shawnessy), Cameron Bancroft (Jed Benton), Jeffrey Meek (Jackie Furst), Terry Hoyos (Blanca), Michelle Jones (Catherine Shawnessy), Nathan Anderson (Sean Shawnessy), June June (Diane), Ann Walker (Dorothy), Seamus Dever (Cricket), Boris Cabrera (Daniel), David Hunt Stafford (Dr. Bennett), Ogy Durham (Tanya), David Parker (Officer), Victor Talmadge (Townsperson), GiGi Erneta (Photographer). 120 minutes.

Why director/screenwriter Rachel Feldman did not credit Cornell Woolrich as the source for her made-for-television film is not clear. She obviously took her material from the two previous Woolrich adaptations, *Mrs. Winterbourne* and *J'ai épousé une ombre*, so the omission is rather flagrant. A synopsis clearly shows that the story follows the same general blueprint.

Instead of the introductory relationship between the unwed mother and her abusive boyfriend in Woolrich's story, Feldman's film begins violently with two men attempting to rape Liddy Carlyle (Tracey Gold). Feisty and defiant, she gets hold of a knife and stabs both assailants, killing one and wounding the other. Whereas Helen had set out on a train, Liddy manages to hitch a ride with two newlyweds, Sean and Catherine Shawnessy (Nathan Anderson and Michelle Jones), who are traveling by car on their honeymoon. During their conversation, Catherine lets Liddy try on her wedding ring—the very moment before the Shawnessy car crashes head-on into a truck. (The automobile accident replaces the train wreck in the Woolrich and earlier film stories.) Only Liddy survives. As in the previous versions, she is recuperating in the hospital when she discovers that the dead groom's parents, in this case Donald (Kevin Dobson) and Maureen Shawnessy (Dee Wallace-Stone, who earlier appeared in *I'm Dangerous Tonight*), mistake her for their as-yet-unseen daughter-in-law. With no prospects and nowhere to go, Liddy encourages their misperception. She accepts their hospitality and begins to enjoy her new life style of carefree wealth. (They own vineyards as the Meyrands do in *J'ai épousé une ombre*.) Sean's best friend (rather than a brother) begins to have romantic designs on the supposed young widow. Catherine, meanwhile, begins to experience bouts of nausea and she learns that she is pregnant. At the same time, the wounded rapist, substituting for the philandering, opportunistic boyfriend in Woolrich's story, runs across Liddy's picture in the newspaper's society column. Because he knows her secret history, he plans to locate her and extort money from her.

The parallels are more than coincidental. Perhaps it proves that a good story, devised by a creative writer like Cornell Woolrich, deserves repeated retelling.

"For the Rest of Her Life"

Short story, first published in *Ellery Queen's Mystery Magazine*, May 1968; reprinted in *Angels of Darkness*, The Mysterious Press, 1978.

In the mid–1930s and into the early 1940s, when Woolrich shifts his literary ambitions from mainstream realistic fiction to the sensational pulps, he tests his new genre with some of the most outrageously bizarre and shockingly offensive situations that he can concoct. Characters display the most despicable sides of human nature or find themselves in the eeriest of predicaments. Live burials ("Graves for the Living," 1937), drug orgies ("Marihuana," 1941), satanic intervention ("I'm Dangerous Tonight," 1937), occult phenomena ("Dark Melody of Madness," 1935), or creatively grotesque murders ("Mind over Murder," 1943) become trademarks of his febrile imagination. His output in the mid–1940s may tone down the outlandishness, but he never really strays far from the seamy side of life, both the external landscape of decrepit neighborhoods and the internal wasteland of degenerate humanity. The dregs of society, the basest of its environs and its people, are what most of Woolrich's writings explore, infringing on restricted physical and psychological areas that most would consider taboo.

Toward the end of his life, Woolrich writes two stories exploiting the most hideously repulsive of human behaviors, incest and sadism. In *Into the Night*, a woman falls in love with the man she had planned to assassinate. In ironic Woolrichian fashion, he turns out to be her estranged brother whom she had not seen since he was a child. The mistake could have been an innocent one, except that the man *knew* who she was and let the romance proceed anyway. Of two novels that Woolrich left unfinished at the time of his death, *Into the Night* is the one more nearly complete, although it lacked a definite beginning and ending and it fell short of the consistently grueling intensity of his more notorious successes. Even so, most of its internal story was intact, and the task of editing and fleshing out the work was given to Lawrence Block. Block is a capable and reputable mystery writer, but he stumbled over the plot line on this one, trying to insert a romantically hopeful ending where it is clear that Woolrich's characters had damnation tattooed all over them.

The second work is the short story "For the Rest of Her Life." This is the last of Woolrich's stories that he sees published before his death on September 25, 1968. It is an astounding excursion into one of those secret abhorrent worlds that people, busying themselves with their everyday septic and sanitary routines, would rather deny exists. The writing recalls the author at the peak of his literary powers, stirring deep feelings of disgust for a husband's cruel perversion and fraying the nerves when the wife tries desperately to free herself from her living hell.

While vacationing in Rome, Linda Harris meets "a personable-looking man," Mark Ramsey. They meet again in New York City and get married. A series of odd events begin to expose him for what he is, a sadist. On their honeymoon at a resort in New Hampshire, he spills scalding tea on a waitress, supposedly an accident. And after he tours the lake in a motorboat, it is discovered that he had dragged a dog on a towline, although he claims the creature must have got snagged in the ropes.

Linda meets Garrett Hill at a New Years party. They become friends and the friendship grows into love. When Garrett makes a few tender advances toward her, she overreacts with revulsion and he quickly realizes the nature of her husband's psychological perversion and what it has done to her. It is obvious that, before she married, Linda had little experience in romance because she thinks any physical show of affection is supposed to have "pain attached to it." Although Garrett tells her to leave Mark for her own safety, she is reluctant, for "she not only feared fear, she feared rescue from fear."

On a Friday, Garrett finally convinces her to run away with him. She returns home to get money and her birth certificate. As a rule, Mark stays in the city during the week and returns to their Pittsfield home for the weekend. He happens to phone while she is gathering her things and his snide comments arouse her fear that he suspects her conspiracy with Garrett. Shortly after, the arrival of a car evokes her intense fear that Mark has come home. She hides in her closet. Fortunately, it is Garrett. He helps her to the car and they set out together, but as he drives, Linda's trepidation inflames her imagination and she believes the car behind them is Mark's. Garrett speeds faster and faster until he loses control and collides with a truck. Garrett is killed. Linda survives, but is left paralyzed from the waist down. Showing no despondency or self-pity, she expects to go into a residence where she will be cared for. The doctor, however, unaware of her situation, gleefully announces that she has a loving husband willing to take care of her at home. In a stupor, partially from drugs, partially from numbed emotions, she looks at her husband as he wheels her out of the hospital and deciphers "in his shining eyes and in the grim grin he showed his teeth in" his unspoken thought, "*Now* I've got you."

On the narrative level, "For the Rest of Her Life" is economically written, with elliptical references that convey meaning without elaborate, graphic description. Garrett (and the reader) interprets Linda's predicament on the basis of a few understated occurrences: her expectation that hurt must accompany a kiss; her fearful withdrawal when he tries to shake her hand; her revulsion when he offers her a cigarette. The nature and extent of those forbidden acts that go on behind closed doors are left to our imaginations. Woolrich also manages to achieve the greatest tension in the most compactly described scenes. The two main suspense sequences, when Linda waits at home for Garrett but fears that Mark has arrived there first, and when Garrett and Linda race along the road to elude the uncertain menace behind them, are skillfully constructed, starting with a simple, mundane event that builds gradually into a terrifying crescendo and ends in an emotion-ripping climax. The denouement is all the more intensely and horribly wrenching because it is described in a flat, impassive tone that reflects Linda's mental state, her mind stupefied by drugs and numbed by depleted emotions, her will shattered with a defeatist resignation to spend the "rest of her life" with her demonic tormentor.

In one respect, Mark and Linda play the reverse roles of Louis Durand and Bonny Castle (*Waltz into Darkness*). Unlike the doting husband who lets idyllic romance with the woman of his dreams blind his eyes to reality, Mark takes total control, beating his wife into submission and using fear to imprison her mind as well as her body. Like Durand, Mark wishes to possess his wife completely; unlike Durand, who finally wins Bonny over with his devotion, Mark has the malevolent personality to accomplish his desire with physical force and psychological ploys. If Durand had more of Mark in him, one wonders if the strong-willed, independent Bonny would have succumbed like Linda.

Woolrich combines three plot elements to enhance the conflict of his story. The first is male dominance: Mark marries Linda to legitimize his control over her, the husband acting as master of the household. The notion that "power corrupts" is one Woolrich has used before, an authority figure overstepping the bounds of humanity and consideration and turning tyrannical. In "Dead on Her Feet," for instance, an overzealous police detective makes a suspect dance with the corpse of a murdered taxi dancer. The ordeal drives the suspect insane, although it is learned later that he was innocent. In "Nightmare," too, Detective Cliff Dodge, when he thinks his brother-in-law Vince is using him, badgers him physically and emotionally as if his position as a representative of the law gives him that right.

A second plot element is sexual deviance. Mark's sadism is one of many types of abnormal behavior that Woolrich inserts when he wants to depict the demented, perverted side of human nature. In "Face Work," Militis's branding his girls with a hot poker shows that he finds pleasure in cruelty and symbolizes his sadistic sexual aberrations. In *Hotel Room* (1958), a deposed gangster revels in watching his henchmen dance with their women in sensuous, provocative ways. Voyeurism is also the character's motive in "Rear Window," although the sexual aspect of the pastime is suppressed. The strongest and most harrowing precedent for Mark's behavior occurs in *Black Alibi*, where police chief Robles turns sexual rape into a sadistically bloody ritual of mutilation and murder.

D.O.A. — Although he may fundamentally be a principled person, the *noir* protagonist earns no reprieve if he commits even the slightest indiscretion. Frank Bigelow (Edmond O'Brien) is guilty of entertaining promiscuous desires when he should have remained faithful to his girlfriend Paula (Pamela Britton, left), and for this momentary lapse into self-indulgence, he pays the ultimate price (United Artists).

The third element Woolrich weaves into his story is one of his most frequently used *noir* conventions, the role of fate in manipulating characters to its arbitrary ends. He broadcasts its role in an overt remark at the very beginning:

> Every life is a mystery. And every story of every life is a mystery. But it is not what *happens* that is the mystery. It is whether it *has* to happen no matter what, whether it is ordered and ordained, fixed and fated, or whether it can be missed, avoided circumvented, passed by; *that* is the mystery.
>
> ... If she had come along the Via Piemonte that day, but 10 minutes later than she did, would it *still* have happened? Therein lies the real mystery. And no one ever knows, and no one ever will.

This is Woolrich again pondering Macbeth's dilemma, inquiring whether events are preordained and will occur with or without one's active participation, or whether one's free will gives one the power to make choices that will influence outcomes. "For the Rest of Her Life" allegorizes fate's harsh injustice by depicting the intersection of two polarized lives, one completely innocent, the other vile and detestable. The incident gives rise to the question Robert Frost asks at the end of his poem "Design" where a flower, spider, and moth come together in a ritual of death

> What had that flower to do with being white,
> The wayside blue and innocent heal-all?
> What brought the kindred spider to that height,
> Then steered the white moth thither in the night?
> What but design of darkness to appall?

If we accept that "all things come alike to all" (Ecclesiastes 9:2), we can accept that Linda, innocent though she is, has to submit to Mark's cruelty for a time. However, we like to believe that suffering will eventually reach an end, that the sufferer will escape her ordeal and redemption will follow. When Linda and Garrett "make plans for her liberation and her salvation," the expectation is that she will at last fulfill her dream and find release from her tribulation and love with a worthy suitor. This is not to be. Garrett dies and Linda's paralysis leaves her even more helplessly bound in Mark's vise-like grasp. Thus, misfortune does not have to have a stopping point; things may go from worse to still worse. If Woolrich is again drawing from Shakespeare, he may have been inspired by the scene in *Macbeth* where the tyrant has ordered the deaths of Macduff's wife and children, innocents killed because of their incidental importance, not because of any guilt that merited retribution. Or Woolrich may have found some ideas in *King Lear* where the characters who deserve salvation never find it. Evil is so rampant and so overwhelming that it moves forward like a juggernaut, destroying its proponents along with its opponents. Nobility and goodness do not make one immune to the destruction that comes from wickedness. Such is often the verdict in Woolrich's *noir* universe.

Film: Martha

1973, WDR (Made for German television). *D:* Rainer Werner Fassbinder. *P:* Peter Märthesheimer, Fred Ilgner. *Cin:* Michael Ballhaus. *Sc:* Rainer Werner Fassbinder. *Ed:* Liesgret Schmitt-Klink. *Mus:* Max Bruch (uncredited). *Prod Des:* Kurt Rabb. Art *Dir:* Lothar Schultz.
  Cast: Margit Carstensen (Martha Heyer/Martha Salomon), Karlheinz Böhm (Helmuth Salomon), Barbara Valentin (Marianne), Peter Chatel (Kayser), Gisela Fackeldey (Mother Heyer), Adrian Hoven (Father Heyer), Ortrud Beginnen (Erna von Skratch), Günter Lamprecht (Dr. Salomon), Ingrid Caven (Ilse Salomon, uncredited), El Hedi ben Salem (The Libyan stranger), Wolfgang Schenck (Mr. Meister), Rudolf Lenz (Porter), Kurt Raab (Secretary), Lilo Pempeit (Lieselotte Eder), Peter Berling, Elma Karlowa, Heide Simon. 116 min.

In the 1920s and '30s, director Tod Browning frequently explored society's sub-cultures, those mysterious substandard recesses to which people were exiled because of behaviors and physical features that marked them as "different." In films like *The Unknown* (1927), *Freaks* (1932) and even *Dracula* (1931, the first film in the Gothic horror cycle), he used German Expressionist techniques and thematic ideas that foreshadowed *film noir*, while he delved into the shadow lives of monsters and grotesques and revealed that they harbored feelings and desires not so remote from those of supposedly "normal" people.

One of Browning's heirs apparent who focused on quirky, idiosyncratic individuals alienated from mainstream society is Rainer Werner Fassbinder, who was a driving force behind the New German Cinema of the 1970s and an avid admirer of Jean Luc Godard and French New Wave techniques. In examining and developing his characters, his "concern was always with outsiders. His is a cinema of losers—criminals, poor people, prostitutes, homosexuals, foreigners, blacks, and other despised people at the fringes of society. His characters are sad and alone. They yearn for love and acceptance in a world obsessed with status, material wealth, and bourgeois respectability" (Gianetti and Eyman 440).

This observation by Gianetti and Eyman provides a concisely appropriate description of the main characters in *Martha*, defining their eccentricities and motivations. Fassbinder uses Woolrich's story as a schematic, then fleshes it out with fuller development of the two principals, Martha (Margit Carstensen in Linda's role) and Helmuth (Karlheinz Böhm in Mark's role). Placing *Martha* alongside "For the Rest of Her Life," we see that Fassbinder expanded Woolrich's story into something even more intensely disturbing, a conflict filled with more ramifications than the original. Although doubtful as a *noir* entry, it successfully adapts Woolrich's plot, theme, and tone and approaches the accomplishments of Hitchcock's *Rear Window* and Tetzlaff's *The Window*.

In Rome on vacation, Martha Heyer and her father (Adrian Hoven) are sightseeing when he has a heart attack and dies. During the commotion, someone steals her purse. She visits the German embassy for help, and while walking up to the building, she passes a handsome but stern-faced gentleman. They do not talk or even acknowledge each other, but the encounter leaves a lasting impression. When Martha returns to Germany, she attends the Salomons' dinner party and learns that her host's brother, Helmuth, is the man she passed that day. Martha feels uneasy with him, but is attracted to him and marries him when he asks her. Quickly, though, he dispels her expectations of a tender, loving relationship when he treats her rudely and contemptuously. Although she tolerates his cruelty and is dotingly dependent on him, in time, she starts to fear him. One night, when he announces that he brought home a gift for her, she interprets it to mean that he intends to kill her. She appeals for help from her former co-worker, Mr. Kayser (Peter Chatel), and he flees with her in his car. Hysterical with fear that her husband is in the car behind them, Martha grabs the wheel and causes an accident. The car that was following them stops on the road, and the driver who gets out to help them is an unwitting stranger.

In the hospital, the doctor tells Martha that Mr. Kayser is dead and that her legs are irreversibly paralyzed. She is content, however, until the doctor tells her that her loving husband plans to take care of her. She screams in terror and has to be sedated. Her husband comes to take her home. In a quietly tense final scene, he steers her wheelchair down the hall and into an elevator while she sits ominously still and complacent, stoically impassive to the horrors she must know are yet to come.

Woolrich establishes the central conflict in his short story by forcing a collision between two basic but affective antithetical positions, Linda's fragile innocence and Mark's perverse sadism. Fassbinder, rather than treat his main characters on this superficial level, endows Martha with a family that gives her a personal history and explains to some extent her abnormal behavior. Unlike in Woolrich's story where the intimate horrors of the husband-wife relationship are implied, we are allowed a peek into the domestic life of Helmuth and Martha, to see the odd ways they interact with each other.

Mr. Heyer is partially to blame for his daughter's odd behavior. When he has his heart attack on the Spanish Steps in Rome, she runs to his aid, but when she tries to cradle him in her arms, his dying words, spoken firmly and coldly, are an order for her not to touch him. Tactile exchange is a kind of wordless communication connoting many possible expressions of intimacy, love, closeness, caring, support, and so on. Mr. Heyer's revulsion for contact has obviously forced Martha to repress this natural urge, and although she hungers for it, she has learned to control it. (The act of touching has similar symbolic meaning in Danny DeVito's 1989 black comedy *The War of the Roses*. After the husband and wife, trapped together on their chandelier, have plummeted to their deaths, the husband makes a dying gesture of reconciliation by reaching out to touch her arm; she slowly and delicately takes his hand—and flings it away.) We soon learn that in addition to his revulsion for affectionate contact, Mr. Heyer was highly critical of his daughter and extremely domineering in his home, forbidding Martha and his wife to drink or smoke.

Martha's seeing Helmuth for the first time is the pivotal coincidental moment of the film: her father has just died and the man who will become her surrogate father quickly moves in to replace him. That fate is an influential factor is implied in Fassbinder's extraordinarily dynamic camera movement to denote the significance of the moment: he rotates the camera 360 degrees around the two figures as they pass each other. The disorienting shot signifies that Martha's life has changed as a result of her father's death, but by traveling full circle, she comes back to where she started, about to live her life with a self-centered man just like her father, who will control her, dominate her, and dictate her behavior. Helmuth is but a variation of Martha's dysfunctional father: he allows her to touch him intimately only when he is in the mood for sex, and when he does, he becomes violent and abusive. Starved for an outward display of affection, she accepts his abuse, unable to discriminate between sadism and genuine lovemaking.

Whereas Woolrich limits his sadist's perversion to sexual abuse, Fassbinder's Helmuth exerts tyranny over every facet of Martha's life. Going beyond Scotty's (James Stewart) obsession to transform an ordinary salesgirl (Kim Novak) into the exotic woman of his dreams in *Vertigo* (1958), Helmuth exercises a slowly progressive plan for total domination. Softly, and then, if she resists, violently, he determines where she should smoke, what books she should read, what music she should listen to, what she should cook, and when she should grant him use of her body. In *Vertigo*, Scotty thinks he is convincing Judy to change her appearance out of love for him, when she really does it out of guilt for having earlier betrayed his love. Helmuth, more aware than Scotty of how to use psychological manipulation, preys on Martha's naïveté, guilt complex, and eagerness to please. At the Salomons' house party, Helmuth asks her why she should fear her mother: "You're a grown woman, aren't you?" She blurts out, "No, I'm not." In truth, her father caused her arrested development, hindered her maturity, made her a perpetual child. She is confused about propriety and priority. On the Spanish steps, she is torn between devoting attention to her dead father and locating her stolen purse. At the German embassy, despite the tragedy of the moment, she feigns complete control of her emotions with trivial banter and harsh high-handed words for her mother. She knows nothing about this horrid life style Helmuth shows her and she assumes she is the one who is wrong because she does not understand it. Experience is a double-edged sword: to acquire it, one must forfeit one's innocence, but once one has it, one is better informed and prepared to deal with the wicked cozeners and grifters who try to take advantage of the uninitiated. Inexperienced in the ways of relationships, Martha pretends to know more than she does, and her flippant façade belies her ability to cope with Helmuth.

Kayser's character differs from Garrett, his counterpart in Woolrich's story, whose love for Linda is his reason for abetting her escape from her husband. Kayser extends his friendship to Martha, but they do not fall in love. When she fears that Helmuth threatens her life, she runs to Kayser because she does not have anyone else. He helps her not out of love, but out of concern for her safety. This recalls one of the possible alternatives in *The Chase*, where Lorna, to escape her vicious husband, could have enlisted Chuck's help out of desperation, not because she sees some romantic future with him.

It appears very likely that Fassbinder consciously crafted his screenplay as a complement to another story dealing with a husband-wife relationship, Henrik Ibsen's *A Doll House*. In Ibsen's play, Nora has lived a narrow, inexperienced life with a father who failed to prepare her for the wider, harsher world outside her door. She moves directly from her father's house to that of her husband who continues to reinforce her sheltered existence, reinforcing her infantilism and stifling her personal growth and maturity. In Fassbinder's film, Nora becomes Martha and Helmer becomes (ironically named) Helmuth, and the two couples' situations are variations on the kind of relationship that develops when one partner dominates the other. Many critics have debated that the slamming of the door at the end of *A Doll House* is a symbol of women's emancipation (validly argued). Fassbinder uses Woolrich's story to suggest that, although Nora's gesture may have been a bold statement for herself as an individual, suppression of women within the household is still rampant among the general population. Whether it be the man or the woman, if one wields the mace of domestic power menacingly over the other, inequality and dictatorial rule will undermine the health and validity of their relationship.

As the source for *Martha*, "For the Rest of Her Life" belongs to a specific category of *film noir* where, instead of the *femme fatale* endangering the male, it is the male who jeopardizes the life of the female. In *noir*, the destructive *femme fatale* can operate without any definite motive; Kathie Moffat, Elsa Bannister, and Phyllis Dietrichson do what they do because they are inherently wicked. When a man turns evil, however, he seems to have some justification. Burt Lancaster in *Sorry, Wrong Number*, for instance, can offset his guilt by claiming a logical, legitimate motive for killing wife Barbara Stanwyck. In other cases, the male is a casualty of war or he rebels against social repression. Sometimes he is simply mad, but the madness is itself a symptom of some social turmoil or imbalance and the male personifies that ill. In films such as *Gaslight, Beware My Lovely, Cause for Alarm, Rage in Heaven, The Secret Fury, The Two Mrs. Carrolls, Shadow of a Doubt*, and *Julie*, a man's sanity becomes clouded by some obsession (jealousy, hate, greed) and he shows an excessive need to control a woman (or women) for his own demented purpose. There are also other films, such as *The Chase*, where the male (Roman, in this case) is not insane, but he is driven nonetheless to manipulate, control, or even kill the female. *Sleeping with the Enemy*, a consideration as a neo-*noir*, has some strong parallels with Woolrich's story and seems a positive variation of Fassbinder's film. Fleming's 1941 *Dr. Jekyll and Mr. Hyde* comes at the very beginning of the classic *noir* cycle and contains definite *noir* characteristics, especially the conflict between guilt and innocence, its central theme. Significantly, its primary relation to Fassbinder's film is the role Hyde (Spencer Tracy) plays as an amoral, unconscionable sadist. He subjects Ivy (Ingrid Bergman) to physical and mental brutalities, turning a carefree street urchin into a cowering child. He imprisons her in their love nest (as Helmuth did with Martha) and beats her into submission, eventually carrying his violence to an extreme and killing her. (The most bizarre irony of the film is that he kills her because she flirted with Jekyll; that is, he murders her because he was jealous of himself.)

An implied question is what drives men to act this way, to demand that their women become totally submissive and strictly follow the rules they have established (a dream evolving finally into the ultimate male misogynistic fantasy, the science-fiction thriller *The Stepford Wives*, 1975). One answer relates to the social upheaval that resulted from World War II. Women were required to replace their absent men in the job force, and when the men returned, they found themselves displaced, the women no longer feeling obliged to return to their traditional domestic duties. Symbolically, then, the *noir* male struggles to reclaim his lost status in the family and community, lashing out at the female who usurped his position and his potency.

Another answer may be contained in the 1952 *film noir*, *Don't Bother to Knock*. Nightclub singer Anne Bancroft severs her relationship with wisecracking boyfriend Richard Widmark because he does not have an "understanding heart." The male has developed a callousness toward life, a cynical, skeptical, inconsiderate attitude that acts as a defense mechanism to protect him against a hurtful world. The fragile male ego, once bruised, becomes suspicious of sentiment. This is Robert Ryan in *On Dangerous Ground* and Victor Mature in *Gambling House*. It could also be Fassbinder's Helmuth Salomon (and Woolrich's Mark Ramsey), but no explanation is offered for his cruel offensiveness toward his wife. Without that explanation, he becomes a symbol of the evil that pervades the world and indiscriminately assaults the innocent as well as the guilty without concern for justice or deserving. In other words, he is wicked without cause, a male version of *noir's* most heinous *femmes fatales*.

Bibliography

Bazin, André. "In Defense of Mixed Cinema." *What Is Cinema?* Vol. 1. Ed. and trans. Hugh Gray. Berkeley: University of California Press, 1967. 53–75.

Benvenuti, Stefano, and Gianni Rizzoni. *The Whodunit: An Informal History of Detective Fiction*. Trans. Anthony Eyre. New York: Collier Books, 1981. Trans. of *Il romanzo giallo*.

Borde, Raymond, and Étienne Chaumeton. *A Panorama of American Film Noir, 1941-1953*. Trans. Paul Hammond. San Francisco: City Lights Books, 2002. Trans. of *Panorama du film noir américain*. 1955.

———. "Towards a Definition of Film Noir." Trans. Alain Silver. *Film Noir Reader*. Eds. Silver and Ursini. 17–25.

Brady, Frank. *Citizen Welles: A Biography of Orson Welles*. New York: Doubleday, 1989.

Christopher, Nicholas. *Somewhere in the Night: Film Noir and the American City*. New York: Free Press, 1997.

Conrad, Peter. *The Hitchcock Murders*. London: Faber and Faber Limited, 2000.

Cook, David A. *A History of Narrative Film*. New York: W.W. Norton, 1996.

Cressey, Paul G. *The Taxi-Dance Hall: A Sociological Study in Commercialized Recreation and City Life*. Chicago: Chicago University Press, 1932. New York: Greenwood Press, 1968.

Dickos, Andrew. *Street with No Name: A History of the Classic American Film Noir*. Lexington: University Press of Kentucky, 2002.

Flinn, Tom. "Three Faces of *Film Noir*." *The Velvet Light Trap* 5 (1972). Rpt. in *Film Noir Reader 2*. Eds. Silver and Ursini. New York: Limelight Editions, 1999. 35–43.

Frank, Nino. "Un nouveau genre 'policier': L'aventure criminelle." *L'Écran Français* (August 28, 1946). Rpt. in *Film Noir Reader 2*. Eds. Silver and Ursini. New York: Limelight Editions, 1999. 15–19.

Gianetti, Louis, and Scott Eyman. *Flashback: A Brief History of Film*. Upper Saddle River, NJ: Prentice Hall, 2001.

Gruber, Frank. *The Pulp Jungle*. Los Angeles: Sherbourne Press, 1967.

Hiney, Tom, and Frank MacShane, eds. *The Raymond Chandler Papers: Selected Letters and Nonfiction, 1909-1959*. New York: Atlantic Monthly Press, 2000.

Hirsch, Foster. *The Dark Side of the Screen: Film Noir*. New York: Da Capo Press, 2001.

Hitchcock, Alfred. *Making Mystery Movies*. Interview on audiocassette, 1964. Los Angeles: Pacifica Radio Archive, 1986.

Hopley, George. *Fright*. New York: Rinehart, 1950.

———. *Night Has a Thousand Eyes*. New York: Grosset & Dunlap (by arrangement with Rinehart), 1945.

Insdorf, Annette. *François Truffaut*. Boston: Twayne Publishers, 1978.

Internet Movie Database. <www.imdb.com>
Irish, William. *The Best of William Irish*. Philadelphia: J.B. Lippincott, 1960.
_____. *The Blue Ribbon*. Philadelphia: J.B. Lippincott, 1949.
_____. *Bluebeard's Seventh Wife*. New York: Popular Library, 1952.
_____. *The Dancing Detective*. New York: Popular Library, 1951.
_____. *Dead Man Blues*. Philadelphia, J.B. Lippincott, 1948.
_____. *Deadline at Dawn*. In *The Best of William Irish*. Philadelphia: J.B. Lippincott, 1960.
_____. *Deadly Night Call*. Hasbrouck Heights, NJ: Graphic Publishing, 1954.
_____. *Nightmare*. New York: Readers-Choice Library, 1950.
_____. *Phantom Lady*. Cleveland: World Publishing, 1944.
_____. *Strangler's Serenade*. New York: Walter J. Black, 1951.
Kaplan, E. Ann, ed. *Women in Film Noir*. London: British Film Institute, 1998.
Lloyd, Ann, and David Robinson, eds. *Movies of the Forties*. London: Orbis Publishing, 1982.
Maltin, Leonard, ed. *TV Movies and Video Guide*. New York: Signet, 2002.
Malzberg, Barry N. "Cornell George Hopley Woolrich." *The Big Book of Noir*. Eds. Server, Gorman, and Greenberg. New York: Carroll & Graf, 1998. 163–166. Rpt. of "Cornell George Hopley Woolrich: December 1903 to September 1968."
McCarthy, Todd, and Charles Flynn. *Kings of the Bs: Working Within the Hollywood System: An Anthology of Film History and Criticism*. New York: E.P. Dutton, 1975.
Michael, Paul, James Robert Parish, John Robert Cocchi, Ray Hagen, and Jack Edmund Nolan, eds. *The American Movies Reference Book: The Sound Era*. Englewood Cliffs, NJ: Prentice-Hall, 1969.
Naremore, James. *More Than Night: Film Noir in Its Contexts*. Berkeley: University of California Press, 1998.
Nevins, Francis M., Jr. *Cornell Woolrich: First You Dream, Then You Die*. New York: Mysterious Press, 1988.
O'Brien, Geoffrey. *Hardboiled America: The Lurid Years of Paperbacks*. New York: Von Nostrand Reinhold, 1981.
Porfirio, Robert, Alain Silver, and James Ursini, eds. *Film Noir Reader 3*. New York: Limelight Editions, 2002.
Ringgold, Gene. *The Films of Rita Hayworth: The Legend and Career of a Love Goddess*. Secaucus, NJ: Citadel, 1974.
Schrader, Paul. "Notes on *Film Noir*." *Film Comment* 8, no. 1 (spring 1972). Rpt. in *Film Noir Reader*. Eds. Silver and Ursini 53–63.
Server, Lee, Ed Gorman, and Martin H. Greenberg, eds. *The Big Book of Noir*. New York: Carroll & Graf Publishers, 1998.
Silver, Alain, and James Ursini, eds. *Film Noir Reader*. New York: Limelight Editions, 1998.
_____. *Film Noir Reader 2*. New York: Limelight Editions, 1999.
_____, and Elizabeth Ward, eds. *Film Noir: An Encyclopedic Reference to the American Style*, 3rd ed. Woodstock, NY: The Overlook Press, 1992.
Sinyard, Neil. *The Films of Alfred Hitchcock*. New York: Gallery Books, 1986.
Smith, John M., and Tim Cawkwell, eds. *The World Encyclopedia of the Film*. New York: World Publishing, 1972.
Spoto, Donald. *The Art of Alfred Hitchcock*. New York: Anchor Books, 1992.
_____. *The Dark Side of Genius: The Life of Alfred Hitchcock*. New York: Ballantine Books, 1983.
Telotte, J. P. *Voices in the Dark: The Narrative Patterns of Film Noir*. Urbana: University of Illinois Press, 1989.
Truffaut, François. *Hitchcock*. New York: Simon & Schuster, 1985.
Woolrich, Cornell. *Angels of Darkness*. New York: The Mysterious Press, 1978.
_____. *Black Alibi*. London: Robert Hale, 1951.
_____. *The Black Angel*. New York: P.F. Collier & Son (by special arrangement with Doubleday, Doran & Co.), 1943

_____. *The Black Curtain.* New York: Books, Inc., 1944.
_____. *The Black Path of Fear.* New York: Ace Books, 1944.
_____. *Blues of a Lifetime: The Autobiography of Cornell Woolrich.* Ed. Mark T. Bassett. Bowling Green, OH: Bowling Green State University Popular Press, 1991.
_____. *The Bride Wore Black.* Franklin Center, PA: Franklin Library, 1989.
_____. "C-Jag." *Black Mask* (Oct. 1940). Rpt. as "Just Enough to Cover a Thumbnail." *Ellery Queen's Mystery Magazine.* Dec. 1965.
_____. *The Cornell Woolrich Omnibus.* New York: Penguin Books, 1994.
_____. *Darkness at Dawn: Early Suspense Classics by Cornell Woolrich.* London: Xanadu, 1988.
_____. "Dormant Account." *Ellery Queen's Mystery Magazine.* May 1953.
_____. "Face Work." *Black Mask* (Oct. 1937). Rpt. as "Angel Face." *Ellery Queen's Mystery Magazine.* Dec. 1946.
_____. *Hotel Room: An Entertainment.* New York: Random House, 1958.
_____. *I Married a Dead Man.* In *The Cornell Woolrich Omnibus.*
_____. *Into the Night.* New York: Mysterious Press, 1987.
_____. *Nightwebs.* Ed. by Francis M. Nevins, Jr. New York: Harper & Row, 1971.
_____. *Rendezvous in Black.* Boston: Gregg Press, 1979.
_____. *Vampire's Honeymoon.* New York: Carroll & Graf, 1985.
_____. *Waltz into Darkness.* In *The Cornell Woolrich Omnibus.*
Yates, Donald A. "Con." *The Big Book of Noir.* Ed. Server, Gorman, and Greenberg. New York: Carroll & Graf, 1998. 166–169.

Index

Abril, Victoria 337, 338
Act of Violence (film) 91, 336, 339
The Adventures of Huckleberry Finn (Twain novel) 97
Aeneas (mythological figure) 137
Aesop 303, 304
Affair in Trinidad (film) 91
An Affair to Remember (film) 233
"After-Dinner Story" 195
After-Dinner Story (collection) 143
Against All Odds (1984, film) 258
Aldrich, Robert 91
Alexander, John 267, 269
All-American Fiction (pulp magazine) 39
"All at Once, No Alice" 17, 57–66, 71, 97, 108, 195, 217
"All It Takes Is Brains" *see* "Crime on St. Catherine Street"
All My Sons (film) 54, 336
All My Sons (Miller play) 54
Ambler, Erik 259
American Gigolo (film) 173
Amick, Mädchen 42, 43
"And So to Death" *see* "Nightmare"
Anderson, Nathan 343
Andrews, Dana 315
Andy Hardy series (film) 318
"Angel Face" *see* "Face Work"
Angel Face (film) 138, 258–259, 280, 300, 301
Angel Heart (film) 183
Angels of Darkness (collection) 345
"An Apple a Day" 41, 46
Argosy (pulp magazine) 12, 57, 68, 107, 120
Armstrong, Charlotte 316
Armstrong, Robert 71, 73, 76
Arnt, Charles 71, 72
As I Lay Dying (Faulkner novel) 315
As You Like It (Shakespeare play) 264

The Asphalt Jungle (film) 84, 232, 284
Astor, Mary 316
Atwill, Lionel 180
Aubert, Lénore 61
Auer, Florence 249, 251
Aurora 205, 206
Azito, Tony 28

Backus, Jim 307
Bagdasarian, Ross 151, 155
Baker, Roy 169
Balsam, Martin 90
Bancroft, Anne 354
Banderas, Antonio 296, 297, 300
Barrett, Tim 318, 320
Barrymore, Lionel 173
Barsha, Leon 34, 35, 37
Bartlett, Benny 151, 155
Barton Fink (film) 235
Barzun, Jacques 9
Basic Instinct (film) 297
Bassett, Mark T. 3, 6, 9
Baye, Nathalie 337
Bazin, André 286
Becker, Harold 321
Beeding, Francis 121
Bell, James 180, 182
Belmondo, Jean-Paul 285, 286, 288, 293
Bendix, William 141, 227, 307
Benetar, Pat 28
Benjamin, Richard 339, 340, 341, 342
Bennett, Joan 121
Berbert, Marcel 285, 289
Berger, William 42, 44
Bergin, Patrick 66
Bergman, Ingrid 65, 121, 253, 307, 353
Berner, Sara 151, 155
Bernhardt, Curtis 141, 226
Berry, John 322

Index

The Best Years of Our Lives (film) 73, 250
Bettger, Lyle 328, 329
Beware, My Lovely (film) 66, 322, 353
Beware the Lady see *The Bride Wore Black*
Beyond a Reasonable Doubt (film) 301, 336
Biberman, Abner 180, 188
Bierce, Ambrose 257
The Big Book of Noir 249
The Big Clock (film) 241, 267, 284, 336
The Big Heat (film) 74, 91
The Big Knife (film) 235
The Big Sleep (novel) 228, 248
The Big Sleep (1946, film) 248
The Birth of a Nation (film) 1
Black Alibi (novel) 60, 70, 78, 135, 175–189, 194, 195, 200, 232, 347
The Black Angel (film) 102, 189, 206, 219–229, 235, 254, 336
The Black Angel (novel) 14, 15, 16, 17, 18, 22, 23, 34, 41, 67, 70, 78, 120, 132, 141, 204, 205, 206, 208, 213–229, 233, 247, 300
The Black Curtain (novel) 16, 17, 18, 21, 57, 78, 130–142, 194, 204, 217, 222, 225, 233, 236, 240, 255
"Black List: Essential Film Noir" 249
Black Mask (pulp magazine) 12, 31, 190
The Black Path of Fear (novel) 16, 22–23, 65, 78, 194, 233, 242–260, 300
Black Series (Woolrich series of novels) 78
Blackton, J. Stuart 8
Blackton, Violet Virginia ("Bill") 8
Blade Runner (film) 91
Bleckner, Jeff 170, 172
The Blob (film) 43
Block, Lawrence 12, 17, 345
Blood and Sand (film) 35
The Blue Dahlia (film) 72, 135, 141, 227–228
"Blue Moon" (song) 80–81
Bluebeard 180
"Bluebeard's Seventh Wife" 17, 67
Blues of a Lifetime (Woolrich's autobiography) 3, 4, 5, 6, 7, 8, 9, 78, 85, 95–96, 143, 177, 215
Body and Soul (film) 84
Body Heat (film) 301
"The Body Upstairs" 10
Bogart, Humphrey 253, 316
Bogdanovich, Peter 250
Böhm, Karlheinz 349, 350
Bohnen, Roman 267, 269
Bohringer, Richard 337
Bolster, Anita 318
The Bonfire of the Vanities (film) 296

Borde, Raymond 19, 22, 249
Born to Be Bad (film) 280
Born to Kill (film) 138, 301–302
Borrowed Crime (collection) 190
Boulanger, Daniel 85, 86
Bouquet, Michel 85, 86, 89, 285, 287
Boxoffice (magazine) 35
"The Boy Cried Murder" 14, 21, 57, 81, 133, 143, 168, 169, 180, 204, 216, 223, 233, 303–323
The Boy Cried Murder (film) 318–322
"The Boy Who Cried Wolf" (Aesop fable) 303, 304–305
"Boy with Body" see "The Corpse and the Kid"
Boyer, Charles 65
Bradley, David 316
Brahm, John 294
Brandon, Marlon 235
The Bravados (film) 91–92
Breakston, George P. 318, 319, 321
Brialy, Jean-Claude 85, 87–88
The Bride Wore Black (film) 84–92
The Bride Wore Black (novel, aka *Beware the Lady*) 15, 16, 22, 23, 26, 27, 39, 58, 77, 78–92, 134, 177, 194, 202, 204, 205, 300
Britton, Pamela 348
Brooks, Jason 42, 44
Brooks, Jean 180, 181, 182
Brown, Charles D. 51, 52, 54
Brown, Phil 318
Browning, Tod 349–350
Bruce, Virginia 267, 268
Buñuel, Luis 121
Burnett, Whit 200, 201
Burr, Raymond 151
Buscemi, Steve 321

The Cabinet of Dr. Caligari (film) 120
Cahiers du Cinéma 85
Cain, James M. 3, 19
Calcutta (film) 267
Calhern, Louis 232
Call Northside 777 (film) 336
Calling Dr. Death (film) 71
Calvert, John 197
Cape Fear (1962, film) 336, 337
Cape Fear (1991, film) 336
Capra, Frank 122
Captive City (film) 30
Carroll, Leo G. 90, 121
Carstensen, Margit 349, 350
Carter, Janis 196
Casablanca (film) 253

Caspary, Vera 315
Cassell, Wally 97, 98, 100
Castle, Don 51, 52, 54, 97, 98, 100, 101
Castle, William 196, 199
Cat People (1942, film) 181
Catch-22 (film) 340
The Catcher in the Rye (Salinger novel) 97
Cause for Alarm (film) 66, 353
Cavanaugh, Hobart 219, 221
"Chance" *see* "Dormant Account"
Chandler, Raymond 3, 13, 14–15, 19, 212, 227, 228
Chanslor, Roy 219, 220
Charlie Chan series (film) 35
The Chase (film) 23, 74, 249–260, 352, 353
Chatel, Peter 349, 350
Chaumeton, Etienne 19, 22, 249
Un chien andalou (film) 121, 242
Children of the Ritz (film) 5, 8, 34, 135, 200
Children of the Ritz (novel) 5, 8, 34, 78, 135, 200, 276
Chinatown (film) 336
Christ figure 113–114, 116, 134, 268, 272
Christensen, Benjamin 200
Christine, Virginia 123
A Christmas Carol (Dickens novel) 263, 334
Christopher, Nicholas 291
Cinderella motif 45
Citizen Kane (film) 1, 55, 233, 288, 315, 336
City Across the River (film) 114
"C-Jag" (aka "Cocaine," "Dream of Death," and "Just Enough to Cover a Thumbnail") 16, 41, 54, 67–77, 107, 132, 133, 225, 240, 255, 300
Clarke, Gage 122, 123
Clash by Night (film) 235, 301
Clift, Montgomery 235
Cloak and Dagger (film) 322–323
Clurman, Harold 234, 235, 239, 254
"Cocaine" *see* "C-Jag"
Cochrane, Steve 249, 250, 251
Coen brothers (Joel and Ethan) 235
Colbert, Claudette 64, 154
Coleman, Dabney 322, 323
Collins, Ray 226
Compulsion (film) 317–318
Conan Doyle, Sir Arthur 149, 220, 261
Conflict (film) 301
Conrad, Peter 153
Conspiracy Theory (film) 65
Conte, Richard 307
Convicted (1938, film) 34–38

Conway, Jack 228
Cook, Elisha, Jr. 71, 72, 117, 205, 206, 209
Cooper, Gary 30
Copycat (film) 180
Corey, Wendell 151, 153, 161
Cornell Woolrich: First You Dream Then You Die (Nevins book) 3
The Cornell Woolrich Omnibus (collection) 1, 143
Cornered (film) 73, 91, 226
"The Corpse and the Kid" 306
"The Corpse Next Door" 20, 21, 25–30, 69, 195, 300
Corrigan, Lloyd 249, 252
Cortez, Stanley 20
Coster, Ritchie 170
Cotten, Joseph 55, 66, 259
Cover Charge (novel) 5, 276
Cowan, Jerome 134, 136, 140–141, 235, 236, 267, 268, 316
"The Coward" (Maupassant short story) 26, 262
Cowl, Jane 328, 330
Crack-Up (film) 73, 74, 226, 250
Crawford, Broderick 219, 221
Crawford, Cheryl 235
Crawford, Joan 66
Cregar, Laird 55
Crehan, Joseph 205, 206
Cressey, Paul G. 233
"Crime on St. Catherine Street" (aka "All It Takes Is Brains" and "One Night in Montreal") 77
Criss Cross (film) 52, 205, 336
Cristofer, Michael 295, 296, 298, 299
Cromwell, John 91
Crossfire (film) 227
Crossroads (film) 228–229
Crowther, Bosley 35
Cukor, George 65
Cummings, Robert 249, 250, 256
Curtis, Alan 205, 206
Curtiz, Michael 300
Cusak, Noel 34, 37

Dali, Salvadore 121
Dale, Esther 328, 331
Dale, Virginia 71, 72
"The Dancing Detective" 70
The Dancing Detective (collection) 93
A Dangerous Profession (film) 307
Daniel (O.T. figure) 134
Darcy, Georgine 151, 155
Dark City (1950, film) 91
Dark City (1998, film) 65, 226

Dark City: The Film Noir (Selby book) 114, 267
The Dark Corner (film) 62, 336, 339
"Dark Melody of Madness" (aka "Papa Benjamin" and "Music from the Dark") 10, 39, 57, 65, 128, 180, 183, 261, 345
The Dark Mirror (film) 205
Dark Passage (film) 336
Dark Side of the Screen: Film Noir (Hirsch book) 3
Darwinism 238, 247
da Silva, Howard 227
Davis, Andrew 66
Davis, Robin 300, 301, 337, 338, 339
Dead Man Blues (collection) 303
Dead of Night (film) 275
"Dead on Her Feet" 347
Dead Reckoning (film) 91
Deadline at Dawn (film) 195, 213, 234–241, 254
Deadline at Dawn (novel) 15, 16, 21, 70, 230–241, 247, 258, 272, 300
"Deadly Night Call" *see* "Somebody on the Phone"
Dean, James 235
Dean, Loren 340
"Death Sits in the Dentist's Chair" 60, 65
Death Takes a Holiday (1934, film) 328
Deceived (1991, film) 66
Demarest, William 267, 269
DeMille, Cecil B. 122, 328
Demme, Jonathan 301
Deneuve, Catherine 285, 286, 288
Denner Charles 85, 86
Denning, Richard 328, 329, 330
Depardieu, Gérard 337
"Design" (Frost poem) 349
Detective Fiction Weekly (pulp magazine) 12, 25, 47, 68, 83, 93, 143, 200
Detective Story (pulp magazine) 12
DeVito, Danny 351
deWalt Reynolds, Adeline 134, 135, 140, 173
Dial M for Murder (1954, film) 66
Diana (mythological figure) 82, 87, 88
Dickens, Charles 31, 263, 334
Dickos, Andrew 3, 12
Dieterle, William 91
Dillon, John Francis 5, 34
Dime Detective (pulp magazine) 12, 34, 143
Dime Mystery (pulp magazine) 128
Dirty Harry series (film) 91
Dix, Richard 60, 196, 197
Dmytryk, Edward 91, 120, 141, 226, 316
D. O. A. (1950, film) 62, 74, 289, 348

Dobson, Kevin 343
Dr. Jekyll and Mr. Hyde (1941, film) 353
Dr. Jekyll and Mr. Hyde (Stevenson novel) *see The Strange Case of Dr. Jekyll and Mr. Hyde*
Dr. X (film) 180
A Doll House (Ibsen play) 31, 352
Domergue, Faith 30, 259
Domestic Disturbance (film) 321
Don't Bother to Knock (film) 169, 354
"Dormant Account" (aka "Chance") 21, 23, 59, 133, 190–199, 244
Double Indemnity (film) 31, 50, 52, 84, 113, 208, 228, 234, 259, 278, 280, 284, 316, 353
Douglas, Donald 34, 36
Douglas, Kirk 258
Douglas, Michael 297
Dowling, Constance 219, 220
Dowling, Doris 227
Dracula (1931, film) 350
Dracula series (film) 120
"Dream of Death" *see* "C-Jag"
Driscoll, Bobby 307, 308, 311, 312, 319
Duane, Michael 61
Duggan, Andrew 92
Dupont, E. A. 142
Duryea, Dan 121, 219, 220, 225, 229

Eastwood, Clint 91
Easy Living (1937, film) 328
Ebert, Roger 296–297
Ecclesiastes 349
Eden theme 42, 327, 328, 333, 336
Edison, Thomas 8
Edwards, Edgar 34, 36
8mm (film) 180
El Dorado 232
Ellery Queen's Mystery Magazine (pulp magazine) 31, 57, 67, 143, 190, 345
Elliot, William "Wild Bill" 34–35
Ellison, Harlan 3
"The Enemy" (Armstrong short story) 316
Erinyes (Furies, mythological figures) 103, 130, 137, 191, 204, 283, 336
Ermey, R. Lee 42, 43
Erskine, Chester 169
Estefan, Gloria 297
E.T.: The Extraterrestrial (film) 323
Ethan Frome (Wharton novel) 153
Evelyn, Judith 155
"Even God Felt the Depression" (in *Blues of a Lifetime*) 8
Everyman motif 113, 115, 126, 275, 307
Eye Witness (1950, film) 212

Eyes That Watch You (collection) 57
Eyman, Scott 350

"Face Work" (aka "Angel Face") 15, 16, 17, 31–38, 41, 53, 70, 71, 77, 81, 120, 135, 205, 213, 215, 216, 218, 222, 247, 347
Fairbanks, Douglas 328
Fall Guy (1947, film) 54, 71–77, 189
Fallen Angel (2000, film; aka *Revenge*) 91
The Fallen Sparrow (film) 74
The Fantastic Stories of Cornell Woolrich (collection) 39
Farewell, My Lovely (Chandler novel) 228
Farrow, John 30, 241, 266, 267, 268, 271, 272, 273, 275
Farrow, Mia 267
Fassbinder, Rainer Werner 349, 350, 351, 354
The Fates (mythological figures) 145
Faulkner, William 315
Faust 245
"Faustine" (Swinburne poem) 278–279
Fax, Jesslyn 151, 155
Fear in the Night (film) 74, 114–122, 122–129, 172, 189
Feldman, Rachel 343
Ferrer, Mel 63–64
Field, Mary 220, 221
Fields, Leonard 34
The File on Thelma Jordan (film) 50, 301, 336
Film Noir: An Encyclopedic Reference to the American Style (Silver and Ward) 19, 129, 139, 226, 267
The Films of Rita Hayworth (Ringgold book) 35
"Fire Escape" *see* "The Boy Cried Murder"
The Firm (film) 65
First National 5, 34
"First You Dream, Then You Die" (title for unwritten short story) 12, 264
Fisher, Steve 9, 51, 52, 53, 55
Fitzgerald, F. Scott 5, 10, 13, 14, 78, 173
Fleischer, Richard 317
Fleming, Victor 353
Flesh and Fantasy (film) 275
Flesh and the Devil (film) 31
Flinn, Tom 3, 208
Fontaine, Joan 280
Foolish Wives (film) 249
"For the Rest of Her Life" 14, 345–353
Ford, John 138
Ford, Wallace 219, 221
Foreign Correspondent (1940, film) 235

The Formula (film) 65
Forster, Robert 170, 171
Forrest Gump (film) 240
Forsythe, John 30
Forsythe, William 322, 323
Foster, Jodie 301
Foster, Norman 259
"The Fountain Pen" (aka "Dipped in Blood") 41, 46, 195
The Fountainhead (film) 128
Fowley, Douglas 71
Frank, Nino 20
Frankenstein Meets the Wolf Man (film) 220
Franklin, Richard 322
Fraser, Brendan 340
Freaks (film) 350
French New Wave (*Nouvelle vague*) 85, 90, 286, 287, 292, 294, 295, 350
Frenchman's Creek (film) 328
Fright (novel) 23, 27, 204
"From Dusk to Dawn" 15, 67, 205
Frost, Robert 349
Furies *see* Erinyes
Fury (1936, film) 132

Gaffney, Veronica "Vera" 6, 59
Gambling House (film) 307, 354
Garbo, Greta 31
Garnett, Tay 66, 316
Gaslight (film) 65–66, 353
The General (film) 1
Gerety, Peter 340
German Expressionism 20, 105, 120, 205, 226, 284, 307, 350
Gia (television film) 296
Gianetti, Louis 350
Gilda (film) 35, 62, 84, 336
The Glass Menagerie (Williams play) 49
The Glass Wall (film) 114
Godard, Jean Luc 350
Going My Way (film) 140
Gold, Tracey 343
Gomez, Thomas 205, 206, 294
Good-bye Columbus (film) 340
Grahame, Gloria 241
Granger, Farley 113
Grant, Cary 90
Granville, Bonita 97, 99, 101
"Graves for the Living" 55, 59, 180, 194, 345
Gray, Billy 316
Great Expectations (Dickens novel) 31
Great Expectations (1934, Stuart Walker film) 318
The Great Gatsby (Fitzgerald novel) 14, 97, 173

Greenstreet, Sydney 117
Greer, Jane 258
Grenier, Marc S. 91
The Group Theater 235
Gruber, Frank 9
Guilfoyle, Paul 197
The Guilty (film) 97–106, 189, 227, 254

Hale, Barbara 307, 308
Hall, Daisy 42, 44
Hamlet (Shakespeare play) 134, 183, 263
Hammett, Dashiell 3, 15, 19
Hannibal (film) 180
The Harder They Fall (film) 2
Harris, Damian 66
Harry, Deborah 28, 29
Hart, Lorenz 80
Hawn, Goldie 66
Hayes, John Michael 28, 150, 152, 155, 168
Hayward, Susan 235, 236, 237, 239
Hayworth, Rita 34, 35, 38, 74, 280
"He Looked Like Murder" (aka "Two Fellows in a Furnished Room") 14, 16, 50, 67, 93–106, 143
He Ran All the Way (film) 322
Hecate (mythological figure) 81
Hedda Gabler (Ibsen play) 31
Heflin, Van 253
Hemingway, Ernest 10, 13, 83
Herrmann, Bernard 85, 90, 172, 300
High Noon (film) 30
High Wall (film) 74, 141, 142, 226, 229, 250
Hillerman, Tony 261
Hiney, Tom 15
Hirsch, Foster 3, 20
His Kind of Woman (film) 267
Hitchcock, Alfred 1, 28, 30 42, 49, 50, 66, 85, 86, 90, 97, 105, 121, 122, 141, 150, 151, 152, 153, 155, 156, 161, 162, 164, 165, 166, 167, 168, 169, 170, 171, 172, 180, 183, 211, 220, 235, 242, 247, 279, 285–286, 287, 288, 289–290, 293, 300, 306, 307–308, 316, 317, 335, 350
Hively, Jack 134, 138
Hlepsa, Yorda 318, 319
Hold Back the Dawn (film) 328
Holt, Jack 249, 254
Homer 97, 263
Hooper, Tobe 42, 43, 45
Hopkins, Anthony 301
Hopley, George (Woolrich pseudonym) 27
Hopley-Woolrich, Genaro (father) 3, 67, 305–306, 306–307
Horner, Harry 66, 322
Hotel Room (novel) 41, 46, 347

The House of Dr. Edwardes (Beeding novel) 121
House of Horror (1929, film) 201
Hoven, Adrian 349, 350
The Human Comedy (film) 140
Humoresque (1946, film) 235
Hurst, Veronica 318
Hurt, William 301
Huster, Francis 337, 338
Huston, John 91, 232, 316

I Love You Again (film) 229
I Married a Dead Man (film) see *J'ai épousé une ombre*
I Married a Dead Man (novel) 14, 15, 16, 20, 23, 50, 204, 276, 297–298, 299, 324–344
I Married a Shadow see *J'ai épousé une ombre*
I Wake Up Screaming (film) 55
I Walk Alone (film) 250, 336
I Walked with a Zombie (film) 181, 183
I Want to Live! (film) 339
I Was a Teenage Werewolf (film) 43
"I Wouldn't Be in Your Shoes" 47–56, 95
I Wouldn't Be in Your Shoes (collection) 47, 107
I Wouldn't Be in Your Shoes (film) 51–56, 69, 195, 240
Ibsen, Henrik 31, 352
The Iliad (Homer epic poem) 263
"I'm Dangerous Tonight" 39–46, 49, 180, 345
I'm Dangerous Tonight (television film) 42–46, 343
In a Lonely Place (film) 241, 336
In Search of Lost Time (Proust novel, former English title *Remembrance of Things Past*) 19
Inescourt, Frieda 134, 136
Ingster, Boris 208
Internet Movie Database (web site) 201
Into the Night (novel) 12, 14, 17, 82, 345
Invasion of the Body Snatchers (1956, film) 30, 65, 127
Ireland, John 142
Irish, William (Woolrich pseudonym) 200–201
Irving, Bill 34, 37
Irving, Washington 336
The Island of Dr. Moreau (Wells novel) 263
Island of Lost Souls (film) 180
"It Had to Be Murder" see "Rear Window"
It Happened One Night (film) 154, 318
It's a Wonderful Life (film) 173
Ivano, Paul 220

Jack the Ripper 180
Jackson, Thomas E. 97, 98
Jaffe, Sam 307
J'ai épousé une ombre (film, English titles: *I Married a Dead Man* and *I Married a Shadow*) 300, 337–339
Jane, Thomas 298, 299
Jane Eyre (Brontë novel) 61
Jazz Age 4, 5
Jewell, Isabel 180
Joe Palooka series (film) 71
Johnny Got His Gun (Trumbo novel) 173
Johnny Guitar (film) 295
"Johnny on the Spot" 41, 83, 219
Johnson, Michelle 91
Johnson, Nunnally 169
Jolie, Angelina 296, 297, 300
Jones, Michelle 343
Journey into Fear (film) 259
Julie (film) 353
Jungle Woman (film) 71
"Just Enough to Cover a Thumbnail" *see* "C-Jag"

Karloff, Boris 52
Kasdan, Lawrence 301
Kasznar, Kurt 316
Keane, Robert Emmett 114, 116, 118, 172
Keats, John 163
Kelley, DeForest 114, 115, 118
Kelly, Gene 240
Kelly, Grace 151, 157, 161
Kelly, Paul 64, 114, 115, 116
Kennedy, Arthur 307, 308, 312
Key Largo (film) 138
The Killers (1946, film) 205, 281, 315, 336
The Killing (film) 284
King, Henry 91
King Kong (1933, film) 1, 76, 180
King Lear (Shakespeare play) 31, 263, 349
King of Kings (1927, film) 328
Kiss Me Deadly (film) 91
Kiss of Death (1947, film) 84, 91, 336
"Kiss of the Cobra" 10, 39
Kiss the Girls (film) 180
Kitty (1945, film) 328
Knott, Harold 3
Knox, Elyse 51, 52, 54
Koschetz, Nina (Koshetz) 249, 253
Krenske, Emil *see* Nigh, William

Labyrinth motif 137, 179, 187, 208, 209, 214, 216, 223, 234, 239, 245, 253, 276, 282–283, 287, 289–290, 291, 292, 294, 309–310, 315, 319

Lacca, Yolanda 249, 253
Lachman, Edward 28, 30
Ladd, Alan 141, 227, 228
Lady for a Day (film) 122
The Lady from Shanghai (film) 31, 35, 113, 120, 278, 280, 281, 284, 316, 353
The Lady in the Lake (Chandler novel) 228
The Lady in the Lake (film) 212
Lake, Ricki 340
Lake, Veronica 227
Lancaster, Burt 281, 353
Landers, Lew 229
Landis, Carole 55
Landry, Margaret 180, 182
Lane, Lola 235, 236
Lang, Fritz 91, 120, 121, 122, 186, 205, 307, 316, 322–323, 326
Langley, Noel 120
The Last Married Couple in America (film) 340
Laughton, Charles 241
Laura (Caspary novel) 315
Laura (film) 284, 315
Lawrence, Marc 34, 35
Lazarus (N.T. figure) 134
Le Borg, Reginald 71, 77
Lederman, D. Ross 60, 62
"The Legend of Sleepy Hollow" (Irving short story) 84, 336
Lehman, Ernest 235
Leigh, Janet 90, 105
Leisen, Mitchell 328, 338, 339
Leonard, Sheldon 134, 135
The Leopard Man (film) 135, 179–189, 252, 254
Leopold, Nathan 317
Lewton, Val 179, 181, 183, 189, 252
"The Light in the Window" 143
Lipscomb, Dennis 28, 29
Litel, John 97, 99, 101
Living Nightmare theme 195
Lloyd, Doris 205, 207
Locke, Sondra 91
The Lodger (1926, film) 180
Loeb, Richard 317
Loncar, Beba 318, 319
Lonsdale, Michel 85, 86
"Lord Arthur Saville's Crime" (Wilde short story) 275
Loring, Teala 71, 74
Lorre, Peter 186, 219, 221, 225, 249, 250–251
Lowell, Robert 51, 52
Lugosi, Bela 51
Lukas, Paul 235, 236, 239

Lund, John 267, 268, 269, 328, 329, 335
Lupino, Ida 66

M (1931, film) 122, 186
Macbeth (Shakespeare play) 31, 96, 107, 110, 130, 134, 245, 263–264, 271, 277, 278, 279, 283, 349
MacGregor, Doreen 34, 36
MacIntosh, Alex 318, 319
MacIntosh, Fraser 318, 320
Mackie, Alison 170
MacLaine, Shirley 340
MacMurray, Fred 113, 228
MacShane, Frank 15
Madama Butterfly (Puccini opera) 4
Male and Female (1919, film) 328
The Maltese Falcon (Hammett novel) 117, 258, 283
The Maltese Falcon (1941, film) 11, 74, 91, 117, 140, 234, 258, 278, 283, 316, 336
Maltin, Leonard 129
Malzberg, Barry N. 3, 9, 13
Man in the Dark (film) 76, 135, 142, 229
"The Man Who Corrupted Hadleyburg" (Twain short story) 336
The Man Who Knew Too Much (1934, film) 122
The Man Who Knew Too Much (1956, film) 122
Manhattan Love Song (film) 5, 34, 135
Manhattan Love Song (novel) 5, 8, 34, 78, 135, 276
Manichaeism 153
Mankiewicz, Joseph L. 91
Margo 180, 181
La Mariée était en noir see *The Bride Wore Black*
"Marihuana" 15, 16, 68, 69, 205, 223, 240, 300, 345
Mark of the Whistler (film) 194, 196–199
Marsh, Ali 170
Marshall, George 226
Martha (1973, German television film) 349–354
Martin, Marion 220, 222
Martin, Richard 182
Mason, James 90
Massen, Osa 235, 236
Massey, Raymond 121
The Matchmaker (1958, film) 42
Maté, Rudolph 289
Mathews, Carole 328, 329
The Mating Season (film) 328
The Matrix (film) 65, 91, 226
Matthews, Junius 220, 222

Mature, Victor 55, 307, 354
Maupassant, Guy de 26, 78, 81, 82, 262
May, Billy 122, 124, 126
Mayo, Archie 120
McCambridge, Mercedes 142
McCarthy, Kevin 30, 122, 123, 127
McCarthyism 295
McCoy, Horace 19
McGill, Everett 28
Méliès, Georges 315
Memento (2000, film) 336
Mencken, H.L. 12
Meredith, Burgess 134, 135, 139, 140
Mermaids (film) 340
Merrill, Gary 169, 317
The Method (acting style) 235
Midnight (1940, film) 328
A Midsummer Night's Dream (Shakespeare play) 263
Mildred Pierce (film) 62, 298
Milland, Ray 241
Miller, Arthur 54
Miller, David 66, 322
Miller, Marvin 235, 236
Milton, John 327
"Mind over Murder" (aka "A Death Is Caused") 50, 55, 195, 240, 345
Minotaur (mythological figure) 164, 187, 223, 310, 320
Minotis, Alexis (Alex) 249, 253
Mirage (1965, film) 141
Miranda, Carmen 206
Mississippi Mermaid (film, French title: *La Sirène du Mississippi*) 85, 86, 285–295, 300, 337
Mr. Wong series (film) 51
Mitchum, Robert 30, 249, 258, 259, 281, 300
"Momentum" (aka "Murder Always Gathers Momentum") 15, 67, 68, 143
Monk, Debra 340
Monroe, Marilyn 169
Montgomery, Robert 91, 212
Moore, Terry 307
Moreau, Jeanne 85, 86, 89, 90–91
Morgan, Henry (Harry) 241
Morgan, Michele 249, 250, 256, 259
"The Morning After Murder" see "Murder on My Mind"
The Most Dangerous Game (1932, film) 180
Mrs. Winterbourne (film) 339, 340–343
The Mummy's Ghost (film) 71
"Murder Always Gathers Momentum" see "Momentum"
"Murder in Wax" 15, 34, 70, 77, 205, 213, 215, 216, 217, 218, 222, 234

Murder, My Sweet (1944, film) 74, 91, 102, 120, 138, 316, 336
"The Murder on My Mind" (aka "Morning After Murder") 16, 67–68, 133
"Murder on St. Catherine Street" (aka "All It Takes Is Brains")
Murders in the Rue Morgue (film) 180
Murders in the Zoo (film) 180
Musuraca, Nicholas 239
My Favorite Year (film) 340
Mystery Book Magazine (pulp magazine) 303
Mystery Digest 67
Mystery of the Wax Museum (1933, film) 180
Mystic River (film) 91

The Naked Kiss (film) 337
The Naked Street (film) 114
The Narrative of Arthur Gordon Pym (Poe novel) 16
Nathan, George Jean 12
Neill, Roy William 219, 220, 222, 225, 228, 254
Nelson, James 200
The Net (film) 65
Nevada Smith (film) 91
Nevins, Francis M., Jr. 3, 8, 9, 12, 13, 25, 28, 29, 50, 55, 95, 143, 151, 177, 180, 201, 220, 222, 264, 281
New German Cinema 350
New Wave *see* French New Wave
Newman, Paul 235
Nigh, William 51–52
"Night and Day" (song) 81
Night and the City (1950, film) 21–22
Night Has a Thousand Eyes (film) 266–275
Night Has a Thousand Eyes (novel) 14, 65, 70, 261–275
"The Night Reveals" 21, 27, 195, 204, 223
"Nightmare" (aka "And So to Death") 14, 16, 17, 21, 57, 68, 70, 95, 107–129, 132, 133, 195, 204, 222, 225, 232, 236, 240, 255, 347
Nightmare (collection) 47, 107
Nightmare (1956, film) 114, 121, 122–129
Nightmare on Elm Street series (film) 43
Nightwebs (collection) 25
No Man of Her Own (1950, film) 328–337, 338, 339
No Way Out (1950, film) 91
Noah's Ark (film) 300
Nora Prentiss (film) 74, 281, 301, 336–337
North by Northwest (film) 90
Notorious (film) 85, 307

Nouvelle vague see French New Wave
Novak, Kim 85, 258, 352
"The Number's Up" 41

O. Henry 78
O'Brien, Edmond 142, 229, 348
O'Brien, Geoffrey 13
O'Brien, Pat 226, 307
"An Occurrence at Owl Creek Bridge" (Bierce short story) 257
Odds Against Tomorrow (1959, film) 84, 258
O'Dea, John 76
Odets, Clifford 235–236, 237, 238, 239, 240, 241
Odysseus 97, 137, 264
The Odyssey (Homer epic poem) 97, 263
Oedipus Rex (Sophocles play) 31, 263
Of Mice and Men (1939, film) 140
O'Hara, Shirley 249, 251
O'Keefe, Dennis 180, 181, 182
O'Leary, Matthew 321
Oliver Twist (Dickens novel) 293
On Dangerous Ground (film) 255
"One and a Half Murders" 17
Original Sin (2001, film) 295–302
Oscillation technique 95, 96
O'Sullivan, Maureen 259
Othello (Shakespeare play) 97, 149
Out of the Past (1947, film) 23, 50, 76, 84, 102, 138, 258, 281, 301, 339, 352
Overman, Jack 71, 72

Pacino, Al 74
Paget, Debra 74
Palance, Jack 66
Panic in the Streets (film) 74
"Papa Benjamin" *see* "Dark Melody of Madness"
The Paradine Case (film) 74, 138, 302
Paradise Lost (Milton epic poem) 327
Paradise Regained (Milton epic poem) 232
Parker, Alan 183
Parker, Corey 42, 44
Parma, Tula 180, 183, 185
Party Girl (film) 84
Peck, Gregory 92, 121, 141
The Pelican Brief (film) 65
Penn, Clifford 71, 73, 74
A Perfect Murder (1998, film) 66
Perkins, Anthony 42–43, 45, 90, 105
"Phantom Alibi" (magazine serial) 15, 200, 201
Phantom Lady (1944, film) 205–212, 235, 336

Index

Phantom Lady (novel) 14, 15, 16, 17, 34, 65, 67, 70, 71, 74, 97, 120, 132, 195, 200–212, 213, 216, 232, 233, 247
Phillips, John 219, 221
Phoenix (mythological bird) 132, 293
Pitfall (1948, film) 50, 74, 102, 138, 259, 302, 336
Planer, Franz F. 205
Platt, Louise 134, 135
Pocket Mystery Reader 67
Pocketful of Miracles (film) 122
Poe, Edgar Allan 13, 16, 25, 26, 57, 59, 78, 149, 175, 194
Poltergeist (film) 43
"The Poor Girl" (in *Blues of a Lifetime*) 6, 59
Porfirio, Robert 129, 139, 249
Porter, Cole 81
Possessed (1947, film) 50, 284
The Postman Always Rings Twice (1946, film) 74, 84, 301, 316
Powell, Dick 120
Powell, William 228
Preminger, Otto 300, 315
"President Eisenhower's Speech" (in *Blues of a Lifetime*) 9
"Preview of Death" 10
Production Code of 1934 180, 253
Proyas, Alex 226
Psycho (1960, film) 30, 42, 90, 105
The Quick and the Dead (film) 91

Quigley, Charles 34, 36

Racing with the Moon (film) 340
The Racket (1951, film) 76
Raft, George 307
Rage in Heaven (film) 353
Raines, Ella 205, 206, 307
Rains, Claude 30, 85, 289
Rand, Ayn 128
Rathbone, Basil 220, 228
"Rear Window" (aka "It Had to Be Murder") 1, 14, 16, 18, 21, 27, 50, 67, 95, 96, 143–174, 198, 204, 308, 335, 347
Rear Window (1954, film) 1, 29–30, 150–169, 170–174, 220, 247, 288, 308, 335, 350
Rear Window (1998, television film) 140, 170–174
"The Red Tide" 95
Reed, Carol 259
Reeve, Christopher 140, 170, 173–174
Reichert, Mark 27, 28, 29, 30
Reinhardt, John 97, 98, 105, 254

Reis, Irving 226
"Remington Portable NC69411" (in *Blues of a Lifetime*) 4, 5–6, 10, 11
Rendezvous in Black (novel) 15, 16, 23, 78, 83
Le Retour de Martin Guerre (film, English title: *The Return of Martin Guerre*) 336, 337
Return of the Whistler (film) 60–66
Rich, Claude 85, 86
Ride the Pink Horse (film) 91
Rideout, Bob 34, 37
Ringgold, Gene 35
Ripley, Arthur D. 249–250, 251, 253, 255
The Ritterlma 151, 163, 288
The Road to Yesterday (film) 328
Roadblock (film) 77, 113, 301
Roberts, Julia 66
Robin Hood (1922, film) 328
Robinson, Edward G. 121, 122, 123, 128, 267, 268, 269, 316
Robinson, Madeleine 337, 338
Rodgers, Richard 80
Roman, Ruth 307, 308, 319
Rooney, Mickey 318
Rope (film) 317–318
Rowland, Roy 169
Rozsa, Miklos 205
Ruben, Joseph 66
Russell, Connie 122, 123
Russell, Gail 267, 268, 269
Ryan, Robert 64, 66, 241, 354

The Saint Mystery Magazine (pulp magazine) 142, 303
Salomy Jane (film) 51
Sanders, George 317
Sandoval, Miguel 340, 341
Santiago-Hudson, Ruben 170
The Scarf (film) 135, 142
Scarface (1932, film) 31
The Scarlet Letter (Hawthorne novel) 84
Scarlet Street (film) 113, 326, 339
Scene of the Crime (1949, film) 102
Schafer, Natalie 42, 44
Schoenfeld, Bernard 205, 206
Schrader, Paul 173
Schwarzenegger, Arnold 229
Scott, Zachary 228
"The Screaming Laugh" 180
The Searchers (film) 1, 91
The Secret Fury (film) 64–65, 142
Selby, Spencer 114, 249, 267
Serie Noire (French crime literature series) 19

Index

Serpico (film) 65
Server, Lee 249
The Set-Up (1949, film) 241
Seven (film) 180
Seven Footprints to Satan (film) 200
The Seventh Victim (film) 183
7th Voyage of Sinbad (1958, film) 1
The Shadow (radio show adapted to film) 196
Shadow of a Doubt (film) 166, 336, 353
Shakespeare, William 31, 96, 97, 107, 134, 183, 233, 263, 266, 349
Shane (film) 1
Shane, Maxwell 114, 116, 172
Sharp, Henry 105
Sherlock Holmes series (film) 220
Sherlock Holmes series (literature) 234, 261
Sherman, Vincent 91, 228
She's No Angel (2001, film) 343–344
Shield for Murder (film) 77, 113, 301
Shoot the Piano Player (film) 85
Side Street (film) 77, 113
Sign of the Cross (1932, film) 328
Silence of the Lambs (film) 180, 301
"Silent as the Grave" 95, 195
"Silhouette" 50, 143
Silver, Alain 19, 21, 139, 226, 249, 267
Silvera, Darrell 239
Simmons, Jean 258, 280, 300
Simon, Simone 181
Simon and Schuster 200
The Simple Art of Murder (Chandler book) 15
Sinatra, Frank 240
Singapore (1947, film) 294
Singin' in the Rain (film) 1
Siodmak, Robert 205–206, 208, 210, 211, 315
La Sirène du Mississippi see *Mississippi Mermaid*
Six Nights of Mystery (collection) 31
The Sleeping City (film) 74
Sleeping with the Enemy (film) 66, 353
Sloane, Everett 173
Smith, Howard 116
"Somebody on the Phone" (aka "Deadly Night Call") 17
Somewhere in the Night (film) 135
Sommersby (film) 236
Sophocles 31, 263
Sorry, Wrong Number (film) 21, 353
Spacey, Kevin 97
The Sparkuhlodor 205
Spellbound (film) 121, 141
Spielberg, Steven 323

Spoto, Donald 152
The Squaw Man (1931, film) 328
Stage Fright (film) 97, 152, 166
Stagecoach (1939, film) 138, 154
Stanwyck, Barbara 169, 228, 253, 280, 302, 317, 328, 329, 330, 331, 335, 339, 353
Star Trek series (film and television) 115–116
Stavrinos, George 28, 30
Steel, Edward 318
Steel, Freddie 220, 222
Steeves, Harrison R. 10
Stengler, Mack 77
The Stepford Wives (1975, film, remade 2004) 353
Stephenson, Bob 267, 270
Stevenson, Robert Louis 148
Stewart, James 151, 157, 161, 173, 257, 352
Stewart, Paul 307, 308, 311
Stone, Milburn 328, 331
Stone, Sharon 297
The Story Press 200
Stout, Rex 147
The Strange Case of Dr. Jekyll and Mr. Hyde (Stevenson novel) 132, 133, 148, 226
The Strange Love of Martha Ivers (film) 102, 253, 280, 284, 336
The Stranger (1946, film) 128
The Stranger on the Third Floor (film) 208
Strangler's Serenade (novel) 177
Strasberg, Lee 235
Street of Chance (1942, film) 62, 102, 134–142, 173, 189
Street with No Name (Dickos book) 3
Sudden Fear (film) 66, 322
Sudden Impact (film) 91
Sullivan, Barry 66
Sunset Boulevard (film) 23, 298, 302
The Suspect (film) 205
Suspicion (1941, film) 279
Svengali (1931, film, remake 1955) 120
Sweet Smell of Success (1957, film) 235
Swinburne, Algernon Charles 278
Swing High, Swing Low (film) 328

Take a Letter, Darling (film) 328
Tales from the Crypt series (film) 43
Tales of Manhattan (film) 46, 275
Talk About a Stranger (film) 316–317
Tallichet, Margaret 208
Tarler, Claire Attalie (Woolrich's mother) see Woolrich, Claire Attalie Tarler
Tarler, George Cornell (Woolrich's uncle) 3
Tarler, Gyorgi (Woolrich's grandfather) 3
Taylor, Robert 141, 226

"The Tell-Tale Heart" (Poe short story) 25
The Tempest (Shakespeare play) 264
The Ten Commandments (1923, film) 122
The Ten Commandments (1956, film) 122, 140
The Testament of Dr. Mabuse (film) 120
Tetzlaff, Ted 220, 304, 307, 318, 319, 323, 350
The Texas Chainsaw Massacre (film) 43
Thailing, William 3, 51, 53, 54, 73, 89, 100, 101, 115, 118, 157, 161, 182, 185, 197, 225, 229, 237, 239, 251, 256, 269, 288, 311, 312, 320, 330, 335
Thaxter, Phyllis 328, 329, 330
"They Call Me Patrice" 15
The Thief of Bagdad (1924, film) 328
The Thin Man series (film) 35
The Third Man (film) 259–260
This Gun for Hire (film) 76, 91, 336
Thomas, Henry 322, 323
Thompson, Jack 298
"Those Who Kill" 15
"Three O'Clock" 195
"Through a Dead Man's Eye" 306
Thunder Road (film) 249
Tierney, Gene 315
Tierney, Lawrence 302
Till the Day I Die (Odets play) 235
The Time Machine (Wells novel) 263, 265
The Time of Her Life (novel) 5
Times Square (novel) 5
The Tin Star (film) 42
Todd, Richard 97
Toland, Gregg 20
Tombes, Andrew 205, 206
Tone, Franchot 205, 207, 210–211
"Too Nice a Day to Die" 23, 233
Toomey, Regis 51, 52, 53, 54, 97, 99, 101, 205, 206
Total Recall (film) 229
Totter, Audrey 229, 307
Touch of Evil (film) 284
Tourneur, Jacques 179, 180, 181, 189, 254
Tracy, Spencer 353
Travolta, John 321–322
Tree Grows in Brooklyn, A (film) 140
Trevor, Claire 134, 135, 138, 139, 228, 301, 302
Trivial Clue Device (Woolrich convention) 17
The Trouble with Harry (film) 306
Truffaut, François 49, 85, 90, 92, 285–286, 287, 290, 291, 292, 293, 294, 295, 296, 300, 301
Trumbo, Dalton 173

Tryon, Tom 90
Turner, Kathleen 301
Tuttle, Frank 91
Twain, Mark (pseudonym of Samuel Langhorn Clemens) 336
Twenty Bucks (film) 46
"Two Fellows in a Furnished Room" *see* "He Looked Like Murder"
The Two Mrs. Carrolls (film) 353

Ulmer, Edgar 250
Ulysses *see* Odysseus
Under the Gun (film) 307
The Unfaithful (film) 228, 250
Union City (1980, film) 27–30
The Unknown (film) 350
Urubu (film) 318
The Usual Suspects (film) 97

Valli (Alida Valli) 259
Vampire's Honeymoon (collection) 39
Van Dyke, W.S. "Woody" 229
Van Rooten, Luis 267, 269
Vaughn, Vince 321
The Velvet Touch (film) 138
Verhoeven, Paul 229
Vertigo (1958, film) 2, 85, 138, 142, 169, 211, 257, 258, 285–286, 289–290, 293, 300, 308, 316, 336, 352
Vidor, King 128
Vincent, June 219, 221, 225
Vitagraph Company 8
Voice in the Wind (film) 250
von Stroheim, Erich 249

Wachowski, Andy 226
Wachowski, Larry 226
Waiting for Lefty (Odets play) 235
Wallace-Stone, Dee 42, 44, 343
"Walls That Hear You" 10
Waltz into Darkness (novel) 14, 16, 17, 23, 50, 85, 134, 276–302, 347
The War of the Roses (film) 351
Ward, Elizabeth 19, 21, 139, 226, 249, 267
Warner, Jack 71
Warren, Phil 235, 236
Wayne, John 154
Webb, Clifton 315
Webb, Richard 267, 269
Welles, Orson 20, 55, 113, 120, 128, 259, 281, 315, 316
Wells, H. G. 263, 265
Wharton, Edith 153
Where Danger Lives (film) 30, 50, 258–259, 267, 301

The Whistler series (radio show adapted to film) 60–61, 195
Widmark, Richard 169, 354
Wiene, Robert 120
Wilde, Oscar 275
Wilder, Billy 205, 316
Wilding, Michael 97
Williams, Bill 235, 236, 237, 239, 307
Williams, Emlyn 142
Williams, Tennessee 49
Wilson, Don 249, 254
Wilson, Flip 233
The Window (film) 2, 169, 220, 304, 307–318, 319, 322, 323, 350
Winston, Irene 155
Winterset (film) 140
Wise, Robert 241
The Witches of Eastwick (film) 296

Witness to Murder (film) 169, 317
The Wolf Man (film) 181
Woman in the Window (film) 121–122, 316
Woolrich, Claire Attalie Tarler (Woolrich's mother) 3, 8, 9, 68, 70, 247, 265
Worth, Constance 235, 236
The Wrong Man (1956, film) 335–336
Wrong Man theme 204, 205, 335
Wuthering Heights (Brontë novel) 61
Wyman, Jane 97

Yates, Donald A. 3
The Yellow Rolls Royce (film) 46
"You'll Never See Me Again" (aka "The Room That Wasn't Restful") 17, 27, 57, 97
Young, Loretta 66
A Young Man's Heart (novel) 5
Zinneman, Fred 91

www.ingramcontent.com/pod-product-compliance
Ingram Content Group UK Ltd.
Pitfield, Milton Keynes, MK11 3LW, UK
UKHW041921140426
5217IPUK00014B/263